Oct 21

MONEY AND INCOME

An Outline of Monetary Economics

AN OUTLINE OF MONETARY ECONOMICS

MONEY
AND
INCOME

A. C. L. DAY *London School of Economics*

STERIE T. BEZA *Princeton University*

New York OXFORD UNIVERSITY PRESS 1960

Preface

This book attempts to give a systematic presentation of present-day monetary economics in a form suitable for an American audience. In the preface of its English prototype, published in 1957 under the title *Outline of Monetary Economics*, the first co-author of the present version wrote that 'the interpretation of the phrase "monetary economics" which is employed is a broad one: the subject is taken to include the whole of what is often called the theory of macro-economics, as well as a discussion of monetary events and institutions. The two major exclusions are that no attempt is made to deal with micro-economics (i.e. the theory of the firm and the industry), nor is any attempt made to deal with the question of economic growth. Inevitably, this has meant that it has not been possible to consider many important questions as fully as one might wish, because they lie uneasily in the half-explored boundary zones between macro-economics and the other two important areas of economic studies. These shortcomings are inevitable in any work whose aim is primarily to present existing ideas systematically, because economists have not yet investigated these boundary zones as carefully and as systematically as is desirable.

'Within the confines of macro-economics itself, no such difficulties present themselves. A useful, consistent, and systematic body of analysis has been rapidly erected since the mid-'thirties; this book attempts to set it out.'

Particular emphasis has been placed on several topics which are of great practical importance, and seem likely to remain so for many years to come. One is the problem of inflation. The attempt we have made to move steadily from the more simple to the more complicated problems means that our discussion of the theory of inflation is found halfway through the book. But the fact is that any satisfactory theory of inflation must be rather complicated. Most economic discussions of inflation tend to be remarkably superficial; we do not claim to have organized all the theoretical problems involved with complete success, but we do claim to have faced up to them more squarely than is usual.

The second topic on which we have laid emphasis is that of stabilization. In doing so, we have brought out from the back room some ideas which are still in quite an early stage of application to economic theory. But we have done so deliberately in the attempt to show the 'limits' to the value of stabilization policies as usually expounded. In support of the need for the relatively sophisticated approach we have followed, we have made a point of presenting the dynamics of the savings-investment adjustment, as well as the comparative statics; and in doing so, we have tried to show how easily cycles can arise during a process of economic change.

The third topic on which we have laid a good deal of emphasis is that of international finance. Throughout the book, we have tried to relate theory and practice, and nowhere is this more important than in the field of international finance, where the theory is complicated and the practice impinges on major international political problems.

Inevitably, in a subject like this, some sections are more difficult than others because they deal with more complicated sets of relationships. In order to make the path of the relatively elementary student as smooth as possible, the book has been written in such a way that the easier chapters can be read through by themselves, without need for reference to the more difficult intervening chapters. The more difficult chapters or sections that can be omitted are marked by an asterisk in the table of contents and in the headings.

Although the basic structure of this book is the same as that of its English precursor, substantial changes have been made for this American edition. Five of the institutional chapters (12-15 and 26) are completely new, and Chapter 42 has been almost completely rewritten to take account of the changes that have occurred since the English book was completed in 1954. In addition, we have made major changes from the original English version in all the chapters describing present-day institutions when they have not been rewritten completely—Chapters 9, 17, 35, and 36 have all been changed in this way. We have also added diagrams at all the places where they seem likely to be useful to many readers, but have resisted the temptation to scatter them about in places where a verbal or arithmetical exposition is more satisfactory.

We have made substantial changes in the exposition of several of the theoretical chapters, notably Chapters 2, 4, 18, 23, and 27. Finally, the opportunity has been taken to correct a number of mistakes in the Mathematical Appendix which were kindly pointed out to us by Mr. J. Black of Merton College, Oxford.[1] We must also thank Mr. K. Klappholz and Mr. R. G. Opie for suggesting certain minor alterations to the English text.

A. C. L. DAY
S. T. BEZA

September 1959

---

[1] For the sake of owners of the English version who happen to see this book, the major mistake was one which crept into the numerator of equations 13, 14, and 27, which should in each case read $\dfrac{m_h}{s_h(1 - s_h)}$ and not merely m_h. The other substantial error is in the footnote of page 542 of the English version, where the word 'divided' should read 'multiplied.'

Contents

ix

---

* Indicates more difficult topics or chapters or sections that may be omitted in a short survey course.

I

INTRODUCTION

1

The Economic Significance of Money

At the very heart of nearly all economic relationships in communities that have attained any considerable degree of economic development lies the institution of money. A large part, indeed some would be inclined to say the major part, of the subject matter of economics is concerned with the functioning and malfunctioning of money.

This central position in economic relationships arises from the two main characteristics of money. In the first place, the majority of debts in developed communities are settled by means of one or other of the various forms of money. Purchases of goods, of services, and of claims (such as stocks and government bonds) are all generally made with the agency of money, as are payments of taxes. As a direct consequence of this, there arises a point which is still more important for our purposes in the following pages. It is that most incomes are received in the form of money. If a worker or a professional man sells his services for money, then it follows that he is receiving his income in money, because his income consists of the payment he receives for selling his services. In the same way, a businessman who buys and sells goods with money also finds that his income, which derives from the difference between the price at which he sells and the price at which he buys, accrues in the form of money.

The second main characteristic of money, which goes to explain its central significance in a large part of economic theory, is that one of the most important ways in which wealth can be held is as money. Nearly everyone who has any possessions at all in an economically developed community owns some money, whereas many people have practically no other possessions at all apart from their clothes. Moreover, wealthy individuals and organizations (such as business firms) generally own a very considerable amount of money, usually in the form of bank deposits.

The Nature of Money

Like several of the other kinds of wealth with which we shall shortly be concerned, money is a claim. This characteristic of money can be seen at two levels, one of which is relatively superficial while the other is fundamental. At one level, some kinds of money are expressed in the form of a claim to other kinds of money. At the more important level, the real significance of money is that it is a claim which can be used by its owner to buy anything. Money is the most convenient way of laying claim to such goods and services as one wishes to buy.

At the less significant level, many kinds of money are expressed as a claim against other money. As important an example of money as the United States one-dollar bill bears on its face the promise that 'one dollar in silver is payable upon demand.' But there is little point to making such an exchange since the silver dollar that is paid out in exchange for a silver certificate contains an amount of silver worth approximately 70 cents. If one should examine a five-dollar bill, that is a Federal Reserve note, there appears on its face a statement that 'this note . . . is redeemable in lawful money at the United States Treasury, or at any Federal Reserve Bank.' If a person tries to exercise this option he will find that all that happens is that he will be presented with a new bill in place of the old.

Lawful money does not have any significance today apart from merely stating that some money is legal tender. Prior to 1933, however, Americans could convert their notes and deposits into gold coin or gold certificates and it could be said for that period that bank notes carried out the functions of money somewhat less perfectly than did gold. This superiority of gold coins did not arise out of any intrinsic superiority of money that has gold backing over fiat money; [1] it arose out of the greater willingness of some people to accept and hold gold money than paper notes.

To some extent this greater willingness arose because at one time

---

[1] The major virtue of money stamped on precious metals was that it was expensive to create, so that there was no temptation for governments to create too much of it.

(before the Civil War) gold (and silver) coins were legal tender, whereas bank notes were not. This meant that a creditor was legally entitled to refuse to accept payment of a debt owing to him if the sum were offered in some form other than gold (or silver) coins. Today legal tender consists of coin and paper money issued by the United States government or by banks under the authority of the United States government.

Payment by check, that is, by an order to a bank to transfer a claim you have against it (i.e. your bank deposit) to some other specified person, is not and never has been legal tender. All the same, it is used for practically all transactions of any substantial amount; in fact, in spite of the law about legal tender, the income tax authorities are inclined to be particularly suspicious of people who avoid using checks for settling large debts (because of the easier opportunities for income tax fraud when there is no record of transactions in a bank's ledger). Yet there are some people, particularly people who do not have bank accounts, who are unwilling to accept checks and prefer to accept cash. So, to a minor extent, Federal Reserve notes and Treasury currency today are a rather more perfect form of money than are bank deposits. Bank deposits are expressed as promises by the bank concerned to pay the amount of the deposit to the bank's creditor (the depositor) in the form of Federal Reserve notes or Treasury currency. Unlike the promise on the face of Federal Reserve notes or Treasury currency, this promise to redeem the bank deposit in another form of money is still of some significance, and is not a mere relic.

A bank's debt to its depositor, which is expressed by a statement on the bank's books that it owes the person concerned a certain sum of money, might be regarded as more significantly distinct from legal-tender money if there were any serious danger that the bank might be unable to redeem its debt in legal-tender money. This danger, in modern American conditions, is for all practical purposes non-existent; it is certain that no government would tolerate the confusion that would result if a number of banks were unable to redeem their debts. Something would certainly be done to help the banks concerned over a crisis, if one arose, but it should be noted that serious bank failures were widespread as recently as 1933 in the United States.

For most practical purposes, then, except where transactions involving rather small sums are concerned, money in the form of claims against banks appears to most Americans to be at least as desirable to use and to hold as money in the form of legal-tender currency. The fact that most money now consists of claims against a particular kind of commercial organization (namely the banks) will prove to be of considerable importance in our subsequent discussion of monetary economics.

The second and more important sense in which money is a claim arises from the fact that money can be used immediately to buy anything. It is a claim by its owner which can be used to obtain any goods, services, or other assets he may require; he can always exchange money directly for anything else at the current market price of whatever it is that he is buying. Anyone will be willing to accept money in exchange for whatever it is he has to sell, because he knows that in his turn he can use money to buy whatever he wants. It is this feature that distinguishes money from everything else. It is a common feature of gold coin under the pre-1933 system, of bank notes, and of bank deposits. If I hold coin, notes, or a bank deposit, I can use my holdings to buy anything in the market, quite directly.

In order to be considered as money, a claim must be exercisable against all other goods, claims, and services, whoever may be selling them. Therefore, a currently redeemable debt of an ordinary individual or of an ordinary business firm does not count as money, because it will not generally be acceptable in payment for other things. Someone who knows the individual or firm concerned may be willing to accept the transfer of a claim against it in payment for something; but such cases will be the exception and not the rule. Banks are very different in this respect, however. Transfer of the debt of a bank by its depositor is usually accepted without any question by someone who is receiving payment from that depositor; this is merely a more formal way of describing check payments, which are taking place daily. Banks, in fact, are those institutions whose current debts are generally acceptable as payment for goods, services, and other claims. Generally speaking they specialize in this sort of business, but occasionally at a rather early stage of development they may have other business activities. Similarly, it sometimes happens, as in some colonies, that the debts of large trading firms are so generally acceptable that they are regarded and used as money. In developed economic systems, however, such as those of twentieth-century Europe or North America, banking has become a highly specialized business.

Other Forms of Wealth

In addition to money, there are other forms of wealth which will be among our major concerns. In the first place, there are many important kinds of claim, other than money. It is obvious, for example, that someone who owns a document on which another person promises to pay a sum of money at some future date is sensible if he regards himself as being wealthier than if he did not own such a claim. Where transactions of lending and borrowing are common, as in all developed economies, such kinds of wealth are very important.

Although in small personal contracts for borrowing and lending the same amount may be repaid at the future date as has been lent today, it is usual when the transactions are large or when they are on a commercial basis for the borrower to pay back to the lender a larger total sum than he borrowed. In other words, interest is usually charged when money is lent. Our immediate concern is to look briefly at the reasons why interest is usually paid on debts and to note the characteristics of some of the principal kinds of interest-bearing claim.

Debtors are willing to pay interest on loans because they think that they can acquire an advantage by being able to use funds immediately and only needing to repay at a later date. The advantage may be purely illusory, as in the case of a spendthrift; usually, however, it is quite real. A businessman may see a profitable opportunity which demands the use of more funds than he himself possesses— for example, he may see that if he goes to the expense of installing a new machine, he will be able to lower his costs of production. In such circumstances he will be willing to borrow in order to install the machine, and pay interest out of the extra profits it earns him. In a phrase, borrowers are willing to pay interest because borrowing allows them to increase productivity. The factors which determine the level of the rate of interest which borrowers have to pay will be our concern in later chapters.

There are two kinds of interest-bearing loan which will be our particular concern in this book. One is the bill, and the other is the bond. A bill is a promise to pay a fixed sum of money on a given future date, commonly three months from the time of issue. The bill bears no explicit statement about interest payable; nevertheless, it is paid, simply by making the promise one to pay a larger sum than the current debt. For example, it may be possible to borrow $990 now by writing out a promise to pay $1000 in three months' time; this implies a rate of interest of just over 1 per cent every three months, or rather more than 4 per cent per annum. We have used the term *bill* to encompass the variety of short-term credit investments that are commonly used to finance trading transactions and short-term government borrowing. In the United States the most important of these instruments are: commercial paper, the promissory notes of prominent business firms; bankers' acceptances, which are used primarily to finance international transactions; and Treasury bills, which are the short-term obligations of the federal government.

A bond is a document which promises to pay a fixed sum of money as interest at regular intervals (frequently annually); the promise may apply for a fixed number of years, at the end of which time the capital sum borrowed is repaid, or it may offer no date when repayment of the capital sum is promised. Undated bonds, which carry no maturity date and hence do not require that the borrower redeem them at fixed values, are used in other countries (notably Britain) but not in the United States. We shall use them in some of our discussion since they simplify the arithmetical computations of bond values and interest yields. Undated securities such as these simply consist of a piece of paper which bears a promise on the part of the debtor to pay a certain sum of money (as interest) at stated intervals (usually twice a year). The legal owner of such pieces of paper has an asset which consists of the right to receive this income indefinitely into the future; this asset has a market value, for which the owner could sell it, and he regards it as part of his wealth.

The differences between the bill and the bond provide examples of both the main kinds of distinction within the family of interest-bearing claim which we need to make. In the first place, there is the distinction between the two kinds of way in which the commitment to pay interest can be expressed—it can be hidden in with the repayment of the loan (as with the bill) or it can be expressed separately (as with the bond).

Secondly, and more important, there is the distinction with regard to the length of time which the lender has to wait before his debt is repaid. The most important distinction here is that between short and long loans. The bill is an example of a short-dated loan. The bond is long-dated, at least when it is first issued—that is, when the loan is first made. But, of course, a loan made for ten years in 1957 will only have a year to run in 1966, and by then can reasonably be classified as a short-dated loan. The division between short- and long-dated loans can conveniently be drawn at twelve months. Practically all bills are issued with much less than twelve months to maturity (typically the period is three months), so bills are short-dated securities throughout their lives.

For some purposes, it is convenient to make the division threefold —into short-, medium- and long-dated loans; the division between short and the others is still at twelve months, but loans with between one and five years to run to maturity may be called medium-dated securities, and all other loans, including undated bonds, are called long-term securities.

So far we have considered claims which give rights to predetermined sums of money. There is also a further broad category of claims, which plays a central role in modern capitalist economies. This is a claim which involves the ownership of a share in the assets of a company, and which gives the right to share in the profits of the company. The share is an uncertain one, both with regard to capital and to income; the success with which the company is run determines how large the income will be, and in extreme cases, whether the capital will remain of any value. Since the successful running of the firm is so important, common stocks, or equities as they are often called, generally include a voting right for the election of directors and for the general control over the running of the business. There are also certain shares of stock which give a prior claim on profits, and so are called preferred stocks (as distinct from common stocks, whose holders take a bigger chance on what is left over); such stocks often have only limited voting rights, and sometimes none at all.

The greater part of the assets of most firms is in the form of real wealth; that is, in the form of things which have physical existence and which are useful for their own sake or for the sake of what they can produce. Examples are factories, machines, and inventories of materials. In addition, real wealth is held by the government in such forms as barracks and museums and by private individuals in such forms as houses. From the point of view of the country as a whole, total wealth consists predominantly of such physical wealth, because claims by one citizen against another or against a firm within the country or against the government cancel out against the corresponding liabilities of the debtors. If I owe you $1, then you have an asset worth $1, but I have a corresponding liability of $1; if we are working out the sum of our joint wealth, this item drops out of the reckoning.

The only claims that do not cancel out when we are adding up the total wealth of a country are claims against foreigners; similarly, liabilities to foreigners must be subtracted from total wealth. In just the same way, if we want to calculate how large is the wealth of a family, we ignore all claims between father and son or between husband and wife, but we count claims against outsiders and claims by outsiders against members of the family.

In addition to money, other claims, and real wealth, there is one more kind of wealth to which we must turn our attention for the moment; this consists of those assets which are not claims and which do not have physical existence; they can be called incorporeal assets. The most important examples are goodwill, patent rights,[2] and skill and knowledge. Strictly speaking, the first two of these kinds of incorporeal wealth should perhaps be ignored in deciding what is the total wealth of a country, because although their value can be measured commercially and they are salable, they are assets which give rights or power over other people and are wealth only from the point of view of the beneficiaries of those rights, and not from the point of view of society as a whole.[3] As for wealth in the form of skill and knowledge, it is best excluded for another reason. Although it is undoubtedly significant, its value is very hard to measure; eventually, we have to draw a line at which we must stop. Where we decide to draw that line, and say that everything beyond that line we shall not consider as part of private or national wealth, is a matter of convenience which is essentially arbitrary.

The Subject Matter of Monetary Economics

Monetary economics, then, is concerned with income and with wealth, because most incomes are received in the form of money,

---

[2] A patent can be regarded as a potential claim against a usurper.

[3] Insofar as goodwill and patents give rights over foreigners, they may reasonably be counted as part of the wealth of the country as a whole.

and because money is one of the most important forms in which wealth can be held. Moreover, several of the non-monetary forms of wealth, which we have described in outline above, are expressed in terms of money. In particular, this is the case with interest-bearing loans such as bills and bonds.

A precise definition of the subject matter of monetary economics is almost impossible, and the attempt to make it is hardly worth while. Income and wealth together form the subject matter of the study of economics as a whole; monetary economics simply lays emphasis on certain aspects of the broader subject, which are particularly closely related to the existence of money. The most convenient way of indicating the scope of our subject, is, therefore, to list the most important kinds of problem with which we shall be concerned.

The problems of the succeeding chapters will be problems concerning levels of income and the accumulation and holding of wealth. Principally, three questions will be our concern. Firstly, what factors are important in determining the level of income of a society? In looking at this question, our concern will not be with the deeper, more fundamental question of why some countries are very rich and others very poor; those are questions concerning long-run developments, which can only be answered by collaboration between the economist, the sociologist, the historian, and the geographer. Our questions about the level of income will be concerned with phenomena that are more subject to change in short periods. We shall be particularly concerned with the reasons why a country may fail to use all the resources it has available as fully as it might, so that its real income is lower than it might be (that is, with the problem of unemployment), and with the causes of rises in the level of money income when real incomes are unchanged (that is, with the problem of inflation).

The second of the three fundamental questions that will be our concern will be consideration of the reasons why people try to build up wealth, that is, why they save, and why they decide to amass real wealth,[4] either financing its purchase out of their own current savings or by borrowing from other people.

The third of our questions is also concerned with wealth, but with wealth that has been acquired in the past, and not with current

---

[4] Such as houses, machines, land, etc.

additions to wealth. This is the question of how people will choose to hold the wealth that they have amassed in the past; whether they will continue to hold it in the form in which they are already holding it, or whether they will try to switch from holding one sort of asset to holding another (as, for example, by selling securities and holding cash instead, or by selling securities and buying a house).

These three main questions will be the heart of our study; their answers will occupy us at length, particularly since we shall find that they are linked inextricably. In looking at the answers to these questions, we shall be concerned with the actions of groups of individuals, groups of firms, and of large organizations such as the government and the banks. Our concern is the income and wealth of nations and of the major economic groups within nations.

SOME SUGGESTED READING

The great debt of modern macro-economic and monetary theory is to J. M. Keynes (later Lord Keynes), on whose work the structure of this book is based. His epoch-making work, *The General Theory of Employment, Interest, and Money* (New York, 1936), is not particularly easy to read, but all serious students of the subject should attack it. In doing so, they will find A. H. Hansen, *A Guide to Keynes* (New York, 1953), a useful ally. *The New Economics,* edited by S. E. Harris (New York, 1947), is a useful guide to the revolution that was carried out by Keynes, as is L. R. Klein, *The Keynesian Revolution* (New York, 1947). D. H. Robertson, *Money,* 6th ed. (New York, 1948), is a remarkably subtle book by another member of the Cambridge school who differed sharply from Keynes but shared much of the same tradition. D. Patinkin, *Money, Interest, and Prices* (Evanston, 1956), is a valuable analysis of the relationship between Keynesian economics and the 'classical' school which it has replaced.

$$ $$

2

The Reasons for Holding Money

The Transactions and the Precautionary Motives

In the last chapter, we saw that money is commonly used for making transactions. A major part of the incentive to hold wealth in the form of money derives directly from that fact—a major element in the demand to hold money is a transactions demand. This demand to hold money is based on two characteristics of money, which can be summed up as convenience and certainty.

Lying behind the attribute of *convenience* are the facts that transactions are normally settled with money, and that the carrying costs of money are negligible: money, unlike most commodities, costs nothing to store. These facts in turn provide a strong reason why the gaps between the receipt of payments from other people and the making of payments to other people should be bridged by holding money. Most transactors do not receive payments at precisely the same time as they have to make them. For example, a salary earner, who receives his income at the end of the month, will want to carry out a large part of his purchases at intervals through the succeeding month. He will not buy all the groceries or meat he needs in that month in one great pile at the beginning of the month; these purchases are spread out. In the same way, a firm may be paying salaries at monthly intervals, wages weekly, and for raw materials at irregular intervals, while receipts for the product it sells may also be coming in irregularly.

There is, therefore, always a strong incentive to hold some money (either as cash or as deposits at a bank) to allow for this irregularity in carrying out transactions. The average amount that a transactor holds may be very small; a wage earner who receives his wages on Friday and has spent them all by Saturday evening has an average

13

holding of money which is small in proportion to his weekly income, and very small in relation to his annual income. On the other hand, businessmen may well hold cash balances that are of the same order of magnitude as their annual income. Most people, therefore, have on an average a positive holding of money, because their holdings cannot fall below zero, and at certain times (usually for most of the time) are greater than zero.

The other characteristic of money contributing to the transactions demand for money is summed up by the word *certainty*. It has been a feature of reasonably normal times that prices of goods and services in general in terms of money tend to be more stable than prices-in-general expressed in terms of anything else. In normal times, individual commodity prices have generally fluctuated more than the average of commodity prices. It is, therefore, more likely that money will have retained its value in terms of whatever one eventually chooses to buy, than if one's income had been held in some other form between the time of its receipt and the time one chooses to spend it. This is true, even though it is likely [1] that modern economies have a tendency toward a slow but persistent price inflation, with the general level of prices rising 1 or 2 per cent a year. Even if money is persistently losing its value in terms of goods, it is still much easier to estimate next year's value of a dollar in terms of goods in general, than of next year's exchange value in terms of goods in general of a bushel of wheat or a ton of copper.

For some purposes, it is convenient to distinguish a second motive for holding money, similar to the transactions motive but not quite identical with it. This is the *precautionary motive;* money may be held in order to be prepared for the sudden arrival of unforeseen contingencies. The difference between this and the transactions motive is that the amount of money held for the latter purpose can safely be regarded as varying in direct proportion to the value of transactions taking place in a given time in the country. In turn, it is a reasonably safe assumption to regard holdings of money that people will desire to have for transactions purposes as varying directly with the national income, that is, with the sum of all the incomes received by all the individuals in the country. Neither of these approximations is absolutely reliable; for example, a change in the method of organization of industry may affect the transactions

---

[1] As will be argued in Chapter 22.

demand to hold money. If, for example, two firms, one of which has been buying from the other, combine to make one firm, the transactions which formerly required money will now be a matter of internal bookkeeping. The total volume of income is unchanged, but the volume of transactions changes. Another case where the volume of transactions might change in relation to income is an increase in financial transactions, that is, in the volume of purchases and sales of various kinds of claim. A stock exchange boom might increase the amount of money used for transactions purposes, without there being any rise in income or in the number of non-financial transactions. Usually all such changes are unimportant when we are looking at periods of a few years, so that they do not seriously affect the assumption that the amount of money held for transactions motives varies directly in proportion to the total of money incomes in the country. This is the assumption which we shall follow henceforward.

The precautionary motive differs in that money holdings for this motive vary significantly with the degree of uncertainty. For example, at a time of financial crisis, such as the onset of a serious depression or at the outbreak of a war, people may prepare for unforeseen contingencies by trying to hold an unusually large part of their wealth as money. Apart from particular stresses at its outbreak, a time of war is inevitably a time of uncertainty; precautionary holdings of money, therefore, are particularly large at such times. This was probably one of the reasons why cash holdings in nearly all belligerent countries were unusually large between 1939 and 1948. Pessimistic expectations as to future income or the experience of wide fluctuations of income are also likely to augment the desire for precautionary balances. For most purposes, however, the precautionary motive for holding money can be combined with the transactions motive, and regarded as varying directly with the level of national income.

So far, we have seen as advantages of holding wealth in the form of money that no carrying cost is involved, that money is immediately convertible into all kinds of claims, goods, and services, and that it has a fairly constant purchasing power over goods and services in general. These last two attributes are often summed up by saying that money is the most *liquid* of all assets. The reader may be tempted to ask why do people not hold all their wealth in the form of money, if it has such virtues? There is a simple answer:

wealth held as money does not provide an income. Money is a convenient and certain form of holding wealth, and does not cost anything to carry; but it does not provide a return as does, for example, a machine, a house, or a bond. A machine can be used to produce something else and so, usually, bring a profit to its owner; a house can be lived in or rented to a tenant; a bond brings in a fixed annual amount of money as interest. Money does none of these things. For this reason people generally prefer to hold only part of their wealth as money and the rest in a form which will provide an income. They may do so by acquiring claims giving the certainty (e.g. a bond) or a chance (e.g. an equity) of an annual money income, in which case no carrying costs are involved. Alternatively, they may acquire an asset such as a machine, which has carrying costs (in the form of maintenance, insurance, etc.) but also has an expected yield in the form of what it can produce which more than outweighs these costs.

In reality the situation is somewhat more complicated than we have indicated. In a fuller treatment of the demand for money we would consider the liquidity and illiquidity of many types of assets and liabilities. There are, for example, short-term assets such as bills which may serve many liquidity needs almost as well as money. Or, if an individual feels that credit facilities are readily available to him, he may consider it safe to reduce the size of the money balance that he carries. But these are complications that we cannot explore at this time, and they do not alter the basic contentions of the analysis.

The position is, then, that transactors usually like to hold part of their wealth, but not the whole of it, in the form of money: they have preference for liquidity up to a certain point, but only up to that point. Their liquidity preference is relative, and not absolute; we can rephrase the question which is being answered in this chapter (namely, what determines the community's desire to hold money) by asking instead, to what is the community's liquidity preference related?

We have already given much of the answer. The desire to be liquid, that is to hold money, will depend partly on the transactions and precautionary motives. In times that are not subject to sudden threats of uncertainty about economic conditions, we can say that the desire to hold money arising from these motives varies directly with the level of the country's money income. This, however, is not the whole of the answer. A third motive, which will play a large part in the analysis in subsequent chapters, is the speculative motive.

The Speculative Motive

People may, and do, speculate about the future level of all kinds of prices, by holding things whose prices they think are going to rise, and by being hesitant about holding things whose prices they think will fall. The speculation with which we are concerned here is speculation about future prices of claims other than money. An observant reader will have noted that, whereas we have talked of transactions as including purchases of goods, services, and claims, when we have talked about the normal stability of the value of money we have merely described it as stability in terms of goods and services. We have not argued that there is any normal tendency for the prices of claims other than money, taken as a group, to be stable in terms of money.

To see what has been implied by this omission, let us take a typical example of a claim other than money—an undated bond. The advantage of choosing an undated bond is that arithmetical problems, which are irrelevant to the main point, will be at a minimum; the advantage of choosing a bond rather than a bill or other short-term paper is that the effects are seen more markedly on long-term paper; the advantage over looking at a share is that we do not find ourselves getting mixed up between rates of interest and rates of profit. It is with rates of interest that we are directly concerned at the moment. Now, the price of any bond varies inversely with the current rate of interest. That arises as a result of the operation of market forces, which themselves are influenced by simple arithmetical calculations. An undated bond is a promise by a debtor to pay at stated intervals and for an indefinitely long period a fixed sum of money to the owner of the piece of paper carrying the promise. If the long-term rate of interest was $2\frac{1}{2}$ per cent at the time it was issued, the initial selling price of a promise to pay $2.50 a year would be $100: that is what is meant by a rate of interest of $2\frac{1}{2}$ per cent. Now, let us consider what happens if the long-term rate of interest subsequently changes to 5 per cent, for some reason which we need not investigate for the moment. Such a rate of interest implies that the market price of the $2\frac{1}{2}$ per cent bond has now fallen to $50; for $100 it is possible to buy a claim to $5 a year, and so for $50 it is possible to buy a claim to $2.50 a year. It also implies that if anyone now wishes to borrow $100 by issuing a new undated bond, he will have to promise to pay $5 a year to its holder. If he is not willing to pay as much as that, no wealth-holder would be willing to buy his bonds; if he were willing to pay more, no wealth-holder would be willing to hold old bonds. The rate of return to the wealth-holder is, therefore, the same whether he owns old or new bonds.

When we consider bonds with a fixed date of maturity (or one which is fixed within limits) the same rule applies as far as bonds which will mature at the same time are concerned. In the case of bonds where the borrower promises to repay a fixed capital sum at the date of maturity the investor will make allowance, not only for the interest earned, but also for the inevitable change in the bond's value from its current price to the maturity value that accrues to whoever is holding it when it matures. This change will involve an improvement in capital value between the present date and the maturity date, if the present price of the bond is less than its redemption value (as will generally [2] happen if interest rates have risen since the time the bond was issued); while if its present price is greater than the redemption value (as will generally [2] happen if interest rates have fallen since the time the bond was issued), the investor has to face a loss in capital value between the present time and the redemption date. If allowance is made for the arithmetical complications such calculation of 'yields to redemption' causes, we find that any two bonds issued by similar borrowers and which are due to mature at the same date, will have prices such that the return to the investor on a $100 worth of one bond will be the same as the return on $100 worth of the other. For example, let us imagine that the United States government issued 2½ per cent bonds at a price of $100 in 1947, due to mature in 15 years, and that it issued in 1952, also at a price of $100, 3½ per cent bonds due to mature in 10 years. Both these bonds are due to mature at the same time. Let us also suppose that both issues will be redeemed at the full issue price ($100) and that at present in 1957, the rate of interest on such medium-dated government bonds is 4 per cent. Leaving aside the further complications arising because we should calculate at com-

---

[2] 'Generally' but not always, because redemption values may sometimes differ appreciably from the original price of issue.

pound interest and not simple interest, the current prices of each bond will be such that an investor can expect $4 per annum from investing $100. The total of $20 income for every $100 he invests he will obtain partly from the annual interest payment, and partly from the inevitable change in capital value accruing to whoever holds until maturity. This means that an investor will be willing to offer $93.75 for a 1947 2½ per cent bond of $100 face value; if he buys one bond at that price, he will receive $12.50 in interest payments in that period (in five annual payments of $2.50; the annual amount promised on the face of the bond); in addition he receives an increase in capital value of $6.25. His total receipts, therefore, are $18.75, which is 4 per cent of his purchase price of $93.75. In other words, he receives the present rate of interest on bonds of that maturity. Similarly, he could receive 4 per cent on his purchase price by buying the 3½ per cent bonds at a price of approximately $97.75; he receives $17.50 in interest and about $2.25 in capital gain, totalling about $19.75, so giving him 4 per cent per annum on his original investment. Similar considerations will influence many other wealth-holders, and therefore will determine these market prices of the two kinds of bond, assuming interest rates are 4 per cent.

These arithmetical computations, which become more complicated when account is taken of uncertain redemption dates [3] (as when a range is given, e.g. 1965-1975) are the bread and butter of many individuals in financial centers. They are for us, however, unimportant complications which tend to obscure the simplicity of the most important relationships from the economist's point of view. For that reason, having pointed out the complications, we can leave them aside and save ourselves a great deal of trouble by assuming all long-term bonds to have no effective redemption date.

We can, then, return to the simplicity of the world where the price of bonds varies inversely in proportion with the long-term rate of interest; in that simple context we must further discuss the speculative motive for holding money. A change in the long-term rate of interest means a change in the market price of all long-term bonds. Methods by which different transactors value their bonds on their books vary, and in some cases such changes in value will not be

---

[3] And also of the facts that many people are not indifferent between capital and income receipts because of the tax laws, and that quoted bond prices take account of interest that has accrued but has not yet been paid.

reflected in changes in the value of such assets in their holders' accounts. Generally speaking, however, such a change in the market value of the security will be regarded as a change in the total wealth of the person or organization concerned. Corresponding to a fall in the rate of interest is a rise in the value of bonds in the same proportion; for example, if interest rates fall from 5 per cent to $2\frac{1}{2}$ per cent, the market price of a $2\frac{1}{2}$ per cent bond will have risen from $50 to $100. If such a change takes place in a year, the total gains which the holder of such a bond makes are $52.50 ($50 in capital gains, and $2.50 in interest on the bond). Conversely, if interest rates rise from $2\frac{1}{2}$ per cent to 5 per cent in the same period, the holder gains $2.50 on income account, but loses $50 on capital account; he takes a total loss of $47.50.

It is obvious that it is a matter of importance to a holder of a bond whether its market price rises or falls while it is in his possession. In particular, if it falls (that is, if the rate of interest rises) the capital loss involved can easily wipe out the interest received, and the holder can be left in a position no better and very possibly worse than originally. Now, if the holder of a bond thinks that such a fall in value is a serious possibility, it is clearly worth his while to try to avoid the loss. Any individual holder can do this by selling the bond and holding money until after the fall has taken place. Holders of bonds who consider that interest rates on the bonds they are holding are likely to be higher in the relatively near future than they are at present will be well advised to sell their bonds and hold cash; they thereby forgo income for the period during which cash is held, but avoid a bigger capital loss. By maintaining their capital intact, they can increase their *future* income by purchasing bonds when their price has fallen. For example, if I have bonds earning $2.50 per year, and the rate of interest is currently $2\frac{1}{2}$ per cent, I can sell them for $100. If I think the rate is going to rise to 5 per cent, I can maintain my capital intact by moving into cash until the rise has occurred; the price has then correspondingly halved, so I can buy twice as many bonds as before with my $100, and double my income to $5 per annum at the expense of forgoing income for the time in which I hold cash.

This is the source of the *speculative motive* for holding money; a demand to hold money additional to the transactions and precautionary demands arises because bonds vary in price. There is always the possibility that by deferring the purchase of bonds the individual wealth-holder may be able to purchase bonds at a lower price (and at a higher yield). There is a great deal of uncertainty concerning the future course of bond prices; but if bond prices are high and interest rates are low, when compared with the levels that the individual wealth-holder considers normal, such a holder is likely to expect an increase in interest rates and a decline in bond prices in the future. The reaction of the wealth-holder to this situation is to move out of bonds, and of the things that he may move into, the most likely one is money. We can generalize this a bit more; for the community as a whole, the lower the rate of interest, the greater will be the number of wealth-holders who consider the rate of interest to be below its normal level, and hence the greater will be the demand for money to hold. It is conceivable, at least in the short run, that there is some low level of the rate of interest (some high level of bond prices) that wealth-holders consider to be a minimum (maximum) and they will be willing to hold a limitless amount of money at this minimum rate of interest, i.e. at this minimum rate of interest the speculative demand to hold money will be extremely large.

Expectations and the Speculative Motive

If we assume the simple position where a wealth-holder has open to him the alternatives of holding his wealth as money or as bonds, it is possible to say a little more about the state of expectations which will lead him to want to hold money for speculative motives. The decision to hold money for speculative reasons will depend on the certainty with which a wealth-holder believes the change in interest rates will take place, the time he expects to elapse before it takes place, the present rate of interest, and the rate of interest he expects in the future. Assuming he is quite certain that a rise in interest rates will occur, and that it will occur within a year, a wealth-owner who is trying to make as large a gain as possible and who is deciding whether to hold money or bonds for the next year [4] will compare the interest he could earn in the year with the loss he expects in the year on the market value of the bond. If the present rate of interest is 4 per cent, he can in a year earn $4 in

---

[4] Usually the decision will be for a much shorter period; then the principle is just the same but the arithmetic is rather more complicated.

interest on an amount of bonds he can at present buy or sell for $100. It is not worth while to hold those bonds for a year if their price at the end of the year will be less than $96; in such a case he would be wiser to sell them now, hold cash for a year, and buy similar bonds in a year's time.[5] A fall to $96 in the market price of a bond which is currently worth $100 and which brings in an annual income of $4, corresponds to a rise in the rate of interest to 4.16 per cent. It can be seen, therefore, that if the rate of interest is expected to rise by more than 0.16 per cent when it was originally 4 per cent, it would be wiser to hold money until after the rise has taken place, and then repurchase bonds at the lower price.

If the present rate of interest is 2 per cent a wealth-owner earns only $2 in a year with bonds which cost $100 on the market. It is preferable in that case to hold money rather than bonds if their price is expected to fall below $98 within the following year. This corresponds to a rise in the rate of interest to only 2.04 per cent. In other words, when the rate of interest is very low, an expectation of a very small rise in it will make it appear more sensible to hold money, while if the rate is high a prospect of a rise which is relatively much greater will be needed to cause a speculative movement into money. A rise from 4 per cent to 4.16 per cent is both absolutely and relatively much greater than a rise from 2 per cent to 2.04 per cent; yet each represents the critical point beyond which an expected rise would, on our assumptions, cause a movement into money.

This is a matter of considerable practical importance, because it means that wealth-holders are likely to be easily alarmed into moving their wealth from bonds to money if the rate of interest is very low, and if the costs of movement between holding bonds and money are relatively small. Fear of a very small rise in the rate of interest will cause widespread unwillingness to hold bonds and a desire to hold cash, if the rate of interest is at a very low level. Added to this is the fact that fears of a rise in the rate of interest are likely to be greater when the rate is low, for the simple reason that the rate can never fall to zero [6] (and historically has never approached that level), so that the nearer it gets to zero, the more

---

[5] This assumes that there are no costs of buying and selling bonds, such as brokers' commission. In practice there will be, so the story is correspondingly complicated, but its fundamentals are not altered.

[6] For reasons we shall examine in Chapter 4.

likely it seems that the next change will be upward. In the post-war years prior to 1951, it was a matter of policy in the United States (primarily at the insistence of the Treasury) to keep the yield on long-term government securities from rising above $2\frac{1}{2}$ per cent. And despite the strong demands for credit, which exerted pressures on the $2\frac{1}{2}$ per cent rate, the line was held, but the price paid was the central bank's surrender of its control over the money supply to the commercial banks and the public since interest rate stabilization depended upon the Federal Reserve's support of the prices of government bonds; this reliance upon Federal Reserve support was especially obvious in the year after December, 1947, when the support levels were scaled down somewhat. The higher ceiling on interest rates evoked expectations on the part of investors of further upward changes in rates, and heavy purchases of long-term bonds by the Federal Reserve Banks were necessary to keep the rate from rising above $2\frac{1}{2}$ per cent.

In Figure 1 the demand for money for speculative purposes is shown graphically. On the vertical axis we measure the rate of interest and on the horizontal axis we measure the quantity of money. The curve expressing the demand for money for speculative purposes is drawn to slope downward from left to right; i.e. the lower the rate of interest the larger will be the quantity of money demanded for speculative purposes. As we have drawn the curve expressing the speculative demand for money, the lower the rate of interest the more elastic is the demand for money (for speculative purposes) with respect to the rate of interest. This can be interpreted as saying that the lower the rate of interest, the greater will be the percentage addition to the quantity of money demanded for speculative purposes with a *given* percentage decline in the rate of interest. And if there is some low level of the rate of interest that is considered to be a minimum (at least in the short run), the curve will flatten out at that minimum rate of interest, i.e. the demand for money for speculative purposes becomes infinitely elastic with respect to the rate of interest. This occurs in Figure 1 when the rate of interest falls to r_M. We should add that the infinite elasticity of demand-for-money case is more likely to be a short- rather than a long-run phenomenon. The reason for this is that the longer the rate of interest remains at or near the 'minimum' level, the more likely it is that people may begin to think that it can go lower, i.e. a change might occur in people's thinking about the 'normal' range of interest rates.

Working contra to this possibility, however, is the fact already discussed that as the rate of interest gets lower and lower, the upward changes in the rate of interest that would cause a loss (taking account of interest income and capital loss) become smaller and smaller.

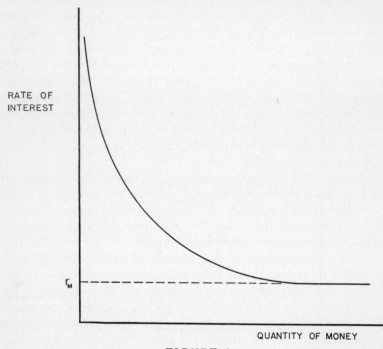

RATE OF
INTEREST

r_M

QUANTITY OF MONEY

FIGURE 1

A further influence reinforces these speculative factors. The lower the rate of interest, the less income does one give up by having large cash holdings for transactions and precautionary purposes instead of holding one's wealth in interest-earning assets. Regardless of expectations about future interest rates, there is a tendency for cash holdings to be larger when interest rates are low.

The demand for money for transactions and precautionary purposes can be pictured quite simply, as we have done in Figure 2. On the vertical axis we measure the rate of interest and on the horizontal axis we measure the quantity of money. If we assume that the transactions-precautionary demand for money varies solely with the level of money income, we can express the relationship in our diagram by a series of vertical lines, each line representing a given level of money income. In our diagram, money income Y_3 is greater than money income Y_2, and so on. The higher the level of money income, the greater will be the quantity of money demanded

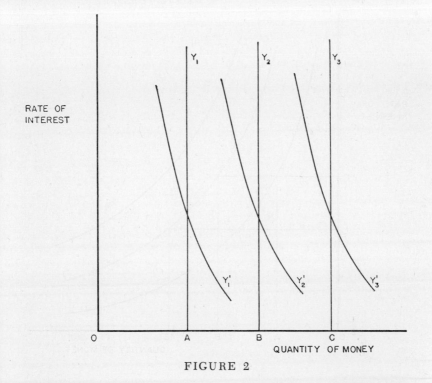

FIGURE 2

for transactions and precautionary purposes. For example, when the level of money income is Y_2, the quantity of money demanded is OB, which is greater than the amount OA, the quantity demanded at Y_1, a lower level of money income. The lines representing the demand for money are, in this case, vertical, indicating that the demand for money for these purposes is not influenced by the rate of interest. If, on the other hand (as was suggested in the preceding paragraph), the transactions-precautionary demand varies both with money income and with the rate of interest, the lines representing the demand for money will slope downward from left to right, as in the lines Y_1', Y_2', Y_3'.

We can show the combined influence of money income and the rate of interest on the demand for money, as in Figure 3. This diagram brings together the analyses of Figures 1 and 2. On the vertical axis we measure the rate of interest and on the horizontal axis we measure the quantity of money. For each level of money

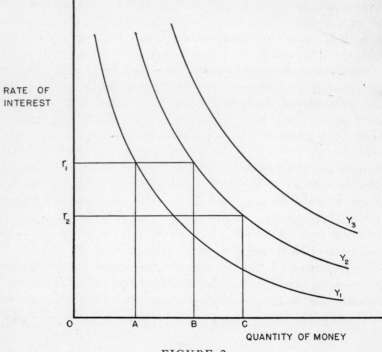

FIGURE 3

income there is a separate curve expressing the demand for money. Money income Y_3 is greater than money income Y_2, etc. If we assume a given level of money income, the lower the rate of interest the larger will be the quantity of money demanded. Along the curve labeled Y_2 (a given level of money income), for example, when the rate of interest declines from r_1 to r_2 the quantity of money demanded rises by BC. Or, if we assume a given rate of interest, such as r_1, when the level of money income rises from Y_1 to Y_2 the quantity of money demanded rises by AB.

The speculative demand for money is usually described in terms of the two alternative ways of holding wealth, as cash or as bonds.

We shall find in the succeeding chapters that it is convenient to assume this limited choice, in order to make our analysis easier; but in the real world, where there are many different ways of holding wealth, similar speculation can take place between any pair of assets. Examples are common on the stock exchange; many people are able to make steady profits out of judicious movements out of shares which are going to fall and into shares which are going to rise; or a holder of long-term bonds who thinks that their price is going to fall may shift his wealth into equity shares, if he thinks their price is not going to fall. Many other examples are to be found; we shall look at similar operations when we investigate the relationship between the long-term rate of interest (on bonds) and the short-term rate of interest (on bills). Speculation involving the future price of any kind of asset may give rise to a speculative demand to hold money; the mechanism outlined above is not limited to the case of bonds. For example, if there is a fear that prices of all shares are going to fall sharply in the near future, their holders would be wise, as far as their immediate personal interests are concerned, to sell them and hold cash instead. If many people take part the effects on the economy of such a flight into liquidity can be shattering; such a flight was a large element in the 1929 stock market crash in the United States, which was a feature of the onset of the Great Depression. It is here that the speculative motive borders closely on the precautionary motive; flight into money at the onset of a crisis may be interpreted in terms of either motive; usually the one reinforces the other.[7]

The Deflationary Motive

When we see that the speculative motive for holding money can operate when a fall is expected in the price of any asset, and not merely of long-term bonds, we border on another motive for holding money. We have seen in Chapter 1 that wealth includes real assets, as well as claims. Wealth can be held in the form of anything which is not perishable. When the price level of goods in general is rising

---

[7] The analytical distinction between the two motives still remains, however. The precautionary motive deals with expected changes whose nature is quite uncertain; the speculative motive deals with expected changes whose characteristics are forecast (perhaps inaccurately, of course) by the transactor concerned.

or falling, another motive affecting decisions about holding money enters the situation. If it is expected that prices of goods in general are going to fall in terms of money (that is, a deflationary situation), then people who want to buy goods but have no immediate need of them would find it in their interests to hold back from purchases until their needs are pressing, and to hold money in the meantime. If a manufacturer will need copper in a month's time, normally he might buy it at once and hold it in stock for the month; that is a convenient thing to do as he can avoid the trouble that will occur if he waits until it is needed almost immediately and then finds delays in delivery. If, however, he believes that the price is going to fall within the month, he believes he can save money by waiting until the last possible minute. If such conditions and expectations are general, an increase in demand for money to hold will result, because it will generally be convenient to hold in a liquid form the wealth that would normally have been tied up in materials. The reverse tendency will be likely when prices are rising; people will prefer to hold more goods and less money than usual. The effect of such operations will show themselves only if there is a general upward or downward movement in the price level. When some prices are rising and some falling, and the general level of prices is approximately stable, operators in some markets will be moving into money and in other markets they will tend to be avoiding money, and so the total effects will cancel out.

This kind of pressure to hold, or to avoid holding, money arises from speculation about future prices of goods; it is convenient to distinguish it from the speculative motive in the narrower sense, which is concerned with speculation about future prices of claims.

To make the difference clear, we can distinguish the *deflationary motive* for holding money,[8] which operates when there is general deflation. Correspondingly there is its reverse, the inflationary motive for avoiding holding money.

It is in times of severe inflation that these influences on the desire to hold money are especially important. When prices are rising rapidly, money is rapidly losing its value and it is unwise to hold any more than the absolute minimum necessary. Any money that is

---

[8] Together with claims whose value is to some extent fixed in terms of money—e.g. bonds, as distinct from shares, whose prices tend to fall as prices (and therefore profits) fall.

earned is spent as soon as possible; attempts are made to hold all wealth in forms that are rising in money value at least as fast as the price of goods in general. In very severe inflations there is a flight into so-called 'real values,' such as the purchase of antiques, stocks of raw materials, equity shares, in fact almost anything whose value is not fixed in terms of money. Correspondingly, just as there is a flight from money, there is an unwillingness to hold claims whose value is more or less fixed in terms of money, such as bonds. Such a flight from money occurs to some extent in relatively mild inflations, such as that in the United States since the war; it has been quite marked at times in the sharper inflations that many other countries have suffered.

Changes in Total Wealth and Liquidity Preference

One last complication still needs to be added to this chapter's analysis of the motives for holding money. So far, we have been implicitly assuming that each transactor owns a fixed amount of wealth. In fact, changes will occur in the total wealth they own, and this will affect their desire to hold money. These changes can come about in two ways—by changes in the money value of the claims and other assets held, and by additions to wealth arising from saving.

The first of these two can easily be neglected. It simply reinforces relationships we have already observed. For example, if bond prices rise (i.e. interest rates lower), total wealth of bond-holders rises. If other things are equal, it seems very likely that a person will want to hold more money when his total wealth is larger: plentiful liquidity is one of the luxuries the wealthy can afford to enjoy. Lower interest rates are, therefore, likely to cause an increased demand for money for this reason, which reinforces the speculative and transactions-precautionary motives for holding more money when interest rates are low. Thus there are three forces at work that cause a larger quantity of money to be demanded the lower the rate of interest: (1) the lower the cost of holding money balances, in terms of interest income forgone, the greater will be the amount demand for transactions and precautionary purposes; (2) the lower the rate of interest, the greater will be the value of each bond, and assuming a fixed number of bonds in existence, a lower rate of interest causes an increase in the wealth of their holders which, other things equal, will increase the quantity of money demanded; and (3) the lower the rate of interest, the greater will be the quantity of money demanded for speculative purposes. This last relationship is generally thought to be the most important, and will be our main concern.

The second of the two effects of changes in total wealth cannot be dealt with quite so easily. A person who has added to his total wealth by saving is also likely to want to increase the holdings of money he was keeping for any or all of the four motives. He is likely to feel he can afford the luxury of bigger transactions balances, so that he has more room for maneuver. He is also likely to increase any money holdings for speculative purposes, if he has added to his total wealth by saving. Similarly, if he was holding cash for precautionary or deflationary motives, the amount he wants to hold is likely to increase when his total wealth is greater.

All of this amounts to saying that the four motives to liquidity apply both to a situation in which a transactor or the community has a *given quantity* of assets that have come down from the past, and also to *additions* to wealth that are made by saving. Liquidity preference applies both to old wealth and to new.

For the most part, our concern in the rest of this book will be limited to the choice of whether to hold old wealth as money or in some other form. In considering this choice, it will be sufficient for most purposes to regard the demand to hold wealth in the form of money as the result of two motives, the transactions motive (which can be looked on as depending directly on the level of money income) and the speculative motive (which depends on expected future changes in the rate of interest). It is not possible, generally speaking, to identify particular parts of a transactor's holdings of money as being due to one motive and other parts as due to another; the position is better regarded as one where total money holdings depend on the combined influence of the two together. For the most part, wealth is held in the form of money for these two reasons and if one becomes stronger while the other remains unchanged, then the amount of money a transactor will want to hold will increase at the expense of wealth held in other forms.

SOME SUGGESTED READING

The reasons for holding money as developed in this chapter are organized in large part along the lines set out by Keynes in Chapters 13-15 of *The*

General Theory of Employment, Interest, and Money (New York, 1936); A. H. Hansen, *Guide to Keynes* (New York, 1953), is a useful aid to understanding this part of the *General Theory*. While the Keynesian formulation was path-breaking in many ways, it also represented an extension of the analysis set out by earlier writers. L. Walras, *Elements of Pure Economics* (1926), translated by W. Jaffe (Homewood, Illinois, 1954), and A. Marshall, *Money, Credit and Commerce* (London, 1923), contain elaborate discussions of the factors that influence the demand for money. Both of these writers attempted to place the demand for money on a footing similar to the demand for other things. Keynes also contributed to what can be called the pre-*General Theory* literature. In his *Tract on Monetary Reform* (New York, 1924) he linked a person's demand for money in real terms to the real value of transactions undertaken, but in his *Treatise on Money* (London, 1930), vol. 1, he began to move closer to the position he took in the *General Theory* by bringing the rate of interest to bear on the analysis of the reasons for holding money.

For the reader who is interested in a survey of the literature on the demand for money, J. C. Gilbert, 'The Demand for Money: The Development of an Economic Concept,' *Journal of Political Economy* (1953) is a useful starting point.

II

THE BASIC THEORY

3

A Description of a Simplified Monetary Economy

To describe fully the important relationships in a complicated monetary and economic system such as that of the United States would be a very difficult, if not an impossible, task. The difficulty arises from the immense number of facts and relationships that would have to be described; the impossibility might derive from our inadequate knowledge of these things. In such circumstances, to attempt to plunge straight into as full a description as is possible would be to ask for disaster. We should find immense complications in trying to give immediate answers to the questions put at the end of the first chapter.

A way in which these difficulties can be avoided is to imagine an economic and monetary system that is much simpler than the real one in which we live, but which approximates to it as nearly as possible. We can then look at the workings of this relatively simple economy; when we have understood them, we can add the complications which bring us to a closer approximation to the actual situation, so that in the end we shall have had, not a complete picture, but at least as complete and as comprehensible a picture of the workings of the monetary system as is possible in a limited space.

This chapter will be concerned with describing the most important features of such a simplified economy, and with giving some justification for the simplifications chosen. Some of our simplifications would be grossly misleading if they were taken to describe the actual features of the U.S. economy, or, for that matter, of any other developed economic system. Their validity is that they help us to isolate relationships that are particularly important in the structure of modern monetary systems, but which need to be simplified in order to be more easily understood. Other of our simplifications are very near approximations to an accurate description of modern eco-

35

nomic systems and we shall not have to modify them substantially later.

The most important of our grosser simplifications concern the kinds of transactor to which we shall pay attention, and the ways in which they receive their income and can hold their wealth. These simplifications will, for the most part, be maintained right through Part II of this book.

We shall consider only three kinds of transactor in our skeleton economy, namely households, firms, and banks. Households include all private individuals, grouped together into family units. Many households consist of only one person; households of more than one person arise where incomes and wealth of the members of the group are pooled and used by the group jointly. For all our purposes, the household will, therefore, be the smallest unit we need consider among private individuals. Firms are manufacturing or commercial units, engaged in buying and selling commodities and services. Banks are the only financial institutions we shall consider, and in this part of the book the role they will play will be very small.

The two largest exclusions from our cast, when we compare it with the real world, are the government and foreigners. Both omissions are highly unrealistic, but we can proceed satisfactorily for a time without introducing them. We are also excluding various other organizations which are important in developed economic systems, for example, public corporations and financial institutions other than banks (such as insurance companies).

Our preliminary simplifications will place some restrictions on the forms in which transactors can hold their wealth. We shall assume that there are only three kinds, namely undated bonds, money, and real wealth (e.g. buildings, materials, machines, land). By restricting the list so drastically, we have only one kind of income-yielding claim in our economy, and so only one rate of interest. We are assuming that there are no shares of stock; that is, no marketable claims to a share in profits.[1]

In addition to this restriction to three kinds of wealth, we shall assume certain limitations about the power or willingness of certain kinds of transactor to hold certain kinds of claim. We shall assume that households can only hold wealth as money and bonds and can-

---

[1] To some extent this is like the position before corporations were introduced; trading companies then frequently financed themselves by issuing bonds.

not hold real wealth, or get into debt (since we assume only firms issue bonds). These limitations [2] can easily be dropped once the main structure of relationships has been established.

Firms in our simplified economy can borrow by issuing bonds which are assumed to be undated and effectively irredeemable. By this assumption we avoid arithmetical complications and also avoid the introduction of several different kinds of bonds; a twenty-year security issued in 1939 is a different thing from a twenty-year security issued in 1949, because one has only two years to run to maturity by 1957, while the security issued in 1949 has twelve years still to run. Equal to the total liabilities of a firm, which are all in the form of bonds it has issued, are its total assets, which we assume may be held either in real wealth or in money, but not as bonds. We also assume that firms do not speculate about the future price of bonds, and so in normal times their only reason for holding money will be the transactions motive.

Finally, brief mention must be made of banks. For the time being we are only concerned with their liabilities, which are employed as money by households and firms. There is no need to concern ourselves with the assets of banks at the moment, since the assumption throughout Part II will be that the banks' position remains unchanged, so that the quantity of money in existence available for use by households and firms does not change, whatever else may happen. For the sake of completeness, however, it may be noted that in our simple economy the assets of banks would be in the form of bonds.

The question to which we can turn next is, how do people receive income? In the first place, in our system incomes are received only by households. They have three ways of making incomes; they can sell the services of their labor to firms, in return for a weekly wage or salary; they can buy bonds with any wealth they possess, and earn interest; finally, they can operate a firm, by acting as a businessman.[3] A businessman, in our economy, operates a firm, which buys and sells goods and services and which finances its holdings of goods and money by issuing bonds. The businessman's income is the profit

---

[2] Which means that households cannot own houses but must rent them from firms, and that purchases of goods by households are always for immediate consumption.

[3] Either alone, or in partnership with other businessmen.

made from the difference between the current expenses of the firm he operates and its current receipts. The current expenses consist of the cost of the goods and services (including wage labor) it buys plus the interest payments on the bonds it has issued, together with any fall in the value of its real assets. Such a fall may occur because the fixed assets (such as machines and buildings) are wearing out and not being maintained, or because the market value of the firm's assets has fallen, or because stocks of raw materials, goods in process, and salable final products have fallen. The receipts consist of the money received from the goods it sells, plus rises in the value of stocks held. The difference between expenditure and receipts is the profit which is made by the entrepreneur, and accrues to him at the end of each week (which we regard as happening on a Friday night) as personal income, in the form of money.[4]

We have now stated the simplifications that will be made in the analysis in Part II that involve a state of affairs substantially different from that in the world as we know it. Our next task is to state the simplifications which probably do not need substantial modification in order to provide as full understanding as is possible of the real world. These concern the reasons for expenditure by households and firms.

Firms spend for two reasons: partly to maintain intact the quantity of assets they are holding, in order to be able to continue the present level of output, and partly to build up their assets to a higher level, in order to increase the level of output (and so eventually of the businessman's profits). The first aim, to maintain assets intact, is a concept which involves difficulties at times when commodity prices are changing; the question then arises whether we are concerned with maintaining the money value of the assets constant, or the actual 'bundle' of real commodities constant in physical terms. In Part II, however, we can avoid this issue by considering only conditions where prices of commodities in terms of money are stable. When we consider inflation, in Part V, we shall have to return to these difficulties. When commodity prices are stable, a firm which is planning to continue running at the same level of output as in the recent past will find it has two things to do. It must maintain and replace things which are wearing out through the ravages

---

[4] If the firm is a partnership the profits are divided between the businessmen concerned, in proportions determined by their partnership agreement.

of time; typical examples are repairs to buildings and replacement of machines. Secondly, it must make purchases to replace those things used up in the process of production; the most obvious examples here are raw material stocks, which have to be maintained if output is to be maintained. All these current expenses are met out of current receipts.

The other reason why firms spend is to raise the level of output. In order to increase output, it will often be necessary to buy more machines and buildings, and nearly always more raw materials will be needed. Additional machines and buildings will not be necessary when output has been running below capacity in the preceding months and years; when this is not the case, money will have to be raised to finance the necessary purchase of the additional machines, etc., and it will always be necessary to finance the purchase of extra raw materials. In our economy, the only way in which firms can do this is by borrowing from households, by making extra bond issues at the current rate of interest. All expansion is thus financed by borrowing by issuing bonds. This is the only way open, because we have excluded other methods of financing (e.g. borrowing from banks, or by short-term bills, or issuing equity shares) and we have assumed an economy where firms do not hold money in excess of the amount they need for transaction purposes; any profits earned are paid over almost immediately to the businessman who is running the firm, for use in his household.

We can now turn to the influences that determine expenditure on goods and services by households. Here the answer which undoubtedly gives most of the truth is quite simple, and at the same time it is of the highest importance in the explanation of the workings of the whole economic system. The modifications that will be needed to move to an explanation of a complicated economy such as the United States' will be quite small. Without question, the overwhelmingly strong factor determining a household's expenditure is its income, either at the moment or in the very recent past. Practically all households will consume more if income rises and less if income falls.

When the level of income is rather low, poverty will be so general that practically every household will spend the whole of its current (or more precisely, very recently acquired) income on buying goods for consumption. A shorthand way of expressing this is to say that the *average propensity to consume* is equal to unity. The average propensity to consume is the ratio between the total expenditure on consumption by a household or a group of households, and the total income of that household or group of households.[5]

Above some minimum level of income a household is likely to decide that it is worth while to put some of its income aside for future use, by adding it to wealth, and to consume only a part of it currently. When income is at or above this level, a household saves; the average propensity to consume is less than unity, and accumulation of wealth takes place. In the simplified economy described earlier, this means that it adds to its holdings of money, or of bonds, or of both.

The other piece of terminology that is relevant in this context is the *marginal propensity to consume*. This measures the proportion of an *additional* unit of income of a household or group of households that it will wish to spend on consumption. Up to a certain level, we have seen, all income is spent on consumption, and none is saved. But when income is higher than this level, part of any further increase in income will not be spent, but will be added to wealth. The marginal propensity to consume is unity up to a certain point, but then falls below unity. The concepts of the average and marginal propensity to consume can be represented by hypothetical figures for an economy, as in Table 1.

This chapter has constructed a simplified economy, with whose aid we shall be able to start our investigations of the most important

TABLE 1

Total household income	Total household consumption expenditure	Average propensity to consume	Marginal propensity to consume
$ thousands	$ thousands		
2000	2000	1.00	1.0
2500	2500	1.00	0.8
3000	2900	0.97	0.8
3500	3300	0.94	0.8
4000	3700	0.925	

[5] Of which the group consisting of all households in the country is particularly important and will be our main concern.

relationships within a monetary economy. We can now proceed to consider the answers to our three main questions asked in Chapter 1 in the context of a plausible, though unrealistically simplified, economy. Our simplifications have been particularly drastic with regard to the ways in which wealth can be held; the reason for this was to ensure that there would only be one rate of interest in the economy, so that the core of the theory of the rate of interest could be laid bare in a plausible and consistent context. Having cleared the way, we can now proceed to a discussion of the factors determining the rate of interest.

4

The Determination of the Rate of Interest

The first part of monetary theory with which it will be convenient to concern ourselves is the theory of the rate of interest. It will not, however, be possible to deal with this problem fully in this chapter, because the rate of interest is so intimately connected with the whole of the rest of economic activity. This means that we shall have to attack this problem in several stages.

Broadly speaking our analysis of interest rate theory involves five stages. We have already seen [1] why borrowers are willing to pay interest: by borrowing they can do things that would otherwise be impossible and that they consider to be worth while. In particular, businessmen can borrow to install new machinery and plant, and so increase the productivity of their firm.

The second stage of our analysis will be the concern of this chapter. We shall be considering, in the context of the simplified economy outlined in the last chapter, what determines the level of interest rates at a particular moment of time, when a given number of bonds and a given amount of money are in existence, and when national income is at a given level.

The third stage will come in Chapter 7, when we shall consider, still in the context of our simplified economy, the interactions between changes in the level of income and the rate of interest. Then in Chapter 8, a closer approach to reality will be made, by allowing for the fact that there will be several different interest rates on different kinds of asset. Finally, in Chapter 17, we shall consider what complications have to be added to our analysis, when we allow for

---

[1] In Chapter 1, p. 7.

the more complicated institutions which exist in reality, particularly the existence of active banking policy.

Despite the complications which make necessary this lengthy series of steps, the basic point about interest rate theory is very simple. It is that the rate of interest on any particular kind of security varies inversely with the price of that security,[2] and that the price of a security, like the price of anything else, depends on demand and supply.

The complications arise because very many forces go to make up demand and supply in the market for securities. Our step-by-step approach gradually introduces more and more of these forces. At the first stage, considered in this chapter, we simply take account of one of the most salient features of the market for securities, which is that they last for a long time (or even indefinitely), so that there is always a large number of old securities in existence which can be bought and sold.

The market for these securities will be in balance only if they are all in the hands of willing holders, and if there are no people who would like to hold more than they have. In this chapter we consider what will be the circumstances in which these conditions are satisfied.

It is clear that they will be satisfied only if each transactor is satisfied with the form in which he is holding his wealth. If, for example, a householder would like to hold more bonds and less money, he will try to buy bonds, which affects their price. The rate of interest is in equilibrium if each transactor is content with the form in which he is holding his wealth.

In the last chapter, when we were describing a rather simple kind of monetary economy, we went to considerable pains to limit the number of kinds of asset we should have to consider. Households hold their accumulated wealth either as money or as bonds. Banks hold part of the stock of bonds; but since in Part II banks are looked upon as being completely inactive, whatever changes may occur in the rest of the economy, the total number of bonds held by the banks is regarded as always being unchanged. Correspondingly, the total quantity of money which consists of debts of the banks is

---

[2] The simplest case being the undated bond considered in Chapter 2.

also unchanged. As for firms, they hold a part of the total stock of money in existence, for transactions purposes. They will, therefore, vary from week to week the amount of money they wish to hold if the level of transactions varies, but not for any other reason. So long as the level of income is constant, the amount of money that firms will choose to hold will not vary from week to week.

The amount of money firms hold will vary during the week, with the ebb and flow of payments and receipts day by day. Total money holdings of firms will be low on the day on which they all pay incomes out to businessmen and to employees. On Friday nights (if Friday is the pay day for all income recipients) firms' total holdings of money will be at low ebb, and then they will recover through the week. This fluctuation within the week need not worry us at all, however, because there corresponds to it an exactly inverse fluctuation in households' total money holdings for transactions purposes. The holdings of households will be at their peak on Friday evening, and run down to a trough at Friday lunchtime. Total transactions holdings of money by households and firms together can reasonably be taken to be constant from hour to hour, so long as the rate of interest and the level of income of the community is constant.

The scene is now set for a preliminary explanation of the rate of interest at any moment of time. Let us look at the situation as it exists at a particular hour on a particular day. A certain number of bonds is in existence, having been issued in the past by firms; all of them, except a fixed quantity in the hands of the banks which we can ignore (since nothing can occur which will alter it) are in the possession of households. At the same time there is a certain amount of money in existence; the quantity is fixed, and is predetermined by action of the banks in the past. A definite quantity of this money is being held by firms and households taken together for transactions motives. The rest of the money in existence is in the hands of households, which are willing to hold it for speculative reasons.

We have seen that the speculative motive for holding money and not holding bonds depends on an expectation that the rate of interest is going to rise in the relatively near future, with the result that losses on the market value of each bond held will wipe out the amount of interest earned. A household which expects the rate of interest to rise appreciably in the near future will hold its accumulated wealth as money. A household which thinks the rate of interest is going to remain practically stationary, or is going to decline, will hold such part of its wealth as remains after the transactions motive for holding money has been satisfied, in the form of bonds; such a household can expect to earn an income in the form of interest which will not be wiped out by capital losses.

The factors which determine expectations that households have about future changes in the rate of interest are numerous and difficult to fathom; but at least one thing is fairly obvious, namely, that the lower the present rate is, the more households are likely to think that it will rise in the future; conversely, the higher the rate is at present, the more households are likely to think that it will fall in the future. If the rate is now 2 per cent, there will be few households who think it will move still further downward; if it is now 8 per cent, there will normally be few who think the next move will be upward.

It follows that we can say two things with some degree of confidence. If the present rate of interest is high, few households expect a further rise in the rate of interest, and many expect a fall; in other words, few expect further falls in bond prices and many expect rises; therefore most householders will be perfectly content to hold their wealth as bonds, and few will want to hold money for speculative reasons. Conversely, if the present rate of interest is low, few households will expect a further fall in rates of interest and many expect a rise; in other words, few expect bond prices to rise still more and many expect them to fall; therefore, many householders will want to hold money for speculative reasons, while few of those who pay attention to these matters will want to hold bonds.

This argument is not disturbed at all by the unquestioned fact that many wealth-holders will pay no attention to such speculative motives and will continue to hold bonds for the sake of the income from the interest, whatever may be happening to the market price. All that is demanded by our analysis is that there should be an appreciable number of wealth-holders who do switch between money and bonds as the rate of interest changes, because of discrepancies between their expectations and the current situation.

To sum up, we can say that there are strong grounds for thinking that the higher the rate of interest the more willing will households as a whole be to hold wealth as bonds, while the lower the rate of interest, the greater will be the tendency to hold money for speculative reasons.

This is reinforced by the other two relationships between interest rates and the demand for money that were distinguished in Chapter 2. One is the fact that the opportunity cost of holding wealth in money rather than in bonds is less when interest rates are low; the other is that when interest rates are low the value of total wealth is higher, so that more money will be held. These relationships are generally considered to be of subsidiary importance [3] and since they always operate merely to reinforce the speculative relationship with which we are mainly concerned, they will not be mentioned explicitly in future, and it will be assumed that the transactions (and precautionary demands) are inelastic to interest rate changes. But it is worth bearing in mind that when we talk of the speculative relationship between the demand for money and interest rates, we should really be talking about all three relationships: the speculative, the opportunity-cost, and the value-of-wealth-held relationships.

Any household which is holding wealth in a form which it considers to be unwise can be expected to set about changing the form in which it is holding its wealth more or less immediately, by buying bonds with money or selling bonds for money. We can reasonably consider that such movements take place with very little delay; it is only a matter of a few minutes to find out what the current rate of interest is and then to buy or sell. We can therefore assume that at the end of each day every household will be holding its wealth in the form which it considers appropriate.

The whole pattern of the argument now falls into place. A given number of bonds and a given amount of money are in existence. Households and firms together need a certain amount of money for transactions purposes; this amount depends on the level of income, so that on any particular day it is already determined by whatever the level of income happens to be. The whole of the existing stock of bonds (except a fixed amount in the hands of the banks) plus all the rest of the money must be held by households; and since each household can change the form of its wealth holdings very rapidly, this money and these bonds must, at the end of the day, be held *willingly* by all households, taken together. But we have already seen that each householder's views about the relative advantages of holding money and bonds depends on speculation about

---

[3] Although this is by no means necessarily true.

the relationship between the present and expected future rates of interest. The higher the rate of interest, the more willing will households be to hold bonds. There will be one rate of interest which will, on any particular day, make households as a group willing to hold precisely the number of bonds and precisely the amount of money that are left over after other demands for money and bonds are satisfied.

As an example, let us assume that all the bonds in existence happen to be a claim to $3.50 per annum for an indefinite period, and are undated, and that there are 2,000,000 such bonds in existence, outside the hands of the banks, on the day we are investigating. We also assume that there is a total of $13,000,000 of money in existence, of which $10,000,000 is needed by firms and households for transactions purposes. Now, if the rate of interest were high, say 4 per cent, relatively few households would be willing to hold money in the belief that the rate of interest was going to rise still higher. Speculative holdings of money might total only $1,000,000 and the total willingness to hold money would be less than the amount in existence. Such a rate of interest would, therefore, be impossible more than very temporarily. If it did exist at the end of the day, some households would be holding more money than they considered desirable; but since they can correct undesired situations very rapidly, they do not accept such a position at the end of the day.

Let us assume that $3\frac{1}{4}$ per cent is the rate of interest at which sufficient households would be of the opinion that a future rise in the rate of interest was quite likely, for total speculative demand for money to equal $3,000,000. At this level of the rate of interest, the total demand for money to hold would just equal the supply in existence; everyone who wanted to hold his wealth as money could do so. At any rate of interest, lower than $3\frac{1}{4}$ per cent, there would be too big a demand to hold money for speculative motives, and once again such interest rates would be impossible.

Alternatively, we can express the same situation by saying that only at a rate of interest of $3\frac{1}{4}$ per cent will precisely that number of households which want to hold their wealth in bonds be able to do so. At a lower rate of interest, there would be some unwilling holders of bonds who would prefer to hold money; at a higher rate there would be some unwilling holders of money who would prefer to hold bonds. But since no household will accept a position it does not want, and since its reaction is very rapid, any position other than our $3\frac{1}{4}$ per cent would not be possible at the end of the day.

We can express the same situation in another way with the aid of a few diagrams; these are shown in Figure 4. In diagrams (A),

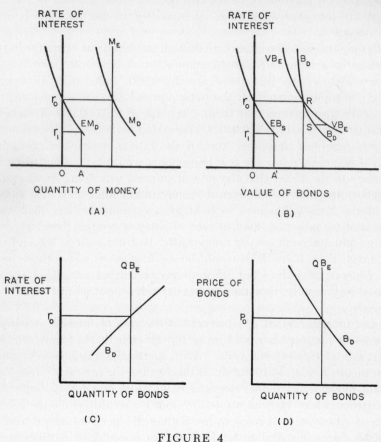

FIGURE 4

(B) and (C) we measure the rate of interest on the vertical axis, and in diagram (D) we measure the price of bonds on the vertical axis. On the horizontal axis we measure in diagram (A) the quantity of money, in (B) the value of bonds, expressed in terms of money and in (C) and (D) the quantity of bonds. We assume throughout that the quantity of bonds and the quantity of money in existence are fixed. (On the other hand, the value of bonds in existence will change inversely with the rate of interest.) In diagram (A) the curve labeled M_D represents the demand for money while the curve M_E represents the unvarying quantity of money in existence. The curve labeled EM_D represents the *excess* demand for money, i.e. it represents the quantity of money demanded that is in excess of the quantity supplied at each rate of interest. At the rate of interest r_0, where the quantity of money demanded is equal to the quantity of money in existence, the excess demand for money is zero. At interest rates higher than r_0, where the quantity demanded is less than the quantity available, the excess demand is negative, or, to put it another way, there is an excess supply of money.

In diagram (B) the curve labeled VB_E represents the value of bonds in existence at each rate of interest. The curve EB_S shows the excess supply of bonds (in value terms) at each rate of interest. This curve is precisely the same as the excess demand for money; the excess supply of bonds must equal the excess demand for money, because the only alternatives open to households are to hold their wealth as money or as bonds. This means that at r_0, where the excess demand for money is zero, the excess supply of bonds must also be zero; and for each rate of interest the excess demand for money is matched by an equivalent excess supply of bonds. At interest rate r_1, for example, the value of the excess supply of bonds, OA', is equal to the excess demand for money, OA in diagram (A).

Now we can proceed to make some use of our apparatus. Since we know the quantity of bonds in existence and therefore the value of bonds at each rate of interest, and since we also know the excess supply of bonds at each rate of interest, we also know the demand curve for bonds. At interest rate r_0 the excess supply of bonds is zero, so the demand for bonds must be equal to value of bonds in existence. From this we know that point R is on the demand-for-bonds schedule. At interest rate r_1 there is an excess supply of bonds so we know that the demand for bonds is *less* than the value of bonds in existence; there is a point S on the demand-for-bonds schedule which is to the left of the VB_E curve by an amount equal to the excess supply of bonds. By repeating this process for each rate of interest we can derive the demand-for-bonds schedule which we have labeled B_D.

This curve is not a conventional demand curve, because neither of the axes of the diagram measures the same variables as in the normal kind of diagram relating (say) the price of sugar to the quantity demanded. Our demand curve may slope downward from left to right (as we have drawn it); alternatively, it may slope upward from left to right; this will happen if the demand for bonds is sufficiently elastic.

The steps to relate our demand curve for bonds to a more conventional one are quite simple. In the first place, we can switch to a measurement of the *quantity* of bonds on the horizontal axis, instead of their money *value*. Now the curve representing the amount of bonds in existence becomes a vertical straight line; we have assumed the number of bonds in existence to be constant. The demand for bonds will be a curve rising from left to right (as in (C) in Figure 4); at interest rates higher than r_0, households demand more bonds than there are in existence; at rates lower than r_0 they demand less bonds than exist.

The other step in moving to a conventional diagram is to measure bond prices on the vertical axis, instead of interest rates. As we have seen, a higher interest rate in itself implies lower bond prices. This means that a line that slopes upward from left to right on a diagram where the vertical axis measures interest rates will slope downward on a diagram where the vertical axis measures bond prices. This can be seen in section (D) of Figure 4, where the demand curve for bonds is of the conventional type, like the demand curve for sugar. The bond price P_0 corresponds to the interest rate r_0.

The important thing about Figure 4 is that all four diagrams represent the same set of facts.[4] In principle, we could work with any of them. In practice, it is usually most convenient to use the first kind (A), where the rate of interest is seen as determined by the demand and supply of money. But anyone who prefers to work with the demand and supply of bonds is perfectly free to do so. He is likely to find his approach seems a little more commonsensical—but is also rather more awkward to handle.

At the heart of this explanation of the level of the rate of interest as we find it at any moment of time is the current state of householders' expectations about the future level of the rate of interest. This may, in itself, seem a little surprising. If so, the realism of the analysis may seem greater if we move for a moment to a considera-

---

[4] For our model where bonds and money are the only choices open.

tion of other markets for durable assets of which a large stock has been handed down to us from the past. An example is the market for pictures; the price of a Cézanne today is strongly influenced by expected future prices of Cézannes. If the owner of a Cézanne thinks that the bottom is going to fall out of the market for Cézannes in a year or two, he may well be tempted to sell at today's price and possibly buy back after the price has fallen. He may not, of course. For one thing, there is a factor which we have not yet allowed for in our discussion of the bond market: expectations are not usually held with complete certainty. A price fall may be expected, but there may be no certainty about its time or extent. Moreover, the owner may get so much pleasure from his Cézanne that he will not sell it, however its price might fluctuate. Nevertheless, there are many people who do speculate in the market for pictures, and that means that the current price of pictures is very strongly influenced by expected future prices of pictures.

Returning to our bond market case and to our simple economy, we must ask ourselves a little more about the factors that influence expectations. We have already suggested that when bond prices are high, more people tend to expect future falls in their prices and less people expect future rises; when bond prices are low, more people expect rises than falls. This argument is not substantially modified if we introduce the influence mentioned in the last paragraph and apply it to our economy; individual households will not generally, and certainly not necessarily, have absolute clear and certain expectations. What is likely is that if bond prices are high (that is, interest rates are low) each household is likely to consider that a rise or constancy in the price is rather improbable and an appreciable fall is rather likely, and therefore to hold a relatively large part of its wealth in the form of money. If bond prices were still higher, each household would be likely to insure even more against the risk of future price falls, as they seem to become more and more likely, and so each household's speculative holdings of money would become still higher. The total effect is the same as in the case we were discussing earlier; households taken as a group tend to hold more of their wealth as money at higher bond prices than at lower; that is, the speculative demand for money is larger at low interest rates.

This is not the full story, however, since the rate of change of interest rates (bond prices) may be, in some cases, more influential than the level of interest rates in the formation of people's expectations about future interest rates. It is conceivable that a rapid decline in interest rates will lead people to expect further changes in the same direction. This tends to make interest rate changes cumulative; falling interest changes may swing people around to the view that future interest rates will be even lower and thus induce a decrease in the demand for money (a shift into bonds), which, of course, does lead to a decline in interest rates, while we can expect, in most situations, that there will be a turn-about in expectations after the movement in one direction has gone on for some time, this type of reaction means that the demand for money is less stable than we have suggested. We have chosen a simple pattern of expectations—that people's reaction to interest rate changes are of the sort that stabilize interest rates—because we find it to be a more manageable way of sorting out some of the more important forces at work in determining interest rates and because we find it not severely inconsonant with reality; the pattern of expectations that we assume is, in effect, the largest single step toward reality that we can take.

A particularly important example of the relationship between the current level of interest rates and the demand for money is the consideration introduced in Chapter 2, when we were discussing the speculative motive for holding money. At very low rates of interest it takes only a relatively small rise in the rate of interest (that is, a relatively small fall in bond prices) to cause capital losses sufficient to wipe out the income that can be earned from holding a bond. This fact reinforces the one upon which we have been laying emphasis in this chapter: that low rates of interest are more likely to be followed by higher than lower ones. A fair description of the situation is that there is some low rate of interest below which all those households which pay any attention to the speculative motive will be quite unwilling permanently to hold bonds; they may be willing to hold bonds for a short time because they may think the rate may temporarily go still lower; but they fear that if they hold bonds for any length of time interest rates will rise substantially and so anyone permanently holding bonds will make bigger capital losses than income receipts from holding bonds. As a result, at interest rates lower than the critical level, these households will want, with the possible exception of very temporary periods, to hold all their wealth as money. At the critical rate, many households are just on the point where they are uncertain about whether to hold some substantial part of their wealth as money or as bonds. Above this rate, although a good number of households will still prefer to hold a large part of their wealth in the form of speculative holdings of money, many households will clearly prefer to hold a large part of their wealth as bonds. We can express this by saying that there is some level of the rate of interest below which liquidity preference becomes absolute; below this critical level of the rate of interest many households would want to hold wealth in liquid form (that is, as money), and relatively few would want to hold bonds. The rate of interest can never get below this critical level, because at rates below that level, an insufficient number of households will be willing to hold bonds. Someone must hold the bonds that are in existence, and at very low rates of interest no one will be willing to hold existing [5] bonds, because of fears that bond prices must fall.

It remains to emphasize that this explanation of the factors determining expectations about the future of the rate of interest is by no means complete. For a complete explanation we must go much farther than simply ask whether the present rate is high or low. For the moment, we can only indicate some of the paths that should be followed. Undoubtedly past experience will be an important guide; it is quite likely that many people's expectations will be based on what they regard as normal. This view of normality may be a very simple one, the expected rate being the average of rates experienced in the relatively recent past. Again, it may be more complicated; for example, if in the past prosperous times have been associated with high rates of interest, then if prosperous times are expected again, high rates of interest may well be expected. If many people expect rather high rates, there will be a strong tendency for high rates to come into existence; for if they are expecting rates higher than those now existing, they will try to hold more money for speculative reasons and to avoid holding the existing stock of bonds. But the existing stock of money and of bonds must be held by willing holders; households become willing to hold the bonds when their

---

[5] It should be clearly noted that we are here considering the holding of existing bonds, and not willingness to take up newly issued bonds. In the whole of this chapter, we are looking at a moment of time when the quantity of bonds in existence is fixed. Circumstances affecting purchase of *new* bonds will be considered in subsequent chapters.

current price falls, that is, the rate of interest rises. Expectations thus create the circumstances that are expected.

This is part of what Keynes meant when he said that the rate of interest is 'a highly psychological phenomenon.' The other thing implied by this statement is the fact that speculation may come to feed on itself. To quote a famous passage from the *General Theory,* the choice of the speculator

> may be likened to those newspaper competitions in which the competitors have to pick out the six prettiest faces from a hundred photographs, the prize being awarded to the competitors whose choice most nearly corresponds to the average preferences of the competitors as a whole; so that each competitor has to pick, not those faces which he himself finds prettiest, but those which he thinks likeliest to catch the fancy of the other competitors, all of whom are looking at the problem from the same point of view. It is not a case of choosing those which, to the best of one's judgment, are really the prettiest, nor even those which average opinion genuinely thinks the prettiest. We have reached the third degree where we devote our intelligences to anticipating what average opinion expects the average opinion to be. And there are some, I believe, who practise the fourth, fifth and higher degrees.[6]

To conclude this chapter, two observations might be made about what has been said so far on the rate of interest. On the one hand, it should now be reasonably apparent why we went to such lengths to see that households could hold only two kinds of asset, and that other transactors (that is, banks and firms) were to keep their holdings of those kinds of asset stable. To have allowed the existence of speculation between more than two assets (for example, money, bonds, and shares) or by more than one kind of transactor would have complicated the explanation very seriously; for example, an expectation of a fall in bond prices might have caused a desire to hold either more money or more shares. We are postponing all such complications until later chapters.

The second observation is that we have been looking at things at one moment of time, when a given number of bonds and a given amount of money are in existence as a result of things that have happened in the past. We have not yet said anything about the process by which wealth is accumulated. That is what we shall be doing in the next two chapters. On the one hand we shall be looking at the factors determining firms' decisions to expand, by buying new

---

[6] J. M. Keynes, *The General Theory of Interest, Employment, and Money,* New York, 1936, p. 156.

machines and other real wealth with money that is obtained by issuing new bonds. On the other hand we shall be looking at the factors determining households' decisions to build up wealth by abstaining from the consumption of all the income they receive, and by using the amount saved either to hold as money or to buy bonds. Among the factors affecting these two kinds of decision, the rate of interest is important. But it is not the most important; therefore in the next two chapters we shall be concerned with conditions where changes in the rate of interest do not enter into our calculations. Then in Chapter 7 we shall come back to the rate of interest, both with regard to its importance in influencing decisions by firms about expansion and by households about saving, and also with regard to the effect of changes in the level of income on the rate of interest.

SOME SUGGESTED READING

The basic outline that we have used in the simplified model of the determination of the rate of interest is quite similar to that which appears in J. M. Keynes, *General Theory of Employment, Interest, and Money* (New York, 1936), Chapters 12-15. These chapters in Keynes merit the attention of the serious student. Those who have difficulties with the *General Theory* can turn to A. H. Hansen, *Guide to Keynes* (New York, 1953), for assistance, although as Hansen has noted in his Preface, his book is meant to be read in conjunction with the *General Theory* and not as a substitute for it.

In this chapter we presented the analysis of the determination of the rate of interest both in terms of money and in terms of bonds. It is difficult to recommend additional readings that are appropriate complements to the treatment that was presented in this chapter, but some may find it useful to read D. Patinkin, *Money, Interest, and Prices* (Evanston, 1956), where the analysis is carried out in terms of both bonds and money.

5

The Determination of the Level of Income

One of the three main questions we asked ourselves in Chapter 1 was, What factors determine the level of income in a country? We must now finish setting the stage on which we shall provide an answer to that question. Most of the matters that are relevant have already been introduced, but they need putting together.

The general principle on which the theory of the determination of the level of income is based is simple. Plans about future economic activity (such as spending, production, and holding of inventories) are made by a large number of different people in the community, acting in isolation from one another, except insofar as they are linked by market forces. There is no reason why these multitudinous and independent plans should be consistent with one another. But if they are not consistent then the inconsistency shows itself up as a failure of some (or all) of these plans to come about precisely as was expected. This failure in turn leads to revision of subsequent plans. The situation must therefore contain the seeds of change unless everyone's plans are consistent. Only when plans are consistent is it possible for the situation to be in equilibrium.

Preliminary Considerations

There are two complications we shall do well to exclude from our analysis for the time being, in addition to those we have already excluded by simplifying the structure of our economy. They concern changes in the price level and changes in the rate of interest. The analysis will be much simpler if we argue in terms of circumstances where neither the price of goods and services nor the prices of

bonds vary. Fortunately, it is easy to imagine plausible circumstances in which both these conditions are satisfied.[1] These arise
when trade is depressed and many men and machines are unemployed. In the first place, for reasons which will become apparent
in Chapter 7, such conditions are frequently associated with low
interest rates; we shall assume a situation in which interest rates
are constant at the lowest possible level.[2]

The second complication we do well to exclude is the possibility
of changes in the prices of newly produced goods and services. A
reasonable explanation of the observed tendency for constancy in
the price of manufactured goods, when the level of output changes
in the range below full employment, can be based on three foundations. The first is the fact that money wage rates do not change
substantially when changes occur in the level of activity below the
level of full employment. This constancy of money wage rates when
there is substantial unemployment is in turn largely a consequence

---

[1] It may be hoped that these conditions, which can reasonably be regarded as
pathological, will not recur; but they have occurred in the past. In any case,
it is useful to approach our theory from this direction, in order to avoid having
to consider everything at once.

[2] If interest rates are at the lowest possible level (i.e., at a level where the
demand for money is infinitely elastic with respect to the rate of interest), many
households are just on the margin of indifference whether to hold a substantial
part of their existing wealth as bonds or money. At slightly lower interest rates
many of them would see a clear advantage in holding money; at slightly higher
rates many of them would see a clear advantage in holding bonds. At this critical rate many of them are indifferent about whether to hold existing wealth in
one form or another. Changes in transaction needs for money can then be coun-
ter-balanced by corresponding changes in speculative demands, without any
change in interest rates. Moreover it seems very likely that the new wealth
that households pile up when they save will have no effect on the rate of interest; this means that we can satisfy the assumptions of this chapter that the
rate of interest is constant, while still allowing fully for the fact that saving is
taking place. The justification for this view is that if households are indifferent
about the form in which they hold *existing* wealth at any moment, it is also very
likely that they will be indifferent about how they will hold any *additions* they
may make to their wealth by saving some of their current income. This is likely
because household savings in any week are small in relation to total wealth of
households, since total wealth is the sum of a very large number of weeks' saving. Therefore, at the critical rate of interest, many households will be indifferent about whether they hold *new* wealth in money or bonds. Thus, by assuming that we are at the critical (lowest possible) level of the rate of interest, we
avoid difficulties arising from the fact that households will be compelled to
choose how they will hold their new wealth, which in turn normally affects
interest rates.

of the attitudes of trade unions and of their quasi-monopolistic power.

The second foundation of this explanation of the constancy of prices is technological. The law of diminishing returns comes to operate to any really noticeable extent in most industries only when full capacity output is almost reached.

These first two foundations together imply that there is a strong tendency for money marginal costs to be practically constant over a wide range of output. Only if the price of some important element in variable cost other than labor should vary substantially is this conclusion upset.

The third foundation of the explanation lies in the actions of businessmen. For one thing it seems to be a reasonable approximation to say that they do not pay very close attention to small variations in marginal costs as output changes. So long as marginal costs are more or less constant they look on average variable costs as an adequate approximation. In the second place their decisions about the prices they will charge are commonly made in terms of a decision to add to average variable cost a percentage gross profit margin that experience has taught them to be appropriate. These margins will vary from industry to industry, and may well vary over time in the case of an individual firm or industry; for our purposes it is sufficient to regard them as constant.[3]

On these three foundations we can easily build an explanation of the constancy of manufactured prices when there is substantial unemployment. As the simplest case (a rather unrealistic one), we can assume that labor is the only element in variable costs in each industry. In this case, the prices of manufacturing output will not vary at all when the level of activity changes below the full employment zone. A change in activity has no effects on money wages, and therefore no appreciable effect on average variable costs. Since percentage gross profit margins are constant, the prices of final output are also constant.

The major modification needed to this theory comes from the fact that primary products are usually needed as raw materials for

---

[3] We can easily express the constancy of selling prices in the face of demand changes in terms of conventional pricing theory by assuming that the demand curve moves in a particular manner. This is that the elasticity of the new demand curve at the old price is the same as the elasticity of the old demand curve.

manufacturing industry. The general tendency in the case of primary production is for there to be considerable price changes when demand varies. In general the result of a low level of demand for primary products is for their prices to be low; the level of output of these commodities usually reacts very little in the short run to changes in the level of demand,[4] For the most part we shall assume in this book that changes in demand for primary products are met solely by price changes, and that their output remains unchanged. In other words, we assume zero elasticity of supply of primary products. This is probably a reasonable assumption, at least for periods of up to a year or two. Of course, if prices remain low for several years together, then output does usually fall substantially; correspondingly if prices of primary products are high, then in time output will rise substantially.

When primary products are part of the raw material of industry, their prices enter into the variable costs of the industries concerned, and variations in primary product prices when the level of activity alters imply variations in variable costs. The consequential changes in the price of manufacturing output will be the larger, the more important primary products are in the variable costs of industry, the larger is the change in primary product prices, and the larger is the percentage gross profit margin that businessmen add to variable costs.

Since we shall be concerned, for the time being, with income determination in industrial economies that have extensive unemployment of men and machines, it will be safe to assume that prices will neither rise nor fall appreciably when the level of output changes to a moderate extent from its previous position. This constancy of prices means that a certain percentage change in money income involves an equal percentage change in real income. Real income represents the power of money income to purchase the things

---

[4] In some cases, especially peasant farming, output may be increased when prices are low, in an attempt to maintain incomes. On the other hand, some kinds of primary production, especially those whose organization is more like that of modern industry (e.g. mining, plantation agriculture) may show considerable reductions of output when prices are low. Such reductions may nevertheless come about very slowly in cases such as tree crops, e.g. coffee, where the product comes many years after the decision is made to plant the tree, and where it is very cheap or physically necessary to collect the crop when it matures. The simple assumptions of the text can also be upset by stabilization schemes, of which more will be said in Chapter 27.

the income receiver wants; it represents the purchasing power of a transactor's income over real goods and services. If, for example, my income in terms of money has risen from $5000 per year before the war to $10,000 a year now, my money income has doubled; but if the prices of the things I buy have also doubled, my real income is unchanged. When the prices of things bought are rising or falling, then changes in real incomes are not the same as changes in money incomes; but when prices are constant, money incomes and real incomes move in step with one another.

We can now start to answer the question which is the concern of this chapter, namely, what are the factors which are most important in determining the level of income?

The total income of our (simplified) economy in any period of time (say, a week or a year) is the total amount received by households for the sale of their labor, plus the amount received by households as interest on bonds, plus the profits received by businessmen. This total is equal to the value of the output of the economy in the same period, if we exclude from output that part of output which is in turn used up in producing other things, and that part of output which is used to restore the condition of machines, buildings, etc., which have deteriorated during the week.

This can be seen if we first look at the incomes produced by the operations of a particular firm in our economy, and then add together the total incomes produced in all firms. Let us take, for example, the case of a baking firm that produces and sells bread. The total income created within that firm consists of the total amount it pays out to households, which is the sum of the amounts paid to labor in wages, to bond-holders in interest, and to the businessman as the residual part of earnings, i.e. profits. This total will be equal to the net output of the firm, that is, the difference between the costs of the raw materials it buys plus the expenses needed to maintain its equipment, and the value of the bread produced.

The same kind of statement can be drawn up for every other firm within the economy. For example, total income created within a flour-milling firm will equal the difference between the costs of wheat, etc., plus the costs of maintaining the plant, and the value of the flour sold.

If we add up the value of the income created in every firm in the country, we find it equals the value of the new goods created during the week in the country as a whole. To this, for completeness, we should add the total value of services sold directly to households, such as those of a domestic servant. In total, we find that the accounts for any period show that in that period the national income (that is, the sum of all household incomes) equals the value of the national output (that is, the sum of all the net outputs of firms, together with the sum of the value of all services sold directly by households to households).

Investment and Saving

We have just seen that if we look at the accounts for any past week, we shall always see that total output is equal to total income. Now, we have already seen that part of households' income is spent on buying goods and services, while part is saved (except when incomes are very low) and is used to increase their holdings of bonds or money. We have also seen that firms may spend in order to increase the real wealth in the firm. In doing this they may increase stocks of materials, work in progress or finished products, or they may install new machines or build new factories. This spending is additional to the amount of spending by firms needed to maintain equipment in good order, and to purchase the labor and replace raw materials used in the course of current production.

Firms, when increasing the amount of real wealth they hold, may spend on two main kinds of purchase. They may spend on purchasing those kinds of real wealth of which the total amount available is fixed and cannot be increased. Alternatively, they may spend on purchasing other kinds of goods (reproducible goods) and on services (with which they can produce reproducible goods). Purchases of land and of second-hand goods which are now no longer made are examples of the first kind of purchase. With the exception of land, practically all purchases by firms come into the second category, and it is with these items that we shall be overwhelmingly concerned.

When a transactor plans to add to his holdings of reproducible real wealth (that is, expenditure falling into the second category), he is said to be planning *investment*.[5] Similarly, when his holdings

---

[5] In national income accounting, net additions of groups of transactors to holdings of irreproducible real wealth are also included as investment. This is done for reasons of statistical convenience; it can rarely be misleading because such transactions must cancel out in the economy as a whole.

of reproducible real wealth have risen, *investment* has taken place.

Three things are worth noting in connection with this terminology. In the first place, it covers only net additions, after allowance for real wealth used up in the process of production or by the effects of age. More accurately, therefore, it can be described as *net* investment. Secondly, it is very important to note that this terminology is different from one that is found in ordinary speech, where 'investment' often includes additional holding of claims (i.e. bonds and shares). For the economist, investment is usually limited to increases in a transactor's holdings of reproducible real wealth.[6] Thirdly, in the simplified economy with which we are at present concerned only firms hold real wealth; consequently, only firms can invest.

Investment can be grouped into two categories; it may be planned or unplanned. A deliberate increase in the quantity of inventories held, and the installation of a new plant, are examples of the former; a rise in the level of inventories resulting from an unexpectedly low level of sales is an example of the latter. (Similarly, there may be unplanned disinvestment if inventories fall because of unexpectedly large sales.)

The other activity with which we shall be closely concerned throughout this study is *saving*. A transactor plans to save when he plans to add to his wealth by putting aside a part of his current income. He is said to save when he actually adds to his wealth. If he saves without having planned to do so, his saving is known as 'unplanned' saving.

Since in our economy all income accrues to households almost immediately after it is earned, only households can save. Moreover, since in our economy households do not accumulate real wealth, all their savings are held as claims (i.e. bonds or money). Both of these characteristics are broad approximations to the real world, which emphasizes the most significant relationships, and which can easily be modified when necessary.

Consumption and saving together account for the whole of income in our simplified economy. It will be remembered that the proportion

---

[6] This rule applies only within a country, and so is perfectly satisfactory in the context of the first five sections of this book. As we shall see in Part VI, the position is different when relations with foreign countries are considered since additions to *claims* against foreigners are classified as investment. Although somewhat illogical, this confusion does not give rise to serious difficulties.

of additional income which households will plan to consume is called the *marginal propensity to consume*. Similarly, we can call the proportion they will wish to save out of additional income the *marginal propensity to save*. In our economy, the sum of these two propensities must be unity, since income must (by definition) be either spent or saved.[7] For example, if the marginal propensity to consume is 0.9, the marginal propensity to save is 0.1. Similarly, the *average* propensity to save is equal to one minus the *average* propensity to consume.[8]

It is now convenient to look in a little more detail at the total accounts for our economy as they are found on Friday night, just after households have been paid their incomes; the accounts describe the total of transactions that have taken place since business started on the previous Saturday morning. The value of the output created in the week will be exactly equal to the total incomes received by households during that week. During the week, households will have saved a certain amount; these savings (or net additional wealth held) consist of two parts. Firstly, there is that part of the incomes received last Friday which households deliberately planned not to spend on goods and services during the week. This part, which is equal to the income received last Friday multiplied by the average propensity to save, will have been used to buy bonds or to increase holdings of cash. Secondly, there is the difference between last week's income and this week's. This element in saving is unplanned, and may be positive or negative. If my income received today differs from that received last week, then, if I am calculating my accounts for the week ending on Friday evening and want to know what the additions are that I have made to my wealth during the week, I should include both the wealth I have deliberately put aside during the week since last Saturday morning, and also the changes in the amount of money in my paycheck compared with last Friday night. For example, I may have received an income of $100 last Friday evening, $80 of which was spent on

---

[7] In economies where there is taxation or foreign trade, this rule no longer applies. On this, see Chapter 16 and Part VI.

[8] It is conceivable for an individual's marginal propensity to consume to be greater than unity; then his marginal propensity to save is negative. This means that a rise in income leads to the whole of the income being spent, *plus* additional spending based on dissaving. Similarly, his average propensity to save may be negative if he spends more than his total income.

consumption during the week and $20 of which was deliberately added to my wealth during the week. If I receive $110 income this Friday, the total additions to my wealth during the week from last Friday night to this Friday night are $30. This consists of $20 planned saving and the $10 increase in my paycheck; the latter is unplanned saving.

The Inevitable Consistency of Realized Saving and Investment

The next thing to notice is that the total of these savings by households in the week ending on Friday night are exactly equal to total investment by firms in the same period. This identity follows necessarily from the way in which we have defined the words saving, investment, and income. In the week a certain output was produced, which gave rise to an income equal in amount. In the first place we can ask, What happens to this income? In the week during which this income was being earned, a certain amount was spent on buying goods for consumption. The difference between this amount spent on consumption and the total income actually earned in the week is saving, as we have defined it above; that is, the amount actually added to households' total wealth during the week. That, then, is one way of looking at the matter—splitting up incomes earned in the week between the amount consumed in the week and the amount saved.

At the same time we can look at the matter from a different direction. We can ask, What happened to the output produced? One part of it was taken up by households during the week for consumption; the rest was added to the real wealth of firms; that is, the rest was invested. Some of the investment might be in increased holdings of buildings and machines; some might be in the form of increased inventories of raw materials, of goods in process, and of finished products; these inventory changes may have been either planned or unplanned.

Since total income in the week equaled total output, and since we find consumption as an item in both ways of splitting up the total, it follows that the other two items are identical in size with one another; that is, saving equals investment. Income that is not spent on goods (i.e. saving) is identical in size with the quantity of goods produced which are not bought with current income (i.e. investment). The proof of this rule, which is fundamental to modern

economic theory and which always applies when we are adding up
the accounts for a past period, can be briefly summed up as follows:

Income	$\equiv$	Consumption plus Saving
Output	$\equiv$	Consumption plus Investment
But Income	$\equiv$	Output
$\therefore$ Investment	$\equiv$	Saving

This rule applies for any period for which we can add up the
accounts. It would be true in our economy, if we looked at another
weekly period, as from a Tuesday to a Tuesday; but the only periods
for which it can be seen conveniently in our economy are periods
of a week, or multiples of a week, ending on a Friday night. Calculation for any other period would be difficult, because we assume
that transactors receive their incomes for weeks ending on a Friday
and do not necessarily know what their income is for a period starting or ending on any other day.

It is possible to see this same identity in another way, in terms of
purchases and sales of new bonds. When a firm is investing voluntarily, by deliberately building new factories or putting in new
machines, or deliberately increasing stocks of raw materials, goods
in process, and finished products, it finances the purchase of the
new real wealth by issuing new bonds. When it finds an involuntary
change in its stocks of finished products, it will find a corresponding
involuntary change in the opposite direction in its holdings of money.
(For example, if it has sold more finished goods in a week than
expected, its stocks of finished goods have declined involuntarily and
its holdings of money have risen correspondingly.) Turning now to
households, all their savings go either into additional holdings of
money, or into additional holdings of bonds. Once again we come
to the conclusion that saving is numerically identical with investment; a demonstration in terms of identities is convenient.

Investment	$\equiv$	Issues of new bonds *minus* firms' increased holding of money (or *plus* firms' decreased holding of money).
Saving	$\equiv$	New bonds taken up *plus* increased households' holdings of money (or *minus* households' decreased holdings of money).
But Increased holdings of money by one group $\equiv$ Decreased holdings of money by the other, since the amount of money is assumed constant.[9]		

Also, all new bonds issued must be taken up by someone.
$\therefore$ Investment $\equiv$ Saving.

---

[9] See Chapter 3.

The Possible Inconsistency of Investment and Saving Plans

This identity between saving and investment is inevitable; but it is to be found only in the accounts for a *past period*. Looking forward, there is no reason at all why they should be equal. *Plans* to save are by no means necessarily consistent with *plans* to invest.

There is no reason at all why plans to save and plans to invest for a future period should be consistent, because the plans are made by different people. In our imaginary economy (and as a general rule in reality) plans to invest are made by businessmen, while plans to save are made by householders. This separation of decisions about saving from decisions about investment is one of the central points upon which monetary theory rests. As a description of modern economic society, it is reasonably accurate. There are some cases where the two decisions come together, and we shall have to look at them later; but for an explanation of mechanisms, we need to emphasize the separation of the two decisions. That is the reason why the simplified economy we are discussing is one where the two decisions are necessarily separated; we have assumed that firms cannot save and households cannot invest.[10]

This possibility of inconsistency between saving plans and investment plans lies at the heart of the explanation of changes in the level of income in a country. When there is inconsistency between the two sets of plans, then one or both sets of plans must fail to be precisely realized, because actual saving must equal actual investment. Such a failure implies the existence of unplanned saving (or dissaving) and/or of unplanned investment (or disinvestment).

Now, when there is unplanned saving or investment (and, of course, their negatives) forces must be at work to change the level of output and income. We can consider them in turn, taking investment first.

Unplanned investment and disinvestment occur when a firm's actual sales of its final products are different from its expected sales; if more goods have been sold than was expected, the firm finds unexpectedly low stocks of finished products on its hands at the

---

[10] We assumed the former by assuming that all profits are distributed at the end of the week, the latter by assuming that households cannot own durable real wealth.

end of the week, and correspondingly it finds unexpectedly large holdings of money. Normally, a firm will react to such changes by changing its output. If sales have proved to be unexpectedly high, then in the absence of any signs of a reversal of the situation, output plans for succeeding periods are likely to be raised. Similarly, if sales have been unexpectedly low, output plans for succeeding periods are likely to be reduced.

At a later stage it will be necessary to look in some detail into the precise characteristics of the reactions of firms to changes in the level of their sales. For the time being it will be convenient to follow the simplest assumption. This is that firms will plan to produce in the next succeeding period a level of output which is equal to the level of sales they have made in the preceding period. (This means that they try to prevent any further changes in their inventories arising from the changes that have already occurred in the level of sales.) On this assumption, unplanned investment or disinvestment is always followed by a change in the level of output and so of income.

We can now turn to the question of why unplanned saving or dissaving leads to changes in the level of output and income. Unplanned saving or dissaving is a reflection of the fact that households do not know precisely what their income is until the end of the week in which it is earned. Households' current plans to save and spend cannot therefore depend on what the current week's income in fact is. What, then, does current expenditure depend upon? We can put two plausible hypotheses forward; for our purpose they come to the same thing. The first is that this week's plans for spending and saving depend upon last week's income. The second is that this week's plans depend upon the level of income that was expected for this week when the plans were made. Now, in some cases, where a change in income is clearly expected at the time when the plans are made, plans based on the second hypothesis will not be the same as those based on the first. But very frequently (and we shall assume always) the expectation will be that this week's income will prove to be the same amount as last week's. In that case, the two hypotheses come to the same thing.[11] We can say,

---

[11] The first hypothesis is closely associated with the name of Sir Dennis Robertson and the second with various Swedish writers. If we follow the Swedish writers and allow that transactors may expect conditions in the next week

therefore, that the existence of unplanned saving or dissaving reflects the fact that actual income was not the same as had been expected. In turn, a failure of actual income to be as it was expected leads to a revision of households' plans for consumption and saving.

Conditions for an Equilibrium Level of Income

We are now getting quite near to an answer to this chapter's question: What determines the level of income? The total income of our community will have no tendency to change from one week to the next, and so can be said to be in equilibrium, if the plans of both households and firms are precisely realized. By precise realization, we mean simply that planned saving equals actual saving and that planned investment equals actual investment. But plans to save and plans to invest for a particular week can be precisely realized only if the two sets of plans were consistent with one another; that is, if total planned saving for the week was equal to total planned investment. This is so, because realized saving must always equal realized investment.

If planned saving for a particular week does not equal realized saving as measured in the accounts at the end of that week, or if planned investment for the week does not equal realized investment, then there are forces at work which will change the level of output and income; the level of income is not in equilibrium. If planned investment is not exactly realized, then firms will change their output plans, and output and income will therefore be different in future periods. If planned saving is not exactly realized, this is an indication that realized income has not turned out to be as was

---

to be *different* from conditions in the preceding week, the analysis becomes rather more realistic but very much more complicated. One reason is easy to see. It is quite possible that there could be consistency of the plans of all the transactors in the economy, without equilibrium in the level of income. At the beginning of this chapter it was said that 'only when plans are consistent is it possible for the situation to be in equilibrium.' But this consistency is only a necessary condition; it is not a sufficient condition under the circumstances discussed by the Swedish writers. For example, if all transactors expect next week's income and output to be 5 per cent higher than this week's, their plans may well be consistent but the economy is not in equilibrium—output and income may well rise as expected. Unfortunately, it is extremely difficult to allow for all the complications that are introduced once we move away from the very simple structure of expectations which is outlined in the text.

expected; as a consequence, household expenditure plans for the next week will be revised, and will be different from those in operation for the week that has just ended. This in turn means that firms will find their sales different from what they had expected, so that they in turn change their output plans.

In either case, therefore, a failure to realize plans leads to changes in the level of output and so of income. The only possible equilibrium level of national income is one where planned savings are equal to planned investment; then only is it possible for both sets of plans to be precisely realized, so that there are no forces working to change the level of income.

We can define this conclusion still more precisely by considering a further point. When the level of output and income is in equilibrium it is reasonable to consider that businessmen have no incentive to add to or reduce their inventories. If a firm's sales are running at a constant level, there will generally be no incentive to reduce or add to inventories, either of raw materials or of finished output. Thus in equilibrium, investment and disinvestment in inventories is zero. This means that the only kind of investment taking place when income is in equilibrium is investment in machines, buildings, etc. (which can be called 'fixed investment' for short).

It follows that, when income is in equilibrium, planned saving must be equal to planned fixed investment. In our simplified economy the only possible equilibrium level of income is one at which this condition is satisfied.

We have already seen that plans for saving depend on the level of income of the preceding week. We can, therefore, define our equilibrium conditions with more precision. If the level of incomes is such that households' plans for saving are just equal to firms' plans for fixed investment, there need be no forces leading to a subsequent change in the level of income; and if the level of income is different from this amount, there must be forces leading to changes in the level of income.

There is, therefore, only one level of income at which equilibrium is possible: that is the level which induces households to plan to make just the right level of savings, so that planned savings equal planned fixed investment. This equilibrium level of income depends on two things: firstly, upon the relationship between income and households' plans to save; secondly, on the level at which firms are planning to make fixed investments. If we assume households' plans

to consume and save happen to be related to income as in Table 1
at the end of Chapter 3, a total income of 3500 leads to total plans
to save of 200. (The figures are expressed in units of money—say
thousands of dollars.) If investment plans by firms are for a steady
weekly rate of investment in buildings, machines, etc. of 200, planned
fixed investment, therefore, equals planned saving when income is
3500. This level of income is the only possible equilibrium. If income
were less than this, say at a level of 3000, plans to save (at 100)
would be less than plans to invest; but since realized saving must
equal realized investment, there would be unplanned saving or
unplanned disinvestment (or both); in less formal terms, households
would find their incomes larger than they had expected and/or firms
would find sales larger than they had expected. In either case there
would be revisions of plans, leading to increases in household expenditure and/or the output of firms; these in turn lead to changes
in the level of national income. Conversely, if income happened to
be more than 3500, forces would again come into operation leading
to a change in the level of income.

The same thing can be seen in another way, by using a simple diagram. In Figure 5 the vertical axis represents total plans for expenditure on the country's current output, either by household consumption or through fixed investment by firms. The horizontal axis represents total national income, which, as we have seen, is equal to total
national output. In equilibrium, the country must be in a situation
where expenditure plans equal total output; otherwise there is unplanned investment or disinvestment in inventories, and producers'
plans are not realized. In equilibrium, therefore, the economy must
be at a point on a line sloping at 45° through the origin; all points
on that line, and no other points, represent positions where planned
expenditure equals actual output.

Expenditure, as we have seen, consists of two parts—consumption
and investment. Consumption plans are determined by the level of
income; all points where consumption plans are consistent with the
current level of income are represented by a line such as CC; at all
other points there is unplanned saving or dissaving. The CC line is
flatter than 45°; a rise in income (a rightward movement) leads
to a rise in plans for consumption expenditure, but by an amount
less than the rise in income. The remainder of income is saved; this
amount is represented by the vertical distance between a point on
the CC line and one on the 45° line vertically above it. For exam-

ple, if income is 3000 and consumption is 2900, saving is 100, as shown in the diagram.

The remainder of expenditure on current output, other than consumption expenditure, is fixed investment. This, we have assumed, does not vary with income and thus can be set at 200. We can

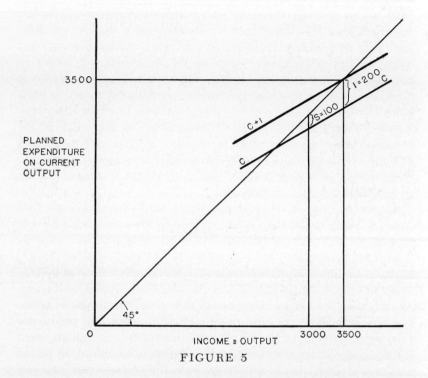

FIGURE 5

represent it in the diagram as a constant (vertical) addition to the CC curve of consumption expenditure, giving a curve representing total expenditure at various levels of income, labeled $C + I$.

The only possible equilibrium position is now apparent. It must be on the 45° line—otherwise there would be unplanned investment or disinvestment. It must also be consistent with the conditions determining consumption and investment plans—in other words it must be on the $C + I$ line. The two lines intersect at one point and that is the only possible equilibrium. At that point, savings plans are equal to the difference between consumption plans and income and so are 200, represented by the vertical difference between the

CC curve and the 45° line; this is the same as the level of fixed investment plans.

Here then is the heart of the answer to the question, What determines the level of income? An equilibrium level of income is possible only if planned saving equals planned investment, because only at this position is it possible for savings plans and investment plans to be precisely realized. The statement that equilibrium demands that savings plans must equal investment plans is therefore a convenient summary. It should be remembered, however, that it is only a shorthand way of expressing the common-sense idea that equilibrium is possible only if the plans of all transactors are precisely realized, so that they are under no pressure to revise their plans in the next period.

Since an equilibrium level of income is possible only where planned saving equals planned investment, it follows that the equilibrium income depends on the relationship between the households' plans to save and their income, and upon the level of fixed investment which firms plan to carry out.

The Multiplier

This set of relationships can usefully be summed up in the theory of the multiplier, which tells us what is the effect of a change in firms' fixed investment plans upon the equilibrium level of income. Again using the hypothetical household expenditure figures given in Chapter 3 (p. 40), where the marginal propensity to save is 0.2 (since the marginal propensity to consume is 0.8), we can ask what is the change in the equilibrium level of income which would follow a change in firms' plans for fixed investment? Suppose, for example, that firms suddenly decide it is not worth their while to carry out more than 100 a week of fixed investment (perhaps because the new technique proves less successful than had been hoped); they carry on maintaining old buildings and machines, and replacing them as they wear out, but they add only 100 per week to their stock of fixed capital. Plans for fixed investment are now 100, instead of the previous rate of 200 per week. Investment plans have fallen by 100. What is the corresponding change in the equilibrium level of income? There can be equilibrium in the level of income only if planned saving is equal to planned fixed investment; that is, if planned saving is 100 per week. Reference to Table 1 shows that at any level of income above 3000, planned saving is more than 100, while at any level of income below 3000 planned saving is less than 100. The only possible equilibrium level of income is now 3000; the equilibrium level of income has fallen by 500, as a consequence of a reduction of 100 in the level of plans for fixed investment.

The first thing to notice is that the equilibrium level of income has fallen by more than the fall in investment plans. This must be so; if income had fallen only 100, then planned saving would have fallen only 20, and so planned saving and investment would not have been equal. The second, and more important, fact to notice is that the fall in the equilibrium level of income is five times the fall in investment, and that five is the inverse of the marginal propensity to save. (The marginal propensity to save is 0.2; $1/0.2 = 5$.) This case is, in fact, an example of an extremely useful general rule. The change (either increase or decrease) in the equilibrium level of income will be a multiple of the change (increase or decrease) in the level of fixed investment; this multiple (the multiplier) is equal to the inverse of the marginal propensity to save.

We can see this more clearly if we now assume a completely different set of household expenditure plans, as given in the following table:

TABLE 2

Total household income	Total household consumption expenditure	Average propensity to consume	Marginal propensity to consume	Marginal propensity to save
$ thousands	$ thousands			
4500	4500	1.00		
5000	5000	1.00	1.00	0.00
5500	5450	0.99	0.90	0.10
6000	5900	0.98	0.90	0.10
6500	6350	0.98	0.90	0.10
7000	6800	0.97	0.90	0.10

Now in these circumstances, if planned fixed investment is 100, the equilibrium level of income is 6000. If planned fixed investment now rises by 100, to 200, the new equilibrium level of income is

7000 (where planned saving = 200 = planned fixed investment). A rise of 100 in investment leads to a tenfold rise in the equilibrium level of income; and ten is the inverse of the marginal propensity to save.

The theory of the multiplier is simply a statement of these relationships. In order to see what will be the effect of a given change in planned investment on the equilibrium level of income, we multiply the change in investment by a 'multiplier' which is equal to the inverse of the marginal propensity to save. The answer tells us the change in the equilibrium level of income.

In summary we can say that the multiplier tells us what change in the level of income will be sufficient to restore a position at which individual transactors' plans are consistent with one another, after a disturbance here taking the form of a change in the level of investment plans. It depends on the fact that plans can be consistent only if plans to use household income for purposes other than the purchase of currently produced goods and services are equal to total plans to use current output of goods and services for purposes other than sales to households; that is, if plans to save equal plans to invest.

SOME SUGGESTED READING

The saving-equals-investment question which we treated in this chapter has an illustrious background. The main discussion began with J. M. Keynes, *General Theory of Employment, Interest, and Money* (New York, 1936), but for the best examples of the discussion in the 'thirties of how saving equals investment, the interested reader should consult the articles by A. P. Lerner and F. A. Lutz in the *Quarterly Journal of Economics* (1938-1939). Lerner's articles were 'Saving Equals Investment' (1938) and 'Saving and Investment: Definitions, Assumptions, Objectives' (1939); Lutz's article was 'The Outcome of the Saving-Investment Discussion' (1938). The first Lerner piece is reprinted in S. E. Harris, *New Economics* (New York, 1947) and the second Lerner piece (1939) and Lutz's piece are reprinted in the American Economic Association, *Readings in Business Cycle Theory* (Philadelphia, 1951).

6

Changes in the Level of Income

In the last chapter we saw that the equilibrium level of income is that at which all plans are realized. The theory we have outlined tells us what is the only level at which income can be permanently maintained—but it is important to note that it tells us nothing about how that level is attained. Nor, for that matter, does it tell us that the level will ever be attained at all.

All that we have done so far is to follow an analysis in terms of comparative statics. The multiplier used in the preceding chapter tells us what will be the difference between the two static positions which are the only possible equilibrium positions before and after some disturbance. This information is important; but it is clear that for many purposes we want to know about the process of movement from one equilibrium to another and (if it be relevant) about the reasons why a new equilibrium may never be attained. This latter part of the problem need not detain us for the moment, but will be relevant in Part V; for the time being we shall follow assumptions that are consistent with the eventual establishment of a new equilibrium.

To solve these dynamic problems of the process of change from one equilibrium to another, more information is necessary than for a solution in terms of comparative statics. We must know, for example, how long are the delays that occur before households or firms react to a failure of their plans to be realized. Since it is possible to make innumerable different assumptions of this kind, there can be an infinite number of different possible paths that can be followed on the way from a given static equilibrium to another equilibrium. Thus, dynamic solutions are, in a sense, more special than comparative static solutions. At the same time they are important, because they give us information about the process of adjustment. After all, the real world is never in an equilibrium position but is always undergoing a process of change; long before a new equilibrium is attained, a new disturbance affects the system and puts it on another path of adjustment.

Among the many kinds of assumption about the dynamic reactions of households and firms to change, we shall find that realism usually involves oscillations in the level of income in the process of adjustment from one equilibrium to another. As a first step, however, it will be easier to trace the changes in income which take place when the approach is smooth, and later to consider the complications that arise from a more realistic situation.

Smooth Approach to New Equilibrium Income

A convenient way of looking at this question is to assume that the economy is at an equilibrium level of income and then to consider the effects of a disturbance which destroys that equilibrium. We can see what process of adjustment follows the disturbance, and what new equilibrium the level of income will eventually reach. Let us consider an economy which is initially in equilibrium—that is, where there is no tendency for the level of output and income to change. In the terminology of the preceding chapter we should find that planned saving = realized saving = realized investment = planned investment. For the sake of arithmetical simplicity, let us assume that saving and investment equal 100, and that the level of income equals 1100. Consumption, therefore, is 1000, and the average propensity to consume is $10/11$.

Let us now imagine that some invention appears which makes it seem profitable for certain businessmen to increase the rate at which their firms are investing, to a weekly rate of 164. A more efficient machine may, for example, produce the same output with less labor; despite the interest charges on the bonds that would have to be issued, the cost reductions might still be sufficient to increase profits. In the succeeding argument, we shall consider what will be the effect on income of such a steady flow of new investment. Without any great loss of realism, we can assume that the firms concerned are versatile enough to produce the new machines with their own raw materials and by direct employment of labor.

We can now trace the chain of events, week by week. We shall not be concerned with the increased share of a given national income that now accrues to the businessmen, or the losses that are suffered by the particular workmen who are displaced by the new machine. Our concern is with the effect on the total incomes of all households together, although the distributive effects are obviously important from other viewpoints.[1]

In the first week in which the new investment is taking place, the total output of the firms concerned is increased. The firm issues new bonds to obtain the money to pay for the new machines; it is also likely to issue some new bonds to obtain some more money to satisfy its additional needs for transactions purposes. These changes will be taking place each week, while investment is under way; we shall, however, not mention them much in this chapter because their effects, if any, will show up in the market for claims by affecting the rate of interest, and we are continuing to assume conditions in which the rate of interest does not change.

Corresponding to the increased output in the week, households will find the incomes received at the end of the week, on Friday evening, larger than those they have been receiving in the past. Households therefore find they have made unplanned savings when they add up their accounts on Friday evenings. In the circumstances we are assuming, planned savings were 100, out of a total income of 1100.[2] Now, however, households find income for this week is larger than that for last week; their expenditure in the week was based on last week's income; the unplanned savings are equal to the difference between the income received last Friday and the income received on this. For example, a household which received, say, $5 last Friday evening and spent it all on consumption goods between last Saturday and this Friday, and then receives, say, $7 this Friday evening, finds that its wealth is unexpectedly $2 greater this Friday evening than last: it has made unplanned savings of $2. For the community as a whole, unplanned savings are 64, which is the difference between last week's income of 1100 and the income actually

---

[1] As we shall see, the consequence of a rise in the level of investment by firms is a rise in the level of output, employment, and income of the community as a whole. It is therefore possible for the men displaced by the machines to be taken into new employment elsewhere: no one need suffer in the process following the rise in the level of investment plans.

[2] Once again, these units can conveniently be regarded as thousands of dollars.

received this week, of 1164.[3] Total savings of the community are, therefore, 164, of which 64 is unplanned and 100 was planned on the basis of last week's income.

During this first week, realized investment is the same as planned investment (i.e. 164). Businessmen who planned to continue output of consumption goods at the old rate would find their final inventories would neither rise nor fall, but would remain at the accustomed level; there is no unplanned investment or disinvestment. There are no unexpected changes in businessmen's inventories because in the first week, since consumption plans, being based on the old level of income, are unchanged.

It will be observed that realized savings for the week equal realized investment (at 164). This identity is inescapable, for reasons already discussed in the preceding chapter.

In the second week during which firms are spending on the new investment, a new kind of disturbance appears. As a consequence of the higher income received on the Friday at the end of the first week, households revise their expenditure plans. They spend part of the increased income on goods, and use part for saving; the proportions put to these two purposes are expressed by the marginal propensities to consume and to save. Now there is no particular reason to expect that firms are prepared for this increased consumption expenditure by households. Although firms started the whole process, by increasing their own spending, it is unlikely that each firm will consider the repercussions of its own spending on itself, since each firm's output is an extremely small part of the output of the whole economy. In the case of most firms, demand for the final product by the firm's own wage earners, etc., is likely to be a very small part of total output; moreover, by no means all firms necessarily participated in the original increase in investment. It is likely, therefore, that firms will not have increased their output of consumer goods, but will have continued to produce the same amount as in the first week after the rise in investment (and all the preceding weeks, before the system was disturbed). The consequence of the increased consumption expenditure by households is that firms find, at the end of the second week, that their inventories of final products are unusually low (while their stocks of money are

---

[3] In units of thousands of dollars, as before.

unusually high). In the terminology used earlier, they find that there has been unplanned disinvestment.

The accounts at the end of the second week, therefore, show realized saving equal to planned saving; there has been no rise in household income for the second week over the first. But the accounts do show a difference between realized investment and planned investment. Total *real* wealth held by firms has not grown as much as was planned, because the unplanned decline in the stock of finished products has offset some of the increased stock of machines.

For the moment, we are assuming somewhat unrealistic reactions by firms to this unexpected fall in their inventories; we wish to describe circumstances in which income moves steadily and smoothly up to the new equilibrium level, and does not oscillate on the way. This smooth movement will occur if firms react by increasing their output to a level that is just equal to the sales made in the preceding week. The limited realism of this assumption is obvious; it means that firms do not attempt to restore unexpected changes in inventories that have taken place, but act only in order to prevent further changes.

The other element of unreality in our argument, which will be retained throughout this chapter and the next, simply in order to make arithmetical explanation of the argument tolerably simple, is the assumption that reactions by households and by firms are simultaneous and take precisely the same length of time to come into effect. In fact, some people will react more slowly than others and, moreover, time is not split into discrete weeks with the sharpness we employ. One consequence of this inevitable rigidity is that we alternate between weeks in which savings plans fail to be precisely realized but in which investment plans are precisely realized, and weeks in which the failure applies to investment plans, while savings plans are realized. In practice, of course, there is overlapping, so that in any week in which there is no equilibrium, both savings and investment plans will usually fail to be realized.

To continue the argument: in the third week firms try to prevent further falls in their inventories and increase the level of their output so that it is equal to the amount of sales made in the second week. This increase in output means, in its turn, that households receive bigger incomes at the end of the third week than they did at the end of the second. This, again, means that household consumption plans for the fourth week rise; as a consequence firms (who had planned output for the fourth week on the expectation that sales would be the same as in the third week) once again find their inventories of finished products unexpectedly low. So the pattern continues; the increased expenditure by firms on machines leads to increased incomes, which lead to increased expenditure by households, which in turn leads to further increases in expenditure by firms in order to build up their output, which in turn leads to still further increases in the incomes of households, and so on.

This sequence of changes does not continue forever, because the adjustments become successively smaller and smaller. Fairly soon, they are so small that they are imperceptible, and for all practical purposes the process of change is over. This level of income at which the adjustments become imperceptibly small is, again for all practical purposes, the equilibrium level of income that we found in the last chapter.

We can follow this sequence of events in more detail if we make an assumption about the numerical value of the marginal propensity to save from any increase of income; it will be convenient to assume that it is 0.5.

As we have seen, households find at the end of the first week that their total income is 1164, compared with 1100 on the preceding Friday. Since expenditure during the week has been based on last week's paychecks, households find that they have made unplanned savings in this first week of 64, and, as we have also seen, total realized saving equals total realized investment, at 164.

Households' plans for the second week are based on the incomes received at the end of the first. Their marginal propensity to save is 0.5; this implies that they plan to save half of the extra income, and spend the other half. In the second week, household consumption, therefore, totals 1132, and planned saving is 132. But firms have developed production plans on the assumption that sales will continue at a level of 1100, as in the first week. Firms therefore find unexpected falls in inventories of finished goods of 32. Planned investment was 164; unplanned disinvestment is 32; realized investment equals realized saving, at 132.

In the third week, firms increase their output of consumption goods by 32, to prevent any further depletion of inventories; this leads to a rise in incomes at the end of the third week by a further 32, to 1196. Households' plans for the third week were based on the second week's income of 1164. Households, therefore, find they have made unplanned savings of 32, as well as the planned savings of 132 that correspond to the expected income of 1164. Firms suffer no unexpected inventory changes, so investment is realized at the planned level of 164. Again, realized saving and investment are equal.

In the fourth week households change their expenditure plans, to put them in line with the third week's income of 1196. Consump-

TABLE 3

(*$ thousands*)

Week	Firms' planned fixed investment	Output of consumer goods (1)	Total output = actual household income (2)	Expected household income (3)	Household consumption	Household planned saving	Household unplanned saving (4)	Firms' unplanned investment (5)	Household realized saving = firms' realized investment (6)
0	100	1000	1100	1100	1000	100	0	0	100
1	164	1000	1164	1100	1000	100	64	0	164
2	164	1000	1164	1164	1032	132	0	−32	132
3	164	1032	1196	1164	1032	132	32	0	164
4	164	1032	1196	1196	1048	148	0	−16	148
5	164	1048	1212	1196	1048	148	16	0	164
6	164	1048	1212	1212	1056	156	0	−8	156
7	164	1056	1220	1212	1056	156	8	0	164
8	164	1056	1220	1220	1060	160	0	−4	160
9	164	1060	1224	1220	1060	160	4	0	164
10	164	1060	1224	1224	1062	162	0	−2	162
11	164	1062	1226	1224	1062	162	2	0	164
12	164	1062	1226	1226	1063	163	0	−1	163
13	164	1063	1227	1226	1063	163	1	0	164
14	164	1063	1227	1227	1063.5	163.5	0	−0.5	163.5

(1) Equals previous week's household consumption.
(2) Equals planned fixed investment plus output of consumer goods.
(3) Equals actual income of previous week.
(4) Equals actual income minus expected income.
(5) Equals output minus (consumption + planned investment).
(6) Equals planned + unplanned saving or planned + unplanned investment.

tion totals 1148, and planned savings are 148. As a consequence of the rise in consumption, firms find unplanned disinvestment in inventories of 16. In the fifth week, they therefore increase output by 16, and this leads to a further 16 of income at the end of the fifth week, to a level of 1212. In the sixth week, this leads to a level of

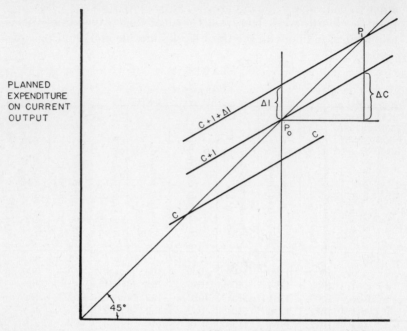

FIGURE 6

consumption expenditure 8 higher than in the preceding two weeks, at 1156; planned saving is now 156. The sequence can be followed further in Table 3.

In thirteen weeks, income has risen by 127. It is obvious, from the trend of the figures, that actual income will eventually reach 1228; income thus rises by 128. This is the result the multiplier theory of Chapter 5 would lead us to expect. The extra investment is 64 and the inverse of the marginal propensity to save is 2; it can, therefore, be expected that the rise in the equilibrium level of income will be 128. The argument summarized in the table shows how the change can take place. Strictly speaking the complete change takes an infinitely long time; [4] but for practical purposes it is over when one is within 1 per cent of the goal, which happens in our example after 13 weeks.

The same sequence can be represented diagrammatically. This can be done on a diagram such as Figure 5 in Chapter 5, but in order to concentrate on the changes that are taking place between

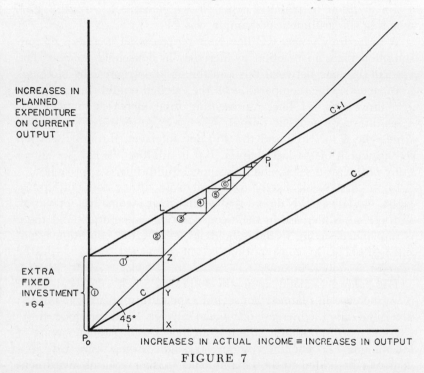

FIGURE 7

the old equilibrium and the new, it is more convenient to use a development of that diagram. In Figure 6, the axes are the same as in Figure 5; P_0 is the original equilibrium as before; then there is a rise in the level of investment plans by ΔI. This induces increased consumption ΔC and the new equilibrium P_1.

In Figure 7 we concentrate on a small part of Figure 6; namely

---

[4] An infinite series of numbers, each of which is a fraction of the preceding one, adds up to a finite total. For the algebra of this, see the Mathematical Appendix, p. 613.

the section north and east of the old equilibrium P_0. The axes now represent additions to planned expenditure and to income and output, compared with the original equilibrium position; the origin of the diagram therefore represents the equilibrium position from which we start, when a disturbance appears in the form of a rise in plans for fixed investment, which is represented on the vertical axis as an addition to planned expenditure on current output ($= \Delta I$, which in the arithmetical example was 64).

We can draw a new CC line, now representing increases in consumption plans in reaction to increases in household income. The vertical distance between this and the 45° line represents increases in planned saving, compared with the original equilibrium. We can also draw a $C + I$ line, representing total increases in plans for expenditure on current output. The new equilibrium position is where the $C + I$ line and the 45° line intersect; this follows from the argument of the last chapter. But in addition we can see something of the process by which this new equilibrium is approached.

In the first week, fixed investment expenditure and output rise by 64; but households do not realize that their income has increased, so there is no increase in their consumption expenditure and there is unplanned saving by households of 64; the CC condition is not satisfied, because consumption is not increased along with the increase in actual income.

This failure is made up in the following week (2) when there is an increase in planned household expenditure of an amount XY, determined by the increase of income in week 1 and the slope of the CC line; correspondingly, there is an increase in planned saving of an amount YZ. The increase in household expenditure can conveniently be added to the (maintained) higher level of investment expenditure as determined by the $C + I$ curve; at the end of period 2 we are at a position L.

This, in turn, is not an equilibrium; planned expenditure on current output is greater than actual output and there is unplanned disinvestment; in terms of the diagram we are not on the 45° line. In week 3 this is put right, by a rise in output which in turn implies unplanned saving; we are not on the $C + I$ curve. This leads to adjustments in week 4 in household expenditure on consumption. And in this way the sequence of events proceeds until the new equilibrium is reached.

* Oscillatory Approach to the New Equilibrium

This explanation of the process by which the actual level of income smoothly approaches the equilibrium level, after there has been a change in the level at which firms plan to invest, suffers from a serious limitation—the rather implausible assumption that has been made about the reaction of firms when sales of their products are unexpectedly high or low. So far, we have been assuming that firms change output until it is equal to the previous week's sales, but that they do not attempt to rebuild inventories to the normal level. In the example in Table 3, this would mean that by the end of the fourteenth week, firms would find that their inventories of finished products had declined by 63.5. Correspondingly, they would find that their stocks of money had risen in the 14 weeks by this same amount.

Obviously, it is very unlikely that firms would permit this to happen. What they are likely to do is to attempt to restore any unplanned changes in inventories that have recently taken place. What we shall assume is that, as well as reacting in the way considered in our first case, firms look back at the end of each four-week period (or month) to see what unexpected inventory changes have taken place in that month and plan to restore stocks to normal at a steady rate during the next month.[5] If, for example, firms' inventories have fallen by a total of 20 in one month, they will plan to make investments in inventories of finished goods of 5 per week in each of the four weeks of the next month.

We can now trace through the sequence of events following a rise in fixed investment, when firms are trying to maintain their inventories of finished goods at a constant level. This is, of course, a much more realistic assumption. Firms hold inventories of mate-

---

[5] We are avoiding the assumption that firms rebuild last *week's* decline in inventories in the succeeding week, because if that assumption is combined with the rigidity of our model, certain additional and violent fluctuations are set up, which have no counterpart in the real world. In the real world, of course, the delays in reaction times of different economic units differ substantially. To allow for this in an arithmetical example is almost impossibly complicated. What we can do is give plausible arithmetical examples which give very much the same solutions as the more complex cases; that is what we are doing here, and that is why we make the assumption that firms plan to rebuild inventories each month and not each week.

rials, goods in process, and finished products for good reasons, and so are likely to want to rebuild them if their levels fall (or reduce them if their levels become excessive).

When we allow for rebuilding of inventories by firms, the process of adjustment to a new level of output is more complicated than the one we have followed in the preceding pages, but the mechanisms are the same, with this one addition of reaction by firms to unplanned disinvestment in inventories.

For the first four weeks, the story is exactly the same as in the example already given; since we started off in equilibrium, there was no unplanned disinvestment or investment in inventories in the month preceding our first month. In the first month under consideration therefore, firms do not plan to add to or reduce inventories. The only planned investment is the 164 per week of fixed investment.

Just as in the earlier example, there is unplanned disinvestment totalling 48 in the first month; firms' inventories of finished goods are 48 below normal at the end of that month. Therefore, in each week of the second month, there is planned investment of 12 in inventories, in addition to the 164 in buildings and machines. In this way, firms hope to restore their inventories by the end of the second month. The effect of this further rise in planned investment is just the same as that of any rise in investment; it causes bigger output than would otherwise have been the case, and therefore bigger incomes, and therefore bigger expenditure by households and so on. These effects are seen in Table 4 in the column representing actual income. In the fifth week, output (= actual income) is 1224, compared with 1212 in the example (Table 3) when firms were not trying to restore inventories. In the sixth week, therefore, households spend 1062, instead of 1056 in the earlier example. This means that by the end of the second month income is 1238; it has considerably overshot the equilibrium level of 1228.

At the beginning of the third month, businessmen look back over the second month and find that their firms have suffered unplanned investment of −21 (or alternatively we can say unplanned disinvestment of 21). They will, therefore, make plans to rebuild these inventories in the third month by a weekly investment in inventories of 5.25. Now the significant fact to note is that the unplanned disinvestment in the second month is less than the unplanned disinvestment in the first, because income has been rising less rapidly in the second month than in the first. This means that planned invest-

TABLE 4

($ thousands)

Month	Week	Firms' planned fixed investment	Firms' planned investment in stocks of consumer goods (1)	Output = actual household income (2)	Expected household income	Household consumption	Household planned saving	Household unplanned saving (3)	Firms' unplanned investment (4)	Household realized saving = Firms' realized investment
0	0	100	0	1000	1100	1000	100	0	0	100
1	1	164	0	1164	1100	1000	100	64	0	164
	2	164	0	1164	1164	1032	132	0	−32	132
	3	164	0	1196	1164	1032	132	32	0	164
	4	164	0	1196	1196	1048	148	0	−16	148
2	5	164	12	1224	1196	1048	148	28	0	176
	6	164	12	1224	1224	1062	162	0	−14	162
	7	164	12	1238	1224	1062	164	14	0	176
	8	164	12	1238	1238	1069	169	0	−7	169
3	9	164	5.25	1238.25	1238	1069	169	0.25	0	169.25
	10	164	5.25	1238.25	1238.25	1069.12	169.13	0	−0.13	169.13
	11	164	5.25	1238.38	1238.25	1069.12	169.13	0.13	0	169.25
	12	164	5.25	1238.38	1238.38	1069.19	169.19	0	−0.06	169.19
4	13	164	0.05	1233.24	1238.38	1069.19	169.19	−5.14	0	164.05
	14	164	0.05	1233.24	1233.24	1066.62	166.62	0	+2.57	166.62
	15	164	0.05	1230.67	1233.24	1066.62	166.62	−2.57	0	164.05
	16	164	0.05	1230.67	1230.67	1065.33	165.34	0	+1.29	165.34
5	17	164	−0.97	1228.36	1230.67	1065.33	165.34	−2.31	0	163.03
	18	164	−0.97	1228.36	1228.36	1064.18	164.18	0	+1.15	164.18
	19	164	−0.97	1227.21	1228.36	1064.18	164.18	−1.15	0	163.03
	20	164	−0.97	1227.21	1227.21	1063.61	163.60	0	+0.57	163.60
6	21	164	−0.43	1227.18	1227.21	1063.61	163.60	−0.03	0	163.57
	22	164	−0.43	1227.18	1227.18	1063.59	163.59	0	+0.02	163.59
	23	164	−0.43	1227.16	1227.18	1063.59	163.59	−0.02	0	163.57
	24	164	−0.43	1227.16	1227.16	1063.58	163.58	0	+0.01	163.58
7	25	164	−0.01	1227.57	1227.16	1063.58	163.58	+0.41	0	163.99

(1) Equals previous months' unplanned disinvestment ÷ 4.

(2) Equals planned fixed investment + output of consumer goods (the latter equals planned investment in stocks of consumer goods plus previous week's household consumption).

(3) Equals actual income minus expected income.

(4) Equals output minus (consumption + planned investment.)

ment in inventories during the third month is less than planned investment in inventories during the second. This in turn means that income rises much more slowly in the third month than it did in the second.

To explain this, let us consider what happens in the ninth week. Expected income, on which household consumption and savings plans are based, is 1238, which is equal to realized income in the eighth week. Actual output and so actual income in the ninth week is not 1238, however; two forces operate on it, one pushing it up and the other pushing it down. Actual output in the ninth week is increased above output in the eighth by 7, because firms sold 7 more to households in the eighth week than in the seventh. (In our terminology, they suffered unplanned disinvestment in the seventh week of 7.) On the other hand, actual output in the ninth week is reduced below that in the eighth, insofar as planned investment in inventories is less in the third month than in the second, because unplanned disinvestment had been less in the second month than in the first. This effect reduces output by 6.75 ($= 12 - 5.25$). The net effect is that output ($=$ actual income) in the ninth week is 1238.25.

This difference between actual income and expected income in the ninth week is therefore very small: it is only 0.25. The revision in household consumption and savings plans in the tenth week is therefore very small. All told, income hardly changes at all in the third month; its total rise is only 0.38. This constancy of the level of income in the third month is only temporary, however. In the fourth month investment in inventories is very small, as there has been very little unplanned fall in inventories in the third month. This has its consequences on the level of income in the fourth month. Output in the thirteenth week is less than that in the twelfth, because of the reduction in the rate at which planned investment in inventories is taking place. This in turn reduces consumption in the fourteenth week. Income falls through the fourth month, and at a reduced rate through the fifth.

The reduced rate of fall in income in the fifth month means that there is a smaller planned reduction in inventories in the sixth month than there was in the fifth. This reduced disinvestment causes a slight rise in income in the seventh month. By the end of that month, the fluctuations have become almost imperceptible, and income has almost settled down at the equilibrium rate of 1228.

We can sum up by saying that when firms attempt to rebuild inventories to the normal level when income is rising from one equilibrium level to another, the temporary re-investment in inventories that takes place makes the level of income shoot past the equilibrium. In turn, when this temporary re-investment in inven-

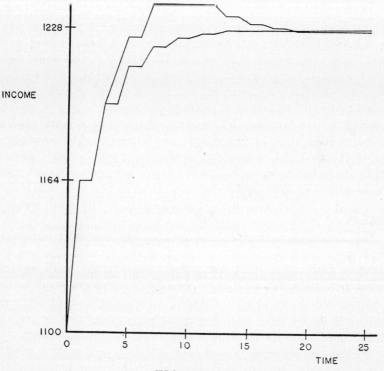

FIGURE 8

tories slows down, the level of income starts to decline, and falls below the equilibrium for a time. This decline causes excessive unplanned accumulation of inventories for a time, and so causes plans to reduce inventories (that is, temporary disinvestment); but these reductions in turn slow down and income starts to rise again. After one or two such fluctuations, the level of income comes very near to the equilibrium. The contrast between this case and the more unrealistic one considered earlier can be seen in Figure 8, representing the development of income over time in the two cases.

When there is a downward shift in the equilibrium level of income, which will happen when fixed investment falls, exactly the opposite occurs; initially the level of income falls below the new equilibrium.

This sequence (technically known as damped oscillations), will always occur when firms plan to rebuild their inventories to a normal level whenever unexpectedly large sales take place, and when they plan to reduce inventories to a normal level whenever sales have been unexpectedly small. It is probably an important cause of the minor fluctuations in the level of activity from year to year or month to month which are commonly observed in practice. These cycles are frequently called 'inventory cycles.'

The sequence of events in these inventory cycles can be summarized by saying there are four stages which are identified by the nature and direction of the predominant inventory changes that are taking place. In the upswing of these short cycles, unplanned declines in inventories predominate; around the height of their boom, planned additions to inventories predominate; in the downturn, unplanned additions to inventories are the biggest element; and in their lowest stages, planned inventory reductions predominate.

A similar sequence, with larger oscillations, is to be found when firms follow what are probably the most common and sensible policies for inventory holding. It is reasonable to assume that most firms hold larger inventories of raw materials, goods in process, and finished goods when the level of output and income is higher than when it is lower. In this case, they have not only to rebuild unplanned reductions in inventories in an expansionary process, but also to build up their desired level of inventories to higher levels. Once again, however, the only possible new equilibrium is the same as in the simplest case; investment in inventories does not affect the equilibrium because no plans for investment or disinvestment in inventories are made in an equilibrium situation.

There are two main conclusions to be derived from the analysis of this chapter. In the first place, when fixed investment changes from one level to another, a chain of events is set into operation which leads the actual level of income to move, over time, toward the new equilibrium. The movement takes time, but fairly soon the actual level of national income will be very close to the new equilibrium. Secondly, whenever reasonably likely assumptions are made about firms' actions, the movement will usually involve fluctuations which temporarily carry the actual level of income beyond the new equilibrium.

* Time Lags in the Process of Income Generation

To conclude this chapter, a little must be said about the corre-spondence between our analysis in terms of time periods and what we know of the real world. Our approach involves several simplifi-cations, which are practically unavoidable and are not excessively misleading. In the first place, the reactions of any one person to a given change will not come sharply, in one step, as we have been assuming. More will be said of this in Chapter 26. Secondly, dif-ferent people (and firms) have different reaction delays. This means that the total reactions to any one change are spread over time, and do not come in one sharp step. This reinforces the point that has just been made, and will also be considered in Chapter 26.

Thirdly, we can now say something more about the average length of the various time lags. In the analysis followed in this chapter, three lags were implicit. The first is the lag between changes in output and changes in income receipts; the second is the lag between changes in income receipts and changes in expenditure; the third is the lag between changes in expenditure and changes in output.[6]

In the sequence followed through in this chapter, the first two of these lags were each equal to about half a week, and together totaled about one week. An increase in output occurring in the week ending Friday leads to an increase in incomes accruing to households on Friday; if the rise in output had occurred at the very beginning of the week, the average delay between the increase in output and the increase in income is half a week. Similarly, if the additional income received on Friday is spent at a steady rate through the following week, the average income-expenditure lag is half a week.

As for the lag between expenditure changes and output changes, this was equal to one week in our model. If household expenditure was running at a higher rate in one week, we assumed that output would be running at a higher rate in the following week.

Such observations of reality as it is possible to make suggest that all these three lags are considerably longer than we have assumed them to be. This means that the changes outlined in the tables would

---

[6] In the more complex (oscillatory) case, we can usefully split this last lag into two parts: the lag between expenditure changes and inventory changes and the lag between inventory changes and output changes.

take longer in practice than the number of 'weeks' in the tables. Moreover, it is probable that the average income-expenditure lag is considerably shorter than the average expenditure-output lag. This might reasonably be expected: it is easier for a household to adjust its expenditure plans at fairly short notice than for a firm to adjust its production plans. It is probably reasonable to regard the income-expenditure lag in the real world as averaging something of the order of a calendar month, and the sales-output lag as being of the order of three to six calendar months.

It is much more difficult to generalize about the output-income lag. To give an average here is probably rather meaningless. The lag for wage-earners is probably quite short—say half a week, since wages are usually paid weekly. On the other hand, profits may be distributed more than a year after they are earned. A full analysis would have to take account of this big difference in lags; in Chapter 9, we shall be able to give it a little more consideration.

In fact, there is a limit to the value of paying attention to the differences between the various time lags involved in the process of income generation. To do so complicates the arithmetic and gives much the same kinds of solution as in the examples followed through in this chapter. The most important point to remember in the switch from our simplified analysis to thought about reality is that our analysis compressed time substantially and that our 'weeks' should be regarded as being considerably longer than a calendar week. In practice, the sequence of Table 3 would probably take a little less than two years to work to a point fairly near to equilibrium, while the sequence in Table 4 should be regarded as covering two to four years.

SOME SUGGESTED READING

The dynamic approach to the problem of the determination of an equilibrium level of income has received a great deal of attention in the literature. A good example of the Swedish approach to this problem is B. Ohlin, 'Some Notes on the Stockholm Theory of Saving and Investment,' *Economic Journal* (1937), reprinted in the American Economic Association, *Readings in Business Cycle Theory* (Philadelphia, 1951). The Robertsonian formulation, which often has been compared with the Swedish approach, appeared in D. H. Robertson's article 'Saving and Hoarding,' *Economic Journal* (1933) and in his review of Keynes' *General Theory* in the *Quarterly Journal of Economics* (1936). The former is reprinted in his *Essays in Monetary Theory* (London, 1940).

Lags in the adjustment process have been explored by E. Lundberg in his *Studies in the Theory of Economic Expansion* (London, 1937) and by L. Metzler in two articles, 'Three Lags in the Circular Flow of Income' in *Income, Employment, and Public Policy,* essays in honor of Alvin H. Hansen, edited by L. A. Metzler (New York, 1948) and 'Nature and Stability of Inventory Cycles,' *Review of Economic Statistics* (1941).

The multiplier analysis has been carefully examined by R. Turvey in 'Some Notes on the Multiplier Theory,' *American Economic Review* (1953), where he develops a less aggregative approach and notes that in addition to distinguishing between firms and households in treating the saving-investment question, it can also be helpful to distinguish between the markets for factors and the markets for goods.

7

Interactions of the Rate of Interest
and the Level of Income

In the last three chapters we have been able to isolate consideration of changes in the rate of interest from consideration of changes in the level of income. We must now pay attention to the facts that, normally, both the rate of interest and the level of income will move simultaneously and that each of them, when it moves, usually affects the other. The theories of the determination of the level of income and of the rate of interest become so much the more complex. The only equilibrium situation which can exist is one which satisfies both the condition that planned saving equals planned investment (as in Chapters 5 and 6) and also the condition that each transactor is holding his assets in the form which most suits him (in particular this concerns the choice of households between bonds and money outlined in Chapter 4).

In other respects, the assumptions of our analysis continue to be rather restrictive. We are continuing to limit our households to holding bonds and money, our firms to holding real wealth and money, and our banks are still inactive, so that the quantity of money is constant. All extra claims which are held must, therefore, be in the form of bonds.

Another point is relevant here. It is probably realistic to assume that the amount of wealth which a person desires to hold as cash increases when his total wealth increases as a result of saving on his part. To combine this assumption with the one that the quantity of money is constant would, however, lead us into profitless complications.[1] By being somewhat unrealistic and assuming no changes

---

[1] When saving is taking place, total wealth of households is increasing. If

in desire to hold money when saving leads to increases in total wealth while nothing else changes, we can postpone these complications until we can deal with them more realistically. We shall do this when active operations by banks (and so changes in the quantity of money) have been brought into consideration.

In order to take account of the interactions which usually occur between changes in the level of activity and income on the one hand, and changes in the rate of interest on the other, we must pay attention to two very important relationships, which so far we have been able to ignore. These relationships are the effects of changes in the rate of interest on investment plans and on savings plans.

Effects of Interest Rate Changes on Saving and Investment

In the first place, we can consider the effects of a change in the rate of interest on savings plans. It should be noted clearly that what we are doing here is considering the influence of the rate of interest upon households' plans *to add to* total wealth, by refraining from consuming the whole of their income. This is a decision which is distinct from the one we were considering in Chapter 4, where we were concerned with the effect of the current rate of interest (together with its relationship to expected future rates) on the form in which households wish *to hold* their wealth; that decision was concerned primarily with existing holdings of wealth, which are the products of past decisions to save.

As far as decisions to save are concerned, we can distinguish two kinds of household which will be affected by changes in the rate of interest in diametrically opposite ways. One kind of household tends to save more of a given income when the rate of interest is high than when it is low; the other kind tends to save less. The

---

total demand to hold money rises as wealth rises, and if the quantity of money in the country is unchanged, this extra demand must be satisfied by reduced demand in some other direction; this can be brought about by reduced speculative holdings of money, through the agency of rising interest rates. Positive saving in a community where the desire to hold cash increases when total wealth increases therefore leads to persistently rising interest rates, if the supply of money is constant. It is our assumption of constant money supplies that leads to this solution, which is rather unrealistic, although in certain circumstances, which will be looked into later (in Chapter 17), these results may be significant. For the time being we will avoid the situation as best we can by assuming that the desire to hold money does not increase when wealth increases.

households which plan to save more out of a given income at a higher rate of interest are those who see that they can get a larger income in the future in return for a given amount of abstention from consumption now, and which will be attracted by that larger future income into making larger abstentions now. If the rate of interest is 5 per cent I can make $5 a year by abstaining from consuming $100; if it is only 2½ per cent the same amount of abstention will give me only $2.50 a year. It is clearly plausible that a household which would only save, say, one-tenth of its income at the lower rate of interest might save, say, one-eighth at the higher rate. This is the reaction which seems most likely at first sight, and it probably predominates in most economies.

The reverse reaction is also perfectly plausible, however. If a household is saving to provide a given income in the future (perhaps to provide an income on retirement) it will be necessary to save less per year when the rate of interest is high than when it is low. In spite of this possibility, it is probable that the first kind of influence on saving usually predominates, and that the total plans to save out of a given national income are rather larger at higher rates of interest, and smaller at lower rates. At the same time, it is more probable that the influence of changes in the rate of interest on plans to save is much less important than that of changes in the level of income. A relatively small change in the level of income can easily have a very large proportional effect on the amount saved; in Table 1, for example, a rise in national income by one-sixth, from 3000 to 3500, led to a doubling of plans to save, from 100 to 200. A very large change in the rate of interest would be needed to produce the same effect on plans to save out of a given income; in fact, it is quite possible that no change in the rate of interest that would be likely to occur in practice could have such a large effect.

Turning now to the effect of the rate of interest on the plans of firms to invest, we must distinguish two kinds of investment, as we did in Chapter 5. These are investment in reproducible *fixed wealth*, such as buildings and machines, and investment in *inventories* of raw materials, goods in process, and finished products.

Plans by firms to invest in fixed wealth are based upon the businessman's expectations that he will be able to increase the productivity of his plant, and so increase his profits. It may be, for example, that he sees a prospective increase in demand for the goods he is selling. Again, it may be that he sees opportunities for new investment arising from the appearance of new productive techniques. Moreover, even when the state of trade in a particular line of business is constant, and even though no new techniques or inventions may be appearing, it is still possible for a change in the rate of interest to influence firms' plans to invest in machinery and buildings. For example, there may already be in existence some technique which is just not profitable enough to introduce when the rate of interest is 5 per cent. Businessmen think that the returns that would be brought in if the new machinery were installed would not be quite sufficient to cover the interest on the bonds they must issue to buy the machines. If the rate of interest now falls to 4 per cent, this means that the annual amount the firm has to pay in interest to people who buy new bonds from it is so much less. If the machine costs $2000, a firm would have had to pay annual interest charges of $100 when the rate of interest was 5 per cent. When the rate of interest falls to 4 per cent, the annual interest charges fall to $80. Businessmen who were unwilling to install the new equipment at the higher rate of interest might well think it worth while at the lower rate.

There are, however, severe limitations to the significance of this analysis. What businessmen must take into account, when they are making decisions about fixed investment, is the total annual charge they will find themselves committed to if they carry out the investment. The annual interest charge is only part of this total; the other part is the cost of maintaining the machine (or building) and replacing it when it is worn out, or of repaying the debt as the machine wears out. If this second part of the total annual capital charge were not allowed for, a continuing debt, with no corresponding real wealth behind it, would eventually result.

When capital equipment is relatively short-lived, these charges needed to maintain capital intact are very large in relation to interest charges. Variations in interest rates then have relatively small effects on total capital charges. For example, if a machine costing $2000 must be replaced in five years, the average annual charges for maintaining the capital intact are $400. If the rate of interest is 5 per cent, the annual interest charges on the bond raised to purchase the machine in the first place are $100. Total annual capital charges are, therefore, $500. With a rate of interest of 4 per cent, the annual interest charges are $80; since the annual charges for maintaining the capital interest are unchanged at $400, total capital charges are now $480 per annum. A decline in the interest rate by one-fifth leads to a decline of only one-twenty-fifth in the level of annual capital charges.

Because of the uncertainties of technical change and of future business conditions, accountants usually recommend that firms assume that new machinery will be worthless within five or ten years. This is done even though the potential physical life of the machine may be much longer; it is a convention which has the support of the income tax authorities, who consider such a rate of amortization charges an allowable expense, necessary for the running of the business. In the case of a very large amount of fixed investment, quite large changes in the rate of interest may make relatively little difference to the level of annual capital charges. There is strong reason to suppose, therefore, that the level of the rate of interest has less influence upon firms' investment plans than might be expected at first sight. In practice, the major determinants of changes in investment plans are to be found on the side of demand rather than of costs; they will be discussed at length in Chapter 23.

In a large group of cases, however, there can be little doubt that the rate of interest has a big influence on plans for fixed investment. These are the cases of investment in such things as buildings, with a long economic life. A house costing $20,000 to build can probably be maintained at an annual charge of $500. The interest on $20,000 at 5 per cent amounts to $1000 a year; therefore, total capital charges at 5 per cent will be $1500. In this case, a fall in the rate of interest to 4 per cent will lower total capital charges to $1300; this is, relatively speaking, a very substantial drop. There can, therefore, be little doubt that interest rate changes have significant influence on plans to invest in long-lived fixed capital.

The other kind of investment we distinguished was investment in inventories of materials. Here, as with the case of short-lived fixed capital, it is rather doubtful whether changes in the rate of interest have very much effect on firms' plans to hold inventories. The convenient level of inventories is strongly influenced by the level of output and sales, and is unlikely to be appreciably influenced by relatively small changes in the costs of carrying inventories. The changes in carrying costs that will result from normal changes in the rate of interest will usually be relatively small, because interest charges are only a relatively minor part of total costs of carrying inventories: the major part usually consists of warehousing costs, insurance, and allowance for deterioration and for risks of loss of value.

The influence of the rate of interest on investment may be summarized by saying that, in all cases, there is some tendency for a higher rate of interest to be associated with smaller plans to invest.

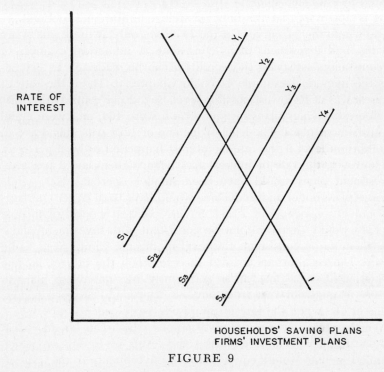

RATE OF
INTEREST

HOUSEHOLDS' SAVING PLANS
FIRMS' INVESTMENT PLANS

FIGURE 9

Only in the case of relatively long-lived fixed capital will changes in the rate of interest show this effect at all strongly. Investment in short-lived equipment will be influenced relatively little by interest changes, and we can safely assume that investment in inventories is also influenced very little by normal changes in interest rates.

The relationship between savings and investment plans and the rate of interest can easily be represented diagrammatically. In Figure 9, savings and investment plans are measured along the horizontal axis and the rate of interest is measured vertically. As the rate of interest falls, investment plans rise, as shown by the *II* line. On the other hand, if the rate of interest falls, we can assume the plans for savings which households will make out of any given income will fall somewhat. For example, out of a fairly small income (Y_1), savings plans at different levels of the interest rate might be those represented by the S_1Y_1 curve; at a rather higher level of income (Y_2) savings plans at different interest rates might be those represented by S_2Y_2; and so on.

It is apparent that the only possible equilibrium situations are those where the SY curves cut the II curve; only at those points are savings and investment plans consistent. A numerical example of circumstances satisfying this condition can be made up, by extending the numerical example given in Chapter 6. There the rate of interest was at its lowest possible level—say, 2 per cent. At that rate of interest, savings plans in equilibrium were 164, and were equal to investment plans. The level of income of 1228 was, therefore, an equilibrium level if the rate of interest happened to be 2 per cent. If, however, the rate of interest had been higher, say, 3 per cent, investment plans would have been smaller (perhaps 160) while savings plans out of a given income would have been larger (perhaps 166 out of an income of 1228). Saving plans at a level of income of 1228 would, therefore, not be consistent with investment plans. For them to be consistent, the level of income would need to be lower. The equilibrium level of income when the rate of income is 3 per cent would need to be sufficiently low for savings plans to be 160. It might be that an income of 1214 would produce savings plans of 160 when the rate of interest is 3 per cent.

We therefore get a series of situations which can be set out in tabular form. The table expresses the levels of income at which planned saving would equal planned investment, if the rate of interest were at various conceivable levels.

TABLE 5

Income	Rate of interest per cent
1228	2
1214	3
1200	4
1186	5

Alternatively we can represent these possible equilibrium positions graphically, on a diagram (Figure 10) where the horizontal axis represents current income and the vertical axis the rate of interest. The *IS* curve on this diagram represents all the pairs of situations in Figure 9 where interest rates and income levels are such that savings and investment plans are consistent.

Interactions of Income Changes and Interest Rate Changes When Interest Rate Changes Do Not Affect Savings or Investment Plans

Although interest rate changes usually have some effects on saving and investment plans, it is quite possible for small changes in interest rates to have no appreciable effects at all. As a starting point in our analysis of the interactions of changes in the rate of interest and the level of income, it will be convenient to assume that the interest rate changes of the magnitude with which we are concerned have no effect on saving or investment plans. (In Figure 9, the *II* curve and the *SY* curves would all be vertical and only one level of income would be consistent with equality between investment and savings plans, whatever the rate of interest might be. Correspondingly, the *IS* curve in Figure 10 would be a vertical line.)

In that case, if we return to the situation discussed in the last two chapters, where there is an autonomous rise in the level of investment, the final equilibrium position must be one at which the level of income and of interest rates are both higher than before the change. In the final equilibrium, savings plans must equal investment plans, and households must be willing to hold their wealth in the form of existing claims, which implies that they must be willing to hold precisely the amount of money left over after satisfying the transactions demand of firms. For equilibrium, both of these conditions must be satisfied.

As far as the equality of saving plans with investment plans is concerned, there is nothing in this situation to alter the solution reached in Chapter 5, since neither is influenced by interest changes, which are the new element in the situation. The new level of income will be higher than the old by the amount of autonomous rise in the investment, multiplied by our familiar multiplier. (In terms of the diagrams, the *II* curve moves rightward and now coincides with a new and higher *SY* curve; the *IS* curve moves rightward correspondingly.)

As far as the asset-holding equilibrium is concerned, the final position must be one with a higher rate of interest. There is additional demand for transactions holdings of money by both firms and households (because of the high level of income and activity). At the same time the quantity of money is unchanged; all the additional claims that have been created have been bonds. This demand for additional transactions holdings of money is satisfied from reduced

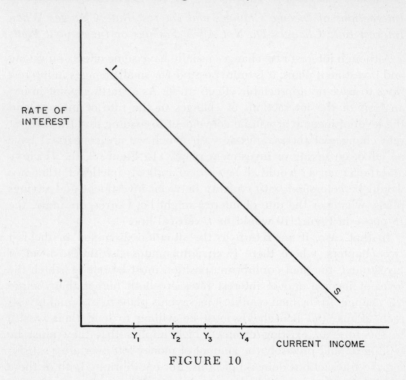

FIGURE 10

speculative holdings, which are made possible by a higher level of the rate of interest. On our assumptions of a constant quantity of money, therefore, a higher level of income implies a higher level of interest rates.

The various possible positions that could satisfy the asset-holding equilibrium can easily be represented diagrammatically. In Figure 11, the vertical axis again represents the rate of interest and the horizontal axis now represents the quantity of money. The vertical MM curve represents the (unchanging) quantity of money in existence; the family of LY curves represent the amount of money transactors will want to hold at various interest rates and various levels of income. As interest rates fall, speculative demand to hold cash rises; as the level of income rises, transactions needs rise.

The only possible conditions satisfying the asset-holding equilibrium are those where the *MM* curve cuts the *LY* curves.

Various conceivable situations, in all of which transactors would

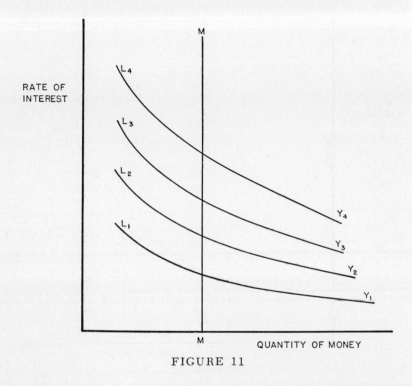

FIGURE 11

be content with the form of their asset holdings, can be set out in tabular form:

TABLE 6

Income	Rate of interest per cent
1125	2½
1150	3
1175	3½
1200	4
1225	4½

In each of these conceivable situations, we can imagine that the rate of interest is such as to absorb into speculative holdings precisely the amount of money that is left over after satisfying transactions needs. These situations can be set out diagrammatically as in Figure 12. The *LM* curve represents all the possible positions of equilibrium in the asset markets in terms of various possible income and interest

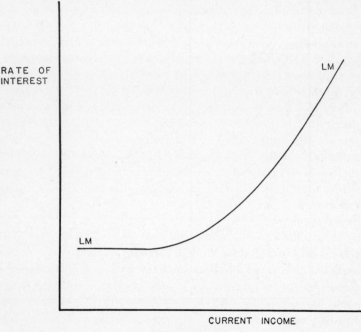

FIGURE 12

rate levels. It can be seen that, as incomes rise, so must the level of interest rates—the conclusion we have already reached verbally.

The process by which the movement takes place from the initial position to the final equilibrium is quite simple. Three influences all operate in the same direction upon interest rates (causing them to rise if investment plans and realized income rise, and to fall if investment plans and realized income fall). Two of them are temporary and last only while the process of adjustment is taking place; the third is permanent in its effects.

As soon as there is a rise in the rate at which investment plans are being carried out, there is a rise in the rate of interest, because the firms which are making the additional investments issue more securities, while households have no immediate reason to increase their plans to save and so to buy securities. The extra holdings of securities are only taken up by households if their prices fall; if that happens some households are willing to make the necessary switch from money to securities. This effect depends on a discrepancy between planned investment and planned saving, since it assumes that firms are issuing more securities to finance the investment while households have not come to realize that their incomes have risen and so do not plan increases in savings and hence in their holdings of securities. The effect therefore persists only while the discrepancy between planned investment and planned saving persists.

The second effect is a logical extension of the first [2] but precedes it in time. If a firm is planning to increase its level of investment, it is likely to take steps to increase its money holdings, in order to prepare for the higher level of transactions, even before the plans are actually brought into operation. It can obtain this money by issuing bonds to households, who exchange some money for bonds if interest rates rise a little. This 'finance-induced' rise in interest rates occurs a little before the firm actually starts spending on additional investment.

The third effect is the permanent one. When transactors (both households and firms) come to find that they are carrying out more transactions, as a result of the higher level of incomes induced by the initial rise in investment, they will want to hold more money than they were holding originally. These extra transactions needs are satisfied by a permanent reduction in households' speculative holdings below the original level, which is brought about by a rise in the level of interest rates.

If the initiating disturbance is a decline in saving arising from a decline in thriftiness, the effects are similar, except that there is no correlate for the 'finance-induced' rise in interest rates. In the first place, the fall in savings implies a fall in plans to purchase bonds, which is not offset by corresponding plans to issue less securities; equilibrium in the security market comes about by a rise in interest

---

[2] Both arise from the sale of bonds by firms before households increase their saving plans; in the first case, because households have not had time to realize that their incomes have risen, and in this case because households' incomes have, in fact, not yet risen.

rates. This effect lasts while saving plans and investment plans are inconsistent. In the second place, there is the permanent effect arising from the increased transactions needs for money accompanying the rising level of income which is induced, through the multiplier process, by the decline in thriftiness.

It is rather likely that another influence would reinforce those we have been considering. If past experience has been that high levels of income are usually associated with high rates of interest (as will be the case if the mechanisms we are considering have been in operation) then when households see incomes rising, most of them are likely to expect that interest rates will rise in the near future. Most households will therefore have strong fears of falls in bond prices; this will lead to a definite tendency to shift into holding money, for speculative reasons, which reinforces the rise in the rate of interest.

Interactions of Income Changes and Interest Rate Changes When Interest Rate Changes Do Affect Savings and Investment Plans

The argument of the preceding section of this chapter assumed that investment and saving plans were not significantly influenced by interest rate changes. More normally, however, there are such influences; both sets of plans are influenced by interest rate changes. When this happens the equilibrium level of income that follows a disturbance (such as a rise in investment plans resulting from the invention of a new machine) will not be the same as when there are no such influences. Moreover, the existence of such influences affects the path followed by the level of income and of interest rates in the movement from the original situation to the new equilibrium. As we have already seen, the path followed by the level of income depends upon differences which occur each week between planned saving and realized saving, and between planned investment and realized investment. Clearly, if plans to save and to invest are changing under the influence of current changes in the rate of interest, the path that will be followed by the actual level of income, as it moves from week to week, will not be the same as that which would have been followed if the rate of interest had been constant.

What we have now is a two-way relationship between income changes and interest rate changes. As was seen in the preceding section, income changes affect the interest rate, through the effects of changing transactions demand to hold money. Now we also see that interest rate changes affect the level of income, through influencing plans of firms to invest and of households to save.

This is the first of many cases where we shall find it necessary to consider a closed loop of influences—cases where a change in A affects B and a change in B affects A. Consideration of the existence of such 'feedback' is rather complicated, but it is inevitable: nearly all the important relationships in practical problems in the sphere of monetary economics are linked up in this sort of way (and frequently in longer and more complicated sets of loops).

Fortunately, even though the relationships are complicated, it is easy to determine the equilibrium situation, by answering three questions in turn: firstly, what situations are consistent with the condition that planned savings must equal planned investment; secondly, what situations are consistent with the condition that each transactor must be content with the form of his asset holdings; thirdly, what situation is common to both these preceding sets, and so satisfies all necessary conditions? We have considered each of these sets of conditions individually, and it is easy to fit them together.

A possible set of situations satisfying the first condition have been set out in Table 5 and in Figure 10. Similarly, a possible set of figures satisfying the second condition have been set out in Table 6 and Figure 12.

The third step is now simple. Table 5 shows conditions satisfying the asset-holding condition and Table 6 shows those satisfying the consistency of savings and investment plans condition. Our equilibrium must satisfy both these conditions; there is only one situation common to both tables, and there could be only one, however detailed they were and however far extended. This is the situation where income is 1200 and the interest rate is 4 per cent.

The same kind of solution can be expressed diagrammatically by putting Figures 10 and 12 together. This is done in Figure 13; the point where the IS and the LM curves cut is the only possible point of equilibrium.

A comparison of this solution with that in Chapter 6, where interest rate changes did not occur, is instructive. The rise in the level of income from the original position is smaller than that in the simple multiplier case; in Chapter 6 a rise in the level of investment plans by 64 led to a rise in the level of income by 128 (from 1100 to 1228); in this example, the same initiating rise in the level of investment plans led to a rise in the level of income by 100. This smaller rise is the consequence of the damping effect [3] of the rise in interest rates, caused by increased transactions demand for money and operating through the level of plans to save and to invest.

The more responsive savings plans and investment plans are to

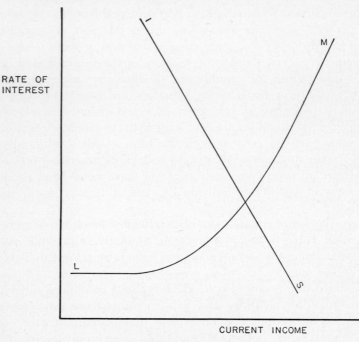

RATE OF
INTEREST

CURRENT INCOME

FIGURE 13

changes in the rate of interest, the less will be the rise in the level of income arising in the multiplier process following a rise in the level of investment plans. This can easily be seen if we change the information in Table 5 to that in Table 7.

This table once again represents the levels of income at which planned saving would equal planned investment, at different possible rates of interest. It assumes that a small rise in interest rates

---

[3] In the terminology of radio engineers, which is rapidly becoming acquired by other disciplines as far apart as physiology and economics, 'negative feedback.'

TABLE 7

Income	Rate of interest per cent
1228	2
1189	$2\frac{1}{2}$
1150	3
1111	$3\frac{1}{2}$

substantially increases planned saving out of a given income and/or substantially reduces investment plans.

If Table 6, which describes the various situations in which transactors will be content with their asset holdings, still applies, the only possible equilibrium is one with an income of 1150 and an interest rate of 3 per cent.

At the extreme is the position where the level of income is unchanged after a change in the level of investment or savings plans, and where the new equilibrium involves a change only in the level of interest rates. As this extreme is approached, the more responsive savings and investment plans are to changes in the rate of interest (the IS curve representing the consistency of savings and investment plans becomes more and more horizontal) and the less willing people are to change the form in which they hold their wealth when interest rates change (the LM curve representing the asset-holding condition becomes more and more vertical). If people are completely unwilling to change the form in which they hold their assets, whatever change occurs in the rate of interest, then there can be no change in the amount of transactions balances which are available—still assuming, of course, that the quantity of money is constant. This means that the level of income must be at the original level in the new equilibrium (because at any other level the need for transactions balances would be unequal to the amount available); this equilibrium is brought about by sufficiently large changes in interest rates to bring about consistency between savings and investment plans without there being any need for changes in the level of income. In our diagram, the LM curve representing the asset-holding condition becomes vertical and no change in the level of income is possible in equilibrium.

This possibility is at the other extreme from the case considered in Chapters 5 and 6, where conditions in the asset market were such that interest rates were unchanged, so that the whole adjustment took place through income changes, in the multiplier process. This can be represented diagrammatically by a horizontal *LM* curve representing the asset-holding condition. In practice an adjustment usually involves changes both in interest rates and in the level of income—hence our need to discuss both interest rate theory and multiplier theory.

Consideration of the process by which equilibrium is reached in the normal, mixed, case need not detain us for long. It involves the superimposition of changes in plans to save and to invest arising from interest rate changes upon the sequence already discussed earlier in this chapter. The main new point of interest is that these changes may very probably take some considerable time to come into effect. In particular it is likely that it is a long time before changes in the rate of interest has any considerable effects on actual purchases of buildings, plant, and machinery by firms. Projects that are already under way when interest rates change will usually not be altered; the changes in the interest rate influence views on projects some months or even years distant in the future. This long time lag may be a further reason why the movement toward the new equilibrium involves fluctuations. The other reactions we have considered may occur so fast, relative to this effect of interest rates on investment, that the level of income is well on its way to the equilibrium that would be established if investment plans were not reduced by the rise in interest rates, before the effects of the rise in interest rates start to show themselves in reduced investment plans. When these effects do finally show, it may transpire that the level of income has overshot the mark.

The same sort of analysis as that followed in this chapter applies when other changes initiate a process of adjustment to a new equilibrium. If there is an initiating fall in investment plans (due, perhaps, to a failure of new inventions to appear), the consequence will be the reverse of that already followed, namely, a tendency for both income and interest rates to decline. Similarly, if there is some rise in thriftiness—if for some reason people plan to save a bigger proportion of their incomes at given interest rates—the consequences will be the same as a fall in investment plans. Both the level of income and of interest rates will tend to fall. Again, a decline in thriftiness tends to cause rising interest rates and income levels.

The upshot of the argument of this chapter is the importance of the two-way linkage that exists between the level of income and the level of interest rates. Normally anything that changes one of this pair also affects the other, and this in turn reacts back on the first. It was only by considering rather special conditions that it was possible in Chapters 4-6 to isolate factors affecting one from the factors affecting the other.

Some Suggested Reading

The classic works on the mutual determination of the level of income and the rate of interest are J. R. Hicks, 'Mr. Keynes and the "Classics": A Suggested Interpretation,' *Econometrica* (1937) and O. Lange, 'The Rate of Interest and the Optimum Propensity to Consume,' *Economica* (1938). Hicks' piece is reprinted in the American Economic Association, *Readings in the Theory of Income Distribution* (Philadelphia, 1946), and Lange's piece is reprinted in the Association's *Readings in Business Cycle Theory* (Philadelphia, 1951). A detailed examination of the Keynesian monetary theory which is in many ways similar to the Hicks and Lange formulations but carries the analysis beyond the point to which it is taken by the earlier writers, is F. Modigliani, 'Liquidity Preference and the Theory of Interest and Money,' *Econometrica* (1944), reprinted in the American Economic Association, *Readings in Monetary Theory* (New York and Philadelphia, 1951).

Other versions of this type of analysis that can be useful to students are in L. Klein, *The Keynesian Revolution* (New York, 1947), and in A. H. Hansen, *Monetary Theory and Fiscal Policy* (New York, 1949).

8

Interest Rates on Long-Term and Short-Term Securities

We can now start to move nearer to reality by abandoning one by one the limitations that we imposed upon the characteristics of our economy in order to make the framework of the problem clear and manageable. In this chapter we shall start to allow for the existence of many different kinds of claim by considering what happens when firms issue short-term securities as well as long.

Once we consider the consequences of the existence of several different kinds of claim our analysis becomes more complicated. We can no longer talk of 'the' rate of interest. There are as many different rates of interest as there are kinds of security.

Moreover, we now have to recognize more kinds of difference between individual claims than when we were solely concerned with the differences between irredeemable bonds and money. In the discussion of the rate of interest in Chapter 4, in terms of liquidity preference, we were concerned with the effects of expected future changes in the rate of interest on the capital value of wealth held. The important new consideration that enters when short-term claims exist is the possibility of changes in the amount of money income received as interest. When wealth is held as an irredeemable bond, the annual income received by its owner is fixed in terms of money. That, at least, is certain. If, however, a wealth-owner holds his wealth in bills, which are repaid (say) every six months, and if he buys new bills to replace the old ones as they are repaid, his income will vary substantially if the rate of interest on bills changes. He may make a loan of $100 by buying a bill at a price involving an interest rate of 5 per cent; this gives him an income in six months of $2.50. When at the end of the six months this bill is repaid, and he immediately proceeds to lend again, he may find the rate of interest on six-month bills is now only 2 per cent; in the second half-year his income is then only $1. His income is subject to big variations as the rate of interest alters; on the other hand, the money value of his wealth is practically assured, since he never has to wait more than six months before being repaid in full by the debtor. Bills are safe in respect of capital value, but the income they provide is risky; whereas irredeemable bonds are certain in respect of income, but their capital value is risky.

For the sake of arithmetical simplicity it will be convenient to continue to assume that one method of borrowing is by an irredeemable bond, while the short-term claim we are introducing is a bill with one year to run from the time it is issued to maturity.

Basically, the forces that operate when more than one kind of interest-bearing claim exist are just the same as when there are only irredeemable bonds and money. Wealth-holders will switch between different sorts of asset if they consider that their future prospects in terms of income and of capital losses or gains will be improved by switching. As wealth-holders try to switch there will be increased pressure of demand on the asset toward which they are switching and decreased demand for the asset from which they are moving. This will affect asset prices, and so will affect prospective returns. The movement will continue up to the point where all wealth-holders are just satisfied with their position. (All this assumes that switching does not cost anything; in practice, of course, there will be some costs involved, which will limit the adjustment when the benefits are small in relation to these costs.)

To this possibility of switching by wealth-holders, which was the operative force in our earlier consideration of a single rate of interest, must be added the possibility of switching by debtors, which did not enter in that case because there was only one kind of debt that could be issued by institutions other than banks—namely, irredeemable bonds. Now, however, firms may switch between issuing bonds and bills, in accordance with the relative advantages of the two ways of borrowing. If other things are equal, they will if possible switch to borrowing in whatever form they expect to be cheaper over the period for which they want to borrow.

The rates of interest on bonds and bills (that is, the long and the short rate of interest) must be consistent with one another, in the sense that there is no pressure upon wealth-holders or upon debtors to switch from one form of wealth or one form of debt to another. This consistency rule implies that, generally speaking, the two rates will move sympathetically with one another. For example, if there is a rise in the level of income, so that long rates tend to rise, for reasons already followed through in Chapter 8, the short rate will usually also rise. If the short rate did not rise in these circumstances, both borrowers and lenders would be tempted to switch between the two markets. Some borrowers who had previously been borrowing at long term would now be tempted to borrow at short term, because of the lower rates; on the other hand, wealth-holders (lenders) would switch the other way; they would wait for their bills to mature and then use the cash they received to buy bonds for the sake of the higher income which could now be earned for each $100 of cash used for buying bonds. There would, therefore, be a particularly large number of new bills coming on to the market, and relatively few buyers; the effect would be a fall in the price of bills—in other words, a rise in the short-term rate of interest. Again, if there is a shift in the views of wealth-holders or of debtors about the relative advantages of short- and long-term securities, there will usually be opposing movements in the two interest rates. Thus, if some debtors come to think that at the existing relationship between long- and short-term interest rates short-term debt is now more advantageous than long-term debt, the tendency would be for more short-term debt and less long-term debt to be issued. But since there is assumed to be no corresponding change in the views of wealth-holders, this will mean that an excess supply of short-term securities appears, and an excess demand for long-term securities. This is met by the normal operation of market forces—long-term interest rates fall relative to short-term rates.

Usually these reactions are very rapid, so that both the long and the short markets usually move simultaneously; operators are prepared for the pressures that would arise if rates did not immediately shift sympathetically and so they speculate on their expectations of such a shift.

Although influences which cause one rate of interest to rise (or fall) are likely to cause a simultaneous movement in the other rate, the magnitude of the change is not the same in the two cases. There is a marked tendency most of the time for the short-term interest rate to be much more volatile than the long-term rate. The reason is that changes in the levels of interest rates are not usually regarded as indicating that the whole future pattern of interest rates is going to alter by the same amount. If, for example, an alteration in circumstances causes upward pressure on the general level of interest rates, what will be the effect on expected future levels of interest rates? Very frequently, at least, there will be no effect at all on expectations about the rates that will be in force a year or more ahead. Sometimes the change will be regarded as being a step on to a new level, which will be the normal level in future; but very frequently the change will be regarded as a relatively minor fluctuation which does not affect the general pattern of expectations of future levels.

For example, we can consider circumstances when forces operate to cause a temporary rise in interest rates; this rise is expected to last for one year only, and then conditions are expected to return to normal. We can imagine that both long- and short-term interest rates were at 3 per cent before the rise, and that the current expectation is that they will both return to that level in about a year's time. Before the change, irredeemable bonds which happen to have been originally issued at 3 per cent sell for $100, similar bonds which were originally issued at 6 per cent sell for $200, and so on. During the coming year, however, rates are expected to be above that level. Let us suppose that conditions are such that short rates rise to 5 per cent. Wealth-owners will be tempted to switch to holding 5 per cent bills during the coming year, while borrowers will tend to switch to borrowing by bonds, unless the long-term rate of interest alters sufficiently to prevent such shifts from being profitable. If the short rate is 5 per cent and the long rate is 3 per cent, a wealth-holder will be tempted to sell any bonds he now owns, buy bills, hold these for the year until their maturity and earn 5 per cent interest on them, and then use the money he receives on maturity of the bills to buy bonds again. If he expects the normal level of the long rate to be 3 per cent, he will expect to be able to buy back 3 per cent bonds at a price of $100. In that case, if he originally owns one 3 per cent bond, worth $100, he hopes to make $5 income in the year (by holding bills) and to maintain his wealth intact; at the end of the year he buys back just what he had before, namely, one 3 per cent bond worth $100. By such a switch he hopes to make $2 more in the year than if he had stayed in bonds all the time and simply earned $3 interest on that bond.

In reality, as we have seen, pressure to sell bonds by wealth-holders at the beginning of the year will depress their prices. If the price of a 3 per cent bond is pushed down to $98, it is no longer worth while for wealth-owners to switch in the manner described in the last paragraph. By the end of the year, the price of the bond can be expected to be back to $100 (because 3 per cent is the expected level of interest rates in the future). Anyone who switches when the price of bonds is down to $98 will find he loses $2 in capital value over the year; to restore his original position he has to make up these $2 from income. In such circumstances, the extra income earned by switching into bills for a year is canceled out by capital losses. At a price of $98, switching by wealth-owners is just not worth while. Such a fall in bond prices implies a rise in interest rates; if a bond which earns $3 in a year can be bought for $98, the interest rate is

$$\frac{100}{98} \times 3 \text{ per cent} = 3.02 \text{ per cent}$$

At this rate, borrowers will also show no tendency to switch from borrowing short to borrowing long; if they do switch, they save this year but have to pay more in every succeeding year; their alternatives are paying 5 per cent for one year and 3 per cent each year indefinitely thereafter, or paying 3.02 per cent indefinitely from the present time. The equilibrium rise in the long-term rate of interest is much less than the rise in the short-term rate, because the influence of the long future life of a bond, in which its price is expected to be at a level which is not appreciably changed by temporary fluctuations, is so very strong.

If, on the other hand, the market thinks that the factors leading to a rise in interest rates are likely to be permanent, then long rates will alter as much as short. If, for example, the market changes its expectations and considers that the rate of interest to be expected as a normal level for an indefinite time to come will be at a higher level than has been expected in the past, bond prices will adjust themselves to this new level of expectations, and the long rate will move as much as the short. In fact it is possible for long rates to rise by amounts appreciably greater than short rates, if a generally rising trend in all rates of interest comes to be expected. The current level of the long rate takes account of all changes in the factors determining interest rates that are expected in the future, while the short rate only takes account of the near future.

So far we have seen that short-term rates of interest tend to fluctuate much more than long-term rates. The other important question is that of the determination of the average level of short rates and the average level of long. Will these levels, over a period of time, tend to be about the same, or will one rate tend consistently to be higher than the other? Experience shows that in some periods and places the average level of short and long rates tends to be about the same; this was the case in Britain during much of the nine-teenth century. At other times and in other places the long rate runs at an average level which is appreciably higher, and it is only quite occasionally and temporarily that short-term interest rates exceed long-term. This is a description of the situation that has ruled with few exceptions in the United States since World War I.

When the majority of both borrowers and lenders are practically indifferent between borrowing or lending short or long if the costs in or the returns from the two markets are identical, then the average level of the two rates over a long period of time will be more or less the same. Whenever borrowing by one method appears likely to be cheaper, for the period for which the loan is being made, bor-rowers will switch to using that method; lenders, on the other hand, will switch to the opposite method. Forces then operate which will tend to bring the two rates back into equality. Temporarily they can diverge markedly, because the long rate takes account of the changes expected in the rate over a long future period of time, while the short rate does not. Over a long period of time, however, the two rates average the same level, because if they did not most lenders would try to go into the more profitable market, and most borrowers would try to go into the cheaper.

There is, however, no reason to suppose that the majority of bor-rowers and of lenders will be indifferent between the two markets when returns or costs in the two markets are identical. In the first place there are the considerations mentioned earlier in this chapter, that short lending tends to involve risks about incomes, while long lending tends to involve risks about the value of wealth owned. Some lenders will be more perturbed by uncertainty about incomes, and others by uncertainty about capital values, when other things (including average income earned and average capital value owned) are equal. If one type of lender predominates, there is a particular pressure to hold wealth of one particular type. It seems likely that there is a tendency for very many lenders to be particularly con-cerned with certainty in the value of their wealth, even at the cost of some uncertainty about their income. They are, therefore, willing to accept a lower average annual income if they are guaranteed certainty about the value of their wealth, which they enjoy when they lend short. Another factor working from the lending side is that many loans are made for purposes such as the installation of fixed equipment, where the borrower cannot give suitable security to a short-period lender. A short lender likes to lend on the security either of an unquestioned name or of a readily salable asset: many borrowers can offer neither.

Like lenders, borrowers also tend to have preferences. They are frequently committing themselves to operations which will take many years to carry through fully (e.g. installing new plant). In making their plans, it may well be convenient for them to know what their annual interest charges will be.

The upshot of these preferences of lenders and borrowers is that there usually tend to be more potential short-term lenders than borrowers, and more potential long-term borrowers than lenders, when the general levels of long- and short-term interest rates are the same. As a consequence the average level of long rates tends to be rather higher than the average level of short rates; this difference brings about balance in both markets.

These conclusions are modified by the existence of financial inter-mediaries such as savings and loan associations, mutual savings banks, life insurance companies, and commercial banks, which borrow short and lend long. It will be one of our main concerns in Part III of this book to consider the work of these intermediaries, notably of the banks.

But, although this work of the financial intermediaries is very im-portant, the costs and risks of these activities, of which we shall see more later, mean that the average levels of the two rates are not brought together. The preponderance of borrowers with a prefer-ence for long-term borrowing and of lenders with a preference for short-term lending is not by any means fully offset, and short-term rates are consequently more usually than not below long-term rates.

The same sorts of consideration apply when we add to the pic-ture by considering a spectrum of interest rates for loans of every possible length of time to maturity. Medium-term loans usually earn higher interest rates than short, and lower rates than long: circum-stances can arise when the position is reversed, however; for exam-ple, if the present conditions are a boom which is expected to last two or three more years, so that interest rates for two or three years are expected generally to be higher than corresponding rates at later dates, a medium-term loan for, say, three years will be at higher rates than a long loan for, say, twenty years. The longer loan takes account of some seventeen years in which rates in general are expected to be relatively low compared with present levels, and therefore the rate offered on it does not rise to such high levels as the three-year loan, which will have been repaid before the general structure of rates falls.

Some Suggested Reading

The literature on the structure of interest rates is not very large, with much work remaining to be done in this area. The difficulty is that most of the work on the interest rate question has been carried out in terms of a *single* rate of interest; the bias has been to treat the question of the structure of interest rates as a subsidiary problem which can be safely ignored. This leaves an awkward gap between macro-economic theory and banking theory since the latter is essentially concerned with the structure of assets and their yield.

There are some works in this area, however, that can be very useful to interested readers. F. A. Lutz, 'The Structure of Interest Rates,' *Quarterly Journal of Economics* (1940-1941), reprinted in the American Economic Association, *Readings in the Theory of Income Distribution* (Philadelphia, 1946), is a careful and highly detailed analysis of the factors that influence the structure of interest rates. In a similar vein is F. R. Macauley, *Some Theoretical Problems Suggested by the Movement of Interest Rates, Bond Yields and Stock Prices in the United States since 1856* (New York, 1938). J. R. Hicks' treatment of the connection between short- and long-term rates of interest in *Value and Capital*, 2nd ed. (Oxford, 1946) has been disputed as a theory that explains interest rates, but it does offer some insights as to the relations between the short and the long rates.

III

THE PRESENT-DAY INSTITUTIONAL

FRAMEWORK

9

The Finance of Modern Business

In Part II of this book we were considering an economy whose description had deliberately been simplified, in order to show up more clearly the basic structure of the workings of the economic system. In Part III we shall move much nearer to reality by considering the activities of other economic agents, in particular the financial intermediaries (of which the banks are the most important) and the government. In addition, we shall move nearer to reality by imposing less rigorous restrictions on the actions of the various kinds of transactor, and by introducing a greater degree of realism into our description of the various kinds of asset that can be held.

In this chapter our discussion of the finance of modern business will be made more realistic. In Chapter 3 it was assumed that firms financed themselves solely by issuing bonds, which offered a fixed annual income. As a stage in our argument this device was useful; nevertheless it is an inadequate description of the methods by which modern business is financed, and our concern now is to give a more accurate description.

The introduction of short-term loans in the last chapter involved one step nearer to reality. In practice an appreciable part of the financing of modern business is done by various kinds of short-term borrowing. The major source of short-term loans for industry and commerce as a whole is the commercial banking system, in the form of bank loans. In addition, individual industrial and commercial firms commonly receive short-term loans from other firms. For example, trade debts are not generally settled immediately, and direct loans may be made from one company to another. Finally, the government usually acts as a source of a kind of short-term

123

loan, because taxes on firms are usually assessed and collected some time after the earning of the profit in respect of which they are paid.

Non-Bank Financial Intermediaries

A second step toward reality is to consider the impact of the non-bank financial intermediaries that were mentioned in the last chapter.

The most important of these non-bank financial intermediaries—life insurance companies, mutual savings banks, and savings and loan associations—account for roughly one-third of the assets held by the private financial intermediaries.[1] Of these intermediaries, the life insurance companies are the most important. The funds that flow into them come largely from the premiums received by the insurance of lives and from the sale of annuities. These funds are used, in the main, to purchase securities (both government and private) and real estate mortgages. Savings and loan associations, next in importance and a sector that has grown rapidly in recent times, obtain funds from the public in two ways. They accept deposits that are quite similar to the time deposits of commercial banks, but, more important, they sell shares in the associations to the public; the purchasers of association shares usually pay for these by making periodic payments to the associations. The prime (almost exclusive) investment activity of the savings and loan associations is the purchase of real estate mortgages. Mutual savings banks, the smallest of the non-bank financial intermediaries that we are considering here, obtain funds from the public through the acceptance of time deposits. These funds are invested largely in real estate mortgages and to a lesser degree in gilt-edge securities.

Unlike the commercial banks, these institutions do not play a direct role in determining the quantity of money available to the community: their debts, unlike those of banks, are not acceptable as money. But they do influence the availability of credit and the course, structure, and level of interest rates and in that way influence the community's expenditure stream. These financial intermediaries issue their own liabilities for funds, which in turn they lend to business firms or households through instruments such as bonds or mortgages. Their effect is to enrich the variety of claims available to

---

[1] See R. W. Goldsmith, *Financial Intermediaries in the American Economy Since 1900,* Princeton University Press, 1958, pp. 73-6.

lenders and the forms in which credit is available to borrowers. Through their borrowing of funds from a large number of lenders and through their purchases of a wide variety of debt claims they provide some protection against risk. These institutions also serve to increase liquidity; the holder of claims of these financial institutions finds it a great deal easier to convert his claim into money than the holder of claims against small and comparatively unknown business firms and households. (And in those cases where the liabilities of the financial intermediaries possess a high degree of liquidity, they serve as substitutes, albeit imperfect substitutes, for holdings of money, thus affecting the demand for money.)

Business Risk

The failure to consider the various kinds of short-term finance and the role of the financial intermediaries was not the main shortcoming in the analysis of Part II, insofar as it concerns the finance of modern business. The major omission in Part II was the failure to consider business risk. Most commercial operations involve considerable risks of various kinds; for example, a process may not be successful, unforeseen events may occur, or sales may not be as good as had been expected. These risks may mean that earnings are not as large as had been hoped, or even that the firm is unable to cover its costs and has to close down.

If the firm has obtained all its finance by issuing bonds, it finds itself in considerable difficulties if any of these risks are realized, because it is committed to fixed annual interest payments, which may be difficult to find. What is more, it is very unlikely that it would be possible to obtain the whole of a firm's financial needs by issuing bonds if the firm's activities involved any appreciable degree of risk. There are two possible ways out of these difficulties. One is to rely for finance on the personal wealth of the businessmen running the firm; the other is to offer a share in the ownership of the firm to outsiders.

One way in which reliance can be placed on internal finance is to create a general partnership. A major disadvantage of a partnership is that it cannot usually raise really large sums of money. It is possible for only a fairly small number of partners to work together, because they are all well advised to take an active part in the running of the business. This is because each partner is legally liable for the debts of the whole partnership. One partner may, therefore, find that he loses all his possessions (including personal possessions such as his house) if his colleagues have been acting unwisely and have run the partnership into bankruptcy.

Some of these disadvantages can be avoided without resorting to the corporate form of business organization by using the legal device of establishing a limited partnership. A limited partnership is made up of general partners (operating under the laws pertaining to general partnerships) and limited partners who are afforded limited liability but who are prohibited from acting as agents for the partnership and from taking part in the management of the partnership. From the point of view of the general partners, this form of business organization does provide the opportunity to expand the size of the enterprise without having to give up managerial control and without having to undertake the liability that would be incurred if they had obtained an equal volume of funds on a loan basis. The limited partnership form enables the limited partner to make financial investments that may bear higher returns than those he could obtain in the securities market, but without having to bear the unlimited liability risk of a general partner. The United States tax system, which levies taxes on corporate income and then upon dividends distributed on the basis of the corporation's income, provides an additional incentive to adopt the limited partnership, which is not taxed as a corporation.

Despite these advantages, the limited partnership has not really taken hold in the United States. The unlimited liability of the general partners limits their number as in the general partnership, while the withholding of managerial authority from the limited partners means that only those who have fairly intimate knowledge of the operations of a firm will accept such a position. So while the limited partnership may make it possible for a firm to expand beyond the bounds imposed by the general partnership form of organization, it still does not solve the problem of how to raise really large sums of money.

To get around these difficulties in obtaining funds, firms have turned to the corporate form of organization. With perpetual life for the organization, limited liability for the stockholders, and easy transference of shares of stock, the corporation can amass large amounts of capital under the centralized control of a body of directors (who are elected by the stockholders). Each stockholder has the hope of a profit and the certainty that his loss cannot be greater than the amount he has paid for his share of stock (plus any unpaid contribution to the share of stock, whose amount, if any, he knows).

The corporation can offer shares of stock (which are ownership shares) for sale to its stockholders and/or to the general public. For many of the large companies these shares of stock will be traded freely on the stock exchanges. In many cases firms market their shares through investment banking firms—firms which are in essence traders in securities and whose earnings stem from the spread between the prices at which they buy and sell. If the corporation is a well-known and reputable firm, the investment banking firm may underwrite the issue, which means that the investment banker guarantees a certain sum of money to the firm and that he, and not the firm issuing the shares of stock, bears any of the risks involved in not being able to market the issue at the price paid to the firm.

The common stock issues of corporations will be the ownership share with which we shall be most concerned in the analysis that follows. This type of share gives a right to a claim on profits, after all prior claims have been satisfied. One group of these prior claimants consists of those people who are the creditors of the company; they include, among others, a bank which has given a loan to a company, and people who hold bonds issued by the company.

Another group of claimants which stand prior to the common stockholders are people who are stockholders in that their claim is, in legal theory, to a part-*ownership* of the business, but who have a preference over other stockholders. They are usually known as preferred stockholders. They have a prior claim over any profits that are earned, up to a fixed maximum; an owner of a 5 per cent preferred stock has an annual claim to $5 out of any profits made for every $100 in nominal value of shares of stocks he owns.

In periods when a business is making profits the preferred stockholder is, therefore, in a position closely allied to a bondholder, even though his legal position is different. In the remainder of this chapter, it can be assumed that the forces influencing the prices of preferred stocks are closely allied to those affecting bond prices, subject to the proviso that allowance must be made for the greater risk of receiving nothing if trade is bad or if the firm closes down.

Some kinds of firm issue a large proportion of preferred stocks and/or bonds to common stocks, while others do the reverse. A high ratio of preferred stocks and/or bonds to common stocks is known as a high leverage ratio; it is used where the risks of the business are fairly small. If the business is highly speculative with chances both of complete loss and very high profits, preferred stocks (and bonds) are rarely issued because they are almost unsalable. This is so because the income which their holder receives is at most the fixed amount stated. Unless this maximum income is impossibly high, it is hardly likely to be sufficient to compensate their holder for the serious risk of complete loss.

This risk that the firm may fail completely is one that every investor must take into account. Other things equal, the greater the risk the greater the compensation he needs in the form of the promise of the possibility of a higher income. This statement applies to both purchasers of stocks and to purchasers of industrial and commercial bonds. Industrial borrowers have to pay higher interest rates than the government when they issue bonds, because the risk of default is larger in their case.

The Determination of Stock Prices [2]

The prices at which each kind of share of stock changes hands vary from hour to hour when active trading is taking place. The principles that determine these prices are just the same as those we have seen to apply in the case of other assets; prices must be such that each share of stock is held by a willing holder, and that there are no people who would like at those prices to hold their wealth in some form other than the one in which they find it. In principle, the analysis is the same as that we have already followed in considering interest theory; in practice, it is more complicated, because there are so many more possibilities open, and because of the number of considerations that have to be taken into account in making the choice.

The possibilities that now lie open to the wealth-owner include bonds issued by various borrowers, of varying degrees of riskiness and with varying maturity dates; short-term securities; money; liabilities of the non-bank financial intermediaries; and all the immense variety of shares issued by many firms in many industries. We can

---

[2] This section is solely concerned with equities; preferred stock prices mainly move with bond prices, and are ignored.

still sum up the wealth-holder's choice by saying that he will hold wealth in the form which he thinks will give him the biggest return commensurate with the risk involved.

In estimating the return on a share of stock, account must be taken of the risk of complete failure of the firm, of the firm's profit-earning possibilities, of any claims to profits that are prior to your own (e.g. preferred stocks), and of the possibility that profits may not be distributed by the directors but may be retained in the firm. If the return, taking account of all these factors and of the particular person's willingness to gamble and take risks, appears to be large in relation to the current market price, such a share of stock is one to buy or to hold. If my judgment is ahead of other operators on the market,[3] the time will come when other people will realize the worth of this particular kind of stock; its price rises, and I have made a capital gain.[4]

The level of the prices of stocks in general depends on similar forces. The main substitutes for stocks in general are bonds and money. It is convenient to look at the question in two parts, as we did when looking at the prices of short- and long-term securities in Chapter 8. In the first place, we can ask what relationships there are between *changes* in stock prices and bond prices—that is, between changes in yields (i.e. rates of return) on stocks and changes in (long-term) interest rates. Secondly, we can ask what determines the relationship between the *general level* of interest rates and the general level of dividends received from stocks.

When bond prices (i.e. long-term interest rates) change there is usually a tendency for stock prices to move in sympathy. The main reason for this is directly parallel in character to one of the reasons why long- and short-term interest rates tend to move in sympathy, namely, the possibility of shifting by asset-holders. If bond prices fall, while stock prices remain constant, it will be worth while for some wealth-holders to shift into holding bonds. They can earn a larger annual income than before from a given amount of money spent on bonds, and they may also hope for future capital appreciation if they believe that the fall in bond prices is only temporary.

---

[3] Alternatively, if one is successful in guessing what the market's delusions will be tomorrow.

[4] And even if I guess wrongly and the price remained unchanged, I still receive an income in the form of whatever dividend is distributed.

There is, therefore, pressure to sell stocks, which tends to cause their prices to fall. If stock prices fall, at a time when dividends that are being distributed by firms are unchanged, then the dividends received, expressed as a percentage of the market value of the share of stock, show a rise. Clearly, therefore, there is in consequence a tendency for this percentage (the yield) to move sympathetically with interest rates.

The argument of the last paragraph has assumed that the dividends that are being paid out by firms are constant. This is by no means necessarily true—for example, profits may be changing. Historical observation suggests that these changes in profits, which lead to changes in the annual income received from existing shares of stocks, frequently tend to weaken the tendency for bond and share prices to vary sympathetically. Booming trade conditions, in which profits and dividends are high, are usually associated with high interest rates.[5] The high level of dividends tends to mean that stock prices are high; if a firm is distributing $50 per year per share of stock, it is clear that the price of its shares will almost certainly be higher than if it is distributing only $5. On the other hand, bond prices tend to be low in a boom, since interest rates are high. There is, therefore, some tendency for bond and stock prices (or alternatively we can say interest rates and dividend yields) to move in opposite directions between conditions of boom and slump. How far this happens depends largely on the monetary policy of the financial authorities with regard to interest rates, and on the possibilities of switching between bonds and stocks, both by lenders and borrowers. (It may be noted that most borrowers have some discretion open to them between bond finance and equity finance; if long-term interest rates are particularly low in relation to current yields on stocks, a firm which is involved in enterprises not involving too great a degree of risk may choose to issue bonds [6] for an unusually large part of any finance it may need.)

The comparison of the general level [7] of interest rates with the general level of dividend yields is also broadly determined by forces of a kind with which we are already familiar. These forces

---

[5] This is partly a matter of policy and partly a matter of the automatic working of the system; on the former see Chapter 25, and on the latter see Chapter 18.

[6] Or, of course, preferred stocks, which we are currently ignoring.

[7] As distinct from their day-by-day and month-by-month movements.

are the possibility of shifting both lenders and borrowers and the views of lenders and borrowers about different kinds of risk and uncertainty. If few lenders are willing to take the risk of fluctuating incomes and of complete loss of their capital, then yields on stocks will have to be rather high. If many firms consider it safe to issue a large percentage of bonds (because their enterprises are not very risky) then there tends to be a large number of bonds in existence, and interest rates tend to be relatively high compared with yields on stocks.

Generally speaking, yields on stocks tend to be higher than interest rates, because of the additional risks involved in holding stocks rather than bonds. Two sets of circumstance are worth mentioning in which the reverse situation may apply, quite possibly for some time together. One is where the general level of prices of goods and services is rising rapidly; the other arises where there is considerable limitation on distribution of profits.

When prices are rising and are expected to continue to rise,[8] bonds are an unsatisfactory way of holding wealth, because the income they provide is fixed in terms of money and, therefore, declining in real terms. On the other hand, equity shares [9] may well be a good way of holding wealth at such times; profits can be expected to rise more or less in line with prices, and so dividends are more likely to be constant in real terms. When, therefore, there is a general expectation of price rises, wealth-holders tend to switch from bonds to stocks, with the result that stock prices rise and current dividend yields may become less than the current rate of interest.

Current yields may also be abnormally low if dividend distributions are held abnormally low, as occurred under wartime legislation in a number of countries during World War II. Instead of being distributed, profits are retained by the firm to a greater extent than usual. Wealth-holders may be willing to accept unduly low current rates of yield in these conditions, both because they anticipate that the dividend limitation will only be temporary, and because they realize that the profits which are being retained by the firm will probably be used eventually to the advantage of the share-

---

[8] A situation that will be analyzed at length in Part IV.
[9] But not preferred stocks, which here again are assimilated to bonds.

holders, either as distributed dividends when the controls are over, or as additional capital equipment which increases the firm's earning power.

Self-Financing by Business

The final characteristic of the financing of modern business which was ignored in Part II, and to which attention must be directed in this chapter, is that much of the finance needed by business is provided by the firms themselves and not by loans from and purchases of stocks by households. In the real world, firms frequently save as well as invest.

In Part II, in order to emphasize the essential dichotomy between the act of saving and the act of investment which lies at the heart of modern economic theory, we assumed that only households saved, while only firms invested. Now that this essential division is clear we can allow for the fact of saving by firms.

It will be remembered that a decision to save was a plan to put aside a part of current income and use it to add to total wealth. In Part II this could not be done by firms, which were assumed to pay all their net earnings over to households (i.e. businessmen) at the end of the week in which they were earned.

We can now make a big step nearer reality by allowing for the fact that firms usually distribute to their owners (in the case of corporations, the shareholders) less than the full amount of the profits they earn; moreover, they sometimes—though much more rarely—distribute more than they earn. The difference represents in aggregate the amount that firms save.[10] How does this affect the theory outlined in Part II?

Fortunately, the complications we must add to the theory are quite manageable. It is necessary to look at two aspects of this feature of modern business finance, which are distinguishable in terms of our analysis but may frequently be impossible to distinguish in practice.

One aspect is that firms generally delay a very long time before they pay out increased profits to their shareholders. If dividend distributions are made annually there must be an average lag of at least six months between the earning of profits by the firm and

---

[10] An amount which may be negative; firms, like households, can dissave.

their payment to shareholders. This lag is very much longer than that between the time at which work is done and the time at which the firm pays over income to the other major factors of production, namely wage and salary earners.

If this were the end of the matter, this long delay could simply be dealt with in the same way as the other lags in the circular flow of income; as has already been said in Chapter 0, our assumption of single-period time lags is a simplification, made for expository purposes. To take account of this long time lag, the arithmetical sequences would have to be made more complex; in a period of rising incomes some households would receive no increase in income until several months after the rise started, and firms would correspondingly be piling up money (or some relatively liquid asset) ready to pay out as profits at the end of the accounting year.

The first aspect is not, however, the end of the matter. In practice many firms do not distribute at the end of an accounting year the whole of the profits earned during the year. Nor can their actions be explained in terms of still longer time lags; for example, by supposing that this year's profit distribution depends on the profits earned in the year before last. In fact, it is difficult to make many useful generalizations about the relationship between profit distribution and profit earnings. Probably three are relatively safe. One is that there is a fairly long time lag between earnings and distribution; this we have already considered. A second is that firms probably distribute a bigger proportion of profits when profits are declining than when they are rising. A third is that firms frequently retain some of their profit earnings permanently.

Our immediate task is to consider the consequences of this third fact. Firms may use the profit earnings that they fail to distribute either to buy claims, or to buy goods. To the extent that they use them to buy and hold claims it is obvious that most firms can hold their accumulated savings in almost any of the different kinds of claim we have distinguished. They can hold money, short-term assets, bonds, and stocks of other firms. All that this implies is that account must be taken of the action of firms when we consider the effects of the choice of wealth-holders on asset prices: that is, on interest rates and yields on shares. The principles determining the choice of firms between different kinds of claim are much the same as those influencing households, and do not need elaboration.

To the extent that firms fail to distribute the profits and use the proceeds to buy goods (such as machines and factories), they are not only saving but also investing; they are both putting aside a part of current income and adding to their total holdings of real wealth. Clearly such simultaneous acts of saving and investment are quite common in practice. Up to this point in our analysis they have been excluded, because the key feature of the economic system is that decisions to save and decisions to invest are frequently made separately, and that the two decisions certainly need not be made together. In fact, a firm's decision to save-and-invest is logically two decisions: a decision to distribute less than the whole of profits and a decision to buy real wealth. Either of these two decisions could have been made independently of the other.

All of this complicates our analysis of the determination of the equilibrium level of income because the total amount of saving plans no longer depends totally on the level of households' incomes. Nevertheless, it does not alter the fundamental analysis.

The conditions for equilibrium in the level of income, when account is taken of saving by firms, are precisely the same as those outlined in Chapter 5. Equilibrium is possible only if planned savings are equal to planned investment. All that is necessary now is to take account of total saving, by both households and firms. Similarly, the multiplier must take account of the marginal propensity to save of firms and of households taken together. This can easily be done; an arithmetical example shows the principle. If profits are 50 per cent of total national income, and if firms distribute four-fifths of total profits and retain (save) the rest, then firms save 10 per cent of total national income. If households save one-fifth of the income they receive, they save one-fifth of 90 per cent of total national income (90 per cent being the sum of distributed profits and of the non-profit element in national income—e.g. wages). Households thus save 18 per cent of national income—the average propensity to save of the community as a whole is therefore 28 per cent. If similar calculations were made for savings out of increments of income, the community's marginal propensity to save would be calculated.

Investment by Households

Just as firms can and do save, we must also take into account the fact that households may invest. In Part II, we assumed that households could buy goods only for immediate consumption. Now we must take some account of the fact that households can spend in order to increase the real wealth they hold. One of the best examples is expenditure made to build a house.[11] The expenditure can be financed in several different ways. It may be financed by borrowing, in which case it is of just the same character as the investment by firms considered in Part II. It may be financed out of current income: in that case, our household is simultaneously saving and investing. Again it may be financed by selling claims [12] that have been accumulated in the past.

The construction of a house or the purchase of a new house is an action by households which is clearly of the nature of investment. Many other purchases by households are much less clearly defined. If we apply in its full rigor the definition of investment that we have been using earlier, then a large part of household expenditure is a simultaneous act of investment and saving. For example, if I buy a new suit I am adding to my total wealth by putting aside some of my current income. Moreover, I can finance such a purchase by borrowing: consumer credit is frequently used to buy things that are as short-lived as clothes; in that case the act is simply akin to investment by firms.

It is, however, usually inconvenient to cast the net of our definitions of investment so wide as to include purchases of durable consumer goods. The point is that it is extremely difficult to find any clear line of distinction between consumption and household investment which is useful. In Part II we defined consumption as household expenditure on goods for immediate use. Convenience now dictates that we should include under consumption all items of household expenditure, even though they are strictly speaking acts of saving-and-investment. There is no really valid line of distinction between consumption and consumer investment that can be drawn anywhere in the spectrum from the purchase of a pound of sugar that will last two weeks, through that of a pair of stockings that will last a month and a pair of shoes that will last two years, to the purchase of a car or refrigerator that will last ten years and a house that will last forty years.

---

[11] A purchase of a second-hand house is a transaction of a kind which we have excluded from the definition of investment.

[12] Including using up stocks of money.

The upshot of this argument is that all expenditure by households on goods is probably best left to be classified as consumption; the only exception that is commonly made is the purchase of houses, which is in a rather special position because of the large size of expenditure involved in relation to income, which means that it is nearly always financed by borrowing or from the sale of other assets. This in turn means that investment is left to cover only increases in real wealth held by firms, plus the special case of additional wealth held by households in the form of houses. Similarly, household saving merely includes incomes set aside to make net additional holdings of claims, together with the special case of additional real wealth held in the form of houses; whereas business saving includes both that part of profits which is set aside to add to firms' holdings of claims and also that part which is used to add to firms' holdings of real wealth.

This use of terms has proved to be the most useful—but at the same time it is important to pay attention to the implications of the fact that much consumption is, in a sense, saving-plus-investment. The major point is that decisions whether or not to purchase durable consumer goods may depend to a very important extent upon influences other than the level of income received in the immediate past. For one thing, these decisions are strongly influenced by the extent to which the household is in debt and by the quantity of claims it possesses. To some extent, this applies to all purchases: if a household owns more wealth but is in the same position in every other respect, it is quite likely to spend more on consumption than if it owns less wealth.[13] But the relationship between households' debtor-

---

[13] This relationship provides the basis of the 'Pigou effect,' which was an ingenious rehabilitation of the pre-Keynesian belief that if wages and prices were sufficiently flexible, full employment is the only possible equilibrium position. The argument is that if there is less than full employment and price flexibility reigns, wages and prices will fall. This will raise the real value of net claims against the government held by households and firms (i.e. of their holdings of government legal-tender money and government bills and bonds). This increases their total wealth and so leads to an increase in their expenditure on currently produced goods and services, so eventually restoring full employment. As a matter of logical analysis this is incontrovertible within its assumptions—but its assumptions are not very useful. Firstly, the fact is that wages and prices do not fall easily in a time of unemployment. Secondly, the analysis is in comparative static terms; if we switch to dynamics it becomes all too obvious that a period of falling prices and wages is likely to induce *reductions* in expenditure because purchasers hold off the market in the expectation that

creditor position is likely to be particularly important in the market for consumer durables, which are generally paid for out of past savings or by borrowing. A household which is in debt is likely both to be less willing and less able to borrow in order to make further purchases. A household which owns a large number of claims (e.g. bonds) is more likely to buy consumer durables than one which is not. it can sell the claims to buy the durable goods or it can use them as security for a loan.

All of this is reinforced by the fact that purchases of consumer durables are much more easily postponable than purchases for immediate consumption. I am much more likely to postpone buying a new car, especially if I dislike the shape of the new models or if I am pessimistic about the general economic situation, than to reduce my consumption of food.

Such influences as these are important examples of the fact that a full explanation of the influences determining the level of household expenditure would be very complicated. The explanation that was used in Part II, that household expenditure is higher, the higher the level of consumer income, is undoubtedly the most important single influence; but others exist, including the rate of interest and the forces just considered.

Some Suggested Reading

We have covered a number of topics in this chapter that can be profitably explored through some additional readings. On the role of the financial intermediaries, R. W. Goldsmith, *Financial Intermediaries in the American Economy since 1900* (Princeton, 1958), offers a wealth of statistical material on the development of the various intermediaries. On business risk, M. Kalecki's article 'The Principle of Increasing Risk,' *Economica* (1937), is still the standard reference, but T. Scitovsky, *Welfare and Competition* (Chicago, 1951) is also helpful reading in this area.

The various forms of business enterprise available to entrepreneurs and the various methods employed by business firms in financing themselves are topics that are covered extensively in books on 'corporate finance.' Of these we mention two that can be useful to those readers interested in pursuing these topics further: Guthmann and Dougall, *Corporate*

---

prices will fall still more. This adverse effect on expenditure is likely to be more important in the short as opposed to the long run: but, as Keynes said, in the long run we are all dead.

Financial Policy, 3rd ed. (Englewood Cliffs, New Jersey, 1955) and A. S. Dewing, *Financial Policy of Corporations,* 5th ed. (New York, 1953), 2 vols.

The consumption-income or saving-income relationship has received a great deal of attention in the recent past, and it has come to be realized that saving cannot be explained by the level of income alone. Two works that are notable in exploring the area beyond the simple saving-income relationship are J. S. Duesenberry, *Income, Saving and the Theory of Consumer Behavior* (Cambridge, Mass., 1952) and M. Friedman, *A Theory of the Consumption Function* (Princeton, 1957).

The 'Pigou effect,' which has come to be a much debated theoretical issue (although hardly anyone considers it seriously as a practical issue), is discussed in D. Patinkin, *Money, Interest, and Prices* (Evanston, 1956) and in an article by the same author, 'Price Flexibility and Full Employment,' *American Economic Review* (1948), reprinted in the American Economic Association, *Readings in Monetary Theory* (New York and Philadelphia, 1951).

10

The Business of Commercial Banking

Up to this point we have been able to avoid consideration of the operations of the banking system. In Part II it was assumed that banks existed, but were quite inactive. Our purpose now is to remedy this shortcoming. In doing so we shall need to pay attention to two major kinds of banking institutions, namely commercial banks and central banks. The former are the banks with which most members of the public have direct dealings; examples are the Bank of America and the Chase Manhattan Bank in the United States and the 'Big Five' in England (Barclays, Lloyds, Midland, National Provincial, and Westminster). Examples of central banks are the Bank of England, the Bank of France, and the United States' Federal Reserve System. As the name implies, there can be only one central bank in each country, although it can be a federation of several banks operating as a unity, as is the case in the United States.

Our discussion of the principles of commercial and central banking systems, in this and the succeeding chapters, will be carried out in general terms. It will, however, have a strong bias towards a description of conditions as they have developed in the advanced industrial countries, in order to provide an introduction to the more detailed analysis of American banking institutions in Chapters 12-15.

Historically, commercial banks appeared long before central banks. The first real central bank was the Bank of England; it was established in 1694, but did not carry out the work of a central bank until well into the second half of the nineteenth century. The Federal Reserve System was not established until 1913. Relatively few independent countries are now without a central bank, but in many cases they have come into effective operation only within the last few years; and it is possible to find important countries (e.g. Switzerland) where the legally constituted central bank has little power of control over the monetary and banking system. Since the fundamental purpose of a central bank is to operate such control, we can still find places where there is no organization which is carrying out the primary central banking function; moreover it is necessary to go back only a generation to find a situation in which very many countries had no effective central bank. On the other hand, it would be necessary to go back two or three centuries in Europe, and to the early days of settlement in most newly settled countries, to reach times when there were no institutions carrying out the essential functions of the modern commercial bank.

Our method of approach, therefore, will be to consider in this chapter the nature of commercial banking, its economic significance, and its manner of operation in the absence of control by a central bank. Then, in the next chapter, we can proceed to consider the ways in which a central bank can control the banking and monetary system, and the purposes for which it operates these controls.

The point of fundamental significance about banks, as far as the economist is concerned, is that, unlike the debts of other private institutions, banks' debts are used by the public as money. That is the reason why we are much more interested in these institutions than in other financial organizations, such as savings banks and savings and loan associations. Moreover, the banking system has a strategic position in the economy, because it can usually increase or decrease the quantity of money in circulation, by increasing or decreasing the amount of debt it owes, which means an increase or decrease in the claims held against it by households, firms, etc.[1]

Our purpose in the next few chapters will be to consider the ways in which the banks use this power. It is a power which can be used only within limits, either of prudence or of law; it is a power which may be used rather actively, with definite aims in view, or it may be used rather passively, with bankers believing that they are simply responding to the needs of trade.

The debts which are owed by bankers and which are used as money by the rest of the community are expressed in two main forms. One is represented by the bank note, and the other by the bank deposit. The former is a claim against the bank concerned, for a given amount, which is printed on a piece of paper and passed

---

[1] Including, of course, the government and foreigners when they come into consideration.

directly from hand to hand in settlement of purchases. The latter is expressed as a claim against the bank which is entered into the account books of the bank to the credit of a depositor, who can transfer this claim (or a part of it) by means of a check, which is an order to the bank to transfer the claim to someone else. In Britain and the United States, bank deposits are much more important than bank notes; the latter are, for the most part, used for only relatively small transactions. In many other countries, including most European countries, the check/bank deposit system is less common; even for quite large transactions; the two kinds of money are broadly of equal importance quantitatively. Generally speaking, checks are safer from risks of theft or loss by fire and are more convenient for payments than bank notes; they can be made payable to one specified person, and for any exact amount. On the other hand they are subject to the risk to the recipient that the person who is paying money by check does not have an adequate bank balance. Moreover, payment by check has the disadvantage, for some people, that individual transactions made in that way can more easily be investigated by the income tax authorities than when payment is made with notes.

In England, the United States, France, and many other countries, the only bank notes that can now circulate are the notes of the central bank.[2] The legal provisions creating this situation imply that the only bank money that can be created by commercial banks is in the form of bank deposits. In the past large quantities of notes issued by commercial banks used to circulate; in some countries there is still a significantly large note circulation issued by commercial banks, but where such a circulation survives, it is usually subject to very strict legal control.

A Primitive Banking System

We can now proceed to look at the operations of a rather primitive banking system, in which there is no central bank, and in which there is, in the first place, only one commercial bank. By tracing the ways in which such a bank might originate and develop the full functions of a commercial bank, and then by considering the com-

---

[2] In the United States, in addition to Federal Reserve notes, Treasury currency circulates and accounts for about one-sixth of the currency in circulation.

plications that are added when a second bank enters the scene, we shall be able to follow the broad lines of the path of development of commercial banking through history, up to the time of the appearance of an effective central bank on the scene; and we shall be able to see the main principles guiding bankers in the development of their activities.

The three main sources to which commercial banking operations can be traced are the merchant, the goldsmith, and the money-lender. Each of these was particularly closely concerned with dealings in money in the days when all money was still in the form of coins made of precious metals. The merchant was concerned with settling debts in distant places; the goldsmith was likely to hold considerable stocks of valuable metals, and so had to take careful precautions against theft; the money-lender was continually concerned with lending and borrowing of the money that was in circulation.

These special circumstances meant that each trade was in a position where enterprising men might see the advantage of using paper claims instead of actual coinage, for carrying out transactions. Merchants took to settling transactions in other cities by sending paper claims,[3] to be settled in coin by a colleague in the other city, in return for reciprocal arrangements; this saved the risk and expense of two movements of coin in opposite directions. In troubled times, goldsmiths might accept deposits of coin in exchange for an IOU (and, no doubt, a payment by the depositor for the risk the goldsmith was taking), the reason being the safer storage facilities owned by the goldsmith. A money-lender might, when lending, give a paper claim against himself to the borrower, stating that the owner of that claim had the right to so much coin from the money-lender on demand, instead of lending coin itself.

In time these paper claims came to be passed from hand to hand, and used as money in place of metal coinage. As long as the merchant, goldsmith, or money-lender who created the claim is willing to convert it into coin on demand, and as long as holders of the claims have confidence that this situation will last, then a paper claim is as useful for monetary purposes as coin. Since, on our assumptions, the person who issues the claim has a reserve of coin

---

[3] Usually in the form of a bill of exchange—that is, a form of claim to payment normally involving a short time delay.

of an equal value in his vaults, he can always pay up the full amount of all the paper claims he has issued. The holders of the claims take no risks, as long as the issuer is honest, and there is no reason why the claims should not freely circulate as money. A certain number of people will be suspicious, of course, and will convert any paper claims of this sort they receive into coin; but the ease and certainty with which the doubters can do this will only serve still more to reassure the rest.

So far there has been no creation of money. All that has happened is that the character of a part of the money in active circulation has altered. A part of the coinage has been sterilized, and is lying unused in the vaults of the merchants, money-lenders, or goldsmiths, awaiting the time when someone thinks coin is preferable to a paper claim. The claims simply stand in the place of coin, replacing coin but not supplementing it. This continues to be the case for as long as the merchant, goldsmith, or money-lender considers it desirable to hold exactly as much coin sterilized in his vaults as there are claims outstanding against himself in circulation. While these circumstances last, his balance sheet may look something like this:

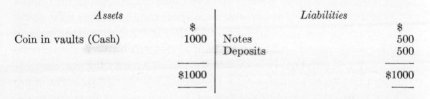

Assets	$	Liabilities	$
Coin in vaults (Cash)	1000	Notes	500
		Deposits	500
	$1000		$1000

On the liability side he has $500 of debts in the form of promises to pay cash that are expressed on pieces of paper (notes); he has also $500 in debts which are expressed in his books as claims owned by other people. On the assets side he has 100 per cent reserves in his vaults, in the form of 'sterilized' coin. The balance sheet shows his capital position, and so does not indicate how he makes an income; this he will do (as far as this part of his activities is concerned) by charging a storage charge on coin deposited with him, by charging for the service of transferring claims from one person to another, or by borrowing at lower rates of interest than those at which he lends.

Our merchant, goldsmith, or money-lender is already carrying out some of the functions of a bank. He is acting as an intermediary in the capital market: he borrows from some people and lends to others. He is also acting as a ledger clerk, who helps keep his customers' accounts and make payments in the convenient form of changes in entries in his books. These are two of the most important functions of a bank; but we have not yet called our man a banker, because so far he has failed to take the final and crucial step. His debts are used as money, but he has not created any money; he has not added to the total amount of money held and used by the general public. So far, all he has done has been to change the form in which some of that money is held.

The next and most important step occurs when he comes to realize that he can safely create more debts against himself than he has coins in his vaults, and still remain in business. He can do this because most holders of his debt (that is, of notes and deposits) are quite confident that they can be changed on demand into coin; therefore nearly all people are willing to accept these claims in payment for goods and services, and very few people rush off to change such claims into coin when they receive them. As long as people are quite confident that the claims will always be useful and will always be convertible into coin, most people will not bother. The banker finds that in any given period only a small proportion of the notes and deposits held by his creditors are redeemed in coin; at the same time other holders of coin will be turning it back into bank money (by depositing coin and taking a claim) because of the convenience of using bank money. This means that most of his 100 per cent reserve is completely idle; a much smaller reserve of coin would be sufficient to take up the fluctuations in demands to change claims into coin that he has learned to experience.

Our banker finds, therefore, that he can lend out more money (that is, create more debts against himself) than he has in reserves of coin, and yet still be in a position to convert any normal volume of claims into coin on demand. Clearly, these are potentially very profitable operations. He can, for example, lend to a businessman who is in need of money for his business. The banker creates a debt against himself, in the form of notes or of a statement in his books to the effect that this businessman now owns a claim against the bank. The businessman can use this claim as money (by means of checks) to pay for materials; he can use the bank notes he receives (or that he can draw from his account by cashing a check) to pay his workmen. The businessman receives the loan he needs, and the quantity of money in circulation rises. The banker also benefits from the situation, of course. In exchange for the debt he has created in favor of the businessman, which the latter uses as money, an equal debt has been created by the businessman in favor of the banker. The banker has, therefore, a legal claim against the businessman; and if there appears to be any risk that the businessman may not repay, the banker may also require security for the businessman's debt (perhaps in the form of a claim over the businessman's inventories of goods which can be exercised if he fails to repay his debt to the banker at the agreed time). Moreover, the banker will charge interest to the businessman for the loan that has been made; out of this interest, the banker earns an income.

After a number of transactions of this type, the banker's balance sheet may look something like the following:

Assets		Liabilities	
	$		$
Cash (coin in vault)	800	Notes	600
Loans	800	Deposits	1000
	$1600		$1600

It will be seen that account has to be taken of the fact that some of the businessmen to whom the banker makes loans will choose to exercise their right of changing their deposits or notes into coin. Similarly, some of the people who receive payments from these businessmen may also claim payment in coin. The total effect, therefore, is that the banker loses some of his cash reserves; in this example, we assume he loses $200 once things have settled down again.

In our example the liabilities of the bank have risen by $600 compared with the previous case; this represents additional money in circulation of $600, which has been created by the bank. (In this particular example, it has been assumed that most of the holders of this new money want to hold it as bank deposits and not as notes.) On the assets side there is an additional item of $800 labeled 'Loans.' This represents the claims the bank now has against businessmen; on this debt the businessmen pay interest, so providing the bank with the incentive to carry out this sort of transaction.

It should be noted that banks also frequently pay interest on their deposits, that is, on some of their own liabilities. Today, payment of interest is the usual rule in the case of 'time deposits,' which can be withdrawn by the depositor only after giving a certain number of days' notice; they are a way of holding assets in a very liquid form which also provides a small income. Sometimes interest is also paid on 'demand deposits'—that is, those which can be withdrawn (by paying over to someone else or by converting into notes or coin) on demand, without any advance notice being given at all. Payment of interest on demand deposits is likely to be particularly common in countries and circumstances where the banking habit is not deeply ingrained, either because of suspicion, ignorance, or habit, and where some inducement is needed to persuade many people to hold their money in the form of bank deposits. The interest that banks can charge on bank loans is always much higher than that given on any kind of deposit: the reasons for this we shall look into shortly.

Normally, then, creation of money by the banks occurs when two opposite transactions occur simultaneously between a bank and a customer, as a part of one contract. The bank increases its debt to the customer by an agreed amount, and the customer simultaneously puts himself into debt to the bank by the same amount. There are the following changes in the balance sheets of the bank and the customer:

BANK

Assets	$	Liabilities	$
Increased loans	100	Increased deposits	100

FIRM OR HOUSEHOLD

Assets	$	Liabilities	$
Increased money held (as bank deposit)	100	Increased debt payable to bank	100

This exchange of debts is significant because one of the debts that is created is money, while the other earns an income for the bank.

It is possible for banks to create new money in circumstances where there is no such interchange of debts between banker and customer. For example, a bank may pay for a new building (or perhaps even for high living on the part of the banker) by creating new money in the form of notes or deposits. In the early days of banking, there can be little question that such things happened;

but for reasons we shall look at in a moment, banks have learned to be very cautious about forwarding their self-interest in this way. Suppose, however, that our banker did decide to create notes and deposits in order to buy himself a new building. Then his balance sheet might be as follows (allowing for a further loss of coin into circulation, because some people prefer coin to notes or deposits, and so change any additional notes or deposits they receive into coin):

Assets	$	Liabilities	$
Cash (coin in vault)	700	Notes	700
Loans	800	Deposits	1100
Buildings	300		
	$1800		$1800

The reason why bankers have learned to be very cautious about such activities (in particular, about creating money in order to spend freely themselves or in order to help other business enterprises run by themselves) is that their whole position depends upon the confidence of the general public. Once a fear develops that a banker cannot pay his liabilities freely on demand, the general public becomes unwilling to hold its money as bank notes and deposits and tries to convert into coin, and there is a 'run' on the bank. If this run persists for long enough, a banker who has carried out the full functions of a banker and has actually created money must be forced to close his doors. This must be so, because his assets are not all in the form of coin: a large part is in the form of advances to businessmen, and it is unlikely that he can easily call for their repayment at short notice. If a part of his assets is also in the form of buildings, realization is likely to be still more difficult.

A prudent banker has only one answer to this difficulty—to make sure that the general public will never lose confidence in him, so that there will be no possibility of a 'run' which will exhaust the reserves that he can realize. One way in which he can avoid the danger of loss of public confidence is to avoid any suspicion that he is using his power of money creation directly to his own advantage. This means that a wise banker will keep his banking activities well separated from any other business he may conduct: or better, that he should not conduct any other business. Moreover, he will be wise to pay for things such as new buildings out of profits as far as possible, so that they do not enter into his balance sheet as a counterpart to notes or deposits.

A second way in which a prudent banker may try to avoid a loss of confidence is to make loans which are repayable fairly quickly; frequently they may be renewed, but the principle that the banker can ask for repayment in a reasonably short time is a good one. In addition, it may be considered that prudent banking demands that loans shall not be made that involve a risk of dragging the banker deeply into the affairs of the firm to which he has given a loan; the bank should try to make loans that can be repaid without forcing a sale of fixed capital assets of the firm. These are some of the reasons lying behind the English banking tradition of the self-liquidating loan (a tradition which has not always been strictly followed in England and which has rarely been operative in many other countries [4]). According to this tradition, the ideal bank loan is one to finance the processing, holding, or carriage of a stock of material; a loan is made to buy the material, such as raw cotton for spinning, on the security of the material, and is repaid out of the proceeds of the sale when the material has been processed or carried to its destination. Such loans are self-liquidating, in the way that a loan to buy a building or a long-lived machine is not, because the whole transaction is completed in a fairly short time, and involves the security of some commodity for which there is almost always a ready market.

Caution about the kinds of loans that are made is not a sufficient guarantee of a banker's solvency, however. The times when there is a particular danger of a run on the bank are times of crisis, such as the onset of a trade depression or the outbreak of war. It is precisely at times such as these that self-liquidating loans may turn out to be almost impossible to repay; stocks of commodities may be salable only at low prices, if at all. The final and most important safeguard of the banker's position is that he should avoid making too many loans; he must always maintain sufficiently large holdings of cash [5] to be able to deal with any conceivable 'run.' What a minimum necessary proportion between holdings of reserve of cash and

---

[4] For a discussion of the attempts that have been made to apply this rule in the U.S., see Chapter 13.

[5] Or near substitutes for cash; on this, more will be said in subsequent chapters.

his total liabilities will be can only be decided by experience. Since the banker makes bigger profits the more loans he makes in relation to his cash holdings, there is always a temptation to allow cash reserves to fall too far; the reckoning then comes with the next general economic crisis. Eighteenth and nineteenth century history is full of bank failures arising simply from imprudence about cash ratios

If experience shows that a suitable minimum cash ratio happens to be one-third of total liabilities, the balance sheet of our bank might look as follows:

Assets	$	Liabilities	$
Cash (coin in vault)	700	Notes	800
Loans	1400	Deposits	1300
	$2100		$2100

With such a ratio, the banker feels confident that he can meet any run that may develop; he is sure that public confidence in him will be such that no more than one in three of the notes and deposits outstanding will ever come up for repayment in coin at any one time. If he has a cash ratio of one in five or one in ten, he can make larger profits (out of interest on advances) but public confidence in him will be less (if the public knows of or suspects the low cash ratio) and he is in a weaker position to meet any run; he will have to close his doors if one in five or one in ten of his liabilities is presented for changing into coin. In many countries, including the United States, legal provisions have been introduced to reinforce the banker's self-discipline and to protect the depositor. By these provisions, bankers must hold a minimum proportion of their total deposit liabilities in the form of some suitably liquid asset (in the United States, as deposits at the Federal Reserve Banks).

All this means that commercial bankers are always very conscious of their liquidity position—much more so than most other transactors. A banker must always have sufficient assets in a form suitable to pay out to customers on demand; in our simple case this is coin. He needs, therefore, an adequate supply of liquid assets: of assets that combine convenience and certainty. They must be in a convenient form, so that they are always available; and they must be certain in value. Thus, most loans are not liquid assets; even though the banker may be confident about receiving full repayment, he cannot get it at a moment's notice. Again, a bond is not usually a liquid asset; it is convenient in that it is always marketable, but its value is far from certain: capital losses may be incurred if it is sold.

At the same time, liquidity cannot be the sole aim of a banker; he could hold a 100 per cent reserve of coin, and be perfectly liquid, but then he would have no source of profit (except insofar as he charged for carrying out the ledger clerk function of making payments on behalf of clients). Since a banker is in business in order to make profits, he also holds some assets that are not perfectly liquid, but which earn interest.

Normally, the banker's choice is not simply one between perfect liquidity plus no profit on the one hand, and low liquidity plus considerable profit on the other. Instead, there is a spectrum of possible assets, with varying degrees of liquidity and varying returns. A banker spreads his asset distribution along this spectrum in what seems to him the best way of reconciling these two conflicting interests. In addition to holding a minimum proportion of cash, he will usually also hold some assets which bring in a low return but can quickly and easily be turned into cash without appreciable risk of loss of capital value. Bills are an example of such an asset.

Relationships Between Two Commercial Banks

The other matter which we still have to look at in this chapter concerns the additional complications that arise when several commercial banks exist, and not merely one. We now have to consider inter-bank relationships; in addition to payments made between customers of one bank, and to people who have no banking account, payments will also be made between customers of the two different banks. Let us imagine that the initial position of the two banks is as follows:

BANK A

Assets	$	Liabilities	$
Cash	1600	Notes	3000
Loans	6400	Deposits	5000
	$8000		$8000

BANK B

Assets	$	Liabilities	$
Cash	800	Notes	2000
Loans	3200	Deposits	2000
	$4000		$4000

Each bank is following a 20 per cent cash-ratio rule. Now let us suppose that a customer of bank A draws a check on his bank to pay a debt of $100 to a person who is a customer of bank B. This customer pays the check into his bank and receives an additional credit on his account of $100. If commercial banks do not hold deposits with one another, then bank B hands the check over to bank A and demands and receives payment in coin. The result is as follows: [6]

BANK A

Assets	$	Liabilities	$
* Cash	1500	Notes	3000
Loans	6400	* Deposits	4900
	$7900		$7900

Cash Ratio 19 per cent

BANK B

Assets	$	Liabilities	$
* Cash	900	Notes	2000
Loans	3200	* Deposits	2100
	$4100		$4100

Cash Ratio 22 per cent

A's cash ratio has fallen below 20 per cent, because both cash and deposits have fallen by the same absolute amount. For similar reasons, B's cash ratio has risen above 20 per cent.

Normally, there is a strong presumption that the position will

---

[6] The asterisks mark the items which have changed in magnitude.

shortly be reversed, by other payments between customers of the two banks. On most days much the greater part of transactions between customers of the two banks will tend to cancel out. (To avoid excessive movements of cash, banks settle only net balances arising out of this large number of transactions; a clearing house is used in most banking systems to work out what these net balances are.) If, however, there is a persistent tendency for customers of one bank to make more payments to customers of the other bank than are coming the other way, the cash ratio of the bank whose customers are paying out will fall, and the ratio of the other bank will rise. In such circumstances, the bank that is losing cash will have to demand the repayment of some loans in order to get its cash ratio back to a suitably prudent level; the other bank will be able to make more loans.

This question of the interrelationships between two or more commercial banks involves a matter of some theoretical interest. In the past, practical bankers have frequently protested that banks do not *create* money, but merely lend money which has already been deposited with them. By looking at the matter from the point of view of the individual bank, it is easy to discern the reason for this 'practical' view but from the point of view of the economy as a whole, there is no doubt that the commercial banking system can and does create money.

An example can demonstrate the contrast. Let us now assume a country with ten commercial banks, each of equal size, and each of which obeys a cash reserve ratio of 20 per cent. Now, if one of those banks receives an additional deposit of coin valued say at $100, it can safely increase its lending operations. Immediately, the increase it sees possible is $80. In that case, its cash reserve ratio remains at 20 per cent, even if all the loan is used to make payments to customers of other banks, or to withdraw coin. The banker is prepared against the worst possible contingency; in doing so he simply sees himself as lending part of the money he has already received.

As is so common in economics, however, the immediate effect is only part of the story. We now have to look at the other banks and so at the commercial banking system as a whole. In a country where the banking habit is well established, most of the payments made out of the $80 of loans to customers of the first bank will be received by customers of other banks, who will deposit them in their accounts.[7] Inter-bank settlement in our simple system is made by transfers of coin; hence, each of the other nine commercial banks finds that it has additional holdings of coin. They in turn use these coins as the basis of further loans; at this second stage, we can see that money is truly being created. Each banker may imagine he is only lending money he has already received; but the system as a whole is using the coin as a basis for expansion of the money supply. This expansion continues through a series of stages; at the third stage, each banker finds he can make further loans, because the loss of cash from his reserves arising from the loans he has made to customers is largely counteracted by an inflow of cash from other bankers, who have also been expanding loans.

There is, therefore, an expansionary process in the money supply whose general characteristics are not unlike those of the multiplier process discussed earlier. The similarity is that a disturbance leads to a change in the plans and actions of one transactor (in this case a bank); this in turn affects other transactors, whose consequential adjustments in turn cause further adjustments.

The process comes to an end when each banker has reestablished a 20 per cent cash ratio and the reactions of each become so small as to have negligible effects on the others. At that position there has been in total an expansion in the supply of bank money which is much greater than the initial deposit of $100.

One of the most important ways in which such an expansion (or contraction) in the quantity of bank deposits can come about is through the initiative of the central bank. It is, therefore, now convenient to introduce the central bank onto the scene.

SOME SUGGESTED READING

The principles of commercial banking are treated rather well in most modern textbooks on money and banking. There are, however, some classic pieces that the serious student may want to consult. C. A. Phillips,

---

[7] A certain number (on average, a tenth of the total) will be received by other customers of the first bank, which will, therefore, find that its fears of loss of cash reserves were rather exaggerated and that some expansion of loans is possible.

Bank Credit (New York, 1926), contains a good treatment of how bank reserves, loans, and deposits are interrelated. Also useful is W. F. Crick, 'The Genesis of Bank Deposits,' *Economica* (1927). For a history of commercial banking in the United States, particularly in the 19th century, see C. F. Dunbar, *The Theory and History of Banking*, 4th ed. (New York, 1922).

11

The Operations of Central Banks

The main function of central banks (such as the Federal Reserve in the United States) is to help control and stabilize the monetary and banking system. In doing this they are subordinate to the government, and operate alongside other organs of the government, such as the Treasury. Normally, central banks are rather more independent of the government of the day than are government bureaus; many central banks are still owned by private stockholders and not by the government, although the recent fashion (followed in England and France) has been to bring the central bank under public ownership. The real significance of such changes has usually been small; those central banks which are still privately owned are not operated with the interests of the stockholders in mind; the earning of profits is always completely subordinated to the interests of the community as interpreted by the board which is in control of the central bank.

The most important foundation of a central bank's power derives from its position as the bank at which the commercial banks hold deposits: from its position as the banker's bank. In the banking system that was described in the last chapter there was no central bank, and the commercial banks held their cash reserves wholly in the form of coin. In a system where there is an effective central bank, however, a part of the commercial banks' cash reserves will be held in the form of a deposit at the central bank. This may be an enforcement required by law (as in the United States) or it may be a generally accepted convention (as in England). For the commercial banks, reserves held in the form of deposits at the central bank are quite as liquid as coin. In fact in many ways they are more convenient, because one of the main functions of cash reserves in a

155

developed banking system is to provide a means for settling indebtedness between the commercial banks; this is most easily done by drawing checks on accounts at the central bank. Reserves at the central bank are as liquid as coin because the central bank is always willing to provide coins in exchange for deposits; so that if a commercial bank suddenly finds a need for coin, it can always replenish its stock by reducing its balance at the central bank.

In the days before the First World War, such recourse to the central bank to replenish stocks of coins was very important, because coins made of precious metals were an important part of the monetary circulation. In the United States gold coins and certificates circulated until 1934, at which time the United States government took over all the monetary gold; but the widespread circulation of gold certificates in the period following World War I reflected, in large part, Federal Reserve policy rather than public demand for gold. When the Federal Reserve Banks' gold reserve ratio rose to very high levels, the Banks retired their own issue (Federal Reserve notes) and issued gold certificates in their place; by this technique the System attempted to control its gold reserve ratio so as to permit itself a great deal of freedom in dealing with the domestic monetary situation while at the same time claiming partial adherence to the gold standard system (under which a rise in the central bank's gold reserve ratio, in theory, dictated domestic monetary expansion). But now only a few primitive countries still use gold coins as part of their internal currency circulation. In most countries the only coinage that remains is for low denominations of the currency. Usually the metal content of such coins is worth much less than their face value; in effect, coins are now merely notes, stamped on metal instead of being printed on paper. The requirements of the banks for such 'subsidiary coinage' are a rather minor matter. Today the greater part of the monetary circulation other than bank deposits is in the form of bank notes. Here, once more, the central bank in nearly all countries is in a strategic position. In the last chapter, we imagined that the commercial banks issued notes; this supposition was reasonable, and corresponded to an important stage of banking history. In most countries today, however, the law has deprived commercial banks of the right of note issue; the only money that commercial banks can create is in the form of bank deposits, and it is nearly always [1] the central bank which now has the sole power of note issue. This monopoly is important, because these notes are commonly the sole legal tender for large payments, now that gold coins no longer circulate. The commercial banks now have to be in a sufficiently liquid position to be able, on demand, to pay out these central bank notes in exchange for their debts (i.e. the deposits owned by households, firms, etc.). Up to a certain point, the commercial banks hold central bank notes in their tills and safes, in order to be ready to pay cash immediately on demand. But cash reserves in excess of such day-to-day needs are, again, most conveniently held as deposits at the central bank.

Central Banking Control

There are four main groups of method of control that a central bank can operate over the commercial banks. Not all of these methods are necessarily used in every banking system, although in the majority of effective systems of central bank control there is at least some approximation to all four. Firstly, there is the control resulting from the power of the central bank to take the initiative in buying and selling existing securities. Secondly, there is the power of the central bank to impose conditions when it is carrying out its duty of helping the banking system out of difficulties. Thirdly, there is the power frequently possessed by central banks to impose reserve requirements upon the commercial banks. Lastly, there are a variety of powers (which in most countries have tended to increase in the last two decades) to give specific orders to the commercial banks about the kind and amount of business they may do. These various control methods may be, and often are, used to reinforce one another; alternatively, it is possible for one to be used in a direction contrary to another, either as a result of bad management, or because of deliberate policy, which has the purpose of satisfying objectives that are partly inconsistent.

---

[1] The United States Treasury issues currency, but the situation described in the text is by far the most common.

Open Market Operations

The first of these four groups of control method relies upon the power of the central bank to buy and sell securities of various kinds in the open market on its own initiative; that is, to indulge in open market operations.

There are two main groups of purpose for which open market operations may be used; in some respects these purposes are mutually exclusive, while in others they are complementary. In the first place, they may be employed to have a direct effect on the prices of the securities in which the operations are taking place; in other words, they may be used to influence the rate of interest on the kind of security concerned. In the second place, the purpose of open market operations may be to alter the reserves of the commercial banks.

The first of these two purposes—that of having direct influence on interest rates—is the more obvious. If, for example, the central bank is willing to buy a particular security in unlimited quantities at a fixed price, then the price of that security cannot fall below that level; the rate of interest appropriate to that security has a maximum level. Similarly, if the central bank is willing to sell a security at a fixed price, and if it possesses adequately large holdings of that security, then in effect a maximum price is fixed for it, and a corresponding minimum interest rate. If the central bank is willing and able both to buy and to sell at a fixed price, then the interest rate concerned is pegged.

Moreover, even if the central bank operates only to a limited extent in the market for a particular type of security, it may well affect expectations in that market, and so affect the willingness of other operators to hold that security, and so have a strong effect on the rate of interest concerned. In addition, operations by the central bank in the market for one kind of security may well affect the market for another kind of security. For example, if the central bank pegs the short-term rate of interest at a low level, the effect may well be to keep long-term interest rates at low level too, as a result of the kinds of interaction between the short and the long markets investigated in Chapter 8.

In order to consider the second possible purpose for which open market operations by the central bank may be used, namely, to influence the reserve position of the commercial banks, we must follow through the effects of such operations on the balance sheets of the two kinds of institution and of the other major transactors in the economy. Let us suppose that the initial position is as follows:

CENTRAL BANK

Assets	$	Liabilities	$
1. Securities (= 13)	8,000,000	2. Deposits of commercial banks (= 5)	3,000,000
		3. Notes (= 4 + 9)	5,000,000
	$8,000,000		$8,000,000

COMBINED COMMERCIAL BANKS

Assets	$	Liabilities	$
4. Cash in tills (notes) (= part of 3)	1,000,000	8. Deposits (= 10)	20,000,000
5. Cash at central bank (= 2)	3,000,000		
6. Securities (= 14)	8,000,000		
7. Loans (= 12)	8,000,000		
	$20,000,000		$20,000,000

GENERAL PUBLIC (HOUSEHOLDS AND FIRMS)
(net)

Assets	$	Liabilities	$
9. Notes of central bank (= part of 3)	4,000,000	12. Debts to banks (= 7)	8,000,000
10. Deposits at commercial banks (= 8)	20,000,000		
11. Securities (Government) (= 15)	10,000,000		
	$34,000,000		$8,000,000
Net claims held by general public	$26,000,000		

GOVERNMENT

Assets	*Liabilities*	
		$
	Securities held by:	
	13. Central bank	
	(= 1)	8,000,000
	14. Commercial	
	banks (= 6)	8,000,000
	15. General public	
	(= 11)	10,000,000
	National Debt	$26,000,000

The accounts representing the claims and liabilities (but ignoring the real wealth) of four sectors of the economy are shown here in a consolidated form. Claims by a member of one sector against another member of that same sector are ignored; this means that claims arising between households and firms are ignored (in contrast with the practice in earlier chapters); here we are concerned merely with the external relationships of the group of households plus firms, taken together. For the first time we are introducing the government to the scene; but its actions are purely passive. It has created a certain amount of debt in the past, which is held partly by the central and commercial banks, and partly by the general public (households and firms). This introduction of the government, in a purely passive role, is necessary because central banks usually hold only government securities. In addition, we have assumed that commercial banks hold only government securities, and no securities issued by private firms. It will be noted that the net claims held by the group of households and firms, taken together, are equal to the net liabilities of the government; this is necessarily so (in the absence of any consideration of foreigners) because both kinds of bank have claims outstanding against them equal in total to the claims they own, and all claims involve a corresponding liability somewhere.

The central bank has total liabilities (in the form of notes and commercial bank deposits) of $8,000,000. Correspondingly, it has $8,000,000 of government securities (bonds and bills) which it acquired when the liabilities against itself were created. The commercial banks have at present a 20 per cent ratio of cash to total deposits; three-quarters of this cash must be held on deposit at the central bank to meet the legal reserve ratio, which has been imposed by the government to protect the interests of depositors and which we shall assume to be 15 per cent. The remaining one-quarter of this cash is held in commercial bank tills in the form of central bank notes and satisfies the 5 per cent ratio of till money to deposits that commercial banks consider desirable on grounds of administrative convenience. The remaining assets of the commercial banks earn them interest, and consist in our example partly of government securities (bonds and bills) and partly of advances made to customers.

Let us now consider the effects of a sale by the central bank of $100,000 worth of securities to members of the public, on the open market. A relatively heavy sale such as this can be absorbed only if the price falls somewhat; in other words, the rate of interest shows an immediate tendency to rise. This is a necessary consequence of open market sales (and conversely with open market purchases). The purpose for which we are now supposing the open market sales to be used, however, is the further one of influencing the cash reserves of the commercial banks. The members of the public who are buying the securities from the central bank will normally pay for them by means of checks drawn against their deposits at the commercial banks.[2] The central bank receives these checks to the value of $100,000 and presents them to the commercial banks, who settle them by reducing their deposits at the central bank by $100,000. The cash reserves of the commercial banks have then fallen by the same absolute amount as the value of the securities sold, because the central bank will only accept settlement by the commercial banks in the form of a reduction in claims against itself. The position then is as follows: [3]

CENTRAL BANK

Assets		Liabilities	
	$		$
*Securities	7,900,000	*Deposits of commercial banks	2,900,000
		Notes	5,000,000
	$7,900,000		$7,900,000

---

[2] It is conceivable, but not very likely, that they will pay with central bank notes; to the extent that they do, repercussions on the commercial banks do not follow; this possibility is so unimportant that we can ignore it.

[3] An asterisk is placed by each of the items which alters.

COMBINED COMMERCIAL BANKS

Assets		Liabilities	
	$		$
Cash in tills (notes)	1,000,000	*Deposits	19,900,000
*Cash at central bank	2,900,000		
Securities	8,000,000		
Loans	8,000,000		
	$19,900,000		$19,900,000

GENERAL PUBLIC
(net)

Assets		Liabilities	
	$		$
Notes of central bank	4,000,000	Debt to banks	8,000,000
*Deposits at commercial banks	19,900,000		
*Securities	10,100,000		
	$34,000,000		$8,000,000
Net claims held by general public	$26,000,000		

GOVERNMENT

Assets	Liabilities	
		$
	Securities held by:	
	*Central bank	7,900,000
	Commercial banks	8,000,000
	*General public	10,100,000
	National Debt	$26,000,000

The commercial banks now find that their legal reserves are deficient by $85,000; their reserves have diminished by $100,000, while the decrease in their deposit liabilities by $100,000 has reduced the reserves that they must maintain by *only* $15,000 (since they must hold 15 per cent reserves). And while the commercial banks could replenish their balances at the central bank by paying $85,000 of notes into the central bank, they are unlikely to reduce their till money holdings by that amount since we have assumed that they desire to maintain a 5 per cent ratio of till money to deposits. The important thing to note is that the sale of securities by the central bank has reduced the commercial banks' total cash reserves from 20 per cent to $\frac{3,900,000}{19,900,000} = 19.6$ per cent approximately. The commercial banks must, therefore, accept the fact that their cash reserves are lower,[4] and must adjust the amount of their assets and liabilities until the ratio of cash reserves to liabilities is back to 20 per cent (the 15 per cent legal reserve ratio plus the 5 per cent till money to deposits ratio desired by the commercial banks).

The commercial banks can reduce their total liabilities in two ways. They can sell securities to the general public; the purchasers pay by running down their deposits at the commercial banks. These sales will be possible only if the banks are willing to accept a fall in the market price of these securities: in other words, there will be further upward pressure on interest rates. Commercial bank sales of securities may be limited by the capital losses that they may suffer by selling at rather low prices. The other way in which the commercial banks can restore their 20 per cent cash ratio is to reduce loans to the public, by demanding repayment of existing loans and by tightening up the conditions under which they will grant new ones. The banks may do this by 'bank credit rationing'; they may no longer be willing to grant credit to perfectly sound borrowers who can pay the current rate of interest, to whom the banks would have been quite willing to lend before they had been put into an illiquid position by the central bank's open market sales. Alternatively, the commercial banks may raise the rates of interest at which they are willing to lend, and so discourage some demand for loans. In practice, the commercial banks frequently combine all of these reactions; in the remainder of this discussion it will be assumed that commercial banks sell securities and reduce loans to the public by equal amounts. The final situation after all these adjustments might then be as follows: [5]

---

[4] The only way in which they could acquire more cash would be to sell securities to the central bank; for a discussion of the circumstances in which the central bank may choose to act in this way, see the discussion of the central bank as lender of last resort (pp. 171-4).

[5] An asterisk indicates the changes from the preceding situation.

CENTRAL BANK

Assets	$	Liabilities	$
Securities	7,900,000	*Deposits of commercial banks	2,925,000
		*Notes	4,975,000
	$7,900,000		$7,900,000

COMBINED COMMERCIAL BANKS

Assets	$	Liabilities	$
*Cash in tills (notes)	975,000	*Deposits	19,500,000
*Cash at central bank	2,925,000		
*Securities	7,800,000		
*Loans	7,800,000		
	$19,500,000		$19,500,000

GENERAL PUBLIC
(net)

Assets	$	Liabilities	$
Notes of central bank	4,000,000	*Debts to banks	7,800,000
*Deposits at commercial banks	19,500,000		
*Securities	10,300,000		
	$33,800,000		$7,800,000
Net claims held by general public	$26,000,000		

GOVERNMENT

Assets		Liabilities	$
		Securities held by:	
		Central bank	7,900,000
		*Commercial banks	7,800,000
		*General public	10,300,000
		National Debt	$26,000,000

In this final situation there is less money in the hands of the general public than originally; the public now holds $500,000 less of bank deposits, as a result of a sale of securities by the central bank of $100,000. There is thus a fivefold leverage on the monetary circulation; this corresponds to the one in five cash ratio being maintained by the commercial banks.

This leverage effect is of the greatest importance. As long as the commercial banks maintain constant cash reserve ratios, a central bank operation in the open market has a greatly magnified effect upon the amount of money in the hands of the general public. In the circumstances now under consideration, the leverage effect follows directly and simply from the size of the cash reserve ratio that the banks are maintaining. If in our example, the cash reserve ratio

COMBINED COMMERCIAL BANKS
Initial position

Assets	$	Liabilities	$
Cash in tills (notes)	250,000	Deposits	10,000,000
Cash at central bank	750,000		
Securities	4,500,000		
Loans	4,500,000		
	$10,000,000		$10,000,000

Immediately after central bank open market sale

Assets	$	Liabilities	$
Cash in tills (notes)	250,000	Deposits	9,900,000
Cash at central bank	650,000		
Securities	4,500,000		
Loans	4,500,000		
	$9,900,000		$9,900,000

After adjustment back to 10 per cent cash reserve ratio

Assets	$	Liabilities	$
Cash in tills (notes)	225,000	Deposits	9,000,000
Cash at central bank	675,000		
Securities	4,050,000		
Loans	4,050,000		
	$9,000,000		$9,000,000

had been 10 per cent (or one-tenth), the final effect on the quantity of bank deposits held by the general public would have been twice as great. This can be seen from imaginary balance sheets (on preceding page) for the commercial banks before and after open market sales by the central bank, which again amount to $100,000.

To return to our original example, with a 20 per cent cash reserve ratio, it will be observed that two changes correspond to the $500,000 fall in the general public's holding of money. In the first place, its holdings of securities have risen by $300,000; in the second place, its debts to the banks have fallen by $200,000. In other words, the public has to some extent changed the form of the claims it is holding by exchanging money for securities; for the rest, it has repaid debt to the banks, reducing its assets and liabilities equally.

To some extent this change in the form of some of the claims held by the public is an essential part of open market operations: the initiating force is the sale of securities to the public by the central bank. For the rest, the decision lies with the commercial banks. As we have seen, they can restore their cash ratios, either by reducing loans or by selling securities to the general public. In the example followed through above, we assumed that the commercial banks did both these things to equal extents.

The observant reader will have noticed that a significant difference still remains between the initial position and the final position in the sets of balance sheets considered above. Initially, the general public held one-fifth as much money in the form of notes of the central bank as it held in the form of commercial bank deposits. In the final position, a smaller proportion of the total money owned by the general public is held in the form of bank deposits, because the whole of the reduction in money holdings has been concentrated on bank deposits: the public's holdings of bank notes is the same as it was originally.

Whether this final situation is in fact the most likely one, it is difficult to say. To the extent that the effect of the central bank's operations have been to cause a shift in the form in which the public holds claims from money to securities, the final situation reached above does seem plausible. When a household or firm reduces its speculative holdings of money, in order to buy securities, it is far more likely that the money will come from bank deposits than from holdings of bank notes. On the other hand, it is quite likely that repayment of bank loans by the general public involves a direct [6] and substantial reduction in its desire to hold money in the form of bank notes; not all the reduction is necessarily concentrated on its holdings of bank deposits.

To the extent that the general public reacts to the effects of central bank open market operations by changing the quantity of its holdings of central bank notes, the size of the change in the total monetary circulation is less than when all the changes are concentrated on deposits at the commercial banks. Why this should be so is easy to see. If, as a consequence of demanding repayment of a loan, a commercial bank receives central bank notes, the recall of the advance has led to some replenishment of the commercial bank's cash reserves; the necessary reduction in its liabilities is therefore so much the less.[7]

It is difficult to estimate how far the general public will reduce its holdings of bank notes as a direct consequence of central bank open market sales, it is probably reasonable to guess that the limits of the range of possibility are, on the one hand complete concentration on bank deposits (as discussed already) and on the other hand, restoration of the original ratio between note holdings and deposit holdings.

It will, therefore, be convenient to consider what final equilibrium situation satisfies this latter reaction on the parts of households and firms. The set of balance sheets on p. 168 represents this new situation.[8]

In this case the reduced holdings of central bank notes by the general public, in order to maintain constancy in the ratio of its holdings of the two kinds of money, have greatly weakened the effects of open market operations on the amount of deposits at the commercial banks. Instead of a fivefold reduction, the amount of

---

[6] As distinct from one which is induced indirectly, e.g. through any induced changes in the level of income, operating as a result of a multiplier process arising from the changes in interest rates, etc.

[7] The same applies if it should happen that a household or firm buys securities from a commercial bank with central bank notes; or, for that matter, if households or firms bank with the central bank and buy securities with their deposits at the central bank.

[8] Asterisks represent figures that are different from those arising when all the reduction in the public's money stock is concentrated on deposits at the commercial banks.

CENTRAL BANK

Assets		Liabilities	
	$		$
Securities	7,900,000	*Deposits of commercial banks	2,962,500
		*Notes issued	4,937,500
	$7,900,000		$7,900,000

COMBINED COMMERCIAL BANKS

Assets		Liabilities	
	$		$
*Cash in tills (notes)	987,500	*Deposits	19,750,000
*Cash at central bank	2,962,500		
*Securities	7,900,000		
*Loans	7,900,000		
	$19,750,000		$19,750,000

GENERAL PUBLIC
(net)

Assets		Liabilities	
	$		$
*Notes of central bank	3,950,000	*Debts to banks	7,900,000
*Deposits at commercial banks	19,750,000		
*Securities	10,200,000		
	$33,900,000		$7,900,000
Net claims held by general public	$26,000,000		

GOVERNMENT

Assets		Liabilities	
			$
		Securities held by:	
		Central bank	7,900,000
		Commercial banks	7,900,000
		General public	10,200,000
		National Debt	$26,000,000

commercial bank deposits falls by only two and one-half the amount of the central bank's open market sales.[9] In addition, of course, there is now the reduction in the public's holding of bank notes; but all told, the reduction in public holdings of money is much less in this case. Moreover, the reduction in bank loans is much less, as is the effect on the securities market and interest rates, since fewer securities move into the hands of the general public.

Up to this point the whole discussion has been in terms of open market sales by the central bank. Exactly the same kind of analysis applies in the case of open market purchases. These lead to falling interest rates and to an expansion in the cash reserves of the commercial banks, and so to an increase in the money supply if the commercial banks hold their cash reserve ratios constant.

Limitations on Open Market Operations

The powers of the central bank to influence interest rates and the supply of money by means of open market operations are subject to three limitations. In the first place the central bank can choose either to fix interest rates or to determine the size of the cash reserves of the commercial banks; but it cannot arbitrarily fix both. If it wishes to fix interest rates, it must accept the consequence that the purchases or sales it makes in fixing these rates will affect the cash reserves of the commercial banks and so the amount of bank lending. For example, if the central bank wishes to fix interest rates at a low level it will probably have to support the correspondingly high security prices by extensive purchases of securities; these purchases will expand the cash reserves of the commercial banks, thereby tending to cause a big expansion in the monetary supplies of the country. Contrariwise, the central bank can choose what

---

[9] This result can be generalized by a simple formula. The total fall in the quantity of deposits at the commercial banks will be $\dfrac{1}{f+g}$ times the size of the central bank's open market sales, where f is the commercial bank's reserve ratio (in this case $\frac{1}{5}$) and g is the ratio between the change in the public's holdings of bank notes and the change in its holdings of bank deposits (in this case $\frac{1}{5}$; in the earlier case 0). As pointed out on p. 159 of Chapter 10, these processes of expansion and contraction in the quantity of money in relation to changes in the banks' cash holdings are closely parallel in nature to the multiplier process; hence the similar nature of the formulae.

level of bank lending it desires to allow, and, within the limits we shall look at shortly, can enforce its will; but in so doing, it has to accept whatever interest rates on securities happen to follow from the existence of this quantity of money it desires.

The second limitation is that the commercial banks may not keep their reserve ratios constant. If, for example, the commercial banks are in such a liquid position that they do not mind a reduction in their cash ratios,[10] open market sales by the central bank may have very limited effects; the second stage outlined above is then the final stage. This can be, and frequently is, a difficulty, but there are two points in favor of the effectiveness of central bank control through open market operations that may be made. Firstly, greatly excessive cash reserves are rather uncommon, because they mean that the commercial banks are tying up assets in an unprofitable manner. Secondly, minimum reserve ratios are in many countries imposed by law, and the minimum can well be at a higher level than that which the commercial banks regard as the minimum tolerable.

The third limitation on open market operations by the central bank arises from the facts that before it can operate in the market it must have something with which to operate, and that there must be a market in which to operate. Under modern conditions, with paper money and no precious metal coins in circulation, a central bank can always buy as many securities as it pleases, by creating further debts against itself. This supposes only the existence of the securities to buy and the willingness of the government to allow the central bank to continue creating money. The central bank can, therefore, cause creation of as much money as it likes: it can reduce interest rates to the lowest possible levels, if it wishes, and it can expand the cash reserves of the commercial banks so that they will be willing to lend on easy terms to any eligible borrower, and will also be willing to buy large quantities of securities. The reverse process, of open market sales, may be limited if the central bank does not possess sufficient securities to sell, or if there are few potential purchasers. The latter limitation has often been serious in relatively underdeveloped countries. The former limitation has less frequently been of importance. For one thing, most central banks do possess very large quantities of salable securities. Secondly,

---

[10] This situation prevailed in the United States in the 'thirties, when commercial banks held reserves far in excess of legal requirements.

relatively small security sales lead to magnified effects on bank lending. Quite small sales by the central bank may limit bank lending and raise interest rates quite substantially. Thirdly, and very important, the central bank can usually put the commercial banks into quite severe difficulties by open market sales. In the first example above, we assumed that the commercial banks would be able to reduce advances rapidly by $450,000, and would also be able to sell $450,000 worth of securities. In fact, it may not be easy for the commercial banks to bring about such changes rapidly. This puts the commercial banks into an awkward position, because meantime their cash ratio is below 20 per cent.

It is at this point where open market operations can put the commercial banks into real difficulties, that we find the link with the duty of the central bank to help the commercial banking system out of difficulties. The central bank fulfils this duty by appropriate lending—but in carrying out its duty it can impose its own conditions.

We have now reached the second of the four main types of control that can be imposed by the central bank on the banking system. In carrying out its duty of stabilizing the monetary system, the central bank must always be careful to avoid a situation arising in which the public loses confidence in the commercial banks; it must prevent a 'run' on the commercial banks from developing. Partly, it may do this by imposing direct restrictions on the activities of the commercial banks, either by order or persuasion; these matters we shall look at shortly. For the rest, the central bank must always be willing to help the commercial banks out of difficulties.

The Central Bank as Lender of Last Resort

The ways in which central banks normally help out commercial banks are by lending to the commercial banking system for short periods and by buying approved commercial paper from it. This aid is given at the request of the commercial banking system. Here lies the fundamental contrast between operations by the central bank as lender of last resort and open market operations. Open market operations are at the initiative of the central bank; operation as lender of last resort is at the initiative of the commercial banks.

In order to prevent the commercial banks from abusing such facilities the central bank imposes rigorous conditions upon its lending. Otherwise the commercial banks could obtain deposits at the central bank to act as a reserve on which to base an expansion of their lending which is not considered desirable by the central bank. Abuse of this kind is prevented either by charging a relatively high rate of interest by the central banks for its loans to the commercial banking system or, alternatively, in the American case, by discouraging continuous borrowing by the commercial banks; it has also been the experience in the United States that commercial banks have been reluctant to maintain a position of being continually in debt to the Reserve System. These non-price restraints are an important element in central bank control over the volume of reserves made available to the commercial banks in the United States, since the rate of interest charged by the Federal Reserve Banks is usually lower than the rate of interest earned by the commercial banks on their loans. Thus a distinction is usually made between central bank operations in the United States and in Britain, where the Bank of England prevents the abuse of its lending facilities by charging a penal rate of interest; aid is received by the commercial banks (indirectly, through the discount houses) at rates of interest which are considerably above the other short-term rates of interest with which they are normally concerned.[11]

In addition to charging a rate of interest on their lending, central banks often require, as a condition of receiving aid, that the commercial banks deposit suitable securities with the central bank to act as a guarantee to repay the loan in case of failure. This requirement is designed partly to discourage the commercial banks, partly to maintain the solvency of the central bank itself. The list of acceptable securities may be quite limited; frequently it only includes bills issued by reputable borrowers (including the government). Alternatively, as mentioned above, the central bank may be willing to buy approved commercial paper from the commercial banks at their initiative; once again, the central bank will take only limited kinds. In this alternative method the commercial banks are said to rediscount the bills.

Important consequences follow the willingness of the central bank to give these facilities to the commercial banking system. One is

---

[11] The American practice on bankers' acceptances—bills of exchange—is, however, quite similar to the British practice; the Federal Reserve buying rate on acceptances is normally higher than the rate of interest charged by the commercial banks for this type of security.

that those bills which are eligible for rediscount at the central bank or as a security for a loan from the central bank are particularly desirable assets for the commercial banks; they may be used to get cash reserves immediately (though in some banking systems at a penal price).[12] The commercial banks will, therefore, always wish to hold some such bills among their securities, and they will be willing to offer particularly high prices (i.e. charge low interest rates) on bills that are eligible by the central bank's standards.[13]

A further consequence of this aid is that when commercial banks are in difficulties and have to borrow from the central bank, they may find that their costs have risen. If so, they have an incentive to increase the rates of interest at which they lend. This leads us to see a way in which the central bank can influence interest rates and commercial bank policy on making loans without indulging in any open market operations. If the central bank alters the rate of interest at which it will lend to the commercial banking system when the commercial banks are in difficulties, the latter have a strong incentive to alter the rates of interest at which they are willing to lend; this may operate irrespective of whether or not the central bank operates on a penal rate system. If, for example, the central bank wishes to see a rise in the interest rates at which commercial banks lend, it may be able to induce such a rise simply by raising the rate at which it will lend to the banks should they run into difficulties. The commercial banks will be inclined to follow, because they never know whether or not they might shortly find themselves with a reserve ratio which has fallen a little below the required (or desirable) figure and so may need to obtain help from the central bank at the new and higher rate. When the commercial banks are actually in debt to the central bank, the sensitivity of their lending rates to changes in the central bank's lending rate is increased. In banking systems where the number of commercial banks is small, so that the banks see a direct connection between central bank policy and their reserve positions, there is an additional inducement to follow changes in the central bank's discount rate, for the banks know that the central bank can always create difficulties for them through open

---

[12] In the United States, the Federal Reserve Banks are permitted to lend to their member banks against any sound assets as collateral, in emergencies.

[13] Currently, American commercial banks use government securities, almost exclusively, as collateral when they borrow from the Federal Reserve Banks.

market operations so long as they keep their reserve ratios stable. In such cases it may be unnecessary for the central bank to enforce its view through open market operations, the changes in the central bank's discount rate being sufficient to persuade the commercial banks to follow. In banking systems composed of numerous commercial banks the willingness of the commercial banks to follow the rate changes initiated by the central bank depends upon the first factor noted above—the possibility that the banks will have to turn to the central banks when their reserve ratios are affected (assuming that the commercial banks are required or try to maintain stable reserve ratios). To the extent that the changes in the rate of interest charged by a central bank alter commercial bank lending rates, these changes in commercial bank rates, in turn, will affect the demand for loans and the rates of interest on all kinds of securities.

If the central bank should rely primarily on open market operations to implement its policy, the discount mechanism may act as a partial offset to the tightening or easing of credit effected by open market sales or purchases if the rates charged by the central bank are not penal rates. The virtue claimed for this arrangement is that it smoothes the impact of open market operations and thus enables the central authorities to pursue open market operations with more vigor since there is less fear that they will move too far in either direction; and if it is coupled with central bank discretion over the volume of rediscounts afforded to the commerical banks, the loss of control by the central bank over the monetary situation need not be too great.

Legal Minimum Cash Reserve Ratios

The preceding argument was based on an assumption that the commercial banks strive to maintain a constant ratio between their cash reserves and their total deposit liabilities. The twin pulls of prudence and of desire for profit may well ensure this, but in many countries it has been considered that prudence may not always be a sufficiently powerful force. In those countries, the law has imposed minimum cash reserve ratios. These ratios may be either the ratios between total cash and liabilities or only between cash held in the form of deposits at the central bank and liabilities.

Such regulations have their disadvantages. A rule that cash must *never* fall below a certain ratio deprives the cash reserve of its function: that of acting as a cushion in times of serious difficulties. It is rather like the (no doubt apocryphal) police commissioner who tried to solve a shortage of taxicabs by making a rule that there must always be one cab at each cab stand. The rule should have some flexibility; for example, a provision that penalties are suffered if the ratio is below the legal minimum for more than a certain number of days together. Another limitation of rules about minimum reserves is that they do not prevent the commercial banks from holding a bigger ratio than the minimum provided by law. They may, in fact, consider it prudent to do so if the minimum is too rigidly imposed. But if the commercial banks hold reserves in excess of the minimum, they have much cash that can be absorbed before open market sales by the central bank need have any effect on their policy. Similarly, open market purchases by the central bank may do nothing to enforce expansion of bank lending, if the commercial banks are willing simply to hold a larger ratio of cash reserves.

In situations such as this the central bank frequently uses this power in an active manner, by altering the level of the minimum cash reserve ratios to which the commercial banks must adhere; these levels can be changed by the central bank. If, for example, the present minimum legal ratio happens to be 10 per cent and the ratio actually held by the commercial banks is 20 per cent, very extensive open market sales will be needed before commercial bank cash reserves are reduced to around 10 per cent; meantime, the open market policy may be quite ineffective. Similarly, a change in the central bank discount rate may be ignored by the commercial banks if they are in such a relatively strong liquid position. All this strength can be removed overnight, however, if the central bank is able to change the minimum legal cash reserve ratio to 20 per cent. Then open market sales or a raising of the discount rate will be effective immediately.

The possibility of an extension of this arrangement to replace the use of open market operations for restricting or allowing the expansion of bank lending activities is immediately obvious. In the example just given, if the minimum reserve ratio is fixed at 25 per cent, the commercial banks will find themselves short of cash, by the new standards; they will have to restrict their lending and probably appeal to the central bank for temporary assistance. Similarly, by reducing the legal minimum cash ratio, the central bank can make it possible for the commercial banks to do more lending.

Changes in legal reserve ratios can, therefore, act as substitutes for open market operations; the latter change the size of the cash reserve available while the former affect the size of the reserve necessary to support a given volume of lending. In some banking systems both open market operations and changes in reserve ratios are used to help enforce central bank policy; open market operations can be used for the more delicate changes, while changes in reserve ratios can be used for drastically large operations. The method of changing reserve requirements comes particularly well into its own, however, in countries where open market operations can be of little use because there is no really extensive security market in which the central bank can operate. This is particularly likely in those countries which are relatively underdeveloped economically.

Direct Instructions to the Commercial Banks

The fourth, and last, of the groups of methods by which the central bank can control the monetary and banking system also consists of the possibility of giving direct orders to the commercial banks about the kind and amount of lending they may do. Restrictions may be imposed by the central bank (either by strict orders or by requests) on certain kinds of bank lending—for example, for stock market purchases or for consumer installment loans. The commercial banks may be compelled, or requested, to lend a certain part of their assets to the government.

This kind of direct control by the central banks has been very important in recent years in a number of countries, concurrent with the large amount of direct control by other organs of the state. How effective it has been in practice is a matter for debate; but it is beyond question that controls such as these are now as much an accepted part of a central bank's armory of weapons as the older methods of control we have considered at length. The short space given to these controls is not an indication of their relative importance, but simply of the fact that there is relatively little that can be said about them in general terms.

The Central Bank as the Government's Bank

We have now reached the end of our discussion of the ways in which central banks can control the monetary system, and with that we have nearly reached the end of our discussion of central banking operations. There remains, however, one aspect of central banking operations which has been a feature of most central banks. We have seen that, as controller of the monetary system, the central bank must inevitably have close relationships with the government. Partly as a result of these relationships, and partly in order to give the central bank prestige (with the consequence that it can more easily impose its will on the banking system) it frequently acts as the government's banker. Banking accounts of the government are usually held with the central bank and not with the commercial banks.

There is one disadvantage that can sometimes arise from such an arrangement. The expenditure and receipts of the government do not move in and out steadily; at some times of the month heavy out-payments may perhaps take place; at some times of the year, tax receipts may well be concentrated. If such fluctuations take place, they affect the cash reserves of the commercial banks in the same way as open market operations. For example, when the government is receiving from the public more than it is spending, the balances of the public at the commercial banks fall, the balances of the government at the central bank rise, and the corresponding settlement between the commercial banks and the central bank takes place by a reduction in commercial bank deposits at the central bank. The cash reserve ratios of the commercial banks therefore fall. If the commercial banks are wanting to hold their cash ratios constant, they have to contract their lending. Such a reaction would be undesirable if the heavy payments to the government were purely a temporary phenomenon. It is not difficult to avoid these undesirable consequences; one technique that has been used in the United States is the deposit of Treasury receipts with the commercial banks until needed for the purpose of making payments. In this way sizable fluctuations in commercial bank reserves not related to monetary control are avoided.

A major advantage of employing the central bank as the government's banker is that the central bank then has close relationships with the parts of the government administration which are concerned with monetary matters; as a consequence, the bank is in a better position to convey advice to the government. This provision of monetary advice to the government of the day is, in practice, one of the major functions of most central banks. In addition, the close relationships between the central bank and the government on the one hand and the financial community on the other has meant that certain other administrative functions, such as the issuance, exchange, and redemption of government securities and transactions for the trust fund accounts, are carried out by the central bank.

Finally, it must be mentioned that some central banks carry out a certain amount of banking business for the general public. Generally speaking, such competition with the commercial banks is thought to be undesirable, because it may reduce the central bank's moral authority over the rest of the banking system; a controller should not also be a competitor. For the most part, such activities are the relic of earlier days, and are tending to decline.[14] To the extent that they are significant, they may have consequences similar to the effects of the central bank as banker to the government. If, for some reason, those members of the public who bank at the central bank are temporarily making more payments to the members of the public who bank at the commercial banks than are moving in the opposite direction, the cash reserves of the commercial banks will be tending to expand; and vice versa when the flow is in the opposite direction. Such tendencies are not very likely, and can usually be ignored.

Some Suggested Reading

It is difficult to find literature on central banking that is not preoccupied with the particular problems of a particular central bank. In a collection of essays by R. S. Sayers, *Central Banking After Bagehot* (Oxford, 1957), there are two chapters that come near to this ideal. They are Chapter 1, 'The Theoretical Basis of Central Banking,' and Chapter 9, 'Central Banking in Underdeveloped Countries.' Also quite useful in this regard is H. P. Willis, *The Theory and Practice of Central Banking*, (New York, 1936). In this book H. P. Willis, an economist who played an important part in the establishment of the Federal Reserve System, examines the nature of central banks and the powers with which they may operate.

---

[14] In the United States, the Federal Reserve Banks do not accept deposits from the general public, but they do afford limited credit facilities to the public. The Federal Reserve Banks have the power to make loans called 'industrial advances' to nonbank borrowers under exceptional circumstances.

12

American Banking Institutions—
I. Banking Prior to the Federal Reserve System

In outline the kind of system described in Chapters 10 and 11 approximates reasonably closely a description of the present American banking system, in which monetary controls reside with the Federal Reserve. In this chapter we will attempt to trace through the development of banking in the United States prior to the adoption, in 1914, of the Federal Reserve System, which was authorized by the Federal Reserve Act of 1913. Experience of the defects and failures of the banking system as it existed prior to 1914 were important determinants of the structure and goals of the American central banking system as formulated by Congress.

Banking Prior to the National Banking System

The first bank to be founded in the United States was the Bank of North America, which was established in Philadelphia in 1782. Robert Morris, Superintendent of Finance during the Revolutionary War, was its chief architect and it was his intention to use the bank to provide financial support to the Revolution. With the aid of a governmental subscription to the capital stock (based on gold received from France) the bank turned out to be a success, achieving substantial support from non-governmental sources. The bank made large loans to the government and did a substantial business in the discounting of commercial paper; throughout this period the bank was able to maintain convertibility of its notes into gold on demand and it appeared that the quantity of money in circulation in the country was adequate. Notes issued by the Bank of North America filled the gap created by the disappearance from circulation of the 'bills of credit' issued by the Continental Congress (Continental currency), and the bank's success in large part rested upon this disappearance of the Continental currency. By 1780 the Continental currency had depreciated to the point where it became worthless and ceased to circulate.

Two other banks were established prior to the formation of the federal government, the Bank of Massachusetts and the Bank of New York, both of which were established in 1784. These banks were supplemented by a number of unincorporated banks, called 'private' banks, which operated under common law.

The next important step in American banking was the founding of the first Bank of the United States in 1791 by Alexander Hamilton, the first Secretary of the Treasury; it was the first bank to be founded under federal charter, and it operated for twenty years as a combined commercial and central bank. The United States government held stock in the Bank and the Bank acted as fiscal agent for the government, but its management was in private hands. By private standards the Bank was a financial success; it paid high dividends and accumulated a substantial surplus. From the national point of view, the Bank was an important source of currency; roughly one-fifth of the note circulation was furnished by the Bank, and it performed as a regulator of the currency. The latter role grew out of the Bank's practice of promptly presenting for redemption in specie, for its own protection, the notes of other banks that came to it as deposits; thus it enforced upon the State-chartered banks higher standards of liquidity and thereby contributed to the maintenance of some degree of uniformity among the various bank notes in circulation.

By the time the first Bank's charter came up for renewal, the Federalist party was no longer in control of the government and the Republican opponents of the Bank made the granting of a new charter a subject of political debate. From its very beginning the Bank's existence had been clouded with doubts concerning its constitutionality and during the debate these doubts were brought to the fore by the Republicans. The question of foreign control over the economy by virtue of the substantial number of Bank shares held outside the country was also injected into the debate. State-chartered banks offered their support in opposition to the granting of the new charter because of their wish to be rid of the competition and regulatory power of the first Bank. By a close vote, Congress decided against renewal of the Bank's charter and in 1811 the Bank was liquidated.

The demise of the first Bank of the United States was quickly followed by the rapid spread and growth of state-chartered banks. In part, the growth of the state banks may be attributed to the vacuum that was created by the removal of the first Bank's competition and the demand for finance that was stimulated by the War of 1812, but an additional contributory factor was the withdrawal of the restraining influence that had been exerted by the first Bank. The state banks embarked upon a note-issuing spree and by 1814 gold and silver specie payments had been suspended by the banks in most parts of the country. State bank notes circulated at varying discounts, and the Treasury found itself carrying out a war with a monetary system that was so disorganized that its deposits in one part of the country were not acceptable for the payments it had to make in another part. Proposals were made that a new national bank be formed to ameliorate the monetary situation, but before the form of the new bank could be decided upon by the Congress the war ended and the need for a national bank no longer seemed so urgent; the national bank measure was accordingly postponed.

The end of the war did not, however, bring an end to monetary chaos, and there appeared but few signs that convertibility into gold and silver would be resumed in the near future. The continuing chaotic state of the country's monetary circulation reduced the opposition to a national bank since it became apparent that some form of a central institution was needed to restore a semblance of uniformity among the various bank notes that were in circulation, and to this end, the second Bank of the United States was established in 1816 under a federal charter which was to run until 1836. Its charter was, broadly speaking, similar to that of the first Bank and one of the main purposes of the new Bank was to force the state-chartered banks to restore the convertibility of their notes into specie. The second Bank began operations in 1817, but for the first two years of its existence it did little to lessen the disorderly currency situation; it not only failed to press the state banks on the matter of redemption but even failed to redeem some of its own note issues. Mismanagement on the part of the Bank's officials almost brought it to ruin, but in 1819, after a change in management, the Bank began to fulfill its promise as a regulator of the currency supply of the country and, shortly, convertibility was generally restored.

The second Bank was not destined, however, to have a long life; as was the case with the first Bank, the second Bank became a political issue. President Jackson, who assumed office in 1829, became a staunch foe of the Bank, and in 1832 he vetoed a bill that considered renewal of the second Bank's charter. In his re-election campaign in 1832 President Jackson made the reissuance of the Bank's charter a major issue, and after his re-election the federal government's deposits were withdrawn from the Bank. This, in effect, spelled an end to the second Bank's activities, and when the Bank's charter expired in 1836, central banking was removed from the American scene for nearly eighty years.

How well had the two Banks performed? By and large it appears that they had operated tolerably well in providing a substantial degree of uniformity among the various bank notes, through their partial success in making the many state bank notes convertible. The Banks were not successful, however, in overcoming the strains placed upon the United States monetary system from the defective coinage system. An inappropriate silver to gold mint ratio drove gold out of the country, and an inappropriate silver content for the dollar foreclosed the possibility that any foreign silver coins, which were circulating in the United States, would be brought to the mint. Late in the life of the second Bank, in 1834, an attempt was made to return gold to monetary use, but the adjustment that was made in the relative prices of the precious metals served to reverse their positions so that gold came into the country and became the standard while, on the other hand, it became profitable to export silver. Neither of the two Banks was effective in promoting changes in the monetary circulation directed towards ironing out seasonal or cyclical fluctuations; commercial and central bank functions were combined and the proper goals of a central monetary authority were, at best, only hazily defined.

Between the expiration of the second Bank's charter and 1863 the American banking system consisted of state chartered banks and 'private' (common law) banks. The growth of the state banks was stimulated by the removal of the second Bank's restraining influence and by the enactment of 'Free Banking Acts' (beginning in 1838 in New York state) which provided that bank charters could be obtained simply by meeting the requirements of bank incorporation laws rather than by securing legislative approval. The New York Free Banking Act was designed to break up the bank monopoly which had come to be associated with corruption and bribery in the issuance of charters; within a short time other states enacted similar statutes, the movement gaining support not only from those concerned with the monopoly issue but also from those who considered it to be a means of producing easier money. This principle of 'free banking' had implications for American banking that extend to the present day, since it has been an important feature of nearly all the banking laws that have been enacted since that time, on both the federal and state level. Easy entry into the banking field combined with federal and state laws that severely limited branch banking have resulted in a large number of unit banks in the American banking system, which differentiates it so markedly from the banking systems in most of the other economically developed countries. Many of the states that passed 'free banking' measures paid little attention to the abuses possible under such a 'liberal' arrangement; bank note collateral requirements and reserve requirements were often woefully inadequate to the task of providing a uniform and safe currency. Bank failures were numerous and the holders of notes and deposits often suffered severe losses. The note circulation was, to say the least, confusing; some state bank notes were redeemable in gold and silver at their face value while others circulated at substantial discounts relative to their face value; convertibility into specie, which had been suspended generally during the panic of 1837, continued into the 1840's, and while the gold discoveries in California helped somewhat to alleviate the situation, area inconvertibility recurred from time to time during the rest of the state banking period.

It is not surprising, therefore, that general dissatisfaction with the banking situation evoked demands for closer governmental supervision of the banks. Steps were taken by a number of states to tighten or impose reserve requirements upon the banks in their areas, and while these reserve requirements were originally limited to notes in circulation, a few states extended the requirements to include deposits. A further development which occurred in this period was the inclusion in a bank's reserves of the deposits it held in a bank situated in a financial center, thus departing from the original practice of counting as reserves only the specie held in a bank's vault. This was one of the early steps in the growth in importance of correspondent balances (which exist to this day) that became an integral part of the National Banking System.

It was also during this state banking period that bank deposits became a more important part of the nation's monetary circulation than bank notes. The growth in the relative importance of transactions that were settled through money payments and payment settlements that involved more distant places, reflecting the trend to larger business units and improved communication and transportation facilities, necessitated a more convenient medium of exchange than that afforded by bank notes; checking deposits filled this need and in 1855 they took the lead, in terms of quantitative importance, which was never again relinquished. Concomitantly, the function of banks increasingly became the extension of credit in deposit form rather than the issuance of bank notes; between 1840 and 1860 the volume of bank notes in circulation about doubled while the volume of bank deposits more than tripled.

Despite the efforts made by the individual states to improve the monetary situation, frequent failures by banks to maintain convertibility of their notes and deposits continued. These excesses connected with state banking provoked frequent demands that the note issue be brought under the federal government's surveillance. Suggestions were made that the federal government enact general banking laws that would draw upon the experience of some of the states that had pursued bank regulation policies rather successfully, e.g. New York and Massachusetts, that note issues be restricted to federally chartered banks and that the volume of such notes be tied to holdings of United States government obligations. The adoption of such a system would mean, in effect, that the circulating medium would consist of national bank notes rather than the varied note issues of the state banks.

Apart from the lack of uniformity among the various types of money in existence and the frequent failure to pay specie upon demand in exchange for notes and deposits, fluctuations in the quantity of money during the state banking era tended to magnify rather than to moderate seasonal or cyclical swings if, indeed, they did not create them. Freed from the checks imposed upon them by the second Bank of the United States, state banks increased their note and deposit liabilities sharply in periods of expanding business activity; in periods of slack economic activity the reverse process of monetary contraction was almost as severe. This pattern of behavior, on the part of the state banks is, of course, not surprising since a banking system operating without a central regulator produces changes in the monetary circulation that tend to be cumulative; increased credit extensions tend to make further extensions profitable while, on the other hand, credit contractions which reduce the volume of spending further reduce the demand for loans, thereby generating further decreases in the quantity of money.

The National Banking System

The National Banking System came into being primarily because of the Civil War. Dissatisfaction with the state banking system that was outlined above played a role in the adoption of the new system, but it does not appear that the change would have come about so soon without the pressures of war finance.

In 1861, Salmon Chase, the Secretary of the Treasury, drew up a plan whereby the note circulation of the country could be made a means for increasing the sales of Treasury securities. Under this proposal the banks would issue notes only if they were backed by United States Treasury bonds; this, it was claimed, would ensure a uniform currency and stimulate the sales of Treasury obligations. In spite of the desire to get the proposal quickly enacted into law so that it could be employed as a means of war finance, it was not until 1863 that Congress passed the first law, the National Banking Act, authorizing the new banking arrangement. In the following year a new law was passed which supplanted the 1863 law and introduced some changes thought to be desirable by the first Comptroller of the Currency operating under the new system.

With the passage of the National Banking Act, the federal government assumed responsibilities in the field of banking for the first time since the expiration of the charter of the second Bank of the United States. Under the Act, banks were able to operate under charters secured from the federal government. These national banks could secure national bank notes by depositing United States Treasury bonds with the Comptroller of the Currency; a national bank could obtain, from the Comptroller, notes up to 90 per cent of par or market value of the bonds deposited, whichever was smaller. An additional limitation was that the total volume of national bank notes any one bank could obtain was not to exceed that bank's capital stock. An upper limit of $300 million was placed on the total national bank note circulation; this limit was changed subsequently and in 1875 it was removed completely.

The other main provision of the National Bank Act was the imposition of minimum reserve requirements against both notes and deposits, the percentage required varying with the location of the bank. Reserve city banks and central reserve city banks were subject to a 25 per cent reserve requirement while the other banks (country banks) were required to maintain a reserve ratio of at least 15 per cent. In 1874 the reserve system was modified so as to eliminate the requirement that reserves be held against notes issued by banks and in its place was substituted the requirement that each bank maintain a deposit with the Comptroller of the Currency at least equal to 5 per cent of its notes in circulation. In addition to prescribing minimum reserve ratios, the National Bank Act set down rules as to the composition of bank reserves. Country banks could meet their reserve requirement by holding $\frac{2}{5}$ of their reserve holdings (6 per cent of deposits) in the form of cash in vault and $\frac{3}{5}$ (9 per cent of deposits) in the form of cash in vault or deposits at reserve city or central reserve city banks. For reserve city banks the ratios were $\frac{1}{2}$ (12$\frac{1}{2}$ per cent of deposits) and $\frac{1}{2}$ (12$\frac{1}{2}$ per cent) in the form of cash in vault or deposits at the central reserve city banks. For central reserve city banks the full reserve (25 per cent of deposits) was to be held as cash in vault.

Other provisions of the National Banking Act dealt with (1) the capital requirements; (2) the regulations concerning bank assets, and (3) the supervision and examination rules that applied to the national banks. Minimum capital requirements were set as follows: $50,000 in cities of not over 6000 inhabitants; $100,000 in cities from 6000 to 50,000 inhabitants; $200,000 in cities over 50,000 inhabitants. The same capital requirements are in force at present for national banks. Before a bank could begin operations at least one-half of the capital subscribed had to be paid in, and the rest had to be paid within five months. The bank was further required to deliver to the United States Treasury registered government bonds amounting to not less than $30,000 and not less than one-third of its capital stock. This provision was subsequently modified and finally dropped. The stock of a national bank was subject to double liability,[1] and 10 per cent of a national bank's profits had to be added to its surplus

---

[1] Double liability meant that bank stockholders could be assessed up to an amount equal to the face value of their bank stocks to pay the debts of the bank in case the bank should become insolvent.

until the surplus account amounted to 20 per cent of the bank's capital stock. The double liability rule was finally dropped in 1937.

Restrictions were placed upon the assets that a national bank could acquire; for example, a bank could not purchase real estate mortgages. This rule has been liberalized considerably over time. Nor could it make loans amounting to more than 10 per cent of its capital stock to any single borrower. To guarantee that the strictures of the system were followed the national banks were subject to examinations by the Comptroller of the Currency's office and were required to send periodic reports of their financial condition to his office.

It was at first thought that state chartered banks would take out charters under the National Banking Act, and that new banks would choose federal rather than state charters, but it soon became clear that the state banks preferred to remain under state-issued charters. To force the state banks into becoming national banks or stop their banking activities Congress imposed, in 1865, a 10 per cent tax on the issuance or use of state bank notes. This measure was sufficient to reduce drastically the number of state banks in existence in the short run, but by the end of the nineteenth century, state banks were once again more numerous than national banks. The national banks were larger on the average, however, and accounted for the major share of commercial bank assets. The declining importance of notes relative to deposits and the less stringent regulations under state charters combined to produce a situation in which state charters were relatively more attractive than national charters to new banks.

Let us turn now to the actual operation of the National Banking System. Typically, the banks in the various classifications held no more cash than the required cash reserves so that when currency drains were felt by the country and reserve city banks, they called upon the central reserve city banks to provide them with cash in exchange for the deposits that they held there. The central reserve city banks held all of their reserves in the form of cash in vault, but since they generally maintained a cash ratio that was close to 25 per cent, any demands for cash placed them in tight straits. These central reserve city banks had to meet their reserve requirements at all times so their holdings of required reserves did not provide any cushion to meet drains.

This correspondent relationship was tailored to order as a creator and transmitter of financial panics. As soon as there was a threat that the central reserve city banks might have to suspend payments in cash because of heavy drains to the country and/or reserve city banks, these banks would intensify their demands that their deposits be transferred into cash, thus accentuating the pressure that was being placed on the banks in the financial centers. Further, under the correspondent relationship system it was expected that country banks could borrow from their respective city correspondents if their reserve positions deteriorated, either because of currency withdrawals or because they had to make substantial payments to other banks in response to the checks that were drawn by their customers. At any one time, a few country banks' demands for loans could be met by their city correspondents; but when the demands, in aggregate, were substantial, the city correspondents could accommodate these borrowers only by drastically curtailing the credit that they had extended to local borrowers. And each time the city correspondents did supply currency to the country banks their own reserves were reduced, thus limiting their ability to meet the credit needs of both country and city borrowers.

Since the central reserve city banks did not have the power to expand reserves and no flexibility in meeting their own reserve requirements, it turned out to be impossible for them to carry out the functions usually delegated to a central bank in fractional reserve banking systems. Reserves tended to be concentrated as a result of the operations of correspondent banking, as they would have if a central bank had existed, but no institution existed that performed the central bank function of 'lender of last resort.' From time to time, funds were borrowed from abroad, thereby expanding the volume of reserves available to the American banking system, but more frequently the volume of reserves tended to remain fairly stable in the short run. The result of all this was that crises recurred rather frequently, with particularly severe crises occurring in 1893 and 1907.

An institution that attempted to ameliorate the difficulties resulting from the absence of a reserve-creating mechanism was the clearing house (an arrangement whereby banks, within an area, meet to settle the net balances arising from the checks drawn against each other). Banks that were members of a clearing house were expected to make prompt payments of their debts to the clearing house, and as a consequence of this requirement, clearing houses developed the power to exert disciplinary pressures upon those banks which pursued policies making them unable to assume these obligations for payment. This arrangement served to protect the members of the clearing house in normal times, but it afforded little protection in periods of crisis that resulted from a general inadequacy of reserves. During general crises an individual member of a clearing house had very little control over the situation, and under such circumstances the improvement of one bank's position usually meant that the general problem of shortage of reserves was passed on to other members of the union of banks forming a clearing house. To cope with this problem of shortage of reserves some of the clearing houses, notably the New York City clearing house, began to issue certificates which could be employed to settle debts with the clearing house. Although these were not legal reserves, they served as substitutes and enabled the banks to economize in their use of reserves. From 1860 on, these clearing house certificates were used during periods of crisis, the important dates being 1873, 1890, 1893, and 1907. At times they also served as circulating media among the general public in the .place of currency which was short in supply. The frequent resort to the clearing house certificate device led to their recognition as important stabilizing instruments, and in 1908 the Aldrich-Vreeland Act legalized their issuance.

Early in the development of banking in the United States, it was realized that the operations of the Treasury produced monetary effects—quite often substantial effects which, in the absence of a central bank under the National Banking System, meant that Treasury activities were important determinants of the state of the money market and consequently of the level of economic activity. Attempts were made to conduct Treasury operations so as to produce as few of these disturbing effects as possible. For example, the Treasury tried to avoid, in its operations, sudden transfers of funds that would produce excessively tight money in one area and abnormally easy money in another area. The Independent Treasury System's operations were designed to involve the withdrawal of money from the community, to be locked in vaults when the Treasury's receipts exceeded its expenditures, and the release of money to the community out of Treasury vaults when expenditures exceeded receipts; the Treasury was supposed to avoid the use of bank deposits in carrying out its transactions, insofar as this was possible. But the policy of independence, to the extent that it was followed, meant that Treasury operations were sometimes stabilizing and sometimes destabilizing. Bank reserves were reduced or increased without consideration for the level of economic activity in the community.

By the time the National Banking System was instituted the destabilizing effects of the Independent Treasury System had been tempered to some extent because the Treasury found it necessary and desirable to make use of the facilities afforded by banks. The Treasury's reliance upon banks continued to grow, with some exceptions, during the life of the National Banking System. Despite these changes, however, the Independent Treasury System did, by the very nature of its operation, raise some serious problems for monetary management.

In time, however, the policy of independence came on occasion to be abandoned deliberately, and not merely under the general pressure of administrative convenience. The Treasury came, at times, to attempt to help in stabilizing the economy; there were numerous cases in which Treasury operations were directed toward alleviating the difficulties that arose in the money market because of the inability of the banking system to acquire necessary reserves and because of the stains that developed out of the correspondent bank relationship. In some instances the Treasury purchased government bonds in order to alleviate tightness in the money market. More frequently, Treasury intervention took the form of increasing or decreasing federal deposits with the banks by varying the funds held in the sub-Treasuries, or by allowing the receipts of the government to accumulate in banks rather than diverting these funds to the sub-Treasuries. The movements of funds to and from the sub-Treasuries affected the volume of bank reserves while the latter policy meant that bank reserves, at least, would not suffer contraction. The limitations on Treasury stabilizing actions were, however, quite severe. Expansionist policies could be pursued only to the extent that Treasury funds in vault were available, while its ability to enforce contractions was dependent upon the size of Treasury deposits with the banks and the size of the budget surplus. Further, the Treasury's authority to intervene in essentially central bank operations was often questioned. If it was not illegal for the Treasury to operate in this fashion, it certainly ran counter to the goals that were set forth at the time when the Independent Treasury System was established.

As a consequence of these confusions over the Treasury's authority to attempt monetary management and because of the limited resources possessed by the Treasury for this sort of activity, the role of the Treasury in the money sphere depended, in large part, upon the Secretary in command at any particular time. Secretaries Gage (1897-1902) and Shaw (1902-1907) were particularly active in their use of Treasury operations to influence credit conditions with an eye to stabilization. Gage relied on the deployment of federal deposits, government bond redemptions, and the prepayment of interest charges to influence the money market. Shaw adopted a policy of offsetting the drains that appeared in the crop-moving season when country banks exerted pressures upon their city correspondents. Indeed, Shaw felt that with additional funds at its disposal, the Treasury could carry out stabilization activities that would compare favorably in results with those of a central bank.

In addition to the frequent difficulties that stemmed from the inadequate volume of reserves, a common complaint against the National Banking System was that the issue of notes was too inflexible. In the years of state banking the circulation of notes with varied discounts attached to them had convinced the proponents of reform in banking that a prime requisite of the new system was the safety of bank notes; safety was achieved, but too little attention was given to the question as to how necessary and desirable changes in the volume of notes might be brought about. Since the issuance of notes was limited to 90 per cent of par or market value (whichever was the lower) of government bonds deposited by the national banks with the Comptroller of the Currency, the supply of notes was related to the state of the bond market. If bonds were selling above par the profitability of issuing notes fell, since note issues were restricted to less than 90 per cent of the cost of bonds purchased. In large part, the supply of notes moved with fluctuations in the government bond market, but the fluctuations in this market did not necessarily coincide in timing and amplitude with what would have been an appropriate course for the supply of notes. This inelasticity of the supply of bank notes in response to the currency needs of business and agriculture became a paramount issue in the demands for a central bank.

The accumulated grievances with the banking system as it operated under the National Banking Act were: the instability of economic activity, which variations in the quantity of money fostered rather than counteracted; the inability of the system to expand the volume of reserves when it was appropriate to do so; and the in-elasticity of national bank notes. In the absence of a central bank many of its presumed functions were assumed by the Treasury, clearing houses, and city banks. These institutions performed the necessary services in an imperfect fashion since they were handi-capped by their lack of authority and their lack of the necessary resources. Clearing houses could create partial substitutes for re-serves but only within narrow limits, and their geographical areas of operations were severely limited. The Treasury's authority to per-form central banking functions was often questioned and it was dependent upon the fiscal position of the federal government. The city correspondent banks did not possess the power to expand the volume of reserves, so that in periods of crisis they lacked the ability to lend in a manner most conducive to stabilization.

The panic of 1907 afforded a focal point for the arguments of proponents of reform in banking and strong support was marshaled in favor of altering the monetary system toward reducing the amplitude and frequency of variations of the supply and availability of money and credit. Congress responded by setting up a National Monetary Commission in 1908 for the purpose of investigating the banking situation and suggesting remedial legislation. The original proposal that came out of the Commission's studies called for a single central bank, but the idea that finally took hold and was embodied in legislation called for regional banks that were to be co-ordinated through a single board that was to be situated in Washington; distrust of centralization dictated this regional arrange-ment for the new system.

SOME SUGGESTED READING

There is an extensive literature on the banking system in the United States prior to the formation of the Federal Reserve System. Much of this material can be found in some of the older textbooks on money and bank-ing. Two of these that warrant mention in this connection are H. White, *Money and Banking*, 5th ed. (Boston, 1914) and C. F. Dunbar, *The Theory and History of Banking*, 4th ed. (New York, 1922).

For an analysis of the theories of banking that were extant prior to the formation of the National Banking System, H. E. Miller, *Banking Theories in the United States before 1860* (Cambridge, Mass., 1927) is a useful source. B. Hammond, 'Historical Introduction' in *Banking Studies* (published by the Board of Governors of the Federal Reserve System, Washington, 1941) offers a convenient summary of the pre-Federal Reserve banking system. In a recent book, *Banks and Politics in America from the Revolution to the Civil War* (Princeton, 1957), Hammond has brought forth an interesting and penetrating survey of banking before the establishment of the National Banking System.

ॐ

American Banking Institutions—
II. The Federal Reserve System

The Federal Reserve System was established by the Federal Reserve Act of 1913. Arguments advanced in favor of the central bank were that it would provide a more 'elastic' supply of currency that would prevent the recurrence of crises when the public wished to withdraw currency, and that it would provide a central reserve which would be available for common use in periods of tight credit. It was hoped that this would correct the situation which existed in the National Banking System, where the scramble by the individual banks for reserves imparted strong deflationary pressures to the banking system as a whole. In addition it was hoped that the new system would facilitate interregional check clearing and improve the banking facilities available to the government. Alterations have been made in the legislative basis for the system, the most important changes occurring in 1933 and in 1935. This chapter is concerned with the structure of the Federal Reserve System and the development of its instruments of monetary control.

The Structure of the Federal Reserve System

At the heart of the Federal Reserve System is the *Board of Governors* (called the Federal Reserve Board before 1935). Surrounding this, the System can be seen as consisting of three concentric circles. In the center, in addition to the Board of Governors, there is the *Federal Open Market Committee* and the *Federal Advisory Council*. Next, to move away from the center, are the twelve *Federal Reserve Banks*, which are located in geographical divisions of the country called Districts. Lastly, tied to each Reserve Bank are a large num-

194

ber of ordinary commercial banks which are called member banks —banks which have fulfilled the requirements for membership in the Federal Reserve System. Most of the connections between the member banks and the System are through the various Reserve Banks.

The Board of Governors of the Federal Reserve System is situated in Washington, D. C. and is made up of seven members, who are appointed by the President for a term of fourteen years; the appointments are not renewable and one term expires every two years. The Board's power was increased by the Banking Act of 1935 and it has come to represent the central authority in the Federal Reserve System. It has general supervisory powers over the governing of the Federal Reserve Banks. It appoints one-third of the directors of each Federal Reserve Bank and it has to approve appointments of the presidents and first vice-presidents of the Reserve Banks; it also requires that the Reserve Banks submit reports on their examinations of the member banks and accounts of their operations. In central bank operations, the Board of Governors has the power to approve or disapprove the discount rates set by the Reserve Banks [1] and to set minimum reserve requirements, within the limits prescribed by law, for the member banks. Maximum rates of interest paid by the member banks on time and saving deposits are set by the Board. In addition, the Board was empowered by the Securities Exchange Act of 1934 to fix the margin requirements for loans on securities; this regulation applies to *all* banks and to brokers. The regulation of consumer credit, when such regulation has been in force, has also come under the authority of the Board of Governors. Finally, but not least important, the members of the Board of Governors are the majority members of the Federal Open Market Committee; their functions in this capacity we shall discuss below.

The Federal Open Market Committee is composed of the seven members of the Board of Governors and five representatives from the Reserve Banks. The New York Reserve Bank, because it is situated in the center of the money market and of the United States government securities market, is always represented by its president, who automatically becomes vice-chairman of the Committee;

---

[1] According to the legal interpretation of the Banking Act of 1935, the Federal Reserve Board has the power to require that the Reserve Banks alter their discount rates if it should so desire.

the other four members from the Reserve Banks are selected on a rotation basis. Open market operations were an instrument of monetary policy prior to the formation of the Committee by the Banking Act of 1933, but the informal open market committee organized by the Reserve Banks left much to be desired in terms of the degree of co-ordination achieved. A further criticism of the informal arrangement was that it gave the New York Bank too much power. The Banking Act of 1933 created the Federal Open Market Committee, but the Reserve Banks were not compelled to follow the decisions made by the Committee. The Banking Act of 1935 centralized and formalized the operations and placed the prime power and responsibility for this task in the hands of the Board of Governors, and made it mandatory that the Reserve Banks carry out the policy decisions made by the Open Market Committee.

The full Committee does not, in practice, concern itself with the finer details of open market transactions but confines itself to the formulation of the more significant policy decisions. Then these decisions are transmitted to the manager of the System Open Market Account (who is a vice-president of the Federal Reserve Bank of New York) and the actual transactions for the system are executed at the Trading Desk which is located in the Federal Reserve Bank of New York. It is the responsibility of the Account Management to keep the Open Market Committee informed of transactions it is undertaking to fulfill the instructions received from the Committee.

The Federal Advisory Council is the third group in the center of the System. One representative is chosen by the board of directors of each Federal Reserve Bank, and these twelve representatives serve as advisers to the Board of Governors. Since this group lacks any executive authority it is difficult to assess its importance and competence, but it does serve to keep the Board abreast of the thinking of the bankers in the Federal Reserve Districts.

These three groups are, in essence, the agencies that formulate the policies to be pursued by the Federal Reserve System. But the actual operations of the System are carried out through the accounts of the twelve Federal Reserve Banks. In each of the twelve Federal Reserve Districts into which the country is divided there is a Federal Reserve Bank; these Banks are located in Boston, New York, Philadelphia, Cleveland, Richmond, Atlanta, Chicago, St. Louis, Minneapolis, Kansas City, Dallas, and San Francisco. A number of the

Reserve Banks have branches within their Districts; at present there are twenty-four such branch banks. New York has the largest Federal Reserve Bank, its assets amounting to more than 25 per cent of the combined assets of all the Reserve Banks, while Chicago, which is next in order of size, holds about 17 per cent of the total assets of the System. New York assumes an importance, however, that goes beyond that indicated by the size of its assets; commercial banks in the New York District that are members of the System, especially the New York City banks, execute transactions for the money market and for banks that have correspondent relationships with them, and these transactions are often of the type and size that affect the monetary situation throughout the country.

The Federal Reserve Banks are owned by the banks that belong to the System, with each Federal Reserve Bank being owned by the member banks in its District. Each member bank has subscribed to stock in the Federal Reserve Bank in its District equal to 3 per cent of its capital and surplus, but the member banks' control over the Reserve Banks is severely limited. Dividends paid by the Reserve Banks to their member bank owners are limited to 6 per cent of the subscribed capital; Reserve Bank earnings over and above this dividend allotment are divided between the United States Treasury and the surplus accounts of the Reserve Banks, the former receiving about 90 per cent of this total. Of the nine directors of each of the Reserve Banks, six are chosen by the member banks in the District. To prevent the large banks from controlling the selections, the banks are divided into three classes according to size, then each class elects two directors. It is further stipulated that of the six directors chosen by the member banks, three must be persons not engaged in banking and are to represent commerce, agriculture, and industry in the Federal Reserve District. The remaining three of the nine directors are chosen by the Board of Governors, and of these three one is named as chairman of the board of directors. The president and first vice president of each Federal Reserve Bank are selected by the board of directors but are subject to the approval of the Board of Governors; the other officers of the Reserve Banks are appointed by the board of directors but may be removed from office by the Board of Governors.

The Federal Reserve Banks perform the routine, day-by-day functions that are entrusted to a single central bank in most other countries; they are banks for the member banks in their Districts.

They hold the legal reserves that the member banks must maintain against their deposit liabilities. They issue Federal Reserve notes, which are the most important part of the currency in circulation. They rediscount eligible commercial paper that the member banks bring to them, and they lend to the banks against acceptable collateral. In actual practice the Federal Reserve Bank lends chiefly against government securities. Open market purchases and sales of securities are made by the Reserve Banks. These transactions come under the control of the Federal Open Market Committee, which was described above. The Reserve Banks since 1933 have been permitted to make direct loans to industry.

The Federal Reserve Banks conduct examinations of the member banks (under the supervision of the Board of Governors), they act as fiscal agents for the United States Treasury, and they are engaged in activities involving the collection and clearance of checks. Important as these activities may be, they are of a routine nature and it is sufficient to say that the quality and efficiency of the banking system has been improved by these activities of the Federal Reserve Banks.

An important final point about the Reserve Banks is that they must hold gold certificates as reserves against their note and deposit liabilities; the ratio of gold to these liabilities cannot fall below 25 per cent. These gold certificates arise from the Treasury's monetization of the gold which it purchases; the Treasury pays for the gold by drawing down its deposits with the Federal Reserve Banks and then replenishes these deposits by issuing gold certificates (against the newly purchased gold) which are exchanged for a Treasury deposit at the Reserve Banks. The gold reserve ratio is not an important factor in current monetary management since the current ratio is above the legal minimum, and this requirement will become important only if the United States should export a substantial quantity of gold and/or the Federal Reserve Banks expand their note and deposit liabilities far above current levels; when the actual ratio approached the minimum permitted ratio, the minimum gold reserve ratio was reduced to the present 25 per cent.

The part of the Federal Reserve System with which ordinary people come into contact consists of the member banks. All banks operating under federal charter (the national banks) are required to be members, and the banks chartered by the states may become members if they qualify and should desire to do so. Of the 13,600 commercial banks in operation in the United States at the present time, about 4600 national banks and nearly 1800 state banks are members of the System. Over seven thousand state banks have either chosen to remain outside the System or have not qualified for membership. The member banks account for slightly less than half of the commercial banks in the United States, but they hold more than four-fifths of the combined deposit liabilities of all the commercial banks; the state banks that have remained out of the System are on the average the smaller banks.

In the past twenty years non-member state banks have diminished in number while the number of member banks has gone up slightly— for the latter group the increase in state bank members has more than offset the decline in the number of national banks. This slight shift in favor of membership in the System stems from the relaxation during the inter-war period of some of the rules that applied to member banks but that were not common in the state banking systems.[2] Still, the flow of state-chartered banks to the System has been extremely slow. In some cases the state-chartered banks have not possessed sufficient capital to qualify for membership, but there is a sizable number of state banks that could meet the capital requirements and yet have decided to continue under state regulations. For one thing, the Federal Reserve System requires 'par clearance.' This means that member banks are not permitted to make 'exchange charges' on checks that the Federal Reserve Banks present to them for payment—the full amount of the checks must be paid. A number of banks consider these 'exchange charges' too important a part of their income to give up in order to become Federal Reserve members. Secondly, the Federal Reserve often places more limitations on the types of assets that the banks may acquire than do the state regulatory authorities. Thirdly, in some states the legal reserve ratios that must be maintained by the commercial banks are lower than those imposed by the System; banks that operate in states where the minimum ratios are low find it to be more profitable to remain outside the System. Fourthly, non-member banks often avail themselves of the check clearing and borrowing facilities provided by the city correspondent banks that approximate the services pro-

---

[2] E.g. the regulations that concerned real estate loans made by member banks were modified in the 'twenties and 'thirties; and the double liability provision for bank stocks was removed in 1937.

vided by the Reserve System but without having to undergo the more stringent regulation that membership entails. It is also possible for non-member banks to use the System's check clearing facilities if they agree to par clearance, and in time of stress non-member banks may borrow from the Federal Reserve Banks. These practices on the part of the Federal Reserve naturally do not encourage membership since they provide important facilities to non-member banks which would gain only the slight advantage of added convenience if they should join the System.

The small share of commercial bank assets and deposit liabilities currently controlled by the non-member banks makes it unlikely that there will be strong pressures to force them to become a part of the Federal Reserve System. If such action should be taken it would probably mean some improvement in the overall standards of banking, but it would mean little in terms of its effects on overall monetary policy.

Federal Reserve Instruments of Monetary Control

The aims of the Federal Reserve System at the time of its inception were to provide for a more elastic currency and to provide facilities for the rediscounting of commercial paper. These provisions were to insure the prevention of crises similar to those which had plagued American banking in the nineteenth and early twentieth centuries. Concern for overall stabilization played only a small part in the thinking of the men most responsible for the creation of the Federal Reserve System. In the light of these rather limited, but not unimportant, goals it is easy to understand the emphasis upon discounting as the main function of the System. It was only gradually that the Federal Reserve expanded its aims and its instruments for monetary management. Open market operations were developed in the 'twenties and reserve ratio changes came to be used for monetary control purposes in the 'thirties. The regulation of margin requirements in stock exchange trading was introduced in the 'thirties and the control over installment buying (which has been used in two periods) was developed in the early 'forties. As the Federal Reserve System became more experienced in monetary management it was willing to assume more responsibility for the control of cyclical fluctuations rather than being content with merely preventing financial breakdowns, the first task to which it addressed itself.

In the rest of this chapter we shall be concerned primarily with the methods developed to control the volume of reserves, the cost of acquiring reserves, and the deposit-supporting power of reserves. We shall also look briefly into the qualitative controls that have been employed by the System. The Federal Reserve makes use of all the four main groups of central bank control that were described in the last chapter, and in basic principle its operations are the same as those described there. In detail, however, they are more complex.

As an introduction to our discussion of the instruments of monetary control, it is useful to examine the factors that determine the volume of member bank reserves. In our system in Chapter 11, the reserves of the commercial banks at the central bank would be increased if the central bank bought securities or lent money to the commercial banks, at a time when other things were unchanged. Conversely, the reserves of the commercial banks at the central bank would be reduced if the public decided to hold more cash (obtaining it by reducing their bank deposits), again assuming other things unchanged. The same situation as that shown on page 159 (before the central bank's open market operations) can therefore be represented in the following way:

COMMERCIAL BANK RESERVES

Factors supplying reserves		*Factors using reserves*	
Central bank holdings of government securities	$8,000,000	Notes of central bank in circulation (with general public and commercial banks)	$5,000,000
		Commercial bank reserves at central bank	3,000,000
	$8,000,000		$8,000,000

If an item on the left declines, and nothing else alters, the commercial banks lose reserves; this happened at the first stage of our open market operations, when central bank security holdings and commercial bank reserves both fell by $100,000. Similarly, if the public takes more notes into circulation, and nothing else alters, commercial bank reserves fall by the same amount.

A similar table for the member banks in the Federal Reserve

System is a little more complicated but is fundamentally the same; a recent example is reproduced here.

TABLE 8

MEMBER BANK RESERVES, RESERVE BANK CREDIT, AND RELATED ITEMS [1]

(*June 30, 1958*)

(*$ millions*)

Factors supplying reserves			Factors using reserves	
U.S. government securities			Currency in circulation	31,172
held by Reserve Banks	25,438		Treasury cash holdings	692
Discounts and advances	41		Treasury deposits with	
Float	758		Federal Reserve	410
Other Reserve Bank			Non-member deposits	
credit	46		with Federal Reserve	689
			Other Federal Reserve	
Total Reserve Bank			Accounts	1,096
credit		26,283	Total of above	34,059
Gold stock		21,356	Member bank reserves	18,784
Treasury currency				
outstanding		5,203		
Total		52,842 [2]	Total	52,843 [2]

[1] *Federal Reserve Bulletin*, August 1958.
[2] Totals are not precisely the same because of rounding.

On the left hand side we have items which, if they increase, tend to increase the reserves of the member banks at the Federal Reserve Banks. 'Reserve Bank credit' includes not only the Reserve Banks' holdings of United States government securities, but also acceptances, discounts, and advances for banks, industrial loans made by the Reserve Banks, and Federal Reserve float (float arises when the Reserve Banks credit the payee bank before collecting from the payor bank—it appears on Federal Reserve Bank statements as the difference between *uncollected cash items* and *deferred availability cash items*). The monetary gold stock means all gold held by the United States Treasury, the only legal holder of monetary gold since 1934. As we have seen, the Treasury issues gold certificates against the gold it buys. Most additions to or reductions of the stock are the result of transactions with foreigners. When a United States bank receives gold from abroad (perhaps in payment for United States exports), it immediately sells it to the Treasury, receiving a deposit at a Federal Reserve Bank in exchange. The remaining item is 'Treasury currency outstanding'; this is the money that has been issued by the Treasury. At present it consists primarily of silver certificates, subsidiary silver coin, and minor coin; the silver-based currency stems, in large part, from the Silver Purchase Act of 1934, under which the Treasury is obliged to purchase all newly mined silver offered to it at a fixed price. Once again, the bank acting as agent for the seller receives a deposit at a Federal Reserve Bank.

It should be noted that the Federal Reserve enjoys direct control over only one of these three sources of member bank reserves—the volume of Reserve Bank credit [3] (excluding Federal Reserve float); the other two lie outside its immediate control.

On the other side of the account are the items which, if they increase, tend to reduce the reserves of the member bank. The item 'currency in circulation' corresponds directly to the same item in our simple example. In the accounts presented here, this item includes both coin and currency held by the commercial banks and the public; it excludes holdings of the Federal Reserve Banks and the Treasury. When Treasury cash holdings rise, and all the other items are unchanged, once again member bank reserves fall. Similarly, if the Treasury's deposits with the Federal Reserve rise, as when a taxpayer pays his taxes by check drawn on a member bank, then member bank reserves fall. The next item ('non-member bank deposits') mainly covers deposits of foreign central banks; settlement of a receipt from a foreigner might commonly be made by reducing this item rather than by the receipt of gold. Lastly, 'other Federal Reserve accounts' mainly covers various capital accounts which do not change very much.

Our discussion of the means employed by the Federal Reserve to affect the volume, cost, and depositing-supporting power of member bank reserves can conveniently be divided into three parts: discount rates and discounting, open market operations, and variations in legal reserve requirements.

The first of these was considered most important when the Federal

---

[3] The Federal Reserve's direct control over Reserve Bank credit needs to be qualified slightly. The Federal Reserve undertakes open market operations at its initiative, but borrowing from the Federal Reserve Banks is at the initiative of the member banks. The Federal Reserve does control, however, the terms and conditions under which it will lend to the member banks.

Reserve System was founded; discounting was to be the principal mechanism employed to attain the objectives of accommodating 'legitimate' demands for credit. When member banks had exhausted their excess reserves through their loan making activities or because the public demanded cash, they could meet further demands for 'legitimate' loans and cash by obtaining reserve funds from the Federal Reserve Bank at the discount rate. This was intended to introduce more elasticity into the banking system than had existed previously; but to ensure that the banks did not abuse the privilege of going to the Reserve Banks for funds, eligibility requirements were imposed on the paper brought to the Reserve Banks for rediscount or as collateral for advances. To be eligible, the paper had to be short-term self-liquidating paper that originated for the purpose of securing funds needed for the production, purchase, stocking, or marketing of goods. Discounts and advances based on such paper could not, it was argued, lead to an inappropriate volume of credit. It was held that if the eligibility requirements were restricted so that loans were made for 'productive' purposes alone, the quantity of money and the volume of output would move together, thus avoiding the dangers of an excessive or insufficient supply of money. This was the 'commercial loan theory' approach to banking which placed emphasis on control over the quality rather than the quantity of credit. The notion that control over the quality of credit was sufficient to ensure that the proper quantity of credit would follow almost automatically did not live up to expectations in its operation. In the first place, control of the quality of paper discounted bears little relation to the total loan activities of the commercial banks: moreover, even those credit extensions which are made for 'productive' purposes in the private sense need not be productive in the social sense. For example, in periods of full employment an expansion in expenditures based on loans would cause prices to rise which might further stimulate the demand for loans—loans that may appear to be productive from the point of view of, say, a manufacturer who now finds that he needs more funds to carry his inventories. Yet from the social point of view it is impossible for real output to rise, since the economy is already at full employment.

While the System in the 'twenties moved to more positive control measures the eligibility requirements remained, and during the banking crisis of the early 'thirties the eligibility requirements hampered the efforts of the Federal Reserve Banks to come to the aid of the commercial banks, since the volume of eligible paper was not in sufficient supply. After this experience the eligibility rules were liberalized considerably; the Reserve Banks can now lend to the commercial banks not only against short-term commercial paper but also against government bonds and, in times of stress, against any other assets of the commercial banks that are acceptable to the Reserve Banks.[4] Today, banks that need reserves usually obtain these funds through advances secured by government securities.

With all the emphasis that was being placed upon eligibility requirements when the Federal Reserve Banks began their operations, there seemed to be little room for discount rate changes as a means for control over the monetary situation. Still there was considerable sentiment among a number of people in favor of varying the discount rates in order to check or stimulate lending, and under the pressures that developed during the post-World War I boom this view took hold and the Reserve Banks began to use discount rate changes as a positive policy measure. The manipulation of discount rates came to be an important part of monetary policy and was used extensively during the 'twenties and early 'thirties. On other matters pertaining to discount rates, the Federal Reserve Banks found it difficult to decide, in their early days, whether or not the type of commercial paper and the geographic areas should be determinants of the discount rates, and whether or not their discount rates should be penalty rates. After some experimentation with a multiplicity of discount rates up to the early 'twenties the tendency was toward a simplification of the discount rate structure, and regional differences in discount rates have tended to diminish. Penalty discount rates never took hold as a part of Federal Reserve policy.

The last point mentioned deserves a little more attention. Since member banks can borrow directly from the Federal Reserve Banks and can then lend these funds at a higher rate to their customers it seems strange at first glance that they do not do more borrowing. The explanation for this lies with both the commercial banks and the Reserve Banks. For one thing, the Reserve Banks discourage continuous borrowing or 'borrowing for profit' by the member banks.

---

[4] Advances secured by assets other than government bonds or eligible paper bear an additional ½ per cent interest charge.

On the other hand, member banks usually do not like to show heavy indebtedness to the Reserve Banks. This combination of factors is what has made it possible to continue to operate without resorting to penalty discount rates and without courting serious inflation.

With the easy money period that began in the 'thirties the member banks came to rely even less on the Reserve Banks for reserve funds; from 1934 to 1951 the discount mechanism was rarely used. Member banks had excess reserves until the early 'forties, and before they felt any deficiency in reserves the stable bond market program was in full swing. Under this, the Federal Reserve Banks purchased government securities in quantities sufficient to ensure that there was no shortage of reserve funds.[5] The stable bond market program was abandoned in 1951 and since that time we have witnessed a return to a more flexible monetary policy under which member banks have had to resort to use of the discount windows of the Reserve Banks to repair deficient reserve positions. The way this usually happens in the United States today is that pressure is put upon the banks (in periods of inflation) by open market operations which force the banks to borrow from the Reserve Banks. Naturally this results in less tightening than would have occurred without the offsetting effects of bank borrowings, but generally this is not considered detrimental to the efficacy of monetary control. In the first place, when member bank borrowings from the Reserve Banks rise they are put under pressure by the Reserve Banks to trim their lending activities and to repay their loans. Secondly, it can be argued that leaving the member banks free to make use of the discount window makes it more likely that open market operations will be carried out on a scale sufficient to ensure success—the Open Market Committee can be much bolder if they know that a safety valve is in operation.

The most important control device currently employed by the Federal Reserve System is that of open market operations. Open market operations include transactions in government securities, acceptances, and any other securities that the Federal Open Market Committee considers acceptable. In practice, securities other than

---

[5] See Chapter 14 for a fuller treatment of this program.

those issued by the federal government have been an unimportant part of total operations.

Federal Reserve purchases of acceptances have some of the characteristics of open market operations in securities and some of the characteristics of discounts and advances. Like discounts and advances they are generally brought to the Federal Reserve Banks by the member banks and dealers, although the Reserve Banks may actively seek to purchase acceptances. But like open market operations they do not add to the indebtedness of the member banks with the Reserve Banks. Bankers' acceptances were at one time important in the financing of international trade, particularly in the 'twenties, but in the easy money periods of the 'thirties and 'forties the volume of acceptances outstanding dropped sharply and few were brought to the Federal Reserve Banks. Since that time there has been some recovery in the use of acceptances and the Federal Reserve Banks are currentiy carrying acceptances in their portfolios, but the volume that they hold is not large.

Open market operations first came into play when the Federal Reserve Banks, in 1922, tried to correct their weak earnings positions through the purchase of government securities. By 1923 the implications of open market operations for monetary conditions were realized, and from then on the size and frequency of open market operations came to be directed by a committee that attempted some degree of co-ordination; full centralization of open market operations that made it mandatory that the Reserve Banks follow instructions issued by the Federal Open Market Committee came in 1935.

In the 'twenties the Federal Reserve Banks discovered that they could exert rather sharp influence upon the interest rates prevailing in the market without large changes in the reserve balances held by the member banks. If the Reserve Banks purchased securities on the open market the member banks would frequently employ the cash they received to reduce their debts at the Federal Reserve Banks, but the mere fact that they were free from debt caused the banks to expand their loans and forced interest rates down. Open market sales created the opposite effect; banks were driven to the discount window to restore their reserves, but this caused some automatic tightening since member banks were reluctant to show indebtedness to the Federal Reserve Banks and hence checked their loan activities in order to repay their debts. Manipulation of open market rates through open market operations was feasible until the Great Depression came along. Prior to the Depression the member banks did not maintain substantial excess reserves, so they were quite sensitive to changes in the direction of open market operations; but once the era of excess reserves began hardly any monetary changes were attempted through the use of open market operations. From late 1933 to early 1937 the Reserve Banks' holdings of government securities remained virtually unchanged at about $2400 million. In 1937 the Reserve Banks did some buying in connection with their support of 'an orderly bond market' (to be discussed later) but since the purpose was to affect the structure of interest rates rather than the level, they sold almost as many securities (but of different maturities) as they bought, simply switching from one maturity to another.

In the 'thirties, when the member banks came to hold large excess reserves, changes in reserve requirements were made an adjunct to discount and open market policies in the exercise of monetary control. Reserve requirements were fixed between 1917 and 1933, but the 1933 emergency banking legislation gave the Board of Governors the power to alter the requirements. This temporary measure was supplanted by the Banking Act of 1935, which gave the Board of Governors the power to alter the reserve ratios within limits. Upper and lower limits for reserve ratios were set, the lower limit being the ratios that had been employed since 1917—for demand deposits 13 per cent in central reserve city banks, 10 per cent in reserve city banks, and 7 per cent in country banks. The upper limit on demand deposits was double these ratios, and the lower and upper limits on time deposits were 3 per cent and 6 per cent. At first, the Board of Governors could not change the reserve ratio applying to a particular class of banks without altering the other legal ratios; this was changed in 1942, leaving the Board free to alter the various ratios independently of each other.

The Board of Governors first used its new power in 1936 when it raised reserve requirements to reduce the volume of excess reserves; the reserves had been swollen by gold inflows from abroad. In 1937 the reserve requirements were pushed upward twice and since that time the required ratios have been maintained at or close to the ceilings permitted by law, with the exception that the reserve ratio that applies to central reserve city banks has been reduced substantially below its statutory limit since 1953. If the Board of Governors is to have the freedom of maneuver to be able to change reserve requirements in both directions, then it will have to reduce the required ratios from where they stand at present, unless it is given the authority to raise reserve ratios above the present legal maximums.

The important thing to note is that changes in required reserves are now an instrument of monetary control and have very little to do with the 'soundness' of the banking system. The latter notion carried some weight at the time of the formation of the Federal Reserve System when the System was viewed, in part, as a common pool of reserves available for emergencies. But few people now look upon the purpose of an increase in required reserves as being designed directly to protect depositors.[6] More significant, from a public policy point of view, is the relationship between the level of reserve requirements and the level of bank earnings, and since monetary goals probably can be attained without varying reserve ratios, reserve requirement changes can be used to regulate commercial bank earnings. But undoubtedly the most important use of reserve requirements is to help control the quantity of bank lending.

We must now look briefly at some of the supplementary methods for controlling the volume of credit, in particular the qualitative controls. First, we should note that the automatically elastic banking system that was supposed to develop after the Federal Reserve System was formed was predicated upon qualitative control—the quality of paper offered for discounting. It was argued that if the Federal Reserve discounted only that paper that reflected genuine commercial transactions, then the monetary circulation would adapt itself to the volume of real output in a most harmonious way. We saw previously that this qualitative approach was generally abandoned in the post-World War I boom and slump.

In the 1928-1929 stock market upswing the Federal Reserve System attempted to employ *moral suasion* (publicly and privately requesting banks to curb some particular activities) to check the

---

[6] Protection for depositors is provided, in part, by deposit insurance. Nearly all commercial banks are members of the Federal Deposit Insurance Corporation, which insures deposits up to $10,000 for each depositor. Banks that are members of the Federal Reserve System are required to belong to the Federal Deposit Insurance Corporation, while membership is optional for other banks.

growth of loans that were being used for stock market speculation. It appears that these exhortations were in part successful at the first step, curbing the volume of loans made by banks to speculators; but it appears that the speculators did not suffer from any shortages of funds since they were well supplied by the funds provided by the customers of banks. One consequence of this failure to control the stock market's movements was the enactment into law, in 1934, of regulations concerning the borrowing of funds for the purchase of listed securities. The Board of Governors was empowered to set margin requirements on such securities; the margin is the part of the cost of a security that must be paid for in cash. Regulations fall under two headings, Regulation T and Regulation U. The former applies to the lending activities of dealers and brokers and the latter applies to commercial bank loans for securities transactions. Since borrowing for securities purchases has come under the regulatory purview of the Board of Governors, the changes in margin requirements have reflected the general credit situation as well as developments associated primarily with the stock market. The justification for this course of regulation has been that if we expect to affect the overall state of the economy, at least marginally, by changes in the rules under which the stock market operates, the state of the economy should be an important consideration in determining change in margins.

Finally, in the recent past the Board of Governors has been empowered from time to time to control down payments and amortization periods for consumer installment loans and residential construction loans. It is probable that both regulations are quite effective (although advocacy of their effectiveness is currently diminishing), but they do raise a number of administrative problems. They also raise the question of discrimination in the credit control system since controls of this sort do differ from the broader instruments of monetary control (such as open market operations and discount rates) in that they are not concerned with the aggregate volume of credit but with its use in certain specific areas. These controls are not currently in use and it appears unlikely that the Federal Reserve will press for their return unless an extremely serious inflationary situation develops.

SOME SUGGESTED READING

There is a wealth of literature on the Federal Reserve System, much of it put out by the Federal Reserve System itself. There is an excellent but simple description of the Federal Reserve System entitled *The Federal Reserve System, Its Purposes and Functions,* 2nd ed. (Washington, 1947). *Banking Studies* (Washington, 1941) contains a number of essays on the nature and operations of the Federal Reserve System. To round out the picture a publication of the Federal Reserve, entitled *Banking and Monetary Statistics* (Washington, 1943), the *Federal Reserve Bulletin* (published monthly), and the *Annual Report* of the Board of Governors furnish an exhaustive set of statistics on the past and present of the banking and monetary situation.

E. A. Goldenweiser, *Monetary Management* (New York, 1949) and *American Monetary Policy* (New York, 1950) are useful in tracing the development of the Federal Reserve's monetary instruments and afford valuable insights on policy decisions that were undertaken by the Federal Reserve in the past. In a similar vein is G. L. Bach, *Federal Reserve Policy-Making* (New York, 1950).

For an excellent treatment of the Federal Reserve open market operations the interested reader should consult R. V. Roosa, *Federal Reserve Operations in the Government Securities Market* (Federal Reserve Bank of New York, 1956).

14

American Banking Institutions—

III. The Federal Reserve System: The Stable Bond Market
Program and the 'Bills Only' Doctrine

In the last chapter we discussed the development of the Federal Reserve's instruments for quantitative monetary control, and we saw that the open market operation is the most powerful method available to the System in its attempts to influence the quantity of member bank reserves. Yet, between 1937 and 1951 this control was in large part surrendered by the System because of its decision to stabilize the price of government bonds and consequently the general structure of interest rates. In this chapter we shall discuss this policy of stabilizing the government bond market and the reasons for its eventual abandonment in favor of a more flexible monetary policy. Soon after the Federal Reserve System regained its freedom in monetary management it imposed upon itself the restriction that open market operations be confined to the short-term end of the government securities market—the 'bills only' doctrine; this new doctrine also merits our attention.

The Stable Bond Market Program

Before 1937 open market operations were conducted primarily to affect the volume of member bank reserves and consequently the nation's monetary circulation, but in that year the maintenance of 'orderly conditions in the government securities market' became an objective of monetary policy, and open market operations had to be tailored to that end. The first active measures taken by the System to support the government bond market came in April and May of

1937 and were designed to halt the downturn in the prices of long-term government securities which had followed the increase in reserve requirements that occurred in March of that year. Purchases were made that amounted to about $100 million for each month, and in turn the Reserve Banks disposed of some notes and bills that they had held, thus concentrating their efforts on affecting relative yields on long-term and short-term securities rather than the aggregate of member bank reserves. The price decline of the long-term government bonds was arrested, but more important in terms of future developments was the initiation of a policy that was directed toward limiting fluctuations in the government bond market by directly influencing prices and yields rather than relying upon changes in member bank reserves to produce stabilizing monetary effects.

When war broke out in Europe in September 1939, government bond prices fell off sharply, and the System's reaction to this break in the bond market was to purchase about $500 million of bonds and to announce that it would lend to member *and non-member* banks on the security of government bonds (at par value); the interest charged on such loans was the same for both kinds of bank. After this spurt of buying, the Federal Reserve System was comparatively inactive in the government bond market until the spring of 1940, when modest amounts were purchased; during the second half of 1940 about $300 million in government securities were sold in an attempt to temper the rise in the price of government bonds that followed the sharp rise in member bank reserves. (Substantial gold imports had increased sharply the volume of member bank reserves during 1940.) For the rest of the period prior to America's actual entry into the war the Federal Reserve did little trading in the market for government securities.

With the outbreak of war for the United States in December, 1941, government bond prices fell in the open market and the Federal Reserve System extended its holdings of government securities by about $70 million, this increase was made up primarily of long-term bonds; this was in keeping with the Federal Reserve's announced aim of 'maintaining orderly conditions' in the market for government securities. Further, the Federal Reserve System announced that Treasury war finance would not be hampered for lack of money. In effect, the Federal Reserve stood ready to underwrite any government financing that could not be achieved through taxation or through borrowing from the non-bank public. The Federal Reserve's support of Treasury finance made it possible for the government to carry out its huge borrowing operations at interest rates that were not only very low but for the longer-term securities at rates that were also declining. The Treasury and the Federal Reserve agreed, in 1942, upon a pattern of pegged rates that set upper limits on the yields for the various maturities—$\frac{3}{8}$ per cent for Treasury bills, $\frac{7}{8}$ per cent for certificates, 2 per cent on medium-term bonds, and $2\frac{1}{2}$ per cent on long-term securities, and the Federal Reserve took steps to guarantee the maintenance of this pattern. The System also stood ready to lend to commercial banks, both member and non-member, at a discount rate of 1 per cent up to the par value of the government securities offered as collateral and at a preferential rate of $\frac{1}{2}$ per cent to member banks for advances secured by government securities that matured within a year. The Federal Reserve's tailoring of its open market operations to the maintenance of this pattern was, however, the more significant measure.

The Federal Open Market Committee, in April 1942, established a buying rate of $\frac{3}{8}$ per cent yield for all Treasury bills offered to the Reserve Banks. Later in the same year the Federal Reserve made it possible for sellers of bills to repurchase the bills that they had sold to the System at $\frac{3}{8}$ per cent yield; in effect, bills became interest-bearing reserves which made it unnecessary for any bank to hold excess reserves to meet unpredictable fluctuations in their balances at the Federal Reserve.

The Federal Reserve posted a fixed buying rate of $\frac{7}{8}$ per cent for certificates of indebtedness (debt instruments with a one-year maturity), and although no specific buying rates were posted for the longer maturities, the Federal Reserve stood ready to buy these securities in quantities sufficient to prevent their yields from rising above the pattern established in the early part of 1942. The upshot of all this was that the Federal Reserve system gave up its control over bank reserves and the money supply; the size and composition of its government securities portfolio was now determined by the Treasury, the commercial banks and the non-bank public. Since practically all government securities prices were supported by the Federal Reserve, the differences between short-term and long-term securities tended to vanish and the commercial banks and the public sold their short-term holdings to the Reserve Banks, adding to member bank reserves, and then used the proceeds to purchase the higher yield long-term securities. Consequently, the Reserve Banks came to hold a substantial proportion of the short-dated securities which carried low yields while other investors were bidding down the yields on the more lucrative long-term government bonds.

The consequences of Treasury wartime financing were a rapid increase in the public debt, which rose from $51 billion at the end of 1940 to $279 billion by the end of 1945, and an increase in the public's money supply from $42 billion to $102 billion in the same period. Between the end of 1940 and the end of 1945 the gold stock declined slightly so that the factors primarily responsible for the monetary expansion were the deficit financing undertaken by the federal government, and the banking system's purchase of the securities issued by the Treasury. War expenditures had brought about a profound transformation of the financial basis of the economy and the public's liquidity had been enhanced markedly.

The ending of the war did not bring to an end the Federal Reserve's program of supporting government securities prices to prevent an upward movement of long-term yields, despite the fact that inflationary pressures were increasing. Easy money conditions were maintained through 1946 and it was not until 1947 that the first major step was taken to dismantle the system of pegged rates. In July, 1947, the Federal Open Market Committee removed the ⅜ per cent buying rate on Treasury bills and switched the initiative on purchases of bills from the market to the Reserve System. Later that same year (in August) the Committee dropped the ⅞ per cent buying rate on certificates and in conjunction with the Treasury's policy of raising, over time, the rate on new issues of certificates to 1⅛ per cent, the rate on bills moved up to the 1 per cent level. This policy turned out to be successful and it enabled the Reserve Banks to reduce their holdings of short-term government securities as commercial banks and other investors bought these securities which now carried higher yields.

Higher yields on these short-term securities coupled with strong demands for loanable funds by the private sectors of the economy put pressure, however, on the longer-term government securities, causing these to fall in price. In response to the increase of yields on the long-terms, which gathered momentum in the autumn of 1947, the Federal Reserve made purchases in the market in November and December, up to the 24th of the month, to dampen this upward movement in yields. But then, on the 24th of December, the Federal Reserve lowered the support level of bond prices and subsequently made heavy purchases to bring the market around to its new pattern of rates.

As in 1947, inflationary pressures continued to be the predominant problem for the economy through most of 1948 and the government bond support program of the Federal Reserve came to be attacked more frequently. The Federal Reserve bought heavily in the long-term government bond market throughout 1948 to maintain the new support level which was instituted in December, 1947. Shorter-term holdings of the System were reduced at the same time but on balance its government securities portfolio rose by about $800 million. Gold imports and a decline in currency in circulation constituted further additions to member bank reserves which rose by about $2.7 billion during the year, but the money supply was kept in check by increases in the reserve requirements for member banks which occurred in February, June, and September of 1948. Late in 1948 economic activity began to turn downward and the problem confronting the Federal Reserve altered.

Between the end of 1945 and the end of 1948 the public's money supply rose from about $102 billion to about $112 billion with the Federal Reserve's ability to control this monetary expansion severely curtailed by its adherence to the policy of supporting the government bond market. The Federal Reserve did succeed, in this period, in reducing its holdings of government securities by selling short-term securities in larger quantities than it purchased long-term. The net effect of these switches in the 1945-1948 period amounted to a reduction of about $900 million in the Federal Reserve's government securities portfolio. Gold imports, which in this period totaled over $4 billion, meant that member bank reserves rose substantially and for the reasons that were noted above the Federal Reserve was not able to check this expansion, except for the reserve requirement changes that took place in 1948. As things turned out, the most important monetary restraint exercised in this period of rising prices came from Treasury operations. Treasury surpluses, particularly in 1947 and 1948, were used to retire Treasury debt and/or to build up Treasury balances, thus exerting modest inflationary pressures.

Why, in the face of the inflationary bias in the economy, did the Federal Reserve and the Treasury continue to support the prices of government bonds after the end of the war? Firstly, it was argued by some that higher interest rates would increase the cost of government. This argument begged the question as to whether *total* costs of government would be increased simply because debt service charges would be increased, since it is conceivable that a more vigorous monetary policy that curbed inflation might reduce other government costs sufficient to offset higher interest charges. Secondly, another argument advanced in favor of the support program stated that higher yields on government bonds would depreciate the prices of these securities, causing serious capital losses to holders of bonds, and for that reason yield pegging should be maintained. This argument raised the question as to the nature of the commitment of the Treasury and Federal Reserve authorities to the holders of marketable government securities, and it avoided the question as to whether the public was better protected by preventing decreases in the prices of bonds or by preventing decreases in the purchasing power of government bonds. It is conceivable that the decreases in bond values might be more than offset by the preservation of the purchasing power of the dollar, which could not be achieved under the fixed yield regime. Thirdly, and probably most importantly, it was argued that a removal of supports from the government bond market would precipitate such a sharp increase in yields that, rather than merely preventing inflation, such a course of action would actually lead to a calamitous business depression. This line of thought was framed in terms of the size and widespread distribution of government bonds which, it was alleged, made the economy extremely sensitive to changes in yields. Implicit in this argument was the assumption of some marked discontinuities in the effect of monetary operations, that small changes would be ineffective while some larger changes would cause a recession. What was not explained was why there was no intermediate point which could have maintained relative stability in the price level. It is true that if too vigorous a policy of contraction led to expectations which were so unfavorable that a cumulative downswing developed which could not be reversed by a turnabout in monetary operations, then one might argue that it would be dangerous to grope for the proper degree of restriction because the costs of making a mistake would be so serious. This type of analysis might have explained the reluctance of the monetary authorities to undertake drastic monetary restraint, but it is hardly an explanation of the policy that was, in

fact, followed—a policy that resulted in the Federal Reserve's providing an infinitely elastic supply of funds at the supported interest
rate levels.

This loss of control over the money supply was a serious concern
of Federal Reserve officials and economists but there is also ample
evidence that the central bank authorities went along with the
Treasury's policy of maintaining the long-term rate at about $2\frac{1}{2}$
per cent. In large part this attitude stemmed from a fear, very widespread in the early post-war years, that the high level of economic
activity would not continue for long. The System was keeping itself
ready to counteract tendencies toward depression, but it appears
that it was not prepared to cope with the expansive character of
the economy such as was exhibited in the 1945-1948 period.

The turnabout in activity which had started in the last quarter of
1948 continued and grew in intensity in 1949. Prices, production,
and employment all declined, and the Federal Reserve's problem
became one of dealing with the recession that was developing.
Reserve requirements for the member banks were reduced and
controls over security loans and consumer credit were relaxed. The
demand for government securities by the private sectors became
extremely active and thus enabled the Federal Reserve Banks to
reduce their government securities portfolio by about $4.5 billion
between the end of 1948 and the end of 1949—the bulk of the
decline occurring in the System bond holdings which were decreased by about $3.8 billion in the same period. Member bank
reserves declined by about $3.7 billion, which was less than the
reduction in Reserve Bank credit because of an increase of over
$200 million in the gold stock and a decrease of about $700 million
in currency in circulation. This change from open market purchases
to open market sales by the System was in keeping with the policy
of maintaining stability in the government securities market, but
it was as inappropriate in a period of recession as it had been in
the previous period of inflation. Federal Reserve and Treasury officials came to be increasingly aware of the fact that the attempt to
maintain a relatively fixed pattern of yield would intensify rather
than alleviate the deflationary pressure, and in June, 1949, the Federal Open Market Committee announced that open market operations were to be partially redirected so as to stress their influence
upon business and credit conditions rather than to aim only for
stability in the government bond market. Shortly thereafter the

Federal Reserve's open market sales tapered off and the decline in member bank reserves was slowed considerably. Some interpreted this rather modest change in policy as a departure from the rigid support program for government securities which the Federal Reserve had pursued for so long, and a return to a more flexible monetary policy.

By late 1949 the recession had ended and the various economic trends pointed upward. Inventories had been worked down to levels which induced some sharp increases in stocks of commodities. With the rapid recovery in production and employment, inflationary pressures were beginning to be felt once again by the spring of 1950. Then war broke out in Korea in June, 1950. Speculative purchases by the civilian sectors, in anticipation of price increases and shortages of goods, accelerated the rise of prices and bank loan extensions.

In the months that followed, the Federal Reserve Banks raised their discount rates and the Board reinstated the regulation of consumer credit. Attempts were made to dissuade banks and other financial lenders from pursuing an easy-lending policy in their issuance of loans. Congress approved an increase in tax rates and wage and price controls were imposed. In January and February of 1951 member bank reserve requirements were raised and during this period the gold stock fell off sharply (by about $2 billion). Reserve Bank credit, on the other hand, rose sharply with the growth of the System's portfolio of government securities. The Treasury's insistence on putting out notes that carried rates no higher than those on issues previously offered, required heavy Federal Reserve support to prevent the failure of the offering and the Federal Reserve's attempt to sell other government securities which it held to avert an increase in its total holdings was not completely successful. The net effect was to increase member bank reserves despite the restrictive effects of other Federal Reserve actions and the gold outflow.

Between the middle of 1950 and March, 1951, sharp increases in consumer and wholesale prices were registered. Federal Reserve officials came to be increasingly restive with the restrictions placed upon monetary control by the agreement to support the government securities market. The basis for open conflict had already been laid in the hearings of the Douglas Committee on Monetary, Credit, and Fiscal Policies, and the report of this committee had questioned the advisability of continuing the support program in view of the destabilizing possibilities inherent in such a policy. The conflict between the Federal Reserve and the Treasury finally broke out into the open, and in March, 1951, a joint statement was issued by the two agencies which officially terminated the dispute. This famous 'accord' freed the Federal Reserve from having to peg the prices of government bonds. The Federal Reserve was freed to pursue a more flexible monetary policy aimed at promoting overall economic stability rather than being preoccupied with the much narrower aim of promoting stability in the government bond market to the virtual exclusion of other objectives.

The 'Bills Only' Doctrine

At the time of the 'accord,' when the pegging program of the Federal Reserve was dropped, the System adopted as one of its objectives the maintenance of 'orderly conditions' in the market for government securities. In the spring of 1953 the Federal Open Market Committee substituted 'correction of disorderly situations' for 'maintaining orderly conditions' as its directive to the committee executing transactions for the System. At the same time, the Open Market Committee adopted the policy of confining its open market operations to short-dated securities, namely, Treasury bills (with an exception for the 'correction of disorderly markets'). These changes were intended as supplements to the policy which was adopted earlier of not intervening in the market for the purpose of supporting Treasury refunding operations. The decision to operate in the short-dated securities, which came to be known as the 'bills only' doctrine, attracted a great deal of attention and in a short time became a controversial issue. Officials of the Federal Reserve Bank of New York questioned the advisability of limiting the scope of the market operations and thus lent a flavor of family discord to the debate. In the end, the views of the Board prevailed and this policy has prevailed since 1953. The Federal Reserve has only entered the long-term market twice (December, 1955, and July, 1958) to correct 'disorderly market conditions.'

The announced purpose of the Federal Open Market Committee in adopting these changes in open market technique was to improve and strengthen the market for government securities. The benefits alleged to follow from such an improvement in this market were, first, and most important, an increase in the effectiveness of monetary policy operations; second, an encouragement of a wider private participation in the government securities market; and third, an amelioration of some of the difficulties confronting the Treasury in its refinancing operations.

How does a policy of 'bills only' contribute to making the market for government securities a more efficient mechanism for transmitting the effects of monetary policy changes? According to the argument presented in defense of this change in open market technique, intervention by the Federal Reserve in the market for securities other than those of short maturity inserts a degree of uncertainty (uncertainty as to where and when the Federal Reserve will intervene) which enhances market risk to a point that deters private investors and security market intermediaries from making a continuous market for government securities. The connecting links in this argument are as follows: bond dealers in the government securities market, when subjected to this additional uncertainty, shy away from taking positions in the market and become mere brokers; they are reluctant, it is argued, to quote prices (to buy or sell), to hold inventories of securities, and to undertake arbitrage operations in the face of risks introduced by the Federal Reserve's intervention. This 'intervention' risk, it is held, is different from 'ordinary' market risk in that the dealers have little basis for forming judgments about movements in the market when it is subjected to the pressure of Federal Reserve open market operations, since (1) the System does not limit its actions because of profit and loss considerations, (2) the System's operations involve larger sums than those encountered by the market in private account transactions, and (3) the System's transactions affect the volume of bank reserves, which in turn may induce further transactions in securities in the attempt to adjust to reserve positions.

With the relegation of these market intermediaries to the status of brokers the market for government securities becomes extremely 'thin' from day to day, i.e. subject to rather severe bond price fluctuations that are in part capricious. Such developments, it is then argued, lessen the attractiveness of government securities to the large proportion of private investors whose holdings are predicated on the availability of a ready market for these securities in the event that they should desire liquidity. Reluctance, as described above, on the part of private investors to enter the securities market adds to the complications confronting the bond dealers and hence re-enforces the 'thinness' of the market.

If the foregoing chain of reasoning is accepted, then it is possible to argue that Federal Reserve intervention in the long-term end of the government securities market by enhancing the risk factor weakens that market with consequences for the transmission of the effects of monetary policy. If market intermediaries are not willing to quote purchase and sale prices and to hold inventories of securities, this will jeopardize the smooth operations of monetary policy conducted through open market operations. If these intermediaries fail to engage in arbitrage, then the spread of the effects of monetary policy through the various sectors of the capital market will to some extent be impeded. Advocates of 'bills only' see little chance that open market operations in short-dated securities will produce similar adverse effects upon the government securities market. The smaller risk attached to bills and the larger volume of transactions that occur daily (since this maturity is commonly used for effecting short-run adjustments) are held to be sufficient to preclude the spread of disruptive influences from Federal Reserve operations in this segment of the market.

Another reason for the appeal of 'bills only' was the desire on the part of a number of Federal Reserve officials to avoid central bank determination of the structure of interest rates. This reflected, in part, a reaction against any open market policy that smacked of the pegged rate regime from which the Federal Reserve only recently had extricated itself. It should be clear, however, that the question is not one of pegging vs. not pegging, and as such there is no necessary conflict in principle in following an open market policy that operates in all maturities but does not attempt to bring about some fixed distribution of interest rates. Rather, the question is whether the Federal Reserve chooses to forego the opportunity of intervening directly in all sectors of the government securities market to affect the entire distribution of interest rates, as opposed to relying on its operations in the short end of the market to achieve the monetary effects that it desires. The System in adopting the 'bills only' doctrine implicitly assumed that it could achieve its monetary goals by dealing in Treasury bills, the nearest thing to money, and allowing the market to transmit the effects of its actions to the medium-term and long-term sectors of the capital market. In terms of administration the new doctrine produced some drastic simplifications, since questions pertaining to the relationships among the various rates could be avoided.

Criticisms of 'bills only' were not slow in coming, and the feasibility and desirability of the new arrangement have been sharply questioned. The following are some of the arguments advanced against the new doctrine, and since they represent dissents from different vantage points they are not necessarily arguments that re-enforce one another.

One argument asks whether it is not possible that the additional uncertainty introduced by Federal Reserve intervention would be discounted in the market. At some discount (increase in yield) the increase in uncertainty would be offset sufficiently to ensure that dealers in the government securities market would take positions in that market. Other people have questioned the whole notion of additional uncertainty as posited by the advocates of 'bills only.' Is it not possible, they ask, that the expectation of Federal Reserve entry will operate not only to increase some risks but at the same time reduce other risks which would be present in the situation where no central bank intervention can be expected? 'Bills only' implicitly assumes some degree of additivity of 'ordinary' market risk and 'intervention' risk when in fact the relationship between these two types of risk may be of an entirely different form. As to the objective of strengthening the government securities market by confining open market operations to the short end of the market, it may be argued that the return to a freer monetary policy in 1951 by itself contained the seeds for such a development. With more opportunities available for profit making from such securities, market operations dealers will step in to perform the functions associated with a freer market and accordingly they will bear the risks attendant upon such activities.

To return to the proposition that Federal Reserve intervention in the long-term end of the securities market increases uncertainty, it is not clear that this is necessarily inimical to the possibility of success for monetary policy. In the arguments for breaking away from Treasury domination over the Federal Reserve, the desirability of restoring to the monetary authorities the ability to create uncertainty was considered as important as the restoration of greater flexibility. Some went as far as to contend that the spread of uncertainty through the money market was fully as effective as changes in the cost of borrowing in achieving monetary restraint. The Federal Reserve, by creating uncertainty in the market for long-term government securities, it has been argued, alters the degree of liquidity ascribed by the commercial banks to their holdings of these long-term securities, and as a consequence the banks are induced to trim their loans to protect their liquidity positions. This creation of uncertainty would, of course, have to be kept within rather narrow bounds; otherwise it would make for disruptive forces in the market for government securities similar to those that the proponents of 'bills only' have claimed existed in the market prior to the adoption of the new doctrine.

More important, however, are questions concerning the effectiveness of this new approach in achieving stabilization goals: the major query being whether or not monetary operations confined in this way can achieve the ends delegated to the monetary authorities. It is possible that in the face of a sharp decline in economic activity (more pronounced than that which occurred in 1953-1954 and 1957-1958) adherence to 'bills only' will produce monetary effects that are insufficient to meet the tasks allocated to the monetary authorities. For example, open market operations restricted to the short end of the government securities market in a downswing may lead to short-term rates being pushed down drastically while long-term rates are affected very little (the experience of the 'thirties is evidence of the possibility of such a break in the connection between long-term and short-term rates of interest). Long-term rates of interest may be affected very little by changes in short-term rates if expectations are that the changes in the short-term rates will not last very long. Yet, if monetary changes are to produce salutary effects in countering a depression, the lowering of the long-term rates of interest is important since expenditure is more likely to be responsive to changes in long-term interest rates than in short.

In the recession of 1953-1954 and during most of the downswing of 1957-1958 the Federal Reserve authorities maintained their adherence to 'bills only.' The Federal Reserve did intervene in the long-term market for government bonds to support some Treasury refunding operations in the summer of 1958, but Federal Reserve officials have not given any indication that they are abandoning 'bills only' as a general policy.

In any event, the new doctrine, 'bills only,' has not been confronted as yet with a really severe test of its ability to bring about the desired effects on the volume of credit and spending. The most difficult test for monetary controls is, of course, a serious decline in economic activity—a decline more serious than the ones that we have faced up to now. The degree to which the monetary authorities affect long-term interest rates does not matter too much so long as downturns in economic activity are largely the result of inventory adjustments, but when downturns result from declines in expenditures on fixed plant and equipment, the matter of how rapidly monetary action can bring down the long-term rates is more important. And it is with the ability of monetary policy based on 'bills only' to cope with the latter type of economic decline that most doubts have been raised.

SOME SUGGESTED READING

While the literature on the stable bond market policy is voluminous, there are a few articles that do a good job of summarizing the main points at issue. L. H. Seltzer, 'Is a Rise in Interest Rates Desirable or Inevitable?' *American Economic Review* (1945) and L. V. Chandler, 'Federal Reserve Policy and the Federal Debt,' *American Economic Review* (1949)—the latter is reprinted in the American Economic Association, *Readings in Monetary Theory* (New York and Philadelphia, 1951)— are excellent surveys of the theoretical and historical aspects of that policy.

At the time the stable bond market policy was in effect, the argument was advanced that only small changes in interest rates were necessary to achieve the desired monetary effects. This argument has come to be known as the 'availability doctrine.' A good example of this doctrine is the view put forth by R. V. Roosa in his 'Interest Rates and the Central Bank' in *Money, Trade, and Economic Growth: Essays in Honor of John Henry Williams* (New York, 1951). The 'availability doctrine' was later examined in two articles by I. O. Scott, 'The Availability Doctrine,' *The Canadian Journal of Economics and Political Science* (1957), and 'The Availability Doctrine: Theoretical Underpinnings,' *Review of Economic Studies* (vol. XXV).

For a review of the more recent Federal Reserve policy of 'bills only,' D. Carson, 'Recent Open Market Committee Policy and Technique,' *Quarterly Journal of Economics* (1955) and P. A. Samuelson, 'Recent American Monetary Controversy,' *Three Banks Review* (1956) are helpful guides. An article by I. O. Scott and D. Fand, 'The Federal Reserve System's "Bills Only" Policy: A Suggested Interpretation,' *Journal of Business of the University of Chicago* (1958) is particularly good in examining the reasons put forth by the System for its adoption of 'bills only.'

15

American Banking Institutions—
IV. The Commercial Banks

Structure of Commercial Banking in the United States

The structure of banking in the United States is markedly different from the structure that prevails in most other economically developed countries; there, the number of banks in each country is small but these few banks provide banking facilities for the whole country through their many branches. American commercial banks, on the other hand, are largely independent units that operate single offices. A number of banks do operate branches, however, and some banks operate through larger organizations called 'groups' and 'chains.'

At the end of 1957 there were 13,566 commercial banks in the United States and they operated a total of nearly 22,000 banking offices. Slightly less than 9000 of these commercial banks operated under state charters (state banks) and about 4600 were under federal charter (national banks). Of the nearly 8000 branches and additional offices in existence, approximately one-half were owned by national banks, the rest by the state banks.

Both federal and state laws define the limits of branch banking, with the rules of federal regulation often depending upon the laws of the state in which the regulation is administered; both forbid the establishment of branches that are beyond the borders of the state in which the parent bank is located. The 34 states which currently permit branch banking differ widely with regard to the secondary regulations governing the establishment of branches; a few states limit branches to within the city in which the main office is located; other states extend this to cover the county in which the main office is located; still others permit the establishment of branches beyond the lines of the county in which the main office is located but stop short of allowing state-wide branch banking; and finally, there are 15 states that permit branch banking to be carried out on a state-wide basis. Federal regulation has tended to become less stringent by its acceptance, over the years, of many state rules that apply to branch banking, but where independent federal control is exercised it is at least as restrictive as the state laws in the region concerned, and quite frequently more restrictive.[1]

The restrictions placed upon branch banking have precluded the establishment of branch systems similar to those in England or Canada. Most American banks that have branches operate only one or two each, with only a few banks operating branch systems that encompass more than one hundred banking offices. Still, limited as the branch banking system may be with respect to area of coverage, an ever increasing number of banks find it worth while to open branch offices. The number of banks operating branches has risen from slightly over 500 in 1920 to about 1900 by the end of 1957, and the number of branches and additional offices operated rose from less than 800 to nearly 8000.

The restrictions encountered on the establishment of branch banking systems have fostered the growth of looser organizations called 'chains' and 'groups' which facilitate multi-office banking. 'Chains' refer to the cases where the operations of a number of banks with separate corporate charters are under the control of one or more individuals; control may depend on stock ownership or interlocking directorates. Group banking, on the other hand, describes the situation in which a number of independently chartered banks are controlled by a corporation [2] (or through some other business organization that is quite like a corporation). No distinction was drawn between 'chains' and 'groups' until the 'twenties,

---

[1] E.g. the capital requirements prescribed for national and state member banks are more burdensome than the capital requirements imposed under the laws of most states.

[2] The way in which a group is usually formed is for a bank holding company to purchase the stocks of a number of commercial banks. If the bank holding company's purchases of stock are sufficient to enable it to name a majority of the directors of the commercial banks involved, it can then exercise control over the policies of these commercial banks.

when corporate control of banks became significant and a distinction between corporate and personal control became meaningful.

Few states have laws that hamper the operations of either chains or groups; but where they do, group banking is usually subject to more restrictions than chain banking, since control is through organizations rather than through individuals. Even then, chain banking is subject to many fewer state-imposed restrictions than is branch banking. Federal law places few restrictions upon chain banking, but group banking is hit more severely. Member banks are not allowed to purchase stocks of corporations, including banking corporations, which makes it difficult for banks to form groups. And since the passage of the Bank Holding Company Act of 1956, bank holding companies can acquire bank stocks only after they have secured the approval of the Board of Governors of the Federal Reserve System. Further, the 1956 Act requires that bank holding companies divest themselves of non-banking interests. Chains are not significant in their command over banking offices on the national scene and are important in only a few states. Commercial banks in chains tend to be small in size and tend to be situated in small towns. Group banking, on the other hand, is much more important in quantitative terms. Included are sizable holding companies such as the Transamerica Corporation (California) and the Marine Midland Corporation (New York). And while both chain and group banks can be found in areas where branch banking does not exist, group banks can also be found in regions where branch banking has taken root. But both chain and group banking will continue as part of the commercial bank structure in the United States so long as branch banking systems are not allowed to cross state lines.

Probably the simplest way to characterize the size structure of American commercial banks is to say that we have a small number of very large banks that would surpass or rival the size of some of the foreign branch bank systems, and from that peak we can move down through the various bank sizes and find some commercial banks at each step along the way. This close succession of banks of different sizes makes it difficult to divide the commercial banks into simple groups such as 'small' and 'large' banks for use in the description of the structure, and we are forced back to statements that try to give some idea of the volume of business done by a particular class of banks.

The banks that are members of the Federal Reserve System, for example, currently account for about 85 per cent of the total deposit liabilities of all commercial banks, although they number less than one-half of all commercial banks in the United States. But the distribution is skewed even more than that suggests; commercial banks in New York City and Chicago which are members of the Federal Reserve System (central reserve city banks) were 32 in number at the end of 1957, yet they held deposits that totaled more than $37,000 million; they constituted less than ¼ of 1 per cent of the commercial banks in the United States but held about 18 per cent of the deposits. The reserve city banks in the System numbered 278 at the end of 1957 which was about 2 per cent of the total of commercial banks, yet they held approximately one-third of all deposits. The remaining 13,000 commercial banks held deposits amounting to slightly less than 50 per cent of the deposits held by all commercial banks. They are not necessarily small banks in comparison with central reserve city and reserve city banks, but most of them tend to be so.

The Business of American Commercial Banks

Commercial bank assets can be broken down into four main divisions: cash, holdings of United States government securities, holdings of other securities (primarily those issued by the state and local governments), and loans. The relative proportions of these assets have not remained stable over time, however, and to see what changes have occurred in the business of commercial banking over the years, we shall examine the distributions of the assets of the member banks for selected years. The years we shall consider are: 1928, a year of prosperity prior to the growth of a large national debt; 1938, a year that is representative of the depressed 'thirties; 1947, a year of prosperity and one of transition from a wartime to a peacetime economy; and 1957, a year of high but not full employment.[3] At the end of 1928 the distribution of the assets of the member banks was as follows: [4]

---

[3] In 1957 production first leveled off and then declined, but prices continued upward throughout the year.

[4] Figures are from Board of Governors, *Banking and Monetary Statistics* (Washington, 1943), p. 72.

	$ Millions	Per cent of total assets
Cash assets	9,952	20.6
U.S. government obligations	4,312	8.9
Other securities	6,217	12.9
Loans	25,155	52.2
Other assets	2,622	5.4
Total	48,258	100.0

The predominance of loans in the member banks' earning assets is easy to see with government securities constituting less than half of the total of investments made by the member banks. As to the breakdown of the loan portfolio into its most important components, the figures available permit only an extremely rough classification. Of the $25,000 million in loans outstanding, nearly $11,000 million were in the category 'other loans' while nearly $10,000 million were in the category 'loans on securities, except to banks.' Taking the latter category first, of the nearly $10,000 million about $3500 million were loans to brokers and dealers and about $6400 million were 'to others.' These 'loans on securities to others' represented primarily commercial, industrial, and agricultural loans secured by stocks and bonds. (At the time that the loan classifications were changed in 1938 the comparison of the loan classifications suggested that about 70 per cent of the 'loans on securities to others' were commercial, industrial, and agricultural loans.) The first category, 'other loans,' consisted mainly of commercial, industrial, and agricultural loans not secured by stocks and bonds; again, from the 1938 comparison of loan classifications it would appear that close to 60 per cent of 'other loans' were commercial, industrial, and agricultural loans. A rough estimate of the total of commercial, industrial, and agricultural loans (including open market paper) would be $11,000 million to $12,000 million or around one-quarter of the member banks' total assets at the end of 1928. As has already been noted, loans to brokers and dealers on securities totaled about $3500 million; real estate loans outstanding were about $3100 million.

By 1938 a number of important changes had taken place although the total of member bank assets remained virtually the same. The distribution of assets for the end of 1938 was as follows: [5]

---

[5] Figures are from Board of Governors, *Banking and Monetary Statistics* (Washington, 1943), p. 74.

	$ Millions	Per cent of total assets
Cash assets	15,490	31.4
U.S. government obligations	13,223	26.8
Other securities	5,640	11.4
Loans	13,208	26.8
Other assets	1,760	3.6
Total	49,330	100.0

Government securities held by the member banks more than tripled in volume between 1928 and 1938, while the volume of loans outstanding declined by nearly 50 per cent. The reduced demand for private credit in the 'thirties coupled with the expanded supply of government securities were the principal factors accounting for this change. Another thing to note is the sharp rise in the ratio of cash to total assets. In part this upswing reflected the higher reserve requirements in force at the end of 1938: $22\frac{3}{4}$ per cent, $17\frac{1}{2}$ per cent, and 12 per cent on demand deposits (for banks in the various classes) and 5 per cent on time deposits in 1938 in contrast to 13 per cent, 10 per cent, and 7 per cent on demand deposits and 3 per cent on time deposits in 1928. But also serving to raise the cash ratio between 1928 and 1938 was the appearance of excess reserves; in 1938 nearly three-eighths of the reserve balances of the member banks represented excess reserves, and while there are no figures for excess reserves in 1928, it is quite unlikely that the member banks maintained large surplus balances prior to the 'thirties. This phenomenon of excess reserves can be explained primarily in terms of the commercial banks' finding private loans to be too risky and government bonds not too attractive as investments; it is quite possible that a number of banks reasoned that the low rates on government securities would not persist for long and on those grounds they found it desirable to remain in cash so as to be able to undertake investments when the interest rate did rise, i.e. the reasons we developed to explain why individuals desire to hold idle balance may be applicable to the behavior of commercial banks in the United States in the 'thirties.

World War II altered the financial situation in the United States considerably; the national debt grew from about $64,000 million at the end of 1941 to nearly $279,000 million by the end of 1945; in the same period the nation's monetary circulation (demand deposits and currency) rose from less than $50,000 million to more than $100,000 million. By 1947, the economy had made considerable progress in the process of switching from a wartime to a peacetime economy but it still reflected the wartime developments to a degree sufficient to highlight their main impact. At the end of 1947 the distribution of assets for the member banks was as follows: [6]

	$ Millions	Per cent of total assets
Cash assets	32,845	24.9
U.S. government obligations	57,914	43.9
Other securities	7,304	5.5
Loans	32,628	24.7
Other assets	1,369	1.0
Total	132,060	100.0

Between 1938 and 1947 member banks' assets rose from nearly $50,000 million to over $132,000 million, with the most significant change being the more than fourfold increase in the member banks' holdings of government securities. The ratio of government securities to total assets rose from one-quarter to three-sevenths while the ratio of loans to total assets remained practically constant between 1938 and 1947. Cash assets fell as a percentage of total assets from above 30 per cent in 1938 to about 25 per cent in 1947; reserve requirements were, on the average, virtually the same for both years, but in 1947 with abundant private loan opportunities and an ample supply of government securities, few banks held sizable surplus reserve funds.

Of the nearly $33,000 million in loans outstanding more than one-half (about $17,000 million) were commercial and industrial loans (including open market paper) with real estate loans of $7000 million and consumer loans of $4700 million next in importance. Agricultural loans were about $1000 million and loans for purchasing or carrying securities amounted to nearly $1900 million. From the end of 1945 to the end of 1947 the member banks expanded their loans by about 50 per cent (from $22,775 million to $32,628 million) and decreased their holdings of government securities by more than $20,000 million (from $78,338 million to $57,914 million);

[6] Figures are from *Federal Reserve Bulletin,* May, 1957, p. 539.

the major part of the liquidation of government securities by the commercial banks had been achieved by the end of 1947, but the postwar growth in loans had barely begun.

Turning now to the situation at the end of 1957, at that time the member banks distributed their assets in the following manner: [7]

	$ Millions	Per cent of total assets [1]
Cash assets	42,746	22.7
U.S. government obligations	47,079	24.9
Other securities	14,324	7.6
Loans	80,950	42.9
Other assets	3,729	2.0
Total	188,828	100.0

[1] Figures do not add up to 100 per cent because of rounding.

Most of the growth in total assets between 1947 and 1957 can be explained by the rise in loans outstanding, which rose from about $33,000 million at the end of 1947 to more than $78,000 million by the end of 1956. Holdings of government securities on the other hand declined by more than $10,000 million during the 1947-1956 period. The ratio of government securities to total assets still remained far above the ratio that prevailed in the 'twenties (less than 10 per cent), but it was quite near to the ratio that held in the 'thirties. The ratio of loans to total assets, however, stood far above the ratios of the 'thirties and the 'forties and approached the level reached in the 'twenties. In addition, the strong demands for loans has induced the commercial banks to depress the ratio of cash to total assets below the ratios that prevailed in the 'thirties and in the period immediately after the war. Reserve requirements in 1957 were quite similar to the legal ratios that held in 1938 and in 1947, but the surplus reserve holdings of banks were practically nonexistent in 1957 whereas in the earlier periods that were considered the banks held excess reserves.

The most important loan categories—commercial and industrial loans (including open market paper), real estate loans, and consumer loans—accounted for about $73,000 million of the $81,000 million in loans outstanding at the end of 1957. Since the 'twenties,

---

[7] Figures are from *Federal Reserve Bulletin,* August, 1958, p. 948.

real estate loans and consumer loans have gained in relative importance while commercial and industrial loans have held their own. Loans for purchasing or carrying securities totaled less than $4000 million at the end of 1957 and have declined drastically in relative terms since 1928; their total at the end of 1957 was not very different from the 1928 total while the sum of all loans more than tripled during that period.

Having traced through some of the major changes that have occurred over time in commercial banking distributions, we turn next to a more detailed examination of the activities of commercial banks as they operate at the present time. We shall be concerned with the structure of the asset and liability accounts of the commercial banks and, whenever it is possible, with some of the factors that account for the relative sizes of the various accounts. For this examination we shall select items from the combined balance sheet of all insured commercial banks; [8] these insured banks currently account for 97 per cent of all commercial banks in operation and 99 per cent of all commercial bank deposit liabilities. At the end of 1957 these insured banks had deposit liabilities of slightly more than $200,000 million. Of these deposits nearly $17,000 million were interbank deposits, which fact demonstrates the significance of correspondent banking. Demand deposits (as the name suggests, payable at the demand of the depositors) other than inter-bank deposits accounted for about $127,000 million, and of this total about $14,500 million were the deposits of federal, state, and local governments. Individuals, partnerships, and corporations held the bulk of the demand deposits, with their total holdings amounting to more than $109,000 million. Time deposits (which are either made for a specified time or are payable at some time after notice is given) made up the rest of the deposit liabilities and totaled $57,000 million; nearly all of these time deposits were in non-governmental hands.

Inter-bank deposits (the correspondent balances) have long been important in American banking. Very early, smaller banks began to hold deposits in the larger banks located in the financial centers, and under the National Banking System many banks were allowed to count inter-bank deposits as a part of their legal reserves. At present, banks that are members of the Federal Reserve System

---

[8] I.e. those with their deposits insured at the Federal Deposit Insurance Corporation—see Chapter 13.

must hold their legal reserves with the Federal Reserve Banks, but many state-chartered banks are still permitted to count their deposits with other commercial banks as legal reserves. In addition, the city correspondent banks often provide their country correspondents with services similar to those provided the member banks by the Federal Reserve Banks; they perform check clearing services, they perform services associated with securities transactions, and they perform international banking services for the country banks.

Turning to the asset side of commercial bank operations, the main thing we shall be concerned with is the commercial banks' loans and investments. At the end of 1957 the insured commercial banks held loans and investments that totaled $169,000 million. The breakdown is as follows: [9]

LOANS	($ Millions)
Commercial and industrial loans, (including open market paper)	40,545
Agricultural loans	4,030
Loans to brokers and dealers in securities	2,569
Other loans for purchasing or carrying securities	1,602
Real estate loans	23,104
Other loans to individuals for personal expenditure	20,200
Other loans	3,526
Total loans net	143,801 [1]
INVESTMENTS	
United States government securities	57,686
State and local government securities	13,733
Other securities	3,911
Total investments	75,330

[1] Loan item figures do not add up to total since they are shown gross (before deduction of valuation reserves).

The largest single item is 'United States government securities,' which accounts for more than one-third of the total of loans and investments. As one might have expected, the commercial banks

[9] Figures are from Federal Deposit Insurance Corporation, Report No. 48, 1957, pp. 6-7.

have tended to hold government securities which mature within a fairly short time and bear less market risk than the longer-dated maturities; roughly 25 per cent mature within one year and another 50 per cent have between one and five years to run. Of the remaining 25 per cent, which have more than five years to run until maturity, slightly more than one-third have more than ten years to run.

Despite the size of the government securities portfolio, the ratio of government securities held to total assets was about the same at the end of 1957, for the insured commercial banks, as in the 1934-1941 period—around 25 per cent. This is in sharp contrast with the situation that prevailed shortly after the end of World War II. At the end of 1945 the insured commercial banks held nearly $89,000 million of government securities out of total assets of $158,000 million, or a ratio of more than 50 per cent. Since that time the commercial banks have moved out of government securities and have acquired instead more lucrative assets consisting of commercial loans, real estate loans, and consumer installment loans. As in the pre-depression period, loans have become, once again, the most important activity of the commercial banks, and the post-World War II lamentations by some persons that the commercial banks were likely to become mere holders of government securities now appear to have been unwarranted.

The relative decline of government securities in commercial banks' portfolios does not mean that the banks have become unimportant in the market for government securities. At the end of 1957 commercial banks still held over 40 per cent of the marketable government securities that were held outside the Federal Reserve Banks and United States government agencies and trust funds. Such a bank share in the market means that the money market and government securities market are closely interrelated, and banks frequently adjust their cash positions by trading in government securities. Most of the very short-run adjustments are made through commercial bank purchases and sales of Treasury bills, the security with a three-month maturity date at time of issue.

State and local government securities are also held by the insured commercial banks; these totaled nearly $14,000 million at the end of 1957. This sector of the investment portfolio has grown rapidly in the postwar years as the states and municipalities have pushed heavy capital programs financed by bond issues. Other securities held by the insured commercial banks total about $3900 million and have changed very little over the years.

Commercial bank loans fall into three main categories: commercial and industrial loans (including open market paper), real estate loans, and other loans to individuals for personal expenditures. The last category includes installment loans or what are often called consumer loans. Commercial and industrial loans (including open market paper) cover some of the following categories: loans to businesses for financing the purchase and storage of inventories; loans to businesses for the purchase of producers' equipment (generally equipment that is amortized over a short period of time—loans issued for this purpose are frequently called 'term loans'); commercial bank holdings of commercial paper, the paper issued in the open money market by well-known firms for short-term financing purposes; and commercial bank holdings of bankers' acceptances—the instruments used primarily in the finance of trade (both domestic and foreign, but primarily foreign). Real estate loans, which are next to commercial loans in size, have expanded sharply in the post-war period and reflect the strong building boom that has continued for so many years. In many cases the commercial banks lend substantial funds to mortgage companies backed by a commitment from insurance companies that they will take over the mortgages as soon as they have accumulated the funds necessary; this practice is called *warehousing* and it enables the insurance companies to commit their expected funds to lucrative investments prior to the actual receipt of these funds. The commercial banks also undertake real estate loans for their own portfolios; some of these mortgages are insured by the Federal Housing Administration and some are guaranteed by the Veterans Administration. Within the consumer loan area the biggest single category is passenger automobile paper, which by the end of 1957 accounted for one-third of the total of consumer loans.

The interest rates earned by the commercial banks on their holdings of open market paper (commercial paper and bankers' acceptances) are quite similar to the yields obtained from Treasury securities with similar maturities (e.g. Treasury bills), the private paper earning slightly higher yields. Short-term business loan bank rates are based on the prime loan rate, which is the rate a bank charges customers who have high credit standings; other customers' rates stand above the prime loan rate. Some regional differences in bank rates on short-term business loans still exist, with rates in the South and West generally being above those that prevail in New York and other Northern and Eastern cities. But a more important differentiation in interest rate charges is connected with the size of the loan rather than with location. The interest rate charged by banks increases as the size of loan decreases, and the difference between rates on $10,000 and $200,000 loans is greater for each region than the interregional differences in rates on any particular size of loan. Real estate loans generally bring a higher gross return but since they are generally for long periods of time the market risk involved is much greater than in the case of short-term business loans. Prior to the guarantee or insurance of real estate loans by the Veterans Administration or the Federal Housing Administration, real estate loans often possessed very little liquidity and were not considered suitable for banks' portfolios; mortgages were often traded only within small regional markets, and it was extremely difficult to dispose of a substantial volume of mortgages within a short period of time without the danger of running heavy losses. Consumer loans probably provide a higher gross return for the commercial banks than any other loans they make, but the net return is reduced substantially below this, since these loans generally involve heavier costs of administration.

The continuance of a generally high level of economic activity and the gradual reduction of the excess liquidity that was carried over from the war years have combined to produce exceptionally strong demands for loans in the past few years. And since the lending capacity of a single commercial bank depends on the size of its deposits,[10] the increased demand for loans has spurred banks to compete vigorously with one another and, to some extent, with other financial intermediaries for deposits. In attracting time deposits, the commercial banks can compete with other financial intermediaries (savings and loan associations, mutual savings banks, etc.) by offering competitive rates of interest, to the extent that the supervisory authorities of the Federal Reserve and the Federal Deposit Insur-

---

[10] This is in contrast to the banking system as a whole, where the volume of deposits depends on the volume of bank loans and investments and ultimately on the volume of reserves made available by the central bank. See pp. 201-3 (above).

ance Corporation permit them to increase the interest rates on time deposits. But to attract demand deposits the commercial banks cannot rely directly on the price mechanism since they are not permitted to pay interest on demand deposits; instead the banks count upon the offer of attractive services to depositors.

We should add that while a single commercial bank's lending capacity depends on the size of its deposit liabilities, it is still the case that a bank's capital determines (by law) the maximum size loan that it can make to an individual borrower. The resuscitation of bank lending on a large scale has heightened the importance of this restriction, and some recent bank mergers and capital flotations might be explained in this light.

Some Suggested Reading

For the factual information on the business of commercial banks the *Federal Reserve Bulletin,* published monthly by the Board of Governors of the Federal Reserve System, is extremely helpful. A detailed discussion of the types of activities that commercial banks undertake appears in Chapter 4 of *Financial Institutions,* edited by E. W. Boehmler.

The structure of commercial banking is examined comprehensively in a chapter by C. E. Cagle in *Banking Studies,* published by the Board of Governors of the Federal Reserve System (Washington, 1941). Information on current changes in the branch banking system appear semiannually in the *Federal Reserve Bulletin* and in the *Annual Report* of the Board of Governors of the Federal Reserve System.

R. S. Sayers in his *American Banking System* (Oxford, 1948) has two chapters on the business and structure of American commercial banking that are extremely helpful.

16

The Role of the Government

The most important institution in a modern economy which we have not yet considered at length is the government; it is the purpose of this chapter to consider the special features that have to be taken into account when we allow for the fact that the government can be (and in recent times usually has been) a powerful actor on the economic scene.

Our discussion of the economic aspects of the government will be narrowly circumscribed; our concern is solely with those aspects which are particularly closely related to monetary economics. Of these, the most important is stabilization policy, which will be our extensive concern in later chapters of this book.[1] In a broader discussion of the economic aspects of government, much more would have to be considered. For our present purpose, the significant point is that economic stabilization is only one of many aims of policy with which the government will be concerned, and it is by no means necessarily the most important. Which choices are made, and which policies are considered most important, will depend on the interplay of political forces. It should be remembered that, while it is necessary to speak of 'the government' as if it were monolithic, in fact government policies are never as simple or as sharply expressed as we shall have to make them appear: in both their political formulation and their administrative application, they are a result of the interplay of personalities, factions, and pressure groups.

In studying monetary economics, there are three characteristics of the government that are particularly significant. It can do anything, within the limits that may be imposed by the constitution

---

[1] See Part V.

or by the operation of political forces; it is large, so that its operations are likely to have much bigger effects than the operations of any other single transactor; [2] and it is much more concerned with the indirect consequences of its actions than are other transactors.

It will be convenient to look at these three points in a little more detail. The power of the government to do anything has two aspects: it can do anything that can be done by any other kind of transactor, and it can do things that no one else can do (except insofar as it delegates its powers).

In the first place, it can do anything that any other transactor can do. It can act like the head of a huge household, receiving contributions from the members of the household and buying goods and services (e.g. school lunches, highways) with the contributions for their consumption. Moreover, like some households but unlike most, it can borrow extensively to finance current consumption. It can operate in the same way as the firms in Part II, by borrowing from the public and buying real resources. It may use these resources in order to make a commercial profit in the same way as firms do, or it may use them for non-commercial purposes, such as making war. It can shift the form in which it holds its assets. It can operate as a bank, and can itself create money.

In addition, however, the government has powers of a kind which are not enjoyed by other economic agents. It can levy taxes or pay out subsidies; and these taxes and subsidies can be directed in any way which is politically acceptable and which appears desirable to the government. What is more, it can issue orders. They may be instructions either to do or not to do certain things. Generally speaking, the latter are the easier to introduce and enforce, and they provide the majority of economic controls.

The second of the main groups of characteristics which distinguish the government from other transactors is that it is very large. A change in the economic actions of the government will have very extensive repercussions. For example, a change in government expenditure policy will have a considerable effect on the equilibrium level of income, in a way that a change in the expenditure plans of no other single transactor can have, because no other transactor

---

[2] In 1957, in the United States, federal, state, and local government expenditure on goods and services amounted to about one-fifth of the gross national product.

is large enough. Similarly, a change in government policy about the form in which it will hold its assets or issue its liabilities will have a large effect on the markets for claims—that is, on the various rates of interest.

The third special characteristic of the government from our point of view is that it is much more concerned with the indirect consequences of its actions than are other transactors. This fact arises partly from the size of the government's economic operations; they are large enough to have substantial repercussions. If an ordinary household or even a single firm alters its expenditure plans, the net effect on the rest of the economy of these changes will usually be very small—in fact, negligible; if, on the other hand, the government changes its plans, the repercussions may well be widespread. This is not the only reason, however, why the government is particularly concerned with the repercussions of its actions. A firm or a household will be concerned with only those results which affect it directly; the government, on the other hand, is more or less intimately concerned with everything that is happening in the country. If a large firm is considering whether to increase its investment expenditure financed by borrowing by, say, a million dollars per year, it will not normally pay serious attention to the fact that this extra expenditure will lead, through the multiplier process, to an increase in the level of activity and income in the country as a whole which is appreciably larger (perhaps much larger) than the initiating one million dollars per year. (This is assuming, of course, that there were unemployed resources available: that the point of full employment had not been reached. If it had been reached, the firm's action will have different, but still extensive, repercussions which we shall consider in the chapters on inflation.) The firm may be aware that its actions will have these expansionary consequences; but except insofar as they reflect back on the firm by the consequential increase in orders for the firm's products (which will be extremely small because the firm makes up a very small part of the economy) the firm will not normally be concerned with these repercussions of its decision. An attempt to raise the general level of activity in a country is not the concern of an individual firm; an ordinary commercial firm is primarily and predominately concerned with making profits.

The government, however, is in a different position. It may, of course, choose to indulge in commercial activities for their own sake (as by running a post office or an electric power plant). It may choose to run an enterprise on non-commercial principles. (For example, the government may provide roads free of charge.) In addition, however, a government will be aware that its expenditure policy in carrying out these activities affects the level of income in the country. By borrowing, and spending money on improving a power plant it owns, it may increase the efficiency and profitability of the plant; to that extent it is following the same sorts of principle as those followed by ordinary business. By spending more money on roads, it may provide direct benefit to the community, by speeding up and cheapening travel. In addition, however, the government pays attention to the effects of this expenditure on the level of activity; such an increase in government investment plans when there is a great deal of unemployment will be likely to be regarded as doing additional good by raising the level of output and income: and this is a matter with which the government is directly concerned. Conversely, in times of full employment, the government may pay attention to the effect of its investment program in increasing inflationary pressure.

The result of these two levels of concern of the government—with both the direct benefits and the indirect effects on the level of activity—is that the government may well act in a different way from an ordinary firm. It may plan to invest, even if the direct returns are very small or even nonexistent, because of the favorable indirect effects on the level of activity. Conversely, in times of full employment, it may choose not to invest, even though investment might have favorable direct effects, because of the wider unfavorable effects of increased pressure on the limited supplies of resources available.

The government, in its concern with the economic state of the country as a whole and so with both the direct and the indirect consequences of its actions, can also try to influence the economy in other ways. As we have seen, it can do almost anything. It can borrow in order to buy goods for current consumption—e.g. uniforms for soldiers or polio vaccine for babies. It is almost impossible for a household to do this except when substantial security can be offered, but governments frequently borrow in order to finance current consumption. The government can also affect the economic situation in other ways. It can influence interest rates by changing the form in which it holds its debt or issues its liabilities; the effect works both directly by changing the amounts of different kinds of asset (such as money, bills, bonds) available for the public to hold, and indirectly by influencing expectations about future prices of various assets, by indicating the directions in which the government is expected to operate. It can also have powerful effects on the economic situation by imposing controls. Most important of all is the power of the government deriving from its ability to tax. It is to the effects of taxation on the level of activity and income that we must now turn our attention.

Taxation and the Level of Activity

As an initial step, it will be convenient to return to relatively simple conditions, in which we can ignore what is happening in the market for claims and so be able to concentrate on flows of income and expenditure. It will be recalled that we did this in the simplified economy of Part II by assuming (in Chapter 5) conditions in which interest rates remained unchanged. For the moment, we shall return to these simple conditions. Later in this chapter, in our consideration of government debt policy, we shall consider changes that occur in the market for claims.

Our need to consider the government separately from firms and households derives from the fact that the government does not act in the same way as firms or households, so that it is not possible to assimilate it to either of these groups. This separate consideration of the government is the most important single example of the need for 'disaggregation' in economic analysis; it is convenient to aggregate only groups of transactors whose motivations and reactions to changed circumstances are sufficiently alike in character to be safely regarded as homogeneous.[3]

In considering the relationship between taxation and the level of activity it will be convenient to consider first the effects of a particular tax system. Then we can proceed to the second stage of considering the effects of changes in the tax system. These changes can conveniently be regarded as being of two kinds. One arises when there is a change in the method by which a given

---

[3] Similarly, therefore, a very precise analysis may demand a disaggregation of households into different groups, e.g. by income.

amount of revenue is raised (e.g. a shift from income tax to excise tax). The other is a change in the total amount of tax gathered.

Let us first consider the effects of a particular tax system, when the same sorts of changes have been occurring as those we considered in Chapters 5 and 6, namely, an increase in investment by firms, which leads to a multiplier rise in the level of income and activity. In the conditions considered in Chapters 5 and 6, the government did not enter into the situation. What difference arises now that there is a government, which is imposing taxes?

In the first place, let us consider what happens if government expenditure remains unchanged. This is quite a plausible assumption; if the government spends all its income on maintaining the armed forces, there is no reason why a rise in the level of activity (with prices constant, as we assumed in Chapters 5 and 6) should lead directly to any increased government expenditure. What the rise in the level of income and activity will almost certainly lead to, however, is a rise in government tax receipts. This happens, whether taxes are on expenditure (e.g. excise taxes) or on income; a rise in the level of activity and income almost invariably leads to the payment of more taxes to the government. The result is that the government's receipts have increased while its expenditure on currently produced goods and services has remained unchanged. If its budget was initially in balance, it now has a budget surplus; we can say that the government is 'saving' all the extra receipts it obtains as a result of this rise in the general level of activity and income: it is not using them to buy currently produced goods and services.[4]

What happens on the side of the households, who are paying the increased taxes out of their bigger incomes? The argument is simplest if we take the case of an income tax paid only by households. The household does not receive as big an increase in disposable income as it would have if the income tax had not existed. Therefore, the householder does not increase his saving or his consumption by as much as if there had been no tax. Let us assume the income tax rate is 20 per cent for all households, and that 50 per cent of the extra disposable income (i.e. after payment of income tax) is saved.

---

[4] This definition of saving is symmetrical with that used for households in Part II; it will be noted that it excludes cases where the government is simultaneously saving and investing (cf. Chapter 9).

Now, for each $1 by which income increases, 20 cents goes to the government, which saves it all. Of the remaining 80 cents, households spend 40 cents on consumption and save 40 cents. The total amount spent out of this extra $1 is 40 cents; the rest (i.e. 60 cents) is saved either by the households or by the government. If, on the other hand, there had been no income tax, then the whole of the extra $1 was spendable by households; on our assumptions, 50 cents of this would be spent on consumption and 50 cents saved.

In this case, then, total leakages into saving are greater when the government imposes taxes: the government saves the whole of its share of the extra income, while the household saves only a part. The consequence, in terms of the analysis of Chapter 5, is quite simple. The equilibrium rise in the level of income following a given initial impulse in the form of a rise in the level of investment plans will be less when income tax is paid and the government saves the whole of the tax receipts, because more is then saved out of any given increase in national income. The new equilibrium, at which planned investment equals planned saving, is one involving a smaller rise in the level of income than when the government does not enter the situation. In terms of the analysis of Chapter 6 (where we considered the sequence of events following an increase in the level of investment), the leakage into savings (by government and households together) at each stage is greater than in the case where the government is ignored; correspondingly less expenditure is passed on to provide more income in the next period, and so the process fades out at a lower equilibrium level.[5]

The nature of the change in the equilibrium level of income can

---

[5] The multiplier which takes account of government expenditure and taxation can be represented by quite a simple formula. The rise in the level of income is equal to the rise in the level of investment multiplied by

$$\frac{1}{s(1-t) + t(1-g)},$$

where s = the proportion of an additional unit of post-tax income that is saved by householders,

t = the proportionate rate of income tax on additional units of income,

g = the proportion of additional tax receipts which is spent by the government on the purchase of currently produced goods and services.

Each of the examples given in the text can be expressed in terms of this formula. For a derivation of this formula and of the others given in this chapter, see the Mathematical Appendix, pp. 613-15.

be demonstrated diagrammatically in a manner similar to that used in Chapters 5 and 6. In Figure 14, the origin of the diagram represents the original equilibrium level of income, before a disturbance in the form of a rise in investment expenditure by firms. The line marked 'Disposable Income' represents that part of any increase

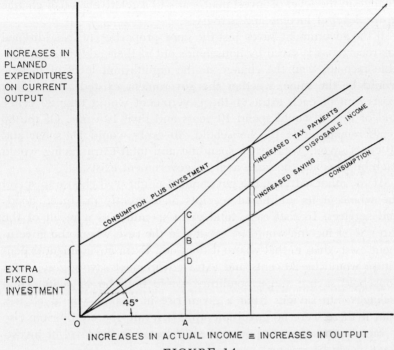

FIGURE 14

in income which is left to households after they have paid taxes; if income rises by OA disposable income rises by AB, while an amount equal to BC is paid in additional taxes. Of this disposable income, a part (AD) is spent on consumption and the rest (equal to BD) is saved. The total induced increase in spending on currently produced output is shown by the slope of the consumption line. This, together with the extra fixed investment, makes up total increases in expenditure plans; where the line representing this total cuts the 45° line, plans are consistent and there is equilibrium. At this point the planned increase in investment is equal to the planned increase in saving plus tax payments.

It is quite possible that government expenditure may be less when the level of activity and income is higher. In this case, the government saves not only the additional tax receipts, but also some of the expenditure it was making when the level of activity was lower.[6] For example, it may have to pay out fewer unemployment benefits. In such circumstances, the multiplier is still smaller: a change in the level of investment leads to a relatively small change in the level of income and activity.

If the government 'saves' just the same proportion of its additional tax receipts as is saved by households out of their additional spendable income, then the change in the equilibrium level of income would be the same, whether the government existed or not. If it exists, out of each extra $1 the government would take 20 cents, and of that it would spend 10 cents and save 10 cents. Of the 80 cents remaining to the household, 40 cents would be spent and 40 cents saved. Total extra spending and total extra saving would each be 50 cents, the same as if no government exists.

At the other extreme, the government might well choose to spend the whole of its additional receipts on currently produced goods and services. In that case, total extra spending as a result of the extra $1 of income would be greater in the case where the government exists than in that where it does not. Extra government expenditure would be 20 cents and extra government saving zero; extra household saving and expenditure would both be 40 cents. Total leakages into savings from a given rise in income would be less than if there were no government; as a result, the equilibrium rise in income consequent upon a given increase in the level of investment would be greater.

We can now proceed to a discussion of some of the ways in which the government can alter the level of income and activity by changing its taxation and expenditure. We are now considering cases where the government is an active disturbing element in the situation and is no longer passive. It will be convenient to consider three sets of cases and to assume the simple circumstances where all taxes are income taxes on households. The first case arises where the government changes its expenditure without changing its tax rates or changes tax rates without changing expenditure. The second

---

[6] In this case, g in the formula in footnote 5 is negative.

arises where taxes and expenditure are altered by equal amounts. The third arises where the total amount of taxes raised from a given national income and of government expenditure made from a given amount of tax receipts remain unaltered, but the incidence of the tax burden is altered.

If the government leaves tax rates unchanged, but alters the amount of its expenditure on currently produced goods and services, the level of income and activity in the country alters. If the government increases its expenditure, financing the purchases by increased borrowing or by reduced debt redemption, then the change is an expansionary force. Increased government expenditure on goods leads to unplanned inventory reductions (disinvestment) by firms and thence to increases in output and household incomes. Insofar as the government increases its expenditure on services (e.g. labor) there is, of course, no preliminary effect on inventories but a direct increase in household incomes.

In the new equilibrium position the usual conditions must be satisfied, that is, all plans must be realized; this demands that all plans must be consistent. They can only be consistent, as we have already seen at length in Chapter 5, if plans to use household income for purposes other than purchase of currently produced goods and services are equal to total plans to use current output for purposes other than sales to households.[7] Now that the government enters into the situation, this condition has a rather more complicated meaning than that planned saving equals planned investment. Instead, it means that

Planned saving plus planned tax payments = planned investment plus planned government purchases of currently produced goods and services.[8]

The left-hand side of this equation lists that part of household income which it is planned not to use for buying current output; the right-hand side lists that part of current output which it is planned should not be sold to households. Just as with savings and investment, this situation is always satisfied for *realized* magnitudes;

---

[7] Here we are ignoring the complications of business saving introduced in Chapter 9.

[8] Alternatively this can be expressed as planned household saving plus planned government 'saving' equals planned investment where government saving equals taxation minus purchases of currently produced output. This approach was used earlier on p. 245.

it is a necessary condition for equilibrium for it to apply for *planned* magnitudes.

It is clear that an increase in government expenditure (on currently produced output), with other things equal, has the same expansionary effect as an increase of investment. In either case, equilibrium demands a higher level of income, at which planned saving plus tax payments will have grown sufficiently for all plans to be consistent. The multiplier formula for the effects of an increase in government expenditure on currently produced output is the same as that for an increase in investment expenditure by the same amount.[9]

It should be noted that the expansionary effects occur whatever the purpose is for which the government buys the goods and services, whether it be to wage war, to distribute goods to the public, or to invest. Similarly a reduction of purchases of newly produced goods and services is a contractionary force. On the other hand, changes in government purchases of irreproducible goods (e.g. land) show their direct effects only on asset prices; any effects on incomes are indirect and operate through changes in asset prices.

We can now turn to the parallel case in which the government reduces tax rates while leaving its expenditure unchanged.[10] In such a case, expansionary forces once again operate on the level of national income. The reduced taxation makes more spendable income available to households, which consequently buy more goods and services. Since the government's expenditure remains unchanged, total demand for goods and services rises. This causes unplanned disinvestment by firms, and so eventually leads to a new equilibrium at a higher level of income.[11]

It is important to note that the change in the equilibrium level

---

[9] The increase in output and income equals the increase in government expenditure multiplied by

$$\frac{1}{s(1-t) + t(1-g)}.$$

For the meaning of the symbols see p. 246n.

[10] In order to do this the government will have to increase its total borrowing or reduce its debt repayments.

[11] Once again the multiplier formula is very like those with which we are becoming familiar—it is

$$\frac{(1-s)}{s(1-t) + t(1-g)}.$$

of income following a given change in taxation is less than the change in the equilibrium level of income following a change of the same size in government expenditure on current output. The reason is quite simple: households usually do not increase their expenditure by the whole of the increase in disposable income they acquire when tax rates are reduced, because they save part. Thus the multiplier expansion following a $1 reduction in taxation is less than the expansion following a $1 increase in government expenditure on currently produced output: the initiating force in the expansion in the first case is smaller by a proportion measured by the marginal propensity to save.[12]

We can now turn to the case where there are equal initiating alterations in the level of taxes and of government expenditure; clearly this case combines the two kinds of change with which we have just been concerned. The most interesting case is that where the government increases or reduces both taxation and expenditure, with the intention of leaving the budget balanced. The two changes then operate in opposite directions. A rise in taxation (with government expenditure unchanged) is a contractionary force; a rise in government expenditure (with taxation unchanged) is an expansionary force. The question that must be answered, therefore, concerns the net result of these two opposing tendencies.

The answer to this question has almost been given in the last paragraph but one. A change in government expenditure on current output has a bigger multiplier effect than a change in taxation of the same magnitude. Therefore, if there is an equal rise in government expenditure on current output and in taxation, the net effect will be an expansion in the level of income, output, and activity.[13]

A particular case of such a change is of some interest. If we

---

[12] This can be seen by comparing the last two multiplier formulas given.

[13] A unit rise in government expenditure on currently produced output leads to an expansion of income by $\dfrac{1}{s(1-t)+t(1-g)}$; a unit rise in taxation leads to a contraction by $\dfrac{(1-s)}{s(1-t)+t(1-g)}$; the effect of both changes taken together is $\dfrac{1-(1-s)}{s(1-t)+t(1-g)}$ which equals $\dfrac{s}{s(1-t)+t(1-g)}$. In most of the literature on the balanced budget multiplier, it is assumed that t and g are both equal to zero; under those circumstances the combined effect of a unit rise in government expenditures and a unit rise in taxation is to raise income by 1.

assume not only that the government spends all the initial increase in taxation on current output, but also that it spends the whole of the additional tax receipts which result from the induced expansion of income on current output, then the expansionary effects of the change depend solely on the initial impulse and on tax rates.[14]

Up to this point we have assumed that the government uses the whole of its additional expenditure to buy currently produced goods and services. This is, however, not necessarily so. It may spend a part of the increase on second-hand or irreproducible goods, such as land. In that case, the expansion induced by the increased government expenditure is so much the less, because the initiating impulse is smaller.[15]

If the proportion of an increase in government expenditure which is used to buy current output is the same as the proportion of a change in household income which is saved, a rise in total government expenditure and a fall in household income by the same amount will cancel one another out. No expansionary or contractionary multiplier process arises from a change in government expenditure and an equal change in taxation;[16] current output is to some extent sold to different buyers, but total sales are the same.

The third way in which the government can use the tax system to influence the level of income and activity is by changing the incidence of taxation. A full analysis of this subject is well beyond the scope of this book; all that can be done is to indicate the kind of thing that may happen. A shift from the use of direct taxes on income to indirect taxes impinging on expenditure may alter the amounts of saving that households will do, and so the equilibrium level of income. Again shifts from taxes impinging largely on capital

---

[14] In this case $g = 1$ and the last formula in footnote 13 becomes $\dfrac{1}{1-t}$; the 'balanced budget multiplier' is always greater than unity; how much greater depends on the size of t.

[15] If h is the proportion of the initiating change in government expenditure which is used for purposes other than purchase of current output, the multiplier expansion following a unit rise in government expenditure is
$$\frac{(1-h)}{s(1-t)+t(1-g)}.$$

[16] This case of a zero balanced budget multiplier can be seen by putting together the equations in footnotes 11 and 15, and assuming $s = h$.

(e.g. inheritance taxes) to those impinging on income and expenditure will undoubtedly influence consumption and savings plans of households. Finally, if the government reduces taxes on the people who save a large proportion of their income (usually the rich) and increases taxes on those who save a small proportion of their income (usually the poor), then the amount of saving that will take place out of a given total income of the community as a whole will increase. This will have the effect of reducing the equilibrium level of income.

It is clear that the operations of the government can have a powerful influence on the economic situation, and that by appropriate actions the government can quite easily set in play forces that lead either to an expansion or to a contraction in the level of income. This power is of the greatest significance in the question of economic stabilization, to which we shall return in later chapters. In most of the rest of this chapter it will be our concern to look at a rule which has been widely invoked to limit this power—the desire for a balanced budget.

Balanced Budgets

It has long been considered by many people that it is unwise for a government to have an unbalanced budget; its receipts should be kept equal to its expenditure, and, in particular, it should avoid spending more than it receives, and so increasing its total indebtedness (the 'national debt'). There is some degree of justification for this view. Historically, serious economic difficulties have frequently been associated with periods in which governments spent more than they received—for example, in times of war. When economic sophistication and understanding were at a lower level than has now been achieved, there was a great deal to be said for the simple and easily comprehensible rule of thumb that governments should keep their budgets balanced. Today, with the greater complexity of the world, such a simple rule is no longer adequate. Our purpose here is to consider the relevance of this rule for modern conditions.

In its simplest form the rule derives from an analogy between the government and households. In the long run few households can spend more than their income, and in the short run, such overspending may well be imprudent. This simple view sees the government as a household writ large. The first shortcoming of this view is that governments can, and nowadays very frequently do, act like firms. (The more logical supporters of this simple view consider that this sort of action is wrong. Be that as it may, every modern government does act to some extent like a firm.) No firm would regard it as an inevitable rule that its expenditure must equal its income. In appropriate circumstances, any firm is willing to increase its indebtedness in order to acquire assets. Correspondingly there is no logical reason why a government should not run into debt in order to acquire assets, such as land, buildings, or electric power plants. Even if the government is following rules of commercial prudence, there is no reason why it should have to acquire durable assets of this kind out of current income.

The second shortcoming of the view that budgets must be balanced is much more fundamental. There is no reason why governments should limit themselves to the degree of prudence either of a household or of a firm. Governments are concerned with the total effects of their actions, including the effects on the level of income and activity. If a government can attain its political aims, such as winning a war, educating children, or maintaining full employment, by running a budget deficit (either by reducing taxation or increasing expenditure), it may well consider such a policy wise. Similarly, it may consider a budget surplus desirable at other times, for example in order to avoid putting too much inflationary strain on the economy. A rule that budgets must be balanced is a way of avoiding the inflationary effects of excessive government expenditure; all the same, a government whose main concern is to maintain full employment without inflation would do much better to choose whatever levels of taxation and expenditure are likely to lead to full employment, rather than rely on the excessively simple rule of thumb. This rule of thumb can involve the abdication of the power that governments now have to influence the levels of activity and of prices. This power is one of the most important results of the development of modern economic theory.

Even if the view is accepted that there is no need for the government to balance its budget, there are limits to the extent to which it is prudent to allow expenditure to exceed income. In the first place care should be taken that there is not a greater demand for resources than there is a supply available; if there is such an excess, prices will rise, as we shall see in the chapters on inflation.

In the second place attention must be paid to the burden of the national debt. This is the debt owed by the government for the most part to its own citizens. The burden of the debt takes the form of the interest charges that have to be paid each year. As the national debt grows, because the government is running a budget deficit, so the government has to pay bigger sums as interest. Insofar as the government has acquired real assets, such as electric power installations which are commercially successful, the income from these assets will cover the interest charges. Insofar as the deficit has been used to finance other kinds of expenditure, there is an appreciable interest burden for the government—the payments must be met either by raising taxation or by still further borrowing. Additional taxation for the sake of these transfers within the community may involve serious difficulties—for example it may reduce the incentive to work.

Fortunately, increasing productivity and in many countries increases in the working population have the result that the level of output and real income that can be achieved in most countries tends to grow as time goes on. It is probably reasonable to assume that the level of income in a country which maintains full employment fairly steadily will grow indefinitely at a more or less constant percentage rate. (Such growth problems are for the most part ignored in this book, but in this context they are highly relevant.)

Now, if income grows at a constant percentage rate, there is strong reason to believe that the transfer burden of raising taxation to pay interest on the national debt will never become intolerable. If the budget deficit which is necessary in any year to maintain full employment is a constant percentage of national income, then the ratio between the total amount of debt outstanding and the level of national income approaches a constant value. This in turn means that the taxes needed to pay interest charges approach a constant proportion of the national income, so long as the rate of interest does not vary. What is more, it seems that this tax burden as a percentage of national income is likely to be a reasonably tolerable one.[17] So long as the maintenance of full employment is

---

[17] The average tax rate needed to service the debt approaches $\dfrac{r}{(g/b) - r}$ where r is the rate of interest, g is the percentage rate of growth of national income, and b is the percentage of the budget deficit of each year to the na-

possible with a budget deficit which remains reasonably constant in relation to national income, and so long as its maintenance makes possible a continuing growth in national income at a more or less constant percentage rate, there seems to be little reason to worry about the tax burden arising from a constant budget deficit.

Government Debt Policy

The last set of questions with which we shall be concerned in this chapter arise from the government's extremely important position in the market for claims. Since governments have, in general, been unable to balance their budgets even over long periods together, most modern governments have extensive debt outstanding. Moreover, since balanced budgets are rare and have no particular economic justification, changes from year to year in the amount of government debt outstanding are quite normal. In addition, governments can change the form in which they owe debt.

In the remaining part of this chapter, we shall be concerned with government debt policy, taken in isolation from other changes. In practice, of course, the problem does not present itself that way: the government has to think simultaneously about the effects of its policies on incomes and their effects on the market for claims. In particular, it must be careful that the two aspects of its policy are not contradictory. For example, a policy to increase the budget deficit by reducing taxation and/or increasing expenditure has been seen to have an expansionary effect on the level of income and output. In the analysis in which this conclusion was reached, no attention was paid to the market for claims. This was a shortcoming, since there must be effects on that market, since the government must increase its borrowing or reduce its debt repayment.

The government's concern with the market for claims can conveniently be expressed as taking two main forms. In the first place there is the government's concern with the health of the economy; it is concerned with the influence on economic events of changes in the level of interest rates and the availability of bank lending, and

---

tional income of that year. (See E. Domar in *American Economic Review*, 1944, pp. 798 et seq.) Plausible figures for each of these three variables might be 4 per cent; the average tax rate then approaches slightly over 4 per cent of the national income.

it is interested in the smooth and efficient working of financial institutions. In the second place there is the government's interest as a transactor on its own account. As a debtor on an enormous scale, a modern government tends to have a strong interest in the existence of low interest rates.

It is convenient to distinguish two ways in which the government may be concerned to take an active part in the markets for claims. In the first place, it will be concerned with seeing that its own operations are carried out smoothly and efficiently. Secondly, it will be concerned with the level of interest rates as a whole and with the structure of interest rates—with the relationship between rates on securities with different maturities.

The first of these occupies a great deal of the time of the officials concerned with the government's financial policy. There is relatively little that can be said about it in general terms, however, and it need not detain us for long. Since the government's operations are on a very large scale, it is necessary that they should be carried out without causing undue disturbance. In doing this the authorities in the United States have the big advantage that the Treasury administers trust funds (e.g. the Federal Old Age and Survivors Insurance and Unemployment Insurance trust funds) which hold large quantities of government debt: one part of the government machine owes money to another part. The form in which this debt is held can be altered, and so the government can help smooth the market by buying and selling its own securities on the market. Such activities often occur in government conversion operations (when the government is offering to convert a maturing loan into a new loan).[18] The Treasury may, for example, allow funds to accumulate in the trust funds as cash for some time, and then use these cash balances to support a loan conversion operation.

The Treasury can also influence the structure and level of interest rates by changes in its debt policy. This it can do in two ways. It can alter the kind of debt it issues or retires; and it can also change the form in which assets are held by the trust agencies under its

---

[18] Transactions between the Treasury and the trust funds are limited to some extent by legal prescriptions which require that the Treasury issue special nonmarketable securities for some of the trust accounts, but the latter are permitted to hold a part of their portfolio in marketable securities.

control. We shall consider Treasury influence on interest rates in more detail in the next chapter.

Some Suggested Reading

There are a number of textbooks that deal with the influence of the government on the level of economic activity. The reader interested in pursuing the subject in more detail than we have done in this chapter can consult H. M. Somers, *Public Finance and National Income* (Philadelphia, 1949), and *Fiscal Policies and the American Economy*, edited by K. E. Poole (New York, 1951).

Another book that deals with a number of the topics that we have touched upon is the American Economic Association, *Readings in Fiscal Policy* (Homewood, Illinois, 1955).

For those interested in balanced budget multipliers, which have received an extraordinary amount of attention, T. Haavelmo, 'Multiplier Effects of a Balanced Budget,' *Econometrica* (1945) is the pioneer article in this area. A recent article by W. J. Baumol and M. H. Peston, 'More on the Multiplier Effects of a Balanced Budget,' *American Economic Review* (1955), cautions against the acceptance of simple analyses of the multiplier effects of changes in the level of balanced budgets.

17

A Synopsis of Interest Rate Theory

A recurring concern in the preceding chapters of this book has been the theory of interest rate determination. It has reappeared on the scene so frequently that it is desirable, now that the main framework of the internal monetary institutions of a modern economy has been described, to make a survey of the different elements lying behind the determination of interest rates.

The central characteristic of the theory is that there is a very large number of forces which influence interest rates to a significant degree; in fact, in a relatively liberal economy, practically all the major economic magnitudes are closely related with interest rates, either as a cause or as an effect, if not as both. As we have already seen, interest rates are closely connected with the level of income of a community, with decisions about adding to wealth, with decisions about the form in which existing wealth shall be held, and with all the intricacies of the banking system.

It is hardly surprising that the consequence is that differences of opinion arise about the relationships upon which emphasis should be laid in explaining the determination of the rate of interest. The most significant cleavage is that between those people who lay emphasis on the relationship between the rate of interest and decisions about adding to wealth (by saving or investing) and those who lay emphasis on the relationship between the rate of interest and decisions about the form in which wealth shall be held.

This difference involves, in the last analysis, judgments about facts.[1] Logically the two positions are perfectly consistent, and

---

[1] It is closely associated with a difference in presentation of the theory. The first group usually explains the theory in terms of flows (e.g. the loanable funds theory) while the second frequently explains it in terms of stocks (e.g. the

sophisticated versions of each pay attention to the forces that are emphasized by the other. All the same, the difference of emphasis is important, because the differences of judgment about facts imply differences of judgment about the consequences of any particular policy or disturbance.

Those who lay emphasis on the relationship between the rate of interest and the process of accumulation of wealth, that is, on the forces of productivity and thrift, tend to believe that a change in the rate of interest has relatively big effects on plans to save and invest and relatively small effects on people's desire to change the form in which they hold their wealth. In such circumstances (as we have seen in Chapter 7) a change in the level of investment or savings plans has a relatively large effect on interest rates and a relatively small effect on the level of income. Moreover, we saw that the effect on income tends to be smaller, the smaller is the willingness of transactors to shift between different kinds of asset when the rate of interest alters.

Those who lay emphasis on the relationship between the rate of interest and the form in which assets are held tend to believe that the relationships between productivity and thrift and interest rate changes are less important. In such circumstances the main effect of a change in the level of saving or investment plans is to change the equilibrium level of income; the simple multiplier process is, for those who lay emphasis on this side, the major element in the adjustment process which follows a change in saving or investment plans.

The approach followed in this book is to lay considerable emphasis on the asset-structure effects of interest rate changes. One justification of this approach is that it is realistic, because it allows us to isolate the theory of income changes from the theory of interest rate changes: interest rate changes do occur in the absence of appreciable income changes, as in day-to-day price changes on the stock exchange; similarly, multiplier changes often occur without the accompaniment of appreciable interest rate changes, either as part of an automatic adjustment process, or because of deliberate policy by the authorities to keep interest rates stable.

---

liquidity preference theory as used here). This difference is merely presentational; any argument that can be presented in terms of stocks can be presented in terms of flows, and vice versa.

A further justification of the greater reality of the approach followed here is that it seems very unlikely that the speculative element can ever be absent in a market such as that for bonds and shares, where there is always such a big supply of old assets that can come onto the market if their prices alter appreciably. Thus it seems reasonable to consider that although cases may quite possibly arise where the predominant effect of a change in the level of plans to save or invest is to change interest rates while leaving the level of income more or less unaltered, they are rather rare. The normal effect, even when there is no question of deliberate monetary policy by the authorities, is to cause a considerable change in the level of income.

The Determination of Speculative Decisions

Since it is the forces which cause switching between different assets when the rate of interest changes that prevent the interest rate from moving far enough after a change in saving or investment plans to restore the original level of income, it is clear that these forces are of crucial importance in the economic system. We have already seen that these forces are predominantly speculative in origin, and in Chapters 2 and 4 have looked at their general characteristics. There we considered what would happen in various circumstances, under conditions of a given set of expectations. What we must now do is to ask what determines the public's expectations about future interest rate changes. In doing so, we must go beyond what we have done so far, and consider what may cause *changes* in expectations. Unfortunately there is remarkably little that can be said in detail about them; for the most part, the economist is forced to leave them locked in a black box marked 'psychological'; only in the context of certain particular problems (such as the study of banking systems) in which motivations are fairly explicit can he say much in detail.

Nevertheless, since these speculative elements are so important, it is worth while to summarize what can be guessed about their main determinants. In the first place past experience must certainly be a major element at work. The level of interest rates, and the changes in rates, that have been experienced in the past undoubtedly are a strong influence on expectations about the future of interest rates. It seems reasonable to assume that the experience of the relatively recent past usually weighs more heavily than more distant experience.

A second set of influences on psychological attitudes to interest rates consists of all the theories, good or bad, which people believe to be relevant to interest rate determination. Even if it were true that productivity and thrift as such were irrelevant to the determination of interest rates, they would be relevant indirectly, through speculative forces, if sufficient people believed them to be relevant. As Keynes once said: if sufficient businessmen believed that the arrival of swallows in the summer is good for trade, then their arrival would be good for trade.

A third influence on the psychology of wealth-holders is their judgment about what they think other transactors are doing and what they are going to do. One aspect of this is the perpetual desire of speculators to make money by being on the mark a little faster than other people. Another is the attempt to foresee the policies of the monetary authorities and to interpret correctly the significance of their current policies. When the government and the banks are taking an active role in monetary affairs, speculation about their actions is very important.

Further aspects of speculation about the future of interest rates are the degrees of certainty and unanimity with which views are held about the size of future changes, and the degrees of certainty and unanimity about their timing. I may, for example, think that rates are likely to rise, but may hold this view with only a rather low degree of confidence. In that case, my actions are likely to be significantly different from circumstances in which I feel quite certain that the same change will occur. Generally speaking I shall be less willing to switch funds in reaction to a change of a given size which I think is rather uncertain, compared with a certain change of the same size. I may also have differing degrees of certainty about the timing of a change. I may be certain that a particular change will occur at some time, but I may be very uncertain about precisely when it will happen. Again, this uncertainty will significantly affect my actions. What are really important are the changes expected in the immediate future; that is, in the period between now and the next time at which I look at the structure of my asset holdings. If this period is short (say a day) while the range of time within which I expect a given change to take place is long (say a year), the expected change may have little influence on my actions today, because the chances of the change occurring before tomorrow, when I can make a new set of plans about the form in which I hold my assets, is very small.

The upshot of all these forces influencing speculation about interest rates is that the determination of choices about asset holding (summed up in the phrase 'liquidity preference') are very confused. In particular it is probable that any attempt to reduce the relationship between the rate of interest and the speculative desire to hold money to a simple form which shows stability for long periods together is not likely to prove very useful. All that theory can do is to indicate the kind of forces that are at work, and to show the directions in which they work and try to make some guess of their magnitudes in terms of particular situations.

This rather limited conclusion is not the end of the matter. Up to this point, in this chapter, we have implicitly been reverting to the relatively simple kind of system discussed in Part II. In fact, however, one has to take account of the existence of many kinds of transactor and of many kinds of asset; we must now concern ourselves with the general implications of this.

Many Kinds of Transactor and of Asset

There are certain legal and conventional limitations on the ability of some kinds of transactor to hold certain kinds of asset; for example, the government does not hold stocks and shares and banks do not hold appreciable quantities of real assets (the exception being their buildings). Similarly, there are limitations on the kinds of liability that certain transactors can issue; these sometimes arise by law, but often are the consequence of inability to persuade lenders to take up certain claims, such as (for the most part) long-term bonds issued by private persons. All the same, these limitations are not sufficient to simplify greatly the practical problems of asset price and interest rate determination.

Corresponding to the existence of many different kinds of transactor there are many different kinds of views about why assets are held, on which choices between holding or issuing different kinds of asset depend. Similarly, corresponding to the many different kinds of asset that exist, there are many different characteristics of different assets. To a considerable extent this wide range of assets and of their characteristics is a consequence of the wide variety of transactors and the consequent variety of their reasons for holding or issuing different kinds of asset; particular kinds of claim exist because they are convenient and desirable for particular kinds of lender and borrower.

One major difference of view about various kinds of asset and liability is the difference between those who are concerned with capital certainty and those who are concerned with income certainty.[2] We have already looked at this in connection with the choice between long- and short-dated securities; we saw in Chapter 8 that short-dated lending or borrowing was associated with capital certainty, while long-dated lending or borrowing was associated with income certainty. This distinction is also of considerable relevance to the choice between holding bonds and money that was discussed in Chapters 2 and 4. There we saw that, if a person thought that long-term interest rates were going to rise appreciably,[3] he would be wiser to hold cash while the fall in bond prices is taking place. In this way he avoids a capital loss and increases his future income, at the cost of foregoing current income. In making this analysis it was implicitly assumed that the person concerned was indifferent between receiving a given sum of money as income or as a capital gain,[4] and that he was indifferent between fluctuations of a given size in the level of income and in the value of capital held. Neither of these assumptions is necessarily correct.

One reason why individuals may not be indifferent between receiving a certain sum as income and as a capital gain is that they do not realize the equivalence of the two. A more important reason may be that institutional arrangements are such that the two kinds of gain are not equivalent. For instance the incidence of taxation may be different on income receipts and on capital gains. In the United States incomes are taxed at progressive rates while capital gains taxes have a ceiling rate of 25 per cent. The contrast is very important for people who pay taxes at the upper end of the progressive tax scale.

---

[2] Or, in the case of borrowers, certainty about the amount to be paid out in interest.

[3] 'Appreciably' meaning, in this context, at an annual rate greater than a percentage equal to the interest rate expressed as a percentage of itself, e.g. a 0.16 per cent rise per year when the interest rate is 4 per cent, a 0.04 per cent rise when the rate is 2 per cent.

[4] Or losing it as a reduction in income or a capital loss.

Another institutional reason why some people may not be indifferent between fluctuations in the value of their capital and fluctuations in their income is the imperfection of capital markets. I may, for example, have certain expenses which must be covered each year; in that case I may prefer a steady income to a chance of bigger total receipts through capital gains if it is going to be difficult or expensive to realize those capital gains.

If I am particularly perturbed by fluctuations in my income and am not particularly perturbed by the risk of fluctuations in the value of my wealth, I may well hold securities even if I think that interest rates are going to rise appreciably. In such circumstances I could maintain my wealth intact and increase my future income by holding money until after bond prices have fallen; but to do so inevitably involves a fluctuation in my income, because I have to forgo income while I hold cash. Moreover, I must be aware that my guesses about the future may not prove correct; if I switch into cash I have the likelihood, but not the certainty, of a capital gain; but if I stay in securities, I am sure to maintain the level of my money income.

Contrariwise, a person who is more perturbed by the risk of fluctuations in his wealth than in his income may choose to hold some or all of his wealth in cash even if he thinks interest rates will probably be stable or even falling. He may not think that the certainty of earning income if he holds securities is sufficient to outbalance the risk that is always present that capital loss may occur when wealth is held in bonds.

These differences in reactions by different people reinforce the effects of the inter-personal dispersion of views that there will normally be about the future of interest rates. Even if three people hold precisely the same view about the future movements of interest rates, they may react in different ways. For example, each of them may think that the rate will rise from 4 per cent to 4.16 per cent in the next year. A man who regards capital and income gains and losses indifferently will be on the margin of uncertainty whether to hold his wealth in cash or bonds; a man who is particularly fearful of income fluctuations will hold bonds, and would need a still bigger rise of interest rates to push him into holding cash; a man who is fearful of fluctuations in the value of his wealth will be quite certain that he prefers holding cash.

In addition to these differences of view between different kinds of wealth-holder about income certainty and capital certainty, there are other important differences of opinion about holding various kinds of asset. For example, some people are more willing than others to take the risk of default—the risk that the borrower may become bankrupt. As we have already seen, the prevalence or otherwise of these various views influences the relative prices of different kinds of asset.[5]

In considering the existence of many kinds of transactor, particular attention has to be paid to banks and to the government. The remainder of this chapter will be concerned with a further consideration of the effects of the actions of these bodies on interest rates.

The significance of the banking system in helping determine the structure of interest rates is that it acts as a capital intermediary and that it can create money. In acting as a capital intermediary, the essential characteristic of the banking system is that it is willing to hold relatively illiquid assets (such as government bonds and advances to industry and commerce), while issuing relatively liquid assets. It thus reduces the quantity of illiquid assets held by the general public and increases their holdings of liquid assets. In the absence of a banking system, the relative prices of different assets would be different from what they now are. It is probable that interest rates would be generally higher; this would persuade the public to hold a bigger proportion of the relatively illiquid assets than they actually do hold, and to discourage borrowers from issuing as big a proportion as they now issue.

Changes in the Level of Activity and Changes in the Quantity of Money

In a period of expanding activity, whether arising from an increased government deficit or from increased investment by firms, the banks are very likely to find additional suitable outlets for lending. Consequently they increase the quantity of money. The assumption of Part II, that the quantity of money remains unchanged

---

[5] And of course the relative importance of the various views depends not simply on the number of people holding the various views, but on the distribution of wealth between groups with different kinds of attitudes. If, for example, the poor are cautious while the wealthy are willing to take risks, risk taking will tend to predominate.

during a change in the level of income and activity is, therefore, unlikely to be justified.

It therefore becomes necessary to consider what happens to the rate of interest when there is a change in the level of activity (once again induced, we shall assume, by a new invention) in circumstances when the banking system operates actively. The central and commercial banks may, for example, take up some of the new bonds or bills issued by a government which has increased its deficit, or they may make additional loans to firms, which are now investing more.

It is now possible for us to drop the simplifying but restrictive assumption, made at the beginning of Chapter 7, that a person will not wish to increase his holdings of cash if his total wealth increases as a result of saving on his part. This assumption was clearly unrealistic; it is almost certain that people will want to hold more cash if their wealth is greater, even if their income, the rate of interest, and all other relevant factors remain unchanged. This additional cash will be held for all four possible motives—transactions, precautionary, speculative, and deflationary. If my total wealth is $1000 I am likely to hold more money for transactions and precautionary purposes than if my total wealth is $10; this is so, even though the amount of transactions I wish to carry out is precisely the same. Similarly, with the two motives involving speculation. For example, if my wealth is $1,000,000, I am likely to switch a much bigger absolute amount into cash when I expect interest rates to rise appreciably, than if my wealth is $1000.

In circumstances where the quantity of money is constant, the consequence of this increase in desire to hold money when total wealth rises is that there is a persistent tendency to rising interest rates whenever saving is taking place; only in this way is the necessary money made available from reduced speculative holdings. In fact, however, a constant quantity of money is not a normal situation. Part of the investment which is taking place is usually financed by the banking system, and there is a corresponding increase in the quantity of money.

The net effect on the rate of interest is quite simple to follow. The rate of interest will be unchanged if the additional desire to hold money at existing interest rates is just equaled by the additional amount of money created by the banking system. In other words, if the proportion of the amount saved in a given period which people wish to hold as money is just equal to the proportion of investment (and of the government deficit) which is financed by the banking system, interest rates will remain constant. If the first proportion is the smaller, interest rates tend to fall; if it is larger, interest rates tend to rise.

It is impossible to say, prima facie, which way these forces will work if the system is left to operate automatically; on the one hand, the attitudes of wealth-holders must be considered, and on the other hand, the relative importance of bank finance. Observation suggests that the usual tendency is for interest rates to rise when trade is active; but the main reasons are probably deliberate controlling action by the central bank, a belief (which is probably exaggerated) by speculators, and possibly by bankers, that productivity and thrift are the chief determinants of interest rates, and the effects on speculators of the past experience that interest rates usually have risen in booms.

If the action of the banking system, either in a change in the level of activity or after any other disturbance, is such that interest rates remain unchanged, the banking situation can conveniently be described as one of 'active ease.' It is 'active' because such a situation can only come about automatically, by chance; normally it involves deliberate policy by the banking system. It is a situation of 'ease' because interest rates are not influencing the economic situation.[6]

Like the banks, the government also has a very powerful influence on interest rates. In the United States, as we indicated earlier, the Treasury's influence on the structure and level of interest rates follows from its ability to change the structure of its debt and from the control it has over trust agencies that hold a sizable portion of the national debt.

The Treasury may, for example, sell long-term securities out of the holdings of the trust funds and use the proceeds to retire short-term securities that are outstanding. This decreases the total supply of short-term securities available and increases the supply of the long-terms. The effect of this will be to raise short rates relatively to long.

The Treasury is also able to exert influence upon the structure of interest rates by varying the proportions of short-term and long-term securities through conversion operations. (We are assuming

---

[6] When this expression is used subsequently in this book it will also be assumed that banks are not changing the degree to which they ration credit.

for the moment that the Treasury's debt is of a given size and Treasury decisions are confined to the structure of that debt.) If the Treasury should, for example, offer long-term securities and then uses the proceeds to retire short-term debt, it will in all likelihood result in a rise in long-term interest rates relative to short-term rates. Treasury issuance of short-term securities in place of long-term securities reverses the situation described above, there will be a tendency for short-term interest rates to rise relative to the interest rates on long-term securities. The impact upon the level of activity in the economy of changes in the maturity distribution of Treasury debt is difficult to assess in quantitative terms, although the presumed direction of effects is comparatively simple. If the Treasury lengthens the maturity of its debt by issuing long-term securities in place of short-terms, it reduces the liquid assets of the community and thus checks expenditures; this assumes that the central bank does not offset the effects of changes in the Treasury's debt structure by changes in its securities holdings. Conversely, a movement by the Treasury to shorten the maturity of its debt increases the liquid assets of the community, thereby stimulating expenditures. In actual practice, treasuries find it difficult to alter the structure of their debt in the short run; and the alterations in debt structure that do occur are generally quite limited and of minor significance for the level of activity.

We have to consider next those situations where the Treasury's debt is not of a given size but is increasing or decreasing. In these situations, how the Treasury places or retires debt can influence the structure and the level of interest rates. Suppose, for example, the Treasury's budgetary position shows a surplus. If the Treasury uses this surplus to retire debt held by the Federal Reserve Banks (assuming that the Federal Reserve does not replenish its portfolio through open market purchases), the combined effect of budget surplus and debt retirement is to reduce bank reserves. The commercial banks lose reserves because the excess of Treasury receipts over expenditures is not returned to them. The quantity of money is reduced initially by an amount equal to the Treasury surplus, and then is reduced further as banks adjust to the loss of reserves. As to the effects on interest rates, there are two forces pulling in opposite directions; the reduction in bank reserves operates to force interest rates upward, while the Treasury's running of a surplus presumably brakes economic activity, which reduces the demand for transactions balances and exerts a downward pressure on interest rates.

The combination of budget surplus and retirement of debt held by the commercial banks and/or the general public, on the other hand, does not affect the volume of bank reserves. Budget surplus together with retirement of debt held by the banks does reduce the actual quantity of money in existence, but since the size of bank reserves is unaffected the potential quantity of money is not altered; and when the debt that is retired is held by the general public the actual quantity of money in existence is not affected. There are two forces that operate on interest rates in this case. Since the Treasury's surplus depresses the level of economic activity and since the Treasury's debt retirement reduces the quantity of securities available to the commercial banks and the general public, the tendency will be for interest rates to decline.

When the Treasury issues securities to the various sectors to finance a deficit, the effects on bank reserves, the quantity of money, and interest rates will be opposite to those we indicated above where we discussed retirement of the national debt.

The conclusion that must be drawn is that it is very difficult to describe a general theory of interest rates, which is really relevant to modern conditions, without taking account of a great complex of factors. In the first place there are all the actions that can be taken by the government and the banks. Secondly, speculation by wealth-holders and by debtors about the future of asset prices has a powerful and inevitable influence on their present level. Lastly, and often (but by no means necessarily) swamped by the other influences, there are the old-fashioned forces of productivity and thrift, which should never be forgotten, but which probably seldom dominate the situation in the short run.

Some Suggested Reading

A substantial portion of the literature on interest rate theory since the appearance of Keynes' *General Theory* has been concerned with the relative merits of the loanable funds (in terms of flows) and the liquidity preference (in terms of stocks) approaches to the theory of interest. In *Econometrica* (1950) there were three articles devoted to this issue: L. Klein, 'Stock and Flow Analysis in Economics,' W. Fellner and H. Somers, 'Stock and Flow Analysis: Further Comment,' and L. Klein, 'Stock and Flow Analysis: Further Comment.' G. Haberler in his *Prosperity and Depression,* 3rd ed. (New York, 1946), attempts a reconciliation of the two approaches.

For a further discussion of the impact of 'Keynesian economics' on interest rate theory the interested reader can consult H. Johnson, 'Some Cambridge Controversies in Monetary Theory,' and D. H. Robertson, 'Comments on Mr. Johnson's Notes,' in the *Review of Economic Studies,* vol. XIX (1951-1952), and R. F. Kahn, 'Some Notes on Liquidity Preference,' *The Manchester School of Economic and Social Studies* (1954).

In a stimulating article, 'Consistency and Consolidation in the Theory of Interest,' *Economica* (1954), R. Turvey demonstrates the difficulties that one encounters when one attempts to incorporate systematically in a theoretical model the effects of open market operations on interest rates.

IV

PRICE CHANGES

18

The Level of Prices: The Quantity Theory

So far we have paid no attention to price changes; this shortcoming will be remedied in this chapter and the next four. The justification of this neglect is largely that it is easier to move one step at a time instead of trying in the first place to discuss the causes of changes in the level of prices at the same time as the causes of changes in the level of output. The particular manner in which we have been able to split up the problem while remaining near to reality is the result of a major characteristic of most twentieth-century industrial economies. This is the fact, which we have already noted, that there is no very marked tendency for changes to occur in the prices of industrial products when trade is depressed and there is a considerable amount of unemployment.[1]

But once we come to circumstances when the amount of unemployment is small, the situation is very different; a tendency develops for wages and prices to rise. In a range of fairly low unemployment percentages (in the United States or Britain perhaps ½ of 1 per cent

---

[1] This book is concerned with the problems of 'macro-economics,' and does not deal with 'micro-economics.' This means that we are unable to enter into a detailed discussion of the theory of the determination of prices of individual commodities. Nevertheless we cannot ignore this theory completely. Changes in the general price level are the result of all the separate changes in individual prices; if the general price level is more or less constant the reason must be that individual prices are not changing, or that such changes as are found tend to cancel out. The latter alternative is the more precise description of what happens; even when the general level of prices is constant, some prices will be falling slightly and others rising slightly, in accordance with demand and supply conditions in the market for each commodity. Nevertheless, since such changes frequently cancel one another out they can be ignored in our analysis. This simplification is an example of the whole approach of macro-economics; it looks at aggregates whereas micro-economics attempts to look at particular cases.

to 4 per cent) the situation is particularly complicated, because in that range both prices and output tend to move at the same time: an increase in effective demand tends to lead both to price rises and to output rises. This is awkward, as we shall see in Chapter 22, because modern political circumstances usually demand that the level of unemployment in industrial economies should be maintained in this very range. When unemployment falls to very low levels (say under ½ of 1 per cent) all the effect of increased demand tends to show itself in price rises; there are so many bottlenecks in the economy that there can be no further rise in output. The remaining unemployed are unemployable in any job, or do not fit in with the pattern of demand for labor, because they do not have the right training or are in the wrong places.

It may be noted that this asymmetry in price and wage changes has largely been a feature of the twentieth century, and may not have been so marked in the nineteenth. As a result of the development of this asymmetry, the emphasis of monetary economics during the interwar period, when unemployment was common in all manufacturing countries, swung away from analysis of price changes toward analysis of the causes of changes in the level of output. This change of emphasis came rather slowly, and for a long time the majority of economists were inclined to interpret monetary events in terms of a theory that was more appropriate to nineteenth-century conditions than to those in the first four decades of the twentieth century. The theory around which this approach centered was the Quantity Theory of Money—or, more precisely, the Quantity Theory of the Value of Money. The value of money, in this context, refers to its purchasing power, i.e. the quantities of goods and services in general which are exchanged for a unit of money. And while the Quantity Theory has been broadened to include the impact of money on other variables in the economic system, its prime concern over most of its life has been with the determination of the level of prices.

The Quantity Theory of Money

The rest of this chapter will be concerned with an investigation of the major forms which the Quantity Theory takes, and of their practical relevance. In particular it will be necessary to consider whether the theory has increased practical validity now that full employment is fairly general and mildly inflationary conditions appear to be endemic. It is possible that we are once again witnessing a cultural lag between events and the theories designed to interpret the events. Just as many economists in the 'twenties and 'thirties laid emphasis on price changes when what was really needed was an explanation of output changes, so it is possible that our theory has now swung too far the other way.

The simplest form of the Quantity Theory is to be found in writings as early as the sixteenth century. It states that the price level varies in direct proportion to the quantity of money. If the quantity of money doubles, so will the price level; similarly they will both fall together. This theory had the virtue of simplicity; but it came to be realized in the latter part of the nineteenth century that other considerations had to be introduced. In particular, account had to be taken of the number of transactions that were being dealt with by the stock of money. The number of transactions using money being carried out within an economy might change, either as a result of the general growth of the economy, or as a result of fluctuations in the level of economic activity.

Once some degree of sophistication is reached in the formulation of the theory, two alternative methods of expressing it have to be considered. On the one hand the theory can be presented as an identity: that is, as a statement of a situation which is necessarily true, because of the way in which the terms used in it are defined. An identity is a statement of the same facts in two different ways; its usefulness depends on whether the alternative presentations give additional insight into the situation. The other method of presenting the Quantity Theory is in the form of an equation. This form expresses causal relationships; its usefulness depends on the ability to say something helpful about the causal relationships represented.

The forms in which the Quantity Theory was developed in the early part of this century can be expressed either as the identity

$$MV \equiv PT$$

or as the equation $MV = PT$.

The meanings of the four symbols can best be seen by examining the identity. This follows directly from the definition of a price. The amount of money that is passed over to settle a particular transaction (for example, the purchase of a quart of milk) is the price paid in that transaction. If we add up the value of all the transactions that have taken place in a country in a year we have a statement of the total amount of money that has been passed over in settlement of transactions in that year. This total amount can be expressed in terms of the number of transactions that have taken place, and the average price at which they have taken place. This is what is done on the right-hand side of the identity. T represents the number of transactions in a year; P represents their average price. PT is thus equal to the total value of transactions.

We can now turn to the left-hand side of the identity. If the total value of transactions that has taken place is \$4 million, and if the total money supply consists of one million dollar bills, then it is clear that on average each bill has passed from hand to hand four times in settlement of transactions during the year. This way of looking at the total value of transactions is represented in MV. M represents the total quantity of money in existence and V represents its average velocity of circulation; that is, the number of times which an average unit of money passes from hand to hand.

Two things may be noted about this identity. In the first place it is V (the velocity of circulation) which is in a sense the residual product: it is the quantity which is less directly observable than the others. Secondly, the immediate usefulness of the statement is not clearly apparent. It is as an approach to the theory expressed as an equation that the identity is most useful.

In using the equation to help explain causal relationships, the tendency has always been to lay emphasis on changes in M and P, to pay relatively little attention to changes in T, and to assume that V is constant. Fisher, for example, did discuss at great length the factors that influence the average velocity of circulation in a community (e.g. the quality of the community's financial organization, the payments system in the community, expectations as to future prices, etc.), but for predictive purposes V was assumed to be proximately constant. Rather similar reasoning applies to their treatment of T; it was realized that T cannot be regarded as a constant [2] but the examination of causal relationships was most frequently carried

---

[2] It is unrealistic to regard T as a constant on two grounds: the long-run growth of an economy means that T is likely to rise over time while an economy's short-run instability means that T is likely to fluctuate.

out in terms of full employment situations which were regarded as the 'normal' state of affairs. Thus, Fisher used the equation to explain the effects of increases in the quantity of money (arising through increased gold supplies) on the price level. He assumed that V was constant as between two equilibrium situations, and did not pay much attention to changes in T. On the assumption that T and V are precisely the same before some disturbance (e.g. new gold discoveries) and after the situation has settled down to a new equilibrium, the price level, P, must have risen by just the same proportion as the quantity of money, M. Subsequent users of the theory came to lay more emphasis on bank money and on the power of bankers to create money; but still the emphasis was on the relationship between the quantity of money and the price level.

Two strong criticisms of this approach are that it laid emphasis on the wrong questions for the problems of at least the first four decades of the twentieth century, and that even to the extent that the questions that were asked were important, the approach provides too little explanation of the mechanisms involved. In particular, the old school of quantity theorists gave very scanty answers to the question why the velocity of circulation could be expected to be constant.

The Cambridge Version

A later form of the Quantity Theory, developed in Cambridge, went some way toward meeting these shortcomings. In doing so it took several steps on the way to the modern theory of monetary economics as set forth in this book. It met some of the weaknesses of the older theory by asking and answering a somewhat different question. Instead of considering the velocity of circulation (that is the speed with which an average unit of money passes from hand to hand), the question was asked, Why does money rest in transactors' hands for a certain length of time before being used?

There need not, of course, be any real difference between the answers to the two questions. If a unit of money passes from hand to hand four times per year, then each unit stays in someone's hands for an average time of three months. Nevertheless, the change in the form of question involved a very important switch of emphasis. An attempt was now made to analyze the motivations involved:

the Cambridge economists asked what were the reasons why people wished to hold the quantity of money they actually chose to hold. The Cambridge version of the Quantity Theory examined the choices and decisions of the individual and analyzed the individual's demand for a cash balance of a definite amount in marginal utility terms similar to those used to analyze the individual's demand for commodities. It was argued by the Cambridge theorists that there is some fraction of their income which people find it advantageous to hold in the form of money. The larger the fraction of their total resources that is held in cash, the easier is the task of bridging the gap between payments and receipts; but to hold a large fraction of one's resources in the form of money means that some other satisfactions (e.g. in terms of consumption foregone) must be sacrificed. The Cambridge theorists envisaged, in effect, a process in which the advantages of holding a larger cash balance were balanced against the disadvantages of foregoing consumption; i.e. it was implied that there is a margin at which the individual would consider himself indifferent to having more commodities and a smaller cash balance. Thus, micro-economic reasoning was extended to the demand for money to hold. Nor was this approach restricted to the analysis of micro-economic situations. The demands for money of individuals were summed up to yield a demand for money for the community as a whole.

In changing the form of the question they asked, the Cambridge economists made a switch of emphasis away from the predominant concern with the causes of changes in the supply of money, toward an equal concern with the causes of changes in the demand for it, thereby putting the determination of the value of money on the same footing as the determination of the value of other things. While the transactions versions of the Quantity Theory did have some things to say about the factors influencing the average velocity of circulation, they did not analyze questions pertaining to the value of money within a demand and supply framework.

The Cambridge version of the theory also included another important new element. Instead of being concerned with the total number of transactions, it was concerned with the level of income. Once again, there is a level at which this change can be regarded as purely formal. The Fisher equation can easily be recast in terms of the level of money income, by multiplying price by output instead of by the number of transactions.[3] It would be wrong, however, to see the innovation purely at this formal level. By introducing consideration of the level of income the Cambridge version concentrated attention on a concept which has proved most useful in the whole of modern economic theory.

The equation by which the Cambridge theory was expressed is:

$$M = KY.$$

In this equation, M represents the quantity of money in existence in the country and Y represents the level of national income.[4] The symbol K simply represents the proportion of their annual income which residents of that country wish to hold in the form of money.

The usefulness of this theory depends on our ability to say something about the determination of the variables concerned. If we know what causes changes in M and K, then we know what causes changes in Y. As far as M is concerned, the main explanation of its changes was the policy of the monetary authorities, together with the workings of the international gold standard.[5] As for K, the view was that in the long run it was rather constant, because the main reasons for holding money are those we analyzed in Chapter 2 in discussing the transactions demand for money. In the short period, however, K might fluctuate in accordance with the state of confidence: the forces analyzed in our discussion of the precautionary motive for holding money then became relevant. For example, in a period of crisis people will tend to want to hold a particularly large quantity of money; if the supply of money is constant, this rise in K means that Y, the level of income, must fall.

Thus the theory went some way toward explaining both short- and long-run changes in the level of money income. In the short run, there might be sharp changes as a result of changes in confidence and so in people's desire to hold money. In the long run, changes in money income would be fairly closely related to changes

---

[3] The velocity of circulation relevant to the money income case would be lower than the velocity relevant to the total value of transactions, because the total value of transactions in a year is greater than the total value of output. Correspondingly, the V of the Fisher equation is greater than $\frac{I}{K}$ where K is the element in the Cambridge equation defined below.

[4] I.e. the total of money incomes received by residents of the country.

[5] On which, see Chapter 39.

in the quantity of money. Included in both these short- and long-run changes in the level of money income might be both price changes and changes in the level of output—the theory did not separate them satisfactorily.

Although the Cambridge version of the Quantity Theory represented a big advance on the Fisher version, it is not in itself an adequate monetary theory. Its weakness is that it is too simple to deal adequately with the complexities of the economic system.

One of its main oversimplifications is that it ignores the speculative demand to hold money. While it would seem to be inherent in the micro-economic maximizing process of individuals that the rate of interest enter in as one of the factors influencing the size of the cash balance held, the Quantity Theorists did not, in general, assign the rate of interest a definite role in their formulations. For one thing, this means that it ignores one of the main reasons why the quantity of money may change without corresponding changes in the level of money income, or why money income may change without corresponding changes in the quantity of money. For another thing, the ignorance of the speculative demand means that the linkage between the theories of the rate of interest and of the level of income through the demand for money [6] was not made.

Modern Reformulations of the Quantity Theory

There have been, in recent times, some reformulations and restatements of the Quantity Theory that deserve attention. These recent developments can be considered under two broad heads. Firstly, there are those who argue that the Quantity Theory is a useful tool in treating the problems of applied economics; their general argument is that it is more fruitful to examine the expenditure flow in terms of M and V rather than by the breakdown into consumption and investment. (This point of view is generally associated with the followers of the Chicago School.) Secondly, there is a strand of thought which argues that the Quantity Theory is theoretically useful and that recent critics of the theory have erred in thinking that the Quantity Theory is applicable only under extremely restrictive assumptions. (This point of view is held by

---

[6] As in Chapter 7.

Patinkin.) It may be a mistake to lump these more recent developments with the earlier versions of the Quantity Theory since the theoretical treatment is more refined and many of the claims made for the theory are modest; still, the allegations made concerning the usefulness of the Quantity Theory are similar enough to those which appeared in the earlier writings to warrant the examination of the newer versions in this context. Those who stress the Quantity Theory as a tool of applied economics operate, at the theoretical level, with a demand for money that is not too different from the ones commonly used in analyses in monetary economics. Rather, it is their view to regard V as practically constant for predictive purposes that makes their position so different from that put forth in this book. They argue that empirically the income velocity of money has exhibited a high degree of constancy over time, and that there has been a close connection between changes in the quantity of money and changes in the price level. The difficulty with this approach is that while V may be considered as approximately constant for predictive purposes in the long run (when looking at periods of ten or twenty years), it is not too useful in the short run. To make use of V for predictive purposes in the short run, adjustments must be made for shifts in the holdings of speculative balances, etc., and that leads us back to considering the factors that we have been stressing in this connection.

The other recent line of thinking on the Quantity Theory is, as we noted, concerned with its theoretical usefulness. There the main contention is that under conditions of full employment an increase in the quantity of money results in a proportionate increase in the level of prices. The reasoning of this approach proceeds as follows. If the community's money supply [7] is increased, the business firms and households of the community will feel wealthier; and this increase in wealth, it is assumed, will lead to increased expenditures on current output. Since, by assumption, full employment prevails, prices begin to rise. And so long as the level of prices does not rise by the same ratio as the quantity of money, business firms and households will be wealthier than they were initially, so they will demand more goods. Thus the inflationary pressure will persist until the level of prices has risen in the same proportion as the quantity

---

[7] The highly restrictive definition of the quantity of money that is used in this model will be discussed below.

of money; when prices do reach that level the community's higher cash balance will be worth no more than the initial cash balance in terms of command over commodities, and the wealth position of the community will be the same as it was in the initial equilibrium situation.

The behavior of the rate of interest in this process needs to be explained. It might be thought that the increase in the quantity of money leads to a lower rate of interest so that the public will be content to hold a larger cash balance on this account and thus obviate the need for prices to change in the same proportion as the quantity of money. According to the reasoning of this model this cannot occur. It is assumed that a lowering of the rate of interest increases investment (and possibly consumption) expenditures and thus contributes to the upward pressure on prices. As long as the rate of interest remains below its initial equilibrium level the inflationary pressure is maintained, and this pressure is removed only when the price level has risen in the same proportion as the quantity of money and the rate of interest is back at its initial level.

Without placing any restrictions on V this theoretical model seems to get the same results that one would by assuming V to be constant. But there are some fundamental difficulties in applying this model to the study of price level changes, even under conditions of full employment. First, the definition of money that is used in the analysis is rather restrictive; money consists solely of the legal-tender money issued by the government. Only in this way is it possible to assume that an increase in the quantity of money increases the net wealth of the private community. If the quantity of what we conventionally label 'money' should increase via the lending activities of commercial banks, it would not register as an increase according to the definition used in the model, since the net asset position of households and business firms would be unaffected: households and firms taken as a whole owe more debts to the banks, which offsets the additional claims against the banks owned by these groups of transactors.

Secondly, the model abstracts from expectations and uncertainty as to the future course of interest rates and prices. It is obvious that these dynamic elements are important in any study of changes in price levels.

We can now give an answer to the problem that was posed on page 277. Even though one of the major problems of the modern world is that of price changes, which was the major concern of most supporters of the Quantity Theory, the fact still remains that the Quantity Theory is an inadequate guide to understanding of the reasons for price changes. The Fisher version was a useful tool in its day, the Cambridge version was an important step on the road to the modern monetary theory, and the newer versions of the Quantity Theory (both theoretical and applied) have contributed to our understanding of the role of money in the economic system. Nevertheless, we need more understanding of the mechanics of price changes than the theory can give. Fortunately the approach we have followed in Part II of this book can usefully be extended to these problems and that will be the task of the next four chapters.

Thus our conclusion is that the Quantity Theory does not help us very much in looking at the problems of monetary economics, and in fact its misleading simplicity may obscure more than it reveals. The weakness of the Quantity Theory in all its versions can easily be summed up. For one thing effective demand for goods and services does not necessarily vary at all closely with the quantity of money. In order to explain variations in effective demand it is much more satisfactory to look in some detail at the causes of changes in expenditure, as we are doing in this book. The size and liquidity of the stock of assets held by households and business firms undoubtedly influence expenditure decisions, and the stock of money merits considerations on both of these counts; but it is erroneous to center our attention exclusively on changes in the stock of money in analyzing the level of the expenditure stream. As far as consumption expenditure is concerned there can be little doubt that the best single explanation of its changes lies in changes in the level of household incomes.

The second part of the weakness of the Quantity Theory is that it pays inadequate attention to the fact that the price level does not necessarily change in proportion with changes in effective demand. Sometimes a change in effective demand may have no effect on prices; in other cases (which we shall look at shortly) the price level can change by a more than proportionate amount.

The fact is that monetary economics is too complicated to be dealt with by theories as simple as the Quantity Theory. The most important conclusion we can derive from it is that big rises in the level of money income are not possible unless there are more or less equal rises in the quantity of money; an inflation can always be brought to an end if the supply of money is limited. This is an important fact, but it is only a small part of the theory of inflation.

Some Suggested Reading

The Quantity Theory of Money has received a great deal of attention in the literature and has undergone a number of transformations over the years. For the earlier versions of the Quantity Theory see Irving Fisher, *Purchasing Power of Money* (New York, 1926) and A. Marshall, *Money, Credit and Commerce* (London, 1923). Fisher stresses the factors that affect the velocity of circulation of money, while Marshall is concerned with clarifying the motives for holding money. For a picture of Keynes' drift away from the Quantity Theory approach it is instructive to look first at Keynes, *A Tract on Monetary Reform* (New York, 1924) and then at his *Treatise on Money* (London, 1930).

For modern versions of the Quantity Theory, D. Patinkin, *Money, Interest, and Prices* (Evanston, 1956) and M. Friedman's introductory essay in *Studies in the Quantity Theory of Money,* edited by M. Friedman (Chicago, 1956) are the best examples. Patinkin's book is an examination of the Quantity Theory under conditions of full employment, and while it is a highly valuable book, its restrictive assumptions (particularly about uncertainty and expectations) confine it to a short step toward a general theory of money and prices. Friedman's essay is an attempt to put down on paper the oral tradition at Chicago on the Quantity Theory of Money. His analysis is concerned primarily with the factors that influence the demand for money.

19

The Nature of Inflation

Comparison of the Theory of Inflation and the Multiplier Theory

There are significant similarities between the theory of inflation and the theory of the multiplier expounded in Part II; but there are also significant differences. The most important source of the difference is the fact that in inflationary conditions full employment has been reached, at least in some parts of the economy. There may be full employment in some parts, and unemployment in others; this possibility will be ignored for the time being and in this chapter and the next two we shall be concerned with conditions where full employment is reached simultaneously in all industries.[1]

Under conditions of completely full employment it is impossible for a rise in demand to lead to a rise in the level of output; the analysis we followed in the earlier chapters can no longer apply. Instead there are three possible consequences of a rise in expenditure. The first is that inventories may be reduced; in this way, sales can exceed current output. This is likely to be a very common immediate reaction, just as it was in the under-full-employment conditions of Chapter 6. Secondly, some purchasers may have to wait longer for the things they want to buy; this happens frequently when firms producing machinery and other fixed capital equipment are working to full capacity; other firms which want to install new equipment have to wait longer for it. (We shall consider such cases at some length in Chapters 23 and 24.) Thirdly, there may be a tendency for rises in the prices of things for which the demand has

---

[1] In the discussion of 'suppressed' inflation, later in this chapter, we shall temporarily assume that full employment has been reached in some industries but not in others.

risen, so that it is now in excess of the supply. This is the reaction which will be our particular concern in this chapter and the next two. The ordinary forces of supply and demand, which are always at work in the economic system, operate in a familiar manner—a rise in demand leads to a rise in price.

Here, then, are the first points of similarity and of difference, in comparing the inflationary process with the ordinary multiplier process. In each case a rise in demand leads to a situation in which plans are incompatible, and once again the result is a rise in the level of income; but in this new case the movement occurs by a rise in prices, and not a rise in output.

In the multiplier case, examined earlier, the initial repercussions on income were not the end of the matter; the rise in output and income led to further repercussions, since it involved a rise in expenditure. Similarly, there are repercussions arising from the rise in prices and incomes that we are now considering. This time, however, we have to take account of two kinds of repercussion, because some people have been put into a less favorable position than before by the price rise. In the simple multiplier case, where there were no price changes, no one necessarily lost as a result of a rise in expenditure,[2] while some people necessarily gained (namely, the households who came to receive higher incomes). In the case we are now considering, however, the process inevitably leads both to gains and to losses.

The immediate gainers are the same kinds of people who gained in the multiplier case—the people involved in producing the things on which the initiating increase in expenditure is being made. These people are now selling their product at a higher price. But now there is also inevitably reason for loss; the losers are the people who now have to pay a higher price for the things they buy. The transactors who were previously buying the things whose prices

---

[2] In the particular case chosen in Chapter 5, where a new machine was invented, some people may have lost, temporarily or permanently—namely the workmen displaced by the machine. This example was fortuitous, however; an example of a case where no one loses in the expansionary process is where the government increases expenditure by borrowing; again, in the case in Chapter 5, it would be perfectly easy to avoid any continuing loss, if these workmen were immediately taken on again in the subsequent output expansion. Such compensation of losers is impossible in the inflationary process; if it is attempted, new losers are created.

rise now find that with a given expenditure in terms of money, they can buy less than they could previously.

Of course, many transactors will both gain and lose simultaneously, as a result of the initial price rise. They gain to the extent that they are selling the things whose prices have risen; they lose to the extent that they are buying things whose prices have risen. In some cases these two effects will just cancel out; but more normally we can expect there to be net gainers and net losers as a result of the initial price rise.

Each transactor whose position is altered by the initial price changes will in turn alter his plans. Any net gainers (i.e. people whose money income has increased more than the prices of the things they buy) will be likely to increase their expenditure in real terms. The people who are neither net gainers nor net losers (because their money incomes and the prices of the things they buy have increased in the same proportion) will probably keep their real expenditure constant; but in terms of money their expenditure rises. Finally, the net losers will be compelled to adjust their plans, and they may well attempt to compensate themselves, by means of defensive reactions, for at least some of the effects of the adverse circumstances. They may try to raise the price of the goods or services (including labor) that they sell, in order to increase their money income; or they may borrow or run down their financial reserves in order to increase their level of money expenditure. These reactions may be more or less successful, but they nearly always occur. In their turn, they put other people into a less favorable position, and so cause those people to try to make up at least some of the effects of their losses. This chain reaction by people who are put in a worse situation by the price rises is an additional element in the series of reactions in the inflationary process which is not present in the multiplier process.

This, then, is the first of three basic differences between the propagation in the multiplier process and that in the inflationary process. In the former case, where prices are constant and output changes, the sole motive force of the process of change following an initiating rise in expenditure is the fact that some people are gaining.[3] In the latter case, where output is constant and prices

---

[3] Similarly, the sole motive force of the process of change following an initiating fall in expenditure is the fact that some people are losing.

change, the motive force of the process involves the fact that some people are gaining while some people are losing.

A second difference between the two processes arises from the fact demonstrated in the last chapter, that there is an asymmetry around the point (or zone) of full employment. A rise in expenditure at full employment leads to a process of rising prices, but a fall in expenditure at full employment does not lead to a process of falling prices. Rather it leads to a downward multiplier process— i.e. a contraction of the level of output and real income. Thus the inflationary process is not to any important extent reversible; there is a ratchet effect in operation. If expenditure falls in circumstances of inflation the effect is only to stop the inflation, and if the fall is big enough, to lead to a fall in output; general price rises, once they have occurred, do not usually reverse themselves.[4]

The third difference between the multiplier and the inflationary processes is that there is almost complete certainty that the multiplier process will come to an end of its own accord. Only in the extreme case when there is no saving out of additional income[5] does the multiplier process go on indefinitely.[6] On the other hand the inflationary process is frequently not self-limiting. If no new outside forces come to operate it may quite conceivably go on indefinitely. It may, in fact, grow on itself and speed up, so that the rate of rise of prices becomes faster and faster. On the other hand it often is self-limiting. What in fact happens depends on the kinds and strengths of the forces at work in particular cases; we shall analyze some of them in the next chapter.

The Nature of Inflation

Now that we have made this preliminary comparison of the inflationary process and the multiplier process we can proceed to look further into the nature of inflation. There are three features of

---

[4] This is only strictly true of manufactured products with no primary products as part of their raw materials; to the extent that this unrealistic assumption is dropped, the argument of the text has to be modified.

[5] Or, of course, no reductions in saving when income falls.

[6] It should be noted that this argument only applied to the simple multiplier process, as considered in Part II. In Chapter 24 we shall see that when other elements are combined with the multiplier there may be no self-limitation within this combined process.

inflation to which we must pay particular attention. It is a process of rising prices; it is initiated by some change which makes it impossible to satisfy the whole of the demand which is forthcoming at existing prices, so that initial price rises occur; and it is propagated by the reactions of transactors or groups of transactors to the initial price rise, so that further price rises are induced.

The first of these three features is that inflation consists of a process of rising prices. This simple definition, which corresponds to the layman's idea, avoids difficulties involved in the more sophisticated definitions that some economists have favored.[7] The main criticism that can be brought against it is that it does not consider 'suppressed inflation' to be an example of inflation, because a fully suppressed inflation does not involve any price rises. At first sight this may seem to be a disadvantage, but closer consideration proves it is not necessarily so, particularly because suppressed inflation has been taken to have a variety of meanings.

Suppressed Inflation

One set of circumstances in which it is useful to employ the phrase 'suppressed inflation' is that in which policies are used which prevent price rises at the present time, but which are piling up forces which will increase expansionary pressure in the future. Wartime controls furnish an example. In order to make resources available for war, and to avoid the harmful effects of rising prices, controls and rationing may be imposed which prevent households and firms from buying as many currently produced goods and services as they would like to buy at existing prices and income levels. Consequently, the transactors concerned may have to save more, with the intention of using the extra savings to buy the desired goods when they become available. Thus, in World War II, many firms built up large liquid reserves (as cash or short-term securities) when they could not replace and expand equipment. Similarly, many households built up abnormally large savings during the war, because they were not able to buy the things they wanted.

---

[7] The prevention of price rises may lead to further difficulties, but these are better regarded as problems of the prevention of inflation rather than problems of inflation as such.

With suppressed inflation of this kind, the longer the controls last, the larger becomes the pent-up demand. The pent-up demand may in time become so great that it makes the controls ineffective; then the suppressed inflation turns into ordinary price inflation. Even if this does not happen, suppressed inflation in the sense in which we are using the term may lead to serious open inflation, if the controls are removed too precipitately, as all the backlog of demand then shows itself more or less at once.

This first use of the word 'suppression' applies to the imposition of controls whose effect is that expenditure on currently produced output is *postponed*. A second use of the word is seen where the effect of the controls is to *divert* demand from one kind of output to another. (In practice, almost any set of controls designed to suppress inflation will partly postpone demand and partly divert it; the relative importance of the two effects depends on the type of control and on the reactions of transactors.)

Diversion of demand from one kind of current expenditure to another may be made in a variety of ways. For one thing, it is almost impossible to ration and control everything. Even in wartime, such things as movie theater seats, books, beer, and cigarettes were relatively freely available. Diversion of expenditure into such channels may not be considered harmful. For one thing it may be that output of these things can still be increased without leading to price rises. It is possible to divert quite a large amount of demand to purchases of goods and services provided by industries where there is normally excess capacity, even when other industries are fully employed, and where the cost of producing an extra unit of output is very small. Examples are theater seats and railway journeys, where queues and overcrowding provide means by which the demand is satisfied up to a point very near the physical limit of capacity.

Controls may also divert expenditure into channels in which the pressure of demand causes price rises, so that there is price inflation; nevertheless, it may be considered by the authorities that such a diversion is desirable, and that if the price rises are confined to certain parts of the economy, the harmful effects are not important. In the final analysis, inflation is an important subject for consideration because of the disturbances caused by price rises. If those disturbances can be limited to certain unimportant sectors of the economy (such as the luxury goods trades) they may not be considered undesirable.[8] Inflation may be measured simply in terms of the prices of commodities in general demand (as by a cost-of-living index); in a useful sense, we can say that inflation has been suppressed if price rises occur but are limited to luxury goods.

Another purpose for which controls may be used to divert demand and so to 'suppress' inflation can be very important where the existing structure of the economy is inappropriate to the demands that are being placed on it. For example, a rearmament drive may involve a very heavy burden on the machine tool industries, or wartime destruction may have reduced the potential output of some key industry (e.g. steel). The inappropriateness of the industrial structure to the demand placed on it means that 'bottlenecks' appear in the economy.[9] This means that the demand for the products of some industries is greater at existing prices than the available supply, while there is still excess capacity and unemployment in other industries. Now it is always possible to deal with these bottlenecks, either by raising the price of the goods concerned relatively to other goods, or by reducing total demand for all goods and services to such a level that there are no bottlenecks. But frequently, both these policies may be considered undesirable. To lower overall demand may involve extensive unemployment in the other parts of the economy, while appropriate relative price shifts may be politically and administratively intolerable. For example, it might involve big rises in the prices of important commodities such as steel, while other prices remained more or less unchanged. The alternative policies that may be realistic would then be either to accept a general price inflation as a result of these particular scarcities, or to control demand for the goods which are particularly scarce. This latter alternative may frequently be the more attractive; by diverting demand, the inflation that would otherwise arise is suppressed.

Controls may be imposed, therefore, either to postpone or to divert demand. Unfortunately, such controls also tend to have effects

---

[8] The danger may well remain that resources will be attracted to the luxury goods trades, so that the supply of essential goods is reduced. Strict controls may be needed to prevent this.

[9] As we shall see in Chapter 22, the appearance of bottlenecks in some industries before others is a normal characteristic of the full employment zone. Some of the inflationary tendencies in that zone can, therefore, be suppressed by appropriate diversion of demand.

leading to increased pressure of demand, because they tend to increase the attractiveness of leisure compared with work; if one cannot buy freely all the things one would like to buy with current income, it may seem desirable to enjoy more leisure. This does not necessarily increase inflationary pressure; there is a reduction in output because less work is done, but there is also a reduction in expenditure because less income is received. If the people concerned do not reduce their saving when these changes occur, then output and expenditure fall equally, and it may be that there is no net additional pressure of demand. Even if this should be so, the effects of these changes may be inflationary if the reduction in output is concentrated in industries where supplies are particularly short (e.g. steel) while the reduction in demand is spread broadly over the whole economy.

We have now seen two senses in which the phrase 'suppressed' inflation can usefully be employed. There is also a third sense in which the term has frequently been used, which is less justifiable. This is the case where 'suppression' simply means prevention, in circumstances where no pressure is being built up for the future, and where there is no diversion of demand.

Suppression is commonly used in this way, as a synonym for prevention, in two kinds of circumstances. In the first place, it frequently implies disapproval on the part of the commentator concerned of the methods of prevention used. Prevention by means considered undesirable (e.g. high taxation) may be called suppression, but not prevention by means considered desirable (e.g. reduction in government expenditure). Such distinctions between approval and disapproval may well be important, but they are probably better not expressed in terms which are apparently objective. The other kind of circumstances in which 'suppression' and 'prevention' are used as synonyms is perhaps more justifiable; it arises when doubt is cast upon the ability to sustain the particular method of preventing inflation under consideration for any long period. For example, it may be thought that the harmful effects of high taxation on enterprise will eventually reduce the supply of goods produced below what would have been possible under a system of lower taxes; in time it may therefore aggravate the problem. Though such points are important, they are probably more conveniently expressed explicitly.

The Initiation of Inflation

Sufficient has now been said on the first feature of inflation—that it is a process of rising prices which may be suppressed by postponement or diversion. We must now proceed to a more detailed discussion of the changes that may initiate such a series of price rises. Quite a considerable amount has already been said about this, in comparing the inflationary process with the multiplier process. There we saw inflation as the consequence of a rise in demand in circumstances when an increase in output was not possible. The main point that needs to be added to this is that the same effects can be brought about by a fall in the supply of goods and services while demand remains unchanged. An excess of demand over available supply may result from either a rise in effective demand or a reduction in available supply.

There are, therefore, two main ways in which an inflationary situation may be initiated; they are changes in demand conditions and changes in supply conditions, in each case either for goods or for services. (In the case of services, the service of supplying labor is particularly important.) Examples of likely initiating changes in demand conditions are increased investment by firms, and increased government expenditure on the basis of borrowing. Examples of likely changes in supply conditions include a fall in the productivity of labor while money wages remain unchanged, and a refusal on the part of labor to do the existing amount of work for present money wages.

The third feature of inflation outlined above was that the initial price rises in turn cause further price rises, because some transactor or group of transactors react to the initial rises. As we have seen, these reactions may be of two kinds. Firstly, people will adjust their expenditure plans to any increases in the money incomes they receive and to changes in the prices of the things they buy. Secondly, people who are worse off in real terms may react defensively, by making an effective, though not necessarily a successful, refusal to accept the worsening in their situation. Their refusal is 'effective' because we are only concerned with it if it has further consequences; we say it may not be 'successful' because the consequences of the refusal may not be the ones that are desired by the transactors concerned.

These refusals may be of two kinds. They may be simply a refusal to accept the effects of the price rise on the quantity of goods purchased, that is, on the level of real expenditure by a transactor. When prices rise, constant expenditure in terms of money implies that the quantity of goods purchased falls. A transactor may well try to prevent such an effect from taking place; in order to do so, he must increase his expenditure in money terms. The government may, for example, try to maintain its purchases by increasing its money expenditure; firms may try to maintain investment in real terms by increasing money expenditure. These transactors can maintain their expenditure by increased borrowing, by drawing down reserves, or by reduced saving.

Households may also try to maintain their expenditure in these three ways; the typical reaction of households, however, in defending themselves against the effects of price rises is to try to increase their money income and so to restore (or partially restore) their level of real income. This they can try to do by raising the price of the thing they sell, for example, by trade union action to raise money wages.[10] This reaction of attempting to restore (or at least partially to restore) real income by raising selling prices can also be made by firms. Something rather similar can also be done by the government, by raising taxes and so increasing its money receipts.

As a consequence of a successful defensive reaction of restoring real income by raising selling prices in terms of money, the transactors concerned will be able to restore real expenditure to the original level (or toward it), without any need to borrow, draw down reserves, or save less than the customary proportion. It therefore follows that both kinds of defensive reaction to price rises involve attempts to restore (or partially restore) real expenditure. The difference between the two is in the path chosen. In the first case, real expenditure is maintained or restored by simply increasing demand in terms of money, on the basis of increased borrowing,

---

[10] Purely defensive actions designed to restore real income assume that the transactors concerned are not following the simple rules of maximization which are outlined in ordinary price theory; that theory assumes that transactors always make the best of the situation in which they find themselves. As we shall see in the next chapter, many reactions which appear to be defensive are frequently in fact reconcilable with ordinary demand and supply analysis and its maximization assumptions. At the same time, there can be no doubt that many income recipients do make purely defensive reactions in inflationary situations.

of reduced saving, or of drawing down reserves. In the second case, real expenditure is restored by increasing selling prices (of labor, of goods, and if one cares to think of it that way, of government services, by raising taxes); as a consequence of this, money incomes rise and so money expenditure is increased and real expenditure restored. One path operates solely on the side of demand for goods and services; the other path operates through the supply of goods and services, and consequently on the demand.

SOME SUGGESTED READING

Although inflation has been one of the major economic problems since World War II, the theoretical literature of the subject is surprisingly meager. There has been a great deal of discussion at the level of political polemics, usually approaching the topic with strong and unyielding prejudices. But the rarity of satisfactory objective studies is something of a reflection on the whole body of professional economists.

A pioneering study was Keynes, *How to Pay for the War* (New York, 1940), which demonstrated how the Keynesian theory could be applied to conditions of overfull employment—that it was not merely the 'economics of depression.' The best theoretical book on the subject is Bent Hansen, *A Study in the Theory of Inflation* (London, 1951), which applies the 'Swedish' approach to macro-economics to this problem. A. J. Brown, *The Great Inflation 1939-51* (London, 1955) is mainly descriptive but has useful theoretical sections. An article which concerns itself with suppressed inflation is E. M. Bernstein, 'Latent Inflation—Problems and Policies' in *IMF Staff Papers,* vol. 1 (1951). The same subject is dealt with in F. W. Paish, 'Open and Repressed Inflation,' *Economic Journal* (1953).

20

The Inflationary Process

The stage has now been set for a consideration of the inflationary process. The questions we shall have to answer in this chapter and the next are much the same as those we looked into in the chapters on the multiplier. In the first place, it is necessary to know whether any new equilibrium level of prices and money income is possible, after an inflationary disturbance. In the second place, it is necessary to know how large a rise in money income must take place in order to reach the new equilibrium, if it exists. Thirdly, it is necessary to consider the path of adjustment; included in this is knowledge of the speed of adjustment.

An inflationary process is initiated by a change in demand or supply conditions, which has as its consequence an initial price rise and rise in money incomes. This price rise in turn provides reactions of two kinds. One kind of reaction is that people adjust their expenditure plans in accordance with any changes in the money income they receive and with the changes in the prices of the things they buy. This can be described as a 'passive reaction.' The other kind of reaction is that the people who are worse off in real terms as a result of the price changes may make what we have described as 'defensive reactions.' [1] It is necessary to simplify the problem in order to make it manageable; in the first place, it will be convenient to assume that there are no defensive reactions; subsequently, we can introduce them.

---

[1] See pp. 295-6.

No Defensive Reactions

There are various possible cases we must consider within this group of cases where there are no defensive reactions. The most useful distinction is that between cases where the initiating disturbance is a change in demand conditions, and that where it is a change in supply conditions. The simpler case to deal with is that where there is an initial change in demand conditions; this will be treated first. The approach we can use is very similar to that employed in Chapter 6.

In Table 9, there is an initial position of equilibrium at full-employment output of 2,000,000 units, each of which sells initially at $1. The disturbance takes the form of a rise in planned investment from $100,000 per week to $200,000 per week. In the first week, this additional demand is met by running down the level of stocks of finished output—there is unplanned disinvestment in inventories of $100,000.

At the end of the first week we assume (just as in Chapter 6) that firms react to this unplanned reduction in inventories; they do so by raising the price of each unit of final output by 5 per cent. At this price, the previous week's total money expenditure is just equal to the total value of output.

If we assume that households base their expenditure plans for the second week on their incomes in the first week and on prices ruling during the first week, then households spend $1,900,000 in the second week. Investment expenditure continues at $200,000. Total money expenditure is $2,100,000; the value of current output is $2,100,000; so demand for goods is equated to supply.

In turn, however, there are changes in plans for the third week. Households find two reasons for adjusting their expenditure plans. For one thing, their money incomes have turned out to be $2,100,000 in the second week and not $2,000,000 as was expected. (There was, therefore, unplanned saving of $100,000 in the second week.) For another thing, they find that the price of each unit of output was $1.05 in the second week, and not $1, which was the price on which that week's expenditure plans had been based.

Now, the consequential revisions of household plans for the third week are reasonably obvious. They find money income has risen 5 per cent and prices have risen 5 per cent, compared with what

TABLE 9

Week	Planned fixed investment ($ thousands)	Total output (thousands)	Price per unit of output ($)	Value of total output = money household income ($ thousands)	Expected household income ($ thousands)	Household consumption ($ thousands)	Planned saving ($ thousands)	Un-planned saving ($ thousands)	Un-planned investment in inventories ($ thousands)	Realized saving = realized investment ($ thousands)
0	100	2000	1	2000	2000	1900	100	0	0	100
1	200	2000	1	2000	2000	1900	100	0	-100	100
2	200	2000	1.05	2100	2000	1900	100	100	0	200
3	200	2000	1.05	2100	2100	1995	105	0	-95	105
4	200	2000	1.0975	2195	2100	1995	105	95	0	200
5	200	2000	1.0975	2195	2195	2085.25	109.75	0	-90.25	109.75
∞	200	2000	2.0	4000	4000	3800	200	0	0	200

they had expected. Real incomes, therefore, have remained unchanged. Households will consequently leave their plans for consumption and saving unchanged in real terms, by planning to use 5 per cent more on each in money terms.[2] Consumption expenditure by households in the third week is, therefore, $1,995,000.

The rise in consumer expenditure in the third week in turn disturbs the position of firms, who find unplanned disinvestment in the third week of $95,000; total money expenditure on goods is $2,195,000, while the week's output, valued at that week's prices, is $2,100,000. Firms therefore react in the fourth week by raising the price of each unit of output to $1.0975. At this price, the total money expenditure of the third week would just equal the value of total output.

In this way a sequence of price rises continues in a manner with which we are reasonably familiar. Each week's rise is smaller than that of the preceding week; but each rise increases household incomes and so leads to an increase in money expenditure, which in turn induces further price rises.

Since each week's price rise is only a fraction of the preceding week's, the process of rising prices eventually becomes imperceptibly small. Given sufficient time, a new equilibrium situation is approached with (in this case) the price level double what it was originally. The significance of this size of increase is obvious, in terms of common sense. When prices have all doubled, $200,000 of investment amounts to the same in real terms as the $100,000 of investment which was carried out in the original equilibrium situation. Savings plans, in real terms, are unchanged in the process under consideration, because real household incomes do not alter between the two equilibrium situations. Thus, with prices double

---

[2] When the real income is constant, the marginal propensity to consume in *money* terms is equal to the average propensity to consume in real terms. Thus if one-tenth of real income is saved, and prices and money income increase in equal proportions, money saving rises by one-tenth of the increase in money income. The formula representing the equilibrium increase in money income is that money income increases by the rise in money investment divided by the marginal propensity to save in money terms. (This can be arrived at in precisely the same way as the real income multiplier, of Chapter 6, as in the Mathematical Appendix.) The formula can therefore also be expressed by saying that equilibrium money income increases by an amount equal to the rise in money investment divided by the average propensity to save.

what they were, real investment and real savings plans are once
again consistent with one another.

This inflationary process, and the new equilibrium position, can
be seen diagrammatically in a demonstration similar to that already
used for the multiplier in Chapters 5 and 6. As in Chapter 5, the two

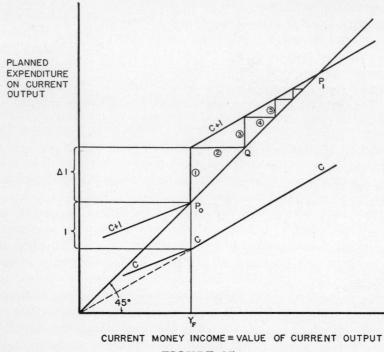

CURRENT MONEY INCOME ≡ VALUE OF CURRENT OUTPUT

FIGURE 15

axes on Figure 15 represent total income and planned expenditure,
and the only possible stable equilibrium is on a 45° line through
the origin; only on such a line can transactors' plans be consistent
with one another. The new feature of the diagram is that we assume
we start at a position of full employment (Y_F) beyond which output
cannot be increased; if planned expenditure increases beyond this
point, money income and the value of money output rise, through
price rises instead of rises in real income.

Up to the point of full employment, the consumption line is as
in Part II; at any point it is flatter than a line through the origin
and that point, because (following the arithmetical examples and

what is probably almost invariably the case in practice) the marginal propensity to consume in real terms is smaller than the average propensity. (The marginal propensity to consume is represented by the slope of the CC line at any point; the average propensity to consume by the slope of a line connecting the point with the origin.)

At the point of full employment, however, the CC line kinks. Beyond full employment, we assume that real saving and real consumption plans are constant; each changes proportionally with the price level. At and beyond the full employment position, therefore, the marginal propensity to consume in money terms is equal to the average propensity to consume in real terms,[3] and the CC line is an extension of a straight line through the origin.

The demonstration of the new equilibrium position after a rise in the level of investment plans (expressed in money terms) from I to a new constant level of $I + \Delta I$, follows familiar lines. The original equilibrium is P_0. In week 1 planned investment rises to the new higher level, and in week 2 firms raise the price of their output so that money income and the money value of current output rise, to Q. This is not, however, an equilibrium position, even though it is on the 45° line, so that planned expenditure is equal to the value of current output. The reason why it is not an equilibrium is that the CC condition is not satisfied, because consumption expenditure, in money terms, has not risen along with the increase in money income.

This failure is made up in week 3, when there is an increase in planned household expenditure determined by the increase in money income in week 2 and by the slope of the CC line (the marginal propensity to consume in money terms). This in turn leads to further price rises in week 4, and so on, until a new equilibrium is reached where prices have risen in the same proportion as the original rise in the level of investment plans—in our arithmetical example, a doubling.

In this process of inflation the eventual losers are firms which tried to invest more. In the final equilibrium real investment is reduced to its original level, although during the process of adjustment it has proved possible to carry out real fixed investment, which, while less than was desired, was more than is possible in equilibrium. An

---

[3] See footnote 2.

important question is, Where have the physical resources come from which have made possible this additional amount of fixed investment? The answer is simply that there has been unplanned disinvestment by firms and unplanned saving by households. Between the two, they have temporarily made available the extra resources for fixed investment.

In practice, of course, things will not work out as neatly as in our model. For example, firms may be unwilling or unable to allow the amount of disinvestment in inventories we have assumed. If they attempt to replace unplanned reductions in inventories, the price rise speeds up, at least temporarily, as did the rise in the level of output considered in Chapter 6.

Exactly the same kind of analysis applies if the initial disturbance is a change in supply conditions. For example, if there is a fall in productivity, household incomes can be expected to fall *pari passu*. This means that household plans to save, expressed in money terms, will be reduced. On the other hand, there is no reason why investment plans (again expressed in money terms) should necessarily be reduced. There is consequently an excess of total demand for goods over total supply. The situation is resolved by price rises which mean that a given amount of investment expressed in money terms becomes less and less in real terms. Equilibrium comes when real investment plans have been reduced to equality with real saving plans.

All this analysis so far has assumed that fixed investment is unchanged in money terms. In other words, people who are investing do not try to defend themselves against the effects of price changes. In practice, however, they may well do so, by increasing expenditure on fixed investment when the price level rises. It is necessary, therefore, to proceed to a consideration of defensive reactions.

Defensive Reactions

As we saw at the end of the last chapter, defensive reactions are of two main kinds. On the one hand, there are attempts simply to maintain real expenditure; and on the other, there are attempts to maintain real income. Maintenance of real income in turn usually involves maintenance of real expenditure out of that income.

In an economy where prices and wages are largely fixed by administrative action, most price and wage rises in an inflation may well appear to be defensive reactions. For example, trade unions justify wage increases by saying that the real incomes of the workers have fallen, because of price increases. Similarly, businessmen justify price increases (perhaps less vocally) in terms of the maintenance of their own real incomes in face of cost increases. To a significant extent, this is correct. As we saw in Chapter 18, there is a large conventional and monopolistic element in wage and price determination. Nevertheless, an explanation based on these forces alone lays inadequate emphasis on the simple forces of supply and demand. The increases in money household incomes that were observed in the sequence of events following a rise in investment plans which was analyzed earlier in this chapter were the direct result of excess of demand for goods over the supply of goods. Yet individual price rises within the general rise might well be regarded as defensive reactions by the people concerned.

This can be seen in two different contexts. In the first place, households include both wage receivers and profit receivers. There is, therefore, a struggle between these two groups to obtain as big a share as possible of the increase in money household income at each stage of the process. To each of these groups individually the situation appears as a defensive struggle to maintain or restore real incomes at the expense of the other. These narrower views may be perfectly correct and perfectly consistent with the fact that the rise in the money income of all households taken together is the result of excess of demand over supply.

In the second place, we have to allow for the fact that, in practice, prices and wages in different industries do not all move to the same extent at precisely the same time. This again may mean that the justification for each price or wage rise in each individual industry may appear to be defensive, although the whole process of inflation is the result of excess of demand over supply. An individual firm or industry may see the situation as one of rising costs of its raw materials, to which it reacts by a defensive rise in its selling price. Taking the broader view, however, the position may well be that there is an excess of demand over supply throughout the economy, which increases the prices of the things an industry is buying and also makes it possible for this industry to sell its output at a higher price. The true *explanation* of each price rise is an excess of demand over supply; the *justification* of many individual price rises may appear to be defensive reactions against rising costs.

The upshot of all this is that it is necessary to look very carefully at an inflationary situation, and not to take things at their face value. Defensive reactions are indeed important as determinants of the prices at which goods and labor are sold, largely because of the quasi-monopolistic position of trade unions and many businessmen. Nevertheless, what may appear to be successful defensive reactions frequently are simply part of the process of adjustment to an excess of demand over supply.

In spite of the fact that defensive reactions are frequently not exactly what they appear to be, it still remains necessary to make an extensive analysis of them. For this, there are several reasons. For one thing, the argument of the last few paragraphs applies only to defensive reactions by those who are attempting (or appear to be attempting) to maintain real income. There is still the important group of defensive reactions where there is an attempt solely to maintain real expenditure. Secondly, analysis in terms of defensive reactions helps our insight into the detailed process of inflation whose basic cause is excess of demand over supply. Thirdly, the existence of effective and genuine defensive actions may be such as to keep inflation going indefinitely.

This last point may be very important in practice. If there is some group which makes an effective attempt to defend itself against the consequences of each round of price increases, then a further round will follow: to restore its position the group concerned will raise its money expenditure or its money income. The process of inflation must continue for as long as circumstances are such that at each stage there is a group (or a single transactor, which to be significant must be large, e.g. a trade union or the government) which effectively refuses to accept fully the effects upon its real income or its real expenditure of the price rises in the previous stage. This must happen if there are at least two groups that are trying to restore their positions; as one group restores its position (at least partially) it harms the other by causing price rises, and a reaction from the other group is provoked. So long as there is such a struggle for incompatible ends, the inflationary process must continue. Of course, the two groups may both satisfy themselves if their struggle and the rising prices it causes have the result that some third group is put in a worse position and is unable to defend itself. For example, wage and profit receivers can increase their real incomes at the expense of people whose incomes are fixed in terms of money. By reducing the real expenditure of a third passive group, the incompatible aims of two actively defensive groups can become compatible.

The inflationary process can also continue indefinitely even if there is only one group which is reacting defensively. This happens because the increased money expenditure of the defensive group will usually increase the money incomes of another passive group. In turn, the money expenditure of the passive group rises, and therefore prices rise. In turn, this causes further reactions by the actively defensive group. An example can be seen from Table 9. If the people doing the fixed investment were defensive, and increased their money expenditure on investment each time the price level rose, there would be no end to the process of inflation.

All this amounts to saying that inflation must continue as long as total planned demand for goods and services exceeds total planned supply at full employment. Our analysis of the process of inflation is no more than an attempt to look a little more deeply into this common-sense statement. Clearly, the number of possible ways in which the process of inflation can develop is practically limitless. We can only trace through a few examples.

Mention has already been made of an example of a case where there is one actively defensive group and a passive group whose money income rises at each stage. This case comes about when investment is maintained in real terms in the modification of the example in Table 9. We can, therefore, proceed to some examples of cases where there is rivalry between two groups.

The number of possible combinations of cases is obviously large. Both groups may be attempting to restore their real income; or both may be attempting simply to restore real expenditure; or, again, one group may be attempting to restore real income and the other simply real expenditure. What is more, it may be that the initiating disturbance continues to be maintained by defensive reactions throughout the process (as in the modification to the example in Table 9 mentioned above) or it may be that the initiating disturbance is not defended (as in the original example in Table 9). The general characteristics of the analysis can be derived from three examples, in which we assume that immediately before the initiating disturbance comes into operation the economy concerned was just at the position of full employment, with prices constant.

Initiation and Defensive Reactions Both Involving Demand Conditions

The first case we shall consider is one where all the active factors operate to change demand conditions. There is an initiating rise

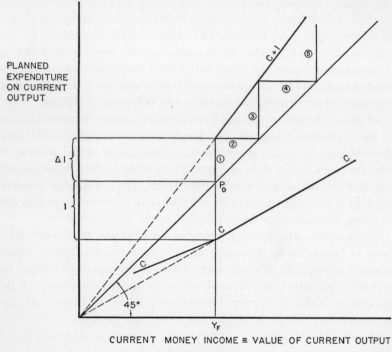

CURRENT   MONEY   INCOME ≡ VALUE OF CURRENT OUTPUT

FIGURE 16

in demand, such as the rise in investment plans assumed in the example on pages 299-304; but we now assume that this initiating change in demand continues to act as a defensive factor right through the process. By this we mean that firms now try to maintain investment expenditure at the new high level in real terms. In this case, there is no end to the inflationary process, as can be seen diagrammatically. Figure 16 corresponds to Figure 15, earlier in this chapter, with the difference that investment plans are raised each time prices rise in order to maintain real investment at the level $I + \Delta I$. This is represented diagrammatically by drawing the

$C + I$ line as an extension of a line through the origin; the vertical distance between the CC line and the $C + I$ line (= planned investment expenditure in money terms) rises in proportion with the price level. In these circumstances, no new equilibrium is possible; prices rise steadily at a constant percentage rate.

Initiation and Defensive Reactions Both Involving Supply Conditions

The second case we shall consider is one where the initiating cause is a change in *supply* conditions, where this initiating change is actively defended right through the process, and where defensive reactions also involve changes in supply conditions, arising from an attempt by sellers (of goods or services) to maintain their real income. In this case, therefore, all changes and reactions are immediately concerned with the conditions under which goods and services are supplied. For the sake of simplicity we shall assume that both groups consume the whole of their income, and that there is no saving or investment in the economy. An initiating factor of this kind might well be one that has been mentioned earlier—a fall in labor productivity. If hourly wages remain constant there is a rise in labor costs to businessmen (whom we can equate, for this purpose, with profit receivers, the other social group in our country); the same amount of money is being paid for less work. In turn, this means that the real income of profit receivers declines: in this initial position they are selling a smaller output at constant prices, so are receiving less money for it, while they are paying out the same amount in wages as before the decline in productivity.

Profit receivers, we can assume, react to this fall in their real incomes by altering the conditions under which they are willing to supply the goods they sell in such a way as to restore their real income to the amount at which it stood before the fall in productivity, by raising their prices. It may be noted that such price increases can be imposed without danger of causing excess of supply over demand, because the price increases involve an increase in the money income of profit receivers, which lead to increases in money expenditure by profit receivers. An individual seller of goods does not increase the money demand for his goods appreciably when he increases his selling price; but if all sellers of goods increase their selling prices, then they also increase the level of money demand for one another's goods.

At this stage all is well for the profit receivers; they have restored the level of real income they enjoyed before the fall in productivity. Wage earners, however, are now receiving a reduced level of real income, because the prices of goods have risen while the level of money wages has not changed. They in turn react by altering the conditions upon which they are willing to supply labor services. If, as we are assuming, they in turn are unwilling to accept any reduction in their real incomes below the level they enjoyed before the fall in productivity, they raise the money wage rate at which they are willing to work to such a level that their money wages have risen by as much as prices. They may be able to do this, because they have a monopoly power and can refuse to supply any labor at a lower money wage rate than the one they choose. Of course, they are not necessarily powerful enough to do this; in such circumstances they may be able only partially to restore their original level of real income. The consequences of such weakness we will investigate shortly.

But even if they are in a powerful enough position to restore their real incomes, the restoration can only be temporary, because profit receivers in turn try to restore their real incomes again, by means of rises in the prices of goods. Profit receivers may, in fact, be willing to grant increased wages rather easily, simply because each of them knows he can rapidly restore his situation by raising prices again. In turn, wage earners try to restore their position by raising wages, and so the spiral of prices and wages continues. Each group tries to restore its own income in real terms by raising the price of the goods or services it sells, only to find the fruits are rapidly snatched away by a rise in the price of the goods or services it buys. This disappointment is inevitable, when neither side will permanently accept any reduction in its real income, because the initial fall in productivity means that there is not as much to go around as before; therefore someone must lose. As long as no one will accept loss, everyone is made worse off by the effects of the process of rising prices.

A geometrical demonstration of this process can be made by using a diagram such as that in Figure 17, where the horizontal axis measures the wage level and the vertical axis measures the price level. Initially the wage level is W_0 and the price level P_0; then there

is a fall of labor productivity. In order to maintain their real incomes, profit receivers raise the prices of the goods they sell to P_1.
Since money wages are unchanged, this means that real wages have
fallen sharply. Wage earners react to this by raising wage rates until
the ratio between wages and prices is the same as it was originally.

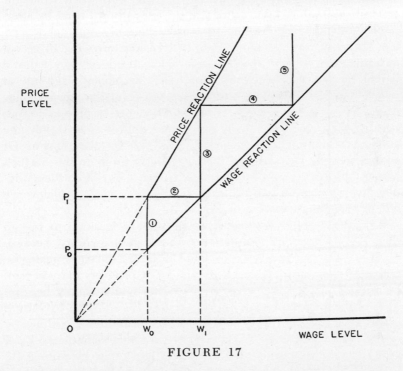

FIGURE 17

The line on the diagram marked 'wage reaction line' represents the
various positions at which wages are in the original relationship to
prices and where real wages are at the original level; since it represents a constant ratio between wages and prices, it is a straight line
through the origin. In week 2, therefore, wages rise to W_1. But in
turn this means that real profits have fallen, and businessmen react
along the price reaction line, which represents all the positions at
which real profits are maintained at their original position, with
prices sufficiently high in relation to wages, to offset the decline in
labor productivity. This price reaction line also passes through the
origin, indicating that prices are maintained in the original relation-

ship to wages; the two reaction lines therefore never meet and the process of alternating wage and price rises continues indefinitely, at a constant percentage rate.

In this example it is assumed that each of the two groups of transactors reacts at the same speed. But it is possible that one group will

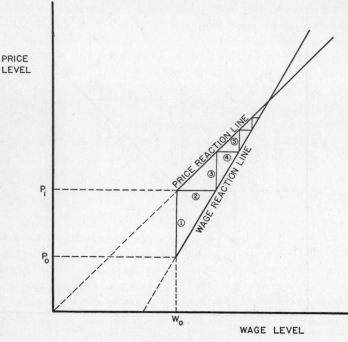

FIGURE 18

react more slowly than the other. If so, the slow reactor takes most of the inevitable burden of loss which is imposed by the rising prices and which results from the fall in productivity; the slow reactor is 'top man' for only a small part of each round (while the other group is making its quick reaction). Correspondingly, the other group gains for a large part of each round.

Another important case arises if one (or both) of the transactor groups is not in a sufficiently strong position to be able fully to restore its real income at each round of the process. In that case, there can ultimately be an equilibrium level of prices and the process does not continue indefinitely. For example, if labor is a weak reactor in this sense, the wage reaction line will not pass through the origin; instead it will be as in Figure 18. In this case, wages rise by a smaller proportion than prices at each round. On the other hand, real profits are fully restored at each round. The rise in wages and prices at each succeeding stage is smaller (in percentage terms) than at the preceding stage, and eventually equilibrium is reached. In this equilibrium real wages have fallen by an amount sufficient to absorb the fall in labor productivity.

In summary, we can say two things about the development of real wages and profits. In the process of adjustment, the faster the group's reactions, the higher is the group's real income. Speed of reactions does not, however, affect the final equilibrium in this model. On the other hand, the strength of reactions affects both the adjustment process and the final equilibrium (if any exists); strong reactors are better off than weak in the process of adjustment and are better off in the final equilibrium.

Defensive Reactions Involving Both Demand and Supply Conditions

A third way in which the process may continue is one where defensive reactions occur on both the demand side and the supply side—where one group is trying to maintain real expenditure and the other is trying to maintain its real income. An example might be one where the initiating factor is a rise in demand, where this rise in demand continues to be a defensive factor right through the process (because the transactor or group concerned wishes to maintain the new, higher level of expenditure), and where the other defensive reactions are on the supply side, taking the imme-diate form of an attempt to maintain real income. Once again, the initiating rise in demand might be a rise in government expendi-ture; this leads to price rises and falls in real income for the people who buy the things whose prices have risen. These people try to restore their real incomes by raising the prices of the things they sell (e.g. if they are wage earners, by refusing to work except for higher money wages). If this happens, the government can maintain its demand in real terms only by increasing expenditure in money terms. This leads to further price rises, and so the process continues.

This case would clearly be difficult to distinguish in practice from the one where each rise in money income is solely the result of increased money demand. In cases such as this, an analysis purely in terms of defensive reactions may seem justified, but (for reasons we have already considered) the reactions of income recipients may well be passive, in the sense that they are no more than a reaction to excess of demand over supply.

SOME SUGGESTED READING

The main contributions to the theory of inflation (apart from the more recent books listed in the reading list for Chapter 19) are skillfully integrated in R. Turvey, 'Some Aspects of the Theory of Inflation in a Closed Economy,' *Economic Journal* (1951). This article makes valuable use of the split into the factor and goods markets referred to in the reading list to Chapter 6. Among the most useful of the other theoretical contributions, see F. Holzman, 'Income Determination in Open Inflation,' *Review of Economics and Statistics* (1950); A. Smithies, 'The Behavior of National Money Income under Inflationary Conditions,' *Quarterly Journal of Economics* (1942); T. Koopmans, 'The Dynamics of Inflation,' *Review of Economics and Statistics* (1942) and J. Duesenberry, 'The Mechanics of Inflation,' *Review of Economics and Statistics* (1950).

*21

The Speed and Ending of Inflation

In this chapter we must look more closely into the questions of the speed of inflation and the conditions in which inflation will come to an end. These are obviously closely related; only if the rate of price rises slows down can the inflation end.

The Ending of Inflation

An inflation can end either because of a change in forces imposed from outside (e.g. a change of government policy) or because its internal momentum runs down. The former case need not detain us; obviously if some outside force reduces expenditure plans sufficiently, the inflation must stop.

About the latter explanation of the ending of inflation, something has already been said in the last chapter. It was said that the inflation must come to an end if there is a passive group whose money income or money expenditure remains constant in the inflationary process, so that this group's real expenditure is reduced sufficiently to make room for the importunities of other groups of transactors. Most of this section will be concerned with the result of the existence of passive groups, which cannot and do not increase their money income or expenditure after a price rise. In addition we must take account of the existence of groups which can increase their money income or expenditure, but not by an amount sufficient *fully* to restore real income or real expenditure to the level enjoyed before a price rise occurred. We must also consider a third force, which might conceivably lead to either a slowing down or a speeding up of inflation; since the former possibility seems the more likely in most practical situations, we are considering it here. It arises from the fact that different groups may have different marginal propensities to consume, so that a redistribution of income between two groups may lead to more or less spending. Finally, we must consider a force that can lead to a slowing down and ending of the inflation which has already been mentioned in the discussion of the Quantity Theory, namely, shortage of money.

The existence of passive groups which do not increase their money income or expenditure is usually one of the main reasons for an inflation coming to an end of its own accord. Passive groups lead to a sort of 'leakage' from the inflationary process, rather like the leakages that slow down and halt the multiplier process. One example has already been considered at some length in Table 9, where money investment remained constant so that the price rise eventually ceased.

It may be noted that it would be a considerable time, in that example, before the rate of price rise would become imperceptibly slow or before the price level was very near its new equilibrium. Even if prices rose for the whole time at the initial speed of 5 per cent every other week, twenty weeks would be needed to reach the new equilibrium; and as we have seen, our 'weeks' are probably considerably longer than calendar weeks. Moreover, the price rise does not continue at 5 per cent per week, but steadily slows down; the total time for the process to work to a near-equilibrium position is therefore quite long.

A similar analysis can be followed in other cases. As an example, we can consider the case of a struggle for real income between profit and wage receivers, following a fall in productivity. As we saw earlier, this process can continue indefinitely if these are the only two groups of transactors in the economy. If we introduce a passive group, whose money income does not increase, the process will come to an end. In Table 10 the sequence of events following a fall in labor productivity by 10 per cent is shown, on the assumption that neither labor nor profit receivers are willing to accept a reduction in their real income, and also assuming that all income is spent on goods and none is saved. In equilibrium, the whole burden falls on the rentier group. In period 1 labor productivity falls 10 per cent, so that output of goods falls to 90, and profits fall to zero, because money wages are constant. In period 2 each businessman raises his selling prices by 11.1 per cent; total profits are now 10, and at the prices ruling in period 1 this would restore total real profits to their old level. But now two groups are disappointed and react. Each businessman finds his real income has not been restored as he had hoped, because the actions of other businessmen in trying to restore their own real incomes raise the prices of the things he buys. At the same time, labor is

TABLE 10

Period	Money income			Total money income	Output of goods in real units	Price index = money income ÷ output of goods × 100
	Profits	Labor	Rentiers			
0	10	40	50	100	100	100
1	0	40	50	90	90	100
2	10	40	50	100	90	111.1
3	11	44.4	50	105.5	90	117.2
4	11.7	46.9	50	108.6	90	120.1
5	12.0	48.0	50	110.0	90	122.2
6	12.2	48.9	50	111.1	90	123.4
∞	12.5	50	50	112.5	90	125.0

disappointed because its wages will now buy fewer goods, and it reacts by demanding higher wages. This leads to further reactions in period 3. Wage rates rise by 11.1 per cent to counteract the rise in prices, between periods 1 and 2; moreover, each businessman raises his selling prices to allow for this wage rise, and also to raise his money profits by 11.1 per cent above the original level, in order to restore his real profits. This means that total money income in period 3 is 105.5, while output is only 90; this involves a rise in the price level rises to 117.2. In period 4, wage earners and businessmen try to counteract this rise in prices between periods 2 and 3 by increasing wages and selling prices still more; consequently prices rise to 120.1. This process continues, with each successive rise smaller; it ends when prices have risen to a level 25 per cent above the original level. This is the new equilibrium level of prices, because the real income of the passive group of rentiers will now have been reduced by one-fifth. Since we are assuming that they spend the whole of their incomes on goods and services and do not save, this means that they are now absorbing only 40 units of output, instead of 50 as originally. This reduction by 10 precisely compensates for the original decline in output which was the source of the inflation.

Similar to the effect of passive groups is the effect of those groups which, while reacting to changes in prices, do not fully restore their real income or real expenditure. It may be, for example, that wage earners succeed in restoring only a half of the effects on their real income of any price rise. Or the government may increase money expenditure, but not fully in proportion to the rise of income. A process of inflation will tend to slow down and come to a stop if transactors only partly restore the preceding situation. Each price rise is only partly compensated, and therefore succeeding price rises are smaller.

A further factor distinguished at the beginning of the chapter as likely to lead to a slowing down of the rate of inflation is the possibility of redistribution of income between different groups. In the process in Table 10, there was a distribution of real income away from the rentier group toward labor and profit receivers. We assumed in that table that all groups spent the whole of their income; now we can modify that assumption and consider that they save, and that the proportionate effects on saving out of a certain percentage change in real income are different for the three groups. If rentiers save a relatively small proportion of their income while the other groups save a great deal, the effect of the concentration of the burden of inflation on the rentiers reduces saving relatively little; inflationary pressure therefore becomes less than in the case where all groups bear the burden evenly. Contrariwise, if a reduction in rentier incomes cuts more deeply into savings than a reduction in other incomes, then the inflation would go farther.

As we saw in the last chapter, in inflations which involve a struggle for income there is usually a redistribution of income between active groups, depending on the relative speed and strength of their reactions. If the weak reactors save a rather small proportion of their income, while strong reactors save a large proportion, a redistribution of income toward the strong reactors reduces total demand, and slows down inflation and stops it at a lower level of prices than otherwise would be the case. If slow reactors save a relatively small proportion of their income, and quick reactors a large part, the process of inflation is slowed down, but the final equilibrium level of prices is uninfluenced, because this redistribution (unlike that between strong and weak reactors) depends for its existence on the continuing presence of price rises.

Generally speaking it is probably right to say that inflations tend to depress the real incomes of the relatively poor, who save relatively little; to the extent that this generalization applies, the redistribution of income effects tend to slow inflation down.

There is one case where this uneven incidence of inflation is particularly significant. If the government relies for a large part of its income on progressive income taxes, then its income rises more than in proportion to the price level, because more and more people are brought into higher and higher income tax brackets as the general level of prices and income rises. It is likely that government expenditure will not rise at this same rapid rate: if that is so the government comes to save more and more in real terms. This is a reduction in pressure of demand for goods and services, which tends to slow down any kind of inflation.

The last factor which may lead to a slowing down and ending of inflation is the one we mentioned in considering the Quantity Theory. Inflation can continue only if there is sufficient money. If the supply of money is restricted, say by central bank action, interest rates will rise and this will encourage saving and discourage investment, leading to reduced pressure of demand. Moreover, monetary scarcity can, if it is extreme, work in other ways; there may not even be sufficient money for transactions purposes at the current level of prices. People therefore try to sell goods and avoid buying them, in order to acquire more money so that their transactions balances become large enough. These forces again operate to reduce prices, or to slow down the rate of price increases. All of this is simply an example of the fact that any appropriate control action by the government or its authorities can lead to an ending of inflation.

The Speed of Inflation

It was convenient to consider the ending of inflation before considering its speed, because it necessarily follows that if inflation comes to an end it must slow down as the new equilibrium is approached. It may also be noted that the forces we have considered which can stop inflation may be too weak to bring it to an end, but may still be able to slow it down.

It remains to be seen what other factors determine the speed of inflation, which is most conveniently measured as the percentage rate of price rise per year. We can start by asking what determines the speed of inflation in its early stages. The actual speed then becomes less and less if the forces leading to a new equilibrium are effective; on the other hand there may well be reasons which lead to an acceleration of the rate of price rises, and we shall have to look into them.

For the moment, we shall ignore these forces leading to an acceleration of inflation. We can then conveniently distinguish five considerations that are of importance in determining the speed of an inflationary process in its early stages. They are, firstly, the size of the initial impetus which set the process going; secondly, the speed with which reactions are made to changes in prices and money income; thirdly, how fully any defensive reactions attempt to restore the original position, and how far the attempts at restoration only go part of the way; fourthly, the size of the groups which are reacting defensively in relation to the total size of the economy; and fifthly, the accounting conventions that are employed by firms in valuing their assets.

The relevance of each of the five influences mentioned above will be fairly clear. In the first place, the size of the initial impetus is of fundamental importance in determining the speed of the inflation, just as it was an essential condition for the existence of the process; it alone determines the percentage rise in prices at the very first stage of all. It is fairly obvious that a bigger initial rise in demand, or a bigger increase in the prices or wages demanded by suppliers of goods or services, or a given percentage increase demanded by a large industry or trade union, will in each case cause a bigger initial disturbance than a smaller impulse of the same kind. This larger impulse means a larger price or wage rise, in terms of the effect averaged out over the whole economy; this in turn means that a bigger adjustment will be made by all those groups which react (either passively or defensively) to the price and income changes.

The next influence also is quite obvious in its effects, at least in principle. If the interval that elapses before reactions are made to changes in prices and money incomes is long, then the rate of rise of price rises will be smaller. This can be seen if we compare two cases where the initial impulse led to a 10 per cent rise in the price level. Now the reaction may well be that all income recipients in the country raise their selling prices by 10 per cent. But a great deal depends on how quickly this happens. If they make this reaction at the end of one month, the annual percentage rate of rise of prices is clearly much greater than if they only make this reaction at the end of, say, six months or one year.

The third influence on the speed of an inflationary process has been mentioned already, but has not yet been given full consideration. This arises from the possibility that defensive reactions may attempt only partially to restore the former level of real income or real expenditure. For example, trade union wage negotiation may be such that wage rises are granted which compensate for part, but not the whole, of the rise in prices which has just occurred. Government expenditure may be increased in money terms as prices rise, but only by a smaller proportion than the price rise, so that expenditure in real terms falls. Firms may not attempt to restore real profits or real investment expenditure fully, but only partially. When these defensive reactions are only partial, instead of trying fully to restore preceding conditions, the price rises that are engendered are smaller, and the process is slower.

The fourth influence on the speed of inflation arises from the fact that some groups may not be able to maintain their real income or real expenditure against the effects of price rises. This is necessarily the case with those groups (rentiers, pensioners, some salary earners) whose incomes are definitely fixed in terms of money. Legal action can frequently lengthen this list—for example, rent control can fix the incomes of landlords in terms of money. The more there are of these groups, the less will be the speed of inflation, because these groups are not raising the prices of the things they sell. The house rent element in the cost of living is constant, so that a given percentage rise in the prices of other things entering into the cost of living means a smaller percentage rise in the total index of the cost of living (including rent). Similarly, the burden on firms of fixed interest payments becomes less; real profits can be maintained without rises in selling prices in the same proportion as rises in labor and raw material costs.

The fifth influence on the speed of inflation depends upon the accounting conventions used by firms. If they value their stock of capital (including both plant and equipment and also raw materials, etc.) at original cost in their accounts when prices are rising, the profits that will be shown in their accounts will be bigger than they are really earning. When the time comes for replacement of the equipment or materials, reserves that have been put by to cover their original cost will be inadequate to replace them. In effect, what happens is that this accounting convention causes certain sums which should logically be put aside for replacement to be regarded as profits. If those profits are distributed, or used for new investment, they lead to a bigger pressure of demand than if other accounting techniques had been followed, and profits had been smaller. Subsequently, of course, the firms which have been following these techniques may find themselves in difficulties because of lack of sufficient liquid reserves. Then their distributions of profits on their investment tend to need to be reduced below what they would otherwise be.

Acceleration of Inflation

We can now proceed to the last big group of questions concerned with the inflationary process: what are the influences that may lead to the process speeding up or slowing down in relation to the initial rate of price rise? The influences that are usually important in practice as causes of an acceleration of the speed of the process of inflation arise from the reactions of the various active groups to their increased awareness of the continuing series of price rises. For the most part this operates in three ways: firstly by the ending of so-called 'money illusion'; secondly by making allowances to an increasing extent for future expected rises in prices; and thirdly by taking advantage of expected price rises.

'Money illusion' is an influence that may operate when relatively small price rises have taken place after a period in which the value of money has been rather stable. In such circumstances, firms and households may have become so accustomed to the constant value of money, that they continue to treat a dollar as buying a constant quantity of goods, even after prices have risen so that it now buys less. A household that has received an income of $100 and spent $90 over a period of years may continue to be content to do the same, even when $100 will only buy what $80 used to buy; and even though a fall in income to $80 with prices constant would have caused the household to spend the whole of its income and to save none; there is the illusion that everything is still as it was before. Such influences soon collapse when big price rises are experienced; the brake which 'money illusion' puts on demand for goods and on demand for higher money incomes disintegrates as experience shows how illusory is an assumption of a constant value of money.[1]

The second group of factors comes about because, as people become accustomed to the existence of steadily rising prices, they speed up their defensive reactions, try to forestall the effects of future price rises on their income and expenditure, and also start to take account of the effect of inflation on the value of the wealth they hold. The adjustments in expenditure and in the prices at which transactors are willing to sell may well tend to be made faster as people come to realize that they are losing for the whole of the time in which they fail to adjust their incomes and expenditure to a new level of prices. What is more, they come to be aware that prices will continue to rise, largely through their action in trying to defend themselves against the last rise; they therefore try to make allowance for these further rises. For example, trade unions become aware that rises in wages lead to further price rises; they therefore try to get still bigger wage rises in order to allow for the expected rise in prices. But, of course, if profit receivers are also unwilling to accept any reduction in their real incomes the consequence is simply that the subsequent price rises are still larger, and the speed of inflation is accelerated.

In addition to this speeding up of defensive reactions with regard to real income and expenditure, another kind of reaction will occur when people come to expect a continuation of inflation. This concerns their wealth.[2] Those forms of wealth whose value or yield is fixed in terms of money, such as bonds and money itself, come to

---

[1] The expression 'money illusion' has been overworked by economists; it is frequently used to describe situations where no illusion exists whatsoever. For example, workers may be willing to accept a 1 per cent cut in their real income as a result of a 1 per cent rise in prices, whereas they would not accept a 1 per cent cut in their money wages, with prices constant. This may well be true, and yet involve no illusion; the reason is simply that contracts are usually made for a money wage and not a real wage, and that it is difficult to break contracts or to ask for their revision in face of relatively small changes in circumstances.

[2] It is the relationship we have already considered in Chapter 2—the 'deflationary motive' for holding money and the 'inflationary motive' for avoiding holding money.

be less attractive ways of holding wealth when it is expected that money is going to lose its value in terms of goods and services. Instead, people tend to try to hold wealth in real forms—e.g. pictures, antiques, buildings. The extreme position of this tendency comes when prices are rising so fast that no one is willing to hold more money than the barest minimum needed for transaction purposes, because money is losing its value hourly. This condition, of hyperinflation, is one in which there is complete collapse of the monetary system. It was experienced in Germany after the First World War, and in China, Greece, and Hungary after the Second World War.

The effect of unwillingness to save is an addition to the pressure of demand, which causes the price rise to go still faster. Even when conditions of hyperinflation have not been reached, and money is still held willingly for transactions purposes, this unwillingness to add to savings in the form of claims may be a serious factor in adding to inflationary pressure: the post-war years in France were a case in point.

This effect on willingness to save is closely linked with the last of the three main groups of ways in which an inflation may speed up—people may take advantage of the inflation and the price rises they come to expect. Speculation about the continuation of price rises becomes an active force; anyone who holds inventories of goods can be fairly confident that he can make a big money profit by reselling them in the future. Such activities are particularly attractive to people who can borrow money (from the banks, for example) to finance speculative holdings of inventories. This is another addition to the pressure of demand: it is an addition to investment. The demand for goods to go into inventories can be a fertile source of pressure which makes prices rise faster and faster.

Finally, it may be noted that these tendencies to an acceleration of inflation may be so strong that they prevent the situation from ever reaching a new equilibrium, even though such an equilibrium appears possible in terms of comparative statics. There may be sufficiently large passive groups whose money income or expenditure remain unchanged, and nevertheless a new equilibrium is never attained. This happens because the process of change itself induces further inflationary forces; it is an example of the fact pointed out in Chapter 6, that comparative static analysis tells us what change in the equilibrium level of income follows a given disturbance, but it does not tell us how the new equilibrium is approached, or even whether it can ever be attained. It may be the case that these accelerating forces are so strong that they keep the inflation going indefinitely.

Some Suggested Reading

The books and articles mentioned in the reading lists for Chapters 19 and 20 are also relevant here. There is also a considerable number of studies of hyperinflation, notably C. Bresciani Turroni, *The Economics of Inflation* (London, 1937), which deals with Germany in the early 'twenties. Another study of the same period is F. D. Graham, *Exchanges, Prices and Production in Hyperinflation: Germany 1920-23* (Princeton, 1930). A theoretical study is the contribution of P. Cagan called 'The Monetary Dynamics of Inflation' to *Studies in the Quantity Theory of Money*, edited by M. Friedman (Chicago, 1956).

22

The Full Employment Zone

In this chapter we shall return to further consideration of a subject that was mentioned in Chapter 18, but which we have avoided in our consideration of the theory of inflation in the last three chapters. This subject arises from the fact that changes in effective demand can simultaneously affect the level of prices and the level of output in a country. In other words it is false to assume there is one precise point of full employment below which the effect of increases in effective demand show themselves solely as output changes (as a result of the operation of the multiplier process), and above which the effects of increases in effective demand show themselves solely as price changes (as a result of the operation of the inflationary process). As an approximation such an assumption is useful; it has allowed us to observe the main features of these two distinct processes, without being swamped by the complications that arise when they are found side by side. But now we must face these complications.

In doing so, it will be necessary to carry on the argument at a somewhat lower level of abstraction than in the earlier theoretical chapters. The reason is fundamentally the one that we have run up against earlier. This is a book on macro-economics and ignores growth theory; the problems we are trying to face here lie in the rather uneasy border territory between micro- and macro-economics and between macro-economic and growth theory.

As we noted in Chapter 5, even when there is a considerable amount of unemployment in manufacturing industry, there is some tendency for the level of prices in general to rise when effective demand increases. This occurs mainly because of rises in prices of primary products, and particularly of agricultural products.

As we have seen, these price rises have two major consequences. They tend to cause some rises in the prices of manufactured products, because of rises in the cost of their raw materials. The price rises, even in this zone where there is still extensive unemployment, spread around the whole economy. Secondly, these price rises make some people worse off. These are the people who were still in employment when the level of activity was very low, and who were continuing to receive an income which would buy a large amount because prices (particularly food prices) were very low. As the level of activity rises, and so demand for primary products and prices rise, these people find the income they are receiving will now buy less. Those individuals who were fully employed even when there was a great deal of unemployment in the economy as a whole are the ones who suffer when prices start to rise. Wage earners who remain in employment even when trade is very bad, and most salary earners, are the most important examples of this group of people, whose standard of living tends to fall when the level of activity rises.

Why is it that these groups do not attempt to defend themselves against falling real income, when there is an upward movement in level of output and income in the country as a whole? The answer is, of course, that to some small extent they do. To that extent, the price rises are still further propagated, and so there is some slight element of the inflationary process of the kind described in Chapter 20, even in circumstances where there is still substantial unemployment in all branches of manufacturing industry. In general, however, such reactions are so slight that they can be ignored, as we in fact did in earlier chapters. Usually no effective defensive reactions are made by these groups until the level of unemployment has fallen rather low. On the side of salary earners strong defensive reactions are not common; traditionally, these earnings are rather sticky in terms of money, and generally speaking large price changes are needed before there is much effect on the level of salaries.

As for the reason why wage earners do not defend themselves against falling standards of living, there are several which are important. One is the existence of 'money illusion,' to which we have already paid attention; little or no reaction may occur to a relatively small change in real income that arises because of a change in prices, although the same change in real income brought about by a change in the money wage rate (with prices constant) would evoke strong reactions. Another reason is that conflicts of interest within the trade unions may often prevent those wage earners who are in employment in times of extensive unemployment from trying to defend themselves against the effects of rises in the general level of activity. In each union there will be one group of wage earners who consider it to be in their interests to press hard for higher wages as output and prices rise, while there will be another group which is uncertain. The members of the former group are those who were in employment even when unemployment was very high; the members of the latter group are those who are less certain of their jobs or who are still unemployed but hope for work. The members of the latter group will be inclined to question the wisdom of a policy of pushing for higher wages, because they may fear that higher wages will make their jobs more precarious. In addition, circumstances will frequently be such that the members of the group who have secure jobs and therefore some interest in pressing for higher money wages may not consider the matter of very great importance. In the conditions we are assuming, price rises will not have been very great, and so real wage rates will not have fallen greatly. At the same time, even this group will often find that it can benefit from such circumstances as ability to earn more overtime pay. All told, the tendency is for trade unions not to press very hard for increases in money wage rates as long as there is still a fair amount of unemployment.

On the side of the demand for labor, there are equally cogent reasons why wages show little tendency to rise when the level of activity rises in the zone where there is still considerable unemployment. Businessmen will in general be unwilling to pay higher wages, because to do so would increase their costs at a time when it is doubtful whether they can increase their selling prices; or at least if they could increase their selling prices it might be unprofitable to do so because the level of sales of the particular products they make could be expected to fall off.

Thus the position below the full employment zone is that there is no appreciable tendency for money wage rates to rise. At the same time, the trade unions are generally sufficiently powerful to resist any wage cuts. The net effect, therefore, is that money wage rates do not vary appreciably below the full employment zone.

The situation becomes very different when unemployment levels in some branches of industry have become very low. Four kinds

of change act in such a way as to make price and wage rises significant. In the first place the rise in primary prices and the induced
rises in the prices of manufactured output continue. Secondly, technological conditions impose sharp rises in marginal costs as full
capacity output is approached. Thirdly, trade unions push more
actively for increased money wages, in order to defend the standard
of living of those at work against rising prices. Finally, businessmen
are more willing to grant wage increases, because market conditions
are such that they believe that they can now easily pass on quite
substantial increases of costs to their customers.

It is clear that when these price and wage rises start to be significant the economy is on the edge of an inflationary situation of
the kind discussed in Chapters 20 and 21: for one thing, price rises
automatically induce further price rises. For another, we see that
both the trade unions and businessmen are in a powerful position
to defend themselves against the effects of rises in the cost of the
things they buy; the one group by demanding and obtaining higher
money wages and the other by demanding higher prices.[1] A cumulative inflationary process is clearly a big danger, once the full
employment zone is entered. We must, therefore, look more closely
at the nature of that zone.

Broadly speaking, a characteristic of an economy in which there
is a reasonable degree of structural balance between the different
industries is that a position of full employment and full capacity
output will be reached more or less simultaneously in all industries.
Even in an economy which has a good structural balance, this will
only be approximately true. For one thing, there is no single position of full employment and full capacity operation for an industry,
or for a firm, any more than there is for the economy as a whole.
Rather, there is a zone in which the marginal cost curves of the
firms in the industry are rising sharply.

Another reason why full employment (even if it can be sharply
defined) may not be reached simultaneously in all industries is
that changing patterns of production and consumption are always

---

[1] Each defensive action is equally responsible for any inflationary process
that is induced. It is an interesting sociological and psychological question why
the defensive actions of trade unions are more usually held responsible for inflation than the defensive actions of businessmen; but as a matter of pure
analysis both groups are responsible.

taking place, so that some industries are declining and some expanding. Since it takes time to change the amount of labor and capital in an industry, some industries will reach full employment rather quickly when there is a rising level of demand for goods in general, while others may stay depressed even when most of the economy is fully employed.

A third reason probably also exists which explains why some industries may reach full employment before others. In an economy where there is a marked trade cycle, with big fluctuations in the level of activity between boom and slump, the tendency is for fluctuations in the level of activity to be particularly sharp in the industries producing capital equipment.[2] One way in which these industries seem to react to the violent swings in their demand is to make their customers wait a long time for deliveries when trade is good.[3] If an economy has become adjusted to such a situation, it may well be that full capacity working is reached earlier in the boom in these equipment producing industries than in the rest of the economy: further expansion in demand for the goods of these industries simply leads to a lengthening of their order books,[4] while rising demand elsewhere still leads to rises in output.

Of course, if the economy of a country is seriously unbalanced (as in post-war Italy and Germany), there may be full employment in some parts of the economy and extensive unemployment in others. Such circumstances make the problem of the full employment zone particularly intractable. In time, they can be dealt with by structural adjustments, as by moving surplus labor to places or occupations where it is short. Such adjustments can be difficult and take a long time. They are not, however, our concern here; we shall only consider countries where these factors do not dominate the situation. There must always be some unemployment in an economy relying on free markets, because of the time taken to move between jobs and because work is not always available in the same places as a surplus of labor. In a structurally balanced economy, such frictional unemployment will be very small—perhaps even less than 1 per cent of the working population. In such an economy extreme

---

[2] An explanation of this fact will be provided in Chapters 23 and 24.
[3] More will be said on this in Chapters 23 and 24.
[4] Which will also prevent some orders from coming forward.

labor shortage in one part of the economy and extensive unemployment in other parts are not to be found simultaneously.

Changes in Prices and Output in the Full Employment Zone

We can consider what happens when the demand for the product of one industry reaches such levels that no more labor is available at the existing wage rate; other industries are assumed not quite to have reached this position. Then businessmen in that industry have two courses clearly open to them. They can either take longer in filling orders or they can demand higher prices for their products. If they choose the former alternative, and lengthen their order books, then they spread the demand over a longer period, and they also choke off some demand (because some purchasers would rather buy something else that is immediately obtainable). Alternatively they may choose to raise prices, by an amount just large enough to choke off the excess demand. If they do so they can afford to pay higher money wages. What is more, they will be under firm pressure to pay higher wages; as unemployment percentages fall to fairly low levels, but even before unemployment has practically all disappeared, pressure from the unions for higher money rates becomes stronger. More and more members of the unions feel that they would benefit from higher wages, and fewer and fewer think that they would lose—the union comes to feel itself in a strong bargaining position.

If the employers in this particular industry with which we are concerned grant increases in money wages of the same proportionate size as the increases in prices they charge, then their percentage gross profit margins remain the same. This means that, in terms of money, profit margins rise in the same proportion as the rise in money wages. Now, as we are assuming that this industry arrived at the full employment position a little before other industries, there are no corresponding rises in other prices and wages. One consequence of this we have already seen: demand for our industry's products is choked off, because its prices rise relatively to other prices. The other major consequences are that the real incomes of participants in this industry (i.e. wage earners and gross profit recipients) rise. Their money earnings rise, while there have been no corresponding rises in prices of goods produced by other industries. Participants in this industry have gained at the expense of the rest of the economy, through the shift in relative prices.

Two implications of this may be noted. For one thing, it encourages defensive reactions on the parts of the losers—i.e. prices and wages tend to rise to some extent in the rest of the economy. Secondly, it is a reason why productive resources tend to be attracted from other industries; labor may be attracted in by the higher real wage rates, and some businessmen may be encouraged to produce the goods of the fully employed industry.

These shifts in productive resources combine with changes in demand and the increasingly strong defensive reactions to cause the price rises to spread throughout the economy. Labor is attracted away from other industries, so that their maximum possible level of output falls. Demand shifts to the products of other industries, so that there is further pressure on their output. Moreover, falling standards of living among those at work in other industries cause a strengthening of their defensive reactions. This, then, is one side of the story. Once conditions of full capacity and very low unemployment are reached in some sectors of the economy, price rises become more marked and show increasingly strong tendencies to lead to other price rises. Experience suggests that this is likely to happen in countries such as the United States and Britain when the average percentage of unemployment throughout industry falls below 2 to 3 per cent. In countries such as Italy, with serious structural problems, the critical percentage may be much larger. Moreover, the critical percentage is not stable. It depends, among other things, upon conditions in the primary producing sector. If harvests are bad, or if primary output is low for other reasons, food and raw material prices will be particularly high, and real wage rates and other industrial sector incomes will be particularly small. These abnormally small incomes may encourage defensive reactions by the groups concerned, in an attempt to maintain or restore their real incomes; this leads to inflationary pressure, which would not have arisen if conditions in the primary producing sector had been more favorable.

It is merely one side of the picture, however, to point out how inflationary price rises may become cumulative in the full employment zone. The other side is that the developments just considered cause the inflationary pressure to spread out more and more evenly over the whole economy. Demand is diverted toward industries where there is some spare capacity available, and supply tends to increase in the industries where price rises are sharpest. If the initial expansionary impulse was relatively small, the inflationary pressure may be contained fairly quickly, by being channeled in such a way as to take up spare capacity.

In addition, increased delays in deliveries may also limit a tendency to inflation which appears in the full employment zone. Those industries which lengthen their order books after a certain point do not pass on increases of demand that they receive; instead they store them up. This will, for a time, weaken inflationary tendencies if the person placing the order holds cash or some other claim until the goods are delivered.[5] Of course, they can only do this for a time. Firms cannot lengthen their order books indefinitely but must at some stage increase their prices, if the excess demand continues for long enough. Moreover, if their order books get too long, some demand may be diverted away from these industries to industries where increased demand does lead to increased prices.

It appears, therefore, that there are four sets of forces at work in the full employment zone. Firstly, increased demand still partly shows itself as demand for products whose supply can still be increased at present prices; the ordinary multiplier process continues. Secondly, increased demand tends also to lead to price rises, which show an increasing tendency to propagate themselves around the system, as unemployment levels become lower and lower and shortages become greater; the inflationary process becomes more and more powerful. Thirdly, there is some tendency for changes in the relationships between different prices to lead to diversion of demand and supply in such a way that cumulative price rises are inhibited, as demand is directed to sectors where supply is available. Fourthly, there may be some storing up of demand as a result of lengthening of order books.

The full employment zone is, therefore, one in which price rises are likely, but do not necessarily lead to cumulative inflation. All the same, if on average, conditions are such that the level of unemployment is so low that the economy is in the full employment zone,

---

[5] The weakening is most likely to be effective in the industries producing capital equipment, etc.; a firm which is planning to invest in a certain kind of machinery is not likely to spend money on something else if the machinery is not immediately available.

the general bias will be toward rising price levels. There is a sort of ratchet effect in operation; when unemployment is somewhat below whatever happens to be the current critical level at which wages and prices would remain constant, then wages and prices rise, but if unemployment is rather above this level, wages and prices do not show a corresponding tendency to fall. Since the level of unemployment certainly cannot always be precisely maintained at this critical level (both because the critical level itself varies and because it is impossible to maintain the level of unemployment precisely constant), there must be some years when unemployment is so small that wages and prices tend to rise, even if unemployment is on the average being kept at the critical level. In other words, there is a bias to secular inflation built into present-day industrial economies, unless the average level of unemployment is maintained fairly high.

This somewhat pessimistic conclusion is reinforced by two features of most modern industrial economics. One is the fact that labor productivity rises much faster in some sectors of the economy (e.g. industry) than in others (e.g. the service trades); in some sectors productivity may not rise at all. It is convenient to assume an economy with two sectors—one where productivity rises and one where it does not rise. Now, if more wages rise at the same rate as productivity in the first sector (so that prices remain constant in that sector [6]), they are very likely indeed to drag up wages in the other sector, through ordinary demand and supply processes. But if that happens prices must rise in the second sector,[6] and the average level of prices rises. Since wages usually do seem to rise at the same rate as productivity in industries where productivity is rising fast, there is clearly a big danger of a bias toward price inflation.

The second feature of modern economies is that trade unions and businessmen realize that the government cannot long survive politically if it fails to maintain a high level of employment. Consequently, they may be insistent in their demands for higher wages or prices, and very insistent indeed in their resistance to wage and price cuts, even in a period of relatively high unemployment—

---

[6] Assuming constant gross profit margins.

because they believe the government will not allow the situation to last.

All of this suggests that some inflation is likely to persist unless unemployment is maintained for long periods at levels which will probably seem intolerably high politically. At this point, the wheel of this chapter has turned full circle, and we are back at the point which we glanced at in the first paragraph—namely, the meaning of the expression 'full employment.' The analysis of the full employment zone that has been made in this chapter has shown the limits of the usefulness of the approximation we had made in earlier chapters, that below a certain level of unemployment, all changes in effective demand showed themselves solely as price changes, and above a certain level of unemployment, all changes in effective demand showed themselves solely as changes in the level of activity. But in addition to the limited (though considerable) value of this approach, it now appears that it is difficult to choose any point at all which can reasonably be described as being *the* position of full employment. When account is taken of the existence of a *zone* of full employment within which both cumulative price and real income changes take place, any choice of a particular point of full employment must be to some extent arbitrary.

This is not to deny that it may frequently be useful to refer to particular conditions as being those of full employment, even though it is accepted that analytically no point can be defined below which changes in demand affect output alone and above which they affect price alone. Generally speaking, however, such choice of a particular set of conditions as being one of full employment usually involves more or less explicit value judgments; there is an implication that 'full employment' in the sense so defined is desirable, while less than 'full' employment and over-'full' employment as so defined are less desirable states.

SOME SUGGESTED READING

This important topic has received very little treatment by economists recently—largely because to deal with it mathematically is extremely difficult. The present-day reader will, however, find some enlightening thoughts on this question in the works of some of the more sophisticated pre-Keynesian writings. The 'classical' economists were mainly concerned with circumstances such as those we find in the full employment zone—a concern which at the time they wrote was frequently disarmingly irrelevant. Examples of the most sophisticated writings are D. H. Robertson, *Money*, 6th edition (New York, 1948) and his *Essays in Monetary Theory* (London, 1940); also K. Wicksell, *Interest and Prices* (London, 1936).

V

STABILITY AND INSTABILITY

23

The Determination of the Level of Fixed Investment

We must now look much more deeply into the factors which determine the level of investment. In Part II, we considered the effects of a new invention on the level of fixed investment plans and we also looked at the effects of interest rate changes, in the context of the very simple economic and financial system within whose framework the argument of Part II was conducted. The time has now come to bring the whole argument much nearer to reality. In particular, we must consider in more detail how the cost and availability of funds will influence investment decisions and how changes in the level of output also affect investment.

It will be convenient to restrict our consideration to fixed investment,[1] and within that, to concentrate on industrial investment. All the same, it must be remembered that there is also a great deal of social and non-industrial investment, such as the building of houses, roads, and schools. Probably the most important determinants of the level of this kind of investment are considerations of the general growth of the economy (including population growth), the rate of interest (because such investments are frequently long-lived), and considerations that can only be described as broadly 'political' (such as general social policy—e.g. slum clearance and government policy for economic stabilization, which will be considered in Chapter 25).

Turning now to fixed industrial and commercial investment, it is easy to provide a formal statement of the factors which determine its level. Investment can be expected to be planned and to take

---

[1] We have already seen, in Chapter 6, something of the effects of output changes on the level of inventories.

place, if businessmen think that the return they will receive (the marginal efficiency of investment) will be at least as big as the marginal cost of raising funds to finance the investment. In itself this statement is not very enlightening—but at least it points to the two main groups of questions with which we must concern ourselves. On the one hand, we must look at the forces determining the demand by businessmen for investment goods and for the funds to finance their purchase. On the other hand, we must look at the supply of these funds.

The Costs of Financing Investment

It will be convenient to consider the supply side first and then later to move over to the demand side. In our simple economy in Part II, the matter of the supply of funds for financing investment by firms was a very simple one. We assumed that all financing of new investment was by borrowing, done by issuing long-dated securities at the current rate of interest; at the same time replacement of equipment as it wore out was financed out of current depreciation allowances. These assumptions were a convenient initial approach to reality—but we can now move much nearer toward it.

One step in this movement is to abandon the assumption of Part II that firms always at least maintained their holdings of real wealth constant; they replaced equipment as it wore out. In such cases 'net' investment may be zero (if no net addition is being made to the capital stock) but gross investment is taking place, to the extent that new machines are being installed for replacement purposes. In this chapter we shall see that firms may not necessarily think it worth while to replace equipment as it wears out. In cases when no capital equipment is being replaced, gross investment is zero. In Part II of this book 'investment' meant 'net investment' in the sense distinguished here. In the rest of this chapter and in the next the expression 'investment' will mean *gross* investment. Correspondingly, 'saving' now comes to mean gross saving, instead of net saving as in earlier chapters; it comes to include depreciation allowances put aside by firms to cover the cost of replacing machines, etc. as they wear out.

The fact that firms need not necessarily make immediate use of their depreciation allowances to finance replacement of equipment as it wears out means that the sharp distinction drawn in Part II between the methods of financing net investment (by bond issues) and replacement (from depreciation allowances) does not apply in reality. Depreciation allowances and bond issues are both sources of funds which may be used to finance any item in gross investment that a firm may think appropriate.

In addition, there are three other main sources of funds which firms may use to finance fixed investment. They may in the first place use earnings which they have accumulated and which have not been distributed to shareholders. Secondly, they might use short-term loans such as bank loans—although (as we have seen) it is not usually considered desirable to do this, and most bankers are unwilling to make short-term loans to buy fixed equipment, except as an interim measure until long-term financing can be arranged. Lastly, a firm can finance fixed investment by issuing new equity shares, either to present shareholders or to the general public.

The most important consequence of this wide range of possibilities is that the simple analysis in Part II of the supply funds to finance fixed investment does, in one respect, provide a misleading picture. In that analysis, the supply of funds was regarded as being perfectly elastic at the current rate of interest, so that if a firm saw very large investment opportunities that would cover interest changes, depreciation allowances, and (one should now add) taxes, it could borrow a very large amount in a very short time to take advantage of these opportunities. But in fact, the supply of funds is not perfectly elastic in this way.

The costs to a firm (in terms of the other opportunities foregone) of using depreciation allowances and retained earnings to finance (gross) investment are relatively small. Broadly speaking, they are equal to the return that would accrue if these funds were used to buy claims, such as government bonds. The cost is, therefore, more or less equivalent to the current long-term interest rate.

When it comes to the point of using outside money to help finance a firm's fixed investment, the effective cost to the firm can easily be substantially more than the market long-term interest rate. For one thing, lenders are not likely to be willing to lend at any one time very large amounts in relation to the total size of the firm's operations. If the venture should go wrong, there are big risks to the lenders in financing too rapid expansion. At best, the firm can only hope to get really large-scale finance, in relation to the current scale of its operations, if it is willing to pay abnormally high interest rates.

In practice, few firms choose to use outside loan finance to expand as rapidly as this. If a firm commits itself to too many fixed charges, in the form of interest payments, it may find that its profits fluctuate to unduly low levels if business conditions turn out to be un- expectedly bad, and it may find that it has to draw heavily on its cash and other liquid reserves to meet its fixed commitments. If business is really bad, it may find itself forced onto the mercies of its creditors, so that the management loses its freedom of action. In the last analysis, too much reliance on loan finance may force it into bankruptcy. For all these reasons, firms are likely to regard the real costs of relying heavily on loan finance for fixed investment as being considerably higher than the actual interest cost. In formal terms, one can say that the elasticity of supply of funds for financing investment is, after a certain point, quite low.

Somewhat similar considerations apply in the case of reliance on the issue of new equity shares to finance expansion. An issue of new equity shares will reduce earnings per share on existing shares unless total earnings per share (both retained and distrib- uted) are expected to have a yield at least as large as the ratio of the firm's average expected future earnings to the issue price of the new shares. Only if management expects an improvement in total earnings per share are they likely to be willing to finance new investment by equity issues. But since total earnings per share are typically much larger than profits distributed per share, the neces- sary return to the firm must be much larger than the current yield to shareholders on equities. As a general rule, firms are probably rather unwilling to use equity finance unless they expect a yield of 8% to 10%—in addition to the costs of floating a new issue.

The total effect of all these considerations is that the supply curve of funds available to a firm in a given period (say of one year) is probably something like the curve in Figure 19. The range OA covers self-finance and depreciation allowances; the range AB covers finance by fixed interest loans; the remainder covers equity financing.

One important implication of all this analysis is that the rate of profits that has been earned by the firm in the relatively recent past is one of the main determinants of investment decisions. For one thing, high profits mean that the market price of the company's shares of stock is likely to be high; this means that further stock issues can be made on terms favorable to the company. For another, high profits make additional investment particularly attractive to a firm, because it can buy additional equipment with some of the

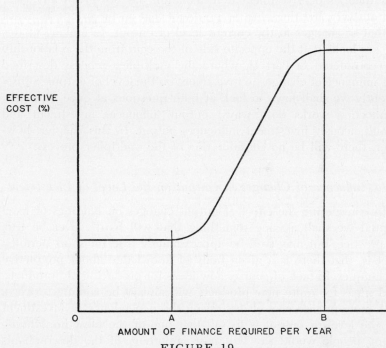

EFFECTIVE
COST (%)

O   A   B

AMOUNT OF FINANCE REQUIRED PER YEAR

FIGURE 19

profits, instead of having to issue bonds or stocks. As we have already seen,[2] such self-financing by large-scale industry has been very important in recent years, while it has always been a major source of expansion for small-scale businesses.

Moreover, there is a direct influence from the rate of profits operating on the side of the demand of firms for investment goods and investible funds, as well as these influences operating on the side of the supply of funds for investment. A high current level of profits is very likely to induce a belief that profits will continue to

---

[2] In Chapter 9.

be high in the future; an atmosphere is created which is conducive to expansion.

This effect of profits on plans by firms to invest is hard to distinguish from the effects of output on investment plans, which will be our concern in the rest of this chapter. Statistical testing of various theories of investment determination has not given any clear cut answers; but there can be no doubt that an important influence is that of changes in the current level of output. In looking at this we are looking at the opposite side of the coin from the relationship we considered in Part II, where the multiplier process described the influence of changes in investment on the level of output. Subsequently we shall have to look at both questions at once, since the connection works both ways: output influences investment and simultaneously investment influences output. In this chapter, however, there will be no consideration of the multiplier process.

The Influence of Changes in Output on the Level of Investment

In considering the effect of output changes on holdings of fixed capital we shall assume something that will hardly ever be true in practice, but may well be approximately true for short periods: that is, that there is a given body of knowledge about productive techniques. In fact, of course, new ideas for producing old products, and ideas for quite new products will always be coming forward.

A more precise way of expressing the dependence of investment on the level of output is to say that one of the most important—many people would say the most important—of the determinants of firms' plans for gross fixed investment is the relationship between their level of output and their stock of fixed capital equipment. With given conditions of technical knowledge and of the other possible variables whose effects we are temporarily excluding, there is some quantity of fixed capital that firms consider is most advantageous for producing a given level of output. By 'most advantageous' we mean most profitable, after allowing for the influence of other factors which no doubt enter into businessmen's decisions, such as laziness and desire for power.

This optimum proportion between fixed capital and the level of output is one which people outside a firm will find difficult to define exactly; fortunately that does not matter for our purpose. It is reasonably certain that it will be one at which available fixed equipment is reasonably fully employed, but not one where it is working right to the limit. Except for quite short periods firms are unlikely to want to produce the maximum that is technically possible from a given plant; such a policy allows no flexibility to allow for sudden temporary rushes of orders or for breakdowns, and it becomes very expensive, by causing excessive strain on the planning ability of management Again, working at such pressure may make regular maintenance work difficult; it may also make labor very expensive, because higher rates have to be paid for overtime.

The consequence is that if a firm's output is so large that the existing plant is overstrained, and is working at a level of capacity which is beyond the optimum, then it will seem worth while to add to the total quantity of fixed equipment; that is, to invest more than is necessary to replace the fixed capital that is wearing out. On the other hand, if output is so small that existing plant is under-utilized, in the sense that it is not being used to the optimum extent, then it is likely that some of the plant will not be replaced when it wears out. Of course, if the present level of output is regarded as a purely temporary aberration, because of a very temporary shortage or glut of sales, fixed investment will not be affected in this way. But in most industries producing consumer goods, the current level of sales or of output usually gives the best single indication to the businessman of his future sales prospects, and so is usually a very strong influence when he decides on the level of his fixed capital equipment.

Industries which themselves produce capital equipment, such as shipbuilding and machine tool making, are in a rather different position; it is quite usual, when trade is good, for them to keep their customers waiting quite a long time: in traders' terminology, their order books lengthen. The length of order books for fixed capital equipment has a strong influence on the investment plans of producers of fixed capital goods. For example, shipbuilders will generally be more inclined to build new shipyards if there are many orders outstanding for ships, than if current output is high but the waiting list is short.[3]

---

[3] This, again, is almost certainly not the whole story; we shall return to this matter of fixed investment in industries producing capital goods later. It should also be noted that not all capital goods industries lengthen their order books substantially when trade is booming; house builders probably do not, although

We can now investigate more fully the influence of changes in the level of output of the consumer goods industries on investment in fixed capital equipment by firms in those industries. Let us first consider what occurs if the shoemaking industry [4] happens initially to be in a position where it owns more fixed capital equipment (in the form of shoemaking machinery, etc.) than is ideally appropriate for the present level of output. In such circumstances there is no reason for the firms in that industry to order any shoemaking machinery. Gross investment by the firms in fixed capital will therefore be zero. Firms own more machinery than they really want: in the absence of changes of technique and the other factors we have already excluded, they will have no reason to install any more machines, even though some are wearing out.

If the same level of output of shoes continues in the next month, once again these firms have no reason to invest in fixed capital. But there is one important change: all the machinery is one month older. Some machines that were almost worn out a month ago, when we first looked at the industry, have now been scrapped. The effect is that in the second month the industry owns rather less fixed capital than in the first month. This has an important consequence. If output is the same in the second month as in the first, the optimum amount of fixed capital is unchanged. Nevertheless, the surplus of actual capital equipment possessed over the optimum amount of capital equipment is less than in the first month. Similarly, if output, and therefore the optimum amount of equipment, remains unchanged between the second and third months, the gap between the actual amount of capital equipment and the optimum amount again becomes narrower.

Before looking at the implications of this, two objections that can be made to this formulation must be mentioned. In the first place, the equipment with which the industry finds itself may be 'bunched' in age; a particularly large part of it may well have been installed during one particular period of time, such as some past boom in shoemaking, or at a time when some new process had just been introduced. In some years, therefore, a great deal of equipment may be wearing out, and in other years, none at all. As far as a

---

in that case there is a similar effect, because it takes longer to get the job finished when trade is good.

[4] As an example of a consumer goods industry.

particular industry is concerned, this may be true and important.[5] What we are really concerned with, however, is change in investment by all industries and in all kinds of fixed equipment. The lives of different kinds of equipment differ so much that it is almost certain that, taking industry as a whole, past equipment is reaching physical old age at a fairly steady rate. Since the shoemaking industry is being taken as representative of all consumer goods industries, we can reasonably look upon shoemaking machinery as coming up for replacement at a steady rate.

The other objection, which can be mentioned only for the moment, is that the life of equipment is not a precise span. Leaving aside the fact that obsolescence is largely determined by technical innovations, there still remains a broad margin of time within which scrapping may or may not seem desirable. Decisions within that margin will largely be based on economic factors, to which we must return later.

Even if these two objections are allowed, the process under description remains broadly significant. What happens is that, sooner or later, so much equipment has been scrapped that the actual amount of capital equipment falls to the optimum amount for the given level of output. After this point, if output continues unchanged, purchase of new capital equipment will be needed to replace the part that wears out. Sooner or later, gross investment will take place, even although output does not change, and however much excess capacity there was originally.

We can now turn to the central point at issue in this chapter— what happens to plans for investment in fixed equipment when there is an alteration in the output of the consumer goods produced with that fixed equipment? In particular, what is the effect on investment in shoemaking machinery if the demand for shoes alters? A change in output, we have argued, usually leads businessmen to expect that the new level will continue, unless very obviously temporary factors are at work. It therefore leads to a change in the same direction in the optimum amount of capital equipment. If output increases, the optimum amount of equipment increases; if output falls, the optimum falls.

Let us consider the latter case first. If, for some reason, output

---

[5] It is probably an important element in cycles in house building.

falls, the optimum amount of equipment falls. This usually means that optimum equipment is less than the amount actually available; the industry finds itself in the position discussed a few paragraphs ago, and will for a time (but only for a time) let equipment wear out without replacing it.

The more interesting case is the effect of a rise in output. It is possible that this will have no immediate effect on purchases of shoemaking machines by the industry; the rise may still leave the level of output so low that desired capital is less than actual. But even in this case, the rise in output to a new level has an important effect: it brings the day so much the nearer when actual capital will equal the optimum (that is, the day when replacement will start again), because less equipment has to wear out before the actual amount of capital equipment sinks to the optimum level.

Frequently, the effects of a rise in the output of shoes on purchases of shoemaking machinery will be more immediate in time. Let us consider circumstances in which output of the finished product of the industry has been running at a steady level for some time, so that the actual amount of fixed capital is equal to the desired amount, and is being held constant by a steady flow of replacement as old equipment wears out. Gross fixed investment is running at a steady rate, which depends upon the amount of fixed equipment owned by the industry, and by its average life span. If the industry owns $4 million worth of fixed equipment with an average life span of 10 years, $400,000 worth will be replaced every year, or $100,000 worth every quarter. This is the level of gross fixed investment; on the other hand, net fixed investment is zero, because the industry is only just maintaining its real fixed wealth constant.

Now, if for some reason output increases, the industry will find itself with less fixed capital than is the optimum amount for that level of output. If the higher level of output is expected to continue, plans will be made to add to the total amount of fixed capital in the industry. It is perhaps reasonable to consider such plans as being made rather less frequently than plans to change the level of output in response to changes of sales [6] and inventories [7]; we can consider conveniently and fairly realistically that plans for fixed investment are made at less frequent intervals than the plans with

---

[6] Which in Chapter 6 we assumed to happen at the end of every week.
[7] Which in Chapter 6 we assumed to happen at the end of every month.

which we have been concerned so far. We can assume that fixed investment plans are revised every quarter, that is every three months or twelve weeks. At the end of the quarter in which the increase in sales and output started, plans are made by the firms in the industry to add to their inventory of fixed capital, in order to bring it up to the level most suitable to the new level of sales.

The amount of new fixed investment that will be planned will depend upon the amount of fixed capital required, under optimum conditions, to produce a given amount of output. If, for example, an annual output of $1 worth of shoes demands (under optimum conditions) $1 worth of fixed equipment, a given rise in output and sales leads to bigger plans for fixed investment than if $10 worth of shoes can be produced under optimum conditions by $1 worth of fixed equipment. The greater the amount of fixed equipment in relation to output, the greater will be the absolute effects of a given rise in output upon plans for adding to fixed capital, and so upon demands made upon the capital goods-producing industries (of which the industry manufacturing shoemaking machinery is taken as representative).

The extra pressure put upon the capital goods-producing industries by the effects of the change of output of finished consumer goods is not solely measured by this absolute size of the effects of the change in output. Increased orders at a rate of $100,000 per month are a much bigger matter for this industry if the preceding rate of demand for replacement of worn-out machines has been a rate of $25,000 per month than if it has been running at a rate of $250,000 per month. In the one case, there is a 400 per cent increase in orders to the capital goods industry; in the other case, there is only a 40 per cent increase. But replacement demand will be the greater, the shorter is the life of the capital goods. We saw that $100,000 worth of new equipment was needed every quarter to maintain a total equipment of $4 million whose life-span was ten years. If the life-span of that equipment had only been two and a half years, four times as big a rate of replacement would be needed. The relative effects of a rise in the rate of final output on the demand for capital equipment, therefore, depends upon the average life of the plant. If the average life is long, demand for new equipment because of higher levels of output has a particularly big relative effect on orders for fixed capital equipment.

To summarize the conclusions of the last two paragraphs: In the first place, the absolute size of the effects of a rise in output of finished goods upon orders for capital equipment (in circumstances when equipment was previously at its optimum level in relation to output) depends upon the value of the optimum amount of equipment needed to produce a given additional flow of finished output. This we can call the optimum capital-output ratio.[8] The *relative* size of the effects upon orders to the capital equipment industry in such circumstances depends upon the average life of the equipment.

In either case the effects of changes in output on the demand for equipment can be very considerable. Take the case of a shoe-producing industry which needs an extra $1 worth of equipment for each extra $1 worth of annual output, in which the average life of plant is ten years, and in which annual output and the value of the plant are originally $4 million. This implies quarterly replacement at a rate of $100,000. If output now rises, so that the annual rate of output is now 5 per cent higher (that is, $200,000 higher) firms in making their plans at the end of the quarter for fixed investment will want to increase the amount of fixed capital by $200,000. They, therefore, give orders for $300,000 of fixed capital, consisting of $200,000 because of the higher level of output and $100,000 for normal replacement. This compares with $100,000 which had been the preceding level of orders, all for replacement—an increase of 200 per cent.

It is reasonable to expect that shoe-manufacturing firms will try to persuade the shoe machinery-producing industry to provide and install this capital as quickly as possible, because in the meantime they are having to overwork their existing machines in order to satisfy the new high level of orders for shoes. In the extreme case, the shoe-machinery-producing firms might be able to satisfy these demands within the quarter, so that when the next date for making plans comes round, firms in the shoemaking industry find they have just the right amount of equipment, unless their level of sales and output has changed once more. On the assumption that these have not changed, but are just continuing at the new high level, firms now have no motive to add to their stock of fixed capital; in their plans for capital equipment purchases in this next quarter, their

---

[8] Strictly speaking, we should talk of the *marginal* optimum capital-output ratio.

demand will once more be solely for replacement of equipment that is wearing out. Orders to the industry producing shoe machinery will fall away again to nothing more than a replacement demand.

The net effect, therefore, is that the equipment-producing industry meets an immense and very temporary bulge in orders when output in the consumer goods industry shows a once-for-all rise; if the equipment-producing industry is able to satisfy these orders more or less immediately, there is a correspondingly large and temporary bulge in investment in fixed equipment by the consumer goods industry. In practice, of course, things do not work out exactly like that. In the first place, fixed capital equipment, by its very nature, takes quite a long time to install, and since it is not generally sold from inventory, there is an additional delay, because time must be allowed for its construction. It may be a matter of years, rather than of a month or two, before orders for capital equipment have been fully dealt with. In the second place, as has already been mentioned, it may be necessary to wait longer for capital equipment when the equipment-producing industries are busy than when they are slack. In times when there is only replacement demand for machinery coming forward, fairly quick installation may be possible. But when there is a big bulge in orders, some purchasers may have to wait a long time. This is necessarily the case if the capacity of the equipment-producing industry is insufficient to meet the peak demand and if, as seems to be commonly the case, manufacturers of capital equipment prefer lengthening order books to raising prices when demand exceeds supply. If in our example the maximum capacity of the equipment-producing industry had been $150,000 per quarter, only part of the bulge in orders could have been satisfied within the quarter after the bulge appeared; out of total orders of $300,000, at least $150,000 would have had to wait over. Although shoe manufacturers would not be entirely satisfied about this, they would not cancel their orders for the machines, as long as orders for shoes continued to come in at the new high rate: their interests would be to get back to the optimum capital-output ratio as quickly as possible. In the next quarter, the usual $100,000 of replacement orders for shoemaking machinery would come in, and be added to the $150,000 left over from the preceding quarter. Once again, not all the orders could be satisfied: this time $100,000 would have to be left over. In this example the excess would be worked off only in the fourth quarter after the bulge in orders.

We can now return to a consideration of some of the consequences of the fact that the life of equipment is not exactly determined. The effects discussed in the last paragraph make it likely that in periods when trade is expanding, capital equipment will have to be maintained in operation when it would otherwise be scrapped. Since firms have to wait some time for their orders for equipment to be satisfied, they will have to make do with what they have in the meantime—this means, among other things, that they will continue to use equipment which would normally be regarded as worn out. This tendency may well be reinforced by other considerations; for example, prices of equipment may well rise when order books lengthen, so that it is worth keeping old equipment in use for longer. Not all the relevant forces operate in the same direction, however; firms may be more willing to scrap and replace in good times because of the general air of confidence; on the other hand, they may tend to continue to make do and mend in bad times.

Whatever may happen in detail, however, it seems reasonable to consider that the general conclusion we have reached is an acceptable one. Because there is some ratio of fixed capital equipment to output which is an optimum, in terms of a particular economic and technical environment, a rise in the level of output will cause a temporary bulge in investment in fixed capital equipment, while a fall in output will lead to a temporary abandonment of replacement of fixed capital. This is a matter of considerable economic significance, and in the next chapter will provide us with an important part of a plausible explanation of the trade cycle.

The Acceleration Principle

This theory we have outlined is basically the same in content as the explanation of capital investment known as the 'acceleration principle.' That theory states that fixed investment depends on the rate of change of output. When output is rising fast, fixed investment will be large; when output is rising slowly, fixed investment will be smaller; when output is falling, investment in fixed capital will be very small or will not take place at all. The assumptions on which this theory are based are usually somewhat narrower than those on which our preceding explanation was based; in particular, the acceleration principle as usually expounded [9] assumes that plans for fixed investment are always fully carried out in the following period, whereas we have seen that there may be considerable and variable delays; but on the same assumptions about these matters, the two explanations are equivalent insofar as they apply to any particular industry.

A further difference exists between the acceleration principle as usually put forward and the explanation of fixed investment we have been following up to this point. We have, so far, explained variations in fixed investment only by firms in industries producing consumer goods, and have not yet considered the determination of fixed investment by firms which are themselves producing capital equipment. We have not, so far, explained the circumstances in which shoe machinery producers will install more plant for making shoe machinery, or in which shipbuilders will put down more shipyards. The usual form of the acceleration principle lumps this question in with the one we have already discussed; it makes fixed investment as a whole (by all kinds of firm) depend upon output as a whole (both of consumption goods and of all kinds of capital goods—not merely of consumption goods).

Investment by the Equipment-Producing Industries

We must now proceed to a more refined consideration of what determines fixed investment by firms in industries producing capital equipment. In what way are their actions so different that it is important to separate them from other producers? To a large extent, the explanation has already been provided. The bulges in orders that can quite easily occur for the capital goods-producing industries may be short and very sharp. If those industries were to react to such increases in demand by substantial increases of their capacity, they would very likely find that when the bulge had passed, there would be serious excess capacity. Experience will, in fact, probably show this to firms in the equipment-producing industries: they tend, therefore, to be rather disinclined to increase capacity when there is a sudden upsurge in orders. They are particularly free to act in

---

[9] At least by relatively recent writers.

this way, and to make their purchasers wait, because the demand by these purchasers cannot easily be diverted into other industries, nor does waiting usually cause their desire for the equipment to diminish. The industries producing fixed capital are particularly wise to act in this sort of way, and ignore temporary booms in orders, because new plant for such industries usually takes a very long time to construct. A new steel mill or shipyard may not be in operation until several years after it has been planned. By that time a temporary boom in orders will almost certainly have passed.

The contrast, in these respects, between equipment-producing industries and consumer goods-producing industries should not be pushed too hard. Nevertheless, there is a broad difference which is significant. Generally speaking, and especially when recent experience has involved big fluctuations in the level of output, the equipment-producing industries are less likely to react to a boom in orders by expanding capacity. Instead, they will tend to overwork existing capacity and make their customers wait. Their direct reactions to booms and slumps in orders may be no more than a tendency to allow their own fixed capital to wear out in bad times, and to concentrate replacement in relatively good times.

What, then, does determine the policies of the capital goods-producing industries in increasing their capacity? Probably the answer is that, because of the long view of the situation firms in such industries must take, their investment in equipment for purposes other than replacement is very largely determined by their view of the long-term prospects of the economy and of their industry. The general growth of the economy will be a much more important influence than temporary fluctuations in orders—even if the fluctuations are several years in duration.

These influences upon fixed investment by firms in the capital goods-producing industries join with the long-run considerations such as population growth which determine housing investment, to create a large category of fixed investment which does not depend to an important extent on the level of output in the recent past. A broad, and not too misleading, summary of the situation is that there are two main groups of influences upon the level of fixed investment, which overlap but for many problems can conveniently be kept separate.

On the one hand, there are these long-run considerations of the growth of the economy; investment plans which take account of such considerations (including investment by the industries producing capital goods and social investment) also frequently pay considerable attention to the rate of interest. On the other hand there are investment plans which depend upon more immediate circumstances, but only to a rather limited extent on the current level of the long-term rate of interest: they depend mainly on the effects of the current and recent level of profits and of quite short-run changes in output on the relationship between desired and actual capital.

Put in this way, the common element in the two sets of influence comes to light. In both cases, changes in the income and output of the economy are of fundamental importance; the difference lies largely in the period to which the planner of the investments pays attention. Moreover, it must always be remembered that technical changes, leading to the introduction of new processes and new products, are very important influences on the timing and magnitude of investment.

SOME SUGGESTED READING

A useful discussion of factors affecting the supply of funds for investment is to be found in J. Duesenberry, *Business Cycles and Economic Growth* (New York, 1958), particularly Chapters 4-6, on which the earlier part of this chapter draws heavily. The literature of the acceleration principle is very extensive and dates back to the early years of the century, in particular to J. M. Clark, 'Business Acceleration and the Law of Demand,' *Journal of Political Economy* (1917); a historical survey is to be found in A. D. Knox, 'The Acceleration Principle and the Theory of Investment' in *Economica* (1952). A mathematical survey is to be found in R. G. D. Allen, *Mathematical Economics* (London, 1956), Chapter 3; rather simpler is the mathematical treatment in W. J. Baumol, *Economic Dynamics* (New York, 1951), Chapters 4, 10, and 12. Other important articles include E. D. Domar, 'Capital Expansion, Rate of Growth and Employment' in *Econometrica* (1946), reprinted in Domar, *Essays in the Theory of Economic Growth* (New York, 1957), and several of the articles dealing with the interaction of the multiplier and acceleration principles which are listed at the end of Chapter 24.

24

The Trade Cycle

In the preceding chapter we looked at the influence of the level of output (and so of real income) on the amount of gross investment taking place in fixed capital equipment. We saw that changes in the level of output normally lead to changes in plans to invest, because of the effects of changes in output upon the optimum stock of fixed capital equipment. It was said at the beginning of that chapter that this relationship between income and investment normally operates at the same time as the multiplier. Normally, therefore, a circular process of causation operates; the ordinary multiplier process and the relationships that were distinguished in the last chapter interact. A change in the level of investment alters the level of income and output through the operation of the multiplier; a change in the level of income and output in turn affects plans to invest. When these changed plans to invest are realized, they in turn influence the level of income.

The cumulative process that this interaction leads to is our subject for investigation in the first part of the present chapter. Subsequently, the analysis of this interaction will be used to provide a plausible explanation of the trade cycle.

The Cumulative Process

A convenient starting point for our analysis is one where trade has been rather depressed for some time. As a consequence firms in the industries producing consumer goods have not been replacing fixed capital equipment as it wears out, because they have more than the optimum equipment for producing the current level of output. In other words, gross investment by firms in those industries has been zero for some time. Sooner or later so much plant will have worn out that the amount of fixed equipment will have fallen to the optimum level for the existing level of output. From that stage onward replacement of capital equipment as it wears out becomes necessary. It is at this point that we break into the situation and begin our story.

We can assume that fixed capital equipment in the industries producing consumer goods has an average life of 500 weeks (or approximately ten years), so that if we find as an initial position that 25,000 units of equipment (each costing $1000) are in existence, replacement at the rate of 50 per week will be necessary in order to maintain this capital intact. We can safely assume this replacement will fall due at a fairly steady rate, even though the installation of the equipment may have been concentrated at certain boom periods in the past; this assumption is safe because there are so many different kinds of asset, with greatly differing lives, contained in the category of 'equipment.' These differing lengths of life can usually be relied on to damp down any tendency for 'replacement cycles' in capital equipment in general, though they may exist in particular industries (e.g. if ships wear out in twenty years, one shipbuilding boom can be expected to follow twenty years after another). We can also assume (again for the sake of argument) that the optimum ratio between fixed capital equipment in the industries producing consumer goods and their output is such that $25 worth of capital equipment most advantageously produces $1 worth of output per week.[1] This fact is reflected in our initial conditions, in week 0, when the week's output of consumption goods is $1,000,000 and capital in existence in these industries is worth $25,000,000; the capital stock is just at its optimum. In each of the succeeding weeks, as $50,000 worth of equipment wears out, it is replaced by gross investment of the same value. The amount of fixed capital in existence in the consumer goods industries therefore remains constant.

The new factor that enters the situation at the point where we break in is that the new gross investment of $50,000 in period 1 has provided unexpected income to the people engaged in producing the equipment concerned. Actual income in week 1 is $1,050,000,

---

[1] If output is expressed at an annual rate, the ratio is therefore about one half.

although expected income was $1,000,000 (it having been assumed by income receivers that everything would stay as it had been in the preceding weeks). There is as a consequence unplanned saving of $50,000.

In week 2 the extra income leads to extra consumption. If we assume that the marginal propensity to consume is 0.8, then in week 2 consumption increases to 1040 thousand dollars.[2] This in turn leads in week 3 to further increases in output and income. The whole sequence follows on in a way similar to that seen in Chapter 6. To save space, however, and to avoid introducing the complications involved in considering unplanned disinvestment in inventories, only a part of the information of the kind given in Table 3 is represented in the adjoining table; the second, fourth, and other even weeks up to the tenth are omitted. The twelfth week is included, however, because the situation in that week is important in determining what follows. Up to the twelfth week, Table 11 represents just the same sort of situation as that represented earlier. A pure multiplier process is in operation, as a result of an initiating increase in investment.[3]

If the process were to continue in this way, eventually there would be a new equilibrium level of income of 1250. (The multiplier is 5, since the marginal propensity to save is 0.2; the injection of investment is at a rate of 50, so the new equilibrium level of income shows an increase of $\frac{50}{0.2}$ or 50 × 5, or 250 above the original level of 1000.) Things do not, however, continue without interruption. At the end of the first quarter in the twelfth week firms review their fixed investment plans, and are producing 1134.6 of consumer goods with a total capital equipment of 25,000. This means that the capital output ratio is below the optimum. They will, therefore, plan to restore the amount of equipment to the optimum level.

In practice, of course, it will take some time to put these plans into operation. Moreover, firms will pay attention to factors other than the level of output reached in the week in which the plans

---

[2] In the remainder of this chapter the units (thousands of dollars) will be omitted for the sake of brevity.

[3] There is, however, the difference pointed out in Chapter 23 that we are now considering investment and income as gross of replacement changes for fixed capital.

TABLE 11

(*$ thousands*)

Quarter	Week	Fixed capital in existence in consumer goods industries	Planned gross fixed investment in consumer goods industries	Output of consumer goods	Total output = actual households' income	Households' expected income	Consumption	Households' planned saving	Households' unplanned saving	Households' realized saving
0	0	25,000	0	1000	1000	1000	1000	0	0	0
1	1	25,000	50	1000	1050	1000	1000	0	50	50
	3	25,000	50	1040	1090	1050	1040	10	40	50
	5	25,000	50	1072	1122	1090	1072	18	32	50
	7	25,000	50	1097.6	1147.8	1122	1097.6	24.4	25.6	50
	9	25,000	50	1118.2	1168.2	1147.8	1118.2	29.6	20.4	50
	11	25,000	50	1134.6	1184.6	1168.2	1134.6	33.6	16.4	50
	12	25,000	50	1134.6	1184.6	1184.6	1147.7	36.9	0	36.9
2	13	25,280.4	330.4	1147.7	1478.1	1184.6	1147.7	36.9	293.5	330.4
	15	25,841.2	330.4	1382.5	1712.9	1478.1	1382.5	95.6	234.8	330.4
	17	26,402.0	330.4	1570.3	1900.7	1712.9	1570.3	142.6	187.8	330.4
	19	26,962.8	330.4	1720.6	2051.0	1900.7	1720.6	180.1	150.3	330.4
	21	27,523.6	330.4	1840.8	2171.2	2051.0	1840.8	210.2	120.2	330.4
	23	28,084.4	330.4	1937.0	2267.4	2171.2	1937.0	234.2	96.2	330.4
	24	28,364.8	330.4	1937.0	2267.4	2267.4	2013.9	253.5	0	253.5
3	25	30,036.4	1721.6	2013.9	3735.5	2267.4	2013.9	253.5	1468.1	1721.6

are made, in formulating the plans. We shall, however, ignore these complications; the general character of the effects they will have is now familiar,[4] and in this chapter we are doing no more than indicate the kind of manner in which economic forces can induce a trade cycle. We shall, therefore, assume that firms plan to build up the amount of fixed equipment fast enough to have sufficient equipment at the end of the second quarter to produce under optimum conditions the level of output attained at the end of the first quarter. To produce an output of 1134.6 under optimum conditions, 28,365 of fixed capital is needed (since the optimum capital-output ratio is such that $25 worth of capital is needed to produce $1 of output per week): this means that 3365 of net investment is needed in the consumer goods industries; if this is spread evenly over twelve weeks, net investment of 280.4 per week takes place. In addition, gross investment of 50 per week continues, for the maintenance of existing capital. Total planned gross investment in the second quarter is therefore 280.4 per week. If capacity is available in the equipment-producing industries, this means that there is a big rise in the level of investment in the second quarter compared with the first.

The consequence of this is that a new impulse is added to the force of the multiplier process which was taking place as a result of the original rise in the level of gross investment. In the first week of the second quarter, actual realized income is 1478.1 compared with 1184.6 in the preceding week. This rise of 293.5 consists of an increase of 13.1 because of the effects of induced rises in consumption still taking place in the original multiplier process, and 280.4 because of the new increase in the level of investment expenditure.

This rise in realized income in the first week of the second quarter leads to a higher level of consumption expenditure in the second week of that quarter. The expansionary process continues, and by the end of the second quarter total output of consumption goods is 1937.0. But by that time although fixed capital in existence has been increased to 28,365 it is once again too small for the optimum scale of operations. Businessmen, therefore, make plans to make up this inadequacy during the third quarter. The optimum amount

---

[4] See, in particular, Chapter 6.

of fixed capital for producing an output of consumer goods totalling 1937.0 is 48,425. Additional fixed capital to an amount of 20,060 is therefore necessary. Still assuming that full capacity output has not been reached in the equipment-producing industry, this involves investment in new plant to an amount of 1671.6 per week, to make up the arrears during the quarter. In addition to this, there is continuing need for 50 per week replacement; total investment in each week of the third quarter is therefore 1721.6.

The consequences of this increase in investment between the second and the third quarters should be obvious. Just as the rise in the level of investment between the first and the second quarters led to a speeding up in the rate of rise of total income (the rise being by 184.6 in the first quarter and 1082.8 in the second), so the rate of rise will be still faster in the third quarter. This in turn leads to a still greater inadequacy in the stock of fixed capital equipment at the end of the third quarter, so that investment plans in the fourth quarter will be still greater.

It appears then, that in the circumstances we are considering, there is a chain reaction by which increased investment leads to greater income, and greater income leads to still more increases in investment. We must now ask what can be said in general terms about these kinds of chain reaction.

Explosive and Non-Explosive Cumulative Processes

There are four possible kinds of chain reaction in the cumulative process; which of these happens to occur depends on the values of the marginal propensity to consume and of the optimum capital-output ratio. The boundaries of each of the four cases depends on the exact nature of the system under consideration (for example, on the relative lengths of the various time lags in the chain of causation); a detailed investigation involves fairly complicated mathematics, but fortunately the general characteristics of the possible developments can be considered verbally.[5]

---

[5] A discussion of the mathematics of the boundaries between the four cases in a very simple kind of economy is to be found in Samuelson, 'Interactions between the Multiplier Analysis and the Principle of Acceleration' in the American Economic Association's *Readings in Business Cycle Theory* (Philadelphia, 1951), pp. 261-9.

If the optimum capital-output ratio and the marginal propensity to consume are both rather small, there is a steady movement towards a new equilibrium level of income. This movement is broadly similar to the simplest multiplier adjustment considered in the first part of Chapter 6. If the optimum capital-output ratio and the marginal propensity to consume are somewhat bigger, there will be fluctuations on the way to the new equilibrium similar in character to those discussed in the last part of Chapter 6, where inventory adjustments by firms were taken into account. The net investment in equipment which is induced by a rise in the level of output causes additional expansion of output, which for a time go beyond the final equilibrium level; but the forces at work are not strong enough to cause explosion; the overshoot is only temporary. These fluctuations are the greater, the larger are the two relevant relationships.

In either of these two cases just outlined, the equilibrium level of income which follows an expansionary disturbance to the system will be somewhat greater than that which would be introduced by the ordinary multiplier process. The additional rise occurs because gross investment (i.e. replacement of worn-out plant) must rise to higher levels when there is more plant in existence because the level of output is higher.[6] Net investment (i.e. installation of additional plant) is, on the other hand, equal to zero when the new equilibrium is attained. This is so because net additions to the stock of equipment are planned only after changes occur in the level of output, because only then are there changes in the optimum stock of equipment.[7] In equilibrium the level of output is (by definition) constant, and so no alterations to the stock of equipment are planned.

The third kind of chain reaction arises when the marginal propensity to consume and the optimum capital-output ratio are still larger. It is very different from the two cases already considered, in that output never tends to level off at a new equilibrium. Instead, the chain reaction is explosive. An expansionary impulse in such a system brings about a cumulative process in which there are no self-limiting tendencies. This case is not immediately explosive; it is akin to the second in that it involves fluctuations. But there is

---

[6] No account was taken of this effect in Table 11, but it clearly must exist.

[7] Assuming that interest rates, techniques, etc., remain unchanged.

the very important difference that fluctuations get bigger and bigger; they are not 'damped,' like all the other fluctuations with which we have so far been concerned, and show no tendency to come to any equilibrium.

The fourth case arises where the marginal propensity to consume and the optimum capital-output ratio are larger still. Here there are no fluctuations in the explosion; the level of income and output rises faster and faster, with no internal limitation whatsoever, as the chain reaction develops through time.

The Nature of the Trade Cycle

The preceding analysis of the interactions of the multiplier and the inducement to invest resulting from changes in the level of activity and output has proved to be the most profitable and convincing line of explanation of the trade cycle that economists have yet developed. Before proceeding to show how it can be so used, it is worth spending a short time in considering the main features of the trade cycle, which has been one of the most clearly marked characteristics of economic conditions in the last century, at least up to the Second World War. The cycle consists of fluctuations in real income, output, employment, and prices which occur with some degree of regularity; they show some tendency to take a period of about ten years to work round from the boom of one cycle to the boom of the next. It is with the fluctuations in the levels of income, output, and employment that we shall mainly be concerned; there seem to be the most important characteristics of twentieth-century cycles.

In earlier theory the tendency was to lay emphasis upon changes in price levels as indications of the stage reached in a cycle. In nineteenth-century conditions, when money wage rates were less sticky downward, this was probably realistic. Currently, however, it is probably largely correct to lay emphasis upon changes in output and real income in the industrial sector of the economy in explaining the cycle, and to regard the price changes that occur as secondary, being induced by inflationary tendencies in the industrial sector in the boom and by the effects of changes in demand on the primary producing sector of the economy. It cannot be said, however, that current economic theory provides an adequate explanation of the role the primary producing sector may play in the trade cycle.

Recent theory has also tended to minimize the importance of such factors as the rate of interest and the operations of the banking system in explaining the trade cycle. Here again there is a contrast with the theory of a generation and more ago, and here again it probably reflects a contrast between the experience of this century and that of the nineteenth century. Inappropriate monetary policies and banking collapse can exaggerate cycles, even in modern conditions; conversely, wise monetary policy can be used as one weapon for helping to control cycles, as we shall see in Chapter 26. Nevertheless, it is probably correct to avoid laying emphasis on these purely monetary matters in explaining the core of the cyclical process under twentieth-century conditions; they can be introduced later as important embellishments that help explain the great differences in detail between individual cycles.

It is conventional and useful to distinguish five phases in the trade cycle; the upswing, the boom, the collapse, the decline, and the depression. The upswing is marked by rising activity, falling unemployment, and slowly rising prices. The boom is marked by low levels of unemployment and sometimes by a certain tendency for an inflationary process to develop; it may be quite a short period or may extend over several years. The collapse involves a sudden downturn in the level of activity, falling prices, and frequently financial crisis (e.g. falling bond and stock prices, and inability by debtors to pay interest charges on bank loans and mortgages). The decline involves steadily falling levels of activity and rising unemployment, together with falling prices. Finally, the depression is the position in which the bottom has been reached, and recovery has not yet started; like the boom, it may be very short-lived or it may last for several years.

It should be remembered that this summary, while valuable, is rather formalized. All cycles met in practice are more complicated than this, so that it is frequently difficult to diagnose at what point one finds oneself. For example, there may well be fluctuations in the level of activity during the upswing or the boom, which over-cautious observers will take to be the outset of the collapse and downswing. The collapse may come as a series of crises, perhaps separated by several months or years. In the depression, false dawns may be seen; the recovery may apparently start, only to fall back again, too weak to get under way.

There are two major groups of possible explanation of the trade cycle which are based on the analysis of the chain reaction outlined earlier. One assumes that the marginal propensity to consume and the optimum capital-output ratio are relatively small, so that there is no tendency to explosion; the other assumes that they are relatively large. They can be described as the explanation in terms of 'weak cycles' and the explanation in terms of 'explosion within external constraints.' Our analysis will concentrate on the latter possibility, so it is convenient to dismiss the other first.

Even if circumstances are such that the economic system will eventually reach a new equilibrium after a disturbance, it is quite possible that history would show an endless series of trade cycles, because in practice there are always new shocks affecting the system. If a series of erratic shocks affects a system which is rather unstable (in that considerable fluctuations occur on the way to the new equilibrium which would follow that disturbance if it were taken alone), then the whole system will show continuing fluctuations. Moreover, it can be shown mathematically that these fluctuations will have a fair degree of constancy in amplitude and in frequency.[8]

The alternative explanation of the trade cycle, in terms of the assumption that the marginal propensity to consume and the optimum capital-output ratio are relatively large, will detain us far longer. The process that was described in the first part of this chapter provides the core of this explanation of the sequence of events in the upswing of the trade cycle. We assume that conditions have become depressed, so that there is for the time being more capital equipment in existence than the optimum amount for producing the current level of output; consequently, equipment is not replaced as it wears out, until eventually a position similar to that in week 0 in Table 11 is attained. At this point the amount of equipment in existence is just sufficient to produce the current level of output in the optimum manner. Thereafter, the position represented in our week 1 arises; firms start to replace capital equipment, and gross investment becomes positive. This leads to a multiplier expansion of income and output, which in turn leads to further increases in investment.

---

[8] This was shown by Professor Ragnar Frisch in his celebrated article 'Propagation Problems and Impulse Problems in Dynamic Economics,' *Economic Essays in Honor of Gustav Cassel* (London, 1933).

In this way a cumulative process of expansion may start automatically without any disturbance from outside the system. Once created, the process feeds on itself and shows no self-limiting tendencies, if the marginal propensity to consume and the optimum capital-output ratio are sufficiently large.

The Full Employment Ceiling

The next question that arises is, what does stop the expansionary movement? If the process is not self-limiting it must be stopped by some external limitation. The limitation which is relevant here is simply the position of full employment. Once this is reached it is impossible for the level of output to rise any higher. Full employment imposes a ceiling to the level of output, and so provides an upper limit to its fluctuations.

We must now consider what happens when this ceiling is reached. Experience suggests that, in the real world, either of two things may happen. The high boom may be very short-lived, and rapidly replaced by a downturn. Alternatively, it may well last for some time (perhaps two or three years); even if this happens, it is unusual for the boom to develop into a serious inflationary spiral. It adds to the plausibility of our theory if it can provide explanations of either of these possible developments.

In the case of the first alternative, the important point is that output ceases to expand. Now, if there has been no substantial lengthening of order books in the industries producing capital equipment, activity soon begins to fall off in those industries. This happens because the cessation of the expansion of the level of output means there is no longer any need to install additional equipment to bring the capital-output ratio up to the optimum. The decline in activity in the capital goods industries has rapid repercussions throughout the economy, in the form of a general contraction. All this happens quite quickly; the high boom only lasts for the very short period in which the expansionary and the contractionary tendencies in the economy are evenly balanced. In this short period there is not sufficient time for any serious inflationary forces to develop. Since the rise in the level of income must be proceeding at a very fast rate when the full employment ceiling is reached (because of the acceleration involved in the explosive cumulative process) there are clearly likely to be strong pressures to inflation at that point. Only if the high boom is very short-lived can sharp inflation be avoided.

The explanation of the second alternative situation (in which the boom may last for some time without causing serious inflation) is, at the same time, more complicated and more plausible. One escape from the need to give an explanation in terms of our theory is to suggest that this situation may arise through successful control policies by the monetary authorities, which for a time successfully hold the balance between inflationary and contractionary tendencies. It is, however, probably more satisfying to provide an explanation which does not rely on such external forces.

The real difficulty is to explain why the powerful expansionary forces that exist prior to full employment do not push the economy over into a sharp inflationary spiral once full employment is reached. How is it that a period of rapid expansion may be replaced by a period of relative stability?

A plausible explanation is the common tendency for the capital goods industries to lengthen their order books substantially rather than increase their prices when they are in the full employment zone. This means that if these industries enter the full employment zone before the consumer goods industries themselves become more or less fully employed,[9] a substantial backlog of orders is likely to

---

[9] As is rather likely if the economy as a whole is in balance. The capital goods industries, both in our model and in practice, suffer much bigger fluctuations in their level of activity than the consumer goods industries. To pile up orders when trade is generally good is a way in which the capital goods industries can compensate themselves for the larger fluctuations, and so attract resources to work in them. Another possible way is to charge higher prices when trade is good. To some extent this reaction (which is the typical reaction of the primary producing sector) also occurs: there is probably a tendency for prices of capital goods to fluctuate more than prices of manufactured consumer goods in a trade cycle. This tendency is not really marked, however; to the extent that it happens, it is probably the consequence of the larger fluctuations of activity in capital goods industries than in consumer goods industries, coupled with the fact (pointed out in Chapter 5 but for the most part ignored in this book) that changes in the level of an industry's activity even below the full employment zone have some effect on the price at which its output is sold.

This chapter does not investigate the effects of relative price changes in the trade cycle on its course. Several theories of the trade cycle have been built round the tendency of the price of capital equipment to fluctuate more than the price of consumer goods. It seems likely, however, that such effects are of relatively small importance. More important, in all probability, are the consequences of changes in the prices of primary products in relation to the prices of industrial goods, and also the consequences of changes in real wage rates and of the

pile up in the capital goods industries. If such a development takes place, two consequences follow. For one thing, there is a slowing down in the rate of expansion of the consumer goods industries. Since fixed investment (i.e. installation of fixed equipment) has now reached the maximum possible level, no further stimulus to the expansionary process comes from rising investment. The multiplier effects of past increases in investment work themselves out, but, as we have seen in Part II, a multiplier process if left to itself levels off. There is therefore a tendency for activity in the consumer goods industries to level out. This may occur rather below full employment for those industries; or they may be pushed into full employment and some price rises may be induced. However, any induced inflationary effects are likely to be rather weak, and so do not get very far before the downturn eventually comes.

The second consequence of the developments we are considering is that some plans for net investment in fixed equipment continue to be made: the level of output in the consumer goods industries is rising, and so their capital needs are rising. Orders therefore continue to flow into the capital goods industries.

For a time, therefore, all is well. Full employment is found in the capital goods industries and is more or less fully attained in consumer goods industries; at the same time there is no marked inflationary pressure. This happy situation may last for some time, if a sufficient backlog of orders has piled up in the capital goods industries.

Unfortunately, the situation cannot be permanent. The fact that output must cease to expand in the consumer goods industries means that a time comes when no new plans for fixed net investment are formulated; when that has happened, and once existing investment plans have been carried out, the only needs are for replacement. For a time the capital goods industries are kept fully employed by exhausting their backlog of orders, and so bring existing investment plans to fruition. Sooner or later, however, this backlog will be worked through, and the capital goods industries have to reduce their level of output drastically: the demand for equipment for replacement purposes is too small to keep them fully employed.

---

share of labor in the national income. It cannot be said, however, that economists have satisfactorily worked a consideration of such changes into the theory of the trade cycle.

The Downturn

We can now continue our explanation of the cycle, from this point at which there is a decline in the output of the capital goods industries to the level necessary for replacement alone. It will be remembered that we had also reached this point in the analysis of the case where there was no substantial lengthening of order books, so that the economy only stayed at the full employment ceiling for a short time. The course of our analysis, which ran in two divergent streams during the discussion of full employment conditions, now runs in one channel again.

At the point at which the level of net fixed investment falls away sharply the crisis appears. The immediate effect of the fall in the level of activity in the industries producing capital goods is unemployment in those industries and a decline in the incomes of people employed in them. As a consequence a downward multiplier process develops. The levels of activity, output, and income in the country fall drastically. Nor is this all. In the first place, there are the various financial strains and crises that have been mentioned, as debtors get into difficulties and as wealth-holders try to move into assets whose value is likely to stay reasonably constant in times of bad trade. In the second place, and more important for our immediate purpose, the fall in the level of income that results from cessation of net additions to the stock of fixed capital means that the existing stock of fixed capital comes to be more than adequate. Replacement of equipment as it wears out therefore ceases, and gross investment falls to zero. This further decline in the level of investment has further effects on the level of income, through a reinforcement of the downward multiplier process. The only possible equilibrium position is one where planned savings equal zero, because only at that level can they be equal to planned gross fixed investment. The contraction takes place in the form of an ordinary multiplier process, whose limit is the level of income at which (gross) savings are zero. This is the lowest possible limit of the cycle,[10] gross fixed investment cannot be negative; at the worst, there is no replacement of old equipment when it wears out. The lower equilibrium which is at-

---

[10] Except if there is disinvestment in inventories taking place; this can only be temporary, but may cause a temporary overshoot of the lower limit of the cycle.

tained at the end of the downward multiplier process is itself only temporary. For a time the depression stage continues, with a low and more or less constant level of activity. Eventually, however, so much capital will have worn out that the capital stock falls to the optimum size for producing the low current level of output; investment for replacement purposes once again becomes necessary. Here the position has worked back to the one at which we started, and the upswing of the cycle starts again.

This, then, is an outline of a plausible theory of the trade cycle. The theory depends upon the interaction of the multiplier and the effect of changes in the level of income on the amount of investment, arising from changes in the size of the optimum stock of capital. It assumes that this circular interaction is powerful enough to be explosive; once an expansion gets under way, it contains no self-limiting forces. The limit to the expansion is provided by full employment conditions. The lower limit is imposed by the fact that gross fixed investment cannot be less than zero; at worst, no new equipment is installed and none is replaced when it wears out. Here, then, are the explanations of the expansion, the contraction, the ceiling, and the floor. The other feature we have also explained; the reversal of the direction of movement at the upper and lower limits of the cycle depends upon the exhaustion of needs for new fixed equipment after the level of output has reached its peak in the boom, and the reappearance of needs for replacement of worn-out equipment when the slump has gone on for long enough.

This theory provides a plausible outline explanation of the trade cycle as it has been experienced in the twentieth century.[11] A cycle caused by factors of the kind considered would show fluctuations in the level of activity and of real income between conditions of full employment and conditions of a moderately high degree of unemployment. It would be a cycle in which production of capital goods fluctuated much more than production of consumption goods; in the rigorous conditions we are assuming, no fixed equipment for the consumer goods industries would be produced at all in the slump. Of course, that is an oversimplified view, which we can easily drop without changing the fundamentals of our system. Even in the slump

---

[11] For the nineteenth century it is probable that much more emphasis would have to be placed on price, wage, and interest rate changes than we have done here.

there would be some investment taking place, because not all investment is induced by changes in the level of activity. To some extent new techniques would be exploited, so that some industrial investment would continue, while investment in the capital goods-producing industries and for non-industrial purposes might also be maintained (or, if interest rates fall in the slump, even be increased) in the depression phase. The boom and the depression phases might be very short, or quite long-lived. The length of the boom would depend on the extent to which backlogs of investment orders had piled up, which in turn depends on the optimum capital-output ratio on the average life of equipment and on the capacity of the capital equipment-producing industries. In all these respects, the cycle that would be created by the forces we are considering might well tend to correspond to those observed in reality.

The duration of such a cycle would depend on the nature of the forces just outlined, and, more generally, on the lengths of the various time lags in the system, such as the lags involved in the multiplier process and the lag between increased output and increased plans for investment. Plausible values for these various reaction times [12] result in a cycle whose length is of the same order as those which have been observed historically: namely, between seven and twelve years.

While this theory of the trade cycle is plausible it is by no means perfect. Some possible criticisms may be briefly mentioned. For one thing it probably pays insufficient regard to the attempts of the government to control the cycle—such attempts are nearly always made, and may modify the form of the cycle, either for good or ill. For another thing too little attention is paid to monetary elements; changes in interest rates and in banking policy can undoubtedly be important influences. Thirdly, description of the reactions of firms is undoubtedly too mechanical. Firms in some industries do not base their investment plans to any great extent on the level of output in the immediate past; and again, as we have seen in Chapter 23, other influences affect the investment plans of all firms. To an important extent, the factors affecting the supply of funds for investment which were investigated in the first part of Chapter 23

---

[12] The time units that have been used in the numerical example are almost certainly too short as descriptions of the actual clock times involved in these processes.

probably damp down the violence of the fluctuations. Since the supply of capital funds to firms is not perfectly elastic, it is likely that they will not expand investment as much as they might otherwise do—and correspondingly a backlog of investment projects may continue for a long time. Nor is the theory too easy to reconcile with the explanation of the constancy of prices of manufactured goods below the full employment zone which was given in Chapter 5; if the upswing starts only when most firms find they have no surplus capacity even although their level of output is very low, it is not immediately obvious why firms find they can rapidly expand output without reaching a range of rising marginal costs.[13] The important point however that has been dealt with in this discussion of a theory of a trade cycle is the demonstration of the kind of instability that may easily develop, and the kind of explanation that can contribute to a fuller theory of the trade cycle.

Some Suggested Reading

The literature of business cycles is immense and forbidding. This chapter has largely been based on J. R. Hicks, *A Contribution to the Theory of the Trade Cycle* (Oxford, 1950). A valuable review article which outlines Hicks' argument and criticizes it cogently is J. S. Duesenberry, 'Hicks on the Trade Cycle' in the *Quarterly Journal of Economics* (1950), pp. 464-76. The interaction of the multiplier and the accelerator were first clearly set out in P. A. Samuelson, 'Interaction between the Multiplier Analysis and the Principle of Acceleration,' which first appeared in the *Review of Economic Statistics* (1939) and is to be found conveniently in the American Economic Association, *Readings in Business Cycle Theory* (Philadelphia, 1949). Another useful collection of reprinted articles is A. H. Hansen and R. V. Clemence, *Readings in Business Cycles and National Income* (New York, 1953).

Earlier books with approaches similar to that followed are R. F. Harrod, *The Trade Cycle* (Oxford, 1936) and M. Kalecki, *Theory of Economic Dynamics* (London, 1954); the latter largely reprints two of his

---

[13] A possible reconciliation is that the new capacity can be installed quickly in the consumer goods industries if there is still excess capacity in the capital goods industries; in the meantime labor is easily available to work existing capacity in the consumer goods industries rather beyond its optimum, so marginal cost curves do not rise sufficiently for firms to notice any appreciable rise in their average variable costs. Again, it may well be that the upturn starts earlier than is suggested by our model because of the existence of long-term forces in the economy leading to economic growth.

earlier books. Cycle theory and the theory of economic growth are linked in R. F. Harrod's *Towards a Dynamic Economics* (London, 1948); N. Kaldor's article 'The Relations of Economic Growth and Cyclical Fluctuations' in the March, 1954 issue of the *Economic Journal;* and in J. S. Duesenberry, *Business Cycles and Economic Growth* (New York, 1958). A sophisticated mathematical treatment of various cycle theories is to be found in R. G. D. Allen, *Mathematical Economics* (London, 1956).

25

Economic Stabilization Policy

The preceding chapters have shown that there is no reason to suppose that the economic situation will be at all stable. Changes in government expenditure and the level of investment can have greatly multiplied effects on the level of output and income, and may also lead to cumulative price changes. The process of movement toward the new equilibrium position is not likely to be smooth; it usually involves fluctuations on the way. More seriously, observation and theory combine to suggest that no equilibrium will be maintained indefinitely if the economy is left uncontrolled, but that the level of output and income is inherently unstable and will perpetually fluctuate in the major trade cycles and minor inventory cycles [1] unless active counteracting measures are taken.

In themselves these theoretical conclusions provide sufficient reason for the economist to interest himself in the problem of economic stabilization. However, he is driven to such an interest still more forcibly by the great concern of the voters in most democratic countries with the need for price stability and for maintaining full employment. Most political parties these days have to pay considerable attention to the demand for price and employment stabilization —a demand which has been the product of the instability we have suffered, especially since the First World War.

Unfortunately, although the principle of economic stabilization is widely accepted, there is still disagreement about what it means. One form of disagreement is very common but is not our concern here: it arises from the understandable desire of particular groups to stabilize their real incomes at a level which is something like the

---

[1] As discussed in Chapter 6.

highest yet experienced. Bargaining by farmers and by individual trade unions in unsettled periods such as that since 1945 tends to be beset by arguments of this kind. The stabilization with which we shall be concerned, however, will involve questions of stabilization of economic magnitudes of broader significance than these. In this sense, stabilization may imply stabilization of the general level of money wages, of prices, or of employment. In conditions of increasing productivity (which we are mainly ignoring in this book but which are obviously highly relevant, since the purpose of net investment in industry is to raise productivity), there is usually inconsistency between attempts to stabilize money wages and prices; stable prices then imply rising money incomes, and stable money incomes per head could only be consistent with a slowly falling price level. If the aim is to have very low levels of unemployment, there is inconsistency between attempts to stabilize employment and to stabilize prices and wages, because prices and wages tend to rise progressively when unemployment is very low. What is more, we cannot be sure that there is any fixed and low unemployment percentage which is consistent, year in and year out, with price stability; for example, in years of good harvests, 2 per cent unemployment may be consistent with price stability, but in bad years, 5 per cent unemployment may still involve cumulative inflationary tendencies.

Analytically, therefore, the problem is difficult. A reasonable practical escape is to consider the policies that would be needed in an industrial country to stabilize unemployment at some level which is reasonably low and acceptable politically (say 2 per cent or 3 per cent), but which is not so low that it is likely to involve unacceptable price or wage rises. Even if such employment stabilization is completely effective (something we shall shortly find we have to doubt a little), some price and wage changes are likely to be induced in some years. Such a situation is probably widely acceptable, however; the danger that is widely feared is of price rises so steady and implacable that confidence in the currency is lost, with the consequence that people become unwilling to hold wealth in money, bonds, or other forms whose value is fixed in terms of money.

It should be emphasized that, in laying emphasis on employment stabilization, we are making a political judgment which probably has the virtue of being widely acceptable, and certainly has the virtue of being rather easier to handle analytically than an interpretation of stabilization as meaning an attempt rigidly to stabilize prices or wages. It is, however, open to anyone to prefer to lay primary emphasis on price stabilization; if he does he is likely to have a much more cautious bias in his policies than in those we shall consider, because of the asymmetry of price changes in the full employment zone: prices rise sharply and cumulatively if unemployment falls to very low levels but do not tend to fall sharply or cumulatively when unemployment is high.

Stabilization Instruments

The next question we have to answer in our discussion of stabilization policy concerns the instruments which are to be used for attaining the objective of stabilization. This question has two aspects, one of which need concern us only very briefly, while the other will detain us for longer.

The first aspect of the question is whether government action can be discretionary or whether a set of legal rules should be set up which say that the authorities shall do prescribed things in prescribed circumstances. This decision is essentially constitutional. To some extent, it is influenced by political judgments (those who doubt the wisdom of governments will be more inclined to favor systems which do not allow them so much discretionary power). Probably still more, it is linked to the nature of the administrative and legislative processes in the country concerned. This is probably the reason why there has been much more discussion in the United States than in Britain of various artificially 'built-in' stabilizers, such as provision for automatic budget deficits in proportion to unemployment percentages when these rise above a given figure. The important thing is that the same general economic principles apply whether stabilization policy is discretionary or legally 'built in.'

The other aspect of the choice of stabilization instruments is more important for our purpose. In a closed economy there are three main kinds of instrument that can be used in attempting to maintain economic stability. There are monetary controls, fiscal controls, and direct controls. Monetary controls are those which operate through the banking system and/or the rate of interest. Fiscal controls are those which operate through changes in the taxation and expenditure policies of the government. Direct controls are controls imposed by the government which expressly forbid or restrict certain kinds of economic activity.

As with all such classifications, there is some fuzziness at the boundaries between the three types. For example, bank credit rationing imposed by government order can be regarded either as a direct or as a monetary control. Again, government manipulation of the long-term bond market can be regarded either as a monetary or a fiscal control. In each case the choice is a matter of convenience and depends on the context.

In modern circumstances, policies for attaining economic stability are likely to include some examples of each of these three kinds of instrument. The choice of the constituents of the mixture depends largely upon political judgments, which are not our immediate concern. Purely technical economic considerations must, however, have an important influence on decisions about the appropriate mixture. We must, therefore, consider some of the most relevant economic characteristics of each of these controls.

The oldest (and for long the only respectable) instrument is that of monetary control, taking the form of changes in interest rates and in the availability of bank credit. This instrument has the considerable virtue of flexibility: it can be rapidly imposed or removed, and the force with which it operates can be adjusted sensitively. Discount rate changes can be made from week to week; open market operations can take place continuously and can be 'played by ear,' while instructions to the commercial banks can be made at a moment's notice. What is more, some of the effects of changes in monetary controls may show themselves quite quickly. Insofar as changes in monetary policy operate through altering expectations and through affecting traders' ability and desire to hold stocks of goods, the effects of changes appear within a few days or weeks. The other side of this coin is the fact that the total possible effects of monetary policy tend to be rather limited, especially for encouraging expansion. The main effects which are possible in the short run probably come from variations in the availability of bank credit. These can come into operation quite quickly, but their total possible magnitude is probably quite small. As for interest rate changes as such, we saw in Chapter 7 that their effect on investment and savings plans is probably relatively weak. Moreover, there is a minimum level below which interest rates cannot fall (as we saw in Chapter 4)—hence their value is frequently very limited as a mechanism for causing recovery from very low levels of activity, because an impossibly low rate of interest might be needed to cause appreciable expansion.[2]

Above this minimum limit, there is one way in which changes in the level of interest rates may have a big effect, but this takes a long time to bring into operation. Plans for investment in long-lived capital (such as houses, railways, and roads) will be significantly affected by interest rate changes. On the other hand such investments usually take a long time to plan, so that the effects of changes in the level of interest rates may not show very much for several years. In this respect, therefore, interest rates are hardly a flexible mechanism.

To sum up, monetary weapons can have a rapid but limited effect operating mainly through changes in the availability of bank credit; they can also have a very slow but quite considerable effect, operating through changes in the general level of long-term interest rates.

Fiscal controls, by which we mean changes in the level of activity imposed by changes in government expenditure and taxation policy, tend to be slow in getting into operation, but are always capable of having very large effects when they are in full operation. The slowness is the result of constitutional factors such as the delay in passing legislation and the convention of annual budgets, administrative delays in transforming decisions into actions, and the fact that even when tax or expenditure changes do get into operation, their effects are spread over a long period and do not all come more or less at once. The convention that budgets normally occur only annually also provides another disadvantage of fiscal control, namely, a certain 'jumpiness.' It may well be that if reliance is placed on fiscal controls alone, nothing is done for several months, and then it is done too violently, in an attempt to catch up.

Some economists would disagree about the ability of fiscal controls to have very large effects, given sufficient time; they point to the risk that a budget deficit may discourage a recovery of private investment. Such reactions may be large enough to matter, but even if they are, it is always possible to make the budget deficit still

---

[2] Moreover, even if this 'liquidity trap' did not exist, interest rates could not be pushed below zero without big institutional changes (such as the 'stamped money' idea that was suggested by several writers between the wars). But even a zero rate of interest might not be sufficient to encourage recovery from very depressed economic conditions.

larger. The opposite action, of making the budget surplus larger and larger to deal with inflation, is one to which more obvious limits attach, because of the difficulty of indefinite increases in taxes or reductions in government expenditure. But in either case, the technical limits to the size of control possible through fiscal policy are very broad; such narrow limits as may exist are the result of political prejudice, in such forms as unswerving belief in the rectitude of balanced budgets, or implacable opposition to any restriction or extension of the field of governmental activities.

It is possible to sum up a great deal of the difference between monetary and fiscal instruments of control quite briefly. Broadly speaking, fiscal instruments of control can do much more than monetary instruments, and in particular they can be invaluable for lifting the economy out of a depression. Monetary instruments, on the other hand, can act more sensitively and less jerkily and can therefore also be useful for the delicate task of maintaining a situation of full employment without inflation.

In fairly normal times at least, direct controls suffer much more than the other two instruments from politically based limitations on the range within which they can be used. While accepting the importance of these limitations, we can point out the ways in which direct controls may be particularly advantageous as weapons for controlling the economy, at least in countries where they can be effectively enforced. This matter of enforcement is an important one: direct controls need a cumbersome administrative organization if they are to work, and even then it is almost impossible to avoid some leakages around the controls. One advantage that direct controls share with monetary controls is that they can be introduced or changed quickly (so long as the administrative apparatus is ready and available), so that the effects of these changes can be rapid. This is a consequence of the fact that direct controls are invariably negative—they stop someone from doing something he would otherwise do. It is always possible for a government with sufficient political power to prohibit anyone from doing anything, almost at a moment's notice. A government could, if it wished, reduce fixed investment to zero almost overnight.[3]

---

[3] On the other hand, direct controls can be much less effective if they have to be tempered with a regard for equity. If a time delay is allowed, so that existing commitments can be fulfilled, the controls work much more slowly.

The fact that direct controls are all negative lies behind another feature they possess which may be very valuable: that these controls can be more discriminatory than monetary and fiscal controls. This may be particularly important at times when big structural adjustments are taking place, such as during or after a war. There may be very serious shortages of certain commodities, such as coal or steel, or there may be a need to divert resources into particular uses. Direct controls can be easily operated in a discriminatory manner; they can favor some industries and burden others, or allow things to be done in one set of circumstances and prohibit them in others. This is not to deny that monetary and fiscal controls may have discriminatory intensions of the same kind (e.g. by taxing particular industries or making credit particularly scarce in particular uses), and still more frequently these controls will have discriminatory effects, by burdening some industries and social classes more than others. All the same, direct controls are particularly susceptible to operation in discriminatory ways.

A further advantage of direct controls is that variation in the intensity of the operation of controls may take up some of the fluctuations in the economy that otherwise would have to reflect themselves in price or output changes. It may sometimes be considered that it is better to have short-period fluctuations in the intensity with which steel rationing is imposed, or in the difficulty in obtaining building licences, than to have fluctuations from quarter to quarter or year to year in the price level or the level of activity.

Despite these advantages, there are also strong economic arguments against too much use of direct controls, especially for too long a time. For one thing, they tend to inhibit innovations, such as new techniques. They tend to freeze activity into existing channels, because it is only with existing channels that the bureaucrat can easily deal. Moreover, like any other economic change, they can easily induce speculation, which may be destabilizing. For example, if it is expected that steel is to be rationed, because of a slight shortage, consumers may try to accumulate abnormally large stocks, which aggravates the shortage.

Another weakness in direct controls is that they may, by putting pressure on one part of the economy, cause increased strain in other parts. This is particularly likely in the case of consumer rationing: if one commodity is rationed, then consumers have so much more of their income left over, with which they will probably attempt to buy more of other goods. In fact, direct controls are very likely to lead to the harmful effects of suppressed inflation, which we looked at in an earlier chapter. These dangers are less likely in the use of investment controls: if a firm is forbidden to build a factory it is not very likely immediately to plan to build a hotel which it would not otherwise have considered building. For this reason, it seems likely that direct controls over investment are more likely to be acceptable in countries which decide to make use of direct controls than are controls over consumption.

SOME SUGGESTED READING

A discussion of the matters treated in this chapter is to be found in most of the standard texts dealing with macro-economics. Beyond this rather conventional level, the literature is surprisingly meager. Several useful articles are gathered together in Part Seven of *Readings in Business Cycles and National Income*, edited by A. H. Hansen and R. V. Clemence (New York, 1953). A. P. Lerner, *Economics of Employment* (New York, 1951) is a useful radical treatment of the problem. A. G. Hart, *Money, Debt and Economic Activity* (New York, 1948) and A. H. Hansen, *Fiscal Policy and Business Cycles* (New York, 1941) are both well worth looking into.

26

Fluctuations and Stabilization Policy in the United States

Historical experience in the United States shows how prone modern economies are to fluctuations; but it also shows how much can be done, by means of automatic built-in stabilizers and by well-directed discretionary policy, to limit these fluctuations. In this chapter, we shall be concerned with two things: with tracing an outline of historical experience of economic fluctuations in the United States since the First World War, and with discussing some of the means by which it now seems likely that we can manage affairs so that we can achieve a greater measure of economic stability than in the inter-war years.

The Historical Experience: The Inter-War Years

The inter-war years can conveniently be divided into four periods. The first is the period of postwar adjustment, ending in the sharp recession of 1920-1921. The second is the period of high prosperity that continued up to 1929, which was only interrupted by minor setbacks in 1923-1924 and 1926-1927. The third period is that of the catastrophic decline and economic stagnation of the Great Depression; and the fourth is the period of recovery which started in the mid-'thirties, marred by a short but sharp recession in 1937-1938, which was in turn followed by recovery with the approach of war.

No one can claim to be able to make a full analysis of all the causes of these fluctuations, and there is plenty of room for disagreement in detail. But in broad outline there can be little doubt that the forces at work were to a very large extent those which we have been discussing in the theoretical analysis of economic fluctuations in earlier chapters of this book. In particular, it is clear that fluctuations in investment have a very great deal to do with the causation of fluctuations in the levels of income, activity, and prices; these fluctuations in investment have included changes in gross fixed investment in manufacturing and other industrial plant and equipment, changes in other construction (notably housing), and changes in inventory accumulation.

As is suggested by our theoretical analysis, the general pattern of causation in United States experience has been for consumption expenditure to vary as a result of changes in the level of income and activity, rather than being a major factor as an initiator of such changes.[1] Of course, once changes in consumption have been induced they have led to further changes in income, through the multiplier process. And in absolute terms, changes in consumption are highly significant, simply because consumption accounts for such a large part of national income. But in relative terms, investment changes are much more important. In several of the minor cycles investment has altered sharply while it is hard to see appreciable changes in consumption, and in the Great Depression, gross investment fell by nearly 95 per cent, while total consumption fell only by about 40 per cent. Again, the failure to achieve a strong recovery in the 'thirties is probably mainly the result of the failure of fixed investment expenditure to recover to its pre-Depression levels. Moreover, there is further evidence for believing that changes in investment (and consumer durable expenditure) have been the main causative factor, rather than changes in consumption: the normal pattern has been for changes in investment to precede changes in consumption.

The effects of government expenditure and of the actions of the monetary authorities was sometimes stabilizing and sometimes destabilizing in the inter-war period: sometimes they countered the changes in income and activity caused by other factors, but on occasion they aggravated the fluctuations. It is therefore now necessary to consider what happened in the inter-war period in a little more detail.

---

[1] Although, as we saw in Chapter 9, expenditure on consumer durables can vary to an important extent independently of income, and such changes may sometimes have been major causative factors in economic fluctuations.

The Prosperity of the 'Twenties

After a very minor flurry of recession in the last months of 1918 and early 1919, as a result of the immediate problems of reconversion from a war to a peace economy, a strong and inflationary boom set in during 1919. Five major elements contributed to this; there was a backlog of fixed investment (such as construction); export sales were high, particularly to Europe; there was a government deficit through the first three quarters of the year; Federal Reserve policy was to keep both long- and short-term interest rates low in order to facilitate the Treasury's borrowing operations; and the boom, rising prices, and easy money all encouraged large-scale inventory accumulations by private business. With all these expansionary forces working together, industrial production and prices rose sharply.

The turning point into the slump of 1920-1921 came at the very beginning of 1920, when industrial production fell sharply; fifteen months later, when the trough was reached, it had fallen by about one-third. The turn in prices came about six months after the turn in industrial production; both the rise and fall in prices lagged behind most of the other changes.

The collapse in 1920 came as a result of a reduction in the pressure to expansion from each of the five forces listed above. Perhaps the most important cause of the reversal was the collapse of speculative investment in inventories. This was partly the result of the reversal of Federal Reserve policy in October, 1919. Rediscount rates charged by all the Federal Reserve Banks were raised at least twice between October, 1919, and June, 1920; this was a deliberate policy, intended to break the speculative boom and to bring prices down to what were regarded as normal levels. The Federal Reserve action was made possible because the Treasury no longer needed to borrow; the government swung into budgetary surplus in the last quarter of 1919; this in itself contributed to the downturn in activity by reducing the flow of expenditure on current output. It is, however, hard to put the primary responsibility for the downturn on Federal Reserve policy; bank loans continued to expand in the first few months of 1920, and there was no severe credit rationing to cause financial panic.

The most important single cause of the downturn was probably simply that inventory holdings were top-heavy and some liquidation was inevitable; this became rapid in the middle of 1920, when prices broke. But there were also probably other forces which helped trigger off the collapse; fixed investment may have declined (building contracts turned down in the latter part of 1919), and in addition exports were lower in 1920 than in 1919. But probably the best way to understand a situation that is not particularly clear (largely because the statistics are inadequate) is that the collapse of 1920 was rather like the collapse of many of the nineteenth-century booms —it was a reaction against an overextended speculative position.

Recovery from the slump started in mid-1921, and from then until 1929 the United States economy enjoyed a long period of high prosperity, which was only slightly marred by two minor recessions in 1923-1924 and 1926-1927. Both of these recessions seem largely to have been due to temporary changes in the rate of inventory accumulation, and so were basically of the same character as the minor fluctuations we saw in the level of activity in Chapter 6. Broadly speaking, the 'twenties saw alternations of about two years of upswing followed by a year of minor recession; the predominance of upswings was largely the result of the fact that the minor fluctuations were around a trend of economic growth.[2]

The first clear signs of the 1921 recovery were a rise in industrial output, from about two-thirds of capacity in mid-1921 to about 95 per cent (or practically full employment) by the early months of 1923. Once again, prices were a much less satisfactory indicator of what was happening; wholesale prices continued to fall until early 1922, again showing a lag before recovery, while retail prices declined about 5 per cent in the early stages of this economic recovery and subsequently altered very little.

One main cause of the recovery in 1921-1922 was an expansion in fixed investment, notably in building construction (largely in reaction to the housing shortage and the high level of rents), which recovered steadily after the summer of 1921[3] and was to be a major factor in maintaining the boom of the 'twenties. The value of total new construction practically doubled between 1921 and the peak of 1926. The other main factor in recovery from 1921 to 1922

---

[2] A subject with which it has not been possible to deal in the theoretical parts of this book.

[3] The index of the value of building permits started to recover even earlier, in January, 1921, and doubled in less than six months.

was a swing back to inventory accumulation after the reductions in inventories in 1920-1921; business inventories rose by $1½ billion in 1922 and $3 billion in 1923. Federal Reserve policy also encouraged the expansion in 1921-1922; rediscount rates were lowered and credit became easier; these changes may well have contributed to the swing in inventory holdings.

The minor recession of 1923-1924 is generally attributed to Federal Reserve policy, made in reaction to fears of inflation induced by appreciable rises in wholesale prices in late 1922 and early 1923, at a time when several continental European countries were suffering from serious inflations. Interest rates started to be raised from February, 1923, and then a concerted policy of open market operations by the twelve Federal Reserve Banks was introduced to reinforce the deflation.

The sharpest change in expenditure at the time of the 1923-1924 recession was in business inventories, which, after rising by $3 billion in 1923, fell by $0.9 billion in 1924.[4] In addition, expenditure on producers' plant and equipment and consumers' durable goods both leveled off or contracted slightly; but construction expenditure continued to expand. On balance, the recession was very slight, and only for about nine months in 1924 did industrial output fall below 90 per cent of capacity.

Recovery in the level of industrial output started in July, 1924, and expanded in line with capacity up to the next peak in the fall of 1926. Price changes were relatively minor; in fact, through the greater part of the 'twenties, relatively full employment did not lead to any persistent tendency to price inflation. The main reasons for this fairly high degree of price stability were probably the rapid growth in industrial productivity and the tendency toward weakness of primary product prices on world markets.

The expansion of 1925 was mainly the result of a swing back to business inventory accumulation (after the opposite movement in 1924) and to the continuing expansion of construction. But already the signs of later trouble were beginning to appear; in 1925, residential construction reached its peak, as a result of an ending of the housing shortage; total construction still expanded a little in

---

[4] It seems possible, although it cannot be proved, that some of the rise in inventories in 1923 was unplanned, as in the downswing of the theoretical inventory cycle in Chapter 6.

1926, but one of the main sources of buoyancy in the 'twenties was starting to disappear. Oddly enough, in 1925, a year of expansion, consumption declined a little; this was the only year in the 'twenties when this happened; even in the slight recessions, incomes were maintained sufficiently for consumption to continue to expand.

The 1926-1927 recession was again minor and industrial production was below 90 per cent capacity for less than a year. The recession was marked by lower rates of inventory accumulation and by a start in the decline of construction. It may also have been exaggerated by the closing down of the Ford plant during a model change—one of the main reasons for the buoyancy of the 'twenties was the growth in demand for automobiles.

Recovery came again in 1927-1928, but with hindsight, it is now possible to see that it was not too firmly based. Total construction expenditure was hovering around its peak level in 1927 and declined appreciably in 1928. In 1928-1929, expenditure on producers' equipment helped keep the expansion going. But the underlying position was increasingly unstable. Construction expenditure had been one of the main bases of the expansion of the 'twenties and it was now declining. Moreover, there was the real risk that markets for consumer durables, which had been largely based on borrowing, would also contract.

Unfortunately, many of the indicators (including those on which economists were at the time inclined to place emphasis) were apparently remarkably satisfactory. In particular, prices were stable, with a slight downward trend. This was regarded as satisfactory; it was not realized that this situation at a time of high industrial activity was largely the result of the increasing difficulties that were affecting the primary-producing sector of the world economy.

The other major indicator of the economic situation, which for a long time was regarded as indicating that prosperity would last, was the level of stock market prices. These prices had been rising steadily through the 'twenties and had been almost completely unaffected by the 1926-1927 recession. For the most part, the Federal Reserve maintained a policy of easy money from mid-1924 to mid-1928, with some minor counter-cyclical stabilizing action. Money was allowed to be particularly easy in early 1927, but then in early 1928 the Federal Reserve became alarmed and interest rates were raised to the highest levels since 1921, and in the first half of 1929 monetary stringency was enforced. But by this point the ability of the authorities to limit the quantity of money and to enforce higher interest rates had little effect on the stock market, which soared away through the summer of 1929 to collapse in the panic of October, which was to wreck the whole of the unstable foundations of confidence on which the later 'twenties had been built.

The Great Depression

The fact that was not realized until the stock market collapse was that the turn-around in economic activity had come a few months earlier; industrial production started to fall after July. But such is the difficulty of economic diagnosis that it would not have been unreasonable to see this simply as another inventory recession of the type already experienced twice in the 'twenties; inventory accumulation was fairly high in 1929 and it would be reasonable to expect much smaller accumulations (or very possibly reductions) in the following year.

In the event, this did happen; inventory accumulation was +$1.6 billion in 1929 and −$0.3 billion in 1930. But much worse was to happen at the same time. Loss of confidence and the exhaustion of investment needs combined to reduce gross fixed investment from $14.2 billion to $10.5 billion—a decline of about 26 per cent; while purchases of consumer durables fell by about 22 per cent, from $9.4 billion to $7.3 billion. The percentage fall in other consumer expenditure was much smaller (less than 9 per cent) but the absolute fall was large, from $69.4 billion to $63.5 billion.

The Federal Reserve tried to meet the situation after the stock market crash by sharply reducing interest rates and by open market purchases designed to lead to credit expansion. But these operations were almost useless to deal with a catastrophe of the magnitude of the 1929 collapse. The only action that could have prevented a serious recession would have been expansionary fiscal policy, using large budget deficits. At the time this was regarded as quite a wrong policy and in fact what happened to the government's budgetary position in the years of decline was a result of pressure of circumstances. In 1930, the government still had a budget surplus; in the next two years, there was a deficit, which (by good luck rather than design) had a very slight effect in counteracting the decline.

Everything was set, therefore, in 1929-1930 for a cumulative contraction of the kind analyzed in Chapter 24, with an interaction of the multiplier and the accelerator. For some months in early 1931, it seemed quite possible that this cumulative process might not run very much farther, but these hopes were quickly to be dashed. Private fixed investment fell by 35 per cent—this was faster than in the preceding year; net inventory reduction increased from $0.3 billion to $1.4 billion; and expenditure on consumer durables fell from $7.3 billion to $5.6 billion. At the same time, other consumption expenditure fell from $63.5 billion to $55.6 billion—a fall by nearly 13 per cent.

The collapse was now well under way. And, unfortunately it was aggravated by financial developments, some perhaps inevitable, but others which could have been avoided. The inevitable effects were that businessmen and many consumers were obsessed by the need to liquidate some of the burden of debt they had built up in the 'twenties. Less inevitable was the action of the Federal Reserve, which reversed the easy money policy in the fall of 1931, after the financial crisis in Europe which had culminated in Britain's abandonment of the gold standard.[5] The European crisis led to foreign withdrawals of funds from New York which led to a loss of gold from the United States reserves. To halt the loss of gold the Federal Reserve raised interest rates and tightened credit. The comparatively large stock of gold in the United States at that time makes the authorities' reaction to the loss of gold seem absurd; but a substantial proportion of the gold stock was at that time tied up as backing for Federal Reserve notes since the other permissible collateral for notes, short-term commercial paper, was in short supply. It was not until the passage of the Glass-Steagall Act of 1932 that the Federal Reserve was authorized to use government securities as backing for notes; and while the Federal Reserve responded to its new freedom by engaging in large-scale open market purchases some damage had already been done. The tightening of credit in the fall of 1931 led to a rush to restore liquidity and caused a further rise of stock market selling which caused even bigger percentage falls in security prices than in the 1929 panic.

The result was that 1932 was a year in which the financial system was in a prolonged state of panic, while the multiplier-accelerator process was leading rapidly toward a situation in which no invest-

---

[5] Discussed below, in Chapters 36 and 39.

ment at all would take place—something like the floor of our model cycle of Chapter 24. In 1932, fixed investment was only $3.5 billion; consumer durable expenditures only $3.7 billion, and other consumer expenditure $45.5 billion—falls of 76 per cent, 60 per cent and 35 per cent respectively from the 1929 levels.

The liquidity crisis came to an end in the spring of 1933, only after the failure of some 4000 banks and the temporary closing down of the whole banking system. The level of national income fell a little more in 1933, but the recovery started because inventories had almost been reduced to rock bottom, so that the rate of inventory reduction fell from $2.6 billion to $1.3 billion. This slight expansionary force more than counteracted a further fall in gross private fixed investment from $3.5 billion to $3.1 billion.

The start of the upswing from the Great Depression was in March, 1933, when the financial crisis ended and the new administration came in with an active recovery program. The main element in this was the NRA (National Recovery Administration), which was largely designed to spread work and prevent price cuts. For a time, its effects were good, and industrial output jumped sharply. This recovery soon came to an end, however, and it came to be realized that the NRA was in the long run doing harm; when it was declared unconstitutional in 1935, there was general relief. The early New Deal policies did some good for a time—but they did not bring the level of activity high enough to lead to much of a revival of private investment; gross fixed investment in 1934 was still only $3.9 billion.

Although the new administration had originally come in pledged to 'economy,' its deficit rose a little as public works got under way; but in total, deficit financing was not much greater in 1933-1935 than in 1932; only in 1936, when the Soldiers' Bonus added $2 billion to the deficit, was much difference really made. 'Keynesian' policies of deficit financing did not have a great deal to do with the recovery of the 'thirties.

By the time of the Soldiers' Bonus, expansion was getting substantially under way; business inventory accumulation started again in 1935 and fixed investment continued to grow, albeit very slowly. By 1936, gross private fixed investment was $7.3 billion—just about half the 1929 figure. New construction was still far below 1929 ($2.3 billion against $8.8 billion); the unsatisfactory recovery from the

Great Depression was largely the result of the low demand for housing and other new buildings.

Looking back, it seems that 1936-1937 were seriously depressed, with unemployment still very heavy. But at the time, conditions almost seemed prosperous, and (remarkably prematurely) there was talk of the dangers of inflation. It was true that commodity prices were rising but only from the very low levels of the early 'thirties, which had caused serious distress to primary producers. Nevertheless, the expansionary policy of the government and the Federal Reserve was reversed; relief expenditure and public works projects were cut and the Federal Reserve raised the reserve requirements of the member banks (although substantial excess reserves still remained). All these moves seem to have been interpreted as implying a sharp deflationary policy; and in any case many firms thought they were holding excessive inventories. The consequence was a remarkably sharp contraction in the levels of income and activity from the early summer of 1937 to the summer of 1938. As in the recessions of the 'twenties, inventory reductions after a period of inventory accumulation explain a large part of the turn-around; but the collapse was much sharper than those experienced in the mid 'twenties, because it was aggravated and in fact largely provoked by government policy, and because of the jittery state of expectations after the experiences of the early 'thirties.

In 1938 the fiscal policies of the government and the monetary policies of the Federal Reserve were reversed, and by the end of the year expansion was again under way and inventory accumulation started again. This recovery was in turn absorbed by the boom which developed as war came to Europe and started to threaten the United States.

Wartime and Post-War Inflation

After Pearl Harbor, inflation became the dominant problem as practically all the unemployed and many people who would not normally be in the labor force were brought into civilian employment or into the armed forces. Moreover, the government's demands for goods and services for the war effort were so great that there was a serious excess of demand over supply, even though taxes were raised to unprecedented levels. The budgetary deficit was more than $50 billion a year at the height of the war in 1943 and 1944: equilibrium between demand and supply would probably have involved impossible levels of taxes.

This inflationary situation was met in two ways: some of it was 'suppressed' [6] while some was prevented by controls.

The suppression was carried out by rationing, controls, and sheer unavailability of many goods; this led firms and households to save more than they would otherwise have done (either in cash or government bonds). Most of this suppression merely amounted to a postponement of demand; in the early post-war years, after suppression had ended, transactors were so liquid that they spent much more than they would normally have done, adding seriously to the post-war inflation of 1946-1947. In addition, patriotic appeals to the public led to particularly large wartime savings—and then to particularly heavy dissaving after the war.

Controls and rationing did not merely suppress inflation; they also did a good deal to help prevent inflation altogether. Each of the main economic groups in the community was in wartime in a strong position to increase the price of the things it sold; labor could ask for higher wages, farmers and businessmen for higher prices. But it was apparent to everyone that this would simply lead to a cumulative price rise; if each group acted defensively to restore its real income and/or expenditure wherever price rises occurred, or if each group merely reacted passively (by increasing its selling price when demand exceeded supply and by increasing its expenditure when its income rose)—if these things happened, prices would inevitably have risen cumulatively. [7]

Price controls and rationing were some of the means used to prevent this cumulative process. They, together with an acceptance of a wage freeze by labor, in effect amounted to an agreement between the main economic groups to share the burden of the loss implicit in the need for military production. Fortunately, this loss was not too burdensome; output rose so much that total consumption (except of durables) was able to increase through the war, and not fall as in most of the belligerent countries.

It was generally expected that there would be considerable un-

[6] See Chapter 19.
[7] See Part IV of this book.

employment immediately after the war, as the armed forces and war workers were released and reconversion of factories took place. In the event, there were no such difficulties and activity stayed at very high levels. But the wartime restraints soon broke down; the major economic groups were soon pushing for all they could get and price control soon proved ineffective, to be abandoned in 1946. Demand was at high levels (both at home and from foreign countries) and inflation was sharp until 1948. Monetary policy was hardly used at all to influence the inflation; the wartime policy of low interest rates was continued, in order to reduce the burden on the Treasury, which owed a great deal of short-term debt coming up for frequent renewal. Fiscal policy was used only to the extent of seeing that demand did not get wholly out of line with supply; but in these early post-war years it was presumably thought undesirable to raise taxes or reduce government expenditure sufficiently to stop the inflation.

Post-War Economic Fluctuations

The great difference between economic policy in the pre-war and post-war years is that economists now have a fairly good understanding of the factors that determine whether there will be excessive unemployment or inflation—and this understanding has been successfully transmitted to Washington. The consequence is that, when there has been substantial inflation since the war, it has been more or less accepted deliberately as the best of various political evils. And, although we have been through two minor recessions since the war, neither of them got out of control. Each of them was mainly an inventory recession of the type experienced in the 'twenties. At the time of writing, we are still in the third of the post-war recessions, which started in the fall of 1957.

The remarkable feature of the post-war period is that there has been no major recession of the type of 1920 or 1937, let alone that of 1929. In the early post-war years, the general fear was that such a recession was inevitable: the unwillingness to deal more toughly with the post-war inflation may have been largely due to a fear of provoking a sharp recession. In the event, however, nothing of the sort happened. When a recession did finally come in 1948-1949, it was both mild and short-lived. Industrial production fell by about 10 per cent between the preceding peak in the fall of 1948 and the trough in the summer of 1949, and in 1949 as a whole it was about 7 per cent below 1948 levels. But once recovery started in the summer of 1949, it was quite rapid and the pre-recession levels of industrial production were again reached by the spring of 1950. In detailed characteristics, the recession was quite predominantly one of re-adjustment from the post-war inflation; the immediate pressures of post-war demand had declined and inventories were for a time reduced. In the fourth quarter of 1948, business inventories were increasing at an annual rate of $9.0 billion, whereas by the third quarter of 1949 they were being reduced at an annual rate of $2.4 billion. This switch around of $11.4 billion explains practically the whole of the $13.0 billion decline in the level of gross private domestic investment between the peak and the trough of this recession; the relatively small remainder of the decline was the result of small declines in investment in plant and equipment by producers other than farmers. Construction expenditure was well maintained, and consumption fell only very slightly, by a little over 1 per cent. In volume, consumption expenditure rose slightly, since consumers' prices fell about 2 per cent during the downswing; they leveled out during the subsequent upswing in activity. Wholesale prices fell more sharply and continued to fall until January, 1950, when the recovery was well under way; by then they were 11 per cent below the 1948 peaks. The biggest falls were in farm and wholesale food prices.

All in all, the 1948-1949 cycle was a classic inventory readjustment cycle. On balance, government fiscal action was stabilizing, with an increased budget deficit, partly because of increased government expenditure on defense and overseas, and partly as an automatic result of the pressure of recession on unemployment compensation and agricultural price support expenditure. These automatic effects of recession are now much more powerful than they were in the early 'thirties because of the greater importance of these built-in schemes for supporting incomes in a recession. They mean that fluctuations tend to be damped out—although not prevented.

The period between the 1948-1949 recession and that of 1953-1954 was marked by the Korean War and inflation. Shortages of raw materials and government stockpiling induced sharp rises in world market prices of primary products, and the situation was aggravated by private speculation. Subsequently, in 1951-1952 these prices fell sharply and have been rather weak ever since. The Korean-induced inflation in the United States was partly met by tax increases and price control—the latter being much less powerful or effective than in the Second World War.

The next recession, which started in the late summer or fall of 1953 and reached its lowest point in the summer of 1954, was largely induced by the process of readjustment after the Korean War and once again was predominantly an inventory cycle, conforming fairly neatly to the pattern described in Chapter 6. It seems quite probable that this cycle was made a little bigger than it might have been by Federal Reserve action in the first half of 1953 [8] in raising discount rates and tightening credit. This timing probably helped the downturn—although it is doubtful whether it provoked it. Subsequently, when the recession was well under way in early 1954, interest rates were lowered.

The importance of inventories in this cycle is shown by the fact that in the second quarter of 1953 they were increasing at an annual rate of $4.5 billion; by the third quarter of 1954 they were declining at an annual rate of $4.9 billion. This swing around of $9.4 billion more than fully accounted for the decline between the two periods in gross private domestic investment of $9.1 billion (at annual rates). Fixed investment actually increased, chiefly as a result of increases in construction expenditure which offset some decline in expenditure on producers' plant and equipment. Consumption showed no signs at all of reacting to the decline in total national income; it rose steadily through the recession, and was about 9 per cent higher at the end of the recession than at the beginning. The reason was that disposable income rose sharply between 1953 and 1954, mainly because of tax reductions, and also partly the result of the built-in stabilizers already discussed in connection with the 1948-1949 recession. The counterpart of this increase in disposable income was an increase in the government deficit from a pre-recession annual rate of $4.7 billion to a peak rate of $12.1 billion in the first quarter of 1954.

The swing in industrial output in this cycle was comparable with that in 1948-1949; the decline from the peak month of May, 1953, to the trough in March-April, 1954, was 10 per cent.

---

[8] Following the revival of active monetary policy in 1951—see Chapter 14.

Just as Federal Reserve action in 1953 may have done something to aggravate the onset of recession, so the action in the summer of 1957 may have had similar effects. All the same, there is still less justification for accusations that the 1957-1958 recession was the responsibility of the Federal Reserve than on the earlier occasion, because in 1957 there were clear signs of incipient recession at the time rates were raised and credit tightened.

The main reason why contractionary monetary policy was used at a time when recession seemed to be coming anyway was that in 1957 the United States had for the first time to face up to all the difficulties in the choice between complete price stability and a low level of unemployment, which were discussed in Chapter 22. The problem of choice did not appear in the early post-war years or in the Korean War years, because a degree of price inflation was more or less deliberately accepted; and it did not appear from 1952 to 1956 largely because food prices were tending to fall, so that the total consumer price index was remarkably stable even though other prices were rising. When the forces which had been weakening farm prices disappeared in 1956, the specter of secular inflation became much more threatening and the problem of choosing between some inflation and a higher level of unemployment became pressing. The Federal Reserve action was largely determined by a belief that secular inflation was an evil that must be exorcised—even at the cost of higher unemployment.

It is still too early to give a full analysis of this latest recession. All that can be said is that it has been somewhat deeper than either of the other two, and, unlike them, has been marked by a fall in fixed manufacturing investment; on the other hand, one of its main constituents has again been a reduction in inventories.

The decline in industrial production, from the peak in August, 1957, to the trough in April, 1958, was 13 per cent. The inventory element in the reduction in expenditure was at an annual rate of $10.2 billion, from accumulation at a rate of $2.2 billion per year in the third quarter of 1957 to inventory reductions of $8.0 billion in the second quarter of 1958. But in total, the annual rate of gross private investment fell by $17.8 billion between these two periods; the difference was mainly accounted for by a decline in purchases of producers' durable equipment by $5.7 billion (a 20 per cent decline) and relatively small declines in new construction.

Once again, disposable personal income and consumption have been very well maintained, hardly altering at all; again the main reason has been that government transfer payments (such as unemployment benefits) have risen. In addition, government (mainly state and local) expenditure on goods and services rose through the downswing of the recession so that fiscal developments were probably once again stabilizing in their effects. The Federal Reserve also undertook open market purchases during the downswing and reduced rediscount rates.

Beyond this, it is still impossible to go on in tracing the history of the latest recession. But the experience of the last year or two shows that real problems of economic stabilization remain with us. We have seen that our recent experience shows that the choice between full employment and inflation can be very awkward. Another of the great difficulties is that although we can quickly recognize the arrival of a recession, but that it is not at all easy to be sure whether it is going to be a minor inventory recession or a major decline. The reader will recall that, until the stock market crash, it would have seemed quite reasonable to regard the 1929 downturn as similar to those of 1923 and 1926. Yet we can now see, with hindsight, that investment opportunities were being exhausted in the late 'twenties, and even in the absence of the blow to confidence induced by the stock market crash, a substantial recession was likely in the absence of firm and rapid counteraction by the government. The big question is, How can we be sure that each time an apparently minor recession appears, it will not rapidly spiral down into something like the Great Depression?

One thing we can do is to try to understand the underlying forces in the economy as well as possible—forces such as the decline of construction expenditure in the late 'twenties. But in these matters there is so much room for judgment that people who predict a sharp decline may for too long be dismissed as pessimists—or that people who predict buoyancy may be regarded as too optimistic. This problem has clearly appeared in 1957-1958, with the varying interpretations of the importance and significance of decline in plans for fixed investment by manufacturers.

But there are further reasons for optimism about avoiding anything as bad as 1929-1933. One is that changes in the financial system,[9] and the very fact of memories of what happened in 1929, mean that the likelihood of financial panic is not now as great as it was. Another is that the multiplier is now much weaker than it was in the inter-war years, so the system is less unstable. It is smaller because of the greater importance of progressive income taxes and of social security benefits and unemployment compensation, so that the budget deficit automatically increases sharply, while consumer expenditure does not decline as much as it might, when incomes and employment fall. But it must be recognized that this merely helps damp out fluctuations and cannot prevent them.

Lastly, the biggest grounds for optimism about the possibility of avoiding a major recession is that we know the right sort of things to do, if one should come. If unemployment is high, we know that the right sorts of policy are large-scale budget deficits and encouragement to private spending.

All the same, it is important to realize the limitations of this prescription. It does practically nothing to prevent minor inventory cycles—and perhaps, indeed, they are inevitable and possibly desirable, as a means of shaking up the inefficient. But it also does too little to prevent minor fluctuations from becoming quite sharp and unpleasant, especially if a number of unfavorable circumstances should happen to coincide, rather unpredictably. We can almost certainly prevent anything like 1929-1933; but it will take delicate and firm action to be sure to be able to avoid anything like 1937-1938. To do that, we must operate the right sort of controls in the right direction; but we must also operate them with the right degree of strength and at the right time.

SOME SUGGESTED READING

The basic materials for the inter-war period can be found in S. S. Kuznets, *National Product since 1869* (New York, 1946) and his *National Income and Its Composition 1919-1938* (New York, 1941). An interesting econometric study is J. Tinbergen, *Business Cycles in the United States of America 1919-1932* (Geneva, 1939). Readable outline histories of the inter-war period can be found in sources such as A. G. Hart, *Money, Debt and Economic Activity* (New York, 1948); M. W. Lee, *Economic Fluctuations* (Homewood, Ill., 1955); R. A. Gordon, *Business Fluctuations* (New

---

[9] Discussed in Chapters 13 and 15.

York, 1952); and A. H. Hansen, *Fiscal Policy and Business Cycles* (New York, 1941). The best history of the wartime and post-war inflation is L. V. Chandler, *Inflation in the United States 1940-1948* (New York, 1951). The best sources on the post-war history are the annual *Economic Reports of the President* (Washington) and the periodical surveys in the *Survey of Current Business,* which is also the best source on very recent developments.

27

The Strength of Stabilizing Action

We saw toward the end of the last chapter that major problems still remain if we are to achieve a high degree of economic stability, even if we successfully apply all the familiar principles outlined in Chapter 25.

One problem is that our choices of policy may not always be consistent with one another. The choice between two aims may frequently be that we can approach nearer to the one if we accept being further away from the other. We saw in Part IV that the choice between full employment and price stability is of this nature; the kind of choice that exists can be represented formally as in Figure 20 (on which the vertical axis measures the percentage of unemployment and the horizontal axis the average annual rate of price change) by the possibility curve, which relates different combinations of unemployment and inflation that can be achieved in practice. If unemployment is very low, inflation will be very fast; if unemployment is very high, prices may even fall persistently.[1] This curve is drawn on the assumption that the economic and political environment is unchanged. In particular we assume no change in collective bargaining methods, no change in the degree of competitiveness in the economy, no change in the rate of growth of productivity, and no change in government interference. If any of these alter, it is likely to affect the position of the possibility curve.

If the community tries to achieve a situation which is not on this possibility curve, it runs into hopeless dilemmas because we want

---

[1] This curve is like a production possibility curve in ordinary micro-economic theory. We have drawn it convex to the origin to express the fact that as the economy gets closer and closer to full employment a given drop in the percentage of unemployment results in greater and greater increases in prices.

to achieve aims which are inconsistent with one another—such as a very low level of unemployment and complete absence of inflation. If we are trying simultaneously to achieve two aims which cannot be consistent, we are likely to make the economic system unnecessarily unstable by alternately chasing after the one and then the other.

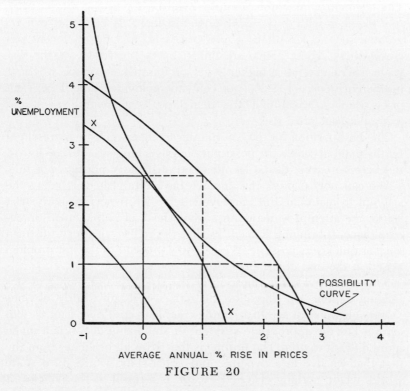

FIGURE 20

Even if the community accepts that it must be on the possibility curve, there are still likely to be disagreements about which position to choose; some people may regard one position as preferable (say one with low unemployment and relatively fast price rises) whereas others may regard another as preferable (say a position with high unemployment but no inflation). Such divergence of views is likely in itself to lead to changing aims of policy, as first one view and then the other is dominant politically; and as policy aims fluctuate, economic instability is likely to be induced. And since many people will in fact vote for positions that are not possible, the two kinds of sources of instability are likely to reinforce one another.

The remaining problems of achieving stability can be highlighted if we assume that the community is unanimous in its views on the choice of the evils of unemployment and inflation. The way in which these views may show themselves can also be seen in Figure 20. The community may, for example, regard a 1 per cent rate of price rise together with 1 per cent unemployment as being an evil no greater and no less than a zero price rise and 2½ per cent unemployment. These points are linked by the curve XX on the diagram.[2] Similarly, at a higher level of unsatisfactoriness, we have indifference curve YY; 2½ per cent unemployment and 1 per cent price rise is no worse or better than 1 per cent unemployment and a 2¼ per cent price rise.

The best position for the community to choose can be represented by the point at which the possibility curve is tangential to the lowest indifference curve; this is the least unsatisfactory position possible.

We can now express the aim we have established as being the attempt to maintain 'full employment,' which means in more strict terms, the attempt to maintain a given level of employment or unemployment, bringing it back to that desired level after a disturbance as quickly as possible. We can now proceed to the last problem raised at the end of the preceding chapter.

This is to decide the question of the strength and timing of stabilizing action. The direction of action is usually fairly obvious (although we shall see that simple common sense may lead us into error); but the appropriate strength of stabilizing action is a much more difficult matter. The problems that arise all originate from the fact that we live in a dynamic and not a static world. In a static world, where nothing changed except as a result of the policies of the government, all would be easy. If, for example, there is too much unemployment and if it is decided that fiscal policies of budgetary deficit are the appropriate control instruments, the necessary increase in the budget deficit can easily be calculated from an estimate of the gap between the present level of income and the full employment level of income and from an estimate of the size of

---

[2] This is an indifference curve, but is concave to the origin, unlike the ordinary indifference curves of economic theory, because it represents indifference to evil, and not to good.

the relevant multiplier, as in Chapter 16. If the gap is $100 million per year and the multiplier is 4, then a budget deficit of $25 million per year will eventually bring the level of activity up to full employment, and then (since we are in a static world) all is well forever after.

In a continually changing world, things are not so easy. New disturbances are always affecting the economic situation, and stabilization is correspondingly more difficult than in a static world. If the world is static, it does not matter much if the correction of an error takes a long time, because once it has been done everything is perfect. In a changing world, speed is much more important; if we correct slowly when disturbances are coming in frequently, our policy in fact does little to stabilize the situation.

The problem of this chapter is, therefore, to see how the chosen stabilization instruments should be used in a continually changing world, in order to stabilize some economic magnitude (in our case the level of employment). In dealing with this problem we must consider whether the instruments are used in reaction to *forecast* changes in the current situation, or whether they are only used after the situation has actually been disturbed. This latter approach can be called the *current error* approach, because there is a difference (an 'error') between the desired situation (e.g. the desired level of employment) and the actual, current, situation.

These two approaches are complementary, and both have a part to play in any satisfactory control mechanism. The forecasting approach involves an attempt to estimate, for a future period (typically of a year) what will be the total demands for resources in an economy, and what will be the total supply coming forth. Total demand in a closed economy (with no foreign trade) consists of demand for consumption, fixed investment, government purposes, and net additions to stocks; total supply consists of the total amount of goods and services currently produced. If the aim of economic policy-makers is 'full employment,' they will try to change the total level of demand so that it is equal to the supply that they forecast will be available at this level of full employment.

This line of approach, using forecasts of the major constituents of total demand and supply, was widely used in economic planning during and after the Second World War. In circumstances such as those arising at that time, this approach is valuable, particularly if changes that are taking place are mainly occurring through the initiative of the government, so that they are (presumably) relatively easy for the government to forecast.

The forecasting approach is, however, by no means tied to the use of instruments of direct control. On the basis of forecasts about future events, decisions may well be made to use monetary instruments. The fact that, historically, national income forecasting has grown at a time when direct and fiscal instruments were widely used does not by any means imply that forecasts are useless for a government which prefers to use monetary instruments.

Nevertheless, there is a tendency for the choice between the two approaches to be closely linked to political judgments. Governments with a *laissez-faire* tendency, which prefer automatic methods of adjusting the economy, must inevitably have a bias to the current error approach, because automatic reactions are only possible to observed events and not to forecast events. On the other hand, governments which are willing to interfere more actively in the economic situation will tend to make more use of the forecasting approach.

Although forecasts are usually a valuable part of the approach to stabilization, they can rarely be adequate taken alone. The main reason is that not even the best economic forecasts can be accurate. Another difficulty in the forecasting approach is that the forecasts inevitably influence the actions of those people who see them. This involves two difficulties. The forecasts have to be made more subtle, to allow for at least the first round of these reactions. Moreover, awareness of the forecasts may have a destabilizing effect. For example, if there is a forecast of inflation, people may tend to build up inventories, which aggravates the inflation. Yet another (possibly major) difficulty in using the forecasting approach alone is the danger of bias in recommendations about when to act, in which direction, and by how much, as a result of bias in the fears of the forecasters. If, for example, they fear unemployment much more than they fear inflation, then they will tend to be more closely watching for signs of unemployment, and particularly ready to offer advice with an expansionary bias. If, in turn, the government concerned has a bias of fears running the same way (as is likely to be the case, since governments will tend to choose sympathetic advisers and forecasters), policy decisions will tend to have a clearly marked bias.

Most important of all, as a weakness of the forecasting approach taken alone, is the fact that some changes are completely unpredictable. There is no point in attempting to forecast such changes; all that can be done is to deal with the disturbances they cause as soon as they appear.

In other words, it is necessary to make appropriate use of the current error approach. This compares the current value of an economic magnitude with that which is desirable from the point of view of economic stabilization. Any difference between the current and the desired situation is an 'error'; in reaction to these errors policies are introduced for their removal. In particular stabilization policy demands the observation and removal of errors between the actual level of employment and the desired level; the aim is to maintain the level of employment as stable as possible.

The Strength of Policy Reactions

We have now seen that policy reactions should be made when disturbances are observed or forecast. It remains to ask how strong should be these policy reactions—how firmly should the instruments of control be imposed.

At a very crude level the answer is very simple: expansionary forces (by means of monetary or fiscal changes, or reductions in the intensity of direct controls) should be set in motion when the level of activity is too low or is expected to fall; conversely, contractionary forces should be set in motion when the level of activity is too high or is expected to become too high (i.e. when excessive inflation is present or is forecast).

To the extent that the size and timing of disturbances in the level of employment are both forecast with accuracy, these simple rules are adequate. If it is forecast that private expenditure will fall to a level of $100 million a year below its present level in six months' time, the government can stabilize demand and so the level of employment by increasing its own expenditure by an annual rate of $100 million, starting in six months' time.

Unfortunately it has proved impossible to achieve such a degree of accuracy in forecasting sufficiently far ahead for the necessary action to be taken to prevent any current disturbance from ever appearing. It is necessary, therefore, to use the current error approach if the maximum possible degree of stability is to be achieved. Here the rules that expansionary forces should be set in motion if the level of employment is too low, and contractionary forces if it is too high, are still valid.

Nevertheless, such simple prescriptions are by no means adequate. Moreover, it is perfectly possible that they may be harmful; attempts to stabilize activity may be so ill conceived that they lead to larger fluctuations in the level of activity than if no such attempts had been made.

Fortunately it is possible to say quite a considerable amount about the control reactions which are necessary to deal with any observed errors in economic magnitudes. A theoretical discussion suitable for this matter has been developed in recent years by engineers, for purposes which are in principle almost exactly the same as those of economists. The kind of problem facing the economist is to describe the strength of the controlling reactions that will be needed to restore the level of employment to some desired level, if an error appears in the form of an observed level of employment different from that which is desired. The need of the engineer is to describe the strength of the controlling reactions that will be needed to maintain the speed of a machine constant, or the voltage of the output of a dynamo constant, in the face of tendencies for these values to fluctuate.

The upshot of this theory is that it is very important that control reactions should be introduced very rapidly, so that there is no long time delay before correction starts, and that the control reactions should be appropriate in magnitude if the disturbance is to be quickly and smoothly corrected.

The significance of rapid reaction is obvious. The longer the delay before the situation is effectively observed and corrective action is taken, the larger the error that has built itself up is likely to be. This means that it will take longer to put the situation right again, and moreover that there is a greater danger that attempts to correct the situation, when they come, will overcompensate and induce fluctuations. Even if things work out very well, the lag between the time when things go wrong and the time when they are corrected is likely to be considerable. The lag can be split into three parts. First, there is the lag between the time when things go wrong and the time when the error is diagnosed. If forecasting is successful, this lag can be negative. But in practice, it is often positive and quite long, because statistics take a long time to be collected, organized, and interpreted. Secondly, there is the lag between diagnosis and action. This may also be long if policy makers are indecisive and the statistics they must use are inconclusive. Lastly, there is the lag between the time action is taken and the time when it has effect. As we have seen, some changes in economic magnitudes (e.g. the change in investment expenditure in Chapter 6) are surprisingly slow in showing their full effects. All told, the case for rapid diagnosis and action is reasonably obvious. The meaning of the phrase 'appropriate in magnitude' is not so immediately obvious, and most of the rest of this chapter will be concerned with elucidating it, on the basis of the theory that the engineers have developed.

This theory has been based on assumptions that are rather different from those we have used so far in considering such economic matters as the multiplier and the trade cycle. In earlier chapters, for the convenience of the arithmetic and of exposition, we used what is known as a 'period analysis with undistributed lags.' This involves an assumption that, insofar as earlier events influence later ones (such as a change in the level of income influencing expenditure), events occurring in one period of time (e.g. a week or month) affect events occurring in a single subsequent period of time. For example, increased income accruing at any time between Saturday and Friday was assumed to affect expenditure plans made on Friday evening and so affect actual expenditure made during the next period from Saturday to Friday.

As a simple approach to reality this assumption has its virtues. All the same, most events both in nature and in economic affairs are in fact linked through time in a rather different manner. For one thing, a 'continuous analysis' is usually rather more accurate than a period analysis. Events occurring on Monday influence subsequent events earlier than similar events occurring on Friday—not at the same time as is assumed in our period analysis (with periods of a week ending on Friday evening). Similarly, events on Monday morning show their effects earlier than those occurring on Monday afternoon, and events at 10.00 a.m. show effects earlier than events at 11.00 a.m.

Secondly, lags are normally 'distributed.' This means that the full effects of events of one period or moment of time do not show themselves in a single subsequent period or moment; instead, the effects are distributed over time. Part of the effects of this week's events may appear next week, another part in the succeeding week, and so on. It is fairly obvious that most economic reactions are of this type. For example, if there is a once-for-all rise in the level of my income it is very likely that the consequent rise in my expenditure will not appear suddenly; it is more likely to appear gradually, with the level of expenditure moving steadily, and not sharply, from the old level to the new. This hypothesis of distributed lags is still more important when we allow for the fact that we are looking at the actions of many transactors, each of whom may have a different length of delay in response to a given change. I may raise the level of my expenditure very rapidly if my income rises; my neighbor may react in the end to the same extent as I, but he may react much more slowly. If we consider the sum of his reaction and mine to a change in our incomes, the rise to a new level of expenditure is spread over a period of time.

Except where otherwise stated, the assumption of the rest of this chapter will be that all reactions are continuous and involve distributed lags. Included in the reactions which we shall consider to have these characteristics are the controlling reactions imposed by the government.

Now that these preliminary questions about the characteristics of the time lags in the system have been dismissed, we can proceed to answer the major question of this last part of this chapter—how can we decide what is an appropriate magnitude of the correctional response to an 'error' in some economic magnitude (of which the level of employment will be taken as the most important example, although the argument can be applied to other magnitudes).

In brief, the answer is that it is desirable to pay attention to three characteristics of the error in judging what is the most appropriate size of control reaction.

In the first place, regard must be paid to the present size of the error. If there is one per cent too much unemployment, a smaller reaction is appropriate then when there is two per cent too much unemployment. This element is that of *proportional control:* one element in the magnitude of the appropriate correction is proportional to the size of the error. (It must obviously also be appropriate in direction; if there is too little unemployment the direction of the reaction will be the opposite of that required if there is too much.) Examples of proportional control are quite common. An automatically working proportionate control has been mentioned frequently in the last chapter; this is the built-in stabilizer of increased unemployment benefits and correspondingly increased budget deficits when unemployment is high. The induced increase in expenditure in each period, of say a month or a year, is proportionate to the excessive amount of unemployment there is, compared with some norm. Many schemes for deliberately building stabilizers into the economic system are schemes for building in proportional control. An example is the much publicized scheme of the Committee for Economic Development, which proposed to permit automatic increases in the budget deficit if unemployment was unduly high and automatic decreases if unemployment was unduly low.

In the second place, regard must be paid to the total amount of error that has accumulated in the past.[3] For example, if there has been one per cent too much unemployment for the last six months, this element in the reaction (known as the *integral control element*) should be twice as strong as if there has been one per cent too much unemployment for the last three months. The control reaction is related to the total number of days of excessive unemployment that have accumulated. As with proportional control, an error in the opposite direction (that of too little unemployment) demands correction the opposite way. A small additional complication enters here; there may have been errors both sides of the desired position since the last time that there was stable equilibrium. In that case we have to cancel out these opposing forces in order to decide how much integral control is appropriate and in what direction it should be used. If, for example, there have been six months with one per cent too much unemployment and six months with one per cent too little, the cancelling out is complete and current corrective policies demand the presence of no integral control element. If there have been six months with one per cent too much, and two months with one per cent too little, the size of the integral element that is appropriate is the same as that suitable for four months with one per cent too much.

An integral control element is quite likely to be introduced into economic policy by ordinary political pressures. While the electorate is quite likely to tolerate rather excessive unemployment or inflation for a certain length of time, political restiveness is likely to grow the longer these conditions last; and the more restiveness grows,

---

[3] In order to avoid going back to Adam and Eve, less attention should be paid to errors arising in the more distant past than in the recent past, and beyond some point in the fairly distant past, errors can be ignored.

the greater is the pressure on the government to do something about them.

Finally, as the third element in an appropriate control mechanism, attention should be paid to the current direction and speed of change of the actual level of employment. If the level of employment is currently declining,[4] there should be a control element (known as a *derivative control element*) introduced which operates to raise the level of employment. The more rapid the rate of decline, the stronger should be this force. Similarly, if the level of unemployment is currently rising, there should be a control element in operation which tends to lower the level of unemployment, and it should be stronger, the greater is the rate at which the level of unemployment is rising.

A derivative control element is one of the hardest to identify in practice, but it undoubtedly does exist, as when the government is unduly concerned when unemployment is at an excessive level and is growing, while it is much less concerned when it is at the same excessive level but is decreasing. A sophisticated example of an integral control element was probably found in the decision of the Federal Reserve to raise interest rates in the summer of 1958, even though unemployment was unduly high, because the level of activity was expanding and it was feared that too rapid an expansion would lead to an overshoot beyond what the Federal Reserve would regard as the level of full employment.

Generally speaking, all these three control elements—the proportional, the integral, and the derivative—should be used at the same time. This may mean that on occasion one element will work one way (tending to expand the level of activity) and another will work the opposite way. For example, if the level of unemployment is currently too high but is currently falling, then proportional and derivative controls will tend to work in opposite directions. In such circumstances, appropriate proportional control will involve a tendency to lower the level of unemployment, because the absolute level is too high; at the same time, appropriate derivative control involves a tendency to raise the level of unemployment, because

---

[4] Strictly speaking, it is possible to observe a rate of change only between two successive observation points; it cannot be observed at a given moment of time. Observation will be the more satisfactory the nearer together in time are two successive observations.

it is tending to fall. It is by this interplay that the desired state of a rapid and smooth return to the desired equilibrium position is most successfully brought about.

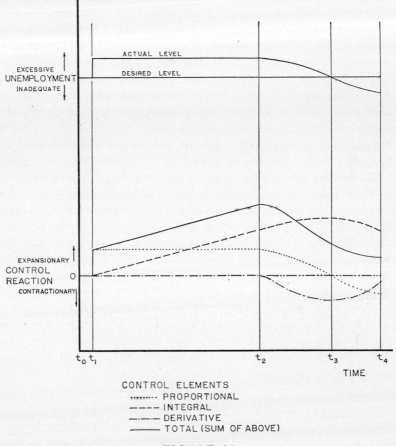

CONTROL ELEMENTS
.... PROPORTIONAL
— — — — INTEGRAL
—·—·— DERIVATIVE
———— TOTAL (SUM OF ABOVE)

FIGURE 21

As an indication of the kind of way in which the three control elements should be used together, Figure 21 shows the sort of control reaction which should be used if it is found that the level of unemployment and economic activity suddenly diverge from the desired level. The upper part of the diagram shows the time-path of the level of unemployment in relation to the desired level; this is assumed to be too high for a time, then later rather to overshoot the mark and for a time to be too low

The lower part of the diagram shows the three control elements and the total strength of control reaction which might be appropriate. The proportional element moves in proportion with the error; the integral element becomes steadily stronger up to time t_3; and the derivative element between times t_2 and t_3 operates in the opposite direction from the other two, because unemployment is contracting even though it is currently too high.

In making the necessary adjustments demanded by the interplay of these three control elements, use can be made of any or all of the three instruments of control distinguished earlier. One instrument may be used to carry out the net adjustment demanded by the three elements, or, alternatively, different instruments may be used to give effect to the different elements.

The reasons why an interplay of these three control elements is needed for rapid and smooth adjustment can be seen intuitively by considering the kind of adjustment that would occur if each control element were used alone. Each element taken alone has serious shortcomings that make it unsuitable as the only control element; at the same time, each has virtues which, when suitably combined with the virtues of the others, gives us the solution we want.

Proportional control taken alone suffers from the disadvantages that it can never provide full correction, and that if it is used too strongly it may induce fluctuations in the level of activity. The former is much the more serious of these disadvantages, and it occurs for the quite simple reason that, since the control reaction depends on the size of the difference between the current and the desired position, the control reaction becomes weaker and weaker as the actual position is corrected toward the desired position. As a consequence, proportional control cannot go all the way to restoring the desired position; it will lead to a new equilibrium level of activity somewhere between the desired level and the level that would have come about if no control reaction had been brought into operation.

Integral control has the advantage that, if it ever leads to an equilibrium, it must lead to an equilibrium at the desired position. Unfortunately this policy taken alone and if imposed at all strongly tends to induce fluctuations around the desired position on the way to the new equilibrium, and if it is imposed too strongly it will lead to fluctuations that become larger and larger, and never settle down. These dangers are particularly great when there are long time delays in reactions to stimuli. The marked tendency to fluctuations and the fact that any stable equilibrium must be at the desired level both arise from the fact that, as long as the actual position continues to be away from the desired position, the strength of the integral control reaction becomes greater and greater. Only when the actual position coincides with the desired position does the error cease to accumulate over time; only in these circumstances, therefore, is there no tendency for the control reaction to become stronger over time. Unfortunately, coincidence of the actual and desired position is only a necessary condition for a stable balance; it is not a sufficient condition. For example, consider an integral control policy which is dealing with circumstances in which outside forces have created a situation in which there is too much unemployment. Integral control policy comes in and operates to reduce the level of unemployment; it operates more and more strongly, the longer the excessive unemployment continues. Sooner or later it brings the amount of unemployment back to the desired level. Unfortunately it may not stop there; the control reaction inevitably operates with a time lag, so that at the point of time where equilibrium is regained, the control is reacting to only a part of the total error in the level of unemployment that has accrued up to that point. Subsequently, the control reacts still more strongly, as it takes into account error that had been excluded from consideration by the time lag; this means that the control reaction may cause an overshoot beyond the desired equilibrium situation. In time, the accrual of days of excessive employment in turn starts to influence the control reaction, and tends to pull back toward equilibrium again.

The upshot of all this is that integral control, if used too strongly, induces fluctuations. If, however, the pure integral policy is not imposed too violently and if time lags are small, the desired equilibrium position is eventually attained, either without fluctuations or because the fluctuations get smaller.

The third type of control element that we distinguished was derivative control. Expansionary forces are introduced if there is a current contractionary tendency, and contractionary forces are introduced if there is currently an expansionary tendency. Taken alone, this kind of control is no use for our purposes. It tends to stabilize the level of unemployment [5] by counteracting any tendency to change; it does not, however, show any tendency to stabilize it at the desired level. Derivative control alone would provide stability of the level of unemployment, but no more.

It should be clear that these three control elements are complementary to one another. For moderate values of control reaction, proportional control tends to pull back toward the desired position but never attains it; integral pulls all the way back but may well induce fluctuations; derivative control damps down fluctuations. A suitable control policy is one that combines all these three elements in appropriate proportions: it is very unlikely that an economic control policy which tries to rely on only one or two of these elements, or which places preponderant importance on one or two of them, can be satisfactory. At the same time it is necessary that the control reactions should not be too strong; all three elements can lead to fluctuations if imposed too violently.

There still remains the more technical question of the precise combination of these three elements which is appropriate. In detail this is a question that cannot be answered here; we can, however, just glance at the major considerations that are involved. These can conveniently be summarized into three groups: the general characteristics of the economic system which is to be controlled, the length of the time lags involved in reactions to changes in that system, and the detailed characteristics of the time lags.

Broadly speaking, the appropriate relative importance which should be given to the three elements depends upon the broad structure of the economy with which we are dealing. An example will indicate the kind of consideration that must be borne in mind. The forces at work in the economy which tend to exaggerate any movement that appears may be very strong or very weak. It may be that any change leads to a strong general expectation of further change in the same direction; alternatively it may lead to an expectation that things will soon return to where they were. In the former case particular emphasis should be placed on a derivative control element, to counteract change as soon as it appears; in the latter case the derivative element can be much weaker.

The second major consideration is the length of the time lags in

---

[5] Except when used very violently, when it may lead to fluctuations.

the economy; here we are including both the lags in introducing and operating changes in the various controls, and the other lags in the system such as lags between changes in income and changes in expenditure, and those between changes in sales and changes in output. The longer all these lags are, the weaker must each element in the control policy tend to be, if we are to avoid creating fluctuations as a result of the operation of the control policies. Here we return once more to the crucial importance of rapid action.

The third major consideration involves matters we have been avoiding so far. We have already seen that lagged responses to changes are likely to be 'distributed' over time: the direct effects of changes taking place today do not all suddenly appear precisely a week or a month from now; some effects may appear at once, more a little later, and so on. Now it is obvious that these effects may be distributed over time in many different ways. It may be that there are some quite strong effects immediately, but the full effects show themselves only over a fairly long time; alternatively (and very plausibly in economic affairs), there may be very little effect for some time, and then after a moderate length of time the effects suddenly come crowding in. If we compare circumstances where the average delay in the response is just the same in each case, but where in one case the first time pattern is found and in the other the second time pattern, we find that instability is much more likely in the second case. The more the various lags in the economy tend to have the second time pattern, the greater is the risk that strong control operations will cause fluctuations.

One last point may be mentioned here. Earlier, we argued that most economic reactions were continuous. This is true; but there are still some important ones that are discontinuous. Crops can only be planted at certain times of the year; government budgets usually come only at a certain time. The more important these discontinuous reactions are in the economy, the more difficult is stabilization policy, and the more difficult it is to get rapidly and smoothly to equilibrium.

The upshot of the argument of this chapter is that stabilization of the level of employment in a closed economy is quite possible, if a suitable stabilization policy is followed. A good stabilization policy is one which uses the forecasting approach to the extent that it is possible to foresee major changes and to allow for them in advance by appropriate use of one or more of the main instruments of policy, namely, direct, monetary, and fiscal controls. It uses the current error approach by using the instruments of policy to apply an appropriate combination of proportional, derivative, and integral correction in the case of unpredicted or unpredictable disturbances. Finally, it may be added, a good stabilization policy diagnoses the source of disturbances and corrects them near the source, whenever that is possible, instead of waiting for disturbances to appear in the level of employment.

SOME SUGGESTED READING

The analysis of the problem of achieving a high degree of economic stability which has been outlined in this chapter is based upon recent work which involves some complicated mathematics. Consequently, there are no books or articles in which the subject can easily be followed further. A survey of the subject is to be found in Chapters 8 and 9 of R. G. D. Allen, *Mathematical Economics* (London, 1956), and an introductory approach is in the same author's article 'The Engineer's Approach to Economic Models' in *Economica* (1955). The most useful article indicating more of the practical significance of this approach is A. W. Phillips, 'Stabilization Policy in a Closed Economy' in the *Economic Journal* (1954). A book which outlines macro-economic theory in terms of this kind of approach is A. Tustin, *The Mechanism of Economic Systems* (London, 1953). For a less mathematical approach to some of these problems of stabilization policy, see the first two essays in Part III of Milton Friedman's *Essays in Positive Economics* (Chicago, 1953).

28

Economic Stabilization in Primary-Producing Countries

In the last two chapters, as indeed in much the greater part of this book, our main concern has been with the problems of an industrialized economy. In this chapter we shall turn for a short time to the special problems of a country where primary production predominates. Our prognosis here is rather less optimistic than it was for an industrial economy; a high degree of economic stability is much harder to attain, and it is probable that as complete a degree of stabilization of incomes as is possible in highly industrialized countries cannot be attained.

The particular problems of economic stabilization in primary-producing countries (and regions) arise from technological factors, and from the ways in which the prices of most primary products are determined. The technological factors are of two kinds: firstly, many primary-producing areas are highly specialized, and secondly, the level of output of many primary products cannot easily be altered quickly.

Specialization is, of course, usually a consequence of geographical and geological factors. Minerals can be mined only where they are found; certain crops can be grown only in certain regions, and often these regions are much less suited to any other crop. As a consequence, many countries are extremely dependent on the fortunes of one or two commodities.

Mining output is not, for the most part, subject to the second of the kinds of technological factor outlined above. Output of agricultural products, on the other hand, cannot usually be altered at all quickly. Animals, crops, and trees take time to mature, which means that a rapid expansion of output is usually very difficult. Moreover, once a crop or tree is planted, only a fairly small additional amount of effort is usually needed to harvest it. Products are rarely left to rot on the ground or on the tree; once the decision has been made to grow a particular thing, its eventual appearance on the market is almost inevitable.

This characteristic of agricultural production (which is, of course, subject to modification in some particular cases) is largely responsible for the peculiar character of the pricing of primary products. The typical situation is for changes in demand for primary products to lead mainly to price changes; output changes, in the short run at least, are frequently small or even nonexistent. The nature of the organization of primary production is often a further reason for this; for example, many agricultural products are largely produced by peasant farmers, whose only source of livelihood is their land, from which they try to get the biggest return possible, which involves producing as much as they can and selling at whatever happens to be the market price.[1]

The contrast with the reaction of most industrial firms to changes in demand (which was outlined in Chapter 5) is obvious. There we saw that industrial prices tend to vary relatively little when demand changes at levels below the full employment level of output; the typical reaction to a change in the demand for an industrial product is a change in output.

In fact, of course, the contrast between the two kinds of pricing policy which we are making is not always so sharp cut. Some primary producers react to a fall in demand by reducing output; similarly, some industrialists (especially in certain countries—e.g. Japan and Belgium) do cut prices substantially if demand falls. Nevertheless, the broad contrast is valid and can be made the basis of useful generalizations.

Price Instability and Income Instability

The consequence of this specialization on a few products, and of the tendency to considerable fluctuations in the prices of most primary products, is that most primary-producing countries inevitably suffer fluctuations in their real incomes. Just as an individual's

---

[1] There may well be, in the long run, a perverse effect of prices on output—more may be produced when prices are low, in an attempt to maintain real income.

income is likely to vary greatly if there are big fluctuations in the price of the things he sells, so with countries.[2] In these countries economic instability shows itself primarily in the form of price changes and not as changes in the level of activity.

This is not to suggest that unemployment may not be a serious problem in primary-producing countries; it frequently is, but its character is very different from that in industrial countries; it will be our task to look at this shortly, in our discussion of 'disguised unemployment.' Nor does it follow that fluctuations in the level of output are unknown in primary-producing countries. One particular form—that of crop changes because of the vagaries of the weather— is often very important in its effects on incomes. These effects may work either way; a bad crop may reduce incomes because there is less to sell, or it may increase them because prices rise more than sufficiently to counteract the decline in output.

The fact that incomes may vary both because of price changes and because of (generally unforeseen) output changes leads to an ambiguity in the definition of economic stabilization in primary-producing countries. This ambiguity is much more serious than that we saw for industrialized countries, in Chapter 25. It concerns the likelihood of conflict between the aims of price stabilization and of income stabilization. A policy of price stabilization makes no attempt to counteract the effects of crop variations on the incomes of primary producers; it simply attempts to maintain constancy in their selling prices, so that the money income of a producer will be constant so long as his output is constant. In turn, his real income will be constant if the prices of the things he buys (which may include both other primary products and manufactured goods) are constant.

A second ambiguity in the definition of economic stability in primary-producing countries is even more important. Price stabilization may imply merely a stabilization of the price received by the producer; or it may mean a stabilization of the price paid by the purchaser. The former aim is easier to achieve; a government or other agency can subtract from or add to the amount paid by the purchaser in order to stabilize the amount actually received by the

---

[2] The observant reader will notice that, in this chapter, we are coming more and more to relax the closed economy assumption; in the next Part of the book we shall look at international monetary relations and abandon the one-country approach completely.

producer. Such a tax/subsidy scheme can be self-liquidating, so that the producers receive in the long run just as much as has been paid by the purchasers, but in the short run receive more or less, with the result that temporary price fluctuations are smoothed out. Alternatively, there may be a permanent tax or subsidy element in the scheme.

More drastic are attempts to stabilize the prices paid by the purchaser as well as those received by the producer. (Income stabilization is a little more complicated, and will not be considered further.) Such price stabilization can be hard to achieve. In the first place it is difficult to introduce suitable policies for achieving stabilization. In the second place it is often difficult, in the short run, to identify whether stabilization is in fact being achieved.

The basic difficulty in introducing policies for this kind of complete price stabilization is that it is impossible to be sure what the price is at which stabilization is possible. Clearly, stabilization will prove successful only if it is at a level which equates demand and supply in the long run; for example, demand may temporarily be greater or less than supply, and stocks may for a time be reduced or accumulated by the stabilizing agency (this is a 'buffer stock' scheme); but in the long run there must be balance.

The difficulty is that it is impossible to tell in advance what price will in fact equate demand and supply in the long run. This intellectual difficulty is in turn likely to give rise to still greater troubles; sellers clearly have an interest in receiving as high a price as possible and buyers, for their part, want to pay as little as possible. As a consequence, prices are likely to be largely determined by the relative power of these groups, and are, therefore, rather unlikely to take adequate account of long-run market forces.

One answer to the problem of keeping long-run demand and supply in balance which is frequently resorted to is to restrict output; most schemes for doing this do harm, by penalizing the more efficient and go-ahead producers. Another answer also usually proves necessary sooner or later—that is to change the stabilized price level. Most stabilization schemes do, in fact, allow for periodic changes of the prices. Stabilization is, in fact, only temporary. This leads to the problem whether temporary stabilization followed by sharp step changes is preferred to continuous slight changes (which cumulatively may become large). The answer is difficult; fortunately, the question does not usually appear in this strict either/or form; intermediate possibilities exist, such as a system allowing price variations within stated limits, which are themselves altered from time to time.

Our conclusion must be that complete price stabilization for primary commodities is very difficult. This leads to a further difficulty: it is often very difficult, in primary-producing countries, to know whether economic stabilization is being achieved.

The problem has frequently presented itself in recent years in the form of inability to identify inflation until it has become quite serious. It is almost impossible to stabilize completely the general price level within a primary-producing country in face of fluctuations in export prices; nor is there reason to think that such stabilization is wanted, granted the almost inevitable acceptance of some export price fluctuations.

Identification of inflation in these countries must, therefore, be made subject to acceptance of some general price fluctuations. The need is to see whether the fluctuations are hiding any long-run tendency to rising prices. The problem is to ensure that there is no marked tendency to emphasize the upswings and minimize the downswings.

In the long run, of course, indices of the general price level and of the circulation of money do provide an indication of secular inflation. But in the short run, where we always find ourselves, these indices only tell us the position we are in. Except in the not uncommon circumstances when a country has been overspending on a grand scale, identification of a tendency to secular inflation is very difficult. Proof of the identification is still more difficult. As a consequence it often happens that the situation gets half out of control before anything is done about it, and then when something is done, excessively violent reactions are needed.

There is no easy way out of this difficulty: it is inherent in the nature of a specialized primary-producing economy. The best that can be said is that we must be aware of the limitations of our analysis, and of the need to identify developments as rapidly as possible, and to act as quickly and smoothly as possible after changes have been identified.

STABILITY AND INSTABILITY

Disguised Unemployment

This difficulty, that it is hard to identify an inflationary situation in primary-producing countries, is aggravated by another characteristic which is to a large extent peculiar to them, and in particular to the 'underdeveloped' countries. This is the existence of 'disguised unemployment.' By this we mean that there are people who are willing to work more than they are currently working, or to do work with a greater productivity than they are currently doing, and that the change would be possible with existing productive equipment. It is 'unemployment' because some people who are willing to produce are not able to do as much as they would like; it is 'disguised' because the people concerned are not completely idle.

Examples of this situation are quite easy to find in both industrialized and primary-producing countries. Compulsory part-time working is an example. A factory manager may choose to employ all his workers for three days a week, rather than employ three-fifths of them for five days a week and dismiss the rest. This is often done in times of temporarily slack trade, with the intention of keeping a labor force together and maintaining good labor relations. Another example arises where a dismissed industrial worker chooses to enter a less remunerative non-industrial occupation rather than be completely idle; examples of such choices are housework, newspaper selling, and part-time gardening.

In underdeveloped primary producing countries the particular form which is usually taken by disguised unemployment is rural overpopulation. It is commonly believed that in many underdeveloped countries at least as much and quite possibly more agricultural produce could be grown on the land which is already cultivated if there were fewer people working on the land. In other words, the marginal physical productivity of labor in these occupations is zero, or even possibly negative. This second and more extreme situation implies that workers are getting in the way of one another. The succeeding argument does not depend on this extreme assumption, and we shall merely consider that the same amount of produce could be grown on the same land, with the use of less labor.

An ambiguity still remains in this statement. It may be that if each of a smaller number of men were to work the same number of hours as before, at the same intensity, then just as much would be produced as before. Alternatively, it may be that the disappearance of some men from the land would mean that the remaining men would work longer hours, or at higher intensity. By this extra effort, made voluntarily, they could quite conceivably produce as much as before. Whether they would, in fact, choose to produce just as much as before the reduction of the labor force would depend on their preference between extra effort and the extra returns they could receive. The important point for our purpose is not this, but the fact that a reduction of the labor force may well evoke more effort from the people who remain.

Whatever may be the form in which disguised unemployment is found, the main problem is to remove it, and so to increase the total output and income of the community. In the case of disguised unemployment in industrial countries the answer is usually fairly simple. An increase in total effective demand, as by an increase in investment or in government expenditure, would tend to attract people back to industry from the less remunerative jobs outside, and it would tend to reduce the amount of part-time working.

In underdeveloped primary-producing countries the solution is frequently not so easy. In the first place, social and legal barriers to movement away from the land may be serious. These we cannot look into in detail, but their existence is often very important. Secondly, in these countries there are economic difficulties which usually exist to a much smaller degree in more advanced countries. Basically, the problem is that it may be difficult to ensure that the extra demand induced by a rise in investment or in other government expenditure is a demand for the kind of goods that can be produced by the surplus labor which is to be attracted away from the land.

The main difficulty is that there are very few sorts of thing this surplus labor can produce. In contrast with an industrialized country in a slump there is likely to be little idle capital equipment, so that it is only possible to produce output needing a very small use of equipment, and if possible it should be simple equipment the surplus workers can make themselves (e.g. baskets for the heads of coolies). Moreover, in most primary-producing countries there is no spare land, apart possibly from completely undeveloped land, which usually needs much capital expenditure. This land shortage, in relation to the labor force, is in fact usually the source of the disguised unemployment. The surplus labor cannot, therefore, be used directly to produce agricultural output.

Fortunately it is possible to ensure that most of the additional demand created is for the things which can be made by the surplus labor. Two things are needed. Firstly, the additional investment or other government expenditure should itself be a demand for things which can be produced by the surplus labor. This is not too difficult. Examples of suitable expenditure are road building, small-scale irrigation schemes, and well digging. The second need is that there shall be as little new expenditure as possible which is *induced* by the rise in investment. In other words, the multiplier should be as small as possible. In this way, an attempt can be made to prevent extra demand from spilling over into the purchase of goods which cannot be produced by the surplus labor (for example, additional food consumption) or into the purchase of imports (with the consequent risk of balance of payments difficulties, of which more will be said in Part VI).

At first sight it is difficult to see how the initial rise in expenditure can be prevented from inducing further rounds of increased expenditure; the marginal propensity to save in these communities is usually very small, so that the multiplier tends to be large.

The answer is to see that both the surplus labor now engaged in the investment project and the labor left behind working on the land consume and spend no more than before. A despotic way of doing this is a forced levy of labor; a democratic way is to encourage community projects, in which the surplus labor does work that will eventually be for the good of all, and is fed in the meantime by the workers who are still on the land.

The relevance of some of the distinctions made earlier between different kinds of disguised unemployment now becomes obvious. It is easier to persuade the labor remaining behind to feed the people working on the investment project if they find they can grow as much food as before with no more effort, than if they have to work longer hours; the persuasion is still easier if a reduced labor force makes it possible to produce still more than before.

It appears, then, that given a suitable political and social climate and sufficient organization, the problem of disguised unemployment can be solved without reliance on very large amounts of outside assistance to provide capital equipment for the use of the surplus labor. Whether rural overpopulation will, in fact, be reduced at all rapidly is uncertain. For one thing it is not at all certain that there is as much disguised unemployment as is commonly believed. Moreover, the process of change must involve considerable disturbance and needs organization; and, unfortunately, organizing ability is a scarce factor of production in many underdeveloped countries.

SOME SUGGESTED READING

Discussion of these topics is usually closely linked with discussion of the economics of development. Four of the most useful of the recent spate of books on this subject are W. A. Lewis, *The Theory of Economic Growth* (New York, 1955); P. T. Bauer and B. S. Yamey, *The Economics of Underdeveloped Countries* (London, 1957); G. Myrdal, *An International Economy* (London, 1957); and C. P. Kindleberger, *Economic Development* (New York, 1958).

All these books are worth looking into, in order to get a fair balance, since they are written from widely varying political viewpoints. A valuable introduction to all these problems and to those discussed in Parts VI and VII of this book is J. Viner, *International Trade and Economic Development* (Glencoe, Ill., 1952). Among the first treatments of disguised unemployment was that by Joan Robinson in her *Essays in the Theory of Employment* (2nd edition, Oxford, 1948).

VI

INTERNATIONAL MONETARY ECONOMICS

29

The Balance of Payments and the Balance of Trade

The most important tool for analyzing the international monetary relations of a country is the 'balance of payments.' Since the expression can be used in a variety of ways, and since confusion can easily arise from its inappropriate use, it is worth while to take a few pages over these matters of definition. That will be the concern of the present chapter.

In the foreign accounts of a country are recorded (in principle) all the payments made by residents of that country to foreigners and all the payments made by foreigners to the residents of that country. If every payment that has been made in some past period (of, say, a year) is included, the accounts must necessarily balance. The total amount paid by residents to foreigners must be equal to the total amount received by residents from foreigners. Full accounts for any past period must satisfy this rule; in a sense, therefore, the balance of payments is always balanced. A simple example will show what is meant by this statement. Let us consider the foreign accounts for a country which imports and exports goods, and where settlement of transactions with foreigners is made in gold. In the simplest case, each and every purchase (either by home residents or foreigners) is paid for in gold. The foreign accounts for a year which had just finished may look like this:

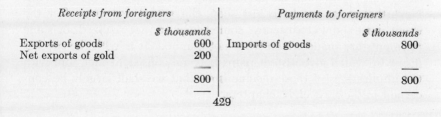

Receipts from foreigners		*Payments to foreigners*	
	$ thousands		*$ thousands*
Exports of goods	600	Imports of goods	800
Net exports of gold	200		
	800		800

Or it may possibly be the case that foreigners make loans to residents of our country, so that the accounts appear as follows:

Receipts	$ thousands	Payments	$ thousands
Exports of goods	600	Imports of goods	800
Loans from foreigners	100		
Net gold exports	100		
	800		800

The same position applies if settlement is in home or foreign currency, instead of gold. Whatever the complication of the details of the accounts, total receipts will still equal total payments in the actual accounts of any past period.

In what senses, then, is it possible usefully to say that the foreign accounts are out of balance—that there is a balance of payments surplus or deficit? The final sentence of the preceding paragraph provides the clue to the two important ways in which we can usefully distinguish the existence of disequilibrium in the balance of payments. In the first place, we may be concerned with accounts other than the actual accounts of some past period. Secondly, we may not be paying attention to total receipts and total payments, but be distinguishing particular items in the total accounts in some manner which can be regarded as significant.

There are two kinds of sets of foreign accounts, other than those for some actual past period, which may interest us; they can be described briefly as *plans* and *forecasts* respectively. The contrast between plans and actually realized results is one which we have already used extensively in discussing the closed economy multiplier in Chapters 5 and 6. Here, in dealing with the foreign accounts, we find precisely the same position as in those chapters. Total plans for payments to foreigners (under a given set of circumstances of prices, incomes, exchange rates, controls, tariffs, etc.) do not necessarily equal total plans for payments by foreigners to home residents. Nevertheless, as we have just seen, the actual accounts after the event must show consistency; some plans are not realized, or some payments are made which were not planned. It is with the mechanisms by which inconsistent plans become consistent fact, and with the implications of those mechanisms, that we shall largely be concerned in the next eight chapters.

It can be seen, then, that the foreign accounts which represent plans for a future period (whether these plans are made by governments, private individuals, or a mixture of the two) do not necessarily balance. In this respect the forecast balance is different from plans; the forecast balance attempts to estimate what the realized accounts for a future period will look like when that period is over. Since it is concerned with what is expected to be realized, the different elements will be consistent; the forecast balance must balance if all items are included. On the other hand it is concerned with the future, and in that respect is closely allied to the set of plans for the future; plans (especially by governments) are likely to be strongly influenced by forecasts of how existing plans will actually realize themselves.

The second major meaning which was distinguished with regard to the expression 'lack of balance in the foreign accounts' arises from the fact that it may be considered useful to separate some items in the foreign accounts from the rest, and to consider that there is disequilibrium in the balance of payments if receipts do not balance payments for the remaining items. There are various ways in which we can disregard certain payments in looking at the accounts for some past period, and consequently find lack of balance in the foreign accounts.

The simplest way in which we can disregard certain items is to disregard all payments other than those made for actual movements of *goods* imported or exported. In this way we get a *balance of visible trade:* quite literally 'visible' because it only includes goods that can actually be seen as they are put on board ship. These are the easiest data to collect, because all countries have customs officers whose job it is to watch and record movements of goods through their ports or over their frontiers. The visible trade account of a country might look as follows:

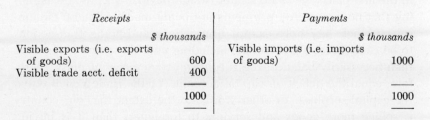

Receipts		*Payments*	
	$ thousands		*$ thousands*
Visible exports (i.e. exports of goods)	600	Visible imports (i.e. imports of goods)	1000
Visible trade acct. deficit	400		
	1000		1000

The main virtue of paying attention only to visible items is the ease of collection of such data. If possible, however, it is much more useful to include 'invisible' trade. This consists of payments and receipts for services by or to foreigners, such as interest on loans, tourist expenditure, banking services, shipping and airline services, etc. Receipts from selling such services to foreigners are very similar in their effects to receipts from sales of goods; they both provide incomes to the people who produce the goods or services concerned. Similarly, expenditure on services provided by foreigners is just like expenditure on goods provided by foreigners. We can, therefore, draw up a *balance of trade,* including both visible and invisible items.

	Receipts		*Payments*	
		$ thousands		*$ thousands*
Visible exports		600	Visible imports	1000
Invisible exports		600	Invisible imports	100
			Balance of trade surplus	100
		1200		1200

In the example given, the whole trading account is in surplus, although the visible accounts showed a deficit, because of the large invisible account surplus.

The other payments items that still remain excluded from this statement of the foreign accounts are capital transactions and 'unrequited payments.' The former group includes loans from and to foreigners, capital repayments from or to foreigners, and purchase of assets by or from foreigners. The latter group consists of receipts such as gifts, where nothing is given in return (unlike receipts for goods and services, where the good or service is given, and unlike capital transactions where an asset, a claim, or a cancellation of a former debt is given in return for the money received).

It is convenient to take each of these two non-trade items in turn; in the first place, we can consider capital payments alone, by assuming that no unrequited payments are being made. In those circumstances there are only capital transactions and trade transactions to be considered. The accounts including both these two items must then necessarily balance; the surplus on trade account must, therefore, equal the deficit on capital account (or the trade deficit equal the capital surplus). In other words, to the extent that our country is selling more goods and services to foreigners than it is buying from them, then residents will be making loans to foreigners, repaying debt to foreigners, and purchasing assets from foreigners. If our country is buying more goods and services from foreigners than it is selling to them, then on balance we must be borrowing from foreigners, receiving repayment of debt from them, and selling assets to them. For example, the position might be as follows:

T<small>RADE</small> A<small>CCOUNTS</small>

Receipts		Payments	
	$ thousands		*$ thousands*
Visible exports	600	Visible imports	1000
Invisible exports	600	Invisible imports	100
			1100
		Balance of trade surplus	100
	1200		1200

C<small>APITAL</small> A<small>CCOUNTS</small>

Receipts		Payments	
	$ thousands		*$ thousands*
Capital receipts (i.e. borrowing from, capital repayments by, sale of assets to, foreigners)	100	Capital payments (i.e. lendings to, capital repayments to, purchase of assets from, foreigners)	200
Capital account deficit	100		
	200		200

It is often convenient to use the expression 'current account' as the opposite of 'capital account.' The capital account deals with payments of debts and claims; the current account deals with payments for currently produced goods and services (including interest earned or paid on claims): it is the same as the balance of trade.

The distinction between the trade or current account of the balance of payments and the capital account is one of which the importance will be seen in the next chapter. The basis of this importance is that current account transactions create or employ current income, while capital account transactions do not. Sales of currently produced goods and services to foreigners involve the creation of income for the producers of those things. Purchase of goods or services from foreigners involves expenditure of current income that would otherwise have been available for purchase of home-produced goods or services. Current account receipts are, therefore, an injection into the circular flow of income in our country's economy, while current account expenditures are a leakage. Capital transactions, on the other hand, do not directly influence income nor are they made out of income: they affect the asset-holding side of the picture.

Unrequited transactions fit into this picture a little uneasily. Some unrequited receipts, for example, are best regarded as income-creating; a regular gift I receive from abroad may appear as a source of income to me. Other unrequited receipts are better regarded as transfers of assets from one country to another. The position is made still more hazy by the fact that an unrequited transaction may be better regarded in the income accounts of one country and in the asset accounts of the other country involved. These difficulties should not be taken too seriously; most unrequited transactions are usually lumped in with capital transactions, although probably the best solution is to give them a third category in the foreign accounts, distinct from both capital and current transactions and intermediate between them.

We have now seen several ways in which particular items in the foreign accounts may conveniently be considered separately, and most of these can provide a useful foundation for saying that there is a surplus or deficit in the balance of payments. In the rest of this book, however, the use of the expression will be based on yet another way in which the foreign accounts can be arranged; in this terminology, a 'balance of payments deficit' means that the country concerned is actually or potentially in balance of payments *difficulties*. These difficulties arise because the present situation, or the present line of development of the situation, is one that cannot continue indefinitely. Sooner or later, the situation will have to change or be changed, because if the present situation continues, sooner or later insurmountable difficulties will arise in the form of the exhaustion of reserves, whether of gold, other foreign currency, or of borrowing power. We can say, then, that a country is in balance of payments difficulties if it is tending to run through an exhaustible stock of reserves. If we present those items in the foreign accounts which represent drafts on (or additions to) exhaustible reserves separately from the rest of the foreign accounts, we have an immediate indicator of whether a country is in actual or potential balance of payments difficulties. This is the justification for separating gold movements and changes in short-term claims and liabilities from the other items in the foreign accounts. It is obvious that a fixed stock of gold or of foreign money is exhaustible; it is also reasonably true to consider potentialities for short-term borrowing as being exhaustible in a way that potentialities for long-term borrowing are not. A large part of total potential availabilities of short-term capital can be mobilized in quite a short period: it is possible to draw on a fund of short loans at a much higher rate than that at which new savings are flowing into the short-term capital market. In the case of long-term borrowing, the borrowing is more frequently at a rate like that at which new savings are flowing in, so that there is less presumption that long-term borrowing may exhaust a fund. There is, therefore, good reason for putting movements of short-term (but not long-term) capital in with movements of international currency and gold in the group of items we distinguish in defining a 'balance of payments deficit' in terms of balance of payments difficulties. We then get a set of accounts which may look as follows:

Receipts		*Payments*	
	$ thousands		*$ thousands*
Visible exports	600	Visible imports	1000
Invisible exports	600	Invisible imports	100
Long-term capital receipts		Long-term capital payments	
(borrowing, etc.)	50	(lending, etc.)	200
	1250		1300
Balance of payments deficit	50		
	1300		

There is a deficit of 50, which is financed by drawing on exhaustible stocks, perhaps in the following way:

Receipts		*Payments*	
	$ thousands		*$ thousands*
Gold export	20	Balance of payments deficit	50
Short-term borrowing	30		
	50		50

In addition it may be noted that governments may sometimes make grants or loans to other countries in order to help them out of balance of payments difficulties; the best example is the Marshall Aid given by the United States to Europe in the late 'forties and early 'fifties. The most convenient way to treat this is to count it as one of the ways of financing the balance of payments deficit just like gold exports or short-term borrowing in the example above. The difficulty arises when governments make grants for purposes which are not so simply obvious—for example a great deal of United States aid to foreign countries in recent years. In such cases, an arbitrary decision has to be made about where the item shall be recorded; it may either be treated like long-term capital or like gold movements in our example.

Our task in the remaining chapters of this Part, now that these basic matters of definition have been cleared out of the way, is to consider how external changes affect the home economy of a country, how changes at home affect the foreign accounts, and how adjustments can be made in order to bring the balance of payments into equilibrium (in the sense of avoiding a situation that cannot be maintained indefinitely).

As a first stage in the analysis of the balance of payments, we shall be concerned in the next four chapters with the relationship between levels of income and prices and the balance of trade. Other things equal, an improvement in the balance of trade is an improvement in the balance of payments, as can easily be seen if larger figures for exports or smaller figures for imports are substituted in the last set of accounts above.

Some Suggested Reading

There are a number of ways in which a balance of payments can be presented and, strictly speaking, the form that is most useful depends on the task at hand. Chapter 2 of J. E. Meade, *Balance of Payments* (Oxford, 1951) has a good discussion of the factors that need to be considered in organizing a balance of payments presentation. On the difficulties encountered in interpreting the balance of payments there are two articles that are extremely helpful: R. Nurkse, 'Conditions of International Monetary Equilibrium,' No. 4 of the *Essays in International Finance* (Princeton, 1945), reprinted in the American Economic Association, *Readings in the Theory of International Trade* (Philadelphia, 1949), and F. Machlup, 'Three Concepts of the Balance of Payments and the So-called Dollar Shortage,' *Economic Journal* (1950).

The interested reader should also consult the International Monetary Fund, *Balance of Payments Yearbook* for the years 1938, 1946, and 1947.

30

The Level of Income and the Balance of Trade

In this chapter we shall be concerned with the reciprocal relationships that exist between the level of income and activity in a country and its balance of trade. Changes in the balance of trade affect the equilibrium level of income, and changes in the level of income affect the state of the balance of trade (and so, in the absence of any countervailing change, of the balance of payments).

The argument of this chapter will run parallel to that followed in considering a closed economy, in Chapters 5 and 6. As in those chapters, it will be assumed that there are constant price levels, interest rates,[1] and quantities of fixed investment in each country, except where the contrary is explicitly stated; moreover, in each country we assume that there are unemployed resources, so that increased demand for the goods of a country (whether the demand arises at home or abroad) leads to increased output and activity and not to price rises. These conditions are likely to be reasonably well satisfied only if each of the countries concerned is chiefly involved in producing manufactured goods.[2] In addition, we assume that there are only two countries in our world, and that the exchange rate between the currencies of the two countries is constant; this means that the price with which one currency can be bought with the other does not vary. This, together with the assumption of constant prices within each country, means that prices of imported goods in terms of home currency in each country do not vary.

---

[1] This assumes a banking policy of 'active ease'; see Chapter 17.

[2] As we saw earlier, primary product prices tend to fluctuate with demand to a much greater extent than prices of manufactured goods. We shall have to consider later the problem of the relationship between the level of income and the balance of trade when one of the trading partners is a primary product-producing country.

The first relationship that needs to be considered is the effect of the level of income (which in conditions of constant prices corresponds directly to the level of activity) on the balance of trade. It is reasonable to consider that the level of income in our country has no influence on the total value of exports, although toward the end of this chapter, some reason will appear for modification of this view.

On the other hand the value of imports into our country certainly must depend on its level of activity and income; the actual value of imports must depend upon plans for imports made some little time earlier. In turn, these import plans depend on the level of income experienced in the period before the plans were made. We have a relationship similar in form to that which, in a closed economy, determined plans for consumption of home goods, and consequently the actual level of consumption of home goods in the subsequent period. Just as we saw in Part II how a change in the level of income leads to a change in plans for consumption of home goods, now we find that we have to take account of another relationship, the effect of changes in the level of income upon plans to buy imports, and so on subsequent actual purchases of imports.

By analogy with the marginal propensity to consume, which relates consumption of home goods to income, use can now be made of the concept of the *marginal propensity to import*. This measures the ratio between a change in plans to import and a change in income. If a rise in income of 100 leads (at current prices, etc.) to plans to purchase 10 more of imports, the marginal propensity to import is $\frac{10}{100}$, or 0.1.

The introduction of this relationship between the level of income and the level of imports (which we can safely assume to be stable when prices, interest rates, and investment remain unchanged) has several consequences for our theory. Firstly, if the marginal propensity to import is greater than zero (as it normally will be in a country engaged in foreign trade) then we are simply saying that the direct effect of a rise in the level of income in our country will be a deterioration in the balance of trade (since imports rise and, as far as the proximate effects are concerned, exports remain unchanged). Similarly, a rise in the level of income abroad will increase foreigners' imports—that is, our exports—and our balance of trade will be improved.

The second consequence for our theory of the existence of this relationship is that expenditure on imports is in the same position as expenditure on purchasing claims (i.e. saving); it is expenditure which does not directly create income in our country. Consumption of home goods provides income to the people who produce and sell those goods; purchases of foreign goods also provide income for the people who produce and sell them, but these people are not in our own country. (We can ignore the profits made by importing merchants by valuing imports at their landed price.) This is important, as will be seen if we consider the consequences of a rise in income in our country (induced perhaps by increased investment plans, as in the cases in Chapters 5 and 6). Some of the increased incomes are spent on consumption of home goods; this directly involves increased incomes for producers and sellers of those goods, who will in turn come to spend more themselves. To the extent that the increased incomes at each round are spent on home goods, there is a direct increase in home income, which in turn pushes the expansion of income still farther. On the other hand, that part of a rise in income which is spent on imports has the same effect, as far as direct consequences at home are concerned, as that part which is saved. It fails to lead directly to further increases of income at home; like savings, it leaks out of the system and provides no direct impulse to a further round of expansion of the level of home income.

Here, then, is one useful analogy: imports are parallel in their effects to savings; they are both forms of expenditure which do not directly give rise to income at home. There is also a similar analogy on the other side of the picture: exports are parallel in their effects to investment. The important feature of investment, from the point of view of the elementary theory of income determination (the 'multiplier') of Part II, was that the level of investment was determined by factors other than the current level of income; investment was determined independently (by such factors as the state of industrial techniques). Similarly, the level of exports from a country does not normally depend directly on the level of income in that country. It is determined by external factors: namely, the level of income abroad. This means that, in the simplest case, changes in the level of exports occur completely independently of what is happening to the level of income within our country; just as in the simplest case of investment, changes in the level of investment occurred completely independently of the level of income. In a word, in the simplest models, changes in both investment and exports are 'autonomous,'

Still more important, a change in the level of exports, when everything else is unchanged, acts in just the same way as a change in the level of investment. It induces a multiple change in the level of activity and income at home. An increase in exports is an increase in the demand for home-produced goods, which leads to increased income for the producers of those goods, and so to more expenditure by them; hence, a multiplier expansion.

More generally, an improvement in the balance of trade of a country, whether as a result of increased exports or reduced imports arising from a shift of demand from imports to home goods, leads to a multiplier expansion of income. Similarly, a deterioration of the trade balance leads, if other things are equal, to a multiplier contraction.

The analogy between investment and exports can be taken further. In Part V we saw that the level of investment was, after all, influenced by changes in the level of income; influences, therefore, work both ways when we look at the fuller and more complicated story. Similarly, we shall see shortly that a full story involves consideration of the fact that the level of exports does depend indirectly on the home level of income, because of repercussions operating through changes in the level of income abroad. For the moment, however, it is better to leave that step out.

The Foreign Trade Multiplier Without Foreign Repercussions

The circumstances which exclude the possibility of these roundabout effects are those in which our country is so small in relation to the other country (i.e. the rest of the world) that any influence of our country on the other is so small that it is negligible, so that no appreciable effect is reflected back to our country.

As in considering the closed economy multiplier, it is convenient to attack the problem in two ways. Firstly, we can consider the conditions that must be satisfied for a stable equilibrium level of income to exist, and secondly, we can look at the process by which economic conditions move from one equilibrium to another, after a disturbance.

The arguments are all extensions of those already used in the case of a closed economy and so can be followed through fairly quickly. As far as the accounts for a past period are concerned, the following identity must always be realized: realized savings plus realized imports equal realized investment plus realized exports. The reasons for the necessity of satisfying this condition may be summed up in a series of statements similar to those in Chapter 5:

Income $\equiv$ Consumption of home goods + Imports + Saving
Output $\equiv$ Consumption of home goods + Exports + Investment
Income $\equiv$ Output
$\therefore$ Imports + Saving = Exports + Investment
or Exports − Imports = Saving − Investment

The first identity describes the ways in which income has been spent; the second describes the various forms of output; the third states the necessary position that total income equals total output. The final statement (that realized exports minus realized imports necessarily equals realized saving minus realized investment) can be seen quite easily in another way. The surplus of realized exports over imports (the balance of trade surplus) is equal to net investment abroad—i.e. to additional net claims against foreigners and fixed assets held overseas. The surplus of saving over investment is the difference between total additional wealth owned by residents of our country, and total additional fixed wealth at home plus additional holdings of stocks of goods at home. That part of additional wealth not held at home must be held abroad, whether as real wealth or as claims against foreigners; common sense and arithmetic both demand that the condition must be satisfied.

Returning to the other form (that imports plus saving equals exports plus investment), it is clear that the condition necessarily applies for *realized* magnitudes, but by no means necessarily for *plans*. If planned purchases of imports plus planned saving do not equal planned purchases of exports plus planned investment for some period, then some plans will not be precisely realized. It is reasonable to assume, as a first approximation at any rate, that home residents' plans to purchase imports and foreigners' plans to purchase exports are always realized (just as we assumed in Part II that consumption plans in a closed economy are always realized). This means that, just as in the closed economy case, failure to realize plans impinges on savings and investment.

From here the argument continues in almost precisely the same way as in the closed economy case. The only stable equilibrium position will be one at which all plans are precisely realized; if they are not realized, plans will be revised and that will lead to changes in the level of income. If there is unplanned saving, because realized income turned out to be higher than expected, then plans for consumption of home and imported goods will be revised upward. If there is unplanned disinvestment, because sales by firms were larger than expected, then output plans will be revised upward. Similarly, *mutatis mutandis*, for unplanned dissaving and unplanned investment.

In the simple conditions we are considering at the moment, where there are no roundabout effects from the current level of income upon plans to invest or foreigners' plans to buy exports, the amount of plans to invest and to buy exports are data. This means that the adjustment to the equilibrium position where all plans are realized [3] involves the appearance of a situation where import and savings plans are together equal to these datum levels of investment and export plans. As we have seen, both import and savings plans depend upon the level of income; there can be only one level of income at which the sum of these plans is equal to the datum level of investment plus exports; this, then, is the only possible equilibrium level of income.

We therefore reach a position which is slightly more complicated than that reached toward the end of Chapter 5, but which is fundamentally the same. An equilibrium level of income is possible only if saving plans plus import plans equal investment plans plus export plans. The equilibrium income, therefore, depends upon the marginal propensity to save (which determines the level of planned saving), the marginal propensity to import (which determines the level of planned imports), the level of fixed investment firms wish to carry out, and the value of exports foreigners wish to buy.

The foreign trade multiplier without repercussions tells us what will be the effect of a disturbance (such as a change in the original level of investment or exports) upon the level of income. Let us assume the following set of relationships between expected income and expenditure on consumption of home goods and on imports. (It will be convenient to assume that all imports are directly used at home, so that exports do not include any imported materials.) The more realistic assumption, that there is an import content in

---

[3] That is, where planned imports plus planned saving equal planned exports plus planned investment, remembering (a) that import and export plans always are realized and (b) that by export plans we mean foreigners' plans to buy our exports.

home output, would complicate the analysis without altering its fundamentals.

Expected income	Planned consumption of home goods	Planned imports	Planned saving	Marginal propensities to:		
				consume home goods	import	save
6000	5000	500	500	0.8	0.1	0.1
7000	5800	600	600	0.8	0.1	0.1
8000	6600	700	700	0.8	0.1	0.1
9000	7400	800	800			

If planned investment is assumed to be 600 and exports 400, the only possible equilibrium level of income is 6000; at that level and that level only, plans are consistent. If either planned investment or exports now rises by 400, the only possible new equilibrium level of income is 8000; at this level plans are again consistent. A rise by 400 in investment or exports leads to a fivefold increase in the equilibrium level of income. The multiplier is 5, which is the inverse of the marginal propensity to save plus the marginal propensity to import:

$$\frac{1}{0.1 + 0.1} = \frac{1}{0.2} = 5.$$

The multiplier now takes account both of the proportion of extra income which leaks into saving and of the proportion that leaks into imports. Here is the real significance of the analogy between saving and imports that was drawn earlier. The larger are total leakages, whether into saving or imports, the smaller is the multiplier.

It should be noted that the formula which has just been used assumes that the whole of additional *investment* expenditure is used for purchasing home-produced goods; the rise in plans to import starts only when consumers' expenditure rises as a result of induced rises in income. If we make the alternative and probably more plausible assumption that some of the investment expenditure goes immediately for buying foreign goods, the internal impulse to expansion at home is so much the less, and the equilibrium rise in income is so much the smaller.[4]

The Foreign Trade Multiplier with Foreign Repercussions

So far we have been ignoring the possibility of repercussions through the foreign country, by assuming our country to be very small. When this is not so, these further complications must be considered. The main point can be seen by considering the expansionary process following a rise in investment at home. This leads to increased imports and a rise in activity and income at home, which in turn involves further increases in imports. These increased imports are an increase in exports by the foreign country; but, as we have just seen, an increase in exports by a country initiates an expansion of the level of activity and income in that country. In turn, this rise leads to increased imports by residents of the foreign country; that is, to increased exports by our country. These increased exports lead to a still further increase in the level of activity and income at home, which in turn increases demand for imports and so the level of activity abroad.

The conditions that must be satisfied by an equilibrium level of income in this case of the foreign trade multiplier with foreign repercussions are just the same as in the simpler case we discussed earlier. The only difference is we now pay attention to the need for the conditions to be satisfied in both countries: in each, planned saving plus imports must equal planned investment plus exports. Moreover, regard must be paid to the fact that the imports of one country must necessarily be equal to the exports of the other.

The equilibrium position that will satisfy these conditions when

---

[4] If, as will be assumed in the rest of this chapter, a given rise in investment expenditure leads to the same rise in imports as an equal rise in consumption expenditure, the multiplier formula becomes

$$\frac{1 - \dfrac{m}{(1 - s)}}{m + s}$$

where m is the marginal propensity to import. The second element on the top line is simply the part of investment expenditure which goes to imports; it is equal to the proportion of consumer *expenditure* (i.e. consumer income minus savings) which goes to imports.

the initiating change is expansionary is one in which the level of income in both countries is higher than it was originally; the argument of the next to the last paragraph includes only expansionary tendencies. Moreover, both during the adjustment process and in the final equilibrium, the balance of trade can never be more favorable and is usually less favorable to the home country than it was originally.[5]

We can also make a number of other general statements about the changes that will be induced when the initiating change is a rise in home investment.[6] In the first place, the change in level of

---

[5] In the final equilibrium the deterioration of the balance of trade of the home country is equal to the initial rise in investment there multiplied by

$$\frac{\dfrac{m_h}{s_h(1 - s_h)}}{1 + \dfrac{m_h}{s_h} + \dfrac{m_f}{s_f}}.$$

When there is no saving at the margin in one or other country, this expression may be equal to zero; otherwise it is positive. For the derivation of this formula and the remaining ones in this chapter see the Mathematical Appendix.

[6] The formulas which represent the equilibrium change in the incomes of the two countries, as a proportion of the initial increase in investment at home, are rather more complicated than the multiplier formula which paid no attention to repercussions. The change in home income is

$$\frac{1 + \dfrac{m_f}{s_f} - \dfrac{m_h}{(1 - s_h)}}{s_h + m_h + s_h \dfrac{m_f}{s_f}}$$

times as large as the change in home investment. The change in income in the foreign country is

$$\frac{\dfrac{m_h}{s_h(1 - s_h)}}{s_f + m_f + s_f \dfrac{m_h}{s_h}}$$

times as large as the change in home investment. (In these formulas s and m represents marginal propensities to save and to import, and the suffixes h and f represent conditions in the home and foreign countries respectively.) It will be noticed that if foreign repercussions are ignored (by making m_f equal to zero) the first of these formulas reduces to the one given earlier, that the change in home income is

$$\frac{1 - \dfrac{m_h}{(1 - s_h)}}{s_h + m_h}$$

times as large as the change in home investment.

income in either country will be relatively large if its own marginal propensities to save and to import are small. If the leakages into savings and imports are small, any given rise in demand for goods of a country leads to a bigger purely internal sequence of expansion. Thus, the rule that has applied in our earlier and simpler multiplier models continues to apply. If the leakages into savings and imports are rather large at home and are rather small in the foreign country, the equilibrium rise in income may be larger in the foreign country than at home because the internal magnification of any given rise in demand is so much greater abroad than at home. Usually, however, the rise in income is larger at home, as is to be expected when the initiating impulse operates there.

Secondly, the rise in the home level of income will be greater than in the case where no account is taken of foreign repercussions; some of the rise in activity abroad is reflected back to cause further home expansion. This expansion through reflection from abroad will be larger, the larger is the foreigners' 'reflection ratio.' This is the ratio of the foreigners' marginal propensity to import to his marginal propensity to save. If the marginal propensity to import is relatively large in the other country and the marginal propensity to save is relatively small (so that the reflection ratio is large), then most of the leakages from internal expenditure in the foreign country benefit the home country.

Other Initiating Changes—A Change in Tastes

In the multiplier example that has just been considered, the initiating impulse was a change in the level of investment in one of the countries. This is, however, not the only possible initiating impulse. Another important initiating change is a switch in demand between home goods and foreign goods.

The process and the characteristics demanded by the new equilibrium situation following such a change are those with which we have become familiar; change continues in each country for as long as the plans of different transactors are inconsistent, and ends when planned saving plus imports equal planned investment plus exports in each country.

The new features of the situation are that the initiating change has a proximate effect on demand for the goods of both countries, and that it has opposite effects in the two; there is an expansion in the demand for the products of one country and a contraction in the demand for the products of the other.

Our analysis needs to consider the way in which the reactions to these proximate effects interact. Some of the induced increases in demand in the country with an expanding level of activity affect its imports, and so prevent the contraction in the other country from going as far as it would otherwise do. Similarly, some of the induced reductions in demand in the multiplier process in the other country affect its imports; this lower level of imports prevents the expansion in the country with expansionary tendencies from going as far as it otherwise would.

In the final equilibrium position, the country which had an improvement in its balance of trade as the proximate effect of the change of tastes always finds itself with a higher level of output than initially and the other country always finishes with a lower level of output. The mutual interference between opposing changes can cancel out but not reverse the changes.

The effects of this on the equilibrium position of the balance of trade between the two countries are also quite simple: the equilibrium change in the balance of trade is less than the proximate change, but the direction of the proximate change is never reversed in the equilibrium position. The induced expansion in the country with an improved balance of trade increases its imports and wipes out some of the improvement in the balance of trade. Similarly, the induced contraction in the other country reduces its imports and wipes out some of the deterioration in its balance of trade. These effects will be the greater the bigger are the changes in imports as a result of a given change in income and the larger the changes in income. This situation arises the bigger are the marginal propensities to import and the smaller the marginal propensities to save.[7]

---

[7] In symbolic terms the equilibrium change in the balance of trade will equal the proximate change multiplied by

$$\frac{1}{1 + \dfrac{m_h}{s_h} + \dfrac{m_f}{s_f}}$$

where the symbols have the same meaning as earlier.

The determinants of the new equilibrium levels of income in the two countries are also fairly simple to follow.[8] In the first place, in line with usual experience, the change (whether upward or downward) in a country's level of output will be the greater, the smaller are its leakages into savings and imports (that is, the smaller are its marginal propensities to save and to import). This is in line with what we have seen in all other cases; when these propensities are small, any given change in demand for home goods leads to a greatly magnified purely internal sequence of expansion or contraction.

In the second place, the reflection ratios are once again relevant. This time, however, we must take account of the fact that output is expanding in one country and is contracting in the other. Therefore, the change in the level of output in either country will be the greater the *smaller* is the other country's reflection ratio; a small reflection ratio means that external forces wipe out only a small part of the internal changes induced in either country. As we have already seen, a small reflection ratio occurs when the other country's marginal propensity to save is large compared with its marginal propensity to import.

Further Considerations

So far, we have been assuming that the marginal propensity to import is constant throughout the range of incomes with which we are concerned (so long as other things, especially relative prices, remain unchanged). This assumption is probably reasonably well

---

[8] In algebraic terms the change in the level of activity and output at home, after a shift in tastes away from the goods of the home country, will be equal to the proximate deterioration in the balance of trade multiplied by the following expression:

$$- \frac{1}{s_h + m_h + s_h \dfrac{m_f}{s_f}} .$$

The change in the level of activity and output in the other country will be its proximate balance of trade improvement multiplied by

$$\frac{1}{s_f + m_f + s_f \dfrac{m_h}{s_h}} .$$

founded, but experience since the war suggests that in conditions of full, or near full, employment, even if relative prices are not changing, extra pressure of expenditure at home may tend to flow very strongly into purchases of imports.[9] This is likely to happen where no spare resources are available at home to produce extra goods there, where this pressure at home does not easily cause internal price rises, and where goods are fairly easily available abroad. In these circumstances the marginal propensity to import may be particularly high in the full employment zone, so that any increased pressure of demand at home has a large adverse effect on the balance of trade.

A further influence on the balance of trade in the full employment zone, apart from any question of price changes, is the effect of a high level of activity on delivery dates, especially of durable goods. As the level of activity moves into and through the full employment zone, there are two influences affecting exports through delivery dates. Export orders cannot be fully satisfied, so delivery dates lengthen; actual exports do not expand as much as foreigners' plans to buy export goods. In addition, this disappointment which is suffered by foreigners may lead them to switch away from buying our goods, even though our goods may be cheaper. A more expensive product with a short delivery date may well be preferable to a cheaper product with a longer delivery date. For both of these reasons, exports tend to fall off, or not to rise as much as the foreign trade multiplier might suggest, when the level of activity moves into the full employment zone, even when price rises are small enough to be disregarded. It appears, therefore, that strong pressure on the balance of trade (and so on the balance of payments) is particularly likely if there is a rise in the level of activity in the full employment zone, because of effects on both imports and exports.

SOME SUGGESTED READING

The relation of national income to foreign trade through the foreign trade multiplier has been widely discussed in the literature. The standard reference is F. Machlup, *International Trade and the National Income Mul-*

---

[9] This may happen even if no price rises occur at home. It is all the more likely if such rises occur; price changes will be discussed in the next three chapters.

tiplier (Philadelphia, 1943), which is carefully written and easy to follow. Also helpful, particularly in interpreting and extending Machlup's analysis, is a review of Machlup's book by L. Metzler which appeared in *The Review of Economic Statistics* (1945).

J. E. Meade, *Balance of Payments* (Oxford, 1951) has a lengthy discussion of foreign trade multipliers that differ according to the domestic and international policies that are followed. Some readers may find an article by Meade, 'National Income, National Expenditure and the Balance of Payments,' *Economic Journal* (1948-1949) easier reading.

R. Nurkse's article 'Domestic and International Equilibrium' in *New Economics*, edited by S. E. Harris (New York, 1947) places a great deal of emphasis on the income elasticity of demand for imports and notes that a low marginal propensity to import does not imply a low income elasticity of demand for imports.

For a critical view of simple-minded applications of the modern income theory to the analysis of foreign trade questions, the reader should consult J. Viner, *International Trade and Economic Development* (Glencoe, Ill., 1952).

31

Exchange Rate Changes and the Balance of Trade

In the last chapter two assumptions were made which ensured that prices would not change while other changes were occurring in our international economic system. We assumed that exchange rates were unchanged, so that if the foreign price of an imported good remained constant the home price would also stay constant; and that there was sufficient unemployment in each country to ensure that a change in demand for the products of either country would not lead to price changes.

Now the consequences of relative price changes must be considered.[1] If we continue the assumption of the last chapter that imported goods are consumed directly and do not form a part of the costs of home production,[2] there are two ways in which relative price changes can come about. Exchange rates may alter, so that the prices of imports alter even when prices of those goods in the countries where they are produced are unchanged; or the internal prices of either country's goods may alter. Except where two changes happen to cancel one another out, either of these changes means that the relationship between prices of home goods and prices of imported goods in each country alters.

In this chapter we shall be concerned solely with the effect of exchange rate changes, while assuming that the prices within each country of all goods produced there remain unchanged. If foreign currency (which we shall call pounds) comes to cost more to home

---

[1] This chapter and the next two will not, however, consider interest rate changes; we continue the assumption of a banking policy of 'active ease.'

[2] A reasonably realistic discussion of conditions where imported goods enter into home production is complicated and does not lead to any clear-cut answers, so it has been ignored.

residents, then the home currency (dollar) price of foreign goods rises, although the pound price is unchanged. Similarly, such a change makes home goods cheaper to foreigners.

The Proximate Effects of Exchange Rate Changes

Except in unusual circumstances, the consequence of a rise in the price of a commodity is that the quantity bought falls. Similarly, a price fall usually leads to bigger purchases of the commodity concerned. The relationship between changes in prices and changes in demand is conventionally expressed by the elasticity of demand; this measures the ratio between a small percentage change in price and the associated percentage change in demand. A large elasticity means that a small price change leads to a big change in demand; a zero elasticity means that a small price change leads to no change in demand. When the elasticity of demand is equal to one, the amount of money spent on purchasing the commodity is the same both before and after a price change, because the rise (or fall) in the quantity purchased just counterbalances the fall (or rise) in price per unit.

The effects of an exchange rate change on the demand in each country for the other's goods, and so on the balance of trade between the two countries, can conveniently be summarized in terms of elasticities which represent the effect on the demand for the other country's goods of a small change in their price in terms of one's own currency (when everything else, including all other prices, remains unchanged).[3] Each is a weighted average of all the individual demand elasticities for all goods imported by one of the countries (including goods that start to be imported when prices fall). It is concerned only with the *proximate* effects of the price changes on demand, and not with any indirect effects through such things as the changes in the level of activity which may arise from the changes in demand. On the other hand, the import demand

---

[3] They include both the income and the substitution effects of Hicks and Allen. They do not, however, take account of the effects of relative price changes on the relationship between saving and consumption. It may also be noted that they are defined in the conventional manner so that they are positive if normal— i.e. as $-\dfrac{dq}{dp} \cdot \dfrac{p}{q}$ where p is price and q is quantity.

elasticities are not solely concerned with the *immediate* effects of the price changes; some changes in expenditure patterns following price changes may not occur at once, which means that demand elasticities may well be higher when more time is allowed for all the proximate effects of price changes to show themselves.

In the case where the balance of trade between the two countries is originally in balance, the relationship between the demand elasticities and the effects of an exchange rate change on the balance of trade is very simple. If the sum of the home elasticity of demand for foreign goods and the foreign elasticity of demand for home goods is less than unity, the balance of trade moves against the country whose exchange depreciates. If the sum of the two elasticities is greater than unity, the trade balance moves in favor of the depreciating country. If the sum is unity, the trade balance remains unchanged. Table 12 presents a number of examples to demonstrate

TABLE 12

PROXIMATE EFFECTS OF EXCHANGE DEPRECIATION ON THE BALANCE OF TRADE,
WHERE TRADE WAS INITIALLY BALANCED

Demand elastic-ities	Ex-change rate	In A's currency ($)			In B's currency (£)		
		Value of A's exports	Value of B's exports	Balance of trade of A	Value of A's exports	Value of B's exports	Balance of trade of A
	4.00	4000	4000	0	1000	1000	0
$\epsilon_f = 0$ $\epsilon_h = 0$	4.04	4000	4040	−40	990	1000	−10
$\epsilon_f = \frac{1}{2}$ $\epsilon_h = \frac{1}{4}$	4.04	4020	4030	−10	995	997½	−2½
$\epsilon_f = \frac{3}{4}$ $\epsilon_h = \frac{1}{4}$	4.04	4030	4030	0	997½	997½	0
$\epsilon_f = \frac{1}{2}$ $\epsilon_h = \frac{1}{2}$	4.04	4020	4020	0	995	995	0
$\epsilon_f = 1$ $\epsilon_h = 1$	4.04	4040	4000	+40	1000	990	+10
$\epsilon_f = 4$ $\epsilon_h = 2$	4.04	4160	3959	+201	1030	980	+50

the working of this rule. The first horizontal row gives the original position, at an exchange rate of £1 = $4. The other rows represent possible results from a 1 per cent depreciation of the dollar (to £1 = $4.04) under varying assumptions about the two demand elasticities, as stated in the first vertical column. For example, the third row shows what would happen if the elasticity of demand of B for A's goods [4] were $\frac{1}{2}$ and the elasticity of demand of A for B's goods were $\frac{1}{4}$. A 1 per cent rise in the price of B's goods to purchasers in A would then involve a $\frac{1}{4}$ per cent fall in the quantity demanded (this is what an elasticity of $\frac{1}{4}$ means). The price in terms of B's currency (pounds) is unchanged; therefore the amount spent falls by $\frac{1}{4}$ per cent to £997$\frac{1}{2}$ (seventh column). The price of B's exports in terms of A's currency (dollars) rises 1 per cent as a result of the exchange rate change; as already noted, the quantity purchased falls $\frac{1}{4}$ per cent; the net effect (fourth column) is that the amount expressed in dollars which is spent on imports of B's goods rises by $\frac{3}{4}$ per cent to $4030. Similar calculations explain all the other figures in the table. It can be seen that the rule described above is satisfied; above a critical sum of the elasticity of unity, A's balance of trade improves; below this critical sum it deteriorates after a small depreciation.

Table 12 also gives examples of a more general rule, of which the rule just outlined is a particular case. The percentage change in the balance of trade directly arising from a depreciation by 1 per cent is

$$(\epsilon_h + \epsilon_f - 1)$$

(where ϵ_h is the home consumers' elasticity of demand for foreign goods, and ϵ_f is the foreign consumers' elasticity of demand for home goods). Strictly speaking, this rule applies only for very small changes, so that in cases such as the last row in the table it is only approximate.

The significance of this formula is quite easy to see. We can break up the consequences of a 1 per cent depreciation into three parts. Firstly, there is the effect on the volume of imports; this will be ϵ_h per cent. (For example, if we say $\epsilon_h = 3$, we are simply saying that a 1 per cent devaluation leads to a 3 per cent decline in the quantity

---

[4] Where A is the home country and B the foreign country.

of imports demanded: this means that foreign currency expenditure on imports falls by 3 per cent.) Secondly, there is the effect on the volume of exports; this rises by ϵ_f per cent in the case of a 1 per cent depreciation. Thirdly, there is the effect on the price of exports: a 1 per cent depreciation means a 1 per cent fall in the price of exports and, therefore, a counterbalancing 1 per cent decline in foreign currency receipts. Here then are the three elements; rises in net foreign currency receipts after a 1 per cent devaluation of $(\epsilon_h + \epsilon_f)$ per cent, and a counterbalancing fall of 1 per cent because of the fall in the price of exports as expressed in terms of foreign currency.

When the sum of the demand elasticities is less than unity, a depreciation causes a deterioration in the balance of trade of the depreciating country. This does not mean that relative price changes cannot bring about an improvement in its balance of trade when the elasticities are low. An *appreciation* in its exchange rate could have this desired effect. For example, an appreciation to $3.96 = £1 in the row in Table 12 where both the home and foreign elasticities of demand are zero would raise the value of A's exports in terms of pounds to 1010 and leave B's exports in terms of pounds unchanged, so that A's balance of trade would improve by £10.

It is often unrealistic to assume that trade is initially balanced when exchange depreciation occurs. Generally speaking, depreciation is much more likely when there is a deficit, the purpose of depreciation then being an attempt to remove the deficit.[5] When the initial position is one of disequilibrium in the balance of trade, with exports not equal to imports, the simple rule no longer applies. It breaks down in two ways. The critical position is no longer so simple. Expressed as a sum of the demand elasticities, it will be somewhere near unity but may lie anywhere in the range from zero to two, getting nearer one or the other of these extreme limits the more unbalanced was the initial position. Moreover, the critical position for the value of the elasticities is no longer the same when we are concerned with the change in the balance of trade measured in home currency as when we are concerned with the change measured in foreign currency. These complications are of considerable

---

[5] This is not necessarily so, however. A balance of trade deficit may be consistent with equilibrium in the balance of payments if there is inflow of long-term capital.

relevance; but they do make the analysis more difficult and do not usually disturb very greatly the conclusions that can be drawn from the simpler assumption of initially balanced trade.

A further complication which needs mentioning at this point is also important; again we can only point it out, and are unable to follow it up. In addition to the proximate effect of relative price changes in causing switches of demand between one product and another, there is another proximate effect which we have not yet considered. As we have seen, the change in exchange rates alters the relationship between export prices and import prices in each of the two countries. This change is known as a change in the *terms of trade;* an improvement of the terms of trade occurs when the terms upon which imports can be obtained in return for exports improve: that is, when import prices fall relatively to export prices.[6] In the circumstances under consideration in this chapter, the terms of trade always move against the depreciating country by the same percentage as the exchange depreciation: exports are unchanged in price in terms of home currency and imports rise by 1 per cent for each 1 per cent of exchange depreciation.

Just as the real income of an individual tends to fall when the things he buys rise in price compared with the things he sells, so with nations. If we compare two situations, in both of which the level of output in a country is the same, the level of real income it enjoys is lower when its imports are more expensive. Therefore, in the depreciating country, where import prices rise, real income is lower if output is unchanged. Correspondingly, there is a rise in real income implicit in the fall in import prices in the other country. This complication may alter expenditure plans and so may affect the critical value of the elasticities.

The Induced Effects of Exchange Rate Changes

We can now proceed to consider the multiplier effects following a change in exchange rates; in doing so, we shall disregard the two sets of complications that have just been mentioned, and assume that trade was initially balanced and that the terms of trade have no effect on total expenditure from a given money income. The

---

[6] Or, of course, export prices rise relatively to import prices.

analysis which has already been followed in the consideration of the effects of changes of tastes at the end of the last chapter can be applied without difficulty to this case.

If the sum of the import demand elasticities in the two countries is greater than unity, the switch effect tends to cause a balance of trade surplus in the depreciating country and a balance of trade deficit in the other country. As we have seen in the last chapter, this leads to an expansion of activity in the depreciating country and a contraction in the other country.

If the sum of the import elasticities equals unity, then the balance of trade remains unchanged in each country. In the home country the value of exports and the value of imports rise by an equal amount. Since saving out of a given money income is (we assume) unchanged, the rise in the value of imports involves an equal reduction in the amount of home expenditure on home-produced goods. Therefore, total (home plus foreign) expenditure on home-produced goods is unchanged, and neither a multiplier expansion nor a multiplier contraction is induced. A similar argument applies for the other country.

If the sum of the demand elasticities is less than unity, there is a deterioration in the balance of trade of the depreciating country, which tends to cause contraction in its level of activity. Similarly, the switch effect in these conditions tends to cause internal expansion in the appreciating country.

The final equilibrium level which arises is precisely the same in nature as that already considered toward the end of Chapter 30, in the discussion of the effects of a change of tastes. In the final equilibrium the country with the proximate improvement in its balance of trade finds it still has an improved trade balance; but the improvement is less than proximately, because its level of activity is higher. Similarly, the other country finds itself with a worsened trade balance (though less than proximately) and a lower level of activity. The relationship between the sizes of the equilibrium changes in the levels of activity and in the balance of trade between the two countries on the one hand and the size of the proximate switch-induced change in the balance of trade on the other is governed by the same factors as those discussed in the last chapter.[7]

---

[7] I.e. leakages into savings and imports determine both the changes in activity and the change in the balance of trade following a given switch in de-

One further induced effect of an exchange rate change may be mentioned. Even if there are no induced multiplier effects, there is still almost certainly a change in the character of output in each country. At the critical position, total (home plus foreign) expenditure on each country's products is unchanged. All the same, there is a switch in composition. The value (expressed in home currency) of imports into the depreciating country rises; therefore, expenditure on other home-produced goods falls. At the same time, the value of exports rises. There is a switch toward the export industries, within a constant total output. In the other country there is a switch away from the export industries. In each case the change in imports probably affects certain industries particularly sharply—these can be called the import-competing industries.

Two consequences may be noted. Firstly, an exchange rate change does lead to disturbances and adjustments, even if the total level of activity is unaltered. This is a particularly important example of something that has had to be ignored in most of this book: that even if the total level of activity is unchanged, some industries may still be expanding and others contracting. Secondly, the income redistribution which is involved (with producers of export goods and import-competing goods becoming better off in the depreciating country and worse off in the appreciating country, relatively to producers of other goods) may affect savings and investment plans, and so in turn may induce changes in the general level of activity. For example, producers of foreign trade goods (i.e. export goods and import-competing goods) in the depreciating country may have larger incomes than the average in their country. They therefore, probably save a particularly large part of their incomes. If their incomes grow and those of other producers fall, total savings tend to rise. This tends, as we have seen, to cause a contractionary process. Again, the rise in the prosperity of the industries producing foreign trade goods may induce big additional investment plans there; these may not be counteracted by correspondingly big reductions in investment plans elsewhere; if not, an expansionary force enters the situation.

---

mand between the goods of the two countries. The formulas indicating the sizes of changes involved are those in the footnotes on pp. 447-8 of Chapter 30.

Limitations of the Elasticity Analysis

The analysis of the effects of relative price changes on the balance of trade (and so indirectly on the level of output) in terms of demand elasticities is subject to limitations; the rest of this chapter will be concerned with them.

The chief limitation is that the analysis is strictly speaking valid only if the exchange rate changes (or other relative price changes) are very small. Very frequently, however, exchange rate changes are large; for example, sterling devalued from £1 = $4.04 to £1 = $2.80 in 1949. This means that there is a considerable disadvantage in our approach, although it is probable that extension of the analysis of small changes to changes of moderate dimensions is rarely hopelessly misleading. The reason for this limitation of our analysis involves a simple mathematical explanation: if very small changes are considered, the formulas representing the effects of these changes can be relatively simple, because certain items which strictly speaking should be included can be regarded as negligibly small, because they are the product of two small fractions, which is a very small number, e.g.

$$\frac{1}{100} \times \frac{1}{100} = \frac{1}{10,000}.$$

Another reason is that our analysis regards the magnitudes of various elasticities and marginal propensities as being independent of one another. This is strictly valid only if the changes we are concerned with are very small.

A further difficulty is that we cannot be at all certain that we know the sizes of the demand elasticities. Statistical investigation made a few years ago suggested that elasticities for the major traded commodities (particularly foodstuffs and raw materials, for which calculation was easier) are typically rather low—often between one-half and unity. This means that the sum of elasticities between two countries exchanging such goods would typically be between one and two. As we have seen, this is in the same range as the critical value. Consequently, pessimism developed about the value of relative price changes as a way of dealing with balance of payments difficulties, because a depreciation might lead to no improvement in the balance of trade, and would at best only lead to a relatively small improvement. It now appears that this pessimism went rather too far. In the first place there are considerable statistical problems in estimating the values of the elasticities, which probably involve a bias toward results with unduly low numerical values. In the second place, it is reasonable to consider that the elasticities will be bigger in the long run than in the short, because time is needed for producers and consumers to make adjustments to the new relative prices.

Despite these limitations the elasticity analysis is the best tool available; even though it may break under strain it remains useful. Even if we cannot know the precise value of a particular elasticity, we can make reasonable guesses about its order of magnitude, and by applying the sort of analysis followed here, we can make the best possible guess about the consequences of a particular change, assuming that there are no changes in internal price levels in either country. If there are such changes, additional considerations have to be brought into account—these will be our concern in Chapter 32.

SOME SUGGESTED READING

A wealth of literature is available on the influence of exchange rate changes on the balance of trade. Some of the more important works in this area are G. Haberler, 'The Market for Foreign Exchange and the Stability of the Balance of Payments: A Theoretical Analysis,' *Kyklos* (1949); J. Robinson, 'The Foreign Exchanges,' in her *Essays on the Theory of Employment* (Oxford, 1947), reprinted in the American Economic Association, *Readings in the Theory of International Trade* (Philadelphia, 1949); A. J. Brown, 'Trade Balances and Exchange Stability,' in *Oxford Studies in the Price Mechanism*, edited by T. Wilson and P. W. S. Andrews (Oxford, 1951); F. Machlup, 'The Theory of Foreign Exchanges,' *Economia* (1939-1940), reprinted in the American Economic Association, *Readings in the Theory of International Trade* (Philadelphia, 1949); and J. Meade's *Balance of Payments* (Oxford, 1951). In an article by S. E. Laursen and L. Metzler, 'Flexible Exchange Rates and the Theory of Employment,' *Review of Economics and Statistics* (1950), income effects and price effects are brought together in the analysis of the effects of exchange rate changes.

An article by A. O. Hirschman, 'Devaluation and the Trade Balance,' *Review of Economics and Statistics* (1949), extended the analysis of the effects of exchange rate changes to cover those situations where the trade balance was not initially zero, an assumption that was frequently made in deriving the elasticity formulas.

S. S. Alexander, 'Effects of a Devaluation on a Trade Balance,' International Monetary Fund *Staff Papers* (1952), puts forth the technique of analyzing the effects of exchange rate changes in terms of 'absorption.' For criticisms of this new approach the reader should consult F. Machlup, 'Relative Prices and Aggregate Spending in the Analyses of Devaluation,' *American Economic Review* (1955).

In his *International Trade and Economic Development* (Glencoe, Ill., 1952) J. Viner raises some doubts as to the usefulness of the analysis of the foreign exchange market in terms of invariant demand and supply curves.

The pitfalls of elasticity measurement are carefully discussed in G. Orcutt, 'Measurement of Price Elasticities in International Trade,' *Review of Economics and Statistics* (1950) and in F. Machlup, 'Elasticity Pessimism in International Trade,' *Economia Internazionale* (1950).

32

Exchange Rate Changes, Internal Price Changes, and the Balance of Trade

In the last chapter we were considering circumstances in which the prices of all domestically produced goods in each country remain unchanged. The time has now come to abandon this assumption. Doing so complicates the issue considerably, and no solution that can be expressed verbally or in the form of relatively simple formulas is really satisfactory. There are two different approaches that we can use that are reasonably manageable; each of them involves simplifications that are regrettable, but each helps to provide some further insight into the situation. The difficulty is that we cannot conveniently consider simultaneously both the indirect effects of exchange rate changes and the fact that prices of different kinds of goods produced at home may not all move in line. One approach we can use is unable to take full account of indirect effects; the other cannot take account of the possibility that prices of different kinds of goods produced within either country may be affected to differing extents.

The first of these approaches involves the introduction of a new concept: *the elasticity of supply of exports*. This measures the ratio between a small proportional change in the volume of exports and the associated small proportional change in the internal price of export goods. When there is general unemployment in a manufacturing country (as was assumed in the last chapter), this ratio will be infinite, because no appreciable changes in prices occur when there is a change in the volume of output.

When supply elasticities are less than infinite, additional exports can be called forth only if the price per unit of all exports rises.

This is likely to be the case when the level of activity enters the full employment zone: extra resources for producing additional export goods are no longer freely available at constant prices. Supply elasticities of exports are also affected by the degree of substitutability in production and consumption within each country between export-type goods and other goods. If, for example, a small rise in the price of export-type goods (while the prices of other domestically produced goods are unchanged) makes it possible to attract a relatively large amount of labor and other resources from other industries, then a small rise in the price of exports makes a big increase in their output possible. This is a high degree of substitutability in production. There may also be a high or low degree of substitutability in consumption in each country. Normally there will be some domestic consumption of export-type goods; if a small rise in the domestic price of export goods (while the prices of other domestically produced goods are unchanged) leads to a big shift away from domestic consumption of these goods, then a small rise in their price makes many more available for export; the elasticity of supply of exports tends, therefore, to be large, even if their output cannot be increased. The relative sizes of the domestic and the export market for export-type goods is also relevant. If the domestic market is relatively large, the elasticity of supply of exports will tend to be large.[1] These examples show that the elasticities of supply of exports are not necessarily particularly low, even in the full employment zone.

Considerable caution must be used in making judgments of policy based on arguments assuming these elasticities to be small, because our analysis looks at only certain limited effects of an exchange rate change. In particular, it must be remembered that we have to assume that prices of other domestically produced goods remains unchanged. This is a serious limitation to our analysis; nevertheless, the consequences of low elasticities of supply of exports in these

---

[1] Consider the case where a 10 per cent rise in the price of export-type goods leads to a 10 per cent fall in the home demand for them. Let us now compare two cases, one where the home market is initially the same size as the export market, with sales of 100 to each; the other where the home market is five times as large as the export market, with home sales of 500. In the former case, a 10 per cent price rise releases 10 units to the export market, and adds 10 per cent to the export supply; in the latter case, 50 units are released from home demand, adding 50 per cent to the export supply.

circumstances are of some importance, and it is therefore necessary to consider them.

Prices of Export-Type Goods Change, Prices of Other Domestically Produced Goods Remain Constant

The circumstances in which exchange rate change leads to changes in the domestic prices of export-type goods but not of other domestically produced goods are fairly narrow. They are rather more likely to apply where the change with which we are concerned involves a rise in the demand for a country's export goods than when it involves a fall; it is, therefore, convenient to consider the first (less restrictive) alternative first. The necessary conditions are that the prices of export-type goods should rise considerably when exports increase, but that prices of other domestically produced goods should not be affected. This is likely to happen when the output of the industries producing export-type goods cannot easily be expanded, and where the rises in the demand consequent upon the depreciation do not lead to rises in prices of other domestically produced goods. The former of these two conditions will be satisfied if little or no surplus capacity is available within the export-producing industries, and if the rise in the price of exports fails to attract substantial quantities of productive resources from other employments. Alternatively it may be that, in the short period, technological conditions are such that output cannot be increased (e.g. crops take time to mature). The second of the two necessary conditions will be satisfied if there is appreciable unemployment in industries other than the export industries. Alternatively, it will be satisfied if the rise in the price of imports and of export-type goods does not lead to any substantial diversion of domestic demand for them to other domestically produced goods, and if any induced multiplier expansion in the domestic level of activity is relatively small.[2]

Clearly, all these conditions are rather limiting. There is an additional limitation in the country which suffers a reduction in the demand for exports as a result of the exchange rate change with

---

[2] This final condition may be satisfied, either because the government follows deliberate policies to prevent such an expansion, or because exports are such a small part of total output that a rise in the incomes of their producers has a negligible effect on the economy as a whole.

which we are concerned. As we have seen, a fall in demand rarely leads to a substantial fall in prices of industrial goods. Low elasticities of supply are, therefore, usually relevant only to cases where there is a *fall* in demand when we are concerned with an exporter of primary products. It is probably a reasonable judgment, therefore, that arguments based on the existence of low elasticities of supply of exports in both trading partners are significant only when at least one partner is an exporter of primary products. This is the more likely, since the necessary conditions defined in the last paragraph are probably particularly common, especially in the short period, in countries which rely on exporting a limited range of primary products and do not produce many goods which are directly competitive with imports.

Having defined the circumstances in which analysis in terms of low elasticity of supply of exports is relevant, we can proceed to analyze their consequences. The new feature that enters the situation when elasticities of supply of exports are low (in fact, strictly speaking, whenever they are less than infinite) is that there are now three forces operating on the relative prices of the goods traded between the two countries. In the simpler circumstances considered earlier, where no changes occurred in the domestic prices of exports, there was only one influence operating to change the relative prices of imports and exports in either country. This was the exchange rate. If the home country depreciated by 1 per cent, imports became more expensive by 1 per cent in terms of home currency, and so were 1 per cent more expensive in relation to exports. In other words, the terms of trade of the home country deteriorated by 1 per cent. Similarly, the terms of trade of the other country improved by 1 per cent.

The two new forces which also affect the terms of trade are changes in the internal price levels of export goods in each country. In the depreciating country the internal price of export goods rises, in reaction to the tendency to increased foreign demand for them consequent on the fall in their price to the foreigner, which arises from the depreciation. Similarly, in the other country, the internal price of export goods falls.

These two forces acting together can be sufficient to more than offset the effects of the exchange rate change on the terms of trade. Together, they can cause the terms of trade of the depreciating (home) country to improve, and the terms of trade of the other country to deteriorate.

This reversal of the ordinary course of events is most marked, and easiest to follow, when the elasticities of supply of exports in both countries are zero: that is, when the supply of exports in both countries is quite fixed, and any increase in demand causes a rise in price sufficient to remove all the increase, while any decrease in demand causes a fall in price sufficient to bring demand back to its original level. In these extreme circumstances the foreign currency price of home exports must be unchanged in the final equilibrium, because any fall would involve some increase in demand, which could not be supplied because the home supply of exports has a zero elasticity. This means that the home currency price of home exports must rise by 1 per cent (the amount of the depreciation). By similar reasoning, the home currency price of foreign exports must be unchanged, which involves a 1 per cent fall in the price of foreign exports within the foreign country. In the equilibrium position, therefore, the price of home exports rises relatively to the price of foreign exports; the terms of trade move *in favor of the depreciating* country by the same percentage as the depreciation.

These internal price changes are always sufficient to cause the terms of trade of the depreciating country to improve to some extent or other, so long as the elasticities of supply of exports in the two countries are low enough. The precise rule is quite simple: if the product of the two countries' export supply elasticities is less than the product of their import demand elasticities, then the terms of trade move in favor of the depreciating country. When the product of the supply elasticities is the greater, the terms of trade move against the depreciating country.[3]

Another equally simple rule concerns the effects of less-than-infinite supply elasticities on the balance of trade. If the supply elasticities are small enough to improve the terms of trade of the depreciating country, then its balance of trade must also improve. This can be seen most clearly in the case of zero supply elasticities. In the final equilibrium position the demand for imports in each

---

[3] The terms of trade improve after devaluation if $\eta_h \eta_f < \epsilon_h \epsilon_f$, where η_h is the home elasticity of supply of exports and η_f the foreign elasticity of supply of exports. ϵ once again represents a demand elasticity.

of the two countries remains as it was before, because the prices of each country's imports in terms of its own currency is unaltered. At the same time, the home currency price of home exports has risen, so that receipts from exports rise; on the other hand, expenditure on imports (again expressed in home currency) remains unchanged.

All of these effects on the terms of trade and the balance of trade in the case where the elasticities of supply of both countries' exports are zero, can be summarized by a numerical example in which the home currency is in dollars and the foreign currency pounds, the original exchange rate was £1 = $4, and there is a 1 per cent depreciation by the home country.

	Original conditions	New conditions
Home price of home exports	$400	$404
Foreign price of home exports	£100	£100
Quantity of home exports	10	10
Foreign price of foreign exports	£ 25	£ 24¾
Home price of foreign exports	$100	$100
Quantity of foreign exports	40	40
Home balance of payments surplus	0	+$ 40
Home terms of trade [4]	100	101

This conclusion, that if the supply elasticities are small in relation to the demand elasticities the terms of trade and the balance of trade of a depreciating country improve, applies even when the demand elasticities are small, where the 'normal' effect of an exchange depreciation would be a deterioration in the balance of trade.[5]

---

[4] An index of the home price of exports divided by the home price of imports.

[5] The effects of a 1 per cent depreciation on the balance of trade of the depreciating country, when we take account of demand elasticities for imports and supply elasticities for exports and where all prices of non-traded goods are unchanged, is that the balance improves by the following percentage:

$$\frac{\eta_h \eta_f (\epsilon_h + \epsilon_f - 1) + \epsilon_h \epsilon_f (\eta_h + \eta_f + 1)}{(\eta_h + \epsilon_f)(\eta_f + \epsilon_h)}.$$

If that expression is positive, a depreciation improves the balance of trade of the depreciating country. All the statements about the effects of depreciation on the balance of trade derived so far in this chapter are implied in this somewhat complicated formula.

As has already been argued, low elasticities of supply of exports, combined with the other conditions sufficient to make our analysis valid, are probably somewhat uncommon. Probably rather more common than conditions in which export supply elasticities are low in both countries are conditions where the elasticity is rather low in one country and high in the other. As an example of this case (which is quite likely to apply in the trade between a primary-producing country and a manufacturing country) it will be interesting to look at what happens when the supply elasticity of exports is zero in one country and is infinite in the other.

In these circumstances the terms of trade between the two countries will be unaltered by depreciation. If the home country is the one with zero elasticity of supply of exports and it depreciates, then the foreign currency price of exports tends to remain unchanged and (correspondingly) their home currency price rises. At the same time there is infinite supply elasticity from the foreign country, so demand changes have no effect on the price of its exports expressed in foreign currency.

When the home elasticity of supply is zero and the foreign elasticity is infinite, the effect on the balance of trade between the two countries depends solely on the home elasticity of demand for imports. The foreign demand elasticity is irrelevant to the solution, because the zero home supply elasticity means that there is no change in the foreign currency price of the home country's exports; its earnings of foreign currency are necessarily unchanged. The effect of the depreciation depends solely on the home demand elasticity; as long as this is more than zero the rise in the home currency price of imports leads to some reduction in the volume of imports and so to some reduction in foreign currency expenditure. This in turn means an improvement in the home country's balance of trade.

These effects suggest one reason why exchange depreciation is often followed by countries which are largely dependent on exporting primary products when they are in balance of payments difficulties. As we have seen, primary-producing countries are very likely to be in the position of the home country in the last two paragraphs. Such a depreciation is likely to be particularly attractive if conditions are generally depressed, when rising prices tend to have a stimulating effect, and the improvement in the balance of trade must lead to an expansionary multiplier process, insofar as there are any unemployed resources in the economy.

Prices of Import-Competing Goods Change, Prices of Other Domestically Produced Goods Remain Constant

It is quite possible that an exchange rate change may show its chief effects on the prices of domestically produced goods in the form of changes in the prices of goods which compete closely with imports, while leaving the prices of other domestically produced goods (including exports) unchanged. The next few paragraphs will, therefore, be concerned with this type of case. It lies at the opposite extreme from the cases which have just been considered, where only the prices of export-type goods altered; it is therefore hardly surprising that it leads to very different conclusions. The depreciating country suffers an adverse movement in the terms of trade by the same percentage as the devaluation, since export prices in each country remain unchanged. At the same time it is quite conceivable that there might be an adverse movement in the balance of trade of the depreciating country.

The conditions in which a big change in the prices of import-competing goods will be associated with a constancy of the prices of other domestically produced goods are precisely parallel to those considered earlier, for changes in prices of export-type goods and constancy of others. In the first place there should be limitations on the possibility of increasing output of import-type goods. In the second place there should either be substantial quantities of unemployed productive resources available for other industries, or the rise in the price of imports and import-type goods must not cause any substantial diversion of demand to other domestically produced goods, nor may any multiplier expansion in the level of activity be substantial.

It will be convenient to consider the extreme case, where the prices of import-type goods rise by the same percentage as the depreciation in the depreciating country and fall by the same percentage in the other country. Moreover, we assume that the prices of all other goods remain unchanged in each country. In these circumstances the terms of trade move against the depreciating country by the full percentage of the exchange depreciation: import prices rise by that percentage and export prices remain unchanged. Correspondingly, the terms of trade of the appreciating country improve by the same percentage.

Although the depreciating country takes a considerable loss in real income in this way, its balance of trade may still not improve; in fact its balance of trade may also deteriorate as a result of the depreciation. How this might happen can easily be seen. If there is no substitutability between import and import-type goods on the one hand, and all other domestically produced goods on the other, there is no reason (in this extreme case where the supply elasticities for import-type goods in each country are zero) why there should be any change in the volume of goods imported by either country. There are, therefore, no changes in the volume of goods traded; at the same time, prices move against the depreciating country by the percentage depreciation. The net result is that the balance of trade moves against the depreciating country, by that same percentage of the initial value of goods traded.[6]

All Prices Tending To Change

The last, and in many ways the most important, case with which we shall be concerned is that where there is a tendency for all internal price levels (whether of import-competing, export-type, or other goods) to alter in the adjustment following an exchange rate change. This is the fourth of the cases [7] we are able to consider; between them they cover the extreme possibilities. In practice, intermediate conditions are likely—for example, bigger changes in some price levels than in others. Very broadly speaking, the conclusions in these cases can be derived from interpolation between the cases we are able to consider.

While we were considering what happened when the prices of some of the goods produced by a country altered while others remained unchanged, it was necessary to confine ourselves to consideration of the proximate effects of exchange rate changes. Now that we are returning to the simplicity of conditions where the price of all of a country's goods move together we can once again consider indirect effects.

The important new consideration we can take into account is the

---

[6] Assuming, as usual, that trade was initially in balance.

[7] Namely, (a) no changes in prices of a country's own goods (as considered in Chapter 31); (b) changes only in export–type goods; (c) changes only in import-competing goods; (d) changes in all prices.

following. If the prices of all goods produced in the depreciating country rise in price and/or if all goods produced in the other country fall in price, the effect on the terms of trade and the balance of trade between the countries, once the final equilibrium is reached, is the same as if there had been a smaller exchange depreciation with no price changes. The effects of the exchange rate change on the balance of trade are the consequence of the changed relationship between home and foreign prices in each country. If overall price changes within each country reduce the change in the relationship between the two price levels, the effect on the terms of trade and the balance of trade [8] is the same as if the depreciation had been smaller and there had been no internal price changes.

Two cases involving changes in the price of all goods produced in one or both countries are particularly relevant to our present discussion. One is an industrial country which is at full employment (which we shall regard as a point rather than a zone). In such conditions an increase in total (home and foreign) demand for its products tends to cause an inflationary process. The other is a primary-producing country, whose prices are likely to be substantially flexible in both directions, in reaction to changes in total demand for its products.

As an introduction to this analysis, it is useful to set forth an important rule, which applies quite generally except in limiting circumstances of a kind that have already been discussed, is that an exchange depreciation which has as its permanent effect an improvement in the balance of trade of the depreciating country will lead to a permanent reduction in the quantity of goods available to that country's inhabitants in return for a given quantity of work. This reduction, which is the normal price of an improvement in the balance of trade which is brought about by exchange rate changes, can be described as a reduction in the standard of living of those at work.

The simplest example of this rule can be seen by returning to the conditions of Chapter 31, in which there are no changes in the prices of each country of the goods produced there. As a proximate consequence of a 1 per cent exchange depreciation, there is a decline

---

[8] In terms of a constant measure—e.g. in terms of a currency in terms of which prices have not altered.

in the volume of imports by ϵ_h per cent and a rise in the volume of exports by ϵ_f per cent. Both these changes are reductions in the volume of goods available at home. Thus, if the quantity of goods produced at home remains constant because the amount of work done is constant, there is a fall in the volume of goods available at home by $(\epsilon_h + \epsilon_f)$ per cent of the original quantity of goods traded.

For the remaining part of the argument it will be convenient to split this volume change into two parts—a change in the value of trade (expressed in terms of the currency of the depreciating country, with which we are concerned) and a change in relative prices. In the simple case considered in the last paragraph, the change in the value of trade is expressed by a formula with which we are familiar: the value of imports falls and the value of exports rises to such an extent that the total value of home plus foreign goods available in the depreciating country falls by $(\epsilon_h + \epsilon_f - 1)$ per cent of the original quantity of goods traded. Added to this is the effect of the change in relative prices: a given value of expenditure [9] on imports buys a 1 per cent smaller volume of imports after a 1 per cent depreciation. In total we come, therefore, to the same result as in the last paragraph: if the effects of value and price changes are added together, the volume of goods available at home falls by $(\epsilon_h + \epsilon_f)$ per cent of the original quantity of goods traded.

Less simple are the cases which have already been considered, where some internal prices change in both countries. As we have already seen, if the prices of export-type goods change sufficiently in each country, and the prices of other goods do not change (or do not change as much), then the terms of trade may improve after a depreciation. If this happens, the relative price changes work in favor of the depreciating country, tending to increase the supply of goods available in return for a given quantity of work. The two effects on the quantity of goods available therefore work in opposite directions, since the value of goods available falls; in any case the balance of trade improves.

In the limiting conditions described by saying that supply elasticities of exports in both countries are zero and where the prices of other domestically produced goods in each country remain constant, the improvement in the terms of trade just counteracts the effects of

---

[9] In terms of the currency of the depreciating country.

the improvement in the balance of trade.[10] The net effect of the exchange rate change on the standard of living of those at work is zero (and, of course, there is the desired effect of evading balance of payments difficulties which, it should be remembered, is usually the basic reason for the changes considered in this chapter).

We can now come to the case where all prices of all domestically produced goods are tending to change in each country. Here, as has already been noted, the total effect is as if there had been a smaller depreciation and no changes in the price of domestically produced goods in either country. Thus, if the home country depreciates by 1 per cent, and then the prices of all goods produced in the home country rise by ¼ per cent and the prices of all goods produced in the foreign country fall by ¼ per cent, the effect is just like a depreciation by ½ per cent accompanied by no domestic price changes in either country: the level of all prices of goods produced in the home country has fallen ½ per cent in relation to the prices of all goods produced in the foreign country. There is, therefore, a deterioration in the standard of living of those at work in the home country, which is half as big as the one that would have arisen if there had been no changes in the prices of goods produced in the two countries. (Similarly, the change in the balance of trade is only half as big.)

This analysis of the deterioration of the standard of living of those at work can now be related to the question of whether cumulative movements in price levels can be expected in the two countries. If there are extensive unemployed resources in the country which has depreciated, the reduction in the standard of living of those at work is unlikely to have noticeable repercussions. Those people who are in employment are not likely to be able to make successful attempts to restore their standard of living to the pre-depreciation level, because the presence of unemployed resources overhanging the market makes it difficult for sellers of goods or services to raise their selling prices. The conditions of the analysis of Chapter 30, where there was a multiplier expansion as a result of the depreciation but

---

[10] A 1 per cent depreciation from an initially balanced situation involves a 1 per cent improvement in the balance of trade (i.e. less value of goods at home, to the extent of 1 per cent of the amount initially traded) and a 1 per cent improvement in the terms of trade (i.e. imports 1 per cent cheaper in terms of the exports sent out to obtain them). (See above, p. 467).

no rises in the prices of home-produced goods, are therefore satisfied.

If there are no extensive supplies of unemployed resources which can easily be brought into employment by additional demand, the situation is very different. The fall in the standard of living now affects most of the community, and there is no supply of unemployed resources overhanging the market which prevents those whose standard of living falls from trying to make defensive reactions of the kind discussed in the chapters on inflation.

In such circumstances of full employment, the reduced value of goods available for use at home and the rise in the home currency prices of imports may act as initiatory forces in an inflationary situation. Our next concern is with the factors that determine the development of this inflation, in which most or all prices tend to rise. If there are passive or impotent groups, who do not or cannot restore any or all of their real income or real expenditure, then the inflation may slow down quite soon; again, limitation of the supply of money [11] or income redistribution may have the same effect. All this is in line with the analysis of Part IV. Alternatively, once again in accordance with that analysis, speculative factors may be set in motion, and an explosive inflationary process may start.

It will be convenient to exclude both of these sets of forces—although in practice one or the other may be very important—in order to concentrate on the most important question on hand. We will, therefore, assume that all groups in the depreciating country are able to restore their old real income or real expenditure, and that there are no monetary limitations and no speculative forces. The rises of money incomes of producers of export goods and the defensive reactions by all those groups of transactors who lose as a result of rising prices lead to a series of rises in the prices of goods produced within the country. This chain reaction continues up to a point where all groups have successfully restored their original positions. It is perfectly possible for such a situation to be reached; the snag is that when it is attained all the effects of the exchange depreciation have been removed. This situation is one where all home prices have risen in the same proportion as the depreciation (assuming no change in internal price levels in the other country). When this has happened, the pre-depreciation relationship between the

---

[11] Which demands abandonment of our assumption of a banking policy of active ease.

prices of home-produced goods and the prices of foreign goods is restored. This means that both the terms of trade and the balance of trade [12] return to their predepreciation values. The standard of living is restored, but the balance of payments situation reverts to what it was. The improvement in the balance of trade (and consequently in the balance of payments) is merely temporary, lasting while the inflationary process is working itself out.

The practical lessons of this analysis are important. An exchange depreciation used to solve a balance of payments problem can be permanently successful only in a country which is at full employment if some or all transactors in that country accept a reduction in their real expenditure. Only in that case can the country prevent these inflationary effects from neutralizing the original change in the exchange rate.

This analysis can easily be extended to primary-producing countries, where a considerable quantity of unemployed resources that are willing to work at existing wages, etc. are not usually available; in a sense full employment is the normal situation. Moreover, in these countries prices and wages are usually flexible downward as well as upward. If a depreciation occurs in such a country, prices and wages tend to rise as various groups try to protect themselves against the fall in their real expenditure and income. If these rises are general, the analysis of the last few paragraphs applies. (We have considered earlier the analysis in cases where the rises are in isolated sectors.) One point is often important; a primary-producing country may deliberately devalue, not solely with the intention of improving its balance of payments, but also to induce an internal price and monetary stability, in face of a fall in the world market price of its exports. If the dollar price of wool halved, Australia might choose to devalue by fifty per cent, to try to maintain internal prices (although, of course, not real incomes). In such cases government policy will not be to oppose the inflationary tendencies normally implicit in a depreciation at full employment. Rather it may be to encourage it, in order to counteract deflationary forces coming from abroad.

If a primary-producing country appreciates, it will experience a tendency to falling internal prices; this movement, insofar as it

---

[12] Expressed in foreign currency, which is a stable measure in the circumstances assumed here.

affects all prices, once again tends to counteract the effects of the exchange rate change. As we have seen, a downward price spiral is rarely as violent as one in an upward direction; nevertheless, it is clear that a depreciation by a fully employed industrial country *vis-à-vis* a primary-producing country might lead quite rapidly to price movements in both countries which could quickly wipe out the effects of the exchange rate change.

SOME SUGGESTED READING

How exchange rate change and internal price changes affect the balance of trade is best presented in J. E. Meade, *Balance of Payments* (Oxford, 1951). In Chapter XVIII of his book Meade presents a four-commodity model that includes a home trade product and a foreign trade product for each of two countries; he then uses this model to analyze the effects of exchange rate changes on the terms of trade. A useful complement to Meade's work is the review by H. G. Johnson, 'The Taxonomic Approach to Economic Policy,' *Economic Journal* (1951).

The question of the effects of exchange rate changes on the terms of trade is also considered by G. Haberler in *A Survey of International Trade Theory, Special Papers in International Economics,* No. 1 (International Finance Section, Princeton University, 1955).

33

The International Propagation of Price Changes

In the preceding chapters we have considered a number of the significant inter-relationships that can arise in international monetary economics. But there still remains a major gap in all this analysis, which it is the purpose of this chapter to fill. This is a consideration of the international propagation of price changes. When there is a change in the level of prices in one country, it has repercussions on the other; these in turn have further effects. It will be convenient to concentrate our attention on two cases: one being trade between two fully employed industrial countries, and the other trade between a primary-producing country and an industrial country which is at a position of less than full employment.[1]

In the first of these two cases output cannot be increased, so any rise in demand must lead to price rises (or rationing, etc., which will be excluded from our consideration). In the second case, a change in demand for the products of one country leads to a change in its output but no change in its prices; a change in demand for the products of the other country results in a change in its prices but no change in its output. In discussing both these cases it will be necessary, for the sake of brevity and clarity of exposition, to assume that the terms of trade do not affect the total amount that people will choose to spend and to save out of a given money income.[2]

---

[1] The second analysis can also be applied to trade between two industrial countries, one of which is fully employed throughout the period under consideration, and the other which is not.

[2] The reader should be warned that some of the results given in this chapter are considerably affected if this assumption is dropped. The arguments of this chapter do no more than indicate the kind of thing that may happen.

The International Propagation of Inflation

The theory of the international propagation of inflation is merely an extension of the theory of inflation discussed in Chapters 19, 20, and 21. A convenient initiating force to consider is a rise in the level of government expenditure in one country, when both of the countries with which we are concerned are already at the position of full employment. Within the country in which the initial expansionary force appears, there are the familiar effects. The increased demand must lead to price rises; transactors react to the effects of these price rises, which in turn induces further price rises.

In addition to these internal reactions, it is necessary to consider what happens in the other country. Some of the initial increase in government expenditure in the first country is likely to involve additional imports—that is, additional exports by the country now under consideration. Since this country is already at full employment, the increased pressure of demand there sets off price rises, which themselves induce further price rises, in the manner discussed in Part IV.

The major additional complication to which we have to pay attention is that the price changes within the two countries are not necessarily parallel to one another. If prices rise faster in one country than in another, a shift in the pattern of trade between the two countries occurs. The country in which prices are rising more slowly shifts into a balance of payments deficit, if the sum of the demand elasticities is less than unity. If this sum is greater than unity, it switches into balance of payments surplus.

The effect of this is obvious. There is an increased inflationary pressure in the country which shifts into balance of payments surplus. This implies a faster increase in prices in that country and a slower increase in the other. When the elasticities sum to more than unity, the acceleration occurs in the country where the rate of rise of prices was tending to fall behind; there is, therefore, a tendency for price rises in the two countries to keep in line with each other. If, on the other hand, the elasticities sum to less than unity, the faster price rise is accelerated and the rise in the other country is slowed down.

If there are passive groups somewhere in the world economy, whatever inflationary process arises in each country will slow down and come to an end. It simplifies matters a little for this purpose if we regard countries as indivisible units. Then we can say that there is a tendency for the inflation to slow down if at least one country is to some extent passive in face of the inflationary process, or if at least one country chooses or is compelled to take steps to slow down the price rise.

Passivity may arise if a country is willing to accept worse terms of trade than at the beginning of the process: this necessarily implies (since output is at its maximum) that the levels of real income and expenditure are lower. Ways in which this may come about are obvious from the earlier discussion of inflation: for example, compression of the real incomes of the rentiers or fixing of government expenditure in money terms and not in real terms.

A country may be compelled to take steps to slow down the price rise, if a consequence of the inflationary process is that its international currency reserves are running out. If such balance of payments difficulties arise, a country may be compelled to take deliberate action (as by monetary or fiscal policy) to prevent prices from rising as fast as in the other country, and so to make its own goods more competitive, and so improve its balance of payments.

Such deliberate action reduces total demand for world resources; this reduction in the country in balance of payments difficulties may go far enough to reduce total world demand to a level compatible with price stability, thus wiping out the effect of the initial expansionary force.

Even if it is not in balance of payments difficulties, a country may still choose deliberately to introduce contractionary policies in order to break the international spiral of inflation. Any reduction in demand anywhere in the world must slow the inflation down, and a reduction equal in size to the original disturbance can be expected to stop it.

Trade between Primary-Producing and Industrial Countries

In our consideration of trade between a primary-producing country and an industrialized country it will be convenient to consider first of all what happens when there is an increase in the total level of demand in one country: this can be assumed to result from increased government expenditure, or from an increase in the level of investment. In either case it is assumed that the increased level of expenditure is maintained, in real terms, throughout the subsequent adjustment process.[3] It will be assumed that in the primary-producing country all labor is fully employed, so that changes in demand show themselves in the form of wage and/or price changes. In the industrial country we assume that conditions of full employment are not reached during the changes under consideration, so that neither prices nor wages have any tendency to alter.

For the sake of simplicity and brevity it is necessary to limit ourselves to a consideration of relatively simple circumstances, and not to follow up some of the complications which must enter into a complete analysis. In particular it will be assumed that imports do not enter into home-produced output in either country, so that we do not need to consider how a change in the price of any import content affects the prices of goods produced in each country. Moreover, it will be assumed that trade and payments were initially in a position of balance.

It is necessary to consider two cases in turn: one where the initiating rise in demand occurs in the primary-producing country, and the other where it occurs in the manufacturing country. In each of these cases we want to know what price changes will occur in the new equilibrium, what changes in the level of activity, and what changes occur in the balance of trade between the two countries. Some of the answers are immediately obvious. Our assumptions are such that there can be no changes in the level of activity in the primary-producing country, and no changes can occur in the level of prices of home output in the industrial country. The remaining changes are not so immediately obvious, however, and it is necessary to look into them. We can consider first what happens if the initiating change in demand arises in the primary-producing country; subsequently we can look at the other case.

Since our assumptions necessarily involve full employment in the primary-producing country, the quantity of goods produced in that country is fixed at the amount that can be produced, with existing techniques, by the existing amount of labor. In equilibrium, just as before the disturbance, precisely this quantity of goods must be bought by someone. But the disturbance we are considering is one where transactors in the primary-producing country are trying to buy more goods than initially: government expenditure (or invest-

---

[3] This is the same assumption as that followed in Chapter 30.

ment) has risen in real terms, and is being maintained at the new high level, while consumption expenditure is also constant in real terms.[4] The only way in which transactors in the primary-producing countries can maintain expenditure at a higher level in real terms, when output is constant, is to run a balance of payments deficit. They maintain real expenditure at a higher level in one or both of two ways. The primary-producing country can buy more goods from the industrial country, and the industrial country can buy fewer goods from the primary-producing country and so release more primary products for purchasers within the primary-producing country. In either case there can only be equilibrium between total demand and total supply in the primary-producing country if its balance of trade deteriorates by an amount equal to the value of the initiating rise in its total expenditure.[5]

The changes in imports and exports which occur during the adjustment process arise from two sources. Firstly, there is the direct effect on the primary-producing country's imports from the rise in its total expenditure. Secondly, there are two kinds of induced effect. One is that changes occur in the level of activity in the manufacturing country. The other is that changes occur in the price level in the primary-producing country, which affect the relative prices of its goods and those of the manufacturing country.

The change in the level of activity in the manufacturing country depends solely in the marginal propensity to save in that country and on the size of the initiating rise in total expenditure in the primary-producing country. We are, in fact, back at the extreme simplicity of the closed economy multiplier: the multiplier formula for the manufacturing country is simply one divided by the marginal propensity to save.[6] The common sense of this solution can be understood by recalling the assumptions of our model of the world economy. If the world economy is taken as a whole, the only 'leakage'

---

[4] Since output is constant and therefore income is constant in terms of home-produced goods, and since we have assumed expenditure to be independent of the terms of trade. It should be noted that our assumptions imply that expenditure in the primary-producing country is held constant in terms of primary products—not of all goods.

[5] For a full proof of this statement, see the Mathematical Appendix, p. 622.

[6] I.e. $1/s_i$ where i represents conditions in the industrial country. For a demonstration of this formula and of the remaining formulas introduced in this chapter, see the Mathematical Appendix.

that occurs when there is a rise in real expenditure in either country
is the leakage into savings in the industrial country. Any change in
expenditure on the goods of the primary-producing country leads to
changes in their prices, and not to any change in the total real expenditure of transactors in the primary-producing country. Thus the
only factors affecting the equilibrium rise in the world's level of
activity (which is wholly concentrated in the manufacturing country) are the initial disturbance (the rise in the primary producer's
expenditure) and the rate of leakage into savings in the manufacturing country.

The direction of change in the level of prices in the primary-
producing country in the new equilibrium depends on each country's
elasticity of demand for the products of the other. If the sum of the
demand elasticities is greater than unity, then a price rise occurs in
the primary-producing country after a rise in demand there. The
common sense of this answer is simple. The effect of both the initial
rise in expenditure in the primary-producing country and the induced rise in the level of income in the industrial country is to increase the total world demand for primary products. Since the supply
of these is fixed the excess demand must be choked off by relative
price changes. In terms of the analysis of Chapter 31, this is brought
about by a rise in the relative price of primary products, if the sum
of the two country's demand elasticities for the products of the other
country is greater than unity. Similarly, if the sum of the elasticities
is less than unity the only possible equilibrium is one where prices
fall in the primary-producing country after a rise in demand there.
The latter result cannot be brought about by the operation of normal
market forces.

The extent of the change in prices in the primary-producing
countries depends on the elasticities of demand of each country for
the products of the other, and also on the marginal propensities to
import and to save in each country.[7] Assuming that the sum of the

---

[7] The change in prices is equal to the initiating change in the total expenditure in the primary-producing country multiplied by the following expression:

$$\frac{1}{I} \cdot \frac{1 + \dfrac{m_i}{s_i} - \dfrac{m_p}{(1 - s_p)}}{\epsilon_i + \epsilon_p - 1}$$

where the suffix i represents the industrial country and p represents the primary-
producing country, and m and s represent marginal propensities to import and

demand elasticities is greater than unity, the price change is the smaller the larger are the elasticities: a relatively small price change leads to a relatively big switch in demand if the elasticities are large. The price change will also be the smaller the larger is the marginal propensity to save in the industrial country (so that the rise in the level of activity there is relatively small) and the smaller is the marginal propensity to import in the industrial country (so that whatever rise in the level of activity does occur has relatively little effect on imports from the primary-producing country). Finally, the price change will be the smaller the greater is the proportion of the initial rise in the primary producers' expenditure which flows immediately into imports (i.e. the larger is $m_p/(1 - s_p)$), thus making corrective induced changes in prices of primary products so much the less necessary.

We can now proceed to the case where the initiating change is a rise in the level of demand in the industrial country. Here the solutions are somewhat simpler and the exposition can be correspondingly briefer.

In this case the balance of payments in the new equilibrium situation must necessarily be at the original position of a zero balance.[8] Output in the primary-producing country cannot change; therefore, in equilibrium, any increase in the industrial country's demand for primary products must be counterbalanced by an equal reduction in the quantity of primary products bought by people in the primary-producing country. Correspondingly, there must be an equal increase in the expenditure of transactors in the primary-producing country on imported industrial products.

As in the earlier case, the changes in imports and exports of the two countries that occur in the adjustment process arise from two sources. Firstly, there is the direct effect on the industrial country's imports of the initiating rise in its expenditure. Secondly, there are two kinds of induced effect. One is that there is an induced change in the level of activity in the industrial country. The second is that there are relative price changes, brought about by a change in the level of prices in the primary-producing country.

The induced change in the level of activity in the industrial coun-

---

to save while ϵ represents the elasticity of demand of each country for the products of the other and I is the initial value of imports.

[8] For a proof see the Mathematical Appendix, p. 624.

try is always in the same direction as the initiating change in demand, and is the larger the smaller is the marginal propensity to save in the industrial country. For the same reasons as those given earlier, no other relationship has any influence on the induced change in the level of activity in the industrial country.[9]

The direction of the price change in the primary-producing country depends, as before, on the value of the sum of the demand elasticities of the two countries for the products of the other. If the sum is greater than unity, prices in the primary-producing country are higher in the new equilibrium; in this way the necessary restoration of the balance of payments to its original position is brought about.[10]

The case where the initiating disturbance is a switch in tastes, leading to a switch in demand from the goods of one country to another, is quite easy to deal with. The initiating change involves no change in the total amount of expenditure in the world economy, but merely a shift in the way in which it is used. This means that no induced changes in the level of activity occur: the marginal propensities to save and to import are, therefore, irrelevant. All that happens is that relative price changes occur which remove the excess demand or supply of primary products; on our assumption that the terms of trade do not influence total expenditure from a given money income, this means that the original quantity of industrial products is also sold, and that the balance of payments is restored to its original position.[11] The whole of the necessary price adjustment is brought about by price changes in the primary-producing country; their direction and size depend upon the size of the demand elasticities. If the sum of the elasticities is greater than unity, prices rise in the primary-producing country if there has been a switch in demand toward its products, and fall if there has been a

---

[9] The change in the level of activity is equal to the change in demand in the industrial country multiplied by $1/s_i$; once again, the simple multiplier analysis applies.

[10] The percentage price change in the primary-producing country which follows a 1 per cent rise in its total demand in relation to its original level of imports is equal to

$$\frac{\dfrac{m_i}{s_i(1 - s_i)}}{\epsilon_i + \epsilon_p - 1}.$$

[11] For a proof see the Mathematical Appendix, pp. 623-4.

switch away from them.[12] If the sum of the elasticities is less than unity, equilibrium can only be restored if prices move in the opposite directions. In either case, the necessary price changes to correct a given disequilibrium are (in accordance with the analysis of Chapter 31) the bigger, the nearer the sum of the elasticities is to unity.

Some Suggested Reading

Modern theories of inflation usually have not been extended to include the international propagation of inflation; hence it is difficult to suggest readings on this topic. A useful start that has been made is G. Patterson, 'Relationships Between Foreign and American Prices,' in *The Relationship of Prices to Economic Stability and Growth: A Compendium of Papers Submitted by Panelists Appearing Before the Joint Economic Committee* (Washington, 1958).

---

[12] In equilibrium the percentage price change in the primary-producing country following a 1 per cent switch in its imports toward the industrial country's goods is

$$-\frac{1}{(\epsilon_i + \epsilon_p - 1)}.$$

The percentage price change in the primary-producing country following a 1 per cent switch in the imports of the industrial country toward the primary producer's goods is

$$\frac{1}{(\epsilon_i + \epsilon_p - 1)}.$$

34

International Capital Movements

International capital movements can take place in many different ways. Capital can move from a country if residents of that country, or its government, choose to acquire claims against foreigners or foreign governments (such as bank deposits abroad, foreign bills, bonds, or shares) or if they acquire real assets abroad (as when a firm builds a branch factory in another country). Similarly, capital can move into a country if these operations take place in the opposite direction.

For our purposes it is convenient to distinguish two main kinds of capital movement, short-term and long-term. It is not possible to draw a rigid line of demarcation between these two, but sufficiently clear distinctions can be made.

There are two distinctions between long- and short-term capital movements that are particularly relevant for us; broadly speaking, they coincide, but in particular cases a transaction may appear to be of one kind if one method of distinction is used, and of the other if the second method is used. One method of distinction is to ask whether the transaction involves short-term claims (with duration to maturity of up to a year) such as bank deposits and bills, or whether it involves long-term claims and fixed real assets. The other method is to ask whether the capital movement is durable or not; if it is likely to be reversed quite quickly it is a short-term movement; if not it is a long-term movement. Broadly these categories coincide, but in detail they do not; temporary shifts of capital may use long-term assets (such as purchases of stocks and shares); relatively permanent movements may use very liquid assets (such as bank deposits).

In reconciling such cases a broad metaphor is helpful for showing
486

in which category it is most convenient to put a particular case. Short-term international capital transactions typically involve the frequent movement around the world of a stock of capital; long-term transactions typically involve the flow of new funds of capital from one country to another. The total volume of transactions involving short-term capital is fairly large in relation to annual accruals to the fund of international short-term capital; the total volume of transactions involving long-term capital is more closely related in magnitude to the annual accruals to the total amount of long-term capital in existence.

Corresponding to these distinctions are distinctions between the purposes and the effects of short- and long-term international capital movements. For that reason it will be convenient for us to treat them separately, and to take short-term capital movements first.

Short-Term Capital Movements

The main reasons for short-term capital movements between countries being made by private individuals and organizations (as opposed to public organizations such as the government and the central bank) can be classified into three main groups: changes in relative interest rates, expected changes in exchange rates, and other relevant expected changes.

When exchange rates are quite stable, with no expectation that they will alter and when no other relevant disturbances are expected, short-term capital movements are made almost solely in response to changes in interest rates in the various countries. If short-term interest rates (such as bill rates and bank lending rates—the sort of rate which is directly affected by discount rate changes) rise in one country, then it is expensive to borrow from that country and advantageous to lend to it. Traders there who want short-term financing of their inventories may find it advantageous to borrow abroad; on the other hand, banks and other financial institutions having funds on hand which they wish to hold in a liquid form which earns as large a rate of interest as possible will choose to lend to the country with high short-term rates. The other influence of interest rate changes on short-term capital movements is familiar. If long-term interest rates rise in a country, there may well be pressure to buy its bonds for speculative reasons, in the belief that the change will shortly be reversed.

This simple position has to be abandoned if the complicating factor of the possibility of exchange rate changes is considered. For example, to take a case of short-term capital movements, involving short-term interest rates, it may be that the three-month bill rate in New York is 1 per cent more per annum (that is ¼ per cent in 3 months) than the three-month bill rate in London. If there is no exchange risk and no appreciable cost of movement, it will be worth while for financial institutions to shift out of London bills and to buy New York bills. If, however, the price of dollars in terms of sterling falls ¼ per cent during the three months in which the bill is held, the interest rate advantage is canceled out, because ¼ per cent of the original amount is lost when the dollars received when the bill matures are turned back into sterling.

Before the First World War, the risks of exchange rate changes were very slight, because of the institutional arrangement of the gold standard. The central banks or treasuries of most countries in the world would buy and sell gold at fixed prices in terms of their own currency and free export and import of gold was allowed. Moreover, there was absolute confidence in the continuation of this system and of the fixed prices. If gold cost nothing to ship from one country to another, if it took no time to ship, and if the buying and selling prices of gold in each country were the same, then exchange rates between the various countries would be precisely fixed. To take an example which is simple numerically: if the British gold price were £5 per ounce and the U.S. price $20 per ounce, the sterling dollar exchange could only be £1 = $4, because at any other exchange rate it would be profitable to buy gold in one country and ship it to the other. In fact these conditions were never precisely satisfied; the buying price in any country was usually slightly lower than the selling price (in order to cover the central bank's expenses) and shipments cost both time (and so loss of interest on the capital tied up) and money; as a consequence slight exchange rate changes were possible. The normal limits of these changes (usually less than 1 per cent apart) were the so-called *gold points*, which were the exchange rates at which purchases and shipments of gold in one direction or the other became profitable.

In these circumstances, interest rate changes were the predominant influence on short-term capital movements. An appreciable rise in the short-term rate of interest could be relied upon to attract funds to the country concerned. In the inter-war period, and especially in the 'thirties, this state of affairs no longer persisted, nor has it been rebuilt since World War II. The experience of exchange rate changes during the First World War and in the early 'thirties, and the abandonment of the gold standard in those years, led to uncertainties about exchange rate movements. A raising of short-term interest rates in a country often came to be intepreted as a sign of weakness and so depreciation of its exchange rate was feared; the effect might well be the perverse one of driving short-term funds away. Once a serious possibility arose that exchange rates might fluctuate substantially and not merely within extremely narrow limits, the effects of interest rate changes on movements of short-term private capital could no longer be forecast with confidence.

In addition, other influences have come to operate on short-term capital movements, particularly fears of political changes, war, and exchange control. However high interest rates may be and however stable exchange rates, short-term capital is likely to leave a country which is subject to political disturbance or which is expected to impose restrictions on foreign payments. In disturbed conditions the position therefore arises that short-term capital movements are mainly influenced by a confusion of fears and expectations; the fund of international short-term capital is liable to wash around the world violently and rapidly in response to fears which are largely outside the control of governments or monetary authorities. In this way arose the problem of 'hot money'—that is, of these unstable and footloose funds—which was so great in the 'thirties and has continued since World War II, despite rigid exchange controls.

The consequence is that the pre-1914 situation, in which changes in short-term interest rates could be relied upon to attract funds from abroad or send them abroad, no longer applies. Formerly, interest rate changes could be relied upon to provide rapid, although limited and temporary, alleviation of the foreign payments position by their effects on the movement of short-term capital; now these effects can no longer be relied upon, and perverse reactions are almost as likely as 'natural' ones. Only short-term capital movements by public authorities (such as central banks) which are deliberately designed to have a stabilizing effect on the balance of payments can be relied upon; private short-term movements are an untrustworthy tool in our disturbed times.

The remainder of our discussion of the effects of short-term capital movements involves discussion of their effects on the banking and financial systems. Discussion of these questions is best delayed until the next chapter; meantime it is necessary to discuss the reasons for and the effects of long-term capital movements.

Long-Term Capital Movements

Long-term private capital movements are also influenced by the factors that we have seen to influence movements of short-term capital. Expectations of exchange rate changes, either in the near or the distant future, affect willingness to acquire claims or take on liabilities expressed in foreign currency. Since the transaction must be expressed in a currency foreign to either the debtor or the creditor, the possibility of exchange rate changes must always enter into rational calculations. Changes in relative interest rates are also relevant; if long-term interest rates rise in one country there is reason for thinking that foreigners will tend to lend more to that country and residents will tend to lend less abroad; this will be a pretty certain result if there is a high probability that interest rates in that country will not go any higher, so that there is little risk of capital losses from falling bond prices counteracting the advantages of the larger income accruing by lending in that country. A rise in interest rates, if it does not induce expectations of still further rises, therefore attracts long-term capital to a country. This effect of the change is likely to be concentrated in a fairly short period of time, quite soon after the interest rate change.

This is not, however, the only effect of interest rates on long-term capital movements. There will be this once-for-all effect, shortly after a *change* in relative interest rates, but there will also be a continuing effect on long-term capital movements arising from the *level* of long-term rates compared with those in other countries, irrespective of whether there has been any recent change in relative rates. If other things are equal, a high level of interest rates in one country is more likely than a low level to attract a large proportion of the new flow of savings into the long-term capital markets of the world. High interest rates relative to other countries provide a *continuing* attraction to capital inflow into a country. (The proviso that other things are equal is important; high interest rates in many poor countries are simply a sign that there are many bad debts there; if this risk is discounted, the rates that can be earned may well be very low.)

It is not only relative interest rates in the two countries that affect capital movements. A large part of the movements are risk capital, which moves in search of an uncertain profit. The more prosperous business is abroad compared with business in the lending country, and the more favorable prospects appear abroad compared with those in the lending country, the larger these movements will be.

Capital Movements and Income Levels

So far in this discussion of the reasons for long-term capital movements we have been concerned with the incentives to movement of funds by private individuals and organizations. In addition to these there are movements by public authorities; these are often induced by other factors, which we must now consider. Broadly speaking, there are two main effects which may be relevant, namely, maintenance or raising of levels of real income and expenditure in the borrowing country and maintenance or raising of real income levels in the lending country.

Levels of income and expenditure in the borrowing country can be maintained or raised in a variety of ways. A foreign loan may save the country from having to reduce its real income and expenditure because of the balance of payments difficulties that would otherwise have arisen from its current policies and economic position.[1] Alternatively, the country may be enabled to increase its total expenditure to levels that would otherwise be impossible without creating balance of payments difficulties. It may be enabled to import more goods for current consumption, or to import more capital goods.

Income levels can be increased in the lending country by making foreign loans if there is less than full employment at home. An outflow of long-term capital is a way in which the lending country can run a balance of trade surplus without the borrowing country running into balance of payments difficulties. A balance of trade surplus is an expansionary force, as we have already seen; it leads to a

---

[1] This matter will be looked at further in Chapter 38; but it has already been seen in Chapters 30 and 32 that an improvement in the balance of trade can frequently only be brought about by a reduction in real income and expenditure, either by a reduction in the internal level of output and activity (Chapter 30) or by the adverse effects of relative price changes (Chapter 32).

higher level of activity and real income in the lending country if full employment has not been reached. Another way of expressing the same idea is that, if suitable opportunities are not available for using the volume of savings that would be forthcoming at full employment for investment at home, full employment can still be maintained if those savings are used for investment abroad.

These two income effects of long-term investment by governments may well provide a justification for foreign investment which would not be worth while if made by private organizations. It may be worth while for a government to lend or even give money for a project in another country from which the commercial return is very low, if the consequence is that income levels are maintained or raised at home or abroad. All the same, if other things are equal, it is a good rule to invest in projects with a reasonably high commercial return.

International lending can, therefore, increase the level of income in both the borrowing and the lending countries when it leads to expenditure that would not otherwise have taken place. It can increase the level of activity in both countries, and make it possible for the borrowing country to enjoy the use of goods it could not otherwise afford.

If the loan does not lead to additional expenditure, or if full employment exists in both countries so that no additional expenditure in real terms is possible, the uniformly favorable results no longer arise. If no additional expenditure takes place as a direct result of the loan,[2] the borrowing country tends to move into balance of payments surplus and the lender into balance of payments deficit. (The current balance is unchanged because expenditure is unchanged; the balance of long-term lending tends to move in favor of the borrower; therefore the total balance of payments does also.) Sooner or later, therefore, the lending country tends to find itself in balance of payments difficulties, and some action has to be taken. As mentioned earlier, solution of balance of payments difficulties frequently leads to a loss of real income for the country in difficulties, because of the policies that have to be taken to solve the problem. So in this case, the lending country tends to lose real income.

---

[2] For example, if it leads to an investment project being financed by foreign savings instead of home savings, or because there is full employment in both countries.

Indirect Effects on the Balance of Payments

We must now look farther into the question of the indirect [3] effects of changes in the level of long-term lending on the balance of payments. We shall be concerned solely with the effects operating through induced changes in income and expenditure, and shall disregard the effects of changes in international lending on interest rates.

If a capital movement amounts to no more than a purchase of an existing foreign asset by a resident of the country which is lending, there are no direct effects on income levels or expenditure in either country. There will be effects on interest rates and the banking structure which will themselves affect income and expenditure; but for the moment we are excluding consideration of these cases.

In other cases, foreign lending may, and usually will, directly affect income and expenditure. Two cases are particularly plausible and interesting. One is the case where the amount of the loan is all spent by the borrowing country on additional investment in home-produced capital equipment; the other is the case where the loan is all used for increased imports by the borrowing country. (An intermediate case arises where a part of the loan is spent on investment in imported capital equipment and part on home-produced equipment; this case clearly partakes of features of both the cases distinguished.)

In the first example, if resources at home are not fully employed, the increase in investment will cause a multiplier expansion in the level of activity in the borrowing country; if the borrowing country spends any of this induced increase in income on imports there will also be a multiplier expansion in the lending country (assuming less than full employment there). The process of interaction is similar to the one discussed in Chapter 30. The net effect is that (assuming there are no further, consequential, changes in home or foreign investment in either country) the balance of trade will always turn against the borrowing country, but never by more than the increase in long-term loans it is receiving. The balance of payments therefore

---

[3] As opposed to the direct effect, which is an improvement in the balance of payments of the borrowing country.

never improves for the lending country and usually moves in favor of the borrowing country.

In the other case, where all the loan is directly used to increase purchases of imports by the borrowing country, the proximate effect is to cause the borrowing country's balance of trade to deteriorate by exactly the same amount as it has received in additional loans; the balance of payments is unchanged. This is not, however, the final position. If there are unemployed resources in the lending country, the improvement in its trade balance leads to a multiplier expansion which in turn causes one in the borrowing country; in accordance with our usual experience, if these conditions last long enough for a final equilibrium to be reached, income will rise in both countries and there will be a further, smaller, shift in the balance of trade which will be unfavorable to the lending country. The net effect will be an improvement in the balance of payments of the borrowing country and a deterioration in its balance of trade. This is the same result as in the case where all the loan is spent on investment in home-produced equipment; it is therefore fairly clear that the consequence of the mixed position, where some of the loan is spent on investment in home-produced equipment and some is spent abroad, also leads to this same kind of final equilibrium.

SOME SUGGESTED READING

The classical discussion of the effects of international capital movements was that between Keynes and Ohlin in the late 'twenties (a controversy in which Keynes was remarkably pre-Keynesian). This controversy and a modern appraisal by Lloyd Metzler is conveniently reprinted in the American Economic Association, *Readings in the Theory of International Trade* (Philadelphia, 1950). Two of the most useful books dealing with capital transfers are C. Iversen, *Aspects of the Theory of International Capital Movements* (Copenhagen, 1935) and A. I. Bloomfield, *Capital Imports and the American Balance of Payments 1934-39* (Chicago, 1950).

35

International Banking Mechanisms—I

In the preceding chapters we were able to ignore the effects of changes in the balance of payments upon the banking systems of the countries concerned by assuming that banks followed a policy of active ease. We must now consider the nature of the movements in interest rates, in bank lending, and in the money supply that would naturally follow international changes, if there were not immediate sterilization by the banking authorities. In answering this question we shall assume that exchange rates are constant and we shall be concerned with three main categories of country.

Firstly, there is the case of a country whose monetary system is merely an extension of the monetary system of another country. Secondly, there is the case (which is the most common) of countries with independent monetary systems. Here, there are two sub-categories which we must investigate. One is the case where payments are being settled in a country's own currency, the second is the case where settlement is in some other currency. Thirdly, there is the case of countries which are international financial centers; we must investigate what happens when one of these acts as a financial intermediary to help settle payments between two other countries.

Any transaction will have effects in at least two countries; the paying country and the receiving. In addition, if it is made through another country which is an international financial center, then that third country will be involved. The total effects of a transaction may, therefore, be very varied; what we must do is split the problem into parts, by considering the possible reactions in each country.

A Dependent Monetary System: The Colonial Exchange System

The simplest case is that in which the banking and monetary system of one country is so closely dependent on that of another that it is best regarded as an extension of the main system. The best example of such arrangements, in which the area covered by a single monetary system extends over several areas which are politically distinct, is the British colonial monetary system; for this system there is no strict counterpart in American monetary experience. Although the trend (as exemplified by the pressure for independent central banks in certain colonies) is toward monetary independence, the current position is still one in which the monetary systems of Britain's remaining colonies are outliers of that of England.[1]

For these dependent monetary systems the most important arrangement is the one involving currency board operations. At present, there are five currency boards in operation—Central Africa, East Africa, West Africa, Malaya and the West Indies. The currency boards are required to exchange colonial currencies for sterling (and conversely, sterling for colonial currencies) at a fixed rate of exchange and for a small commission. English sterling which has been earned by a colony (by sales either to Britain or to another country [2]) can be transferred into colonial currency by selling the sterling to the currency board appropriate to the colony concerned. The currency board then has a liability of a colonial note that it has issued and an asset of English sterling. It generally holds rather less than half in liquid assets (e.g. Treasury bills) and the rest in longer-term securities, all of which earn an income.[3] Part of this income goes to a reserve fund, so that the currency board has more sterling assets than liabilities in notes; the rest goes to the governments of the colonies concerned. Apart from this profit, the currency

---

[1] Almost all the major colonies are now rapidly moving toward complete political independence; when this is achieved (as recently by Ghana and Malaya) there is a rapid movement away from the colonial currency system toward a fully independent system, albeit still within the sterling area.

[2] If a colony earns dollars (or other non-sterling currencies), the dollars will be sold to London for sterling.

[3] Since the end of 1954 they have been entitled to hold up to 30 per cent of their assets in local securities. This change is the first step toward an independent monetary system.

board system makes no real difference to the monetary systems of the colonies; in every other respect, the position is just as if Bank of England notes circulated.

The total monetary circulation of a colony consists, however, not only of local currency but also of bank deposits. If the same banks were to operate in the colonies as in Britain and if those banks operated with the same ratios of the various kinds of assets to total liabilities in both areas, then there would be no difference between an inter-county payment made within England and a payment from a colony to a county in England. In practice, however, there are some differences. Firstly, the most important banks operating in the colonies are the imperial banks; most of them have head offices in London, and each of them operates in several colonies. These imperial banks are independent of the English commercial banks, although some have close relationships with one or another of the English banks. There is also a considerable number of local banks operating in individual colonies, but these are usually rather small, less involved in overseas trade than the imperial banks, and have less close ties with London. Secondly, the banks which operate in the colonies work under different legal rules from those in England and operate with reserve ratios that are different from those customary in English banks. With different reserve ratios a monetary transfer does not result in a monetary expansion (contraction) in a colony that is equal to the monetary contraction (expansion) in England (both measured in sterling).

Generally speaking, a colony's balance of payments surplus or deficit affects the size of the monetary circulation within the colony only to the same extent as the size of the balance of payments surplus or deficit. In the case of a deficit, sterling or foreign currency is bought from the colonial banks with local notes or with bank deposits. To the extent that the purchase is made with local notes, the bank can immediately use these to buy sterling from a currency board, and the bank's position is unchanged. To the extent that the purchases are made with bank deposits, the bank finds that its liabilities (a deposit) and its assets (liquid sterling funds in London) have declined equally. If the bank were working anywhere near a critical cash ratio [4] this would be serious, as it would involve a

---

[4] Or other reserve ratio.

fall in the ratio, and so necessitate a contraction of loans and advances. In fact, however, the imperial banks cannot make as many loans and advances as they would like (because they cannot find enough borrowers whom they consider good enough risks) and they are, therefore, not near any critical position. A multiple contraction of loans and advances is therefore unnecessary.

It is conceivable that such a contraction would be needed if many colonies were simultaneously running an adverse balance of payments; then the imperial banks might find their liquid reserves in London becoming uncomfortably low. In that case advances would have to be reduced and there would, therefore, be a multiple contraction of the monetary circulation in the *whole area* covered by the imperial bank concerned. Even in this case, however, the reductions in loans and advances might not occur primarily in the colonies with the big adverse balances, because the imperial banks, in their colonial operations, do not generally attempt to match local liabilities and local assets in each colony but simply make loans and advances wherever they are profitable.

So far we have been concerned with the effects of balance of payments changes on the money supply of the colonies. There is nothing to say here concerning the other question to be answered in this chapter: the effects of balance of payments changes on interest rates. Interest rates in the colonies depend completely on London's policies; at present Kenya has no more of a separate money or capital market than Wales, and interest rates in both countries are equally dependent on London's policies.

Independent Monetary Systems

We can now proceed to discuss the effects of foreign payments and receipts on the banking system of a country with an independent monetary system. In modern conditions this generally implies the existence of a central bank, so we shall presume this to be the case.

In answering our primary question, of the effects of international changes on the internal monetary circulation, we must first ask whether or not the international payments we are considering are settled in terms of the currency of the country with which we are concerned. Common examples of both systems can be found. Britain settles all her transactions with the overseas members of the sterling area in sterling. A considerable proportion of British transactions with other countries is also settled in sterling. Moreover, very many of the transactions of sterling area countries with non-sterling countries are settled in English sterling, as also are a considerable number of transactions between two countries neither of which is in the sterling area. (Denmark, for example, may make payments to Brazil with sterling.) Most American and a large proportion of French transactions with other countries are settled in dollars and francs respectively. Clearly, when one country settles a transaction in its own currency, the other concerned cannot be using its own. Thus, Brazil's transactions with the United States are practically always in a currency foreign to Brazil. Dollars also are frequently used for making transactions in which the United States is not directly involved, for example, in settlements between the member countries of the European Payments Union. Dollars are not the only means of settlement used in this particular case; there is also a purely inter-central bank 'currency,' consisting of debts to or claims against the Union, which is used for making parts of the settlement. Gold is another common means of settlement; while the U.S. Treasury is willing to buy gold from and sell gold to the central banks of other countries at a fixed price ($35 per ounce) gold and U.S. dollars are in effect interchangeable, as far as foreign countries are concerned.

Transactions Settled in Home Currency

The first case to be discussed is the effect on the home monetary circulation of transactions with foreigners which are settled in terms of home currency; within this group two types of case need to be distinguished. The first is the case where foreign banks operate by varying their holdings of home currency in home commercial banks; the second arises where overseas banks make settlements by drawing checks on the home central bank. (In this latter case most of their holdings may well be in liquid assets such as Treasury bills, but changes in their holdings are made through deposits at the central bank.)

The first of these two cases can easily be dismissed. If a balance of payments deficit [5] occurs in these circumstances, deposits in home

---

[5] The analysis of this chapter will be in terms of balance of payments deficits; the same analysis applies, *mutatis mutandis*, for a balance of payments surplus.

commercial banks are transferred from the ownership of home residents to that of foreign banks. There is a change in the ownership of bank deposits, just as when one home resident makes a payment to another; that is the end of the matter and there are no repercussions on the home banking system.[6]

In the second of these cases, where the foreign banks have accounts at the home central bank, some examples are the British relationships with much of the sterling area outside of British colonies, and the relationship of the United States with many countries. To simplify matters let us assume a case where there are only two countries, the United States and a country in the dollar area, which holds all its international currency reserves in dollars, and that all residents of the United States hold all their money in deposits with American commercial banks.

If in any period residents of the United States are paying out more to residents of the dollar area country than they are receiving, there will be two sets of consequences. In the first place, residents of the United States will come to own less money in the form of claims on their banks, while dollar area residents will come to own more. As an immediate consequence of the payments the monetary circulation of the United States declines by the amount of the payment, and that of the dollar area country rises. In the second place, the American banks with which the residents of the United States hold their banking accounts will be making more payments to dollar area banks than are being received from the opposite direction. The net balance has to be settled between the American banks and the dollar area country's banks. This is done in the same way as net settlements between American banks: checks drawn on the Federal Reserve Banks are paid over to the dollar area country's banks (which may be either the central bank or a commercial bank). The reserves of the American banks at the Federal Reserve decline, and those of the dollar area country's banks rise.

This is not the end of the matter. The reserve ratio of the American banks is down, because reserves and deposits liabilities have declined by equal absolute amounts. What the precise nature and conse-

---

[6] Minimum cash or other reserve ratios may possibly be raised slightly, if a commercial bank is holding an unusually large quantity of foreign deposits: such a situation may be considered risky, because such deposits may all be withdrawn simultaneously.

quences of the reaction to this situation will be depends on whether or not the American commercial banks are holding reserves in excess of the legal requirement, and upon the way in which the Federal Reserve System is operating. If the American commercial banks are holding excess reserves they may not attempt to restore the reserve ratio to its original position. If they do not possess excess reserves or if they desire to maintain a fixed reserve ratio higher than the legal requirement, they will act to restore their reserve ratio, probably in the first instance by disposing of some of their government securities holdings (mainly bills). In the first situation described above (where American banks, because of their holdings of excess reserves, permit their reserve ratio to decline) there is no multiple effect on the quantity of money in the United States; bank deposits (i.e. their liabilities) fall by just the same amount in the period under consideration as the balances of payments deficit that accrues in that period. If the American commercial banks did not start with an excess of reserves, and if the Federal Reserve Banks are not willing to take measures to augment the volume of reserves, then there will be a tendency to multiple contraction of the monetary circulation in the United States as a result of the banking reactions to the effects of a balance of payments deficit. And as the American commercial banks sell securities and/or restrict loans, interest rates in the United States tend to rise.

So far we have assumed that the dollar area country's banks hold their newly acquired dollar assets in the form of deposits at the Federal Reserve Banks, but it is probable that they will be willing to hold some portion of their increase in assets in U.S. Treasury securities. They will be willing to do this because of the interest they can earn, leaving only small working balances at the Federal Reserve Banks. If the dollar area country's banks should decide to invest the whole of the increased dollar holdings in United States government securities, all funds paid into their accounts at the Federal Reserve Banks are paid out for the purchase of securities, thereby restoring American commercial bank reserves to their original level; i.e. checks drawn on the Federal Reserve Banks that are paid over to the dollar area country's banks are matched in amount by checks drawn on the Reserve Banks that are paid over to the American commercial banks. As a consequence, the American monetary circulation can be restored to the level that prevailed before the deficit occurred, unless the American banks choose to hold excess reserves. If we assume that the central bank does not undertake any neutralizing operations, interest rates in the United States will tend to decline, particularly in the short end of the government securities market, where foreign holdings will, in all likelihood, tend to be concentrated.

We have considered so far two extreme cases: one where foreign banks hold their larger holdings of dollar assets as deposits with the Federal Reserve Banks and the other where the foreign banks hold their larger holdings of dollar assets in government securities. There is, however, another possibility. The foreign banks may divide their increased holdings of dollar assets between balances at the Federal Reserve and government securities. Such a division will reduce the commercial banks' reserves and will lead to a contraction in the quantity of money in the United States (assuming that the banks have no excess reserves). But the contraction in the money supply will not be so great as in the first case we discussed, where the foreign banks held *only* deposits with the Federal Reserve Banks. There is one special case that deserves further attention; in this case, the decline in the quantity of money in a given period is precisely the same as the country's balance of payments deficit in the same period. This occurs when the ratio of Federal Reserve deposits to government securities acquired by the foreign banks is equal to the constant reserve ratio being maintained by the commercial banks. The reason for this is that a decline in the quantity of money reduces the reserves that commercial banks must hold, if they are to hold their reserve ratio constant, by an amount equal to the reserve ratio multiplied by the decrease in the quantity of money. If this amount is exactly the same as that which the foreign banks wish to add to their deposits at the Federal Reserve, there is no reason why there should be any further reactions. The foreign banks have taken up precisely the amount of deposits at the Federal Reserve which the American commercial banks no longer need, after their customers' deposits have fallen by an amount equal to the balance of payments deficit. Another way of viewing this last case is to think of the foreign banks as new banks that enter the picture and draw away some proportion of the deposit liabilities and reserves of the existing banks.

So far we have been considering what happens when the United States moves into a balance of payments deficit with a dollar area country. The analysis of a movement into a surplus can be dismissed very quickly. If the American commercial banks allow their reserve ratio to rise (assuming that foreign banks make settlements by drawing on their balances at the Federal Reserve), there are no multiple effects on the American banking system. Alternatively they may restore the reserve ratio to its original position, by a multiple expansion based on purchases of investments and increased loans. If foreign banks make the majority of their settlements through changes in their holdings of Treasury securities, then the impact upon the money supply in the United States will be reduced and the prime effects will be upon the money market rates of interest.

One final point should be made in connection with the effects of a balance of payments deficit: we must pay explicit attention to the effects of the change in the quantity of money which usually takes place in the United States on the liquidity position of the general public, and so through this roundabout route on interest rates. To do this we must compare the changes that occur in the quantity of money with changes in the public's demand to hold money.

Let us consider the case where the balance of payments deficit arises because there has been a shift in tastes which results in fewer American exports to a dollar area country. As we saw in Chapter 30, there will be induced multiplier effects on income at home and abroad, which will lead in time to a new equilibrium in which the level of activity will be lower in the United States, and there will be a continuing balance of payments deficit for the United States. This lower level of activity will cause a reduced transactions demand for money and so a tendency for falling interest rates if the quantity of money were to remain unchanged.

As we have seen, the quantity of money remains unchanged if we are in the extreme position where all the increased foreign holdings go into United States government securities and if the American commercial banks hold constant reserve ratios. We have also seen that, in that case, interest rates in the United States fall. The two effects of the public's transactions demand and the actions of the foreign banks therefore work together to push interest rates down.

But, as we have seen, the quantity of money remains unchanged only in these extreme circumstances; generally it may be expected to continue to fall. Suppose, for example, that whenever residents of the United States are paying more to overseas residents than the other way, foreign banks add the whole of their dollar receipts to their deposits at the Federal Reserve Banks. Then the quantity of money in the United States falls indefinitely, and falls in each period by some multiple of the balance of payments deficit (assuming that the commercial banks do not have excess reserves to cushion the impact of the deficit on the quantity of money). Sooner or later, this fall overtakes the fall in transactions demand for money arising from the lower level of activity, because the level of activity falls to a new equilibrium level. Sooner or later, therefore, the quantity of money falls by more than the transactions demand for it, and the rate of interest tends to rise. This reinforces the tendency we have already noted for interest rates to rise in the United States when the foreign banks put all their receipts into the Federal Reserve.[7]

SOME SUGGESTED READING

The literature of the subjects covered in this chapter is not very extensive. The best treatments, all from a British or a sterling area viewpoint, are in R. S. Sayers, *Modern Banking* (4th ed., Oxford, 1958), in *Banking in the British Commonwealth,* edited by R. S. Sayers (Oxford, 1952), and P. W. Bell, *The Sterling Area in the Post-War World* (Oxford, 1956), especially Part 2. A study of a dollar exchange standard is G. F. Luthringer, *The Gold Exchange Standard in the Philippines* (Princeton, 1934).

---

[7] It may also be noted that for a still fuller analysis, the effect of these changes in interest rates on the level of activity and the changes thereby induced in the balance of payments should also be worked into the story.

36

International Banking Mechanisms—II

Transactions Settled in Foreign Currency or Gold

The case we must now consider is that where settlement of foreign payments is made in foreign currency or in gold. There are many variants of this case; three of the most interesting will be followed up here. The first is the gold standard system. The second includes various systems in which settlement is made in foreign currency and in which considerable repercussions on the banking system follow from changes in the balance of payments, unless specific offsetting policies are employed (examples include the gold exchange standard and the position of the independent sterling area countries today). The third variant is the Exchange Stabilization Fund system, in which settlement is made in foreign currency or gold, but in which institutional arrangements are such that the relationships between the internal banking situation and the balance of payments are to some extent peculiar.

The Gold Standard

A full discussion of the operation of the gold standard system will be found in Chapter 39; for the moment we are simply concerned with its legal prerequisites and with the effects of changes in the balance of payments on the banking and monetary situations of countries adhering to the system.

The legal requisites for a gold standard system are quite simple. The central banks or treasuries of member countries must be willing to buy and sell unlimited amounts of gold at fixed prices; these prices must be practically the same for purchases and sales; moreover, free import and export of gold bullion or coins must be permitted. These requisites can be satisfied in a number of different ways: one is the gold specie standard, where gold coins of fixed weight circulate freely (as in the United States before 1933); another is the gold bullion standard, where bars of gold can be bought from or sold to the central bank, but where no gold coin circulates. Closely related, and (as we shall see) an important element in both the pre-1914 world, when the gold standard was in its heyday, and in the revived system of the inter-war years, is the gold exchange standard, in which the monetary authorities are willing to sell or buy bank deposits in a country which is itself on the full gold standard. This system has attractions for poor countries, since interest can be earned on reserves held as bank deposits or other liquid assets in another country which is on a full gold standard.

It was long believed that the 'classical' way in which the gold standard worked before 1914 was that described by the Cunliffe Committee. This committee considered the form that should be followed by the British monetary system when it was re-established after the First World War. In principle, the 'classical' system is delightfully simple. If a country develops an appreciable balance of payments deficit the deficit is settled by a flow of gold out of the country; it is as if some people who have debts to pay to foreigners settle by sending gold coins or gold bullion which they can buy at fixed prices.[1] Similarly, a surplus country will receive a gold inflow.

At this point comes the essential link in the chain; the banking mechanisms of countries operating the gold standard according to the classical rules should be such that a gold inflow leads to an expansion in the total monetary circulation, while a gold outflow leads to a contraction. The change in the monetary circulation occurs at two points: the change in the quantity of legal tender money (i.e. coin and central bank notes) and the change in the amount of deposits at the commercial banks. There are three main ways in which the former change may come about. Firstly, gold coins themselves may circulate, or notes may be issued each of which represents the same value of gold stored in the vaults of the central bank. This is the *100 per cent reserve principle*. Secondly, the central bank may issue bank notes in a fixed proportion to the amount of gold

---

[1] In practice, of course, the shipments are made by specialist bullion dealers acting on behalf of the banks.

it holds. If the proportion of $3:1$, then $1 more gold held means that $3 more notes are issued. This is the *proportional reserve system*. Finally, a certain number of notes (the amount of which is fixed by law) may be issued without any corresponding gold reserve; any additional notes issued demand 100 per cent reserves. This is the *fiduciary system* (the unbacked notes are the 'fiduciary issue').

The other point at which the relationship between changes in the amount of gold in the country and changes in the monetary circulation operates is on the amount of deposits at the commercial banks. In the first place, changes in the amount of central bank notes that may be issued in turn affect the commercial banking system; as we saw in Part III, there is a limit to the possible expansion in the amount of commercial bank money if the amount of the note issue is limited. In addition, the gold flows have a much more direct effect on the commercial banks. This can be seen if we consider, say, the country with a balance of payments deficit, which is losing gold. Importers pay for the import surplus by buying foreign exchange from their banks; their banks get the foreign exchange by buying gold from the central bank and exporting it. The public's deposits at the commercial banks and commercial banks' cash reserves at the central bank fall by equal amounts. The reserve ratio of the commercial banks therefore falls. In the ideal gold standard system, the commercial banks have no surplus reserves; therefore, in the new equilibrium, they must make multiple cuts in their investments and loans and so in their deposits. Similarly, there will be a multiple expansion in the quantity of money in a country which is receiving gold if its commercial banks are maintaining constant reserve ratios.

The contraction of commercial bank deposits in a country which is losing gold is likely to involve rising interest rates and increased bank credit rationing; correspondingly, interest rates tend to fall and the severity of any bank credit rationing is reduced in a country gaining gold. These are all automatic effects of the system that follow so long as the central bank is purely passive; they become more and more powerful for as long as the gold flow continues. For the classical gold standard, however, such passivity was not considered enough. The 'rules of the game' demanded that the central banks should react positively to gold flows; the discount rate is raised or lowered according to whether a country is losing or gaining gold. Such action clearly reinforces and speeds up the automatic changes in the quantity of bank deposits we have just been considering. It also provides a palliative for the situation; the change in relative interest rates causes short-term capital movements which in turn cause some reduction or even reversal of the gold flow.

There is obviously strong pressure on the country losing gold to raise its discount rate; something must be done to solve the balance of payments difficulties that show themselves as a tendency to exhaust a limited gold stock. The incentive to lower the discount rate in the other country is much less strong; it may well be that the only incentive it has is a desire to maintain the gold standard system by preventing exhaustion of the reserves of the other country. (Indeed, it may be noted that if the gold flow was due to an increase in its trade surplus, there will be an expansionary multiplier or inflationary process there which it may be considered desirable to curb by *raising* the discount rate.)

In fact, the gold standard system never worked as simply and clearly as this. Gold flows were often offset, particularly if they were expected to be temporary. (The Bank of England had, before 1914, an armory of devices for this purpose.) Some central banks (e.g. France) did not often alter the discount rate in reaction to gold flows. Nevertheless, the outline above applies as a fair but extremely simplified picture of the banking effects of gold flows in the pre-1914 system. As a description of banking mechanisms in the system that was re-established in the 'twenties it is much less accurate. Particularly in the United States (and also in France) the central banking authorities generally rejected gold flows and central bank reserves as the prime governors of monetary policy.[2]

Foreign Exchange Standards

A foreign exchange standard is generally defined as a system in which countries with independent monetary systems undertake to maintain a fixed rate of exchange between their currencies and the currency of a center country which is taken as a standard, and where holdings of the center country's money (notes and deposits) are their international reserves and means for effecting international payments. The sterling area which developed after Britain left the

---

[2] It should be noted, however, that Federal Reserve open market operations in 1924 and 1927 were directed not only to the domestic situation but also toward helping to restore the gold standard.

gold standard in 1931 is an example of a foreign exchange standard; in this case a sterling exchange standard since the central banks of the independent members of the sterling area hold their foreign exchange reserves in the form of sterling. Another example is the dollar exchange standard of the many countries which do most of their international banking in the United States. If the center country is on the gold standard, then the countries tied to her currency are said to be on the gold exchange standard.

In discussing the banking repercussions of a change in the balance of payments under a foreign exchange standard, it is necessary to look at two groups of cases: one where foreign exchange is being held by the commercial banks and the other where it is held by the central bank. Both of these cases can be dealt with quite briefly, because they are similar to others we have already considered. Where a country's international currency reserves are held by the commercial banks, as was common up to the 'thirties, the situation is rather similar to that of a dependent monetary system. A balance of payments surplus implies that the commercial banks' holdings of foreign exchange are increasing; these holdings they regard as liquid reserves and they are willing and usually able to use them as a basis for a multiple expansion of credit and the monetary circulation.

The situation which is the more common today, where the central bank holds most of a country's international reserves, involves an internal banking mechanism on the foreign exchange standard which is in principle very like the automatic part of the internal mechanism on the gold standard. To take the case of a balance of payments surplus, the commercial banks are buying more foreign exchange from their customers than they are selling to them, and consequently they sell the balance to the central bank. This increases their deposits at the central bank and makes possible a multiple expansion of their lending and so of the amount of money in circulation. The similarity to the gold standard rarely follows through to the second, non-automatic part of the gold standard mechanism (the obedience to the 'rules of the game'); when an active part is taken by a central bank in a country which is operating an exchange standard, the central bank more usually neutralizes the effects of balance of payments deficits and surpluses than it emphasizes them. Such neutralization can be made by the various methods that are now familiar, such as open market operations and changes in reserve requirements.

* Exchange Stabilization Funds

The third main type of mechanism we shall consider in which settlements are made in terms of foreign currency is the Exchange Stabilization Fund system. This was first introduced in Britain in 1932 (British Exchange Equalization Account) and similar institutions were set up elsewhere. Exchange Stabilization Funds can best be described as agencies of governments holding assets that enable them to intervene in the foreign exchange market for the purpose of preventing undue fluctuations in the rates of exchange. The British Exchange Equalization Account, at the time of its inception, was supposed to allow those exchange rate changes to take place that were not due to seasonal influences or speculative capital movements. Other Exchange Funds that were formed in the 'thirties were more explicitly designed to limit exchange rate changes even if these changes should reflect forces other than those of a short-run or speculative nature; and as a matter of practical operation the British Account evinced increasing interest in promoting exchange stability irrespective of the source of stress upon the exchange rate. Today, the purpose of most Exchange Stabilization Funds is to maintain exchange rates that are pegged within narrow limits.

Another main purpose for which Exchange Stabilization Funds were used is still relevant, although its significance has been greatly exaggerated; that is the insulation of the internal monetary system from the multiple repercussions which might otherwise occur through changes in the balance of payments. This attempt at insulation through the use of Exchange Stabilization Funds was, in many respects, merely an extension of central bank 'sterilization' activities (offsetting gold flows) that frequently occurred under the gold standard arrangement. To carry out a policy of insulation, Stabilization Funds were usually given an initial endowment of gold and/or newly issued government securities. The British Fund was originally predominantly a securities fund; the United States Fund had an initial endowment wholly in gold. The nominal source of the endowment of most of the Funds were the gold 'profits' resulting from the devaluations of each of the currencies concerned that preceded the establishment of all the major Funds; devaluation meant that there was a rise in the home currency value of the stock of gold held by the monetary authorities. And since gold 'profits' and newly issued securities were the creations of governments and not of the banking systems, the ability of government authorities to intervene in foreign exchange markets and to affect domestic monetary situations was enhanced.

Next, we shall trace the operations of a Fund that is attempting to insulate the domestic economy from the consequences of speculative capital movements. We shall assume that the Fund we are considering currently possesses resources both in the form of government securities (which we assume to be bills) and of gold. We also assume that it converts into gold any foreign exchange that it might acquire in its transactions. When an inward flow of funds develops and foreigners demand the domestic currency,[3] the Fund sells securities for domestic balances, which it then sells to foreigners for foreign exchange. The foreign exchange thus acquired is then converted into gold, and since the gold is held outside the banking system no repercussions can follow from it. If the foreign funds coming into the country are held in the form of bills, the policy of insulation is completely successful in attaining its objectives, the net result of the changes being an exchange between the Fund and foreigners of bills for gold.

If, however, foreigners should desire to hold all of their increased dollar assets as deposits at commercial banks, two possibilities arise that must be distinguished. In the first place, if the 'bills' sold by the Fund are purchased by the commercial banks, the inflow of gold results, paradoxically, in a tendency toward contraction; this arises from the fact that commercial banks will have expanded their deposit liabilities without any increase in reserves, and if the banks are maintaining legal or customary reserve ratios their holdings of other assets will have to be reduced. In such cases, short-term rates of interest tend to rise. The second possibility is that the bills sold by the Fund are purchased by the customers of commercial banks. The net effect of this operation is that the customers of the banks exchange their deposits for bills, their deposits being taken over by the foreigners. Again, short-term interest rates tend to rise since the quantity of bills outside the hands of the monetary authorities has been increased, and this extra amount will have been taken up only if more favorable terms are available to their purchasers.

---

[3] We shall assume that the domestic currency is the dollar.

In practice, we are likely to have an intermediate case; foreigners will be likely to divide their increased holdings of dollar assets into bills and deposits at commercial banks, the bills not taken up by foreigners are likely to be taken up partly by the commercial banks and partly by the banks' customers. The net result of these changes is that commercial banks will have to reduce some of their other assets because the expansion of their bill holding and deposit liabilities will leave them deficient in reserves. Moreover, short-term interest rates will also tend to rise since the quantity of bills outside the hands of the monetary authorities is increased.

When foreigners withdraw funds from a country, the process outlined above is reversed. The Fund sells gold in order to acquire foreign exchange, which is in turn used to make purchases of the domestic currency that is offered for sale by those which wish to transfer funds abroad. These domestic balances are then used by the Fund to purchase bills. As we indicated above, there is a variety of possibilities as to the distribution of these bills among foreigners, commercial banks, and banks' customers. We shall consider here only two cases; one is where the bills purchased by the Fund were formerly held by foreigners and the other is where the bills were divided among the three groups that we have taken into account. In the first place, if the Fund purchases bills held by foreigners, the domestic money market is completely isolated from the transaction since the net result is simply an exchange between the Fund and foreigners of gold for bills. When the Fund purchases bills from all three groups, the net effect is that the bill holdings and deposit liabilities of the banks will diminish by equal amounts and the banks will be in the position of holding excess reserves. If the banks maintain a constant reserve ratio they will expand their holdings of other assets and their deposit liabilities. The outflow of gold in this case will result in a decline in short-term rates of interest since the quantity of bills outside the hands of the monetary authorities will have been reduced.

The operations described above could be carried out only by a Fund that possessed both gold and securities. If a Fund has only gold, it can insulate the domestic economy only when funds are flowing out of the country. On the other hand, a Fund that has only securities can undertake insulation only when funds are flowing into the country.

The Stabilization Fund of the United States proved to be in large part ineffective because it was not able to operate on both sides of the market. It was initially set up with claims to part of the Treasury's holdings of gold, originating from a part of the 'profit' that resulted from the increase in the price of gold in 1934. This substantial stock of claims to gold placed it in a good position to meet any drains of gold in a manner that would prevent the gold outflows from producing repercussions on the banking system. But when it was faced with capital inflows, the U.S. Fund was practically impotent, because it had no (substantial) holdings of securities. Foreign demand for dollars in the 'thirties forced the Fund to sell gold to the Reserve System since this was the only way that it could obtain the domestic balances it needed. This provided the commercial banks with increased reserves which raised the level of demand deposits that they could maintain and produced the internal monetary effects that the Stabilization Fund was supposed to prevent from happening. Whatever sterilization of gold inflows that did occur in the United States in the 'thirties depended upon Treasury and Federal Reserve efforts and not on the Stabilization Fund; at times the Treasury sold securities to pay for the gold that came into the country and the Federal Reserve raised the reserve requirements of the commercial banks and in this manner affected the abilities of the banks to support deposit liabilities.

Exchange Stabilization Funds were primarily designed to isolate the domestic monetary situation from the pressure of balance of payments forces, but it was often the case that their success was dependent upon central bank intervention. It is, in fact, almost impossible to isolate completely an internal monetary system from balance of payments changes by means of a purely automatic mechanism, unless the internal system is one which cushions out internally induced changes as well.

* International Financial Centers

Finally, we must give brief consideration to the effects on the internal banking system of a country which is acting as an international financial center of changes in the volume of transactions taking place between two other countries which are using the center as an intermediary. There are two cases that demand consideration. One is where both of these other countries use the currency of the center for settling transactions (as both Brazil and Venezuela use dollar balances). The other is where our country will settle only in some form other than the currency of the center country with which we are concerned. In situations where the United States is the center that is being considered, the second case is not important, since most other countries are willing to accept dollars in payment; but it does arise when Britain (London) has to settle the deficit of a sterling area country with the United States, since the United States does not usually settle in currencies other than its own.

In the first of these cases where the United States acts as an intermediary, there is simply a transfer of dollars from the balances held by one country's banks (say, Brazil's) to those held by the banks of the other country (say, Venezuela). So long as each country's banks holds its dollar reserves in the same form (e.g. both at the Federal Reserve, both in government securities, both at the commercial banks), there are no repercussions on the banking system in the United States.

In the other case, where Britain, for example, has to settle on behalf of a sterling area country that is making payments to the United States, there can be repercussions on the English banking system, but they are likely to be minor since the British Exchange Equalization Account (Stabilization Fund) cushions the impact of the disturbance. What usually happens is that the sterling area bank purchases the necessary dollars in London by reducing its holdings of British Treasury bills. At the same time, these bills are taken up by the British Exchange Equalization Account, as the counterpart to its reduced holding of United States dollars. The net effect on the English banking system is then negligible.

SOME SUGGESTED READING

On banking policy under the gold standard, see R. G. Hawtrey, *The Gold Standard in Theory and Practice* (4th edition, London, 1939), W. E. Beach, *British International Gold Movements and Banking Policy 1881-1913* (Cambridge, 1935) and the last two essays in T. S. Ashton and R. S. Sayers, *Papers in English Monetary History* (Oxford, 1953). For a detailed study, see W. A. Brown, *The International Gold Standard Reconsidered 1914-1934* (New York, 1939) and the *Report of the British* (Macmillan) *Committee on Finance and Industry* (U.K. Command Paper Number 3897).

The best source on the working of exchange stabilization funds is the League of Nations publication *International Currency Experience* (Princeton, 1944). See also F. A. Southard, *Foreign Exchange Practice and Policy* (New York, 1940). A more detailed study of the British exchange fund is N. F. Hall, *The Exchange Equalization Account* (London, 1935).

37

Direct Controls and the Balance of Payments

In the last few chapters we have been considering three of the forces that can affect the balance of trade and payments of a country, namely, real income levels, relative price levels, and interest rates. The government can control all of these by appropriate expenditure and taxation policy, by controlling the banking system, and by controlling the exchange rate; the government, therefore, has powerful tools with which it can indirectly affect the balance of payments.

These, however, are not the only ways in which the government can influence the balance of payments. It can also influence the foreign payments situation *directly*. It can directly control (or at least attempt to control) the foreign payments situation by controlling all expenditure made abroad.

It is not possible to make rigid classifications of the various kinds of direct control that will be satisfactory for all purposes; nevertheless, a broad classification into exchange controls, physical controls, and fiscal controls is useful. Exchange controls are controls over payments to foreigners, whether for goods, services, or capital items. Some exchange control systems are designed to control capital movements only, but, except when the control is very broad, this limited aim generally demands some surveillance of current transactions, because otherwise it is easy to disguise capital items as current. Physical controls are controls over the movements of goods, as distinct from the movement of money. For example, importation of certain goods may be forbidden, or only a certain quantity may be allowed to enter (the quota system). It can be seen that exchange controls and physical controls do largely the same thing, and can be used to reinforce one another. It makes little difference if a

Britisher is forbidden to use dollars to buy an American car, or if he is forbidden to import an American car; if both these rules are in force the British authorities can make doubly sure.

Fiscal controls over the balance of payments are the most prone to overlap with the other kinds of control considered in the preceding chapters. They involve the application of taxes or subsidies to imports (or certain kinds of import) and exports (or, again, certain kinds of export). As far as trade in goods is concerned, there is no difference of principle between a 10 per cent depreciation and a 10 per cent tax on all imports which finances a 10 per cent subsidy on all exports. (There is the difference, however, that it is difficult to apply the tax-subsidy system to invisible items in the foreign accounts, whereas exchange rate changes affect these directly.) Again, a prohibitive tax on a particular commodity is practically the same in its effects as a direct exchange or physical control forbidding its purchase.

It is clear that one characteristic of direct controls is that they can operate in a discriminatory manner, unlike the other controls (such as exchange rate changes, deflation, etc.) that we have been considering earlier. By discriminatory controls we do not merely mean controls that impinge unequally on different kinds of transaction; any change is likely to do that. For example, an exchange depreciation or a general import duty will lead to a bigger reduction in imports of those commodities with elastic demand than of those with inelastic demand; these changes will, therefore, impinge more sharply on imports from countries supplying us with goods for which our demand is relatively elastic. Discrimination implies more than this, however; it implies that stronger restrictions are deliberately placed on some kinds of transaction than on others.

Discrimination may be by commodity; a tax or a restriction may be placed on imports of some kinds of commodity but not on others. It may be by use; imports of a particular commodity may be allowed for some purposes but not for others. It may be by origin; stronger restrictions or higher duties may be imposed on imports from some countries than from others. Similarly there may be discrimination in exports (as by export controls and subsidies) and on invisible items. A particular control may ostensibly involve one kind of discrimination, but effectively imply another. For example, a prohibitive tax in Britain on very powerful motor cars might have practically the same effect as a prohibition on the import of American cars, because the only powerful cars that people would want to import are American, and all American cars are powerful.

The kind of discrimination that leads to the biggest problems is that by origin; the most important example in recent years is that associated with the 'dollar problem.' This problem involves the placing of more stringent controls on many imports from the dollar area (mainly comprising the countries of North and Central America) than on imports from other countries: the countries in the non-dollar world tend to discriminate against dollar goods and services in favor of goods and services produced in other non-dollar countries. For the time being, however, it will be convenient to ignore this discrimination by country and to consider direct controls that are nondiscriminatory in the sense that they do no more than discriminate by commodity or use. We can easily do this by continuing the assumption of a two-country world which has been followed so far; discrimination by country (often simply called discrimination, for short) demands the existence of at least three countries.

Proximate Effects of Direct Controls

There are three main questions we have to answer in considering the effects of direct controls. Who obtains the 'revenue' arising from the control? What are the effects on the balance of trade? What are the effects on the terms of trade?

In the first place, who gets the 'revenue'? The simplest case is in the case of a tariff; the government in the country imposing the tariff receives a revenue which consists of the difference between the price of the imports received by the foreigner and the price paid by the home purchaser. In the case of exchange and quantitative controls, there is a similar benefit which passes to someone or other, but it is more difficult to identify. If restrictions are imposed on the supply of imports available on the home market so that less are available than would be bought in a free market at the existing price, then there will be a tendency for a rise in home prices of imports. If this rise occurs, someone receives the difference between the price at which the article is produced abroad and the price at which it is sold at home. This 'revenue' may be received by a foreign exporter (who may mark up the prices at which he sells), by a government official (if he accepts bribes in return for granting licenses), or by a trader at home. It is also possible that the home price of the imports is not marked up; prices may be held down either by government control of prices or by a choice on the part of traders not to take the profits which are available to them. In this case, the excess of demand over supply is dealt with either by organized rationing or by the first-come-first-served principle. Some home purchasers are better off than they would otherwise be, because they get supplies of the commodity at less than the market price which would result if free competition followed the restriction; they get a kind of 'revenue' themselves.

From our point of view, the important question in all these cases is whether the 'revenue' is received by someone at home or someone abroad. There are two main rules that determine which way it will go, in the case of exchange or physical controls. (In the case of tariffs it always comes to the home government.) If authority to make the imports that are permitted is granted directly to traders at home, then they will be in the powerful position and able to take it themselves (unless price control gives it to home consumers). If the authority is given directly to foreign exporters, then they are in a position of power and may be able to impose scarcity prices themselves. The other rule is that traders who are in a monopolistic position are in a strong position to take the 'revenue'; a situation where competitive home importers face a powerful monopoly of foreign exporters, the 'revenue' may be received by foreigners.

If a part of the 'revenue' goes to foreigners, direct controls lead to a deterioration in the terms of trade; if, in addition, the home elasticity of demand for the restricted imports is less than unity, direct controls which limit the volume of imports also lead to a deterioration in the balance of trade. For example, let us suppose that cars cost $1000 each to produce abroad and the free market demand for home imports is 5 and that restrictions are imposed which allow only 4 to be imported. The home demand will be reduced to 4, let us suppose, if the price rises to $1500 (i.e. we assume, for the sake of argument, a demand elasticity considerably less than unity). Four cars are now imported and sold for $6000; there is a 'revenue' of $2000 (the difference between the cost of production abroad and the home selling price). If this all accrues to foreigners, the control is ineffective in its aim of improving the balance of payments, because the balance of trade has deteriorated by $1000 and the terms of trade are also worse, since the price paid to foreigners for cars has risen by 50 per cent. It is possible to avoid the adverse shift in the balance of trade if permission is granted for imports of a certain total value of imports (e.g. a total of $4000 worth of cars). If this is done, the terms of trade are made still worse, because the only way in which home demand can be choked off to this level is by a still higher price.

Normally, restrictions are likely to be imposed in such a way that most of the 'revenue' accrues to someone in the country imposing the restrictions. This aim is not difficult to achieve; tariffs can always be relied on to keep it all at home. The rest of this chapter, therefore, will assume conditions in which all the benefit stays at home, because there is no tendency for the foreign price of imported goods to rise. In those conditions one of two things must happen; either a gap develops between the price paid to foreigners for imports and the price paid by home users (in addition to the normal gap resulting from shipping costs, normal profits of importers, etc.), or some sort of rationing develops at home.

These consequences make it possible to improve the balance of payments without any adverse movement taking place in the terms of trade.¹ Home demand for imports is reduced either by the rationing or by the rise in home prices. If foreigners leave the prices at which they sell unchanged when the demand for their exports falls, after the home country has imposed import controls, the price paid to the foreigner per unit of imports remains unchanged, and so the terms of trade are also unchanged. At the same time, the quantity imported has been reduced, so the balance of trade improves. If foreigners reduce their prices when the demand for their exports falls,² the terms of trade improve as a direct result of the direct controls. In these circumstances, the balance of trade improves to a still greater extent; less is paid for unit of imports to foreigners, for a smaller total quantity of imports.

These proximate effects of direct controls may be compared to the proximate effects of exchange rate changes used for altering the balance of trade. In Chapter 31 we saw that we could split up the consequences of an exchange depreciation by, say, 1 per cent into

---

¹ Alternatively, the terms of trade can be improved without any deterioration taking place in the balance of payments. This alternative is the one usually followed in treatises on the 'real' theory of international trade. Both formulations come to the same thing. Clearly, an intermediate position is also possible, with some improvement in both terms of trade and balance of trade.

² I.e. their elasticity of supply of exports is less than infinite.

three parts: the effects on the volume of imports, on the volume of exports, and on the price of exports.[3] The first two of these effects improve the balance of trade after the depreciation (by $\epsilon_h + \epsilon_f$ per cent in the case of a 1 per cent depreciation); the third works the opposite way (by 1 per cent in the case of a 1 per cent depreciation). Now if direct controls on imports are used, this last, perverse, effect can be avoided; no change is made in either the price or the volume of exports.

This means that a given improvement in the balance of trade can be brought about with a smaller total reduction in the volume of goods available to the residents of a country if direct controls are used than if exchange depreciation is used. For example, if the home elasticity of demand for imports is 3, a 1 per cent depreciation leads to a 3 per cent decline in the volume of imports; if the foreign demand elasticity is 3, a 1 per cent depreciation leads to a 3 per cent increase in the volume of exports. In this case, a 1 per cent depreciation leads to a reduction in the amount of goods available at home equal to 6 per cent of the total initial volume of trade. It also leads to a 5 per cent improvement in the balance of trade ($\epsilon_h + \epsilon_f - 1 = 5$). Alternatively, this 5 per cent improvement in the balance of trade could have been brought about by a 5 per cent reduction in the volume of imports, by imposing direct controls whose 'revenue' all stays at home. Direct controls, therefore, involve a smaller reduction in the amount of goods available at home than exchange depreciation. The saving is the same percentage of the initial quantity of trade as the percentage depreciation which is necessary if that weapon is used (in this case, 1 per cent).

Clearly this is particularly significant when the demand elasticities are rather low; for example, if their sum is 2, a 1 per cent depreciation leads to a 1 per cent improvement in the balance of trade, at the cost of giving up an amount of goods equal to 2 per cent of the amount originally traded. The same result could be brought about by direct controls leading to a 1 per cent reduction in imports; then the cost involves giving up only 1 per cent of the total amount of

---

[3] We were assuming, as in the following argument, that prices remain unchanged within each country, and that trade was initially balanced. The argument is more complicated if internal prices change, but as we have seen in Chapter 32, it is only in fairly peculiar circumstances that an effective depreciation involves no deterioration of the terms of trade.

goods traded; that is, only half as much as when depreciation is used.

An important assumption of this comparison is that import goods and home-produced goods of equal values are of equal 'importance' to society. This is a reasonable assumption when relatively small restrictions are being imposed where none existed before. The case is different where some direct controls already exist, and the question is whether to impose still more controls or to depreciate the exchange rate. In that case, the government may well consider that to forgo spending one dollar on imports is a bigger burden on the economy than to send out an additional dollar's worth of exports. For example, restrictions may already have been placed on all 'non-essential' imports and only 'essential' imports may remain; or in the case of tariffs, the fact that consumers already pay a substantial tariff as well as the price paid to the foreigner is an indication that goods for which one dollar is paid to the foreigner are more important to the consumer than home-produced goods selling for one dollar.[4]

If the government regards imports of a certain value as more important to the economy than exports of the same value, it may well be unwilling to follow policies that put all the burden of improving the balance of trade on restricting the quantity of imports and none on increasing the volume of exports. If the foreign elasticity of demand for our exports is greater than zero, exchange depreciation will give some assistance to the balance of trade through an increased value of exports; then exchange depreciation may be preferred to import controls.

Further Effects of Direct Controls

Up to this point, we have been concerned solely with the proximate effects of tariffs and other direct controls on the balance of trade and terms of trade. We have still to consider the further effects that these changes may induce. The simplest case, which is the only one which will be considered, is that in which prices of home-produced goods in each country remain unchanged, so that there is

---

[4] On the other hand, if controls exist over home purchases of export goods, export goods also may be considered more important than purely home-trade goods of the same value; the story then becomes somewhat more complicated but the same kind of analysis can be followed.

no change in terms of trade. In these circumstances, if induced effects on investment and interest rates are ignored, the improvement in the balance of trade leads to increased expenditure on home-produced goods and so to an expansionary process at home; correspondingly, the deterioration in the balance of trade of the other country leads to a contractionary process there. These two processes interact in a manner similar to that outlined in Chapter 30, when the multiplier process following a change in tastes was considered. In the final equilibrium, the level of activity will have risen in the country which has imposed the restrictions and fallen in the other, but the balance of trade will still show a movement in favor of the country imposing the controls. The equilibrium improvement in the balance of trade will, however, be less than the improvement immediately arising from the controls; some of this improvement is canceled out by the effects of changes in the level of activity in the two countries.

In addition to direct controls over trade, controls may be (and very frequently are) imposed over capital movements. These controls, therefore, must be briefly considered.

It is widely believed that control over at least one kind of capital movement is necessary; namely, that over short-term movements of 'hot' money in response to political and economic fears. These can so easily cause violent disturbances that there is often good reason for preventing them. The same results can often be brought about by neutralization of these movements through the banking mechanism and an exchange equalization account, as described in Chapters 36 and 40. This alternative solution is of no use to a poor country, which may not have sufficient official holdings of foreign currency reserves to throw into the balance when there is a speculative outflow; on the other hand, it avoids the need for an extensive exchange control apparatus, which is necessary for any but the most cursory control of capital movements. Control over long-term capital movements may be justified in similar terms to control over short-term movements; it prevents quasi-permanent movements of 'flight' capital, such as the movements in the 'thirties from Europe to the United States because of political fears.

More generally, control over capital movements can be justified because it allows the country concerned to have a more independent monetary policy. For example, it is very difficult for a single country to run a cheap-money policy when interest rates are high in the rest of the world, if capital flows occur easily.

Discriminatory Controls

It is now necessary to abandon the assumption that has been followed so far and allow for the existence of a world of many countries. The main consequence is that we have to allow for the existence of controls which discriminate between different countries.

Such discrimination may involve imports, exports, and capital movements. In the analysis which follows, the argument will be concerned with discriminatory import restrictions, which have been much the most important in practice; the analysis of discriminatory controls over exports and capital movements is very similar.

Discriminatory controls may be imposed in many different ways. It is quite possible for a control which is non-discriminatory in form to be discriminatory in intent. For example, particularly severe restrictions may be imposed on the goods, or on detailed sub-categories of goods, which originate in the country against which discrimination is being enforced. Frequently, however, more obviously discriminatory devices are used. For example, the currency of one country may be available for the importation of a particular commodity, but not the currency of another country. Another device is that of multiple exchange rates; this has been common in countries with a weak administrative system. For example, if a country wishes to discriminate in favor of sterling goods and against dollar goods, its banks may sell dollars at higher prices in relation to sterling than would be indicated by the official sterling-dollar exchange rate.

The major question that remains to be answered is, why countries choose to impose discriminatory controls? Some of the reasons need only to be mentioned, since they are not our concern in a discussion of international monetary economics. Discriminatory controls may be imposed for purely political purposes; for example, it may be considered desirable to favor political allies in imposing economic controls, or colonies may be compelled to discriminate in favor of the parent country. Again, controls that are apparently discriminatory may only have a minor discriminatory intent; for example, it may be that the main purpose behind the import restrictions on some U.S. manufacturers in countries such as Australia may have been to protect Australian industries, and not to favor European exports;

the effects would be the same as an overall restriction if European goods were not really competitive with Australian goods while U.S. goods were.

Leaving aside these cases, it is convenient to distinguish two sets of reasons why a country may use discriminatory import controls. The distinction between them is that in one case a single country may consider it worth while to discriminate, even if all the other countries act in a non-discriminatory manner, while in the other case the policy demands that another country also imposes discriminatory controls. The second of these two cases is the more important; it is, therefore, convenient to start by dismissing the first.

A country may choose to discriminate, even if no other countries are doing so, if discriminatory controls are likely to be more beneficial to its balance of payments than controls which are non-discriminatory.

The most important example arises when a country is in a stronger bargaining position *vis-à-vis* some suppliers than others. For example, if a country is consuming most of the world supply of a particular commodity, and if the suppliers of that commodity in one foreign country cannot find anything else to do with their productive resources, while producers in another could easily switch over to producing something else, there may be a strong incentive to the importing country to discriminate. It can drive a strong bargain with one group of suppliers but not with the other. By discrimination it can get the best of both worlds. Suitable discriminatory devices would be bulk buying or imposition of a discriminatory duty. In these ways, it can improve its balance of payments without loss on the terms of trade,[5] in contrast with the situation following the imposition of non-discriminatory controls, and so *a fortiori* with the situation following exchange rate changes designed to bring about this improvement.

We can now turn to the second and more important group of cases, in which a country may voluntarily choose to discriminate; these assume that there are other countries which are also imposing discriminatory controls. The important proposition in this case is that countries can maintain their volume of trade at higher levels if they impose discriminatory controls than if they use non-discriminatory

---

[5] Or improve its terms of trade while leaving the balance of payments unchanged.

controls to deal with balance of payments difficulties. At the same time, the favorable effects of controls compared with exchange rate changes as a method of dealing with balance of payments difficulties still apply; they avoid the terms of trade loss that is usually inevitable when adjustment is made by relative price changes. These virtues of discriminatory controls are important; it is clearly better to maintain a higher level of trade than a lower, if other things are equal; by doing so, greater advantage is taken of the benefits of international division of labor. Nevertheless, it must be admitted that other things are not always equal; this is a point to which we shall have to return.

A simple numerical example can be used to demonstrate the proposition that discriminatory controls can be used to maintain a higher level of trade than non-discriminatory controls. We can imagine an initial situation of two deficit countries and one surplus country, and assume that trade is to be balanced purely by the imposition of import controls; we ignore the effects of changes in any country's exports on its level of activity and prices, and so ignore any effects through these on the level of imports. The initial position may be regarded as that in Table 13; data related to countries acting as importers are represented by columns, and data representing countries as exporters are represented by rows. Thus, the first row represents the fact that country A exports nothing to itself, 8 to B, and 16 to C. The first column represents imports by A of nothing from itself, 8 from B, and 4 from C. A, therefore, has an export surplus of 12, which is represented by +12 in the column on the right. Total trade taking place is 60; this is shown below.

TABLE 13

Exporting countries	Importing countries			Trade balance
	A	B	C	
A	..	8	16	+12
B	8	..	8	−8
C	4	16	..	−4

Total trade = 60.

If non-discriminatory controls are used by B and C in order to deal with their deficits, they can be expected to impinge both on imports from each other and on imports from A. It will be convenient to assume that when a country is imposing non-discriminatory controls, it makes an equal percentage reduction in imports from each of its suppliers. When this happens we can say that, for each country, imports from each of its suppliers are equally 'important.' [6]

The solution to the balance of payments difficulties of B and C, when non-discriminatory controls are used, will then be as in Table 14a.

TABLE 14a

Exporting countries	Importing countries			Trade balance
	A	B	C	
A	..	4	8	0
B	8	..	4	0
C	4	8	..	0

Total trade = 36.

If B and C use discriminatory controls it is possible for the total reduction of trade to be by only 12 units, instead of a reduction of

---

[6] The decision about which goods are in fact to be regarded as more 'important' is primarily a political problem, and there is little that one can say on it in general terms, unless one is constructing a normative system, which is not our purpose here. If the supply elasticities of all traded goods are infinite, if prices in each economy are proportional to marginal social costs and marginal social benefits, and if all the 'revenue' which results from the restriction of imports accrues to home residents, then it is reasonable to regard one imported commodity as being more 'important' than another if the percentage of 'revenue' to the price paid to the foreigner for the first commodity is greater than for the second. This can be modified to cover cases where the three conditions summarized in the first part of the last sentence are not satisfied. For our purposes, however, it is probably more suitable to adopt a positivist rather than a normative definition of 'important'—things are 'important' which the government regards as important, and therefore restricts less rigorously. This view is followed in the text.

24, when non-discriminatory controls are used. The pattern of trade which involves this minimum reduction is that represented in Table 14b.

TABLE 14b

Exporting countries	Importing countries			Trade balance
	A	B	C	
A	..	0	12	0
B	8	..	8	0
C	4	16	..	0

Total trade = 48.

This solution, while passing the test that the reduction in total trade shall be the minimum possible, suffers from the serious disadvantage that B's imports from A are reduced from 8 to zero; whereas in the non-discriminatory case, they are only reduced to 4. If A-goods and C-goods are equally 'important' to B, it is most unlikely that B will be happy if it loses all its imports from A, even though its imports from C are cut only a little. Some A-goods are likely to be essential for keeping B's economy running.

A solution more favorable to B would be that represented in Table 14c.

TABLE 14c

Exporting countries	Importing countries			Trade balance
	A	B	C	
A	..	4	8	0
B	8	..	8	0
C	4	12	..	0

Total trade = 44.

B's imports from A are kept at the level it could enjoy under non-discriminatory controls and its total trade is above the level under that system. C is also better off than under a non-discriminatory system, because its total trade is reduced by less, and its imports from A are as big as under that system. Nevertheless, C may not be satisfied with this solution, since it imposes on C a bigger reduction in total trade and a bigger reduction in imports from A than in the solution of Table 14b.

We can generalize the results of our argument up to this point by saying that the solution which gives the least reduction in total trade may not be acceptable to both of the countries imposing controls. There is a conflict of interest between those two countries with regard to their sharing of the reduction in imports from the surplus country, and so with regard to the total amount of trade which they regard as the optimum.

The result of this conflict of interest depends upon the views the countries have about these questions, and upon their relative bargaining power. Some of the forces that help determine the latter must be discussed shortly. Before doing that, it is necessary to consider a couple of elaborations of the preceding analysis.

One concerns the possibility that goods imported from the surplus country and those from the other deficit country may not be equally 'important.' This is quite likely to be the case, but it does not alter the essentials of the preceding argument. The significant point is that the solution in the non-discriminatory case is not then the same as when each kind of import is equally 'important.' A non-discriminatory control over imports would reduce each country's imports from the country whose goods were more 'important' by a smaller proportion than its imports from the other country. This must alter the final solution in the non-discriminatory case; if the surplus country's goods are the more 'important,' the total reduction in trade must be greater, because there have to be bigger reductions in trade between the deficit countries to match the necessary reduction in their imports from the surplus country. The differing 'importance' of the various kinds of imports may also affect the discriminatory solutions. If it does so, the effect will be in the same direction as the effect on the non-discriminatory solution; for example, if the goods of the surplus country are more 'important,' each deficit country will be less willing to take a share in the reduction of imports from the surplus country, and so the necessary reduction in trade between the two deficit countries may well be greater.

The second elaboration of the preceding analysis concerns the relevance of the size of trade between the deficit countries. If such trade is initially small, the difference between the discriminatory and the non-discriminatory solutions becomes relatively small. This can easily be seen by making up numerical examples; the reason is simply that discrimination helps to maintain the volume of trade taking place between the deficit countries, and, if this is relatively small anyway, the favorable effect of discrimination compared with non-discrimination is inevitably rather small.

We can now proceed to discuss some of the forces which determine the actual structure of discrimination, in view of the conflict of interests between the discriminating countries. One which is very important can arise from the pattern of world trade and payments. It may well happen that a country chooses to discriminate, even though it does not benefit from the existence of the discriminatory system, and even though it might choose not to impose any sort of controls at all, if it were left to its own devices. Nevertheless, it may choose to discriminate, given the existence of the discriminatory system, because discrimination is the less unpleasant choice which is actually open to it. This case arises where a country is given the choice either of discriminating or of enduring discrimination against its goods.

The most important example of this choice arises where currencies are inconvertible; in a non-discriminatory system a country (e.g. Argentina) might like to use some of its receipts from one country (e.g. England) to make payments to another (e.g. the United States), but this is impossible if the necessary conversion of sterling into dollars is not allowed. Argentina then has two alternative policies open to it: it may discriminate or it may permit discrimination to be imposed against itself. It may discriminate in favor of England by restricting its dollar expenditure to its dollar receipts, and allowing sterling goods in more freely, so using up the sterling. Alternatively, it may insist on payment in dollars for its exports to England, in which case England is likely to impose restrictions against imports from Argentina and to discriminate against Argentinian goods in favor of those of a fourth country (e.g. Australia).

Argentina's choice will be based on a balancing of advantages and disadvantages. Entering into the calculation are the relative prices of English and American goods, the strength of discrimination that may be imposed against Argentina, and the volume of trade that will be maintained in the two cases. Here, bargaining with England is likely to be implicit in the situation; it is in the interests of England for Argentina to discriminate in her favor, because then England's overall balance of payments situation is thereby improved. This may mean that England will give Argentina concessions if she appears to be wavering in her choice.

In practice things are usually still more complicated than this. Even those countries whose position in the chain of payments is such that they are under strong pressure to discriminate may still reap some benefits from the existence of the discriminatory system. They may, for example, be able to maintain their total trade at higher levels than would arise in a world of non-discriminatory controls: this may afford some consolation.

The fact is that the discriminatory systems which arise in practice in the real world of many countries are determined by the resolution of many clashes of interest between different countries. Some of these clashes are between countries both of which benefit from a discriminatory system but bargain about the sharing of its benefits and burdens. Other clashes are those between countries which benefit and those which do not, but who nevertheless must accept the consequences of their weak bargaining power arising from their position in the structure of world payments.

From the process of implicit and explicit bargaining, many different results are possible. This is particularly the case since countries may discriminate for bargaining purposes: that is, in order to persuade another country to discriminate in their favor. Very little can be said in general terms about the upshot of these clashes of interest and the process of bargaining. But it is possible to say something, and the final paragraphs of this chapter will be concerned with summarizing what can be said.

For one thing it is probably correct to say that organized discrimination is usually less harmful to all concerned than unorganized discrimination. The reason is quite simple: if discrimination is unorganized, and each country is struggling for its own benefit regardless of what other countries are doing, many of the efforts will be contradictory. By working as a team the group of deficit countries can probably do better than if each fights individually.

Secondly, there may well be some losers as well as some gainers in the discriminating group of countries, the losers being those who bargain badly or are in a weak position. Nevertheless, it is in principle possible for each country in the discriminatory area to benefit from the existence of the system. Whether that is the upshot of discrimination in practice is more doubtful and may well be unprovable.

Finally, and much more generally, it should be remembered that the use of any kinds of control over foreign trade is very likely to reduce the benefits to the world as a whole deriving from the international division of labor. The familiar arguments for free trade, based on the advantages of maximizing the income of the world as a whole, can often be very powerful arguments against the use of direct controls.

SOME SUGGESTED READING

Much of the argument of this chapter is a monetary application of the 'real' theory of the optimum tariff as set out in places such as T. Scitovsky, 'Reconsideration of the Theory of Tariffs,' reprinted in the American Economic Association, *Readings in the Theory of International Trade* (Philadelphia, 1950). S. Alexander's article 'Devaluation versus Import Restrictions' in *IMF Staff Papers* (1951), which has been used as a major source for this chapter, is essentially such an application.

The matrices showing the virtues of discrimination are based on R. Frisch's article 'On the Need for Forecasting a Multilateral Balance of Payments' in the *American Economic Review* (1947). Other important articles are G. D. MacDougall, 'Notes on Non-Discrimination,' *Bulletin of the Oxford Institute of Statistics* (Vol. 9) and M. Fleming, 'Making the Best of Balance of Payments Restrictions on Imports,' *Economic Journal* (1950). The argument of the latter is developed in J. E. Meade, *Trade and Welfare* (Oxford, 1955), Chapter 34; see also J. E. Meade, *Balance of Payments* (Oxford, 1951), Chapters 28-31.

VII

INTERNATIONAL MONETARY

EXPERIENCE

38

The Reconciliation of Internal and External Balance

The conclusion that was reached at the end of our discussion of an industrial country which had no economic relations with others was moderately optimistic. It was that we possess sufficient knowledge of the mechanisms at work for a government which can act quickly, and is willing to do so, to be able to maintain a considerable degree of economic stability, in the form of a relatively stable price level and a high and fairly stable level of employment. Since this conclusion was reached (at the end of Chapter 27) we have been concerned with the very considerable complications that must be taken into account when a country has economic relationships with foreigners. The subject of this final section of the book is a consideration of the problems of countries which are trying to maintain both internal and external economic stability. The present chapter is concerned with setting forward the main theoretical problems involved: to a large extent this means pulling together many of the threads of the argument which have so far been separate. Finally, Chapters 39-42 will look at some of the more important institutional arrangements which have been used or suggested as ways of obtaining internal and external stability.

Unlike internal balance, external balance is in the long run inevitable. There is no compelling economic force which makes it inevitable that a country should be at full employment or should maintain a constant general price level. (There may well be powerful political pressures at work, but that is a different matter.) On the other hand, it is in the long run inevitable that a country should maintain external balance in the sense in which we used the phrase in earlier chapters; a country cannot continue indefinitely running into balance of payments difficulties. Sooner or later, if it is in deficit, its fund of foreign currency reserves becomes exhausted, and foreigners are unwilling to lend any more short-term capital; and then the existing situation cannot continue any longer and so policies have to be altered. Similarly, a surplus cannot be run indefinitely, because the country's trading partners then run into difficulties.

Of course, in another and broader sense, balance of payments difficulties can continue indefinitely; in order to prevent any tendency to an exhaustion of foreign currency reserves, unpleasant policies may have to be imposed. It is quite reasonable (although a little confusing) to describe these unpleasant policies as 'difficulties.' To make a simple analogy with an ordinary person: living within one's income is often unpleasant and frequently involves difficulties; but the sense in which we have been talking of a deficit, we were concerned with the difficulties that are being piled up by temporarily living beyond the level of one's receipts. This is something that can be done for a time, but not indefinitely, either by individuals or by countries. It will be convenient to continue to limit the use of the word 'difficulties' to a description of a situation that is not permanently maintainable.

The analogy with private individuals (which, let it be said, can be dangerous and should be used with caution) can also be used to express the contrast between the long-term inevitability of external balance and the voluntary character of internal balance. An individual cannot indefinitely live beyond the level of income he can earn from others (including gifts and loans continuing steadily through time); in the long run he must be in external balance. There is, on the other hand, no compulsion for him to use his own capacities to the utmost; he may be lazy or inefficient or unwilling to acquire new skills; his own resources need not be fully employed.

Up to this point we have meant by external balance a situation in which a country is neither in surplus nor in deficit in balance of payments. In the long run this condition must be satisfied. In addition, a country may consider that the restoration of balance demands something more than avoidance of exhaustion or the indefinite expansion of its currency reserves; external balance may also be regarded as involving the holding of some optimum stock of currency reserves. Thus, when reserves are less than this optimum, for a time external balance demands a balance of payments surplus; when reserves are more than the optimum, external balance demands a deficit.

This interpretation is undoubtedly more realistic than one which means by external balance simply a situation where there is no current balance of payment surplus or deficit. A country which has suffered a big draft on its reserves will not be satisfied by stopping any further drains: it will want to restore the loss, to give itself room for maneuver. This additional consideration, however, does make the situation more complicated. It may result in a perpetual tug-of-war if the sum of the optimum reserves required by all countries together is greater than the total available supply of international currency. Such a tug-of-war takes the form of attempts to get unattainable balance of payments surpluses; there will be a struggle for surpluses, using the various methods to be outlined shortly. This struggle may continue indefinitely, and add considerable instability to the situation.

Four Methods of Attaining External Balance

Almost every chapter in Part VI was largely concerned with different ways in which a country can move toward external balance, by improving its balance of payments if it is in deficit or by causing its balance of payments to deteriorate if it is in surplus. It will be convenient to summarize these various methods and to consider some of their disadvantages and limitations. As a useful classification we can say that there are four main methods of deliberately creating external balance, if there is no automatic tendency to attain it. It must be remembered that most of these four methods can be brought into operation in a number of different ways, and that many ways of bringing one of them into operation also brings in one or more of the others. These four methods are: firstly, changing the level of activity within the country; secondly, changing the relationship between prices of home-produced and foreign-produced goods; thirdly, changing the flow of long-term lending; and, finally, changing the intensity of controls (including the introduction of controls where they did not exist previously).

1. CHANGE IN THE LEVEL OF ACTIVITY

The first of these methods of attaining external balance can itself be brought about in a variety of ways, which were looked at when we were discussing internal policy. They were then classified into the three groups of internal monetary controls (e.g. banking and interest rate changes), internal fiscal controls (e.g. changing the tax structure or the budget surplus), and internal direct controls (e.g. investment controls). If one country alone is trying to improve its balance of payments by these methods, it must lower its level of activity; similarly, to cause its balance of payments to deteriorate it must increase its level of activity.

The obvious characteristic of this method of attaining external balance is that it has an undesirable effect on the internal situation if internal balance already exists or if the external situation suggests a shift still farther away from internal balance. On the other hand, the internal shift may be one that is desirable for its own sake. While this effect on internal balance may be either advantageous or disadvantageous, it is not peculiar to this method of adjustment. Each of our four methods of attaining external balance has some repercussion on the internal situation.

2. CHANGE IN RELATIVE PRICES

The second method for attaining external balance is to change the relationship between prices at home and prices abroad, either by changes in exchange rates or in internal price levels. A variety of mechanisms can be used to alter exchange rates; at one extreme limit of the range is a change in rate which is wholly administered by the government or central bank; at the other limit is the case where the rate is determined solely by the interplay of demand for and supply of foreign exchange on a free market. In practice, there is nearly always some degree of intermixture between these two. Administered rates frequently allow for a small range of market fluctuation (for example, the range between £1 = $2.78 and £1 = $2.82, which is possible under current British arrangements); on the other hand, governments seldom completely abdicate their power to interfere in a free exchange market. Arrangements which allow a considerable element both of administrative decision and of free market forces will be considered in subsequent chapters.

There are two major disadvantages about changing relative prices in order to attain external balance; exchange depreciation (or a reduction of export prices by internal deflation) does not always alleviate balance of payments difficulties and it usually leads to a deterioration in the terms of trade. The former trouble usually arises when elasticities of demand for imports are low [1] or when the pat-

---

[1] See Chapter 31.

tern of demand elasticities is such that, although the depreciation improves the balances of trade and payments, it throws another country into balance of payments difficulties, and when this second country deals with its difficulties, the first country finds itself in difficulties once again. In principle, this can be avoided; if exchange depreciation causes a deterioration in the balance of trade, then appreciation of the exchange rate may be expected to cause an improvement in the balance of payments. Moreover, appreciation will normally lead to an improvement in the terms of trade, by making exports more costly in relation to imports. Policies of exchange appreciation, in order to deal with a balance of payments deficit, have been seriously suggested on occasion; it is possible that they might work, but they do involve difficulties. In the first place a free market, or a system depending primarily on free market forces, will never lead to exchange appreciation when there is a balance of payments deficit; on a free market prices do not fall when demand exceeds supply. Secondly, acceptance of such a policy demands a certain degree of theoretical sophistication, and a certain degree of confidence in one's judgments about the smallness of the demand elasticities. This sophistication and confidence must be particularly hard to insure if two or more countries must appreciate simultaneously for the policy to be successful. Thirdly, there remains the difficulty that if the sum of the demand elasticities is rather near to the critical value (of unity in the simplest case), then neither exchange appreciation nor depreciation will have much effect on the balance of payments; a very large exchange rate change is needed to get a relatively small effect on the balance of payments.

3. CHANGES IN LONG-TERM LENDING

The third method of restoring external balance that has been used is a change in the amount of long-term lending taking place, or (what for this purpose amounts to the same thing) a change in the level at which grants are being made from one country to another. Such changes may occur through changes in relative interest rates or profitability; these changes in turn involve changes in the level of activity in the country where the change is taking place, and therefore involve the problems of adjustment through changes in the level of activity that have already been discussed. Changes in the flow of lending may also be made possible by means such as the removal of barriers to (or the grant of special favors to) foreign investors, and the provision of government guarantees to lenders (either by the government of the lending or the borrowing country, or by an international organization).

Short-term lending (by definition) cannot solve balance of payments difficulties; like any other process of drawing on an exhaustible stock, it can provide only temporary alleviation. All the same, such alleviation may be extremely valuable, by providing a cushion while the changes that can provide a permanent remedy are brought into operation. As we shall see, this consideration is very important in making the choice between a fixed exchange rate system and one with flexible exchange rates.

4. CHANGES IN CONTROLS

The fourth method of restoring external balance—that of changing the intensity of controls—also has the virtue of acting quickly, with the additional advantage that it can be used to provide a permanent remedy to any balance of payments problem, however large. These advantages explain why this method has frequently been used in times of serious disturbance, such as wartime and the post-war period. At the same time there are serious disadvantages. There are the disadvantages in terms of reduced benefits from the division of labor, possibilities of retaliation, and the reduction of competition spurs to home industry, which are the familiar (and important) effects of moving away from a free trade world.

Internal Repercussions of Changes Introduced for the Sake of External Balance

Each of these four methods of moving toward external balance, by removing a balance of payments surplus or deficit, must inevitably have repercussions on the internal situation. These effects are important for two reasons. They may in turn cause reactions on the balance of payments situation and throw the country out of external balance again. Secondly, they may disturb an internal balance that formerly existed, or may throw the internal situation still farther away from balance than it was initially. The first of these dangers has already been discussed, and we saw that after a balance of payments improvement internal developments generally cancel out some of the improvement and may possibly cancel it all, restoring the original state.[2]

It is with the second danger that we must more immediately be concerned. It is a danger that is not necessarily serious. The authorities may not be concerned about these internal effects. Foreign trade may be so small a part of the economy of the country that the internal consequences of changes made to deal with the external situation may be negligible. Alternatively, the authorities may not be trying to maintain internal balance. We can, however, ignore these conditions and assume that the authorities wish to remedy both the external and the internal unbalance which exist in the initial position. In that case, it is always possible for some single remedy to improve both situations.

Two kinds of policy normally cause internal expansionary tendencies when a balance of payments deficit is dealt with, and internal contractionary tendencies when a balance of payments surplus is being reduced. They are exchange depreciation[3] and changes in the intensity of controls. The other two kinds of policy involve the other possible pairings of results, where internal contractionary tendencies are associated with reducing a balance of payments deficit and internal expansionary tendencies are associated with reducing a surplus.

At first glance, it seems that reconciliation of desire for both internal and external balance is rather easy. If external deficit is combined with internal underemployment, or if external surplus is combined with internal overemployment, then exchange rate changes[4] or changes in direct controls can provide a movement toward both internal and external balance. If external deficit is combined with internal overemployment, or if external surplus is combined with internal underemployment, then changes in the internal level of activity or in the level of foreign lending can provide a movement toward both internal and external balance. Provision seems to be made for all possible cases; unfortunately, this is not the end of the matter.

So far, we have been able to say only that one or other remedy

---

[2] As when internal inflation cancels out all the effects of an exchange devaluation.

[3] When the sum of the demand elasticities is large enough.

[4] If the demand elasticities are suitable.

will move the situation *toward* internal and external balance. We have not been able to say that any one remedy will take both the internal and external situation all the way. In fact, it will only be coincidental if this should be so; generally speaking, restoration of one situation to balance is likely to leave the other on one side or the other of equilibrium.

For instance, we can consider an initial situation of external surplus combined with internal unemployment. As we have seen, internal expansionary forces will then cause both the internal and external situations to move toward balance. Let us imagine that expansionary forces are employed which bring the internal situation just to the position of balance (i.e. of full employment). It will be a very fortunate coincidence if, at this point, balance of payments equilibrium is precisely restored. Usually, either a situation of a (smaller) balance of payments surplus will exist, or the expansion will have gone so far that the balance of payments has swung over into deficit. In the former case, external balance seems to demand still more internal expansion—but that will throw the internal situation into inflation. In the latter case, considerations of external balance seem to suggest that internal expansion has gone too far. In a sentence, reliance on the single remedy of internal expansion to deal with both the internal and external lack of balance must almost inevitably be inadequate. Something else must be brought in to complete the adjustment; the obvious answers are relative price changes or changes in the intensity of controls.

This conclusion can be generalized: it is only by chance that a single remedy can bring both the internal and the external situation to balance, although there is almost always some single remedy that will bring both situations nearer to balance.

What, then, is the necessary basis for a policy designed to introduce and maintain both internal and external stability? The minimum requirement is that at least two of the four methods of adjustment outlined above should be used at the same time. As an example, we can once more consider the case where initially a country is suffering external deficit and internal unemployment. A combination of policies for internal expansion (e.g. increased budget deficit, lower interest rates) and of changes in exchange rates would then be one way of leading to a new equilibrium. We can imagine there is internal expansion (by changes in internal monetary, fiscal, or control policies) until there is internal balance; then the remaining lack of external balance (whether still in deficit or now in surplus) is dealt with by exchange rate changes. This in turn throws the internal balance out again, so more internal changes are made; this again demands external adjustment, and so on. In this way, the new equilibrium could be approached.

It is also possible to come to the new equilibrium by other pairs of methods of adjustment, some of which will be much more sensible than others; to attempt to use some controls in pairs would be very inefficient. What is needed are pairs of methods that are complementary to one another; the members of the pair should have effects which differ substantially in character and magnitude; two methods that are too much alike are too akin to one method, which, as we have seen, is usually inadequate. Generally speaking, this means that the best pairs have as members one method which, if taken alone, causes internal expansion and increased external deficit (or the opposite if used the opposite way), and another method which, if taken alone, causes internal expansion and reduced external deficit (or the opposite if used the opposite way). This means that, generally, the best combination of methods uses changes in the internal level of activity or changes in lending plus relative price changes or changes in controls.

This need for a combination of two methods of adjustment in order to achieve the two aims of internal and external balance is not the end of the matter. Regard must also be paid, in the reaction to the error between the current and the desired situations, to the principles elucidated in Chapter 27. There, we saw that if control reactions were made simply in proportion to the size of the current error, full correction could never occur; that if reactions were made solely in accordance with the integral of the error, serious fluctuations might be caused; but if they were avoided the desired equilibrium must be attained; and finally, that derivative control can be used to damp down fluctuations.

These principles also need to be applied to the adjustment process toward the dual aims of internal and external balance. The absolute minimum requirement is that there should be either an automatic or a deliberate integral control element in the adjustment process. In other words, at some point reactions to errors away from the desired situation of balance must become larger and larger the longer the error persists.

This is only a minimum requirement. For rapid and tolerably

smooth adjustment there must be reactions (which may be built into the system and therefore automatic, or which may be made as acts of deliberate policy) which are related to the proportional size of the error and to whether it is getting larger or smaller. A satisfactory adjustment process demands a careful balancing of these elements.

A part of the analysis of Chapter 25 can also be extended to these wider problems which are now our concern. We saw in our discussion of internal balance alone that it would be frequently desirable to combine monetary policies, fiscal policies, and changes in direct controls, because of their differing characteristics. The same thing applies to the various methods of bringing about international adjustment; some [5] work more rapidly than others; some may work powerfully if given long enough to work themselves out.[6]

It may also be noted that short-term capital movements can play a big part in bringing about smooth and rapid adjustment to changes, just as they can avoid the need for making any adjustment when disturbances are merely transitory. Short-term capital movements can never deal completely with balance of payments problems, because they depend upon an exhaustible stock; but they can always play a valuable role in the adjustment process by acting as a cushion to absorb the immediate effects of changes until the slower acting adjustments which can be permanent in their effect are able to come into play. They can, in fact, act as a stock which can be used to provide a temporary cushioning during changes, just as inventories of goods held by firms help cushion firms against changes that cannot be forecast, and so make possible rapid adjustment to change.

Retaliation by Other Countries

Mention should also be made of a further consideration involved in the choice of methods of attaining external balance. It may well be that some methods, in some circumstances, may provoke retaliation by other countries, which cancels out the benefits achieved or leads to harmful effects in other ways. These possibilities are particularly serious in the cases of exchange rate changes and of direct controls. Thus, exchange depreciation may be regarded as an attempt

---

[5] E.g. direct controls, at least in some circumstances.
[6] E.g. very frequently, relative price changes.

to 'beggar-my-neighbor,' by depriving him of export markets, and provoke a depreciation by him in turn. Still more serious are the risks of retaliation when direct controls are used. In such circumstances, it is quite possible to get a series of retaliatory actions which leave all countries worse off than before, because of a reduction in the benefits of international division of labor. This risk can be a very strong argument against the use of direct controls to deal with balance of payments difficulties.

SOME SUGGESTED READING

The basic approach followed here is that of J. E. Meade, *The Balance of Payments* (Oxford, 1951). A similar approach is that of J. Tinbergen in 'Four Alternative Policies to Restore Balance of Payments Equilibrium,' *Econometrica* (1952), and in his book *On the Theory of Economic Policy* (Amsterdam, 1952).

39

The Gold Standard

The gold standard was the dominant international monetary system in the last third of the nineteenth century and the first third of the twentieth. Up to the First World War it operated in such a way as to achieve a tolerable degree of internal and external balance in the world; after its restoration in the 'twenties it worked much less satisfactorily.

The legal requisites for a gold standard system were outlined in Chapter 36. The central banks or treasuries of the major trading countries must be willing to buy and sell unlimited amounts of gold at fixed prices which must be practically the same for purchases and sales; moreover, free import and export of gold bullion or coins must be permitted. As a consequence exchange rates are almost precisely fixed by the authorities.

The Gold Standard Adjustment Process

These legal arrangements, together with institutional conditions which will be outlined in the course of this chapter, provided the foundations of an adjustment process which could lead to a return to internal and external balance after a disturbance. In favorable conditions the system could adjust itself to any kind of disturbance, whether it affected internal or external balance, or both. Here we shall consider the adjustment process following a shift in taste which reduces the demand for the home country's goods and increases the demand for the goods of the other country. The analysis of this problem will indicate the way in which adjustment occurred after other kinds of change.

The two forces that set the gold standard adjustment process in motion have already been indicated in general terms; they are the banking reactions discussed in Chapter 36 and the multiplier-induced reactions discussed in Chapters 30, 32 and 33.

As far as the banking reactions are concerned, we have seen that the outflow of gold that arises from a balance of payments deficit causes an automatic contraction in the monetary circulation of the country concerned, and an automatic tendency to rising interest rates and restrictive bank lending policies. In the country gaining gold the reverse tendencies occur. Moreover, in the 'ideal' gold standard system, when countries are following the 'rules of the game,' their central banks reinforce these automatic tendencies by raising the discount rate when gold is lost, and lowering it when gold is being gained.

These banking reactions have certain palliative effects on the situation. Higher interest rates tend to attract short-term capital toward the country losing gold, thus slowing down or even reversing the gold flow. Moreover, higher interest rates and reduced availability of bank credit tend to cause some reduction in inventories held by traders and manufacturers; there is consequently a reduced demand for imports. In the country with higher interest rates the opposite tendencies occur.

Both of these effects come about quite rapidly, but they are only a palliative because they affect stocks, which are exhaustible. There is only a limited amount of short-term capital which can be moved from country to country, and there is a limit to the extent to which traders and manufacturers can alter their inventories of goods.

In addition, the changes in the monetary situation have a durable effect on the situation. Rising interest rates tend to cause a reduction in the level of activity in the country losing gold; in the other country the level of activity tends to rise. This effect continues to become stronger and stronger [1] so long as the gold flow continues. As more and more gold is lost, more and more banking contraction becomes necessary; hence the level of activity tends to fall lower and lower.[2]

The other force that sets the adjustment process into operation

---

[1] At least in the deficit country. In the country gaining gold, interest rates may fall to the minimum level possible and come to the limit of their power to affect the level of activity.

[2] This, then, is an automatic integral control element; the longer the balance of payments is away from the desired position of zero balance, the bigger is the interest rate reaction on the level of activity.

also operates to reduce the level of activity in the country losing gold. In the case of an industrial country (which will be our sole concern for the moment) this is the familiar multiplier process. The change in the balance of payments itself has a direct effect on the level of activity in each country. In the country which is losing gold there is a multiplier contractionary process, because its balance of trade has deteriorated and its residents' incomes have declined; in the other country there is a multiplier expansionary process which is induced by the increase in incomes its residents enjoy. As was seen in Chapter 30, these two processes interact and tend toward an equilibrium situation in which the level of activity is lower than originally in the country against which demand has shifted, and is higher than originally in the other country.

In general and in the long run the banking forces and the multiplier forces operate together.[3] Both forces lead to a change in the level of activity, which is an essential stage in the adjustment process in gold standard conditions in industrialized countries: there must be an increase in unemployment in the deficit country and a reduction in unemployment in the other country. These changes in the level of activity become larger and larger, so long as the gold flow continues. Even though the multiplier process works itself out to a new equilibrium, the changes in interest rates, etc., and therefore the changes in activity that they induce, continue while the gold flow lasts.[4]

A direct consequence of the change in the levels of activity in the two countries is that their imports alter; in the country where the level of activity declines, imports fall, while they rise in the other country. This leads to a reduction in the gold flow from the deficit country. How far this improvement in its balance of payments goes depends on the size of the changes in the level of activity. Insofar as the multiplier-induced changes are concerned, the answer

---

[3] In the short run the hardening of interest rates and bank credit availability in the deficit country might well be inhibited by reduced transactions demand for money and reduced need for bank loans arising from the multiplier process, while it is working itself out; similarly in the other country.

[4] Because, as we have seen, the reaction through gold flows and interest rates involves an integral control element. The reaction through the multiplier effect is a proportional control element; part of the error in internal and (as will be seen in the next paragraph) external balance is damped out by this automatic reaction, but not all.

has already been given in Chapter 30. These changes in the level of activity will not, by themselves, restore equilibrium in the balance of payments, except in the limiting case where the marginal propensity to save in either country is zero. In all other cases the balance will still remain unfavorable to the deficit country. On the other hand, the declines in the level of activity induced through banking reactions continue for as long as the gold flows continue; they, therefore, cause an improvement in the balance of payments of the deficit country, which continues until such time as external balance is restored.

In this way the two forces we have been analyzing lead, more or less quickly, toward a restoration of external balance. But in so doing they cause a serious disturbance in internal balance in both countries. The next question concerns the manner in which this internal balance is restored. The method used is that of changes of relative price levels in the two countries; thus the whole adjustment process under the gold standard depends on one of the pairings of two unlike methods, as we saw to be necessary in Chapter 38.

This adjustment in relative prices is brought about as a consequence of the changes in the level of activity in the two countries. In the 'ideal' adjustment process, wages and prices tend to fall in the country with the lower level of activity, and rise in the country with the higher. This causes a shift in demand, in both countries, away from the goods that are becoming more expensive, toward the cheaper goods. If the demand elasticities are high enough, this means that total expenditure on the goods of the country with the lower level of activity rises; the reverse happens in the other country.

This makes either of two things possible. The balance of payments between the two countries can move nearer to balance without the necessity for any further departure from internal balance. Alternatively, each country can move nearer to internal balance without causing any deterioration in the external balance; for example, the amount of unemployment might be reduced in the depressed country without causing any deterioration in its balance of payments.

What is probably most likely in practice is that the relative price changes would cause some improvement in the level of activity and some improvement in the balance of payments in one country; correspondingly there would be some deterioration in each in the other country. The precise proportions in which the mixture would appear depends both on the central bank policies being followed and on the very subtle and complicated interplay through time of the different forces at work.

At this point another complication has to be taken into consideration. Changing price levels will alter the transactions demand for money. The rate of interest in each country will come to depend (subject to central bank action) on the level that transactions demand has reached at any time, in relation to the amount of gold (and so of money) in the country. Once again the precise situation reached at any time depends on the precise interplay of the various forces through time.

Although nothing can be said in general terms about the detailed characteristics of this adjustment process, we can be certain of one thing: if the situation reaches equilibrium it will be at the position of internal and external balance. Only at external balance are there no gold flows, and therefore no forces acting to alter the internal situation of the two countries.[5] Only at internal balance in each country is there no tendency for prices to alter and so to disturb the external situation.[6] The only possible equilibrium, therefore, is one where both internal and external balance are restored in both countries; while either kind of balance is absent, forces are at work to move conditions away from the existing situation.

Up to this point our analysis has been particularly appropriate to industrial countries, where (even in the nineteenth century) substantial unemployment has always been necessary before appreciable price falls could occur. In primary-producing countries the stage of changes in the level of activity has usually been short-circuited; the direct effect of reduction in the demand for the exports of such a country is a fall in their price. Internal balance in the sense of full employment [7] is usually maintained more or less permanently in such countries, while (as we saw in Chapter 28) internal balance in the sense of price stability is almost impossibly difficult to define or achieve.

Conditions for Full Adjustment

Although the only possible position of full equilibrium under the gold standard adjustment process is a situation of internal and

---

[5] Through interest rate changes.
[6] And also the level of interest rates through changes in transactions demand.
[7] Or possibly a constant degree of underemployment.

external balance, there is no guarantee that *any* position of equilibrium will be achieved. Still less is there any guarantee that the position will be attained smoothly and quickly (and if it is not attained tolerably quickly, it may well be as bad as if it is not achieved at all, because new disturbances are always coming along to upset the situation). It is, therefore, necessary to consider the conditions for attaining equilibrium, and the conditions for attaining it smoothly and quickly.

As far as the conditions for full adjustment are concerned, the first point that may be made is that a change in the level of activity is an essential stage in the adjustment process in industrial economies, and that full internal balance cannot be restored until the very end of the adjustment process. These facts arise from the dependence of the relative price shifts (which alone can restore full equilibrium) on the absence of internal balance in one or both countries. The classical explanation of the adjustment process tended to ignore the significance of this stage. Only if prices and wages are extremely flexible (as is typically the case in agricultural communities) can the stage of changes in the level of activity be short-circuited.

A second point is that adjustment to equilibrium, if it is possible at all, will eventually take place, even if the 'rules of the game' are not played. Automatic multiplier-induced and automatic monetary-induced contractions in the level of activity and so in the price level occur in the deficit country, and the reverse in the surplus country, even if central banks are completely passive.

What is more, the adjustment will take place eventually, even if there are no changes in the monetary situation in either country (for example, deliberate policies of 'active ease,' so that interest rates and bank credit availability remain unchanged). The reason is that the changes in income and activity induced in the multiplier process in each country cause a change in the price level in each country which continues until internal balance is restored.[8] These continuing price changes have effects on the balance of payments that grow larger and larger over time. Sooner or later, if the other

---

[8] The integral control element of the effects of gold flows on interest rates is not necessary, because there is still the integral element of the effects of internal unbalance on prices. The rule that there must be some integral element in the adjustment process is still satisfied.

conditions shortly to be outlined are satisfied, they cause such an increase in the demand for the goods of the deficit country and such a reduction in demand for the goods of the surplus country that internal and external balance are restored in each country.

A fourth point is that the adjustment will not take place if price changes lead to exaggerated expectations of further price changes. If a falling price level in the deficit country leads to expectation of still further falls, purchasers may hold off the market and reduce their demands for its products; this reduction induces further price falls, which justify the expectations and create expectations of further falls. Such 'perverse' expectations can make it impossible ever to attain equilibrium, but instead may cause perpetual oscillations around it, which may be explosive.

A fifth point is that the process of adjustment may fail to reach equilibrium if marginal propensities to import in the two countries are very large. A simple case arises where in each country the marginal propensity to import is larger than the marginal propensity to spend on its own goods.[9] In that case the reduction in home demand caused by rising interest rates and reduced availability of bank credit mainly affects demand for goods made in the other country; similarly, the corresponding expansion in the foreign country mainly affects demand for home exports. The net effect is that rising interest rates at home and falling interest rates abroad lead to a perverse effect; they cause expansion of the level of activity at home (the country originally in balance of payments deficit) and contraction abroad. This, in turn, means that prices *rise* in the country losing gold and *fall* in the other country. It is probably reasonable to consider that marginal propensities to import sufficiently large to cause these effects are not usual; much expenditure is upon goods and services (such as hairdressing and house building) for which a local producer has an overwhelming advantage. Nevertheless, the perverse case may occasionally apply.

A final point is that the adjustment process described above may be impossible for reasons with which we are already familiar—the sum of the price elasticities of demand may be too small. The adjustment process involves falling prices in the deficit country and

---

[9] The general rule is that the critical position is where the sum of the marginal propensities to import in the two countries is greater than the sum of the marginal propensities of each country to spend on its own goods.

rising prices in the surplus country, which cause a shift in demand from goods of the surplus country to those of the deficit country. If the sum of the demand elasticities in the two countries is too small, such a shift in demand may still involve more money being spent on the goods that are becoming more expensive and less money being spent on the goods that are becoming cheaper. This would involve deflationary pressure in the country whose prices have fallen, and cause its balance of payments to deteriorate; the movement is then farther away from the full employment position and from balance of payments equilibrium instead of nearer to them; similarly, it increases inflationary pressure in the other country.

Conditions for Rapid and Smooth Adjustment

Even if conditions are such that equilibrium will eventually be restored, the process may be very slow and may involve serious fluctuations. Most of the conditions for rapid adjustment should be apparent from the preceding discussion. Obedience to the 'rules of the game' is probably a necessary condition for reasonably rapid adjustment. Automatic influence can work in time, but they are likely to be slow. Appropriate interest rate changes induced by the central banks help evoke short-term palliatives, and they lead to more rapid and in time to considerable changes in the level of activity, upon which the whole adjustment process rests.

In addition, adjustment is likely to be rapid if prices and wages are very flexible in both directions, so that relatively small changes in the level of activity cause big price changes. Adjustment is likely to be particularly rapid if one of the countries between which adjustment is being made is a primary-producing country, so that price adjustments come very rapidly. It is also desirable that the demand elasticities should be high, so that comparatively small relative price changes lead to big shifts in import and export demands. Finally, it is very desirable that price changes should not lead to expectations of further price changes, so that perverse speculative effects are as small as possible.

The conditions for smooth adjustment are much more difficult to define. For one thing, it is difficult to say unequivocally what one means by smooth adjustment. Does it mean as little disturbance as possible to the internal situation or the external, to one country or to both? It is reasonably certain that substantial fluctuations on the way to the new equilibrium are undesirable. This means that care should be taken not to allow too much emphasis to be placed on the integral elements in the adjustment process. Since these integral elements are essential, they cannot be removed altogether. Their harmful effects can, however, be damped by a use of derivative control elements. Perhaps the most important rule is that the central banks' discount policies should take account of the rate of change of reserves and the rate of change of the level of unemployment, in order to damp out these fluctuations and still permit rapid adjustment.

The Gold Standard in Practice

It now remains to ask to what extent the actual gold standard system in the real world ever approximated to the description that has just been given, and to what extent the much greater success that attended the workings of the gold standard before the First World War compared with the inter-war years can be attributed to the fact that conditions before the war approximated more closely to those just outlined as necessary for its successful working.

It has already been mentioned that there was a serious theoretical gap in the classical explanation of the adjustment process: no emphasis was placed on the essential and practically unavoidable stage (in manufacturing countries) of adjustment through changes in the level of activity. Moreover, there is a still more important failing in that explanation: the gold standard system never depended (either before 1914 or after) upon obedience to the 'rules of the game,' which lay at the heart of the classical explanation of the adjustment. This statement is subject to the significant modification that in the last few years before 1914, the Bank of England did approximate in its actions fairly closely the classical prescription; but, generally speaking, the rules of the game were rarely followed at all closely, even in those years. For example, changes in discount rates by the Bank of France were exceedingly rare; and even the Bank of England did not follow at all consistently the rule of raising the discount rate when gold was flowing out and lowering it when gold was flowing the other way. The period can be crudely described by saying that sometimes there was this deliberate isolation, but generally the rule was one of passivity on the part of central banks except when disequilibrium became very large; then, and only then, was classical discount rate policy used, and only by certain central banks. This does not deny that several of the elements in the adjustment process described above did operate; balance of payments changes did affect the level of activity through multiplier and automatic monetary mechanisms, and the level of activity did affect price levels. Nevertheless, it is difficult to explain why the adjustment process before 1914 appears to have been so smooth and rapid, if adjustment had to rely upon such slowly working mechanisms.

To some extent the explanation is the quite simple one that adjustment before 1914 was not as rapid or as smooth as appeared to observers in the disturbed inter-war years. There were commercial crises and periods of unemployment before 1914, and they seemed serious enough at the time. Moreover, there may be a geographical shortsightedness, as well as shortsightedness over time, in our view of the situation before 1914. The countries and classes which suffered particularly severely in the adjustment process were probably frequently the least vocal politically (e.g. tropical dependencies) or consisted of willing risk-takers (e.g. settlers in new countries). As we have seen, agricultural countries typically short-circuit the second stage of the adjustment process; this makes it rather likely that they took up a particularly large part of the adjustment of relative prices. Moreover, most of the major adjustments needed in world trade in the pre-1914 world were probably adjustments between primary-producing and manufacturing countries. There is no evidence that the system had to take up major adjustments between the manufacturing countries, of the type that had to be made in the inter-war period.

All the same, this geographical shortsightedness is not the only explanation. There are further and substantial reasons why the pre-1914 system worked relatively smoothly. Since they help explain the contrast with the inter-war years and provide lessons for our present situation, it is necessary to consider them. It is convenient to do this by asking two questions. Firstly, why did the cyclical fluctuations that did occur before 1914 not do excessive harm to external balance in the world? Secondly, why were there no serious technical strains in the system (in contrast with the inter-war years)?

Probably the strongest reason why the fluctuations that did occur did not seriously upset external balance in the world arose from the fortunate pattern of trade and of long-term lending in cyclical fluctuations before 1914. Our analysis of the 'ideal' adjustment process

INTERNATIONAL MONETARY EXPERIENCE

did not consider the flow of long-term lending; all the same, it seems very probable that here lay a favorable element, in marked contrast with post-war experience. Britain was the predominant long-term lender before 1914, particularly to non-European countries. Two complementary features of Britain's overseas payments were that when British long-term lending declined, in periods of crisis and depression, her imports did not decline as much as her exports: her marginal propensity to import was relatively small, largely because she imported essential foodstuffs; on the other hand many overseas countries had large marginal propensities to import, since their imports were largely capital equipment financed by long-term loans. In consequence, while depression tended to throw the British balance of payments into surplus because long-term lending declined, there was a simultaneous tendency for the balance to be thrown into deficit because exports declined more than imports. There was, in fact, a tendency for the British balance of trade and balance of long-term lending to move in opposite directions in cyclical fluctuations. Since British trade and lending were of predominant importance at that time, there was a basic tendency toward stability in the external balance of the whole world.

Another element of stability may have arisen from a complementarity between British short-term and long-term lending. As we have just seen, there was a tendency for long-term lending by Britain to decline at time of crisis. In itself this is a factor which would cause instability to spread through the borrowing countries. This did happen to some considerable extent, but its effects were reduced by the efficiency of the short-term capital market in London, which was almost always in a position to help tide over the situation with short loans—at a high price. In times of crisis, it has been said, London's facilities were always such that it could shift the burden of overseas lending from the 'long' to the 'short' shoulder.

Confidence in the gold standard system and more broadly in the whole political system helped its smooth working. Perverse speculation was certainly much rarer than in the inter-war years, when belief in the self-correcting character of the system came to receive rude shocks. It is also probably true to say that prices and wages were more flexible before 1914, so that the 'ideal' adjustment process could work more smoothly. Finally, it must be emphasized that although the system as it was worked in the decades before 1914 did not closely follow the rules of the game, nevertheless interest rate policy was used in the right direction if serious external un-balance threatened. The classical explanation did not describe the actual workings precisely, although it has been suggested that it did describe the system that would have developed if there had been no war. Yet it was not a travesty of the system; if the need was great enough the rules came into operation.

The second of our questions about the working of the pre-1914 gold standard concerns the absence of technical strains, which were to become so common in the inter-war years. The important features that need consideration here are the extent to which the pre-1914 system was centered on London and the extent to which the rela-tions of the monetary systems of many of the 'newer' countries to London was similar to the relationships of the present-day colonial empire to London. Many of the newer countries, including areas that are now independent members of the Commonwealth and countries that have always been independent of Britain politically, were very closely tied to England in their monetary relationships, largely through their use of banks centering on London. The effect of inter-national changes on their banking systems was not unlike that described for the present-day colonies. A very large part of the pre-1914 world was little more than an extension of the English monetary system, following passively the policy of the Bank of England.

Equally important, those countries (e.g. in Europe or North America) with independent monetary systems accepted unquestion-ingly the predominance of London. The City of London was the undoubted apex of the world's monetary system. In a significant sense, the pre-1914 system was a sterling exchange standard, not a gold standard. International transactions were typically settled by means of bills of exchange drawn on London; commodity markets, the gold market, foreign exchange markets—all centered on London.

The Inter-War Gold Standard

After the First World War the conditions for a smoothly working single-centered international monetary system no longer existed. The gold standard was restored (in England in 1925), but it was a different system from that existing before 1914, and it never worked as satisfactorily. One explanation of this was that the system no longer had a single center: New York now rivaled London as an international financial center. British trade was becoming a less overwhelmingly important part of world trade, while New York was becoming a major source of long-term capital. As a result London's position became relatively weaker, and it no longer had the same 'deposit-compelling power' that it had before 1914; it was no longer so essential to channel international monetary transactions through London, and so there was no longer the same compulsion for foreigners to hold reserves there.

Another structural change that came after the war was the extension of the gold exchange standard to include many European countries; their reserves would be held as bank deposits or short-term securities in London or New York (or, later, Paris). The aim was to economize in the use of gold and to earn interest on the deposits. Unfortunately, the extension of this system added to strains; some of the countries which adopted it did so only temporarily (e.g. Germany, France) while those who regarded it as a more permanent policy caused difficulties when crisis came with the Depression, either by withdrawing funds from the center countries and increasing their gold holdings, or by switching reserves from one center country to another.

The shortage of gold that the gold exchange standard was designed to meet was frequently discussed at the time. The fundamental reason for its existence was that gold reserves were becoming less and less a means by which external changes were transmitted through to affect the internal monetary situation, and more and more a means by which the monetary authorities could cushion the internal situation from the effects of external changes. In the 'ideal' gold standard a loss of gold is an indication that a contractionary policy should be followed; in the passive system which was common before 1914 it was still a means by which a gold loss leads to some contraction. In the restored gold standard, on the other hand, the tendency became more and more common for attempts to be made to prevent a balance of payments deficit or surplus from having any influence on the internal situation; a gold loss was frequently accompanied by deliberate expansionary internal policy. This meant that not even the automatic parts of the monetary adjustment process described earlier were allowed to operate.

Obviously there is a limit to the possibility of bringing about such isolation: sooner or later reserves run out in the country losing gold. The advantage of large reserves in this situation is that the isolation of the internal situation from the external when there is a balance of payments deficit can continue for longer. Correspondingly, if the gold receipts are 'neutralized' when there is a balance of payments surplus, the internal situation is undisturbed, and most of any adjustment toward external balance that takes place is thrown on the shoulders of the gold-losing countries.

This deliberate sterilization against the internal effects of gold flows was largely a consequence of the growth of national sovereignty and desire for autonomous control over economic affairs. Complete autonomy is, of course, impossible without isolation: but it is possible to accept that this is true and still be unwilling to accept the internal effects of the 'ideal' or automatic gold standard systems.

In comparison with the pre-1914 system, there were many other strains with which the restored gold standard had to deal. Among them were firstly the disturbances caused by war, such as German reparations and the concentration of many years of economic change into a few years; secondly, increasing internal rigidities in many countries, which reduced price flexibility and made the complete adjustment back to internal and external balance extremely slow; and thirdly, the choice of inappropriate gold parities at which some countries returned to the gold standard, which made additional adjustment of internal price levels necessary. Still more generally, most of the fortunate harmonies of the pre-1914 system disappeared. For example, there was no longer a harmony between changes in the balance of long-term lending and changes in the balance of trade when depression came. The United States, which was becoming increasingly important as a trader and lender, cut its long-term lending drastically in the Depression, but tended to run into balance of trade surplus; this threw immense balance of payments burdens on the rest of the world. Moreover, there was no longer the same world-wide automatic tendency to full employment, largely, no doubt, because of the disappearance of the frontier of geographical expansion.

It is probably as fair a summary of the situation as is possible to say that the restored gold standard failed because far too much was expected of it. It was not realized how greatly the success of the pre-1914 system had depended on circumstances which no longer existed, and not upon the legal institutions and rigid rules of which the gold standard was believed to consist. The major lesson of the inter-war period, which will be further discussed in the next chapter, is that the maintenance of internal and external balance in the modern world is a very difficult task which cannot be left to the automatic working of simple institutions operating under simple rules.

SOME SUGGESTED READING

The pre-1914 gold standard is remarkably little understood, but a fair understanding can be pieced together from a number of scattered sources. On the adjustment process, see J. Viner, *Canada's Balance of International Indebtedness 1900-1913* (Cambridge, 1924) and Joan Robinson, 'The Pure Theory of International Trade' in the *Review of Economic Studies*, vol. XIV and reprinted in her *Collected Economic Papers* (Oxford, 1951). P. B. Whale's article on the 'Working of the Pre-War Gold Standard' which is reprinted in T. S. Ashton and R. S. Sayers, *Papers in English Monetary History* (Oxford, 1953) is also an important source; Sayers' contribution on the gold market in the same volume is also important, as is his book *Bank of England Operations 1890-1914* (London, 1936). R. G. Hawtrey, *A Century of Bank Rate* (London, 1938) is also helpful. On the role of sterling, see B. Tew, 'Sterling as an International Currency' in the *Economic Record* (1952). A useful summary of a great deal of research which has never been published appears in the introduction to W. A. Brown, *The International Gold Standard Reconsidered 1914-1934* (New York, 1939).

40

International Monetary Lessons of the 'Thirties

It is not intended to attempt to provide in these final chapters a full history of international monetary affairs in the twentieth century, but only to indicate some of the features of the institutional arrangements that have been tried. The nineteen-thirties are interesting in this respect; they were a period of substantial change and experimentation, following the collapse of the restored gold standard. New control mechanisms were developed, since the gold standard was found wanting and beyond hope of easy repair.

The collapse of the restored gold standard came in two stages: its abandonment by Britain in 1931 and by the United States in 1933. After 1933, there remained a group of 'gold bloc' countries centering around France which contrived to maintain the form of gold standard arrangements until 1936, but the death blow had already come. In September, 1931, Britain was compelled to abandon the system and to allow sterling to depreciate in relation to gold (and, therefore, to the currencies remaining on the gold standard). The system might possibly have survived this shock, but the end came in 1933, when the United States depreciated the dollar, not because of the unavoidable pressure of external circumstances (as had been the case with Britain) but for rather minor reasons. The gold standard system had been a state of mind as much as a set of legal institutions; its smooth working relied largely on the absence of perverse speculation and on a generally accepted belief that the existing gold parities would continue. The British abandonment of the system must inevitably have shaken this belief; the United States' decision destroyed it completely, and introduced an era in which no one can be perfectly confident that any country's exchange rate with the rest of the world will continue unchanged in the future.

The United States' decision was mainly determined by three purposes. There was a desire to introduce an expansionary banking policy at home; when this had been tried a little earlier it had resulted in a tendency to external deficit which was regarded as an important matter even though the gold reserves were large. More important, there was a desire to raise the internal level of prices and activity. A depreciation of the dollar was expected to raise import prices and so the price level in general; at that time economists laid much more emphasis on relatively small price changes as indicators of the economic health of a country than they do today.[1] Finally, dollar depreciation was expected to increase American exports, by removing the competitive advantage that Britain had gained by her depreciation.

The forces that had led Britain to depreciate had been much more compelling. Fundamentally, they arose from the differences between the pre-1914 world and the world in which the restored gold standard attempted to operate, which were investigated in the last chapter. More immediately, there were two obvious difficulties. In 1925 sterling had been restored to the gold standard at the pre-war parity; it was realized that this parity somewhat overvalued sterling, so that British exports were unduly expensive, causing a tendency toward balance of payments deficit. It was believed that a reduction of the internal price level in Britain would soon correct this overvaluation; this belief was not justified by events, and in the late 'twenties Britain seemed more or less immovably stuck in the middle of the 'ideal' adjustment process, with abnormally high short-term interest rates and with much more unemployment than in most other countries, but without any marked tendency for this unemployment to lead to reductions in wages or the prices of British goods.[2] The situation was aggravated by conditions in other countries; for example, France returned to gold at an under-valued parity but was unwilling to permit inflation, while several primary-

---

[1] Even though prices are a much more significant indicator today, when most countries are in or near the full employment zone, so that inflation is always a danger.

[2] British wages and prices had fallen sharply in the early 'twenties, and it was therefore not wholly unreasonable to expect that they might fall a little further. The main reason why prices fell in the earlier period was probably that pre-war price levels were regarded as a norm (from which wartime and immediate postwar inflation had been a temporary aberration).

producing countries were already running into difficulties. In addition, the interest rate structure led to an unhealthy position for Britain's external capital accounts; the tendency was for Britain to be borrowing short-term capital and lending at long-term.

It was this situation on the capital account which provided the immediate cause of collapse in the summer of 1931, when the Depression was causing world-wide trading and payments difficulties and creating a situation of uncertainty in the financial world. Britain's creditors could easily withdraw their deposits and other short loans in Britain, while British long-term loans abroad were largely frozen or withdrawable only at considerable loss. A broader view of the situation, however, is more accurate; it shows that the collapse of Britain in 1931 represented the general inadequacy of the restored gold standard to cope with the problems with which it had to deal; the failure came in Britain because Britain provided both the weakest and the most important link in the chain of international financial relationships.

The Origin of the Sterling Area

The changes in exchange rates that came about with the abandonment of the gold standard led to the appearance of a phenomenon whose roots can be traced deep down in the history of the gold standard, but which only became important in the 'thirties. This was the system of currency areas, of which the sterling area was, and still is, the outstanding example. When Britain left the gold standard a number of other countries (chiefly the members of the Commonwealth other than Canada) decided to maintain their exchange rate stable with Britain and to allow their currencies to depreciate in relation to gold, dollars, and other currencies. Subsequently, a number of other countries (particularly the Scandinavian states) joined this sterling group, all of whose members held a substantial part of their foreign exchange reserves in sterling. The Commonwealth members all had close banking, trading, and lending relations with Britain, in addition to their close political ties. The foreign members were all countries that were closely dependent upon trade with Britain, particularly in their exports.

In addition to this sterling group, a number of other currency groupings came to be more or less clearly defined. After the United States left the gold standard, a number of currencies in Central and

South America followed the alterations in the value of the United States dollar. At the same time a number of European countries, led by France, maintained a gold bloc until 1936. These countries refused to depreciate their currencies until circumstances compelled them to do so; in the meantime their currencies were expensive in terms of pounds and dollars. They maintained their balance of payments in a tolerable equilibrium by continuing to accept a low level of activity after recovery from the Depression was well under way in Britain and the United States.

There were also a number of countries who started, mainly in the early 'thirties, to use direct controls in order to keep their balance of payments in equilibrium. Many such countries were to be found in Latin America, but the most important member of this group was Germany, which maintained the external value of the mark by exchange controls, by depreciated exchange rates for certain kinds of transaction, and by bilateral trading and other agreements, which in effect created a discriminatory bloc centered on Berlin.

In the sterling area of the 'thirties, discriminatory intentions existed, but were not as strong as they were to become in the more closely knit sterling area of the 'forties and 'fifties. There was a gentlemanly discrimination with regard to capital flotations in London, which favored the members of the area; there was also some degree of trade discrimination under the Imperial Preference arrangements introduced in 1932 (which also included Canada) and under trading agreements with countries such as Denmark and Argentina. It must be emphasized, however, that until the outbreak of war these discriminatory purposes were limited and that there was no discrimination imposed by any sort of exchange control: the sterling system was still basically liberal.

The advantages of membership of the sterling area in the 'thirties were mainly those of convenience and stability. The advantages of convenience were mainly the same as those before 1914, when the whole world was in a sense in the sterling area, looking to London as the apex of its monetary system. By the 'thirties it had become quite clear that this was no longer so, but a fairly clearly defined group of countries made its appearance, whose members continued to make most of their foreign payments through London and held most of their international monetary reserves in the form of sterling.

The other advantage of sterling area membership in the 'thirties arose from the relative stability its members gained through attaching themselves to the British economy, which was less sharply affected by the slump than any of the other major manufacturing countries.

This process of creation of currency areas was one way in which limitations were imposed upon the use of fluctuating exchange rates to bring about external balance, even after the rigid exchange rates of the gold standard had been abandoned: the currencies of very many countries were pegged to those of a center country. There was another important limitation upon the use of fluctuating exchanges, except for very short periods; even the center countries, which permitted their currencies to take an independent line (and also the 'sandwich' countries, such as Canada, which tended to take a course intermediate between those taken by two center currencies) did not generally allow free operation of market forces to determine their exchange rate. The monetary authorities in these countries no longer committed themselves to a fixed gold price, and so to a fixed exchange rate with any other country following the same policy; nevertheless, they did not completely abandon control over the exchange rate for any considerable period.

Flexible Exchange Rates

In the case of Britain, free market forces were allowed to operate for a few months after the abandonment of the gold standard in September, 1931. In June, 1932, however, the Exchange Equalization Account came into operation. Its three main purposes were: to demonstrate the power of the Treasury over the international monetary situation; to insulate the internal monetary system from multiple repercussions of changes in the balance of payments; and to prevent the completely free operation of market forces on the exchange rate. The first of these three purposes was primarily political and administrative, and is not our concern here; the techniques of insulation of the internal banking situation have already been discussed; our purpose in this chapter is to look into the operations of the Account in the foreign exchange market.[3]

The British Exchange Equalization Account was originally intended to prevent fluctuations in the exchange rate which arose

---

[3] It should be emphasized that these three purposes of the Exchange Equalization Account system are logically and practically separable.

from speculative movements of short-term capital or from seasonal fluctuations in the balance of payments; on the other hand it was apparently intended that there should be no attempt to resist 'general trends' in the exchange rate as a result of changes in the balance of payments between the group of sterling area countries and the rest of the world. The Account would exchange sterling for gold (or for some currency with which it could buy gold) to the extent that speculators were moving funds in the opposite direction. If there was a speculative movement of short-term capital into Britain, the Account sold sterling in exchange for gold or foreign currency and if the movement was the other way, gold or foreign currency was sold in return for sterling.[4] If, on the other hand, there was non-speculative (and non-seasonal) excess of demand for or supply of foreign currency, the intention was that the excess should be allowed to operate on the price of foreign currency in the same way as in any free market; for example, an excess of demand for foreign currency over supply would raise its price, by causing sterling to depreciate.

The desire to isolate both the exchange rate and the internal monetary situation from the influence of speculative capital movements arose from the realization that such movements were frequently very disturbing, and had lost the justification they had had under the gold standard system. So long as confidence in existing exchange rates was unimpaired, short-term capital movements were generally made in reaction to changes in interest rates; by appropriate action they could be evoked as a temporary palliative for balance of payments difficulties. Once confidence in the continuation of the existing pattern of exchange rates collapsed the main economic determinants of short-term capital movements were fears of exchange depreciations and hopes of appreciations. In addition, political factors came to play a powerful role in determining the movement of capital; in particular, there was the huge flight from Europe to the United States as war came nearer.

It may be noted that international capital movements in reaction to interest rate changes did continue in the 'thirties, but that they

---

[4] In 1932, when the Account came into operation, short-term capital was moving into Britain, and so it was able to acquire a stock of gold with which to operate subsequently, in addition to the gold it took over from the Bank of England.

no longer had the cushioning effect on foreign currency reserves that they had under the gold standard. The reason was that most people who were shifting capital from one center to another to take advantage of higher short-term interest rates would cover the exchange risk by purchasing the currency they wanted at the maturity of the loan by means of a forward exchange contract. Thus, an American who was attracted into sterling by high short-term interest rates in London would lend for, say, three months in London and simultaneously buy three months' forward dollars for sterling.

In this way he knew precisely how many *dollars* he would have in three months' time: a forward contract is an agreement made now to buy or sell at a date in the future at a price fixed now. The bank which sold the forward dollars would usually in turn cover its exchange rise by buying actual ('spot') dollars at once, and holding them until the three months were up. Thus, the inward capital movement from the United States would not help Britain's official dollar reserves, because it would be offset by a purchase of dollars by a British bank.

It may also be noted that the ordinary forces of supply and demand usually caused closely sympathetic movements in the forward exchange rate when the relationship between short-term interest rates in two centers altered. If short interest rates rose in London, forward dollars tended to become correspondingly more expensive in terms of sterling.[5]

In practice, largely because of the difficulty of identifying speculative movements, it was found difficult in the operation of the Exchange Equalization Account to avoid taking a position in the exchange market and influencing general trends of the exchange rate; still more, it was difficult to avoid accusations of doing this. The United States and French Exchange Stabilization Funds were never intended to be passive in relation to non-speculative and non-seasonal changes in demand for and supply of foreign currency; they were definitely intended to influence trends as well. The primary aim of the U.S. Fund was to 'defend' the dollar against competitive depreciation by other currencies and, in particular, sterling. Broadly, the intention of the United States was that sterling should not be allowed to be cheaper in relation to the dollar than it had

---

[5] These characteristics of the forward exchange market appear to be re-establishing themselves in the 'fifties.

been before 1931. But since the U.S. Fund kept its purchase and sale prices close to the U.S. Treasury's prices, it was the latter institution's policy of maintaining fixed gold prices that was the most important factor in the exchange stabilization efforts made by the United States. At the same time the British authorities appear to have been unwilling to allow any substantial appreciation of sterling in relation to the dollar.[6] The net effect was that from the time of the establishment of the U.S. Fund up to the disturbances in the last year or so preceding the outbreak of war in Europe in 1939, the Exchange Stabilization Fund system did not use exchange rate changes to any great extent to bring about substantial balance of payments adjustments between the two major trading areas of the world.

Nevertheless, there is good reason for discussing the workings of the flexible exchange rate system as a mechanism for obtaining international adjustment by permitting non-speculative changes in foreign payments and receipts to have an immediate and full effect on the exchange rate while partially isolating the banking system from the effects of external events. For one thing there were some fluctuations in the sterling-dollar rate, even after the United States undertook exchange rate stabilization measures and before the disturbances associated with the approach of war. In the second place it is worth while discussing this adjustment process, even though it has probably never operated freely for any considerable length of time, because it has been widely advocated.

It is useful to look at the way the adjustment process works in two cases: firstly, where all countries are trying to maintain internal balance, and, secondly, where one country or group of countries is trying to maintain internal and external balance in the face of unemployment abroad.[7] (The case of a country trying to maintain internal and external balance in the face of inflation abroad involves a similar analysis.)

When both countries in a two-country world are trying to maintain both internal and external balance, the adjustment following

---

[6] In any case, it is extremely doubtful whether such a move would have been appropriate.

[7] In the 'thirties the search for internal balance in the sense of full employment was neither as purposeful nor as well directed as today; because of the relevance of present-day needs for full employment, the aim of internal balance will, nevertheless, be assumed.

a particular disturbance involves much the same changes in the relative positions of the two countries in the final equilibrium position as with the gold standard mechanism. In the final position, external balance has been restored, in both cases, by relative price changes. On the other hand, the ways in which this final position is reached differ greatly. Under the gold standard, changes in the level of activity are the essential condition for adjustment; [8] in the flexible exchange rate mechanism internal balance can, in principle, be maintained right through the adjustment process by internal fiscal, monetary, or direct controls, while external balance is obtained by the effects of exchange rate changes.

These differences mean that the path of adjustment is completely different in the two cases; this is important in practice, because we are always adjusting toward a new equilibrium and never reach it before a new disturbance comes along; moreover, it means that the conditions necessary for attaining satisfactory adjustment are different in the two cases.

The process of adjustment is in principle simple, although in practice it demands flexible and careful administration. The exact description of the process depends upon the initiating change that has to be dealt with; once again it will be convenient to consider a change in tastes which lowers the world demand for the products of the home country and raises it for the products of the other. This tends to cause depression at home and inflation abroad, and causes a balance of payments deficit for the home country. Internal balance is restored by expansionary fiscal, monetary, or direct control policies at home and contractionary policies abroad; these, in themselves, aggravate the home balance of payments situation.

The manner in which external balance is restored depends upon whether we are concerned with disequilibrium between two industrial countries or between an industrial country and a primary-producing country. Since the whole burden of adjustment to external balance can be thrown on to a primary-producing country, it will be convenient to dismiss the case where such a country is involved, before proceeding to the symmetrical case.

In a primary-producing country a shift in demand has an immediate effect on prices while leaving the level of activity more or less

---

[8] Except in cases where all the burden of adjustment is thrown on a primary-producing country.

unchanged. The price changes in themselves help to counteract the changes in demand, and as was seen in Chapter 33,[9] they can restore external balance without any exchange rate changes and without need for any adjustment in the level of activity in the industrial country. If exchange rate changes do occur they make internal price changes in the primary-producing country so much the less necessary: internal price changes and exchange rate changes are substitutes for one another. All this has a significant consequence: the flexible exchange system is quite workable so long as the demand elasticities are sufficiently large, even if primary-producing countries peg their exchange rates to a manufacturing country's rate (e.g. the sterling area of the 'thirties).

Where external balance has to be restored between two industrial countries, the adjustment process under consideration almost inevitably demands adjustments in exchange rates between the two countries. Changes which are appropriate in direction and amount must wipe out a balance of payments disequilibrium.[10] To the extent that these adjustments affect internal balance in the two countries, the situation is put right by appropriate internal policies; to the extent that these react again on to the external situation, further exchange rate adjustments are necessary.[11]

One disadvantage of arrangements by which the authorities leave the exchange rate completely free to the pressures of non-speculative demands and supply of foreign exchange is that there can be no equilibrium if the sum of the demand elasticities is too small. Probably more important in practice is that if the sum is large enough to lead to an eventual equilibrium there is the disadvantage that the exchange rate is likely to fluctuate considerably on its way to the new equilibrium; in particular it is likely to overshoot the new equilibrium for a time. Correspondingly, there will be sharp fluctu-

---

[9] Pp. 484-5. The argument here assumes that the sum of the demand elasticities exceeds unity.

[10] Whatever the sum of the demand elasticities.

[11] In carrying out all these adjustments, attention must be paid to the fact that inappropriate control reactions can lead to serious fluctuations and a long time lag in the restoration of equilibrium. In both the internal and the external policies there must be an appropriate mixture of the various control elements. On the external side, this means that regard must be paid to the size of the balance of payments deficit or surplus (a proportional control element), to the size of the exchange reserves (an integral element) and to whether the deficit is increasing or decreasing (a derivative element).

ations in the terms of trade and in the effects of external changes on the internal situation. These fluctuations, which may well be considered undesirable, arise because the burden of restoring external balance rests solely on relative price changes, and, as we have seen, demand elasticities are likely to be smaller in the short than in the long run, so that larger relative price changes are needed at first than will eventually prove sufficient to fill a given balance of payments gap.

This tendency to fluctuations in the exchange rate (and so in the terms of trade, real income, and the burden of internal adjustment) justifies two modifications to this 'pure' adjustment process. Stabilizing speculation may be permitted, and the Exchange Stabilization Fund may act to prevent these temporary exchange rate fluctuations. One of the best ways of allowing stabilizing speculation is to permit a forward exchange market to operate. If an adjustment involves a temporary depreciation of sterling to, say, $2, although the eventual equilibrium (once demand substitution starts to operate to its full extent) will be $2.50, then speculators can make a profit by buying sterling now at a low price and making contracts to sell it in a few months' time at a higher price. This raises the current demand for sterling and prevents the exchange from falling as far as $2; correspondingly, the transactions somewhat delay the rise to $2.50. Informed speculation of this kind can smooth down the violence of exchange fluctuations—so long as it is well informed.

The fluctuations can also be smoothed down if the authorities are willing to enter the market, not merely to counter perverse speculation, but also to prevent excessive exchange rate fluctuations. The Exchange Stabilization Fund in the home country in our example would sell a certain amount of foreign currency to satisfy non-speculative demands until demand substitution came fully into operation. Of course, once the authorities go this far they are very near to taking a permanent position in the exchange market; the more so since they will presumably want subsequently to restore their foreign currency holdings to some optimal level.

The speed and success with which the authorities in each country act to restore internal balance has an important effect on the process of adjustment to external balance. If they are both perfectly successful, so that no changes occur in internal prices or levels of activity, the burden of external adjustment tends to be relatively large. No temporary alleviation to the external situation is provided by the automatic tendency of a balance of payments deficit to lower the level of activity (and of a surplus to raise it).

If, on the other hand, the restoration of internal balance is rather slow, this is a temporary alleviation of the external situation. There may also be a permanent cure, if price changes occur within either country because of the temporary absence of internal balance. In industrial countries of the type we have under consideration, the only appreciable changes in the price of home output can be inflationary price rises. If inflation occurs for a time in the surplus country, its prices rise. Restoration of internal balance there does not imply restoration of the original price level, but merely a prevention of further price rises. There is, therefore, a 'ratchet' effect on prices. This helps restore external balance between the two countries, so long as the demand elasticities are large enough. Temporary absence of internal balance can, therefore, act as a substitute for exchange rate changes if conditions are appropriate.

This case is an example of a more general rule: the longer the delay in reacting to lack of internal balance, and the less regard is paid to internal balance, the more similar does the adjustment process under consideration become to that of the gold standard. Another example of this rule arises from our discussion of adjustment between a primary-producing country and an industrial country. Primary producers cannot usually maintain internal price stability; therefore they always adjust to external changes by internal price changes: the distinction between the gold standard system and the flexible exchange rate system is relatively unimportant for them. For such countries the choice between the two systems is based mainly on the rather secondary matter of deciding which is the best way to absorb and distribute the internal burden or benefit of the relative price changes that are in any case the main part of the adjustment process.

For industrial countries, particularly in their adjustment with one another, the choice between the flexible exchange system and the gold standard system is more fundamental. In the latter system, internal balance must be absent while the adjustment process is taking place; in a flexible exchange rate system, an attempt is made to maintain internal balance (in the sense of full employment with price stability) for the whole of the time. Not that there are no internal disturbances—terms of trade changes affect the prices of imports and so affect the real incomes of those at work; moreover, some temporary effects on the level of activity are almost inevitable. It may be noted that the different character of the adjustment process under flexible exchange rates means that the necessary conditions for the mechanism to work are different from those needed by the gold standard. In many respects this system is less demanding. In particular, inflexibility of internal prices and wages does not matter, because the mechanism does not rely on changes in internal price levels. This adjustment process suffers from the same limitations as the gold standard process that it can only work automatically if the sum of the demand elasticities is sufficiently large; if market mechanisms are being used they can only work successfully if a rise in the price of foreign currency does reduce the excess of demand for foreign currency over the supply. On the other hand, if the authorities deliberately alter exchange rates they can move them in either direction as circumstances demand.

Up to this point our concern has been with a fluctuating exchange rate system as a means of attaining internal and external balance in all countries. Another purpose for which it may be used is to make possible the restoration of internal balance in one country in the face of depression in the rest of the world, while maintaining external balance. Exchange depreciation is necessary to maintain external balance as the demand for imports rises because of the restoration of full employment at home, while the demand for exports remains low because of the continuance of unemployment abroad.

Three important conditions may be pointed out if such policies are to be successful. In the first place, it is better if an internal expansion in the level of activity has a small effect on the quantity of imports: that is, if the marginal propensity to import is small. Secondly, it is better if the demand elasticities are high, so that a balance of payments deficit is solved by a relatively small depreciation and so by a relatively small loss of income through an adverse shift in the terms of trade.[12] Thirdly, this policy is likely to be more

---

[12] It may be noted that this adverse turn in the terms of trade might be so large that a rise in the level of activity would be accompanied by a fall in the level of real income of the nation as a whole; this would happen if the marginal propensity to import were large, and if the sum of the demand elasticities were not much greater than unity. This can be expressed in terms of the notation of the Mathematical Appendix, using equations 9, 10, 11a and 12, assuming $t = 0$, $\bar{q}_h = \bar{q}_f = 0$ and a disturbance of $^s d_h$. We can define r = change in real

successful if it does not provoke accusations that the country is indulging in beggar-my-neighbor remedies for its unemployment, by undercutting its neighbors' markets.

The Devaluation Cycle of the 'Thirties

It is now possible, after this lengthy excursion into theory, to complete our discussion of the 'thirties. In practice, the main consequence of the three major exchange depreciations of the 'thirties (by Britain in 1931, the United States in 1933, and France in 1936) was to make possible a partial satisfaction of the aim considered in the next to the last paragraph—an expansion in the internal level of activity without risk of loss of external balance through loss of gold reserves. In the case of Britain this was certainly not the intended reason, and in the case of the United States the strength of her gold reserves gives rise to doubt whether internal expansion would have been a serious threat to her external position.

The net result of all these changes was a final position, in 1936, in which the exchange relationships of the three major blocs were little different from those existing before 1931. A cycle of depreciations had taken place, starting in the country in the weakest situation and ending in the most stubborn, which left the final pattern of exchange rates much as it had been. This was so largely because of the policy of the United States in resisting 'competitive depreciation'; it was possible, because the situation of Britain was no longer as obviously weak as in the late 'twenties, largely because of the introduction of the mild discriminatory devices whose nature has already been noted. The old exchange rate pattern had become more consistent with a reasonably settled equilibrium,[13] at least until the disturbances leading up to the outbreak of war.

Only to a limited extent did the system that had developed by

---

income = increase in production minus the worsening in the terms of trade multiplied by the amount of trade—i.e. $r = q_h - Iv$. Then simple algebraic manipulation gives

$$r = \frac{{}^s d_h}{s_h} \left(1 - \frac{m_h}{(1 - s_h)(\epsilon_h + \epsilon_f - 1)} \right)$$

[13] Although almost certainly the position was not at all well balanced; Britain was selling foreign assets at a very considerable rate in the late 'thirties, and France's position was still more obviously unstable.

the late 'thirties make use of the exchange rate adjustment process described above. There were elements of these arrangements in the system, but for the most part the arrangements as they had developed involved a much higher degree of management of exchange rates than would be consistent with the working of the system described. The initial impulse to this state of affairs was the United States policy already outlined; the working of a system in which exchange rates vary in accordance with non-speculative pressures demands that the governments of *all* the major financial countries should be willing to let commercial forces work freely. Once one government refuses to accept the rule of the market but tries to manage its exchange rates with the other leading centers, then the governments of the other center countries must either accept the leadership of the first government or co-operate with it in deciding together on exchange rates that are mutually advantageous. If one major country 'manages' its exchange rate (in the sense that the rate does not simply follow the trends of non-speculative demand and supply), then the other countries must either accept the management of the first or actively manage their own; if they choose the latter course they cannot manage in a way which is inconsistent with the policies of the others.

Once managed currencies are introduced they therefore tend to spread, and they tend to make international co-operation necessary. These are the main lessons of the middle and late 'thirties. The recognition of their validity came clearly with the Tripartite Monetary Agreement between Britain, France, and the United States in 1936. This was immediately concerned with technical matters of co-operation between the Exchange Funds of the three countries, but more fundamentally, the Agreement was important in that it accepted the need for effective international co-operation in a managed exchange rate system. That this lesson was learned well but not applied too wisely in the immediate post-war monetary arrangements will be one of the themes of the next two chapters, which are concerned with post-war institutions and with the mechanics of the post-war managed exchange rate system.

SOME SUGGESTED READING

The best introduction to inter-war currency history was published by the League of Nations, almost in its last breath. It is called *International Cur-*

INTERNATIONAL MONETARY EXPERIENCE

rency Experience (League of Nations Number II, Economic and Financial, 1944 II.A.4). H. W. Arndt, *The Economic Lessons of the Nineteen Thirties* (London, 1944) is an excellent book written from a radical viewpoint. For the early 'thirties, see W. A. Brown's monumental *The International Gold Standard Reconsidered, 1914-1934* (New York, 1939). The role of the United States, from certain points of view, is discussed in the U.S. Department of Commerce, *The United States in the World Economy* (Washington, 1943). See also A. H. Hansen, *America's Role in the World Economy* (New York, 1945). The case for flexible exchange rates is powerfully argued by M. Friedman in his *Essays in Positive Economics* (Chicago, 1953), pp. 157-203.

41

Post-War International Monetary Experience [1]

The international economy that emerged from World War II was characterized by the widespread use of exchange controls, bilateral payments agreements, and discrimination in the control of imports, with all the major trading nations, except for the United States, making use of these direct controls. Further, direct controls appeared to be gaining acceptance as permanent features of the trade and payments system; this line of thought was particularly prominent in 1947, when acute payments problems, especially with the dollar area, were faced by many countries. In this context, regional arrangements that provided greater freedom in the movements of goods and in making payments with a certain area—but that at the same time enabled that area to practice discrimination against outsiders—assumed tremendous importance. In this chapter we shall examine two such arrangements, the sterling area and the European Payments Union; the link provided by Britain between these two groups served to build up a larger area within which relative freedom of payments has obtained. We shall also look into the dollar problem which was the most important factor in stimulating 'regionalism' in the post-war period.

The Present-Day Sterling Area

The outbreak of war in 1939 necessitated drastic changes in the character of the sterling area. In the 'thirties the boundaries of the group had been ill defined, and membership depended solely upon

---

[1] This chapter and the next take account of events up to the end of December, 1958, which date was an important watershed in post-war international monetary history.

the policies of the monetary authorities of the member countries. The difficulties and fears of the last months of peace resulted in practically all the non-Commonwealth members leaving, so that on the outbreak of the war the effective members could be fairly clearly defined as most of the Commonwealth (the major exception being Canada) plus one or two other countries such as Egypt. It was at this point that a fundamental change in the character of the sterling area appeared; for the first time its boundaries were clearly defined, by the passing of United Kingdom legislation. This situation has remained as a continuing feature in the post-war period.

Within the sterling area, both during and since the war, no major restrictions were placed by the United Kingdom upon payments either for current transactions or for capital movements.[2] Restrictions have been imposed by some of the outer members, but in general they have been moderate,[3] so that the sterling area has been a group within which payments have been relatively free and uncontrolled. This has provided a strong contrast with most of the rest of the world; outside the United States and a few other countries with a secure balance of payments position, exchange controls over payments made to and received from other countries have been the general rule since the war—although it is important to remember that they are now much less important than in the early post-war years. The sterling area system made it possible for Britain and the other members to avoid these controls in their transactions with one another, although they have had to employ them in their relationship with non-member countries.

The main advantages of membership of the sterling area system since 1939 have been those of convenience and discrimination. The advantage of convenience has basically been a continuation, within a narrower framework than ever before, of the advantages (including the advantage of economy of reserves) of a centralized payments and financial system, with London at its heart. Since 1952, with the

[2] The exceptions were the temporary blocking of excessive wartime sterling accumulation of certain countries, and Capital Issues Committee control over access to the London capital market similar to that imposed on English borrowers.

[3] Most independent sterling area members outside the United Kingdom have imposed some control over current transactions, and several have imposed restrictions on exports of capital and over tourist remittances to other sterling area countries.

slow but steady dismantling of the discriminatory system shortly to be considered, the relative importance of this advantage has been increasing. Gradually since 1952 the tendency has been for the sterling area to be less and less an exclusive club, with rights and duties attached to membership, and more and more a banker-customer relationship between the United Kingdom and the other members. By 1958 the amount of trade discrimination within the sterling area was quite small. Many of the members did not discriminate at all against dollar goods or in favor of sterling area goods; and those that did (such as Australia and the United Kingdom) did it to an extent which was much smaller than was commonly realized.

Nevertheless, the most powerful justification for the sterling area during most of the post-war period has been that it has been a discriminatory bloc, with regard both to capital movements and to trade. The discrimination has been imposed by a 'ring fence' of controls around the area, which are enforced by the authorities of each member country, and which have been broadly similar in characteristics and intensity in each case. With regard to capital movements the discrimination has been quite simple; broadly speaking, capital can move freely within the area while capital movement from within the area to non-members is (in principle) closely controlled and frequently has been almost wholly forbidden.

The pattern of discrimination in trade has been more complicated and more changeable. Broadly speaking there used to be three tiers, consisting of trade with other members, trade with non-members outside the dollar area, and trade with the dollar countries. A broad description of the pattern as it existed around 1950, when the sterling area was most tightly organized as a discriminatory bloc, was one of strong discrimination in favor of imports from other members and strong discrimination against imports from dollar countries, while imports from other countries were in an intermediate position. But since about 1952 this picture has been steadily modified. In the case of trade in many commodities (e.g. British raw material imports, and imports of manufactures into several overseas members) there has for several years been practically no discrimination; again, in the case of most independent members of the sterling area the distinction between sterling and non-sterling non-dollar countries has become very small since 1952. As the importance of trade discrimination has declined, the traditional banker-customer relationship between the United Kingdom and the other members has once again become the principal characteristic of the sterling area.

The sterling area countries have not been alone in their indulgence in discrimination: practically all countries outside North and Central America have made use of discriminatory trade and currency controls since the war. In detail, a very complex pattern of discrimination arose in the early post-war years. Its two main features have been a proliferation of bilateral trade and currency arrangements, and the existence of the 'dollar problem.' The rest of this chapter will be concerned with these two features; in particular it will consider the techniques that have been used in Western Europe to reduce the need for bilateral arrangements, and the broad characteristics of the post-war dollar problem.

The European Payments Union

Up to about 1950 the European situation was marked by a very complicated pattern of trade discrimination. The failure of the hopelessly overambitious attempt to make sterling convertible in 1947 [4] was followed by a regression into a system using a large number of bilateral trade and payments agreements. Under many of these, pairs of countries tried to balance trade bilaterally. As a consequence, each European country discriminated in favor of some other European countries and against others. This system almost certainly reduced the volume of trade within Europe to levels well below what was possible, and caused serious distortions in the pattern of trade which were generally considered to be harmful.

It was only in 1950 that real success was attained in destroying the bilateral system by the establishment of the European Payments Union. The remarkable success of that organization was largely the result of Europe's relatively rapid recovery from the effects of the war, which in turn was very largely the product of the massive assistance given by the United States, in the form of grants (and to a smaller extent, loans) under the European Recovery Program. Another important contribution to the re-establishment of the position of Europe in world trade was the competitive fillip provided by the exchange devaluations in most European countries in 1949.

---

[4] Made in obedience to the Anglo-American Loan Agreement of 1946.

In its turn, the success of the European Payments Union contributed to the continuing growth of the European economy in the 'fifties.

Before the establishment of the European Payments Union other attempts had been made to provide institutions to break down the bilateral trading system. For example, some slight alleviation to the system was provided by the British Transferable Accounts system. Certain countries belonged to a group which was allowed to use sterling for payments to other countries placed in the same group, as well as to Britain and other members of the sterling area. Transferability was, in fact, a limited form of convertibility; the major limitation (which survived until the very end of 1958) being that the use of sterling for payments to dollar countries was not allowed. Thus, within rather narrow limits, the Transferable Account system provided multilateral payments channels, and reduced the tendency for trade and payments to be forced into bilateralism. Unfortunately the system's membership was limited in the late 'forties, and the hopes that general freedom of trade and payments within the non-dollar world might be based on the use of transferable sterling were not realized.

Much more successful was the European Payments Union,[5] which was established in 1950 under the aegis of the Organization for European Economic Co-operation and survived until the last few days of 1958, when it was wound up at the time when sterling and the other major European currencies became convertible. The membership of the Union was the same as that of the OEEC, namely, all European countries outside the Soviet bloc except Spain, Yugoslavia, and Finland. The effective membership was even wider, since the associated monetary areas of the members made use of the Union through the agency of their parent country; of these areas, the sterling area is by far the most important, while the French franc area is also very significant.

The purposes lying behind the foundation of the European Payments Union were the prevention of discrimination by European countries against one another and the encouragement of trade liberalization between them. To assist in these aims additional reserves of international currency were artificially created; these helped to

---

[5] It had been preceded by the moderately successful and much less ambitious Inter-European Payments System.

absorb temporary fluctuations in the balance of payments between each member and the rest of the group taken as a whole.

There were two sets of administrative devices by which the purposes of the Union were carried out. In the first place, specific agreements were made (and altered from time to time) which provided that each country should refrain from imposing restrictions on at least a specified percentage of its imports from other members. Moreover, members could not use import restrictions to discriminate between other members in the importation of those goods which were still controlled. In the second place, monthly settlements were made covering practically all the current payments of each member country with the other members taken as a group. Every month each member country reported its bilateral payments situation with every other member. The reports were made to the Bank for International Settlements, which added up the total of each country's bilateral surpluses and deficits; this sum represented a country's surplus or deficit with the rest of the members of the Union, and was known as the month's accounting surplus (or deficit).

Each member then settled this accounting surplus or deficit with the Union. It is clear that, since settlements were made with regard to a country's position with Europe as a whole and not with individual members, no country was under any pressure to discriminate in favor of some members and against others. It made no difference to France whether it spent a certain sum on an import from Britain or the same amount on the same import from Germany; in either case its month's settlement with the European Payments Union was pushed into debt by that amount. This situation was in marked contrast with that existing before 1950, when many countries were compelled to settle bilaterally with many others. Thus, in addition to prohibiting discrimination between members [6] the Union created conditions in which countries were not forced to discriminate.

We must now consider how each country's monthly surplus or deficit was settled. In doing that we shall see how the Union created international currency for use between the members, and so made it possible to permit bigger fluctuations in their trade with one another; this, in turn, meant that intra-European trade liberalization was easier to maintain.

---

[6] Although not discrimination against outsiders—the dollar problem still remained through the life of the EPU.

Settlements of each country's deficit or surplus were generally made, partly in gold or dollars and partly by credits granted to or received from the Union. In 1957-1958, for example, a country which had an accounting deficit in a particular month paid three-quarters of it in the form of gold or dollars to the Union; the other quarter it paid by an increase in a book debt to the Union or by a reduction in a book credit against the Union. This 75-25 gold or dollars credit settlement ratio was introduced in August, 1955, and represented a 'hardening' in the settlement basis, since in 1954-1955 settlements had been made on a fifty-fifty basis.[7]

The amount of credit that the Union would give to a country was limited to a prearranged amount which was called the country's quota; outside this limit, settlement was 100 per cent in gold or dollars. Within this limit the credits were granted and received automatically; they therefore increased the international reserves on which a country could draw when it was in balance of payments deficit with other members, taken as a group.

The assumption behind these borrowing and lending facilities was that each member would balance its payments with the other members taken as a group, if a sufficiently long period of time were allowed. From month to month, or from year to year, some countries might swing into deficit and others into surplus. In the long run, however, there must either be balance or some means of further settlement. Otherwise, some countries must have run their credit-drawing rights to the limit and then could make no further use of the Union, while others would find they had given large credits to the Union which were of no use to them.

To a considerable extent there was balancing out between the members in the long run; some countries (such as Germany) swung into deficit and then into surplus, while others (such as Britain) did the reverse. In practice, however, this process of balancing

---

[7] In the earlier years of the Union's life the arrangements for granting and receiving credit were more involved. The ratio between the amount of a deficit or surplus that was settled in gold or dollars and the amount that was settled by book debts was not fixed. Instead, it was on a sliding scale; a bigger proportion of any month's surplus or deficit was settled in gold or dollars, if a country had already run up a big debt against the Union. On the other hand, all settlements with countries which were creditors of the Union were made 50 per cent in gold or dollars and 50 per cent by changing the credit against the Union for all but the first 20 per cent of its quota, which was settled entirely by credit.

over time was sufficient, and from the summer of 1954, arrangements were made from time to time for some of the debts and credits of various countries to the Union to be settled outside the automatic mechanism, when they had been outstanding for some time. This meant that the automatic credits provided by the EPU system were often of limited duration.

The European Payments Union, in its operations, successfully applied two principles. The first is that of an organization which has provided international channels of payment and created international currency. The second is the principle of regional organization—a principle with a long history in the history of the sterling area, but one to which little attention was paid in the international monetary plans made during the war. Even though the European Payments Union was replaced at the end of 1958 by the much weaker and less significant European Monetary Agreement, the successful working of these two principles by explicit international co-operation has been a valuable experience.

The European Monetary Agreement of July, 1955, was designed to supplant (automatically) the European Payments Union when countries comprising 50 per cent or more of the EPU quotas made their currencies convertible. In December, 1958, the most important members of EPU (Britain, France, Germany, the Low Countries, etc.) made a joint move to convertibility and the European Monetary Agreement came into force. The main provisions of the EMA were the establishment of a European Fund with a capital of $600 million and the institution of a multilateral system of settlements to replace the clearing functions of the EPU. European Fund loans which are to replace the credits formerly granted by EPU carry a maximum maturity of two years and are available to members on a nonautomatic basis; in each case the conditions attached to these loans are decided by the Fund. Under the multilateral system of settlements members are obliged to establish buying and selling rates for dollars, to provide specified amounts for interim finance between the monthly settlements, and to pay or accept in dollars at the monthly settlement any net debts or net claims that have accrued during the month. Since members are not obliged to clear their accounts in the monthly settlements and since transactions in the monthly settlement are settled at the lending country's buying rate for dollars, which is the most unfavorable rate possible for the borrower, countries are unlikely to borrow through this mechanism and they will ordinarily elect to clear their accounts with others in the foreign exchange market.

In contrast with the EPU, under the arrangements of the EMA, the clearing mechanism will seldom be used, interim finance is strictly limited in amount, and the creation of credit is not automatic.

The Post-War Dollar Problem

The hardening in the settlement basis of the European Payments Union, culminating in its replacement by the European Monetary Agreement, was made possible by the decline in the post-war dollar problem, which was formally indicated by the restoration of convertibility of the major European currencies. In the first post-war decade the most important single feature of the international monetary situation had been the existence of a serious world dollar problem. With the exception of the countries in North and Central America, whose economies are very closely tied to that of the United States, every trading nation of any importance in the world had a dollar problem in the post-war years.

The immediate symptom of this problem was that such countries (or in certain cases, e.g. the sterling area, groups of countries) paid particular attention to their balance of payments with those countries which demanded payment in dollars, and in general discriminated against dollar imports and other payments to the dollar area. Some countries were compelled to do this, whether they desired it or not. These included countries whose trading and payments pattern tended to involve a balance of payments surplus with non-dollar countries and a deficit with dollar countries; in general it was not possible for them to convert the surplus earned in non-dollar countries to settle a dollar deficit, and they were under strong pressure to discriminate even though the existence of the discriminatory system was not necessarily in their interest. There have also been countries which were compelled to discriminate: these have included some colonial territories which have been under such close political control that they have not been able freely to follow their own economic interests. Since many of them earn a dollar surplus, they probably would not have discriminated if they had been free to choose. Yet it is in some of the colonial territories that some of the most powerful discrimination against dollar goods still persisted at the end of 1958.

These reasons explain why certain countries were, and in some cases still are, under strong pressure to discriminate, but they do not go to the heart of the problem. They do not in themselves explain why such countries have had a dollar problem imposed upon them. Still less do they explain why countries not subject to these constraints have chosen to discriminate.

There are, in fact, three levels at which we can use the expression 'dollar problem.' At the shallowest it simply means that decisions by some countries may prevent other countries from spending as much on dollar goods as they might wish. At a deeper level it describes the view of the objective conditions in the world which helps to decide whether to try to follow discriminatory or non-discriminatory policies. At the most fundamental level it describes the fact that a choice was made for discriminatory controls rather than for a 'liberal' solution. Such a choice depended on a view of objective conditions, on judgments about the desirability and political acceptability of one kind of solution rather than another, and upon the power of the countries making the decision to enforce their views.

The explanation of the existence of the post-war dollar problem therefore lies in understanding why countries that have been in a position to do so chose to discriminate and to impose a discriminatory system on others. The dollar problem, in the sense of the problem that each country had to pay special attention to its payments with the dollar area and in particular with the United States, has arisen because some countries consider that objective circumstances are such that they benefit from the existence of a discriminatory system.

The reason why they have thought this is that they believed that a solution to their balance of payments problems by non-discriminatory controls would probably have involved a very serious reduction in the volume of their trade.[8] Alternatively, a solution by means of the market mechanism would have resulted in drastic declines in their incomes:[9] an exchange depreciation would probably have caused a serious loss through adverse movements in their terms of trade, while solution through deflation of prices and/or the level of activity would have involved serious unemployment.

The initiating balance of payments problem to which this discriminatory system was a reaction took the form of the difficulties

---

[8] And consequently of their real incomes.
[9] And very probably in the volume of their trade.

that most countries outside North America had in balancing their foreign payments in the immediate post-war period. Only in America were the goods freely available which most countries needed urgently; at the same time many countries were able to earn less than before the war from North America.

For a time the problem was met by running down reserves; but that could only be temporary. A more durable solution was that of using discriminatory controls, and these were imposed with vigor. It is, in fact, reasonable to say that such controls were, in the early post-war years, the only method by which countries could maintain an approach to external equilibrium. Indeed, even they only went a part of the way, and had to be supplemented by massive special grants and loans, of which the assistance from the United States under the European Recovery Program was the most important example.

Without this assistance and discriminatory controls it is extremely doubtful whether there could have been any solution to the balance of payments difficulties of the immediate post-war period which would have been politically practicable. Solution by exchange rate changes might have been quite impossible; the necessary devaluations would almost certainly have been very large and would have induced internal inflationary pressures that would have been very hard to control. Moreover, such a solution might well have been impossible because demand elasticities were probably rather low (which might possibly have meant that devaluation would have aggravated the situation), while agreement to appreciate the currencies of deficit countries would have been hard to bring about. Solution by a reduction in the level of activity was still less conceivable. In this initial post-war period, therefore, countries had very little choice practically open to them. In the choice between discriminatory controls and extreme political troubles, few governments could have hesitated for a moment.

Gradually, however, conditions improved, and the decision about the desirability of the discriminatory system came to be more and more a real choice. The alternatives came to present themselves more and more clearly, to the countries in the discriminatory bloc, between continuing the existence of the discriminatory arrangements and allowing them to lapse and accepting any consequential losses.

In fact, of course, the choice has presented itself in more complicated forms than this. For one thing, it has not been an either/or choice; the practical choice has generally been whether to extend or contract the discriminatory system. For another thing, the choice has been deeply intermingled with the process of bargaining between the various discriminating countries to get a fairly high proportion of the benefits of discrimination and a fairly low proportion of the costs. Some countries have done very well in this bargaining process; even in the years when discrimination was widespread and powerful, there were countries which did not discriminate in their imports but which received the benefits of other people's discrimination in their export trade. Lastly, some countries have a much more powerful influence on the effective choice that is made than others; at one extreme lies Britain, for reasons that will be looked into further shortly; at the other extreme lie the countries whose political position or whose location in the network of world payments is such that they have no effective voice.

Broadly, then, the existence of the discriminatory system depended on a real choice by some of the countries in the discriminatory bloc. At existing prices, exchange rates, and levels of activity the abandonment of a system of discriminatory controls would have involved some or all of these countries in balance of payments difficulties. If effectively working discriminatory controls had been abandoned, other methods of maintaining external equilibrium would have been necessary.

In reality, what has happened through the nineteen-fifties has been that countries outside the dollar area have found it possible to abandon most of the discriminatory system. This has happened slowly and quietly, and even now it is not a process that is complete. But in the world as a whole, import restrictions designed specifically to limit imports from North America are now relatively unimportant. The dollar problem, in the sense of the need for and the decision to impose special restrictions over dollar imports, is no longer the dominant feature of the world economy that it was shortly after World War II.

SOME SUGGESTED READING

A general introduction to the topics covered in this chapter is B. Tew, *International Monetary Cooperation, 1945-1956* (London, 1957). The post-war literature of the sterling area is plentiful; mention may be made of A. R. Conan, *The Sterling Area* (London, 1952), which is mainly statistical; of P. W. Bell, *The Sterling Area in the Postwar World, 1946-1952* (London, 1956), which is mainly concerned with banking and with broad policy questions; and A. C. L. Day, *The Future of Sterling* (Oxford, 1954), which is mainly concerned with policy, as is (from a very different viewpoint) Sir Dennis Robertson, *Britain in the World Economy* (London, 1954). More specifically, European experience in the early post-war years is well treated in W. Diebold, *Trade and Payments in Western Europe* (New York, 1952); for a treatment bringing the history more up to date, written by someone who had a major role to play in policy formation, see R. Triffin, *Europe and the Money Muddle* (New Haven, 1957).

Two representative analyses of post-war international problems from an American point of view are R. F. Mikesell, *United States Economic Policy and International Relations* (New York, 1952) and J. H. Williams, *Postwar Monetary Plans and Other Essays* (New York, 1947). For two widely differing views on the post-war dollar problem, see T. Balogh, ultra-dirigiste *Dollar Crisis—Causes and Cure* (Oxford, 1949) and the ultra-liberal article of F. Machlup called 'Three Concepts of the Balance of Payments and the So-Called Dollar Problem,' *Economic Journal* (1950).

42

The Developing Situation

The Decline of the Dollar Problem

A remarkable, and an encouraging, feature of the international currency experience of the nineteen-fifties has been the decline in the seriousness of the world dollar problem. In the late 'forties and early 'fifties it dominated all discussion of international monetary problems; it may, indeed, very well come to do so again; but presently it is not at all serious. Indeed, in 1958 a great deal of opinion swung around the other way, and people started to ask whether the United States might not have difficulty in maintaining the external value of the dollar.

The explanations of this change lie in two directions. On the one hand, the countries outside North America which had formerly discriminated strongly against North American goods have come to realize that there are real disadvantages to themselves in the discriminatory system, and they have shown themselves more and more inclined to use other methods of adjustment to their international monetary difficulties. On the other hand, objective circumstances have changed greatly since the late 'forties, so that the world as a whole outside the United States [1] has had no great difficulty in maintaining a satisfactory balance in its payments with the United States; and instead many people are now asking whether the United States might not find it difficult to maintain a satisfactory balance of payments. All this switch-around in circumstances has in turn had its influence on other countries' attitudes to the use of discriminatory controls to deal with balance of payments difficulties. If the greater part of the world had some difficulty in balancing its

---

[1] Or the world as a whole outside the dollar area as a whole.

payments with the United States, it was reasonable for any country which found itself in balance of payments difficulties, whatever their cause might be, to impose particularly heavy restrictions on imports from the United States. But more recently, it has been harder for any individual country which found itself running into balance of payments difficulties to interpret them as a manifestation of a world dollar problem, it has, therefore, had much less justification in meeting its difficulties by means of discriminatory controls. We can therefore sum up by saying that sentiment has turned against the use of discriminatory controls; that objective conditions have made such controls less necessary; and that the change in objective conditions has made discrimination seem less justifiable.

There are two main reasons why a shift has taken place in attitudes toward the use of discriminatory controls, given the objective circumstances (such as the intensity of the balance of payments problem to be dealt with and the ease or difficulty of dealing with it in other ways). One is that it has come to be more widely realized that discriminatory controls (and for that matter, any controls over foreign trade) can be inefficient and wasteful. They are not easy to administer. They reduce the advantages of international division of labor. Moreover, they can easily provide a shelter behind which inefficient industries can survive; if controls are removed these industries are either compelled to become more efficient, or they disappear and the resources they have employed go into more productive uses. None of these arguments is in itself conclusive; but they do provide good reason for always approaching the use of discriminatory controls with a healthy scepticism about their usefulness.

The other reason for the switch in sentiment has been that it is difficult to achieve a satisfactory and stable apportionment of the benefits and burdens of discrimination between the countries in the discriminatory bloc. As has already been seen, it is possible to have a very large number of ways of apportioning these benefits and burdens; consequently, when doubts start to develop about the need for discrimination, they are often likely to show themselves as a belief that one's own country is taking an unfair share of the burdens and getting an inadequate share of the benefits. Except within broad limits, such assertions are very difficult to prove or disprove; but if a considerable number of countries do think they are getting a poor bargain, there are strong disruptive forces at work.

One way in which these have shown themselves in the last few years has been for some countries to abandon discrimination in their own import policies; to the extent that they do this, they reduce the benefits of the discrimination system to other members of the discriminatory bloc.

While these changes in attitudes have been important, the really significant change in the dollar problem in the 'fifties has been in the objective circumstance—and in particular of the balance of payments of the United States with the rest of the world.

In 1947 the United States had a current account surplus with the rest of the world of $11.5 billion. Other countries financed this excess of purchases from the United States over their earnings there mainly by grants and loans from the United States government of $8.9 billion and by reducing their gold reserves by $2.2 billion—as can be seen from Table 15.

By 1950, the position had improved sufficiently for the rest of the world to be able to acquire gold and short-term dollar claims from the United States; but some of this improvement and its continuation in 1951 was the result of the Korean War. Moreover, the world was able to acquire these dollars only because United States government aid was still between $3 and $3.5 billion—and this aid was still mainly designed to help other countries surmount their payments difficulties.

Since about 1952, aid has averaged around $2.2 billion, and has only to a limited extent been designed to finance the balance of payments difficulties of other countries. Ideally, to give a true view of the situation, we should put most of the aid after 1951 or so in Table 15 in the same category as gifts and pensions; it is an item enjoyed by foreign countries regardless of their balance of payments position. The money is received as a result of the political and diplomatic policies of the United States.

If this switch is made, the improvement in the balance of payments of the rest of the world vis-à-vis the United States becomes all the more remarkable. In spite of receiving only very little aid for the purpose of avoiding balance of payments difficulties, the rest of the world has been able to acquire large amounts of gold and short-term balances from the United States in every year since 1952, with the sole exception of 1957, when there were heavy abnormal expenditures in the United States largely as a result of the closing of the Suez Canal.

This swing in the dollar accounts of the rest of the world is more

TABLE 15

UNITED STATES BALANCE OF PAYMENTS, 1946-1958

(excluding military supplies and services transferred under grants)

(millions of dollars)

	1946	1947	1948	1949	1950	1951	1952	1953	1954	1955	1956	1957	1958
Exports of goods and services	+14,735	+19,737	+16,789	+15,851	+13,901	+18,863	+18,105	+17,081	+17,949	+20,003	+23,518	+26,476	+23,199
Imports of goods and services	−6,991	−8,208	−10,349	−9,702	−12,098	−15,142	−15,760	−16,644	−16,088	−17,937	−19,810	−20,707	−20,951
Balance on goods and services	+7,744	+11,529	+6,440	+6,149	+1,803	+3,721	+2,345	+437	+1,861	+2,066	+3,708	+5,769	+2,248
U.S. private capital	−413	−987	−906	−553	−1,265	−1,068	−1,158	−369	−1,619	−1,211	−2,980	−3,211	−2,844
Foreign capital (except short-term)	−347	−98	−172	+119	+994	−477	+443	+124	+252	+875	+407	+309	+55
Gifts, pensions, etc.	−625	−715	−617	−630	−523	−457	−545	−617	−615	−585	−337	−694	−707
Balance of payments surplus which was financed by:	+6,359	+9,729	+4,745	+5,085	+1,009	+1,719	+1,085	−425	−121	+1,145	+98	+2,173	−1,248
U.S. Government grants and loans[1]	−5,298	−8,866	−4,918	−5,649	−3,640	−3,191	−2,380	−2,055	−1,554	−2,211	−2,521	−2,576	−2,577
Gold transfers (U.S. purchases (−))	−623	−2,162	−1,530	−164	+1,743	−53	−379	+1,161	+298	+41	−306	−798	+2,275
Changes in short-term liabilities to foreigners	−633	+363	+524	−47	+918	+1,055	+1,169	+1,023	+1,210	+579	+1,437	+325	+1,109
Errors and omissions	+195	+936	+1,179	+775	−30	+470	+505	+296	+167	+446	+602	+876	+441

Payments to the U.S.—positive; payments by the U.S.—negative.
[1] Excludes military supplies and services.

remarkable when it is remembered that in the late 'forties discriminatory controls were suppressing a great deal of foreign demand for United States goods, whereas the amount now suppressed is quite small—a very rough guess might be an amount under $0.5 billion a year, and possibly well under that figure. There are many reasons for the swing, and it is hard to assess the relative importance of each of them. But ultimately they all stem from one set of causes —namely the remarkable post-war recovery and growth of production in Europe and in the other parts of the world which had been most closely affected by the war, and the accompanying increase in the competitiveness of producers in those countries compared with producers in the United States.

The recovery of production in foreign countries, and its continuing expansion to levels far higher than those achieved before the war, has meant that these countries are no longer heavily dependent on the United States for basic supplies needed to keep their economies working. In the early post-war years, large parts of the European economy would have broken down completely if supplies of coal, wheat, and other basic necessities had not been available from the United States. In the last few years, this dependence has been much reduced; supplies of these commodities are still bought from the United States, especially in years when European activity is particularly high or when harvests have been bad there; but this is simply a market of normal commercial relationships rather than the difference between life and death.

The recovery of production has also affected foreign demand for less essential imports from the United States. In the early post-war years there seemed to be an almost insatiable demand in the rest of the world for United States manufactures—including both consumer goods and investment goods. Gradually as production has grown and as European countries have been able to develop new products and new techniques, this demand has fallen to manageable proportions. Most of the primary-producing countries of the world now allow United States goods to enter as freely as European —and in the great majority of cases, European producers find they can very well hold their own in competition with the United States. Again, those European countries (such as Germany and Belgium) which allow equally free entry to United States and other European goods find that United States goods show no tendency to swamp the market.

The other important aspect of the increased competitiveness of foreign producers is their growing successes in the United States market. The growth of sales of small European cars is only one particularly dramatic example of a tendency that has been very powerful in the last few years. This is not to deny that there is a strong case for a much more liberal United States tariff policy, and a willingness to tolerate much bigger balance of payments deficits than in recent years. But at the same time it must be accepted that the United States balance of payments now has something of the characteristics which should be expected of a good creditor nation.

There can be little doubt that one of the main reasons why the rest of the world has been reasonably successful in its competition with the United States in the last few years has been the competitive advantage given to most foreign countries by the exchange rate adjustments of the fall of 1949. At that time, sterling was devalued sharply in relation to the dollar, from the old rate of $4.03 to £1 to a new rate of $2.80 to £1. This devaluation was the signal for a world-wide adjustment of exchange rates; all the sterling area currencies (except Pakistan's) immediately followed sterling and most other currencies followed sterling part or the whole of the way. The immediate effects of these changes were not very obvious; they were hidden first by the effects of the recovery from the minor United States recession of 1949 and then, within nine months, by the disturbances caused by the Korean War. Moreover, part of the competitive advantages to Britain and other European countries came to be wiped out by a faster rate of inflation there than in the United States, some of which was undoubtedly induced by the devaluation; moreover, European countries were not able to take full advantage of the price competitiveness because suppressed inflation meant that many of the delivery dates offered by European producers were very long delayed. All the same, the indications are that the devaluations have had the effects that might be expected in circumstances when the demand elasticities were at least moderate in size; as we saw in Chapter 31, the demand elasticities are probably somewhat larger in the long run than in the short, so it is to be expected that devaluation will take some time to have its full favorable effects. But comparing the situation in the mid-'fifties with pre-war, we have all the changes that might be expected from a successful devaluation; there has been a big rise in the volume of Europe's exports to North America, a reduction in Europe's dependence on imports from

North America, and a large increase in intra-European trade as European countries have bought more from one another and relatively less from abroad.

The Convertibility of Sterling

All these changes that have led to a reduction in the intensity of the dollar problem have come about quite slowly and often almost imperceptibly. Correspondingly, the movement toward sterling convertibility, which is one of the most important indicators of the absence of a serious dollar problem, has been equally slow. Sterling is said to be 'convertible' for any given holder when he is free to convert it into any other currency for any purpose he likes. The most likely form of conversion is into dollars, simply because dollars and sterling are by far the most important international currencies. During the war and the first post-war decade, holders of sterling were not, in general, given free rights of convertibility by the British authorities.[2] This meant that a country earning or holding more sterling than it wanted was not free to buy dollars with it and thus buy goods from the United States. This compelled many countries to discriminate against dollar goods, because their trade pattern tended to show a balance of payments surplus with Britain or with the sterling area as a whole, and a deficit with dollar countries. For example, the traditional position of London was that of supplier of dollars to continental European countries in exchange for their surplus sterling earnings.

All this meant that a choice on the part of the British government to re-establish sterling convertibility for any particular group of countries would go a long way toward removing the incentive to those countries to discriminate. Sterling convertibility would inevitably be accompanied by erosion of the post-war discriminatory system.

Shortly after the Conservative Government came to power in late 1951, there was serious consideration of a rapid restoration of sterling convertibility. To have done this sharply would probably have led

---

[2] The central banks of the independent sterling area countries were in law given the right; but by gentlemen's agreement they used it with great restraint and discriminated strongly against imports from the United States, Canada and other dollar area countries.

to big disturbances, because the discriminatory system was very powerful at the time. In the event, the risk was not taken, and it was decided to move more slowly and cautiously. The movement in practice has been quite slow, and, generally speaking, each step has only been taken when it seemed fairly safe, so that sterling convertibility has done no more than move in step with the decline of the dollar problem, rather than dramatically providing the opportunity for its destruction.

The most important single step was that taken in February, 1955, when the British authorities announced that they would henceforward operate in the market for transferable sterling.

As we saw in the last chapter, transferable sterling was, in the late 'forties and early 'fifties, a kind of sterling with limited convertibility. By the mid-'fifties, practically every country other than those in the sterling and dollar areas was a member of the transferable accounts system. This meant that anyone in those countries who earned sterling could use it to make payments to any country in the world other than one in the dollar area. This made world payments appreciably more free than they would otherwise have been. For a long time, however, the British authorities did their best to prevent the use of transferable sterling for payments to the dollar area. These controls were never fully effective, and 'black' markets developed in a number of financial centers outside the sterling area (notably in Zurich and New York), where transferable sterling could be bought into dollars at a price a good deal below the official sterling-dollar rate. Gradually the British authorities abandoned the attempt to prevent funds from flowing into these markets. Then in February, 1955, the major step was taken of announcing that in the future, the British authorities would themselves operate in these markets for transferable sterling. From that time up to the end of 1958, the British authorities always bought transferable sterling with dollars from the British reserves, whenever the transferable sterling rate showed signs of falling more than about 1 per cent below the official sterling-dollar rate. This meant that any holder of transferable sterling was free to use it to buy dollars at a very small premium of about 1 per cent—assuming, of course, that his own exchange control would allow it.

The significance of all this was that in the period 1955-58 transferable sterling was more or less fully convertible into dollars. Some holders of transferable sterling may have been unwilling to pay a premium even as low as 1 per cent; to that extent convertibility was not fully effective for the countries in the transferable account area —but the truth is that sterling convertibility was, in 1955, very nearly fully established for those countries.

The final stage of this movement came at the end of December, 1958, when the British Government announced that all sterling currency held by residents of countries outside the sterling area would be freely convertible into any other currency including dollars, at the official exchange rate. The *de facto* situation of 1955-58 now became a *de jure* situation of full formal convertibility, and the 1 per cent difference between the transferable rate and the official dollar-sterling rate disappeared.

Sterling area residents do not, however, yet enjoy full convertibility. All the same, in the period 1955-58, convertibility became fairly fully established for countries in the sterling area—at least as far as concerns current account transactions by the politically independent members. The monetary authorities in these sterling area countries have always had formal rights of convertibility, subject to a gentlemen's agreement not to misuse these rights. Quietly but steadily, the gentlemen's agreement is becoming more and more laxly interpreted, and in many of these countries, dollars are now as freely available to importers as sterling or continental European currencies. Britain itself has also moved in the same direction— nowadays only a limited and diminishing range of goods is subject to strict dollar import control. In some of the colonies, on the other hand, dollar discrimination is still fairly powerful, but that position is unlikely to last much longer, partly because Britain cannot long deny rights to the colonies which her own citizens enjoy, and partly because nearly all the important colonies will very soon be completely independent politically.

The controls over dollar payments that do remain throughout the sterling area apply to capital transactions, such as the purchase of dollar stocks from the United States. In practice, these restrictions were for a long time ineffective, and large purchases were made through the Persian Gulf sheikdom of Kuwait, which is in the sterling area but which has no effective exchange controls. Measures were taken in the middle of 1957 to close this leak. Subsequently the purchases ceased, but it is quite possible that some new leak may develop when Wall Street booms again or dollar securities seem an attractive political hedge for sterling area residents.

In summary, therefore, the position is that sterling convertibility has been fully restored for non-sterling area residents and more or less fully restored within the sterling area for most holders and for most purposes. There are two main reasons why the final steps have not been taken. One is that Britain's reserves as an international banker are disturbingly inadequate; her short-term sterling liabilities to other countries are around three times as large as her reserves. The other is that there is still a lurking fear that there may be a resurgence of the dollar problem.

The Future of the Dollar Problem

When we look at the future of the dollar problem, we find a great deal of room for disagreement. There are many people who think that future developments of the world economy are likely to involve conditions of trade and payments between North America and the rest of the world which will provide strong temptation to other countries to follow discriminatory policies. On the other hand, the recent experience of United States balance of payments deficit has made many people come to believe, perhaps prematurely, that in the future the main difficulties will be those of the United States.

One version held by the people who are pessimistic about the ability of the rest of the world to balance its payments with the United States, is the view that there are secular forces in United States economic development which are tending to increase the strain on the balance of payments or the terms of trade of the rest of the world, or of significant parts of it. For example, increases in productivity in the United States may be concentrated in the industries producing import goods, and there may be no corresponding increases in productivity in the industries producing those goods outside the United States. Again, rises in incomes in the United States may involve relatively small additional expenditure on imported goods, whereas rises in incomes abroad may involve big increases in demand for United States goods. Again, there may be a tendency for particularly big increases in United States productivity in industries producing certain kinds of goods, which are closely competitive with the main exports of an important group of countries in the rest of the world (e.g. finished manufactures, which involve competition with Europe). If these rises in United States productivity are not shared abroad, the group of countries which is competing in exporting tends to lose exports and suffer balance of payments pressures, or terms of trade losses if the balance of payments pressures are met by exchange depreciation, etc. This group of countries may try to retaliate by discriminating; if it is in a sufficiently powerful position it may organize an extensive discriminatory bloc against the United States.

The other main version supported by the people who foresee dollar problems in the future is the view that the United States economy is particularly unstable, and that when there are downswings in the level of activity in the United States, the rest of the world suffers seriously because of its loss of exports to the United States. Again, it is suggested, there may be a strong incentive to meet this by discriminating against the United States, particularly at times when trade is depressed there.

There is still good reason to think that even a minor United States recession could do a great deal of harm to the economy of the rest of the world; and there can be no doubt that a major recession in the United States could have catastrophic effects. But the experience of the 'fifties has been that minor recessions do not inevitably lead to serious trouble for other countries. In both the 1953-1954 and the 1957-1958 recessions the balance of payments of the rest of the world vis-à-vis the United States had sufficient underlying strength for the harmful effects of the recession on their balance of payments to be fairly easily absorbed. Moreover, it does seem quite plausible on the basis of the experience of these two recessions, that structural changes have taken place in the United States economy which mean that a recession of a given magnitude now has less sharply adverse effects on the rest of the world—for example the marginal suppliers of certain raw materials are now perhaps in the United States rather than abroad.

It is, nevertheless, questionable whether it is correct to extrapolate from the recent favorable experience of the rest of the world and say that in the future it is the United States which will find itself in perennial payments difficulties, rather than overseas countries. The way in which the pessimistic forecasts made a few years ago, about the inevitability of a world dollar problem, have proved to be very questionable should also make one cautious about extrapolating recent trends indefinitely into the future. The fact is that there is a good deal of self-correction in the international payments system; just as the improvement in Europe's competitiveness has helped deal with the dollar problem, so the basic economic strength and adaptability of the United States economy is likely to belie predictions that the United States balance of payments situation must inevitably deteriorate over time—or even that the United States will be compelled to follow restrictive policies (of internal deflation or increased import restrictions) in order to balance her external payments.

The most sensible position to take, therefore, is to be agnostic about the future of the balance of payments position between the United States and the rest of the world, but to be more optimistic about the chances of avoiding serious disequilibrium than seemed reasonable a few years ago. We must be prepared for the possibility that discrimination and the dollar problem may once again dominate the international currency scene, just as we must be prepared for the chance that the United States might find herself in serious deficit—but we need not be sure that things will turn out so badly. For the first post-war decade, the world was dominated by the dollar problem to an extent that very few people had predicted. But there is a fair chance that things will be much more manageable in the next ten years.

The International Monetary Fund

One of the major consequences of the unexpected seriousness of the post-war dollar problem was that the plans made at the end of the war for organizing the international monetary system were very slow in coming into any effective sort of existence. Of the new institutions planned at that time, the International Monetary Fund was to be the most important. In practice, it had relatively little influence on events in the post-war decade, and it is unlikely that it will ever work exactly in the way intended by its founders; but its significance has increased substantially since about 1955 or 1956.

The Fund was established [3] at Bretton Woods in 1944 by international agreement and operates in Washington as a Specialized Agency of the United Nations. The background to the thinking which established the Fund was the currency experience of the 'thirties; on the negative side the background was one of fears of the harmful

---

[3] Along with its twin, the International Bank for Reconstruction and Development.

effects of fluctuating exchange rates (by causing general uncertainty and provoking speculative capital flights of hot money), and fears of competitive exchange depreciation; on the positive side, the background consisted of beliefs in the virtues of a liberal international economic system, in the need for maintenance of internal balance in each country, and in the need for explicit international monetary co-operation. In these respects, particularly with regard to exchange rate policy and explicit co-operation, the forerunner of the Fund can be seen to be the Tripartite Monetary Agreement of 1936.

Some of the earliest schemes for international monetary arrangements, which never got beyond the stage of paper dreams in Washington, bore still closer family resemblance to the arrangements of the late 'thirties. The Fund was regarded as an international correlate for the national exchange stabilization funds; superior to it there was to be an International Central Bank which was to deal with the generally feared problem of lack of effective demand in the world. These plans never reached maturity—it was soon realized that national sovereignty had to be accepted—but they influenced the final form taken by the arrangements.

In the final version the intention still remained that the International Monetary Fund should work alongside a number of other organizations concerned with economic matters. Of these, the International Bank for Reconstruction and Development survives and has done valuable work in the field of international investment. Its resources consist of subscriptions by member countries, nine-tenths payable in each country's own currency and one-tenth in gold or dollars; of these subscriptions, only one-fifth has actually been called up, and the rest remains uncalled, as a reserve. The Bank can lend its own resources, it can increase them by issuing long-term bonds to private lenders, and it can guarantee loans made by governments or private lenders to suitable borrowers. Its loans or guarantees are made in connection with reconstruction and development schemes which the Bank thinks worth while; in making up its mind on borrowers' creditworthiness the Bank has done valuable work in investigating the economies of underdeveloped countries.

The other major organ, the International Trade Organization, which was intended to organize a world with few tariff barriers, with strictly limited use of import controls and with full employment in each country, was stillborn. It was succeeded by the General Agreement on Tariffs and Trade (GATT), which has done valuable but limited work in helping negotiate tariff reductions or the freezing of tariffs at existing levels.

The principles upon which the International Monetary Fund were based can be summarized quite briefly. It was intended to form part of the institutional framework of a liberal world economic system, in which there were (in general) to be no exchange controls over current payments (although controls over capital movements were to be allowed). Exchange rates were to be pegged and (again, in general) altered only after consultation with the Fund. Exchange rate alterations were only to take place when a country's payments position was in 'fundamental disequilibrium.' Finally, additional reserves of international currency were brought into being which were to be made available to countries in balance of payments difficulties.

The Fund system can be regarded as an attempt to combine some of the virtues of the gold standard system and of the system of the 'thirties, while avoiding some of the disadvantages of both. By establishing stable exchange rates it was hoped to reap the advantage enjoyed under the gold standard, that speculators did not speculate against existing exchange rates, because they had confidence that they would be maintained. By this means, and by controls over capital movements, it was hoped to avoid the hot money movements that had been so disturbing in the 'thirties. Again, the provision for international consultation about exchange rate changes derived from a fear of a repetition of 'competitive depreciation'—that is, the cycle of exchange depreciations that took place through the 'thirties.

On the other side it was hoped to avoid the disadvantage of the gold standard system, that the adjustment process depended upon a period of internal disequilibrium in the adjusting countries. Here, one of the features of the 'thirties was to be followed—namely, a high degree of insulation of the internal economic system from external changes. The internal level of activity in each country was not to vary under the pressure of external forces. Instead, each country was to maintain a high and stable level of employment.

Even if every country in such a system successfully maintains internal balance, its satisfactory working must depend on the existence of large and widely distributed reserves of international liquidity. Since in the Fund system exchange rate changes come only infrequently, and then after fundamental disequilibrium in a country's balance of payments have been diagnosed and internationally agreed, it is clear that quite a large loss of reserves may occur before anything is done to correct the situation. In the meantime the other corrective forces at work are weak; internal levels of activity and of prices are held constant, and direct controls are only to be used within agreed limits.[4]

It seems clear, then, that the Fund system demands much bigger reserves of international currency than either the system of the 'thirties or the gold standard system. The system of the 'thirties had greater flexibility through continuous changes in exchange rates; the gold standard had flexibility because internal balance in the participating countries was not considered to be essential.

The Fund has gone a little way toward provision of additional liquidity by acting as a sort of mutual aid fund. Each member has contributed a 'quota,' whose size is related to the country's economic importance; this quota also determines the country's voting rights in deciding Fund policy. Three-quarters of the quota is contributed in the country's own currency and one-quarter in gold or dollars. Each country can buy, with its own currency, any other country's currency from this pool. These purchases may not (in general) exceed one-quarter of a country's quota in a year, and are not (again in general) available automatically. Moreover, total accumulated purchases that are permissible are also limited: the Fund will not hold an amount of a country's currency greater than twice its quota. Charges are made for these services, as a percentage of the amount of purchases outstanding; the percentage increases, the larger the amount of purchases outstanding and the longer they are outstanding. There is, therefore, an incentive to repurchase your own currency from the Fund with the aid of foreign currency; the assistance is only temporary.

The technical method by which a pattern of fixed exchange rates was established in the Fund system was the declaration by governments of each currency's 'par value.' This measures a currency's price in terms of gold, and so relates it to other currencies whose

---

[4] How wide those limits should be has never been really clear. A strict interpretation of the Fund Agreement could imply that the limits would be very narrow; but it is probable that most countries (with the exception of the United States) regarded the *temporary* use of direct controls as being both legitimate and likely to be necessary.

par values have been fixed. Once a par value is established, it should, according to the Fund agreement, only be altered [5] if a country is in 'fundamental disequilibrium.' The meaning of this has never been defined, but it seems reasonable to suppose that a country would be in this state if it had a persistent balance of payments deficit which seemed unlikely to reverse itself, or if it could maintain its foreign accounts in balance only by the use of direct controls over current transactions or by extensive unemployment.

Generally speaking, a country may change its exchange rate (i.e. its par value) only after consultation with the Fund. There is, however, a dispensation that changes of up to a total amount of 10 per cent from the original par value have to be notified, but the Fund cannot object, while for a further 10 per cent the Fund is given only seventy-two hours in which to express its views. The exact meaning of the clauses making these provisions in the charter is not at all clear; this is probably unimportant since very many currencies are already at least 20 per cent away from their original par value, and in any case, consultation has not proved effective.

These provisions for exchange rate changes and for temporary assistance from the Fund were designed to deal with most cases of balance of payments deficits that could not be met from a country's own reserves or from its power to borrow from other countries. In one important set of cases, however, another weapon is permissible: these arise under the 'scarce currency' provisions of the Fund's charter.

One case of scarcity of a particular currency is that when the Fund observes a *general* scarcity of a currency; in such a case the Fund can make a report and recommendations. An appropriate subject might well have been the post-war dollar problem, but in fact no such report was made.

More important is the case of *technical* scarcity of a currency, which arises when the Fund's holdings of a particular currency have fallen to low levels, because so many other countries have made purchases of it with their own currencies and have not yet repurchased their own currencies from the Fund. In such circumstances the Fund can declare the currency formally 'scarce.' When this has

---

[5] Apart from permission for variations within the narrow range of 1 per cent on either side of the fixed rate.

been done, other countries [6] are entitled to impose temporary discriminatory controls over payments to the country whose currency is 'scarce.' [7]

The inclusion of this clause represents a realization that circumstances may arise when the solution of balance of payments problems by occasional exchange rate changes is not appropriate. The circumstances in which the use of the clause has usually been envisaged have been those of an American slump, against which the rest of the world is trying to defend itself. Since such discrimination harms the country whose currency is scarce, it puts it under some pressure to carry out policies to improve the situation; the clause does, in fact, reflect admission of the British view in the Bretton Woods negotiations that external disequilibrium imposes obligations on the creditor countries as well as on the debtors. The clause in effect amounts to saying that controls may be used by all (or at least, several) countries against one, although they may not be used by one country to correct its position *vis-à-vis* all the rest. Controls are not permitted for correcting disequilibrium if the shortcomings are your own, but it may be possible to use them to correct difficulties arising from the shortcomings of someone else. A basic assumption of the International Monetary Fund system is that each country will try to maintain internal balance; insofar as some countries fail to do this and fall into unemployment, there is this provision for seeing that other countries suffer relatively little.

It may also be noted that the International Monetary Fund Charter also allowed controls over current payments in the post-war transition period. This was intended to end by 1952, but in fact such controls were still very powerfully enforced at that time. In the first decade of its operations, the Fund suffered from the fact that post-war difficulties have been much bigger and lasted much longer than was expected, and that too few countries were willing to regard the liberal aims of the Fund as being matters of sufficient priority. Moreover, the post-war difficulty that was most feared in

---

[6] Whether all countries or merely those in balance of payments difficulties remains uncertain; an important political question masquerades as a legal doubt. The United States appears to prefer the narrow interpretation, and most other countries the broad.

[7] In the International Trade Organization Charter there was a similar and corresponding escape clause which has been carried over into the GATT.

1944 (namely, a world-wide depression) is one of the few economic difficulties that the world has not suffered since the war.

It was realized at an early date that the resources of the Fund were inadequate to help European countries with their balance of payments problems in the immediate post-war period. When the European Recovery Program (Marshall Aid) was introduced, the Fund announced that its resources would not be available to participants.[8] This meant that the Fund avoided having most of its resources tied up in loans to Europe; on the other hand, it has meant that it had little hand in dealing with the biggest international financial problems of the post-war decade, and has instead spent a great deal of time on minor and peripheral problems.

In addition to these difficulties arising from the environment in which the Fund had to work in the post-war years, serious criticisms have been made of its structure. One criticism is that the Fund structure regards all currencies as legally equal. No special provision is made for any currencies which are extensively used internationally. It has frequently been argued that the Fund would have been more successful if it had followed the 'key currency' principle, by explicit recognition in its constitution of the nodal position of the dollar and of sterling.

This legal equality of all currencies, together with the desire to give all countries full representation, has led to an unwieldy administrative structure. It has also meant that the provisions for consultation before exchange rate changes are introduced have proved to be a dead letter. In particular, it led to the unwillingness of the British authorities to have any effective consultation with the Fund before devaluing sterling in September, 1949, because it was feared that leakages of the secret would have occurred because so many national representatives on the Executive Board would have had to participate; and speculation against the pound might have been encouraged through these leakages of information.

The absence of effective discussion before the exchange rate changes of 1949 represents the Fund's most glaring failure. Before that there had been others, for example, the adoption of multiple exchange rates by France in 1948-1949, and the refusal of Canada

---

[8] This decision is believed to have been imposed against the wishes of many members, largely through the power of the weighted vote of the United States.

to prohibit gold sales at a price higher than her parity, followed by her adoption of a flexible exchange rate.

The failure of the Fund to do what was hoped of it goes much deeper than any of these individual failures. In origins it goes back to the fact that the two main protagonists at Bretton Woods (Britain and the United States) never really came to full agreement about how the Fund should work. In particular, the British view favored, and has continued to favor, much more automatic working of the Fund provisions than the United States, and the British have been much more worried about the need for applying scarce currency provisions.

The Fund went a considerable way toward meeting the criticism that its resources were not automatically available to members who were in need, by means of a number of administrative changes made in 1954-1955. Most of these were concerned with the power of countries to buy foreign currencies from the Fund, and were designed to reduce administrative delays. For example, the Fund is now willing to enter into 'standby arrangements' with certain countries to help give support to their currencies when they become convertible, without any further discussion.

Subsequently, in the Suez crisis of 1956 and in the payments crises that affected Britain, France, and India in 1957, the Fund's resources were made available to help these countries through their difficulties. In turn, these operations have shown up one of the major inadequacies of the Fund—that its resources (of which the gold and dollar element, amounting to about $3.8 billion, is the most important) are almost certainly inadequate to deal with a major international strain, unless very strong controls were allowed under the scarce currency provisions. The resources made available in 1956-1957 to these three countries absorbed about $1 billion (or 26 per cent) of the Fund's total gold and dollar resources. Even in 1945, the Fund's resources were by no means overgenerous; and the subsequent rise in prices and in the volume of world trade has meant that the Fund can only make a relatively limited contribution to the world's supply of internationally acceptable liquid assets.

A good deal has now been done toward dealing with this problem as a result of the decision made at the 1958 meeting of the Fund in New Delhi proposing that member nations' quotas should be increased by 50 per cent. This decision, and the simultaneous decision to increase the lending resources of the International Bank, represented a welcome, albeit belated, recognition of the handicaps under which these agencies had worked as a result of the serious limitation on their financial resources. There is still, however, no explicit recognition that it will be necessary to increase the quotas as the value of world trade rises.

The major question which remains concerning the future of the Fund system concerns the structure of exchange rates. Opinion on exchange rate changes has, in the last few years, been sharply polarized. The original IMF proposals for infrequent step changes in exchange rates did not go to either of the extremes of permanently fixed rates or of perpetual fluctuations. But now there is, on the one hand, an important group of people who argue that exchange rates should be much more flexible than they are, and on the other there is a group which would prefer even greater rigidity.

The supporters of flexibility point to the stabilizing virtues of a free market, to the inadequacy of international currency reserves, and to the fact that exchange controls and the fixed exchange rate system have not succeeded in preventing movements of speculative capital. These movements can occur in many ways; and when speculators become convinced that a step change in an exchange rate is imminent, there is a very strong incentive to move funds: a movement out of a currency which is about to depreciate assures a certainty of a considerable profit.

Not all people are convinced that the existence of these speculative movements proves that exchange rates should be flexible; it is also widely held that they indicate the dangers of any exchange rate changes.[9] For example, the belief that sterling might devalue and that the mark might appreciate in the fall of 1957 led to very heavy speculation against sterling, partly by movement of funds and partly by delaying commercial payments due in sterling, in the hope that they might be made later on more favorable terms, while on the other hand commercial payments from the sterling area to other countries were speeded up. The lesson drawn by many people is that exchange rates should once again be regarded as completely immutable—that something like a 'new gold standard' should be established.

Certainly the actions of many foreign governments suggest that

---

[9] Apart from the narrow swings already permitted—e.g. between £1 = $2.78 and $2.82 for the sterling-dollar rate.

some such ideas are in their minds. In the fall of 1957 both the British and the West German governments were completely unwilling to change their dollar exchange rates, although there was a strong case for altering one or the other if the attempt was being made seriously to operate the IMF adjustable peg system; this was a good occasion for a step change. But there is one major reason why a 'new gold standard' system is hardly likely to work indefinitely —it is simply that there are fairly narrow limits within which any modern government will find it expedient to abandon internal balance and allow excessive unemployment in order to maintain a given exchange rate. So far this problem has not come up, because the countries which have had balance of payments difficulties in recent years have also had fairly fast rates of inflation. The balance of payments difficulties have, in fact, been largely the result of the inflation. But the important point is that balance of payments difficulties can arise, even if inflation is no faster than in other countries or even if it is stopped completely. For example, productivity may rise more slowly than abroad, so that a country does not have up-to-date goods for export; or again, tastes may be such that rising real incomes in one country, as productivity rises there, may lead to much larger rises in its demand for imports than the rise in the demand for its exports induced by rising prosperity abroad.

The Uncertainties of the Future

At this point, we must be brought to a stop by the uncertainties of the future. The aim of these last four chapters has been to consider how the various possible ways of trying to attain internal and external equilibrium have been combined in the past. How they will be combined in the future remains to be seen. All the same, the experience of the last few years can provide a few pointers.

The really important lessons are two. Firstly, it is impossible to maintain a reasonable degree of internal and external balance without a great deal of conscious management. Automatic mechanisms are not enough in themselves—although wise policy will make conscious and deliberate use of them. Secondly, the process of management will involve a high degree of eclecticism, using a mixture of methods of control, in proportions which change substantially over time.

It is reasonable to see the intended form of the International Monetary Fund system as a part of this movement toward eclecticism; it attempted to combine the virtues of the gold standard and of the system of the 'thirties, without their disadvantages. Whether the Fund system will ever come into full operation remains to be seen; but whatever happens, the Fund's charter is in line with the trend toward the use of several different methods of control, instead of depending solely on a single set of simple rules. Moreover, the Fund approach paid full attention to the need that is generally accepted today for maintaining both external and internal balance.

The fact is that the satisfaction of this dual need (together with the satisfaction of all the other needs and political pressures that have not been our concern in this book) is not possible by following a simple body of rules: the world economy is too complicated. The instruments that can be used are many and varied; the choice between them depends both on judgments about economic forces, and on judgments about what is desirable from a political point of view. In detail, therefore, prediction is impossible. But it can be reasonably expected that if the major countries of the world do contrive to maintain internal and external economic balance, it will be by a subtle, complicated, varying, and well-informed combination of the various instruments outlined in this book. To this need for well-informed action, the preceding chapters are dedicated.

SOME SUGGESTED READING

A moderately pessimistic analysis of the future of the dollar problem is to be found in G. D. MacDougall, *The World Dollar Problem* (London, 1957). At the moment, majority opinion (particularly in the United States) is that his analysis is too pessimistic; only time can tell. A valuable theoretical discussion of the relationship between productivity and the dollar problem is in H. G. Johnson, 'Increasing Productivity, Income-Price Trends and the Trade Balance' in the *Economic Journal* (1954). The history of the move toward the re-establishment of sterling convertibility is found in R. F. Harrod, *The Pound Sterling 1951-1958* (Princeton, 1958) and in A. Shonfield's *Britain's Postwar Economic Policy* (Harmondsworth, England, 1958). For a more orthodox discussion of the devaluations of 1949 than found in this pamphlet of Harrod's, see J. J. Polak's article 'The Contribution of the 1949 Devaluations to the Solution of Europe's Dollar Problem' in *IMF Staff Papers* (1951). European developments in general are well discussed in R. Triffin, *Europe and the Money Muddle* (New Haven, 1957). For an excellent analysis of the negotiations leading up to the foundation of the IMF, of the intentions of its founders, and of the reasons for its early failures, see R. F. Gardner, *Sterling-Dollar Diplomacy* (Oxford, 1956). The idea of a new gold standard is discussed in F. W. Paish's article 'The New Gold Standard' in the *Transactions of the Manchester Statistical Society* (1957).

* Mathematical Appendix

No knowledge of mathematics is necessary to understand this book or to follow up the ideas in it. Nevertheless it is useful to see the derivation of the formulas which summed up the arguments that were expressed verbally in the text. This applies particularly to the somewhat complex cases discussed in Part VI, and this appendix will show how they can be derived.

The simple multiplier formula which appears in Part II is merely the sum of an infinite geometric progression in accordance with the rule that

$$1 + (1 - s) + (1 - s)^2 + (1 - s)^3 + \cdots = \frac{1}{s} \quad \text{when } s < 1.$$

An alternative proof of this simple multiplier case, which is the basis of all the proofs of more complicated cases given below, is simply

$$\Delta S = \delta V,$$

$$\Delta S = s\Delta Y,$$

$$\therefore \quad \Delta Y = \frac{\delta V}{s}.$$

In these formulas, S represents saving, V investment,[1] Y income, and s is the marginal propensity to save, and Δ represents the induced change in the relevant item, while δ represents a small initiating disturbance. The first equation follows from the definitions of saving and investment and from the assumptions of the simple economy in

---

[1] V used to represent investment, because I is used later to represent imports; the more common notation is to use I to represent investment.

Part II. The second equation states the dependence of changes in saving on changes in income.

This proof can easily be extended to the cases considered in Chapter 16, where government expenditure and taxation enter into the analysis. The extension can be shown as follows:

$$\Delta S + \Delta T = \delta V + \Delta G,$$

where T is taxation and G is government expenditure on currently produced goods and services. This equation follows directly from an extension of the income identity; this extension can be expressed verbally by saying income not spent by households on goods and services $(S + T)$ is identical in amount with output not sold to households $(V + G)$. To continue the proof:

$$\Delta S = s(1 - t)\Delta Y.$$

This merely states that households increase saving by s times the post-tax increase in their income, where t is the proportion of an increase in income paid in tax.[2]

$$\Delta G = g\Delta T,$$

where g is the proportion of an increase in tax receipts which the government spends on currently produced goods and services.[2] Finally, we assume

$$\Delta T = t\Delta Y.$$

Combination of these four equations gives the result

$$\Delta Y = \frac{\delta V}{s(1 - t) + t(1 - g)},$$

which is the multiplier formula on p. 246.

Where the initiating disturbance is a change in something other than investment, the formula is correspondingly modified. For example, when the disturbance is a change in government expenditure on goods and services (δG) the first of these four equations becomes

$$\Delta S + \Delta T = \Delta G + \delta G$$

and the equation becomes

---

[2] As with s, both t and g are assumed not to be greater than 1.

$$\Delta Y = \frac{\delta G}{s(1 - t) + t(1 - g)},$$

which is the formula on p. 250, fn. 9.

If the disturbance is a change in taxation of δT, the position is a little more complicated. Such a change also, in itself, involves a disturbance in the level of saving of $-s\delta T$. The total initiating disturbance is, therefore, $(1 - s)\delta T$, so that the first equation is

$$(1 - s)\delta T + \Delta S + \Delta T = \Delta G$$

and the solution becomes

$$\Delta Y = -\frac{(1 - s)\delta T}{s(1 - t) + t(1 - g)},$$

which is the formula on p. 250, fn. 11.

When the change in government expenditure on currently produced goods and services is $(1 - h)$ times the total change in government expenditure $(\delta G')$, the next to the last solution becomes

$$\Delta Y = \frac{(1 - h).\delta G'}{s(1 - t) + t(1 - g)}.$$

To deal with the formulas in Part VI, a rather more complicated analysis is needed. As far as all the formulas in Chapters 30, 32, and 33 are concerned they can be derived from a set of equations representing the changes in the equilibrium situation in our two-country world after various kinds of disturbance have occurred.

Since a considerable number of symbols is needed to represent quite a simple system, careful organization is necessary.[3] The following arrangement is used:

(a) Suffixes are used as earlier; h represents the home country and f represents the foreign country.

(b) Capital letters represent the absolute magnitude of some variable before disturbance appears—e.g. Q_h is the total quantity of goods produced at home in the initial situation.

---

[3] The notation and general approach used is a modification and simplification of that employed by J. E. Meade in the *Mathematical Supplement* to his *Balance of Payments* (*The Theory of International Economic Policy*, vol. i, Oxford, 1951). Apart from several changes in the symbols used, the main differences from his terminology are in the definitions of the marginal propensity to import and the elasticity of demand for imports; the latter is defined in the conventional manner. In each case, the linkage with Meade's usage is shown.

(c) Small letters represent (in general) changes in some magnitude which arise as part of the adjustment from one position of equilibrium to another—e.g. q_h is the change in home output between the equilibrium positions before and after a disturbance.

(d) There are two exceptions to the rule in section (c); m and s represent the marginal propensities to import and to save, as used in the main body of the book.

(e) A bar above a letter represents the measurement of a price— e.g. $\bar{q}_h$ is the change in the price of home output in the adjustment between two equilibrium situations.

(f) A letter s prefixed to a small letter represents that the change is a spontaneous disturbance to the system, arising from causes not defined within our system—e.g. $^s i_h$ represents a spontaneous change in the imports of the home country. Our analysis will be concerned with the reaction of our system to these spontaneous changes. Similarly, a letter i prefixed to a small letter represents an induced change, arising from causes within our system.

The symbols with which we are concerned are the following:

Q_h is the quantity of goods produced at home in the initial situation.

$\bar{Q}_h$ is the price of goods produced at home in the initial situation; we define Q such that this equals unity.

I_h is the initial quantity of goods imported by the home country. We assume trade is initially balanced, so $I_h = I_f$, and so can omit the suffix and simply write I.

E is the initial exchange rate; units are defined in such a way that it equals unity.

q_h is the change in the quantity of goods produced at home which is induced by some small spontaneous disturbance.

$\bar{q}_h$ is the change in the price of goods produced at home which is induced by the disturbance.

$^s d_h$ is a small spontaneous change in the home country's domestic expenditure—i.e. in the expenditure of the home country's residents, whether on imports or home-produced goods.

$^i d_h$ is the change in the level of the home country's domestic expenditure which is induced by some disturbance.

d_h is the total change in the level of the home country's domestic expenditure following some disturbance, including both the change which is induced by the disturbance and any spontaneous change in the home country's domestic expenditure (i.e. $d_h = {}^s d_h + {}^i d_h$).

$^s i_h$ is a small spontaneous change in the home country's imports.

$^{i}i_h$ is the change in the level of imports of the home country which is induced by some disturbance.

i_h is the total change in the quantity of imports by the home country, including both the change which is induced by any spontaneous disturbance in the system, and any spontaneous change in its imports (i.e. $i_h = {}^s i_h + {}^i i_h$).

m_h is the home country's marginal propensity to import—i.e. the proportion of additional income which is used for buying imports.[4]

s_h is the home country's marginal propensity to save.

$^c\epsilon_h$ is the expenditure-compensated elasticity of demand for home imports. It is concerned with the pure substitution effects of a change in the price of home or foreign goods on the demand for imports; i.e. it concerns the proportional change in demand for imports which would follow a price change if the total funds available for domestic expenditure were so adjusted as to enable the old set of commodities to be bought at the new prices.

ϵ_h is the elasticity of demand for home imports, conventionally defined—i.e. the proportional change in the demand for imports as a ratio of the proportional change in the relative prices of home and foreign goods, on the assumption that money income is constant and taking into account both the pure substitution effect and the income effect.[5]

---

[4] This equals Meade's marginal propensity to import (π) multiplied by unity minus the marginal propensity to save, i.e. $m = \pi(1 - s)$. Unlike Meade, we assume consumption to be the only kind of induced expenditure; we have no induced investment and the government is ignored.

[5] It can be seen that $\epsilon_h = {}^c\epsilon_h + \dfrac{m_h}{(1 - s_h)}$.

Define $\chi_h = \dfrac{\partial I_h}{\partial \bar{Q}_h}$ and $\chi_f = \dfrac{\partial I_h}{\partial(Q_f.E)}$,

and continue the assumption that $\bar{Q}_h = \bar{Q}_f = E = 1$. We can split these χ terms into their expenditure and substitution effects (cf. Meade, op. cit., p. 19) as follows:

$$\chi_h = -(Q_h - I_f)\frac{m_h}{(1 - s_h)} + \chi'_h,$$

$$\chi_f = -I_h\frac{m_h}{(1 - s_h)} + \chi'_f,$$

where the χ' terms represent the pure substitution terms on the assumption that total funds available for domestic expenditure have been adjusted so as to enable the old set of commodities to be bought at the new prices. By the standard characteristics of the substitution terms,

(Footnote continued on p. 618.)

e is a small change in the exchange rate, in the form of a depreciation of the currency of the home country.

v is the change in the terms of trade—a negative value is an adverse movement for the home country.

t is the change in the balance of trade of the home country, valued in terms of home currency.

The suffix f attached to the expressions in place of the suffix h above represents conditions in the foreign country. We shall not, however, consider cases where spontaneous disturbances arise in the foreign country; this is unnecessary, because the results are symmetrical.

Our system can be represented by eight equations, as follows:

$$d_h = q_h - i_f + i_h + \bar{q}_h(Q_h - I) + (\bar{q}_f + e)I. \qquad (1)$$

$$d_f = q_f - i_h + i_f + \bar{q}_f(Q_f - I) + (\bar{q}_h - e)I. \qquad (2)$$

$${}^i d_h = d_h - {}^s d_h = (1 - s_h)q_h + \bar{q}_h Q_h. \qquad (3)$$

$$d_f = (1 - s_f)q_f + \bar{q}_f Q_f. \qquad (4)$$

$$\chi'_f = -\chi'_h.$$

Moreover, from the definition of ${}^c\epsilon_h$,

$$\chi'_h = I_h {}^c\epsilon_h.$$

From the last three equations, it follows that

$$\chi_f = -I_h\left(\frac{m_h}{(1 - s_h)} + {}^c\epsilon_h\right).$$

But from the definition of ϵ_h

$$\left(= -\frac{\partial I_h}{\partial \bar{Q}_f . E} \cdot \frac{Q_f E}{I_h}\right)$$

and the second equation above, it follows that

$$\chi_f = -I_h \epsilon_h.$$

$$\therefore \ \epsilon_h = \frac{m_h}{(1 - s_h)} + {}^c\epsilon_h.$$

A similar demonstration can be used to show that

$$\epsilon_f = \frac{m_f}{(1 - s_f)} + {}^c\epsilon_f.$$

$$i_{i_h} = i_h - {}^s i_h = \frac{m_h d_h}{(1 - s_h)} - \bar{q}_h \frac{m_h}{(1 - s_h)} (Q_h - I)$$

$$+ \bar{q}_h I^c \epsilon_h - (\bar{q}_f + e)I \left({}^c \epsilon_h + \frac{m_h}{1 - s_h} \right). \tag{5}$$

$$i_f = \frac{m_f d_f}{(1 - s_f)} - \bar{q}_f \frac{m_f}{(1 - s_f)} (Q_f - I)$$

$$+ \bar{q}_f I^c \epsilon_f - (\bar{q}_h - e)I \left({}^c \epsilon_f + \frac{m_f}{1 - s_f} \right). \tag{6}$$

$$v = \bar{q}_h - \bar{q}_f - e. \tag{7}$$

$$t = i_f - i_h + I\bar{q}_h - I(\bar{q}_f + e). \tag{8}$$

The first two equations both spring directly from the definition of a country's domestic expenditure, which is equal to the quantity of goods bought by its residents, multiplied by the price of those goods. The equations show that the change in a country's domestic expenditure can be broken down into a quantity change and a price change. The quantity change is the change in the amount of goods produced at home, less the change in the amount exported, plus the change in the amount imported. The price change consists partly of a change in the price of the country's own goods and partly of the change in the price at which it can obtain the imported goods; each change is multiplied by the quantity of the respective kinds of goods bought in the original situation.

The second pair of equations represents the dependence of the induced changes in domestic expenditure on the change in the level of money income in the country concerned.[6] This change in money income can be broken down into a change in the quantity of goods produced, and a change in the prices of those goods. If the quantity produced rises, domestic expenditure rises by a smaller proportion, because of the leakage into savings. If the price level of home output rises, domestic expenditure rises in proportion.

The third pair of equations represent the dependence of the induced changes in imports on the change in the level of money income in the country concerned and on the prices of the two kinds of goods. In

---

[6] It is assumed that the terms of trade have no effect on the amount of expenditure from a given money income.

each equation the first expression on the right-hand side represents that the change in the volume of imports varies with domestic expenditure; the expression $m/(1 - s)$ represents the proportion of a rise in expenditure which is used for buying imports. The second and third expressions on the right-hand side reflect the effects of changes in the country's own price level on its imports. This effect is broken down into a pure substitution effect and an income effect. The latter, which is measured by the second expression, represents the effect of the change in real purchasing power which occurs when the country's price level alters and money expenditure there remains unchanged.[7] There is a loss of real purchasing power in these circumstances when the price level rises—hence the expression is negative. Similarly, the last expression on the right-hand side of the third pair of equations represents the effect of a change in the price to you of the other country's goods. Once again this includes a pure substitution effect and an income effect.

The seventh equation simply defines the change in the terms of trade as the sum of the changes in home and foreign prices and in the exchange rate. The last equation defines the change in the balance of trade in terms of changes in the volumes of goods traded and of their prices.

This system of equations has set out the causal relationships involved and the definitions that are being used; but it is still unnecessarily complicated for getting the results we want. Fortunately, it can easily be simplified down [8] to a form which gives the answers employed in Chapters 30 and 33; in those chapters, exchange rates we assumed unchanged, so $e = 0$. The simplified formulas are as follows:

$$q_h s_h - t = {}^s d_h. \tag{9}$$

$$q_f s_f + t = 0. \tag{10}$$

$$v = \bar{q}_h - \bar{q}_f. \tag{11}$$

---

[7] For a full discussion of this application of the Slutsky equation, see Meade, op. cit., pp. 19-21.

[8] A convenient method is to substitute equations 5 and 6 in equation 8, and then to substitute from equations 3 and 4 into the resulting equation. In turn substituting equation 7 into the result, and modifying with the results in footnote 5 we reach equation 12. Equation 9 can be obtained by substituting 8 in 1 and then substituting from equation 3; similarly 10 can be obtained by substituting 8 in 2 and then substituting from 4.

$$t = m_f q_f - m_h q_h - \frac{m_h{}^s d_h}{(1 - s_h)} - {}^s i_h - vI(\epsilon_h + \epsilon_f - 1). \tag{12}$$

In this simplified system we have six unknowns (q_h, q_f, t, v, $\bar{q}_h$, $\bar{q}_f$) and four equations. We therefore have two degrees of freedom which we can utilize by imposing different pairs of restraints on the system. For example, by assuming $\bar{q}_h = \bar{q}_f = 0$ (i.e. constant prices—the assumption of Chapter 30) we have a determinate system with six equations and six unknowns. We can use this system of equations to solve for different variables after spontaneous disturbances of either of the two kinds for which our system makes allowance.

GROUP I

Constant prices in both countries.

($\bar{q}_h = \bar{q}_f = 0$) (cf. Chapter 30).

Case 1. Disturbance ${}^s d_h$ (Chapter 30, pp. 444-6) (i.e. spontaneous rise in domestic expenditure of home country. Some of this additional expenditure is on home goods and some is on imports). Substitution in equations 9-12 gives

$$t = -{}^s d_h \frac{\dfrac{m_h}{s_h(1 - s_h)}}{1 + \dfrac{m_f}{s_f} + \dfrac{m_h}{s_h}}. \tag{13}$$

From this, substituion in equation 10 gives

$$q_f = {}^s d_h \frac{\dfrac{m_h}{s_h(1 - s_h)}}{s_f + m_f + s_f \dfrac{m_h}{s_h}}. \tag{14}$$

Similarly, substitution in equation 9 gives

$$q_h = {}^s d_h \frac{1 + \dfrac{m_f}{s_f} - \dfrac{m_h}{(1 - s_h)}}{s_h + m_h + s_h \dfrac{m_f}{s_f}}. \tag{15}$$

Equations 13-15 have already been presented in footnotes to Chapter 30 on p. 445. (There it was assumed that ${}^{s}d_{h}$ was equal to unity.)

Case 2. Disturbance ${}^{s}i_{h}$ (Chapter 30, pp. 446-8) (i.e. spontaneous rise in home imports, while home domestic expenditure is initially unchanged. This is a switch in expenditure from home goods to imports). Substitution in equations 9-12 gives

$$t = -{}^{s}i_{h} \frac{1}{1 + \dfrac{m_{f}}{s_{f}} + \dfrac{m_{h}}{s_{h}}}. \tag{16}$$

From this, substitution in equation 10 gives

$$q_{f} = {}^{s}i_{h} \frac{1}{s_{f} + m_{f} + s_{f}\dfrac{m_{h}}{s_{h}}}. \tag{17}$$

Similarly, substitution in equation 9 gives

$$q_{h} = -{}^{s}i_{h} \frac{1}{s_{h} + m_{h} + s_{h}\dfrac{m_{f}}{s_{f}}}. \tag{18}$$

Equations 16-18 have already been presented in footnotes to Chapter 30 on pp. 447 and 448, on the assumption that ${}^{s}i_{h}$ was equal to unity.

GROUP II

Variable prices and fixed output at home.
Variable output and fixed prices abroad.

$$(\bar{q}_{f} = q_{h} = 0.)$$

This corresponds to the cases in Chapter 33 where the initiating changes occur in the primary-producing country; the home country is here a primary producer.

Case 1. Disturbance ${}^{s}d_{h}$ (Chapter 33, pp. 480-83).

It follows immediately from equation 9 that

$$t = -{}^{s}d_{h}. \tag{19}$$

It also follows directly from equations 10 and 19 that

$$q_f = \frac{{}^s d_h}{s_f}. \tag{20}$$

Finally, substitution in equations 9-12 gives

$$\bar{q}_h = \frac{{}^s d_h}{I} \cdot \frac{1 + \dfrac{m_f}{s_f} - \dfrac{m_h}{(1 - s_h)}}{(\epsilon_h + \epsilon_f - 1)}. \tag{21}$$

These last three equations correspond directly to those given in pp. 481-2 of Chapter 33; equation 19 is merely presented verbally in the text, while equations 20 and 21 are presented algebraically in footnotes. In Chapter 33 it is assumed that ${}^s d_h = 1$, and the suffixes representing the two countries are altered: h is replaced by p (since the home country is a primary producer) and f is replaced by i (since the foreign country is an industrial country).

Case 2. Disturbance ${}^s i_h$ (Chapter 33, pp. 484-5).
It follows immediately from equation 9 that

$$t = 0. \tag{22}$$

It follows from equations 10 and 22 that

$$q_f = 0. \tag{23}$$

Substitution in equations 11 and 12 gives

$$\bar{q}_h = - \frac{{}^s i_h}{I(\epsilon_h + \epsilon_f - 1)}. \tag{24}$$

These equations are the same as those given verbally or algebraically on p. 484-5 of Chapter 33, subject to changes in suffixes similar to those in Case 1 and to the assumption that ${}^s i_h = 1$.

GROUP III

Variable prices and fixed output abroad.
Variable output and fixed prices at home.

$$(q_f = \bar{q}_h = 0.)$$

This corresponds to the cases in Chapter 33, where the initiating disturbances occur in the industrial country; the home country is here an industrial country.

Case 1. Disturbance $^s d_h$ (Chapter 33, pp. 483-4).
It follows immediately from equation 10 that

$$t = 0. \tag{25}$$

It also follows immediately from equations 9 and 25 that

$$q_h = \frac{^s d_h}{s_h}. \tag{26}$$

Simple manipulation of equations 9-12 gives

$$\bar{q}_f = \frac{^s d_h}{I} \cdot \frac{\overline{\dfrac{m_h}{s_h(1 - s_h)}}}{(\epsilon_h + \epsilon_f - 1)}. \tag{27}$$

These last three equations correspond to results given on pp. 483-4 of Chapter 33. In this case the home country is industrialized, and the foreign country is a primary producer, so in the switch of suffixes i replaces h and p replaces f.

Case 2. Disturbance $^s i_h$ (Chapter 33, pp. 484-5).
The results are simply

$$t = 0, \tag{28}$$

$$q_h = 0, \tag{29}$$

and
$$\bar{q}_f = \frac{^s i_h}{I(\epsilon_h + \epsilon_f - 1)}. \tag{30}$$

Exchange Rate Changes

So far, all the results we have derived have assumed exchange rates to be constant. We can now proceed to consider the effects of changing them. The simple case considered in Chapter 31 can easily be derived by substituting in equations 1-8 above, assuming that e is no longer zero; equation 11 then becomes

$$v = \bar{q}_h - \bar{q}_f - e \tag{11a}$$

Then if $q_h = q_f = \bar{q}_h = \bar{q}_f = {}^s d_h = {}^s i_h = 0$

(as in Chapter 31), we get from equations 11a and 12

$$t = eI(\epsilon_h + \epsilon_f - 1), \tag{31}$$

which is the same as the equation in Chapter 31.

For the case considered in Chapter 32, where not all prices move in line, our model is no longer adequate, since it does not distinguish between different kinds of goods in each country. It will also be convenient to consider circumstances when trade is not necessarily initially balanced. We therefore need the additional symbols:

I_h is the original quantity of home imports.
I_f is the original quantity of foreign imports.
η_h is the elasticity of home supply of exports.
η_f is the elasticity of foreign supply of exports.

Our system can be represented by the following six equations:

$$i_h = -I_h \epsilon_h (\bar{q}_f + e). \tag{32}$$

$$i_f = -I_f \epsilon_f (\bar{q}_h - e). \tag{33}$$

$$i_h = I_h \eta_f \bar{q}_f. \tag{34}$$

$$i_f = I_f \eta_h \bar{q}_h. \tag{35}$$

$$v = \bar{q}_h - \bar{q}_f - e. \tag{36}$$

$$t = i_f - i_h + I_f \bar{q}_h - I_h(\bar{q}_f + e). \tag{37}$$

The first pair of equations relates changes in demand for imports solely to changes in their prices, on the assumptions of Chapter 32 that we do not pay attention to spontaneous changes in tastes ($^s i_h = 0$), that we ignore indirect changes such as changes in the levels of domestic expenditure ($d_h = d_f = 0$) and that we assume conditions where prices of domestically produced goods other than exports do not alter.

The second pair of equations introduce the supply elasticities, while the third pair are similar to those already introduced.

By substitution in 32-37, we can obtain

$$v = -e \frac{\eta_h \eta_f - \epsilon_h \epsilon_f}{(\eta_h + \epsilon_f)(\eta_f + \epsilon_h)} \tag{38}$$

and

$$t = eI_h \left(\epsilon_h \frac{1 + \eta_f}{\epsilon_h + \eta_f} + \frac{I_f}{I_h} \epsilon_f \frac{1 + \eta_h}{\epsilon_f + \eta_h} - 1 \right). \tag{39}$$

From these equations it is possible to derive the results given in Chapters 31 and 32.

It will be remembered that t is the balance of trade valued in terms of home currency. If t' is the balance of trade of the home country measured in foreign currency, equation 37 can be rewritten

$$t' = i_f - i_h + I_f(\bar{q}_h - e) - I_h\bar{q}_f. \qquad (37a)$$

From 32-36 and 37a we can derive

$$t' = eI_f \left(\frac{I_h}{I_f} \epsilon_h \frac{1 + \eta_f}{\epsilon_h + \eta_f} + \epsilon_f \frac{1 + \eta_h}{\epsilon_f + \eta_h} - 1 \right). \qquad (40)$$

Index